THE CATHOLIC
REFORMATION

Henri Daniel-Rops: *History of the Church of Christ:*

1. *The Church of Apostles and Martyrs* (A.D. 30–397)
2. *The Church in the Dark Ages* (397–1050)
3. *Cathedral and Crusade* (1050–1350)
4. *The Protestant Reformation* (1350–1564)
5. *The Catholic Reformation* (1500–1622)

Translations of the following are in preparation:

6. *Le Grand Siècle des Âmes*
7. *L'Ère des Grands Craquements*

THE CATHOLIC REFORMATION

by

H. DANIEL-ROPS

TRANSLATED
FROM THE FRENCH BY
JOHN WARRINGTON

LONDON: J. M. DENT & SONS LTD
NEW YORK: E. P. DUTTON & CO. INC.

H. Daniel-Rops: *Une Ère de Renouvenu: la
Réforme Catholique*, first published in France
by Librairie Arthème Fayard, 1955

TRANSLATOR'S NOTE

M. Daniel-Rops dealt with the period 1350–1622 under the general title *L'Église de la Renaissance et de la Réforme*, in two volumes, from the second of which, *La Réforme Catholique*, this volume has been translated.

CONTENTS

*

MAPS

CHAPTER I

THE AWAKENING OF THE CATHOLIC SOUL: ST IGNATIUS OF LOYOLA

1. RENASCENCE, NOT COUNTER-REFORMATION

THE series of events which form the history of Catholicism in the mid sixteenth century are most often depicted as follows. A violent shock causes the very foundations of Christendom to tremble, and whole sections of the Church's ancient edifice are swallowed up in heresy. Her rulers then drag themselves from their lethal indifference; they determine to oppose the Protestant menace, and at last take steps that should have been taken long ago.

Such is the pattern implied by the word 'counter-reformation.' The term, however, though common, is misleading: it cannot rightly be applied, logically or chronologically, to that sudden awakening as of a startled giant, that wonderful effort of rejuvenation and reorganization, which in a space of thirty years gave to the Church an altogether new appearance. What happened was a true renascence in the fullest etymological sense, more impressive from a Christian point of view than the Renaissance of art and letters upon which contemporary Europe was priding itself. The so-called 'counter-reformation' did not begin with the Council of Trent, long after Luther; its origins and initial achievements were much anterior to the fame of Wittenberg. It was undertaken, not by way of answering the 'reformers,' but in obedience to demands and principles that are part of the unalterable tradition of the Church and proceed from her most fundamental loyalties.

I have remarked elsewhere [1] that in the second half of the fifteenth century every Catholic worthy of his salt, all who were alive to the situation, clamoured for reform, sometimes on a note of furious indignation, but more frequently as an act of faith in the eternal destiny of Mother Church. At the time of Luther's birth this longing for reform had begun to wear the look of agony. In the three departments of faith, morals and ecclesiastical discipline the Council of Trent did no more than supply answers to questions raised at least a century earlier, and even adopted some of those solutions which the more distinguished intellects had long since proposed. To say this is not to deny that

---

[1] *The Protestant Reformation*, Chapter IV, section: 'Forces that Still Remained, and the Anguish of Reform.'

Protestantism played a part, dialectically, in the Catholic renascence. *Oportet haereses esse*, as St Paul says; and heresy obliged the Church to devise an exact statement of her doctrine upon certain points, to establish her position more securely than she would, in all probability, have been led to do, had she not been confronted with the challenge of error.[1] But the impetus which enabled her to join battle with her enemies was generated long before the Lutheran assault, and can in no way be considered a result of the upheaval caused by that event.

A general view of the history of the Church makes it clear that the sixteenth-century Catholic reform is not essentially different from other reforms, which have applied an irresistible law and thus serve as milestones on the road of time. The work of Cluny in the eleventh century, the achievements of St Norbert, St Bernard and others in the twelfth, the heroic undertakings of St Francis and St Dominic in the thirteenth —all these monumental and unending labours are of the same spirit and the same significance as those accomplished by the Popes and the Fathers of Trent, and by the religious founders of that period. Here indeed we have one of the most permanent features of Christianity, one of the most certain evidences of its divine origin and of the reality of those promises which it claims to have received. For ever dragged downward by the weight of original sin, the baptised soul repeatedly falls back into darkness. Nevertheless, with equal regularity, there springs from her very depths, where primeval defilement cannot altogether mask, much less destroy, the supernatural resemblance, a force that impels her once more upward to light and life: a force whose name is Grace. Suspended for a time by such human events as the 'Babylonian Captivity,' the Great Schism and the Hundred Years War, this sublime game of seesaw was resumed in the sixteenth century, and the necessary reform was carried through exactly as in the past. If the means employed seem more drastic, the result more decisive, that is because the remedy had been long postponed and had therefore to act upon a sickness proportionately graver.

Whereas Protestantism marks a complete break in the history of Christendom, the most grievous and most tragic there has ever been, the Catholic reform stands in the direct line of ancient tradition. It is itself, in fact, the rediscovery of living Tradition. From whatever point of view it is considered, the same permanency is observed. The reforming decrees of Trent are in perfect harmony with the Gregorian Bulls, while those concerning faith look back constantly to the ancient conciliar decisions, to the decretals of the popes, to the Fathers and Doctors of the Church. Likewise in the moral sphere: Tauler, Suso and

---

[1] In this respect the term 'counter-reformation' is justifiable, especially after the Council of Trent, when Pius V and Sixtus V applied coercive and repressive means which can be hardly described as the noblest elements in the work of Catholic reform.

the great medieval mystics form an obvious link between St Ignatius of Loyola and the *Imitation*, as do the Fraternities and Oratories of Divine Love between St Philip Neri and St Catherine of Genoa.

The Catholic reform, then, was in no respect a 'counter-reformation' in the chronological order; nor was it any more so as regards the process of its development. Those who promoted it had no intention of combating Protestantism and halting its progress. St Ignatius would have been very surprised, on that feast of the Assumption when he took the vow of Montmartre, had he been told that many historians were going to represent him as the man who recruited a body of shock troops entrusted with the elimination of heresy; and even the great bishops who, twenty or thirty years before the Council, took steps to reform their clergy were not primarily concerned to parry the furious Lutheran assault. The true reform was not directed *against* an enemy; it was undertaken *for* God, *for* Jesus Christ, as a protestation of unwavering loyalty. Before emerging as a body of doctrine, a disciplinary canon, an ecclesiastical code, it was an immense and prodigious movement of fervour, which uplifted the Christian soul almost everywhere (more especially perhaps in Italy and Spain), a kind of spiritual sublevation operated by the saints.

Here indeed is an altogether inexplicable phenomenon; it reminds us once again of the secret designs of Providence that guide the unrolling of history's scroll. For two hundred years there had been a sorry lack of effective witnesses to truth and justice, such as had arisen during the great centuries of the Middle Ages, in the hour when they were needed most. Why did they begin to reappear, in such numbers and so well suited to the times, early in the sixteenth century? What would have happened if men like St Ignatius, St Pius V and others had lived immediately before the tragic drama of the Schism? Things would certainly have been quite different. Again, why did God leave His Church to wallow for so long in slimy darkness before shedding His light upon her? Bossuet himself, aware of this enigma, could supply no answer.

At the critical moment when the Catholic, Apostolic and Roman Church was about to recover possession of herself and regain her rightful aspect, it was as it had always been; her authentic history is written by the saints. The reform was brought about by means of a spiritual rebirth, that is to say, by a deepening of faith, a return to vital sources. The practice of prayer put an end to doubt and laxity, to the divorce between faith and life. It is characteristic that the really decisive personalities of the Catholic reform were all mystics, whose primary and indeed sole purpose was to know God, to love Him and to serve Him. Captain Iñigo, wounded at Pampeluna, wrote no treatise on anti-heretical strategy, but *Spiritual Exercises*; nor was it rage against the Lutheran thesis, but love of God, that lit up the face of St Cajetan before the crib in Santa Maria Maggiore on Christmas night 1517. That the Catholic renascence originated in prayer is of profound significance. The whole difference between Catholic reform and Protestant 'reformation' is summed up in these words uttered by a monk of shining faith, Giles of Viterbo, in 1512: 'Men must be changed by religion, not religion by men.' 'Seek ye first the kingdom of God and His justice,' said the Master, 'and all these things shall be added unto you.'

The most surprising feature of this interior movement, of this effort to obey the Gospel precepts of repentance and self-renewal, is the fact that it was not limited to the domain of conscience, where every man can, if he so wills, be sovereign. In the troubled years of the fifteenth century, mysticism retired within itself, isolating itself from the world of men; [1] the *Imitation*, for example, proposed the monastic enclosure or the more secret region of the heart as the proper field of spiritual endeavour. But the mystical leaders of the sixteenth century practised a form of spirituality directed to the science of God and to the demands of charity—a momentous change of outlook, the causes of which defy analysis. While fashioning a body of religious men dedicated to prayer and renunciation, they were almost unconsciously training an army of seasoned troops for the great battles in which the Church would find herself engaged. They became the most successful opponents of those heretics whom they had at first ignored; and the reform which they began by accomplishing within themselves overflowed and radiated its vigour in the larger realm of institutions.

It is this movement of renascent fervour, this tremor of awakening faith, that allows us to consider the sixteenth century, for all its blasphemy and bloodshed, as one of the fairest in Christian history. At a moment when the mind of man was everywhere scintillating with high intelligence and even genius, the human soul burgeoned also with sublime exaltation, in acts of faith, hope and charity. It was indeed the pressure exerted by this distinctively religious phenomenon upon the Church's rulers that determined the reform of morals, institutions and theological education, just as, by altering the climate of the period, it enabled the greatest of all councils to assemble and the Tridentine canons to become the lifeblood of a reborn Catholicism.

2. RELIGION A WAY OF LIFE

'The evolution of Christian spirituality is often represented falsely in Protestant circles. . . . We may say that on the eve of the Reformation

[1] See *The Protestant Reformation*, Chapter III, section: 'Mystical Theology Comes into Its Own'.

religion had become a way of life.' These words, written by an eminent Calvinist,[1] are of deep significance, expressing an incontrovertible truth. Protestants had no monopoly of the desire to make direct contact with God through faith, to drink at the Gospel sources without being tied to external usages and formal devotions, to understand the word of God in all its fullness. Long before Luther translated the Bible into vernacular at the castle of Wartburg many editions of the sacred books had been published:[2] Cardinal Ximenes Cisneros had devoted immense labour to his Polyglot, and the French version by Lefèvre d'Étaples had proved a great success. As regards that craving for a purer religion, at once more exacting and more interior, which inspired the Augustinian of Wittenberg, it had been experienced well before his time by innumerable steadfast Catholics from Tauler to Ruysbroeck, from Suso to the unknown author of the *Imitation*.[3]

Would it were possible to describe in detail the tremor coursing through so many souls at the end of the fifteenth and beginning of the sixteenth century, a tremor that was to have so many different consequences! But the phenomenon will not yield to analysis; it is complex, contradictory, often ambiguous. The Christian conscience was examining itself, sometimes indiscreetly, and the prolonged silence of Rome allowed certain minds to go astray. The seeds from which the Protestant harvest later sprang did not at first seem very different from the fertile grain that would restore life to the Catholic Church. Before the hardening of attitudes and the erection of barriers that would soon be insurmountable, it was the whole body of the baptised, or at least the better members thereof, that sought to rid Christianity of all pollution and disfigurement. A general trend is clearly discernible; but there are notable contrasts of detail. One might just as well try to give an exhaustive account of the manifold processes of an orchard's blossoming in spring time to produce a whole variety of flowers and fruit.

This reawakening was apparent in all countries and in all classes of society; we can cite only a few names by way of example. In the ranks of the episcopate, and even of the Sacred College, we find Cisneros, Sadolet, Aleandro, Giberti, Carafa, Lippomano; in those of the secular clergy and the religious orders Cajetan, Zaccaria, Jerome Aemilian, Serafino da Fermo, Matteo di Bassi, Battista da Crema. Many intellectual laymen also were anxious to promote the interior reform, particularly such champions of Christian humanism as Marsilio Ficino and Vivès, Erasmus and Sir Thomas More. Of the women who played a large part in the spiritual ferment, some, including Marguerite

[1] E. G. Léonard, *Calvin et la réforme en France*, 1944.
[2] See *The Protestant Reformation*, Chapter V, p. 307.
[3] M. Daniel-Rops does not accept the attribution of this work to Thomas à Kempis.—Tr.

of Navarre and Renée of Ferrara, were suspect; most, however, were true Catholics. Outstanding among these was Vittoria Colonna, the confidante of Michelangelo, of Reginald Pole and of Valdès. There was also her friend Catherine Cibo, who learned Hebrew and Greek with a view to the better understanding of Scripture, and the saintly Louise Torelli, Countess of Guastalla. But the same fervour is observed among the rank and file: the annalist Tassini gives us a picture of common folk discussing faith and dogma in the streets and squares of many an Italian town.

In many places there grew up small associations of the faithful, whose purpose was to study these grave problems, to read the Scriptures and to discuss theology and mysticism. Such groups were to be found at Alcala, Burgos, Palencia and even at the courts of Charles V, François I and Henry VIII. Another flourished at Naples under the aegis of Juan de Valdès, a Spanish mystic who sowed tares along with good grain, but died a Catholic. Giberti established others at Verona, in the Calabrian palace of Donatello Rubbo as well as beneath the arches of San Giorgio. The Oratory of Divine Love at Rome was founded by Gregorio Cortesi not long afterwards; and the circle formed by Briçonnet at Meaux was originally one of many such coteries, of which the Church had no reason to complain. Each of these small groups,[1] whose influence was considerable, may be compared with 'La Chesnaie' in the great days of Lammenais.

Another mark of spiritual effervescence was the proliferation of religious books and methods of prayer. Fresh editions of the mystics, as well as new treatises, published between the end of the fifteenth century and about 1530, form an imposing catalogue. The *Imitation* was continually reprinted; so were Ludolph the Carthusian's *Life of Christ* and St Augustine's *Soliloquy*. Harphius's *Mirror of Perfection* was translated into several languages; while the Charterhouse at Cologne specialized in the distribution of earlier works, an undertaking in which they were rivalled by the diocese of Granada and the abbey of Montserrat in Spain. It was at Montserrat also that Garcia de Cisneros published his *Exercises of the Spiritual Life*, which was afterwards studied by Ignatius of Loyola during his residence in the neighbouring city of Manresa. Meanwhile John of Avila's *Audi Filia* and Louis of Granada's *Guide of Sinners* found their way across the Franco-Spanish

---

[1] Many of them had offshoots in the shape of charitable confraternities similar to those which grew up during the second half of the fifteenth century. The most famous was the Charity of St Jerome, named after the church in Rome which was the centre of its activity. To it Cardinal Giulio dei Medici (afterwards Pope Clement VII) extended his patronage; and persons of all degrees, from members of the Sacred College to humble students, helped it to care for the sick and needy, visit prisoners and social outcasts, and bury the dead who had no relatives. A quarter of a century later the church of St Jerome became the nucleus of St Philip Neri's apostolate.

frontier. Other methods of prayer, drawn up by the Brethren of the Common Life and the canons of Windesheim, attracted the most fervent souls. In France Louis of Blois (1606–66) was the author of many treatises, outstanding among which is the *Institution spirituelle*; and Catherine of Bologna's *Traité des armes spirituelles* enjoyed widespread popularity.

This passionate and uncontrolled ardour led in some cases to reprehensible extremes. Until the imposition of firm principles and the restoration of discipline by the Catholic reform, the Christian soul appeared to be feeling its way, groping hither and thither, in desperate longing for the light of certitude. Consider Spain. Under Philip II she emerged as the most impregnable fortress of the 'counter-reformation,' as the training-ground of St Ignatius, that great soldier of the Pope, as the school of St Teresa and St John of the Cross, those two most orthodox heralds of the mystical experience. But turn back the pages of history a mere thirty or forty years, and what a different scene, reminding us perhaps of molten metal! The idea of a return to genuine Christianity derived from Erasmus, according to whose 'Philosophy of Christ' religion is to be 'lived, not debated.' And now the tide of his doctrine had swept over the peninsula: all 'advanced' Christian intellectuals appealed to it, and the University of Palencia, quickly followed by that of Seville, became its centre. In Spanish Flanders, first at Louvain and then at Bruges, Erasmus found a rival rather than a pupil in the lofty mind of Luis Vivès (1492–1540), who later became one of the pioneers of educational theory. His *Enchiridion Militis Christi* ('Manual of the Soldier of Christ') circulated everywhere: its influence is apparent in the works of Luis de Leon and St John of the Cross, who read it in the celebrated translation by Alonso Fernand. Many souls were overwhelmed with joy on reading this manifesto of the Christian life, so hostile to any kind of formalism; but the Franciscans and Dominicans were alarmed by its seeming unorthodoxy, and the Inquisition intervened. Diego de Zuñiga attacked the views of Erasmus in a pamphlet entitled *Blasphemy and Impiety*; but it cannot be denied, as Maldonado and the two brothers Vergara bear witness, that the Dutchman's philosophy was a true spiritual leaven.

There was yet another movement, affecting the rank and file no less than the intelligentsia of the universities. Illuminism, as it was called, included among its votaries simple laymen, parish priests and religious of both sexes. It was also favoured by such distinguished individuals as Juan de Valdès (before his flight to Naples) and Servetus, a future victim of Calvin's stake; and it won the approbation even of Cardinal Carranza. Illuminism, like Erasmianism, sought a more interior, a more spiritual type of Christianity, and rested its claim upon the vivid awareness of sanctifying grace. The guiding principle of its less exaggerated forms is explained in the *Third Primer* of Ossuna, a Franciscan. This was to create an absolute void in the soul, which God would then visit undisturbed and fill with His light. But contemplative teaching of this kind points the way to a doctrine of abandon, whereby men convince themselves that the conscience, illuminated by God, will no longer sin—a doctrine perilously close to Lutheranism. And indeed we find some peculiar fish among this haul of *Alumbrados*. There was Maria de Santo Domingo whose ecstasies lasted for hours at a time, with complete suspension of her faculties, and who, though ignorant and almost illiterate, held her own against the most eminent theologians. There was also Magdalena de la Cruz, a Poor Clare who made a pact with Satan! The brothers Vergara too, among other Erasmians, were attracted by these doctrines, while Blessed Maria Cazalla spoke of Luther with remarkable forbearance. In some respects the movement bordered upon spiritual aberration; in others it seems to have promoted an esoteric system for the use of certain high initiates. Still, its aim was the regeneration of souls, and it encouraged the desire that Christianity might conform more nearly to Christ. The Inquisition may often have had good cause to censure its adherents; but it is none the less true that without the uncertain strivings of Illuminism St John of the Cross might never have developed and soared so far above it as he did.

Such phenomena reveal the pressure brought to bear by fervent souls upon the Church, whose leaders were thus at last compelled to shoulder the duty of reform. But they prove at the same time how urgent it had become to adopt clear-cut, uncompromising principles. It was no isolated danger that arose from the offensive conducted by Luther and other Protestant reformers and against the Roman Catholic Church. If the Holy See were to remain silent and inert, if authority would not decide to take in hand all those complex movements and to define the relationship between faith and life, there was no knowing into what wild thickets innumerable souls might not be led astray. Let Rome but speak, and all would be made clear; the voice of Rome, and no other voice, could bring order out of chaos. Notions which might originally have paved the way to misunderstanding would cease to be dangerous when circumscribed and defined by the Church; the partnership of truth and falsehood would be dissolved. This was the message proclaimed by Erasmus when, having broken with Luther, he declared: 'I rely for certitude upon nothing but the sure judgment of the Church'; and the decisive steps towards reform were taken by those who 'thought wholeheartedly with the Church.' A period of intense spiritual unrest would terminate in an act of loyal obedience.[1]

---

[1] It is precisely this spirit of loyalty which has led the Church to admit certain formulae while rejecting others scarcely distinguishable therefrom. We read, for example, in St Ignatius's fourteenth 'Rule for thinking with the Church': '. . . it is quite true that no one

It was indeed this ferment of ideas that produced men whose thought was in completest harmony with the Church, men of lofty spiritual aspirations but who never for one moment envisaged reform as a change of religion rather than a renewal of the human heart. They were firm in their allegiance to Mother Church, notwithstanding her unkempt appearance here and now. Most illustrious among them was St Ignatius; Pope Adrian VI might have been another had he lived longer and possessed a little more ability. Others, however, there were —many others; and it was due to their very numbers that the whole Church was at length imbued with their longing, and accomplished her own reform.

Gaspar Contarini (1470–1542) is a particularly attractive example ot this spirit. A Venetian senator, and consequently one of the governing body of the Most Serene Republic, he had represented his country in Rome and at the court of Charles V. He was also a distinguished humanist, a learned Greek scholar, and a friend of all who counted in European literature at that time. But he was no less a man of God, whose tender piety and exquisite charity remind us of St Francis of Sales. His soul was haunted by yearning for the reform of Christendom, and he supported Valdès, Sadolet, Reginald Pole and Giberti in their efforts for the same cause. None had a closer view of Rome's corruption, of the decadence into which the See of Peter had lapsed; and yet he was a devoted son of the Church. He wished that the spiritual awakening which he endeavoured to inspire should take place within the framework of Tradition: it was for the Church herself to accomplish the necessary reform. After the death of his wife he was created cardinal, and became one of the most influential advocates of that reform.

Here is another example: and this time we meet a group of fervent Christians, or rather a whole collection of such groups, from whose ranks a number of great reformers would soon emerge. The Oratory of Divine Love used to meet, between the years 1510 and 1520, in the little church of SS. Sylvester and Dorothea in the Trastevere district of Rome. It included persons of all sorts and conditions: clerics and laymen, devout burgesses and classical scholars. The original idea

---

can save his soul unless he be predestined, and have faith and grace.' Now these words, taken at face value, are reminiscent of Calvin; but their sequel proves beyond a shadow of doubt that the founder of the Jesuits was in perfect harmony with the mind of the Church and had no part in the extravagances of the *Christian Institute*. So too with Seripando, General of the Augustinians from 1539 to 1551, and afterwards a member of the Sacred College and Papal Legate: his propositions on the role of faith seem to re-echo Luther. But as Canon Pasquier writes in the *Dictionary of Catholic Theology*: 'We must not be perturbed by the different treatment accorded by the Church to the ideas of these two men [Seripando and Luther] . . . At every stage of her history the Church has reacted differently to theories expressed in very similar terms.'

which brought them together can be traced to the 'Fraternities of Divine Love,' which, as we have seen, arose towards the end of the fifteenth century, thanks largely to the efforts of St Catherine of Genoa. The oratory adopted St Jerome as its patron, and among its principal members were St Cajetan, Giovanni Pietro Carafa, Lippomano and Fr Giuliano Dati, rector of the church where they assembled for prayers and meditation, as well as to study Scripture and the Fathers. Their first concern was to improve their own lives before thinking of ecclesiastical reform, to make of their own souls a fertile soil in which the grace of Christ might flourish. Their example was quickly followed, and similar Oratories of Divine Love were established at Venice, Brescia and Verona. These energetic associations produced founders of religious orders, e.g. St Cajetan, a future pope in the person of Carafa, and Lippomano, who would one day preside in the Council of Trent. They were societies without statutes, a way of life without fixed rules; but their history affords a perfect illustration of the manner in which the reform itself took root in the Catholic soul. Their programme is well expressed in the sublime prayer taught to his little orphans by St Jerome Aemilian, whose sole purpose was to bring about the reign of faith and charity: 'Lord Jesus Christ, we implore Thee by Thine infinite goodness to re-establish the whole of Christendom in that state of sanctity which shall be most pleasing to Thy Divine Majesty.'

3. EPISCOPAL REFORMERS [1]

'To re-establish Christendom in the most perfect state of sanctity' was in fact the major preoccupation of many individuals long before the Council of Trent and subsequent papal decrees. Nor was that preoccupation confined to persons whose only weapon was prayer; it was found also among men whose duties enabled them to give effect to their purpose. The official Roman reformation was thus preceded by minor reforms in particular dioceses, abbeys and priories. These isolated movements prepared the way for the greater achievement, and in some cases supplied the means. True they were sporadic, often limited to the boundaries of a single diocese, more exceptionally to the frontiers of a kingdom. True also they depended on the life of one man, and were consequently of uncertain duration; but they are of considerable importance as signs of what was afoot.

It has been so often necessary to speak of unworthy bishops, greedy for prebends and leading far from exemplary lives, that we have not yet had the pleasure of showing that all heads of the Catholic hierarchy

---

[1] In the fifteenth century there were printed a great number of treatises on the episcopal ideal, e.g. those of Henry of Haguenau, Gerson, Denys the Carthusian, Laurence Justinian and Antoninus of Florence.

were not of this type. On the contrary, many of them derived from their faith a lofty conception of their duties, and tried to lead their clergy and people to a better understanding and more dutiful practice of true religion. They were very numerous and existed in all countries. Some were gentle, others violent in their methods; some were fortunate, others unsuccessful in the results which they obtained; but together they formed the vanguard of Trent.

One such precursor was the celebrated Cardinal Ximenes de Cisneros (1435–1517). He accompanied the Catholic sovereigns against Granada in 1492,[1] and used to say that he enjoyed the smell of gunpowder as much as that of incense. But it would be wrong to think of him merely as a prelate in armour. He died in 1517,[2] having devoted much of his tireless energy to the work of bringing back Christianity to its pristine holiness; and it is interesting to note that he shouldered this work not for theoretical reasons, but in consequence of a spiritual experience, an awakening within himself of religious fervour, as we find happening to many of his contemporaries. He was a secular priest and administrator of the bishopric of Siguenza when, at the age of forty-eight, he renounced the world and assumed the habit of the strictest Franciscan observance in the friary at Castañar. For more than ten years he lived a lonely and penitential life, dwelling in a wicker hut which he had built for himself in some desert place; and it seemed that he was destined to be no more than the ideal hermit whose virtues had quickly become famous far and wide. At length, however, he was summoned from his retreat by the queen, who made him her confessor and gave him the archbishopric of Toledo. He at once adapted himself to his new duties, and was soon able to devote an immense weight of authority to the service of God's cause. He personally visited each of the Castilian monasteries, urging them to reform, and strove to fashion the priests of his diocese into a model clergy. Realizing at the same time that the Church could play no effective part in the new world that was coming to birth unless she employed appropriate means, he endeavoured to make culture and humanism the allies of Christianity; while the University of Alcala, which he founded and which numbered as many as 12,000 students, was entrusted with the formation of a Catholic *élite* in Spain. The six-volume Polyglot Bible was edited by a team of specialists, including Lopez de Zuñiga and Nuñez de Gusman, under the close supervision of the archbishop, who thus erected a monument of Catholic erudition anterior to the Protestant Bibles and the works of Erasmus. Nor did Ximenes relax his efforts until his death at the age of more than eighty years, though he had been exalted to the

---

[1] See *The Protestant Reformation*, Chapter IV.
[2] Luther was then embarking on his career; the Council of Trent lay twenty-five years ahead.

rank of Cardinal, Grand Inquisitor, Primate of Spain, Governor of Castile and Vicar of the Empire. It would of course be idle to pretend that he was everywhere successful. When, for example, he tried to force the common life upon his canons by obliging them to build houses near the cathedral, the new apartments remained empty, and the canons, in defiance of episcopal authority, went so far as to imprison the nuncio, Ortiz, who had come to excommunicate them. On the other hand it was due largely to his influence that Spain was able to resist Protestant encroachment, and the terrible Cardinal of Toledo set an example to the whole Church.

Such facts must not be overlooked. In Spain itself the current of reform initiated by Ximenes continued to flow after his death. In Andalusia, where John of Avila, a former student of Alcala, began his labours ten years after the cardinal's disappearance from the scene, the bishops showed themselves eager to continue the good work. For instance, when Pedro Guerrero, Archbishop of Granada, was summoned to the Council of Trent, he invited the apostle of the peasants to accompany him.[1] Again, St Thomas of Villanova (1488–1555), Archbishop of Valentia, was the founder of charitable institutions to which he gave all the revenues of his benefices, and even his own bed. In addition, not only was he a great scholar and so eloquent in the pulpit, that Charles V appointed him court preacher, but his success as a reformer caused him to be surnamed in his lifetime 'The New Apostle of Spain.'

The Iberian Peninsula occupies a foremost place in this movement, but it was not the only part of Christendom to be stirred thereby. Italy was likewise affected. We tend to judge the entire Italian episcopate of that time by the worldly (and even more pernicious) character of some Medici, Farnese and Borgia cardinals. Yet it included many diocesan bishops whose lives were irreproachable, whose spiritual quality and achievement we cannot but admire. One man may suffice to represent all that was done, in many places, to rescue Mother Church from the bad example set by the Papal Court, and in view of his manifest sanctity it is surprising that he has never been canonized. I refer to Giberti (1495–1543), Bishop of Verona, 'Master John Matthew, most revered and most rare,' whom the Barnabite chronicler, Lorenzo Davidico, places in the front rank of the vanguard fighting for Catholic reform. Giberti is indeed a splendid figure: a mystic, a contemplative in high places. As a boy he had dreamed only of cloistered silence; and although circumstances obliged him to assume the responsibilities of ecclesiastical office, his constant purpose, wherever he might be, was to implant in men that Gospel teaching which was the well-spring of his own life and activity. Placed by his father, the Grand Admiral of

[1] On John of Avila see Section 5 below.

Genoa, in Cardinal Giulio de Medici's secretariat, he was entrusted with some delicate missions by Pope Leo X, and later became *Datarius* (i.e. virtual prime minister) of Clement VII, his former patron. But these onerous duties notwithstanding, he led the same fervent life of renunciation which he had once hoped to lead in the cloister; and the Oratory of Divine Love welcomed no more regular attendant at its meetings. His titles and honours weighed heavily upon him; and when at last, after the sack of Rome, he obtained the Pope's permission to resign them, he went to reside in his diocese of Verona, where in the space of about fifteen years he accomplished a remarkable transformation. Preaching by example, renouncing all his benefices and living like a monk in his palace, where a spiritual book was read aloud during meals, he managed to reimpose morality and discipline upon a clergy whose behaviour had been far from commendable. Journeying continually, visiting all the parishes of his diocese in turn, dismissing unworthy priests, encouraging the lukewarm and sluggish to do better, he revived faith and religious observance throughout his jurisdiction; and *vicars forane* were charged with the execution of his orders after he had gone. His regulations were printed and distributed to all parish priests; they were so perfect that many of their articles were afterwards embodied word for word in the canons of Trent. The religious orders were likewise an object of his constant solicitude, a fact which was not to the liking of all their members, particularly of certain refined ladies who appealed (unsuccessfully) to Rome. Mendicant friars were asked to moderate their zeal. There was scarcely a field left uncultivated by this amazing bishop. To develop piety among the faithful he established the Confraternity of the Blessed Sacrament, a forerunner of similar institutions. The liturgy was restored with all its dignity in the diocese of Verona, whose example was followed by others.[1] Preachers were invited not to abuse the claims of eloquence, to curtail the length of their sermons and not to revel in Latin quotations. The bishop was also a highly educated man, and gathered around him a study circle known as the 'Gibertine Academy.' Social and charitable, as well as a disciplinarian and moralist, he founded many orphanages, almshouses and hostels for poor girls and Magdalens, while his *Societas Pauperum* foreshadowed our Confraternity of St Vincent de Paul three centuries before Ozanam. It is hardly necessary to add that these results were not achieved without fury, uproar and conflict; but it must be said to the honour of the popes that all of them strongly supported the Bishop of Verona, whom Clement VII had appointed legate. John Matthew

---

[1] The Church owes to Giberti the custom of reserving the Blessed Sacrament in a tabernacle on the high altar, of ringing a little bell at the Elevation and the rule that priests must wear choir-dress and stole while hearing confessions. Many authorities also attribute to Giberti the invention of confessionals as used today.

Giberti died too early, too young, to witness the triumph of his ideas at the Council of Trent, but he had opened up the road; and the Carmelite Castiglione, who pronounced his funeral oration, had good reason to exclaim: 'Our bishop lived and died as a saint.'

Giberti was by no means the only one of his kind. What he accomplished at Verona—where Lippomano continued his work with unrivalled energy—others were doing elsewhere, or would do later: Cornaro at Brescia, Ridolfi at Vicenza, Ercole Gonzaga at Mantua, Contarini at Belluno, Vida at Alba in Lombardy, Pisani at Padua, Aleandro at Brindisi, Doria at Genoa, Cles at Trent. Results varied and in no case attained the same level as at Verona; but it was significant that so many dioceses were handled in this way. The same trend was noticeable everywhere, more or less impetuous, more or less effective. In Germany, where all the bishops did not attain the stature of Hermann von Wied or Rupprecht von Simmern, the movement was nevertheless headed by holy prelates such as Johann von Eich, Friedrich of Hohenzollern and Berthold Pirstinger. Excellent bishops followed one another in the See of Basel, among them Cristof of Utenheim, ably assisted by some energetic auxiliaries. England had John Fisher, than which no more need be said. In Poland, too, Stanislaus Hosius, Bishop of Cholm and a future cardinal, fought Protestantism not only with his pen but also by his example. Nor indeed must we omit from this concise and incomplete list the team of French bishops whom we have already seen at work, deriving from the deep wells of fervour strength to contend for the reform of their dioceses. Two in particular come to memory: the radiant Sadolet of Carpentras, and Briçonnet of Meaux. The latter's doctrine was momentarily suspect, but no one ever criticized his moral eminence or the courage with which he strove to regenerate the Church.[1]

4. REFORM OF THE OLD ORDERS: THE CAPUCHINS

Parallel with this episcopal reaction against the forces of decay rose another, which had long been part and parcel of ecclesiastical history: reform of the religious. In every crisis experienced by the Church in course of centuries, it had been the monastic Orders that had embodied the forces of resistance; and it remained to be seen whether these ancient organizations were capable of doing once again what had formerly been accomplished first by the Benedictines and Cistercians, then by the Franciscans and Dominicans. Outwardly at least they seemed to retain plenty of vigour. There were still numerous abbeys of both black and white monks; the Friars Minor continued to exercise a

[1] See *The Protestant Reformation*, Chapter VI.

strong influence upon the people; and it was to the Dominicans that Paul III entrusted the restored Roman Inquisition. Generally speaking, however, as is only too well known, these old Orders had declined sadly from their primitive fervour. True they still included in their ranks a number of pious religious. But these existed side by side with a host of dubious companions, who had been admitted to vows by an inadequate system of recruitment. Obliged to live among brethren whose conduct was often unedifying, the better elements came to feel themselves altogether ineffective, and the resulting situation gave rise to frequent discord and even violent conflict. The question was whether the good could prevail over the bad, whether those who observed the rule and the traditions of sanctity would manage to convert the others; a question all the more grave because these old Orders were to become the object of the most furious assault by Protestant critics, while new Orders rose up alongside, full of energy and ready to supplant them.

There was a strongly marked tendency, which later became an integral part of the Catholic reform, to subject the religious Orders more strictly to ecclesiastical authority: to the Holy See as represented by the Congregation of Religious, and to the bishops by reducing various monastic privileges. In 1516 Pope Leo X placed all religious, even the Mendicants, under episcopal jurisdiction when ministering outside their own houses; and on the many occasions when conflict arose between reforming bishops and the monks—e.g. at Verona in the time of Giberti—the Holy See invariably upheld the bishops; this policy foreshadowed not only such Tridentine decrees which terminated abuses, made the black Benedictines a congregation, and regulated the official poverty of the Minors, but also the stern measures taken by Paul IV against gyrovague monks, who were sent to the galleys or to prison.

These conciliar and papal measures would have been useless if a sincere and spontaneous will to reform had not existed at the heart of the Orders themselves. Exist, however, it most certainly did; in fact, it had never disappeared. In the worst days of the fourteenth and fifteenth centuries, the deepest loyalties had produced reforms of which some had been efficacious.[1] St Colette, St Catherine of Siena, St Andrew Corsini, St John Capistran, St Antoninus and many more had striven courageously; but the task had once again to be resumed, for human nature is such that even when sustained by the triple vow, it repeatedly falls back.

There was hardly one of the old Orders that did not give striking signs of revival during the forty years preceding the Council of Trent. In all, or nearly all, as in the case of diocesan bishops, men and women

[1] See *The Protestant Reformation*, Chapter III, section: 'Will the Church Reform Herself?' and Chapter IV.

found in themselves the strength to war against everything that imperilled not only their respective Orders but also the very bases of their spiritual life. This revival among the regular clergy is one of the most impressive aspects of the 'pre-reform' which heralded the official reform and prepared for it both strategy and troops. Almost everywhere the process is identical. A man of God establishes within the bosom of an old Order, which has become more or less degenerate, a new congregation or community resolved to live in complete fidelity to the rule. After various difficulties the small nucleus survives, prospers and is joined by many fresh units; sometimes indeed the whole or a substantial majority of the older body transforms itself accordingly.

We should pay homage to those brave men who rekindled the fire; they are less renowned than their contemporaries—St Ignatius and St John Capistran, for example—who founded new institutes. Their memory was not preserved by the zeal of young formations anxious to obtain a protector in Heaven, with the result that few of them have been canonized, though they richly deserved the honour.

Among the Benedictines there was the magnificent effort of the Congregation of Bursfeld in Germany, heir to the impulse given by St Nicholas of Cusa. At the head of the famous Spanish abbey of Montserrat, near Barcelona, stood a great mystic who was to influence St Ignatius of Loyola: Garcia de Cisneros (1455–1510), nephew of Cardinal Ximenes, who restored the splendour of the divine office as well as monastic discipline. The noble humanist Gregorio Cortese (1488–1548), first at Mantua, then at the ancient monastery of Lérins, and finally at San Giorgio in Venice, revived, together with religious fervour and good order, a taste for intellectual studies, which exercised a profound influence on his brethren of Monte Cassino. He was appointed Bishop of Urbino and created cardinal by Paul III.

Among the Camaldolese, the venerable order of St Romuald, the movement was headed by Blessed Giustiniani (1476–1528).[1] First in the Apennines and later in the plain of Ancona, his spiritual sons lived their austere lives in small separate huts, like true hermits; their example was such that the entire Order quickly followed suit, and under his relative, Pietro Giustiniani of Bergamo, Monte Corona on the upper Tiber afterwards became the centre of reformed Camaldolese.

We find the same stirring, the same will to be reborn, among the various orders of Mendicants. If the Dominicans lacked outstanding reformers at this period, it was because their Order had already been reformed since 1493, by the celebrated congregation of San Marco at Florence, which was fostered by the archbishop St Antoninus, and also perhaps because the work of Savonarola, despite his ultimate defeat,

[1] He belonged to the same Venetian family that gave the Church the holy patriarch St Laurence Justinian and the Benedictine *venerabilis* Nicholas.

had continued to make itself felt long after his ashes were thrown into the Arno. The Black Friars, however, possessed a man of wonderful energy in the person of Battista da Crema, whose voice was scarcely less powerful than that of Friar Jerome; while at Pavia and Alba, Prior Ghislieri (afterwards Pope St Pius V) was distinguished by his immense authority. It was rather on the intellectual plane, in conformity with their vocation, that the sons of St Dominic laboured for reform. In Spain, for example, Francisco de Vittoria (1480 or 1492–1546), master of Salamanca,[1] put new life into Thomism by discarding its scholastic subtleties, and was followed on this road of positive dogmatics by his pupils Melchior Cano and Domenico de Soto.

The Augustinians, upon whom Luther was to confer such unpleasant notoriety, included in their ranks some remarkable men, no less preoccupied with spiritual life and reform than was the monk of Wittenberg himself, but never thinking for a moment of leaving the Church. Giles of Viterbo (died 1532), an outstanding humanist and fascinating preacher, delivered a sensational address in the Lateran Council, scourging the vices of the Church and proposing a real programme of reform. His disciple Jerome Seripando (1494–1563), a member of La Carbonaria, the most austere branch of the Augustinians, was of such exemplary life that he was appointed its secretary at the age of twenty-one. He later became General of the whole Order, and visited all its houses as far afield as Spain and Portugal, bringing them back to a higher standard of morality, ridding them of Lutheran influence and breaking all resistance. Among those who profited by his unwavering support was Thomas of Villanova. Another was Gaspard Casal, future Bishop of Coimbra, who was ultimately appointed Archbishop of Salerno; created cardinal, he served as Papal Legate at Trent, and was one of the most vigorous personalities of his age.

There is scarcely an Order, congregation or institute of religious in which we do not find the symptoms of this ferment; the 'reformers' were acquainted one with another and influenced one another without regard to differences of rule or degrees of enclosure. Thus, for example, Fr Serafino da Fermo introduced the Canons of the Lateran to the ideas of Battista da Crema. At Bologna another canon regular, Pietro de Lucca, did similar work; while the Premonstratensians of Spain and Lorraine became imbued with notions of reform that were realized immediately after the Council of Trent.

But in no Order did these notions give rise to such dramatic incidents or to such determined opposition as among the Franciscans, the most numerous and decidedly the most influential Order at that time. Masters in almost every university, preachers in every pulpit, the sons of St Francis displayed their familiar habit throughout Christian

[1] He is the father of international law, and is still much quoted in the universities.

Europe. It is useless, however, to pretend that they were not the target of criticism that was often no less justified than severe. The skill with which they wormed money from the faithful was proverbial, their moral conduct not always beyond reproach. Cardinal Nicholas of Cusa and St John Capistran had frequently complained of them, and in Spain they were severely treated by Ximenes. It is well known that since the morrow of the founder's death two tendencies had been apparent in the Order of St Francis: one favoured a strict interpretation of the Poverello's Rule and Testament; the other demanded some relaxation, without which, they argued, no great Order could function. This cleavage had resulted in the famous crisis of the 'Spirituals.' [1] Having been soothed and reorganized the party of Strict Observance was represented mainly by the Celestines (1294), or Clarenines, in Italy; by the Colettines (1406) in France; by the Amadeans (1457) in Savoy; in Spain by the Brethren of the Cowl (1487). During the mid fifteenth century Bernardine of Siena, John Capistran, James of La Marche and Bernardine of Feltre all belonged to the Strict Observance, which therefore seemed to be the party of the saints. Under its influence there began to flow within the Order a current directed to the recall of lax convents to the Rule and thus to the reunification of the great Franciscan family. In 1516 Leo X allowed himself to be persuaded that circumstances favoured a decree which would suppress the old denominations and bring all the sons of St Francis under the single name of 'Friars Minor.' The attempt, however, failed; a certain number of houses declined to renounce collective ownership. Leo X yielded, and gave official recognition to the Friars Minor Conventual, who thenceforward wore black. The Order as a whole was sadly disappointed, but disappointment here had one good result: it whipped up the energy of individuals, and there began to appear in many sectors of the Franciscan world a host of men determined to apply the principles of St Francis in all their rigour and to live in heroic poverty. Among the most famous of these was St Peter of Alcantara (1499–1562), an austere Spanish ascetic, whose lofty mysticism caused King John III of Portugal to summon him to court, and St Teresa to take him as her adviser when she contemplated the reform of Carmel. Under his direction, too, the 'Alcantarines' enjoyed great spiritual advancement and numerical increase. Their custom of establishing 'houses of recollection' or retreat for the periodical or permanent residence of those who felt the urge to asceticism became widespread; and in France these members of the Strict Observance became known as Recollects.

At about the same period an analogous design for returning to the original observance begat yet another type of Franciscans, whose unfamiliar habit caused them to be known by a new name. 'Capucini!

[1] See *Cathedral and Crusade*, p. 556 f.

Capucini!' the street urchins of Camerino used to shout when they caught sight of these odd, bearded monks, strolling along in their rough habits with fantastic square hoods. The nickname 'Capuchins' passed into usage and still denotes one of the three branches of the Franciscan Order. But the humble Matteo di Bassi (1495–1552) certainly had not the least idea of founding a new congregation when, in 1525, he came down from his friary at Montefalcone to beg Pope Clement VII, with gentle obstinacy and simple heart, for leave to wear a habit which he maintained was the authentic dress of St Francis. He begged also to be allowed to go and preach throughout the world, exhorting all, by example rather than by word, to turn their steps into the paths of God. Son of humble parents though he was, Matteo was already known as a model religious. He had distinguished himself by his devoted service to the plague-stricken during an epidemic in 1523, and was admired by the virtuous Catherine Cibo, Duchess of Camerino. It was rumoured that St Francis had several times appeared to him: 'I want my Rule observed literally; yes, to the very letter!'; and since on these occasions the founder wore the quadrangular hood as used by the peasants of Ancona, Matteo had adopted it notwithstanding criticism and even an express prohibition on the part of his superiors. He won Clement's approval; but it was given by word of mouth only, and the good friar, who had now been joined by two companions, met at first with strong resistance from his Order, even to the point of excommunication. However, Louis of Fossombrone, one of his disciples, had heard tell that Giovanni Pietro Carafa, a future pope and at that time influential in the Curia, was a resolute supporter of anyone working for reform. He therefore went to Rome, and prevailed upon Carafa to obtain a papal Bull which withdrew Matteo from Franciscan jurisdiction and made him subject to his firm friend the Bishop of Camerino. Such was the origin (1528) of the Franciscan hermits, called thenceforward Capuchins. The new formation quickly proved its worth. The strange houses of these new Minors began to arise on all sides, with doors so low that one had to stoop to enter, and narrow windows devoid of glass. The friars themselves ate nothing but bread, fruit and herbs, drank nothing more tasty than water, while their habit was made of coarsest fustian. But they also emerged from their convents, especially into heavily populated districts, and, as we learn from the *Mémoires* of Castelnau, were 'frequently met travelling through towns and villages, visiting private houses to reprimand the occupants . . . reminding the people of the excellence of the Catholic faith,' renewing in brief the far-flung and fruitful apostolate of the earliest Franciscans. Their charity was inexhaustible, in flagrant contrast to the rapacity of some other Mendicants, and earned them much goodwill. After the sack of Rome, when Italy was ravaged by the soldiery, then by famine and epidemic, they rose to magnificent heights; and the Hospital for Incurables, in the Piazza del Popolo, preserves the memory of their generosity. Having been organized as a congregation under the kindly and little more than nominal jurisdiction of the Conventuals, and with their Constitutions approved by Rome in 1529, the Capuchins seemed destined for nothing but success. Severe trials, however, awaited them. First to launch a violent attack were the Friars Minor Observant, maddened by the zeal (somewhat excessive at times) of the new-born institution. The attack failed, and some of the most celebrated Observant preachers actually joined the Capuchins. A second offensive from the same quarter was thus provoked, and the fact that it did not succeed was due entirely to the influence of Catherine Cibo and Vittoria Colonna. Paradoxically assisted by the Conventuals, the Capuchins were able henceforward to live almost independently under their own vicar-general.

Alas, however, a worse misfortune lay in wait for the hermits. The most illustrious of their recruits, whose arrival had been hailed with such delight and who had been quickly promoted to the rank of vicar-general, was none other than Bernardino Ochino. This wonderful man, this born leader, this splendid orator—'he would move stones,' Vittoria Colonna used to say—went over to Protestantism. The scandal of his departure may be imagined. The head of the Capuchins become a Lutheran, and married! It was enough to lay the whole edifice in ruins beneath the blows of its adversaries; and Paul III, hearing the news, went so far as to exclaim: 'Soon there shall be no Capuchins at all.' But the devoted protectress of the congregation intervened once more, helped by Giberti and Cardinal San Severino. A careful inquiry revealed that Ochino's was an isolated case. Could one condemn so many on the strength of one man's error? And so the Capuchins, saved from the pontifical thunderbolts, were enabled to go ahead and prosper. A hundred years later they numbered 30,000, in 1,400 houses; and to these were subsequently added the Sisters of the Passion, founded by Maria Laurentia Longa and known commonly as Capuchines.

Such was the magnificent process whereby the old religious Orders were regenerated and made ready to enter fully into the effort for which the Church would soon call upon her sons. That process, however, was as yet far from complete: it would assume larger proportions on the morrow of Trent,[1] receive fresh impetus and produce many another saint. Even while Rome recovered herself and prepared to undertake reform on a world-wide scale, Teresa of Avila, afire with mystic love, was already contemplating the reform of Carmel and laying the foundations of her great achievement.

[1] When the Observant Franciscans had no fewer than 165,000 members.

5. Birth of New Orders: the Clerks Regular

It appeared that revival and reorganization of the old Orders was insufficient for the end proposed. A new formula was required to meet new demands, and was found in the institution of clerks regular. This, however, was an institution that evolved quite naturally from earlier beginnings. Long ago, in the thirteenth century, the Franciscans and Dominicans, laying much less emphasis than their predecessors on cloistered contemplation, had made close contact with the faithful, particularly through the medium of preaching. The new leaven introduced into the Christian lump by the Mendicants had undoubtedly caused it to rise; but the results of their labour had not been as decisive as could have been wished. Their many examples of priestly virtue had been far from consistently followed by the parochial clergy, and it appeared, generally speaking, that in order to be a good priest one needed to join a religious Order. Surely it was possible to go a stage further by establishing a body of priests with the same spiritual quality as the regulars, and equally subject to vows, but living as part of the ordinary clergy, wearing their dress and leading their life. These 'clerks regular' would help the parish priests in their task and devote themselves to the same ministry, but they would also provide the faithful with a living example of priestly virtue in the world. Trained to methods of prayer and thus deepening their spiritual life, but exempt from the choral office to which even the Mendicants were still bound, these new priests would labour to make their faith an integral part of life. It was a momentous innovation, one that would play an important part in the work of ecclesiastical reform; and it continues fruitful to this day.

The first of such bodies was that of the Theatines, an offshoot of the Oratory of Divine Love. It resulted from the meeting of two men whose characters were entirely different. One of them, St Cajetan of Tiene (1480–1547), was a refined and devout soul, of retiring disposition, full of meekness and moderation. The other was Giovanni Pietro Carafa (1476–1559), 'a Calabrian firebrand,' who afterwards displayed the same temperament on the papal throne, but also those gifts of leadership which had revealed themselves in the years of his early manhood. The idea was Cajetan's. Having attended many meetings of the Oratory of Divine Love, he decided that the pious exercises of that closed circle were having no influence upon the Church, whereas its methods of spiritual perfection might well prove more effective if adopted by an army of zealous priests. He dreamed therefore of creating a sacerdotal community whose members would forgo honours and lucrative positions, bind themselves by vows similar to those taken by

B

religious, and work in collaboration with the rank and file of the secular clergy. The gentle mystic must inevitably have failed without the backing of Carafa's more practical qualities. But agreement between them was not easy. Cajetan did not altogether trust the other's impulsive nature; and having embraced a state of poverty he suspected that the episcopal benefices held by his destined ally might prove a serious obstacle to the realization of his plans. There is a story that Carafa fell on his knees before the future saint, begging him to accept his services, whereupon the astonished Cajetan knelt in turn and embraced him, weeping. Be that as it may, the two men were thenceforward close associates. In 1524, thanks to Giberti, who was at that time head of Clement VII's chancellery, they obtained permission to found a society of clerks regular, and secured the privilege of its dependence upon the Holy See alone. Carafa magnanimously resigned his two bishoprics, but as he had been titular of Chieti (Latin *Theatinum*) in the Abbruzzi, the members of the new Institute soon came to be known popularly as Theatines. Except for their white stockings and larger tonsure, they were in no way distinguishable from other priests; but they strove to be present wherever there was need of preaching, charitable work or other form of service. Their undertaking very quickly prospered. Obliged to flee after the sack of Rome, they forgathered at Venice, whence they were summoned to Naples by the patriarch Caracciolo. Back once again in the Eternal City, at the church of St Nicholas of Tolentino, they gave public proof of their holiness and zeal during months of famine and misery. Within a period of about twenty years the Theatines spread over the whole of Italy, and from there to Spain, Poland, Austria and Germany. The election of Carafa as Pope Paul IV contributed greatly to their success, and they became a regular nursery of bishops, more than two hundred of whom issued from their ranks. They also produced some distinguished preachers, among whom was St Andrew Avellino, and mystics such as Lorenzo Scupoli. The Theatines were once on the point of incorporation with the Jesuits, to whose rule their own, though less exacting, bore some kinship. The proposal never materialized, and their influence steadily declined; but we ought not to forget the work that they accomplished.[1] The canonization of St Cajetan in 1671 was the Church's official homage to an initiative which had opened up for her a new road on the eve of the Council of Trent.

Along that road, or along parallel roads, others quickly set out. A young doctor at Cremona, St Antony Zaccaria (1502–37), was disturbed

[1] St Cajetan and the Theatines are credited with various customs and devotions, which were introduced first at Naples and became universal. These were the Forty Hours, the Christmas Novena, popularization of the crib (invented by St Francis of Assisi), wearing of the surplice by preachers, segregation of men and women at Mass. This last custom is extinct in France, except at funeral Masses, but is still quite common in Germany.

by the sight of his people's misery and increasing immorality; he was already active before his ordination to the priesthood, insisting upon the need for penance, like St Paul, with whose doctrine he was deeply imbued. He was soon joined by a number of disciples; and the citizens of Milan and other towns beheld these new preachers marching through the streets, with ropes around their necks, carrying enormous crosses, and halting at crossroads to proclaim the love of God. The movement gradually became organized. Ludovica Torelli, Countess of Guastalla, told Zaccaria about Cajetan and the Oratory of Divine Love, and a small community was formed, to which a papal Brief (1533) granted the same privileges as those enjoyed by the Theatines. So began the 'Clerks Regular of St Paul,' known popularly as Barnabites because their first house in Rome stood on the site of an ancient church dedicated to St Paul's fellow apostle. The Barnabites differed somewhat from the Theatines in their taste for liturgical splendour (which appealed so strongly to St Aloysius Gonzaga), in their use of such devotions as Perpetual Adoration, and in their work as teachers. They too spread, despite the premature death of their young leader at the age of thirty-five; and it was to them that St Francis of Sales had recourse when he planned to reorganize the education of his diocese.

The radiance of the Oratory becomes once more apparent in yet another of its disciples: Jerome Aemilian [1] (1481–1537), founder of the Congregation of Somascha. He likewise adopted the system of clerks regular when he decided to gather round him a body of men equally obsessed with the general misery and resolved to fight it with the charity of Christ. Orphanages, hospitals, refuges for prostitutes—all that could render the sufferings of mankind less cruel was their domain. Approved in 1540, the 'Clerks Regular of St Mayeul' were thus named after their house at Pavia; but they subsequently established themselves in the little town of Somascha, between Milan and Bergamo, and were thenceforward known more commonly as Somaschi. A fresh field soon opened to their apostolate, and they devoted themselves to the education of youth a hundred years before John Baptist de la Salle.

Theatines, Barnabites and Somaschi: those names are far from representing the whole creative activity of which the Church gave evidence at that time. The idea of 'clerks regular' was so plainly in the minds of all that it took concrete shape almost everywhere, without any apparent influence of one such institution upon the next. In various parts of Christendom, and distinct from the larger formations, a number of priests would meet together for prayer and for mutual instruction with a view to the impending struggle on behalf of Christ; and some such groups even bound themselves by religious vows. The history of these small nuclei is obscure and will probably never be written; but we

---

[1] This was his name in religion. His father was Girolamo Miami, a Venetian senator.

know, for instance, that Cardinal Sadolet was at the head of one at Carpentras, and Cardinal Fisher of another in England. One of the most energetic was formed in Spain by John of Avila (1500–69), author of the mystical treatise *Audi Filia* and a tireless apostle of the spoken word. In the cities and even the poorest villages of Andalusia he and his companions, forerunners of our rural and factory missions, spent themselves without counting the cost. The whole country was familiar with their threadbare cassocks, the burning eyes in their shrunken faces, which put to shame the harshness of the rich and the weakness of proud prelates. Huntsmen of Christ, they ran down such game as Louis of Granada, John of God and Francis Borgia. In the Sierra Morena they built churches which can be seen today, and anticipated by fifteen years the first endeavours of St Ignatius and his companions.

John Ciudad, a young Portuguese, is one example of the profound influence exercised almost everywhere by initiative of this kind. Returning to his home at Evora, after distinguishing himself in a long series of campaigns, he heard John of Avila preaching in nearby Andalusia, and was converted. Known thenceforward as John of God (1495–1550), he determined to form a group of laymen, like himself, who would take vows and lead the same sort of life as the clerks regular. Thus there was born at Granada, in 1540, the little Congregation of John of God, dedicated to the hardest tasks in the hospitals and asylums. In France its members came to be known as Fathers of Charity,[1] in Germany as Brothers of Mercy. Their selfless generosity continued to spread, and is still in evidence today.

Women were somewhat less prominent in this movement, but far from inactive. Female congregations were established whose principles were in many respects identical with those that had given rise to the clerks regular. Instead of their traditional confinement to the cloister, where they were limited to the necessary but exclusive work of contemplation, female religious were now more practically engaged in the daily combat of the Church, assisting the clergy in works of charity, education and even of apostleship. The appearance of these 'secular nuns' provoked surprise and resistance. 'Women need a husband or a cloister,' was a common saying; but the innovation was destined to bear good fruit.

The 'Angelicals of St Paul,' for instance, owed their existence to Ludovica Torelli, and were fostered by St Antony Zaccaria and his Barnabites. They devoted themselves to the care of orphans and penitent girls; and it was largely upon them that St Francis of Sales afterwards modelled his Order of the Visitation. Reorganized by Pope Benedict XV in 1919, the Angelicals are known today as Sisters of St

---

[1] At Paris they founded the Hôpital de la Charité, in the Rue des Saints-Pères; when his was laicized they moved to the Rue Oudinot.

Paul, and flourish particularly in South America. Somewhat later, again thanks to Ludovica Torelli, appeared the Daughters of Mary; they were concerned mostly with education, and were commonly called 'Guastallines.' [1] Thirdly, there was the female branch of the Theatines, established at Naples by Ursula Benincasa. But none of these institutions was destined to so glorious a future as was that founded at Brescia in 1535 by St Angela Merici. As a young woman still living in the world, but favoured by God with ecstatic visions, she beheld in the sky a Jacob's Ladder upon which virgins holding lilies ascended and descended. She therefore resolved to form an association of girls, who, though bound by monastic vows, would continue to live in the world, striving to bring God into the lives of men. The new institute took St Ursula as its patron, and was so successful that it was obliged before long to assume a more official character, to accept constitutions [2] and to become step by step a fully fledged religious order. This was the origin of the Ursulines, who received papal approval in 1544, and afterwards did for the Christian education of girls what the Jesuits did for that of boys on the morrow of Trent. The order spread far and wide, until it included no fewer than 10,000 religious. We shall find them later, in the person of Mary of the Incarnation, riding with the king's officers through the dread forests of Canada, to plant the Cross beside the fleur-de-lis.

Such then was the prodigious quickening that became apparent in many sectors of the Church, long before the Holy See undertook to direct the work of reform and determined to summon a council which would embody the results of that work in social and ecclesiastical institutions. An intense spiritual fervour revealed itself in the manifold achievements of evangelization and charitable endeavour no less than in the sphere of discipline. Countless men and women of goodwill were offering their services, and effective means were already available. This reawakening of the Catholic soul, this return to 'a religion become life,' as Léonard calls it, was undeniably rich with promise. To effect the synthesis of all those efforts and aspirations, to confer upon the resurrected Church her dowry, was the heroic destiny of a genius, of a mystic who was also an administrator—St Ignatius of Loyola.

6. IÑIGO THE BASQUE IS CALLED BY GOD

During the spring of 1521 war was resumed between France and Spain, that is to say, between François I and Charles V. The French troops, under Comte André de Foix, crossed the Pyrenees without

---

[1] Ludovica Torelli was Countess of Guastalla.

[2] Even today the 'Angelines' of Brescia observe usages that date from the time of Angela Merici; they have not accepted the Ursuline constitutions.

mishap, for their adversaries had been called away by a revolt of the grandees of Castile. Their purpose was to recover Navarre,[1] and restore it to King Jean d'Albret. The fortress of Pampeluna was ill defended: the garrison amounted to no more than a single company of pikemen and arquebusiers, under the command of a thirty-year-old captain. Finding themselves encircled by such powerful forces, the city fathers at once began to talk of opening their gates; but the young military comman-dant would not agree. The Duke of Najera, as viceroy, had entrusted him with the defence of this place, and he would not surrender without a fight, however unequal the contest might prove to be. Shut up in the citadel with a handful of loyal troops, he had held out for six days, as a matter of honour, when a bullet suddenly ricocheted off a wall and struck him in the legs, one of which was gashed and the other broken. With him resistance collapsed. His name was Iñigo Lopez de Recalde; he was born at the castle of Loyola, in the heart of Guipuzcoa, one of the Basque provinces.

War in those days had its peculiar refinements. The French officers behaved with great gallantry towards their brave prisoner: they got an army surgeon to dress his wounds and make some sort of an attempt to reset the broken bone; then they had him carried in a litter along the rugged roads of Navarre to his birthplace, where the grateful victim presented his escort with some fine specimens of inlaid armour. But the body set down by its bearers in the ancient hall was indeed a sorry thing. The wounds showed no signs of healing, and the broken tibia, so badly set, had been displaced by the jolting of the litter. It was unthinkable that a Spanish officer should be thus permanently dis-figured, and the wounded man gave orders for a second operation, which he endured with clenched fists but without a groan—'sheer butchery' as he afterwards described it. Moreover it was unavailing; for the bone, broken a second time and reset, continued to protrude below the knee. So they had to saw off the point, then stretch the shortened leg with boards, ropes and weights, while Iñigo de Loyola suffered in stoic silence.

What had been his motive? Pride and concern for his appearance no doubt. What good is an invalid soldier, a well-bred captain become bandy-legged and lame? Providence, however, apparently intended to oppose a barrier to his vain desires, and he was soon obliged to bow before the inevitable. He would never again be the handsome cavalier with his embroidered doublet and gleaming breastplate, the cynosure of female eyes. He had dreamed of life in the style of *Amadis des Gaules*, full of doughty deeds, but must now reconcile himself to being no more than a cripple. But physical suffering, and this kind of humiliating

[1] Ferdinand the Catholic had seized it nine years earlier, while Louis XII was preoccu-pied with his Milanese adventure.

experience which deprives a proud man of bodily strength, are often the means employed by God to bring him back to a sense of moderation and requisite humility. Iñigo's long convalescence within the frowning walls of the ancient *castillo* was quickly transformed into a spiritual retreat. At first he felt a stirring of rebellion against his absurd fate, against a future devoid of hope. Haunted by idle dreams of a worldly life, of love and battles, his thoughts turned to the lady of his heart, for, like every *hidalgo*, he was devoted to a lady, and his was of most illustrious birth. He asked himself 'what he would have to do in her service, what words he would speak to her, what feats of arms he would accomplish on her behalf.' But stern reality dragged him from such fantasies. All that was finished: never would he enter the distant castle and rescue the Infanta Catalina from her dismal fate, unhappy Catalina, daughter of Joanna the Mad, whose secluded life she was condemned to share. What then? What destiny awaited him? It was at this point of his journey that Christ lay in wait for him, to conquer and enlighten.

In his father's library, to which he hobbled along the corridors, he had exhausted all the romances of chivalry. A few books still remained on the niggardly shelves, pious treatises covered with dust. He took them down: *The Flower of the Saints*, a Spanish adaptation of Jacobus de Voragine's *Golden Legend*; Ludolph the Carthusian's *Life of Christ*, which Cardinal Ximenes had had translated into Castilian. Opening these volumes simply because he had nothing better to do, the invalid was surprised to find himself absorbed. He was, as it were, locked in conflict with himself: two currents of thought opposed one another, two contrary dreams fought for mastery of his soul. The history of St Dominic and St Francis, above all, roused in him a strange sense of exaltation. Why should he not do what the saints had done? Might not divine assistance enable him to satisfy that thirst for greatness which he could not quench by human means? It was the first summons of the ineffable Voice, as yet ill defined and unobtrusive. 'God was beginning to overcome the devil in my soul,' he afterwards said of this period. It was not spiritual anguish, such as had ridden Luther, that was driving him to seek a new road, but a sort of inverted pride, of native arrogance. The ways of the Lord are incomprehensible. In the fine summer nights of 1521 Iñigo de Loyola, having climbed to the summit of the castle, would spend long hours watching the sky with its myriads of stars; and there he came to understand that a force more powerful than his will had taken charge of his life. He knew he had been called.

It would be false to say that he had not been hitherto a Christian. In his country at that time there was no one who did not stand fast by the Christian faith, even when faith did not exclude the gravest moral shortcomings. A man is no true Spaniard unless he is a Catholic, and in that land, where the Reconquista had been completed only thirty years earlier with the capture of Granada, the faith was such an integral member of the national conscience that a young knight, swashbuckler and libertine though he might be, would simply not have understood the question if asked whether he believed. The cripple of Loyola was a typical product of his race as well as of his country. Though a son of the Basques, who while attaching themselves to Spain had kept their pride and the certitude of accomplishing a great individual destiny within the Iberian kingdom, he was yet a brother of those crusaders who, in the course of centuries, had rewon their country from the Moors, brother likewise of those conquistadors who were even then winning new worlds for their king, as well as of those mystics who, at the same time, were undertaking the perilous ascent of the high peaks of the soul. His Christian name, Iñigo,[1] was that of a venerable Benedictine abbot who had governed a monastery in the neighbourhood of Loyola. His family, long rooted in the vale of Urola—in its stony hillsides rather than among the maize and apple-trees of the plain—had been from time immemorial a nursery of soldiers. The seven red bendlets of their arms recalled the exploits of their ancestor, Juan Perez, who, with his seven sons, had spent a lifetime in the battlefield. Iñigo had eight sisters and four brothers. Of the latter, one had fallen before Naples, another before Mexico City, while a third was later killed fighting against the Turks on Hungarian soil. His childhood was similar to that of many boys of his rank : his early education was backed with liberal use of the rod; his parents vaguely intended him for the Church, but he was soon driven to embrace a career of arms and placed in the service of a high personage. None of those factors, however, had prepared him for his ultimate destiny. The pious influence of his mother had been withdrawn too early, and he used to say that he had found little among the whole warrior class but traditions of sin; only one of his brothers took holy orders, and his conduct was far from edifying. Yet it was precisely from these elementary fidelities, in this brand of faith confused with the sense of honour, in this ancestral violence on behalf of just causes, that he would derive the strength which urged him forward along a new road. The crusading spirit which he had inherited was leading him, more determinedly than he himself was aware, towards the crucial decision he was about to take. All his life he would remain a soldier, but henceforward a soldier of God.

The interior debate was resolved. 'The discernment of spirits' took place little by little, not in the gloomy resignation of an invalid disgusted with life, but in the choice of a new vocation more exacting

---

[1] He afterwards abandoned it to call himself after the great martyr St Ignatius of Antioch—a name better known throughout the world and more significant perhaps of his own designs.

than that which Iñigo renounced. All the attractions of life in the world appeared to him insipid compared with those he was beginning to discover in another life. Copying 'lovingly' whole pages of the spiritual treatises he was reading—the words of Our Lady in blue, those of Christ in red—praying ceaselessly, with ever-growing fervour, he came to feel within himself the operation of a silent decision, a tranquil obedience to the summons he had heard. Heaven itself assisted him. 'Lying awake one night,' he later told a friend, 'I saw clearly an image of Our Lady with the Child Jesus. From this vision, for a considerable space of time, I received such consolation as to be completely overwhelmed. And immediately I experienced such disgust with my past life, especially with my wickedness, that I seemed to feel my soul scraped clean of all that had been so deeply imprinted there.' All that he had found strongest within himself—the warlike spirit, sexual temptations, the pride of a nobleman and a soldier—was henceforth transformed and directed to other goals. As yet he knew not how he would employ these new forces, whether on crusade or in the extreme asceticism of the Charterhouse; but he was determined to 'perform those great feats which the saints have accomplished for the glory of God.'

Caballeria a lo divino, divine chivalry: Christ's cavalier was now inwardly prepared. So he left the castle that had been his home, 'dressed according to his rank, armed and accompanied by two servants.' After spending a whole night in prayer in the church of Our Lady of Aranzazu, dear to the folk of Guipuzcoa, he set out for the celebrated Benedictine abbey of Montserrat, in Catalunya, one of the main centres of Spanish loyalties. An unfortunate incident on the road made him realize how far he still was from the love of God. A Moslem gentleman, with whom he travelled part of the way, called in question the virginity of the Mother of Christ. Iñigo's first reaction was to challenge him to a duel and kill him; second thoughts, however, stayed his hand, and he knew not what to do. From this embarrassment he escaped by the pleasant expedient of leaving it to his horse, like another Balaam's ass, to show him the will of God. At the next crossroads he allowed it to choose whether it would take the same route as the Moor or follow another path, and the animal chose the way of meekness. God's cavalier had still to learn, among many things, the charity of Christ.

The old Adam still clung to him, but was sloughed off at the end of a short retreat, which, though it lasted for only three days, was conducted with exemplary thoroughness and determination. On that fantastic mountain whose Wagnerian rocks might have concealed the Holy Grail, at the feet of that statue of Our Lady which was said to have been miraculously preserved during the Moslem invasion, young men kept vigil before their admission to the ranks of knighthood. So too did

*B

Ignatius of Loyola—not to gird on arms at break of day, but to put them by once and for evermore. He laid his sword and dagger before Our Lady of Battles, divested himself of doublet, breastplate, all the trappings of this world, and donned the humbler garb of a pilgrim—sandals, staff and all. He handed a written confession, detailed and exhaustive, to one of the monks (a Frenchman named Jean Chanones), and at last obtained peace of mind. His new guide gave him in return Garcia de Cisneros's *Exercises of the Spiritual Life*, a book that would lead him faithfully on the road he wished to follow.

What was that road, and through what country would it pass? As yet he did not know, and he sought it in a strange direction. Having, like some anchorite of the Thebaïd, assumed the dress of a penitent, with long beard, hair and nails, he went and took up his abode at Manresa, a large market-town of Catalunya. Here he spent a year of terrible asceticism—he who was afterwards so moderate, so prudent in this respect—endeavouring to carry renunciation and mortification to a degree seldom attained. He would not accept the hospitality of the Dominicans, who had welcomed him with open arms; he would not even shelter beneath the roof of the hospital where he devoted himself to caring for the worst cases. For weeks on end he lived all alone in a cave near the River Cardoner, eating scarcely anything, kneeling seven hours at a time absorbed in mental prayer. This régime caused his health to deteriorate and he fell sick. At the same time, however, new certainties dawned upon his mind, and it was God Himself who roused him from his reverie. Here now is his own account, taken from the impassioned *Pilgrim's Narrative*, wherein, long afterwards, he described the graph of his spiritual experience. 'One day I was going to pray in a church about a mile from Manresa, on a road which follows the bank of the Cardoner. I sat down, with the river flowing deep before me, and there the eyes of my conscience began to open. It was no vision that was granted me, but an understanding of many things—of the mind, of faith, of human knowledge—and in so clear a light that all seemed renewed from top to bottom.' What had he understood in that moment of inspired insight? He had learned that God had not called him to the eremitical life, that he was destined for other tasks which Providence would lay upon him in its own good time. He therefore decided to eat meat again, to comb his hair and bring to man the fruits of his experience. A new man came forth from the cave of Manresa.

This time of superhuman trial was by no means wasted. In long hours of silent meditation Ignatius had discovered the secret of the most difficult of conquests, the victory which every man must gain over himself. First for his own use, and later with the idea of helping others too, he recorded its elements in minute detail. 'The pilgrim,' he says, 'saw such and such a thing in his soul, then such and such another, deciding that it was useful; and so, in the belief that he would be helping others, he wrote a book.' This book, with whose precious leaves Ignatius would never part during the remainder of his life, this little book which sprang from the depths of one soul's personal experience, and which would become one of the master-works of the age, the most effective manual of warfare and conquest ever possessed by the Church, is known as the *Spiritual Exercises*.

7. A METHOD OF PRAYER BECOMES A CODE OF ACTION

In order fully to penetrate the significance of the *Spiritual Exercises*, to understand them above all in relation to the author, we must place ourselves as far as possible in the climate in which Ignatius lived during those months of unimaginable tension, where in solitude and penance he saw himself at once the battleground and the stake in a terrible conflict between good and evil, between Christ and the Devil, and where by a clear effort of will he made his choice. We have, in one of his favourite phrases, to 'make the composition.' Each paragraph, every one of those formulae whose elliptical simplicity is sometimes baffling, sums up an experience, denotes a vital means to victory discovered by the writer himself. No Christian book—not even the *Imitation*, infinitely more moving though it is—gives so poignant an impression of direct experience as does this slender volume with its atmosphere of a military manual written at the height of battle.

When Ignatius of Loyola quitted Manresa, he certainly carried with him the matter of the *Spiritual Exercises*. The form may have left much to be desired; its shape, as we have it now, is not that of the original. During the twenty-seven years between the saint's conversion and the publication of his book [1] the text was constantly retouched and enriched. Meticulous scholiasts claim to have detected traces of St Bernard, St Bonaventure and such moderns as Fray Alonzo of Madrid, with whom the author cannot have been acquainted until later. All that, however, is mere detail: it suffices to read the book itself, better still to follow its teaching, in order to feel that it was written in a climate of fire—in the Santa Cueva, the cave on the banks of the Cardoner.

Innumerable specialists have analysed the 'sources,' trying to discover from what books the hermit of Manresa derived the living sap of his own. Certainly and above all from the Gospel, whose most striking passages he had copied out and kept always by him; from such works as *The Flower of the Saints* and the Carthusian Ludolph's *Life of*

---

[1] He would not allow its publication until 1548, but by that time it had been recopied and translated by a host of retreatants.

Christ, which had first given him food for thought during his convalescence; from the *Imitation of Christ*, with which he is known to have nourished his mind during the year of his retreat; doubtless also from Cisneros's *Exercises of the Spiritual Life*, to which he had been introduced by Dom Chanones at Montserrat; and an echo has even been detected of Battista da Crema's *Self-Conquest*. Each of these books may have done something to set in train the mysterious process accomplished in the soul of Ignatius, but none has left a direct imprint of any importance. Literary exegesis gives no account of the unique originality of the *Spiritual Exercises*.

It was not in books but in the depths of his own soul that Ignatius found the essence of what he had to say, and that fact alone is quite remarkable. Considering how difficult it is for any man seeking self-knowledge to express himself in writing, one may well ask how a young officer, who could do little more than read and write, and who had only just abandoned the world and a career of arms, was able to advance so far in the most intimate knowledge of the soul and to formulate his discoveries in terms so clear, so powerful and so profound. The key-word is contained in this short precept: 'Study yourself, analyse what goes on within you, for there you have the lists where the spirit of good confronts the spirit of evil.' It was by thus analysing himself, noting his particular difficulties and the means whereby he had managed to overcome them, writing down his examination of conscience, that Ignatius eventually produced his book. Even so he must have had an extraordinary sense of inward sovereignty, of the spiritual drama, of the call uttered by God in the secret place of every man's soul, and of the mysterious means set in operation by grace. Genius he certainly possessed, but he also enjoyed divine inspiration, the direct working of the Holy Spirit on a human intellect. Ignatius himself admitted that he had on several occasions benefited by supernatural enlightenment, and a tradition confirmed by papal authority states that it was *dictante Deipara*, at the dictation of the Mother of God, that he wrote that 'perfect code of every good soldier of Jesus Christ.' [1]

Materially the *Exercises* form a very small volume, a mere booklet running to no more than a hundred pages, one-third the length of the *Imitation*, four times less than the *Christian Institute* in its original form and a mere nothing in comparison with the final edition of Calvin's monumental work. But a soldier is used to expressing himself briefly. The *Exercises* were written first in Castilian, the rugged and uncouth Castilian of the Basques, heavy with obsolete or inaccurate words, but alive at the same time with forcible phrases, concise and unforgettably to the point. Subsequently, in 1534, Ignatius translated his book into Latin, after which he adjudged his own version unsatisfactory, and

[1] Pius XI, *Letter Apostolic to the General of the Jesuits*, 3rd December 1922.

entrusted the work of preparing another to Père André de Freux. This final recasting of the *Exercises,* however, has no literary appeal: it seems calculated rather to discourage simple curiosity.

As we have it today the book is divided into four parts. But the fourth, consisting of a set of rules on the discernment of spirits, on the giving of alms, on scruples and on the manner of 'thinking with the Church,' is evidently much later than the Manresa period; it reveals the cares of a spiritual director, of a religious ruler, while the concluding section on orthodoxy appears to reflect the decrees of the Council of Sens (1528). The three fundamental elements of the work are the 'Annotations,' the 'Exercises' properly so called and the 'Meditations.' Without any wish to please his reader, Ignatius begins by explaining in great detail how he must 'acquire some understanding' of the Exercises and put them into practice. This advice runs to no fewer than twenty pages; nothing is left to chance. After a brief, closely packed and all-important passage entitled 'Principle and Foundation,' which summarizes the meaning of Christian life and experience, the Exercises begin. They are intended to cover a period of four weeks. During the first week the reader's attention is directed to the ultimate ends, and having learned the rules of self-examination and meditation, he will concentrate his mind on Sin and Hell. In the second week he will place himself in the presence of Christ and His kingdom, so that, by fully understanding the achievement of the Incarnate Word, he may 'make choice' of a life faithful to His principles, to which he will be led on the final day. The purpose of the third and fourth weeks is to constrain the soul to set out without further delay upon the chosen road, by meditating the sorrowful mysteries of the Passion, then the glorious mysteries of the Risen Christ, all of them pledges of the Creator's infinite love for His creatures. The third part of the book, called 'Meditations,' is in fact a series of rather dry formulae, devoid of comment, each element of which contributes material for a comprehensive meditation on the life of Christ, step by step from His birth to His glorious Resurrection, and thus provides as it were the skeleton of mystical experience, or the evangelical index of a spiritual treatise.

So much for the externals, the schema of the book; but it would be a mistake to call a halt at this point in the belief that it has been adequately summarized. The *Spiritual Exercises* were not written to be read, however carefully, but to be translated into reality and lived; they came from the pen of one who had himself been first to practise and live them with his whole soul. They require a man who would follow their method to give much of his own being—or rather his whole self. All the powers of the soul, heart, intelligence and sensibility must come into play. Each of the meagre formulae of which the several chapters are composed seems austere, dry and often abstract; but if one manages

to charge it with sufficient spiritual passion it becomes the gateway to
a whole world of imagination, to a whole field of meditation. And so
to make the *Exercises* properly it is not enough to read the paragraphs
one after another in order to understand their meaning; one must
release within oneself such powerful stirrings—love or hate—that
every word produces thereafter in the conscience a driving force which
urges the will irresistibly along the chosen road. The soul which has
accustomed herself to seeing Christ, hearing His words, tasting the
sweetness of His presence and sharing the atrocious sufferings endured
by Him in expiation of the iniquities of men will be restrained from
yielding to evil by the very love she has cultivated within herself;
and if she is not entirely preserved from sin she will be the less willing
to incur its guilt when she considers the horrors which await a sinful
soul—hell-fire, everlasting corruption, the malediction of the damned.
Thus accustomed to bathe in love or freeze in terror, according as she
looks upon light or darkness, the soul will be trained to confront life
with its dire risks and daily temptations, and she will be able to emerge
victorious from the combat.

For here indeed there is question of combat; the word 'exercises'
must be taken in the strictest of military senses—that of training for
battle. This little book, presented as a treatise on prayer, is more
properly a series of 'regulations,' a code of strategy for the waging
of a terrible war whose issue is nothing less than eternity. Captain
Iñigo, now become the hermit Ignatius, still thinks and writes as a
soldier. For him Christ is the king who calls upon men to enlist in
His army, in order to fight nobly at His side. The climax of the four
weeks' retreat is reached on the fourth day of the second week, with
the meditation on the 'Two Standards.' Here Ignatius shows us the
two hostile armies confronting one another: that of Christ 'in the great
land of Jerusalem' with all those who serve under His banner, and that
commanded 'in the great land of Babylon' by Lucifer 'seated on a kind
of lofty throne of fire and smoke.' The true Christian is he who has
given Christ the King his total loyalty and fights on His behalf. His
offensive weapon is the particular examination of conscience repeated
twice daily, by means of which the vices will be vanquished one by one.
Strict discipline is enforced; there must be no faint-heartedness.

This notion of combat is fundamental in Ignatian spirituality; it
presupposes and underlies a whole system of theology diametrically
opposed to that of the Protestant reformers. What would be the use of
expending so much effort in order to teach Christians the laws of combat if, in fact, the result depended solely upon God, without any co-
operation on the part of man? Ignatius certainly declares that God,
in his omniscience, knows what the result will be, and that without
grace human strength is incapable of victory. But to the quietistic

fatalism of Luther and the predestinationism of Calvin he opposes a spirituality of effort which is the main characteristic of his doctrine. Molina afterwards fashioned it into a theological systemization when dealing with the relationship of grace and free will,[1] but the principles are apparent in Ignatius's own book. One of his confidants tells us that he often used to say: 'We must work as if success depended on ourselves and not on God.' Though no less stern with men than Calvin —'without Christ,' he said, 'all would go down into hell'—Loyola believed in the possibility of curing the sick soul of renewing it by means of interior labour co-operating with grace. There you have the essence of his message, a lucid and constructive optimism which has proved to be one of the most effective weapons ever wielded by the Church.

Thus it is completely wrong to consider the *Spiritual Exercises* as an instrument employed by Catholicism in the war against Protestantism. Although substantially anti-Protestant, the thought of St Ignatius owes nothing to dialectical reaction against that of the 'reformers' of Wittenberg, or later of Geneva. 'By the favourite word "reform" he means nothing else than the necessity for everyone to change himself before wishing to change the world .... Loyola passes no judgment on the profane and complicated questions that were troubling the whole world; rather he seems, with his advice to "think with the Church," not to be concerned with the external aspects of religion— doctrine, hierarchy, liturgy, sacraments, ecclesiastical customs .... While Calvin begins his reform in the opposite direction, by a general revolution of the whole structure of the Church, Loyola is content to effect a reformation in the depths of her soul. ... Far from hypnotizing him, the confessional struggles seem for a long time to have occupied no more than the background of his thought. The effort of conquest, implied by submission of the whole world to the 'eternal and universal King,' pursues as its unique object the individual salvation and liberation of souls, of *all* souls, by the sole arms of sacrifice, humility and charity in Catholic truth,'[2] No career shows us better than does that of St Ignatius what the Catholic Reformation really was—a fundamental movement of spiritual rebirth, not a counter-attack upon the Protestant positions; none demonstrates more convincingly that it was not at first a 'counter-reformation,' but a revival proceeding from the deepest loyalties.

What was the ultimate goal of this combat in which, according to St Ignatius, the Christian is engaged? Only one answer is possible: the glory of God; all the rest is vain and laughable. On the threshold of the *Exercises*, in the first line of the 'Principle and Foundation,' we

[1] See Chapter V, p. 345.
[2] A. Favre-Dorsaz, *Calvin et Loyola*, 1951.

read this tranquil and categorical assertion: 'Man is created to praise, adore and serve God Our Saviour, and thereby to save his soul.' The two purposes are inextricably linked: interior reform, the means of salvation, is at the same time a testimony rendered to God in His perfection. Like Calvin on this point, Ignatius was literally haunted by the rights of God, by the adoration of His power, by the recognition of His sovereignty, by His glory which must for ever increase. *Ad majorem Dei gloriam:* the celebrated phrase flows constantly from his pen; in his writings and correspondence it occurs at least a thousand times. But the difference between Calvin and Loyola is that the former conceives God in fear and trembling, and causes man to cringe beneath the rod of a terrible master, while Ignatius, on the contrary, wishes gently to subject human freedom to 'infinite Goodness, the divine Mercy, eternal Wisdom and Love, the charity of Christ Our Lord.' This man, who has so often been represented as hard, unyielding, pitiless, sums up his doctrine in three lines of a letter to the scholastics of Coimbra. He speaks neither of discipline nor of the holy fear of God, but simply says: 'Above all, I want to arouse in you the pure love of Jesus Christ, the desire for His honour and for the salvation of souls redeemed by Him.'

It remains to say to whom he addressed this little book, and to what classes of souls he thought it would be 'useful.' Theoretically, I think, to all Christians. 'Exercises,' runs the subtitle, 'to lead man to conquer himself, to detach himself from all inordinate affection, to lead a Christian life.' Such a programme is exactly that which every baptized person must set before himself; and it is indeed true that *everyone*, provided he holds the Christian faith, finds in the *Exercises* something wherewith to nourish his religious life, to help him to a better understanding of himself and to control over his own soul. Upon whatever rung of the spiritual ladder one may stand, one can derive much profit from this teaching compounded of interior joy, self-discipline and obedience to high principles. For four centuries, too, the method has been used in countless ways and for the most varied purposes, giving rise to 'closed retreats,' 'Manresas' and 'Treatises on Meditation.' If innumerable saints from Francis Xavier to Alphonsus Liguori, from Charles Borromeo to Vincent de Paul, have expressed their gratitude to this little book, there is no Catholic who, though perhaps unconsciously, is not indebted to it for having taught the world the importance of recollection and silence, the necessity for spiritual concentration, and for having given him that warmth of communication with the supernatural world without which there is no true religious life.

In practice also then—and herein lies their richness—the *Exercises* are addressed to all souls without exception. They do good to the most ordinary, to those who possess neither great spiritual ambition nor a wealth of means. They also help those who have already 'made choice' to conform their lives to their vocation, and it is thus that St Francis of Sales, in his treatise *On the Love of God*, advises bishops, priests and religious to use them. More important still, as Henri Bromond had rightly observed, far from being a mere method of asceticism, they can guide the most earnest souls to the highest summits of mystical experience; they lead by way of prayer to contemplation and even to the unitive life; and it is no accident that so many contemplatives, from St Francis Borgia to Père Surin, from Balthazar Alvarez to Père Lallemant, became what they were by the simple practice of the Ignatian method. But this glory itself, this universal extension, is liable to obscure the true goal of their author. It was unintentionally, and because he carried within him the fire of exceptional genius, that St Ignatius was able to make himself understood in so many ways. His initial purpose was not so ambitious. 'As he wrote them,' says Père de Grandmaison, 'the *Exercises* had a definite end in view; their purpose was to enable a man, still free to dispose of his life and excellently endowed for the apostolate, to hear clearly and follow generously the call of God.' All good prayer should be translated into action, and the contemplative must be at the same time an apostle. Such is the logical conclusion of the spirituality of effort.

Thus, it seems, by working simply to reform the interior man, St Ignatius created a type of man of action whose effectiveness proceeds directly from the effort accomplished first at the level of conscience. Corneille's principle, 'I am master of myself as of the universe', might well sum up the purpose of that cripple who was going to produce new men to the service of God and of the Church. Or perhaps he would have said rather: 'I shall master the world to the extent that I first master myself. Even so, while the ancient world collapsed around him St Benedict intended his Rule as a method for training monks to be perfect servants of God, whereas in fact he also proposed a body of heroes who would reconstruct Western society during the 'Dark Ages.'

When he left Manresa Ignatius carried with him, probably without knowing as much, the instrument which would enable him to endow Catholicism with the most efficient of her troops. He would now put it to the test, and gather around him the first of those innumerable men who would answer the summons issued by God through his voice.[1]

---

[1] Like everything connected with St Ignatius and the Society of Jesus, those permanent signs of contradiction, the *Spiritual Exercises*, have been heavily attacked; and not only by such unbelievers as Michelet and Quinet, the last of whom said that they professed 'to create ecstatic automata in thirty days.' Catholics too have found fault with them, possibly because their rigorous method of reform interfered with too much comfortable routine, but perhaps also because the precision of that method exceeded anything else

8. PILGRIM AND STUDENT

It often happens that an idea is slow to find its objective, that the genius who forged it gropes among a variety of means and must await the hour and the event appointed by Providence. So it was with Ignatius of Loyola. Leaving Manresa at the end of February 1523 he thought of pilgrimage to the Holy Places, after the manner of St Francis of Assisi, as prelude perhaps to some kind of crusade. It was long before he finally abandoned this medieval dream.

Accordingly he took ship at Barcelona. Travelling by way of Gaeta and Rome, where he was received in audience and encouraged by the austere Pope Adrian VI, he reached Venice, which was the usual point of departure for Palestine. His health was none too good, but Ribadaneira informs us that it was improved by seasickness which 'got rid of the humours.' Six months of this stern therapy set him on his feet once more. Landing at Jaffa he performed the customary round of a pilgrim: a night of prayer at the Holy Sepulchre, visits to Bethany, Bethlehem and the Jordan ford where John baptized. Was this where God wanted him? Ought he to remain and carry the faith to Jew and Moslem? When he broached the subject with the Franciscans who looked after the Holy Places, they quickly discouraged him, unwilling that this strange Spaniard should hunt in their preserves. The Islamic authorities, they assured him, would never agree to his proposals. So Ignatius once again took ship; Christ had not called him to convert the Infidel.

What next then? He tells us in the *Pilgrim's Narrative* that 'he frequently asked himself what he ought to do; and in the end he came to the conclusion that in order to be useful to souls he would first have to study.' And so, as an elderly scholar at the age of more than thirty-three, he bravely applied himself to grammar at the University of Barcelona, leading of course at the same time a life of prayer and penance, and trying his hand at the apostolate—with more courage than moderation. It was at this time that there occurred one of the most charming episodes in his career. The fervent Basque, having found some lax nuns, won these ladies back to better ways and the observance of strict enclosure—but got beaten up by their admirers for his pains. Then, at Alcala, he devoured with frenzied but over-hasty joy all that he could of philosophy, literature, science and theology, meanwhile

---

of the kind and thereby roused jealously. When their influence began to be felt they incurred such hostility that in 1548 St Francis Borgia asked Pope Paul III to examine them. That Pope's explicit approval was the first of many which have since emanated from Rome. One of the most famous is that of Pius XI, who in 1929 wrote to Cardinal Dubois that he himself had experienced 'the holy benefits of the *Exercises*.'

visiting hospitals and religious houses, and talking to his fellow students so ardently of life in God that four of them became his inseparable companions. Here again his zeal was too impetuous, and questions were soon being asked about these strange young men who always wore brown homespun, like hermits, and who went about preaching although they were not priests. When a rumour began to circulate that they were 'Illuminati,' the ecclesiastical authorities bestirred themselves. Ignatius was arrested and held in custody for forty days, and though examination of his doctrine discovered nothing reprehensible, he was forbidden to dress like a religious or to give public instruction. Things were hardly better at Salamanca, the intellectual centre of Spain, which was controlled by the Dominicans. These latter were even more seriously alarmed by the Basque preacher: twelve days after his arrival Ignatius was apprehended and brought before the Inquisition, doubtless on suspicion of being a secret *alumbrado*, if not a Lutheran or an Erasmian. After three long weeks, during which the *Exercises* were subjected to careful scrutiny, the judges announced that they could find no trace of error in the thought or life of the student and his companions, who were therefore authorized to continue preaching and teaching the catechism within prescribed limits. These trials, however, had determined Ignatius to look beyond the Spanish border for a field in which liberty of thought and action would be less precarious. Notwithstanding the remonstrances of his friends, who pointed out the dangers that lay in wait for him in a distant country, of whose language he was ignorant and which was even then at war with Spain, he set out for France and eventually reached Paris.

His sojourn in the French capital was decisive. The great city was in the throes of intellectual and emotional ferment: the humanism of Guillaume Budé was opposed to the old scholasticism; Luther's books were passed from hand to hand and eagerly read, despite their condemnation by the Parlement and the Sorbonne. It was said that François I and his sister Marguerite were sympathetic towards the new ideas. The Collège des Lecteurs Royaux was about to open its doors alongside the Sorbonne, the Collège de Navarre, and the Franciscan and Dominican schools. It was not, however, to this intellectual excitement that Ignatius responded, but to the more solid element of sober wisdom in the life of Paris. The climate of the Île-de-France exerted a moderating influence upon the fiery Spaniard, and rid the medieval hidalgo of his wilder dreams. He came to realize that the spiritual knowledge he had acquired in solitude at Manresa must be associated with other forms of learning, such as are obtained by study and hard work. At Alcala and Salamanca he had been in too much of a hurry. Embarking therefore upon a regular course of studies, and attending the Dominican classes at Saint-Jacques as well as those of the

Lecteurs Royaux, he set himself to follow the same way of life as that led by students half his age. He registered as a day pupil, first at Montaigu, the famous college of which Béda was president, and then at Sainte-Barbe, which provided a more thorough course in philosophy. Despite his maturity he had the wisdom and strength of mind to spend no fewer than seven years rebuilding his foundations. At a later period this long and meticulous preparation seemed to him so necessary that he made it obligatory when drawing up the Constitutions of the Society.

9. IGNATIUS AT THE AGE OF FORTY

Let us now take a look at this ageing scholar as he limps through the narrow streets of La Montagne Sainte-Geneviève. Some of his young class-mates were already beginning to see him as a leader, but it was certainly not to the prestige of money or of birth that he owed this increasing ascendancy. A younger son from Guipuzcoa had no standing in Paris; and during these seven years Ignatius remained as poor as he had been when, with his few belongings loaded on a mule, he climbed from the banks of the Seine in search of board and lodging. In order to earn his daily bread and defray the cost of his studies, he had to make do as best he could, and was obliged on days of utter penury to go begging like the Franciscans. In the summer, for at least two years running, he betook himself to Flanders and even to England, where some Spanish merchants took pity on him and loosened their purse-strings. He was actually so destitute of means that after obtaining his B.A. in 1533 he had to wait a year before receiving the doctorate, because he could not pay the necessary fees, let alone provide the customary banquet. No one would have guessed that this needy student, who had to share his room with another, was already destined to a most glorious future.

His outward appearance was equally unimpressive. Apart from that poor leg whose shortened bone gave him a permanent limp, he was far from what is commonly called 'handsome.' He was not tall, and seemed at any rate to be devoid of strength; one could only describe him as a little fellow from the mountains, gnarled and lean, his face sunburnt and deeply furrowed. Yet his countenance was remarkable, perhaps on account of a lofty brow whose effect was heightened by his lameness; perhaps because of those strange ears, or the blood vessel that throbbed at his temples. Most surprising of all were his eyes, half veiled by heavy lids, and which, in the astonishing portrait by Sanchez Coello,[1] gave so powerful an impression of looking into the beholder, of considering only the inner man.

[1] In the cathedral at Madrid.

He was not a 'good speaker', as the words are used of an orator or a skilful dialectician. Even in Spanish he retained the accent of his native province, its manner of speech and even many of its peculiar phrases. His Latin was clumsy; when speaking French or Italian he lapsed quickly into patois. And yet in private conversation, or when addressing a small gathering or a crowd, he held the attention of his hearers from the very start. A countryman, used to slow and solitary reflection, he was able to condense the fruits of his thought into the most striking sentences. As Cardinal Carpi observed, 'he could hit the nail on the head.' It is in these brilliant flashes that his intelligence is revealed, an intelligence, however, more solid than sparkling, more original in substance than in appearance.

There was nothing of Calvin in Ignatius of Loyola. He was not one of those towering geniuses who move with sovereign grace among ideas and forms, and upon whom the gifts of intellect seem to have been conferred by destiny. In order to learn and to understand he needed patient research, conducted with modest means and suspicious of intuitive perception. One thing, however, he possessed in common with Calvin, with Luther, and indeed with all the most influential figures of history. This was an enormous, an unlimited, capacity for work. He could spend the whole day attending lectures, helping his neighbours, discussing the most abstract themes—and then pass most of the night reading and writing in the circle of his lamp. We possess no fewer than 6,742 letters from his hand; they fill twelve large volumes, and doubtless represent less than one-half of his entire correspondence. As General of the Society he was never more devoted to his task than as a student at Sainte-Barbe or Montaigu.

It must be admitted that when we of today approach these letters with our twentieth-century outlook, they seem rather cold and slightly dull. Yet, though they lack the impetuous flash of Luther, the hidden flame of Calvin, we must admire their sovereign calm, their logic and their *moderation*. Here perhaps we have the epithet most characteristic of Ignatius. He is serene, firm, wonderfully self-controlled. Luther was prone to ungovernable rage; and it has been said of Calvin by Doumergue, his most enthusiastic panegyrist, that 'he gave way too frequently to hysterics.' The *Spiritual Exercises* would not be what they are if their author had not possessed a conscience absolutely self-assured, trained to army discipline and capable of applying military principles in the spiritual domain. 'Ignatius,' says one witness, 'was never heard to abuse anyone or use a scornful word. In adversity he showed only joy. Later on, when he found that the Archbishop of Toledo was endeavouring to destroy his work in Spain, Ignatius merely said: 'This trial proves that the Lord expects great things of us.' There is no trace of umbrage, rancour or envy, any more than of fear, doubt or excitability. 'He seemed,' Ribadaneira tells us, 'to be free of all interior trouble, of all that can disturb the soul.' When Pope Paul IV attacked him with merciless criticism, Ignatius only smiled and said: 'Let us remember Pope Marcellus, who was a saint and loved us.' The same moderation is evident in his personal relationships. One of the Society's first historians wrote of him with perfect truth: 'He loves his sons, but with good sense and reserve; he is roused, but with prudence and discrimination; he punishes, but with calm and moderation.'

He has been accused of 'hardness,' and hard indeed he was if that word is taken to mean that he never gave way on fundamental issues. He was hard as a soldier must be, for it was no easy war that he was called upon to wage. As head of a great institution he would have to eliminate without fear or favour every doubtful element, all who were weak, hesitant or rebellious; and it was these measures, together with penances which seem to us unfair, that drove Zapata to exclaim: 'I would rather obey fifty superiors than one Ignatius.' But this kind of hardness involved no hardness of heart, from which he was as far removed as it is possible to be. One of his companions took advantage of his confidence and robbed him; yet when Ignatius heard that the thief had fallen sick, he hurried to his bedside, embraced him and forgave him. When, as head of the Jesuits, he learned of the apostasy of Ochino, General of the Capuchins, far from making fun of the affair and giving vent to bitter mirth, as did so many others, he wrote to assure the miscreant that if he desired to return to the Church, he (Ignatius) and all his brethren would be there to welcome and assist him. The charity of Christ is no empty phrase for one who conceives 'the greater glory of God' as an extension of love and justice. 'It is not in words but in deeds that love must first express itself,' he says in the *Exercises*. This notion of charity undoubtedly goes far to explain the radiance of his personality and his ascendancy over others. Later one of his spiritual sons, Gonzales de Camara, paid him this tribute which certainly represents the common opinion: 'Our Father Ignatius is so universally loved that there is no member of the whole Society who does not love him and who is not sure of being equally loved by him.'

But the mysterious prestige of this little gnome-like man rested upon something more than beauty of character; it arose chiefly from the manifest quality of his soul, as is testified by all who knew him well. Once in his students days, while begging in Spanish Flanders, he was received and assisted by the great humanist Luis Vivès, who murmured on parting from him: 'That man's a saint; one day we shall see him at the head of a new Order.' His young fellow student Pierre le Fèvre exclaimed: 'Through this man Our Lord has enabled me to see deep down into my own conscience.' No truer word was ever spoken. In his company a man felt raised above himself, placed quite naturally in a climate of heroic greatness—the selfsame perhaps (on a spiritual level) as that of Spain under the Catholic sovereigns and Don Quixote, the climate of St Teresa and St John of the Cross. Because he himself was filled with God, Ignatius radiated God and the Spirit which animated him; and if he loved any man, any one of his brethren, it was only 'in order to make him serve and glorify God.'

Such was the secret of Ignatius, a poor student at the age of forty, in whose unfurnished room there gradually assembled two, three, and soon six or seven, enthusiasts. He talked to them all; but he did more than talk. In order to teach them how to live he allowed them to copy his first written work, with which he never parted. Surely indeed it was there that the secret of his influence lay, there in those hundred or so pages of military regulations. As soon as a man had understood the lesson and absorbed its substance, he was launched upon a new way of life. The Inquisitor at Paris, having had occasion to examine the little book, was so filled with admiration that he begged the favour of a copy. The *Spiritual Exercises* form a single entity with the personality and very soul of Ignatius: they are inseparable. And it was thus that there gathered round the crippled Basque of Montaigu and Sainte-Barbe a nucleus from which would spring the Society of Jesus.

10. The Vow of Montmartre and the Bull of Paul III

On the morning of 15th August 1534, the feast of Our Lady's Assumption, along an arduous and stony road that lay through vines and rabbit warrens, seven men, nearly all of them young, were climbing the slope of that isolated hillock situated about one and a quarter miles beyond the city wall and known to Parisians as Mont des Martyrs. Having left Mont Sainte-Geneviève at first light, they had walked for nearly two hours reciting prayers, while about them hung an air of mystery and urgency. On the summit of 'Montmartre,' as if to show them their goal, the windmills turned white sails in the rising sun. These seven students were bound for the crypt-like chapel in the ancient Benedictine Abbey, which commemorated the Holy Bishop Denys who was supposed to have been beheaded on this spot. Lameness notwithstanding the eldest among them was in the lead.

The little band represented a fair cross-section of society: it included rich and poor, sons of peasants and noblemen of high rank. Pierre le Fèvre, a Savoyard, had been sent by the Bishop of Geneva to study for the priesthood at Paris, and he had just celebrated his first Mass. His room-mate at Sainte-Barbe, Francisco de Yasu, a native of Xavier in Navarre, was noticeable because of his aristocratic bearing. There were also three Spaniards: Diego Laynez, son of a tradesman at Almazan and a former student of Alcala; Nicolas, surnamed Bobadilla from his native village, more wealthy in brains than in hard cash; and little Alonzo Salmeron, whose precocious learning could not obscure the gaiety of his nineteen years. Lastly there was the Portuguese Simon Rodriguez, a man of noble descent, obsessed with the dream of vast lands to be won for the Gospel along the routes opened up to his countrymen by Henry the Navigator. All of them acknowledged as their head the lean, limping man who was now showing them the way, and who was senior to the eldest of them by fifteen years. They were indebted to him for the grand design which directed their steps to the chapel on Montmartre.

He had won them over one by one, in the course of passionate arguments such as have been beloved by students in every age. It is a strange sight, and one that says much for the reputation of Ignatius, to see these brilliant youths, many of them rich and all talented, bow before an elderly student and receive from him words of command that would decide their vocation. One after another he had taken them in hand, picking out with unerring sagacity those who would be able to appreciate his design, and displaying the ability to talk to each one in the language that would appeal most to him. Having first shaken them out of complacency, he had gone on to explain his famous method to them, requiring them in turn to perform the *Exercises*; and in each case the effect had been conclusive. Pierre le Fèvre, hitherto unsure of his vocation, had determined to receive Holy Orders. Francis Xavier, obsessed with temporal ambition, had come to understand the Gospel saying that it profits a man nothing to gain the whole world if he loses his soul. Thus was formed this little band, linked together by love of the interior life, a fraternal group without rule or formal obligations, wherein each would strive to help the other in the difficult warfare against self, pooling their slender resources, their knowledge and their prayers.

This small circle, formed for the purpose of mutual aid in the spiritual field, had no idea whatever of constituting themselves a body of shock troops, that fanatical army for the crushing of heresy, which too many historians have pretended to discover in the Society of Jesus. It was much more like one of those small associations which the Oratory of Divine Love was even then establishing in many villages up and down Italy, though perhaps with the additional clear-cut aim of evangelization. The seven companions seemed to pay little attention to the dramatic events precipitated by religious issues in the French capital. There is no mention in their writings and correspondence of the first executions of Lutherans and that of the humanist Louis de Berquin in 1529, of the vitriolic sermon preached on the feast of All Saints 1533 by the rector of the university, or of Calvin's flight; nor do they refer

to the tragic affair of the Placards which broke out two months after
the vow of Montmartre.[1] No, these young men had nothing to do with
the various groups of Evangelicals, Bible punchers and Lutherans who
were beginning to swarm throughout the kingdom. On that point they
had satisfied the Inquisition, which, though momentarily suspicious,
had approved their life and teaching. If they had any share in the
strange religious fervour which troubled so many souls at that time, it
was not with a view to altering the foundations of the Church, but to
labouring 'for the greater glory of God.'

As to the precise manner in which they would employ their vocation,
they had as yet reached no final decision. The plan which Ignatius had
formed is described in the *Memoirs* of his Portuguese companion,
Simon Rodriguez, the fellow countryman of Bartholomew Diaz and
Vasco da Gama: 'Having all decided, in a wonderful outburst of
spiritual joy, to devote themselves even unto death to whatever might
increase the glory of God, they agreed unanimously that they would all
start for Jerusalem, leaving the decision to Him.' Several years, however, and a wealth of experience were necessary before they came to
understand that old Europe offered the heralds of the Gospel as vast a
field as pagan territory. Before climbing Montmartre they had resolved
to take a vow binding themselves as champions of Christ in distant
lands.

In that tiny chapel, remote from the crowds, they heard Mass. Pierre
le Fèvre, the only one of them as yet ordained, was the celebrant. Just
before receiving Communion, Ignatius, in the name of them all,
pronounced the triple vow to observe evangelical poverty and perfect
chastity, and to go to Jerusalem in order to labour for the conversion of
the Infidel. But in obedience to what must have been a supernatural
intuition he added that if their efforts to reach the Holy Land had
proved unsuccessful at the end of a year, they would go to Rome and
place themselves unreservedly at the Pope's disposition. It was this last
vow which, though they knew it not, would direct them to their true
path. 'They spent an entire day in boundless fraternal joy, assuring one
another of their common desire to serve God; and at sunset they
returned home, blessing and praising Him.' On that memorable day,
15th August 1534, the Society of Jesus may be said to have been born,
although it had to wait some time before receiving its name and official
Constitutions.

It remained to be seen how the seven companions would employ
themselves, whether they would obey their missionary vow or invite

[1] The only point at which it is possible to detect an influence *a contrario* exerted by
current ideas on the little Ignatian group was their unanimous undertaking that they would
never, as priests, accept stipends for their Masses or other sacerdotal functions; 'Not,'
says Simon Rodriguez, 'that they considered the practice illicit, but in order to shut the
mouths of heretics.'

the Pope to make use of them. Ignatius was unable to set out at once for Italy on the first stage of the journey to Jerusalem and the goal of their desire. He had been taken ill, and had been ordered by his doctors to seek a change of air at Loyola, his home. Here humility forbade him to revisit the ancestral castle; he lodged in the Magdalen hospital, resuming his former life of almsgiving, penance, visits to the sick and preaching. Once again too there were snarls, suspicions, and even importunate entreaties on the part of his family, who disapproved of their shabby relative. As soon as he was able therefore he resumed his travels, turned his back on ungrateful Spain, which he never revisited, and made for Venice where he would be able to rejoin his friends.

The latter, despite his absence, had deviated no whit from the line he had appointed. So deep was the impression made upon them by their leader and by the *Exercises* that it would never have entered their heads, in the words of Laynez, 'to abandon the rule left by our Father and Master Ignatius,' which was administered in his name by 'the excellent Master Pierre le Fèvre.' They held frequent meetings at which they encouraged one another in their spiritual effort, and helped one another to the necessities of life. The little company actually increased: on 15th August 1535, when they solemnly renewed their vows for the first time, Le Fèvre introduced his compatriot Claude le Jay. Next year two new recruits were admitted: Paschase Broet, from Picardy, and the Dauphinois Jean Codure. Life was a gay and joyous experience. In the autumn of 1536, notwithstanding cold, hunger and the insecurity of travel in time of war, they set out through eastern France, southern Germany and Switzerland—regions full of Lutheranism—preaching wherever they could. So grave and modest was their bearing that a peasant of Lorraine, who saw them pass, called out in his expressive lingo: 'They're off to put some furrin place to rights.'

At Venice they rejoined their leader, who had been waiting there for eighteen months and had made some useful conquests: Pietro Contarini, nephew of the cardinal; Gaspar de Doctis, an auditor at the nunciature; John Helyar, an Englishman, secretary to Cardinal Pole; and, above all, three Spaniards, Diego de Hoces and the brothers Eguia. The reunion took place in January 1537. Some months later Ignatius and those of company who were not yet priests were ordained at Venice; and the officiating bishop afterwards declared that of all the ordinations which he had ever conducted none had made so deep an impression upon him as had this.

The critical hour was at hand. War was raging. The Mediterranean, a prey to Barbary pirates, was also the scene of conflict between the imperial navies and those of Genoa in the service of France. Ignatius had withdrawn to a tumbledown house at Vicenza, seeking in prayer and contemplation an answer to his problem. Thither he summoned his companions, who suggested that, while waiting to start for Palestine, it might be useful for them to enter the universities so as better to prepare themselves for the great tasks of the apostolate. Though separated from one another they would be none the less united by their vows, by fraternal love and by the very organization imposed upon them by their leader.

This was all very fine; but the grand project of missionary work in Palestine was proving unrealizable, and Ignatius was beginning to see that they would have to fall back upon the final clause of their vow. At this juncture too he experienced another flash of enlightenment such as he had had years ago at Manresa, on the banks of the Cardoner; it came to him one day as he was praying in the church of S. Pietro in Vivarolo at Vicenza. Accordingly he set out for Rome, and as he neared the journey's end he distinctly heard two phrases ringing in his ears: 'I want you to be My servant.' 'Go, I will be favourable to you at Rome.' These messages could surely proceed from none but Him in whose name the Apostle had established the Church upon the Seven Hills. Moreover, as we learn from Bobadilla, Pope Paul III had said to some of his companions who had arrived in the Eternal City ahead of him: 'Why are you so anxious to go to Jerusalem? Italy is just as good as Jerusalem if you seek to benefit the Church of God.'

The problem was now solved. These soldiers of Christ, so faithful to their vow and determined to place themselves at the service of the Pope, could not but listen to the call of a pontiff who had been roused by the reiterated appeal of the entire Church, who was anxious to begin the work of reform regardless of all the obstacles in his way, and who would at long last summon the oft-promised Council.[1] Besides, the Holy Father was using the companions of Ignatius in confidential missions even before their status had been canonically established by papal Bull. In 1539 he sent Fr Broet to reform a monastery at Siena, Fr Bobadilla to pacify the island of Ischia, Frs Laynez and Le Fèvre to inspect the city of Parma and then to teach in the recently founded College of the Sapienza. Next year Fr Le Jay was entrusted with a mission to Brescia. Soon afterwards Fr Le Fèvre accompanied the diplomat Pedro Ortiz as official theologian at the Diet of Worms; and while Frs Francis Xavier and Simon Rodriguez started on their missionary undertaking in the Indies, at the invitation of King John III of Portugal, there was a question of appointing Frs Salmeron and Broet apostolic nuncios in Ireland and Scotland. It was a curious situation: a religious institute which as yet had no canonical existence and included a mere handful of men was nevertheless already playing an important rôle in the Church.

[1] See Chapter II, section 2.

Success of this kind inevitably failed to please everyone. Ecclesiastical jealousy is well known to be inventive, and care for God's glory often adopts the most extraordinary forms. The fame of their sermons —particularly those delivered in Spanish by Ignatius at the church of S. Maria de Montserrat—did not win the unqualified approval of the Dominicans and Franciscans. The infant order of Theatines, after briefly considering amalgamation with these vigorous newcomers, proved no more friendly; one of its leaders was the powerful Carafa, with whom Ignatius had dealt somewhat brusquely in an open letter. Even the commission of cardinals [1] entrusted by the Pope with preparations for reform and the summoning of a council looked with a jaundiced eye upon the emergence of a new religious order, especially one that rejected choral office and wore no distinctive habit.

Eventually, however, the various obstacles were removed. By skilful use of all the powerful friends he could muster,[2] and by procuring the celebration of three thousand Masses for the success of his cause, Ignatius held his ground and finally won the day. Constitutions were drawn up, creating an apostolic order to be governed by an elected superior in a spirit of military discipline, which would undertake to serve no end other than the will of the Pope. 'Thus,' wrote Bobadilla, 'Divine Providence had changed the vows of Montmartre into others more fruitful.' Paul III saw clearly what a marvellous instrument had been offered him for the tasks he meant to undertake. On 27th September 1540 the Bull *Regimini militantis Ecclesiae* canonically established the Society of Jesus. In the written oath taken by this new organism it was said that the members engaged themselves to go wherever the Pope might send them, either among the Turks or other infidels, or among heretics and schismatics, as well as among the faithful. The Church could henceforward rely upon this *corps d'élite* in the struggle that lay ahead.

11. THE CONSTITUTIONS

The elements of organization submitted to the Pope were merely an outline: more detailed Constitutions were indispensable. Ignatius was unanimously elected head of the Society by his friends in 1541, despite the reluctance inspired by his humility, and he now bent himself to a task which was to take him ten years. First he carefully studied the rules of other Orders, meditated the lessons of experience, having in view the work which already occupied his spiritual sons in various fields, and listened to the objections and suggestions which many of

---

[1] It included Contarini, Sadolet and Reginald Pole.
[2] Pietro Contarini interceded with his uncle, and Ortiz, hitherto mistrustful, showed himself a firm supporter.

them put forward. Then, with the help of Fr de Polanco, his secretary, he drew up a body of regulations at once so firm and so moderate, so simple and so clear, that a Protestant historian [1] has seen fit to pay him this tribute: 'As an organizer, its author is undoubtedly one of the greatest geniuses that have ever lived.'

Created by a soldier for the purpose of spiritual warfare, the Society had several elements of a military nature. We must not of course over-estimate them, as has been done by certain of his enemies, who have compared his spirit with that of Prussian militarism; but they are none the less apparent. Ignatius himself used to say: 'I do not consider myself as having retired from military service, but only as having come under the orders of God.' As in the army then, his essential principle was obedience. The Constitutions declare that anyone desiring to enter the Society 'must strip himself of all earthly affection towards his family, in order to love them only with that well-ordered love required by charity; for being dead to the world, he lives only for Our Lord, who has taken the place of his parents, brethren and all else besides.' He must incline his whole will, submit entirely to his Superior, 'out of respect and love for Jesus Christ, whom he represents. He must be utterly docile in the Superior's hands, must abandon any and every occupation at his command, leaving unfinished even a single letter of the alphabet. He must obey his orders promptly, earnestly and with interior joy; he must be convinced, in brief, that in living under obedience one ought to allow oneself to be led by the will of Divine Providence, through the agency of the Superior, like a corpse—*perinde ac cadaver*—which can be carried anywhere and handled in any way, or, rather, like a staff which an old man holds to use at his discretion.' [2]

Perinde ac cadaver. These celebrated words have given rise to much debatable comment. To attribute them exclusively to St Ignatius, either as praiseworthy or as reprehensible, is equally absurd. The neces-sity for obedience is in full accord with the most ancient tradition as represented by St Basil, St Augustine and St Benedict; and it was probably from Franciscan tradition, perhaps from Thomas Celano's charming life of the Poverello, that the founder of the Society of Jesus derived the idea that subjects 'humiliated, moved from one place to another, ill-treated or honoured, must remain, like corpses, imperturb-able in their humility.' It may also be asked whether the terms of the Constitutions quoted above are any more severe than those of Christ Himself, which bid a man 'leave his father and mother,' to consider himself 'dead to self' and 'to lose his life in order to save it.' Absolute dependence, in the view of St Ignatius, was a free obedience based upon

---

[1] H. Böhmer, *Les Jesuites*, Paris, 1909.
[2] Thomas of Celano attributed these words to St Francis.

the man's will to conquer himself, to reform himself, and to give himself entirely to an ideal which transcends him. Though a reaction against the individualism preached by the spokesmen of the Renaissance, the Jesuit discipline tended to the highest of all human attainments—the clear-sighted and resolute sacrifice of self. Far from being a slave in the hands of more or less unknown masters, as many still profess to believe,[1] the Jesuit was a man raised above himself in order to serve of his own free will.

Ignatius devoted a large part of the Constitutions to this matter of selection and training. 'As regards recruitment,' says Böhmer, 'perhaps no other congregation has shown itself so cautious as the Society of Jesus in the reception of new members. Ignatius considered no one fully qualified unless he were healthy, in the prime of life, of good personal appearance, intelligent and of a disposition at once energetic and serene.' Just so, an army will accept none but vigorous and healthy men. The Constitutions are devised to exclude those who are faint-hearted, hesitant, excitable or mediocre. Above all, the Jesuit must be well balanced, moderate, prudent, mistrustful of exaggeration in any form. Likewise Ignatius refrained from imposing rigorous asceticism and long fasts of the Cistercian type, or privation of sleep; he feared that excessive austerity would enfeeble the body and occupy much valuable time, so that the Fathers would be unfit for work 'and spiritual fervour grow cold.' For the same reason, with a view to making full use of all their faculties in whatever work they might undertake, he would not have his spiritual sons bind themselves to choral office, sung or recited. Their training would have to be such that they might profit by the teaching of the breviary without communal psalmody, and unite themselves month by month with the Life and Passion of Christ without communal participation in the ceremonies of the liturgical cycle.

This training assumed capital importance, and it must be admitted that no Order or Institute has ever envisaged anything so solid or detailed. The fundamental idea was such as can be discovered in the *Spiritual Exercises*, that the most efficient man is he who is most completely master of himself. It was for this absolute mastery that the future

---

[1] This and other still more ridiculous fables derive from a pamphlet entitled *Monita Secreta Societatis Jesu*, written about 1612 by one Jerome Zanorowski, a Pole who had been expelled from the Society and sought a contemptible revenge through the medium of the printing press. According to the *Monita*, the Society is governed by a small clique whose members hold certain secrets and are bound to one another by terrible oaths. Zanorowski also declares that the Jesuits have orders to win the favour of the powerful and the confidence of the rich, in order to impose their influence and to amass useful wealth. 'It is unfortunate,' says the Protestant Harnack, 'that falsehoods such as the *Monita Secreta* are still used to denigrate the Society.' But the practice continues. Many an honest man still believes in the 'Secrets of the Jesuits,' as well as in the 'black Pope' who controls the white Pope and even gets rid of him if he resists.

soldiers of Christ must be prepared; nor did the wise founder think seventeen years an unnecessarily long period for the formation of a perfect Jesuit. The postulant would therefore spend some weeks or months under observation, after which he would be admitted to the novitiate; and this novitiate would last for two years, as against the twelve months required by most other Orders. During it he would be trained in spiritual exercises, in examination of conscience and in meditation, as well as being subjected to trials or 'tests'—in the kitchen, for example, or the infirmary—in order to see whether he were capable of adapting himself to all circumstances. At the end of this period of probation the novice would pronounce simple vows of poverty, chastity and obedience, like all other religious, and then begin his scholasticate, during which he would receive his training properly so called. This would involve two years of classical studies, three of philosophy, four of theology and lastly several years (five at the most) of practical testing, generally in one of the Society's educational establishments. Meanwhile, having completed his theological studies, the future Jesuit would be ordained priest, at the age of about thirty to thirty-five; but he would still have to undergo a final period of probation, the 'third year,' in a special novitiate. He would not be a fully fledged Jesuit until the solemn and public renewal of his vows. Even then he would be only what the Constitutions called a 'spiritual coadjutor'; higher still there would be a select few, numbering perhaps one Father in every thirty or forty, who would take a fourth vow of total obedience to the Pope and be known as the 'Professed of Four Vows.' Naturally such training could be given only to subjects of the highest quality, with outstanding intellectual gifts. The Society, however, did not close its doors to men who, though less richly endowed, might wish to serve as soldiers of Christ. Ignatius admitted them as 'temporal coadjutors,' bound by the three vows. They would act as door-keepers, gardeners or cooks, and would look after the material needs of the community; but the Constitutions laid down that they were 'forbidden to learn more than they knew on joining the Society.'

This admirable logic and methodical genius appear yet again in the organization of the Society. Once more like an army, it was to have a clearly defined system of command, but the whole hierarchy of officers was established with a view to action, to warfare in God's cause. At its head would be the General, or rather, since Ignatius thought of the word as an adjective rather than a noun, the *praepositus generalis*: 'superior-general.' He was to be elected for life by an absolute majority of the General Congregation, itself consisting of the Provincials and two Professed from each province. Helped by five or six assistants, he would be the truly monarchical head of the Society, but a monarch whose authority was clearly defined as intended to be exercised in a paternal spirit and in full agreement with the whole body of members. Personal power and oligarchic power must control and balance one another. On the administrative plane the Society was divided into provinces, to be governed by Provincials appointed for three years and assisted by Counsellors. Jesuits were forbidden to accept positions of authority outside the Society; they must be 'at the service of the Holy See, and not usurp its place.' Hierarchical relationships were to be both confident and strict. The inferior must at regular intervals make 'manifestation of conscience' to his superior, 'that is to say, he must reveal the whole of his interior life, his temptations, difficulties and progress'; and the Constitutions even provide for an *admonitor* on the staffs of the General and the Provincials, specially entrusted with the sanctification of others and having for this purpose access even to the 'manifestations' made to superiors.[1] It is hard to imagine a stricter organization, a closer centralization, a securer discipline. Most recent of the great religious Orders, the Society of Jesus appeared to discard as far as possible the ancient characteristics of monachism. Broadly democratic, it showed none the less, in its will to perfection, as well as in its firm determination to serve God above all, those essential tendencies to which in the course of centuries monachism had owed its development.

The hierarchical system and discipline of the Jesuits were destined to speedy and violent criticism, which has persisted into our own day. Michelet has said that the Jesuit is a mere cog in the enormous machine of the Society; but that is to misunderstand the spirit in which St Ignatius conceived the whole gigantic system. Far from being a prisoner of the hierarchical and administrative framework the Jesuit feels himself all the more free because that very framework protects him against danger and temptation. Within the principles laid down by the Constitutions, and freely accepted, he enjoys a considerable degree of autonomy that may sometimes appear surprising. Sent into the world, he preaches, teaches and campaigns in the way that seems to him most appropriate to his purpose and best adapted to his temperament, without the presence of an immediate superior to direct and control him; government is exercised at a higher level, in the sphere of more ultimate responsibility.

Perfectly trained, the soldiers of Christ as recruited by Ignatius obeyed no other criteria than zeal for souls, with the essential motive for which their leader could feel confident of having equipped them. United by a grand overall design, they would adhere to the strict discipline imposed by their Society, sure that they were serving a cause

---

[1] These two regulations have done more than anything else to provoke criticism of the Society by those who refuse to understand the spirit of charity and faith with which they were to be applied.

which transcended them all, and which had been expressed once for all by their founder in the phrase *Ad majorem Dei gloriam*.[1]

12. THE MEANS OF PEACEFUL RECONQUEST

The Society of Jesus, thus established, was intended for action in the service of God. Its members, outwardly indistinguishable from secular priests,[2] were destined to mix with the people and rub shoulders with those to whom they had to deliver their message, obeying, in short, the celebrated commandment of St Paul which is the motto of every missionary undertaking: 'A Jew among the Jews, a Gentile among the Gentiles.' They were an immediate success—too much so perhaps for the liking of some. It is well known that the outstanding qualifications of the Jesuits are no less proverbial (and decried) than their ability to adapt themselves to circumstances and the readiness with which they can find common ground with every sort of mentality. So also in the matter of their iron discipline: it has provided material for countless tales which have been going the round of ecclesiastical circles for the past two or three hundred years. It was by agreeing to share in everyday life (which incidentally raised for them a number of very real problems) that the sons of St Ignatius exercised their widespread influence. They were daunted by no task or difficulty. Their apostolate was no less pliant than universal. We shall find them later on serving as astronomers and geographers in China, adopting the manners of men of caste in India,[3] but mixing just as easily with the slaves of America in the person of St Peter Claver. Writers, preachers, lecturers, professors, missionaries—they were all these things, and much else besides, according to the precept of St Ignatius: 'You must above all offer yourselves generously for the tasks in which charity also plays its humble part.'

The efficiency of the Jesuits quickly manifested itself on the strictly religious plane, where they had at their disposal a remarkable weapon forged by St Ignatius. I refer, of course, to the *Exercises*. The Fathers gave the *Exercises* wherever they were sent, and on many occasions

---

[1] It must be observed that St Ignatius never made provision for a female congregation. 'Women,' wrote St Francis Xavier, 'would be more trouble than profit to confessors; I advise you always to concern yourselves rather with their husbands.' Between 1543 and 1547 a few communities of female Jesuits tried to establish themselves in Italy, Spain and Portugal, but without success. One at Barcelona, under a certain Isabel Roser, turned out so badly that Ignatius brought an action against the foundress. It was not until much more recent times that religious Orders of women adopted the Ignatian spirituality and the substance of the Constitutions, e.g. the Helpers of the Holy Souls, the Ladies of the Cenacle, the Ladies of the Sacred Heart and the Society of the Holy Child Jesus.

[2] Less even than the Theatines, who retained certain small details of dress peculiar to themselves.

[3] See pp. 292–5 on Fr de Nobili.

C

made truly miraculous draughts. Novices of excellent quality soon flowed in: Italians, Spaniards, Portuguese; then Frenchmen, Belgians and Germans. Wherever Le Fèvre, Jay, Bobadilla or Francis Xavier spoke, souls on fire with this ideal offered themselves without reserve. Such was the Dutchman, St Peter Canisius, afterwards the apostle of Germany. Such too was the Spanish grandee and viceroy of Catalunya, St Francis Borgia, who became third General of the Society and whose holiness washed away the disgrace incurred by others of his name.

But in addition to those who actually became Jesuits, many others experienced the influence of that enchanting little book. It was at this period that there emerged and gradually developed the custom of 'retreats' (analogous to the sojourn at Manresa), during which the soul withdraws into solitude and silence, to consider its last end and its hope of salvation. Individual retreats at first, then collective, were preached ever more frequently, summoning their hearers to conversion. The practice of an annual eight-day retreat soon established itself in religious houses and seminaries, and eventually was made obligatory for all priests. When the decrees of the Council of Trent became part of the Church's life, this use of the *Exercises* became one of the principal means employed by numerous monasteries in the work of reforming themselves and developing a life of prayer among their members.

The Jesuit influence exerted itself far beyond the cloister, reaching out to persons living in the world. Spreading everywhere the practice of frequent confession, and installing in all their churches a newly invented piece of furniture known as the 'confessional,' which guaranteed absolute secrecy, the Fathers began to refine the very technique of confession. This they did by examination of conscience, and also by the use of 'casuistry,' an art much decried by their opponents, but which enabled them to apply with more flexibility, more moderation, and consequently with more justice, the great principles of Christian morality to particular cases that were often extremely complicated. Thanks to their intellectual eminence, it was not long before the Jesuits supplanted the seculars and Mendicants as confessors to princes.

Their activity in the purely spiritual domain made use of devotions and practices which cannot be described as original, but to which they gave new emphasis. The meditation on our Lord's life in the *Exercises* helped to exalt the love of God made Man and the sacrifice of Calvary, a love which soon found expression in devotion to the Sacred Heart. Linked with the worship rendered to her Son, the Blessed Virgin was also held in high honour by the Jesuits; so much so that in the following century St John Eudes paid them this tribute: 'Among all the religious Orders none shows more zeal or more ardour than does the Society of Jesus for the honour and service of the Queen of Heaven.' These two forms of devotion, to which St Bernard had owed much of his success in the twelfth century, contributed also to that of the Jesuits. Among their principal labours was the encouragement of frequent communion, which had fallen into disuse and which St Ignatius strove energetically to restore. In several of his spiritual letters he lays great stress upon the importance of the Eucharist and the advantage of receiving the Holy Sacrament very often.[1] The profound change thus inaugurated by the Jesuits added to their prestige. When Teresa entered the convent at Avila, in 1534, the hundred and fifty Carmelites were not allowed to communicate more than six times a year, or at the very most once a month. Eight years later, thanks to her Dominican confessor, she obtained permission to do so every fortnight, and in 1554 the first Jesuit whom she met advised her to communicate each morning.

Of all the activities pursued by the Jesuits, from the earliest days of the Society and in the lifetime of St Ignatius, that which they favoured most was the work of education. It was not peculiar to them, for it had already been undertaken by such institutes as the Barnabites and Ursulines; but they made such advances in the science of teaching and youth training that within a hundred years of their foundation they held, if not a monopoly, at least a marked predominance in this field. The educational work of the Jesuits was carried on at two wisely chosen levels. First, they left elementary instruction to others, and concentrated upon the religious formation of children in every class of society as well as of illiterate adults, a task all the more indispensable because it had been badly neglected. The first Jesuits, and St Ignatius above all, were zealous catechists. St Peter Canisius's *Summary of Christian Doctrine*, compiled in three stages adapted to the pupil's age and proficiency, was an enormous success: published in 1555, it was reissued four hundred times in a century, and translated into twelve languages, including Japanese and Ethiopian. It was surpassed, however, by the catechism of Bellarmine, with its fifty translations (six or seven in India alone) and world-wide circulation. After the Council of Trent there was talk of making one of the Jesuit catechisms the official catechism of the Church.

The second and very different level of Jesuit education was the formation of a social *élite*, that is to say, the development of a new type of teaching. Here again their interest was not original. The Brethren of the Common Life had been making serious efforts in this direction for more than a hundred years, and their success was apparent in the flourishing Collège de Montaigu at Paris. Their teaching methods, however, remained archaic, scholastic and often brutal, if we may believe Erasmus, Calvin and Rabelais. The new Jesuit educational

---

[1] He experienced such emotion when celebrating Mass that he used to prolong the ceremony far beyond the half-hour prescribed for his subjects. Sometimes he was so overwhelmed that he would not ascend to the altar.

system, taking account of contemporary trends, gave the ancient languages pride of place in the curriculum; at the same time, while maintaining strict discipline and morality, it made use of a technique of encouragement and rewards to stimulate rivalry among pupils, paid attention to cleanliness and physical exercise, and undoubtedly enjoyed greater success than the forbidding schools that were normal at that time. This idea formed no part of St Ignatius's main plan; but when he saw its good results he adopted it. The earlier Jesuit colleges were simply the lodgings of the Society's scholastics who were attending university courses. Soon they began to take in young men who were not destined for membership of the Society; then these college seminaries became regular homes of learning. St Ignatius understood so clearly the importance of this matter that he inserted in the Constitutions a body of rules governing education.

Thus, long before Calvin founded his notorious academy at Geneva,[1] the Jesuits erected so many colleges that by the end of the sixteenth century three-quarters of their houses were schools, and four-fifths of their own number were teachers. This new type of educational establishment spread to every country of Europe and even to India: Coimbra in 1542, Alcala in 1543, Valencia in 1544, Barcelona in 1545; but others were founded simultaneously at Gubbio, Messina, Perugia, Bologna, Ferrara, and also at Goa. The first Jesuit college in France was opened at Billom in Auvergne (1550); others followed at Pamiers, Tournon, Mauriac, Dôle and Dijon. The Collège de Clermont, founded at Paris in 1565 through the generosity of Guillaume Duprat, Bishop of Clermont, afterwards became the famous Lycée Louis le Grand. Elsewhere in Europe the Society reorganized the high schools at Vienna, Ingolstadt and Dillingen; they settled at Louvain, where, despite fierce resistance, they subsequently did much to revive the celebrated university; at Douai and Rheims they founded special colleges for English Catholics who were determined to bring back their country to the Roman faith. In the Eternal City itself the German College aimed at producing zealous and well-educated priests for Germany; while the Roman College, founded in 1551 and now the illustrious Gregorian University, became the model seminary. The goal of Jesuit pedagogy, then, was twofold: to train priests for their tasks, and to produce Christian gentlemen who would exert a beneficial influence in their various walks of life. The Jesuits borrowed their technique from contemporary humanism, but not its anti-religious and unduly individualistic spirit. It is impossible to overestimate the part which they thus played in the revival of Catholicism. Attracted by the quality of their teaching and by the novelty of their methods, as well as by the free instruction offered in many cases by the Society, children thronged

[1] See *The Protestant Reformation*, Chapter V, p. 431.

these 'good houses,' [1] to the great scandal of the synods. Jesuit Colleges were in process of turning out a new Christian *élite*, such as we shall find throughout most of the Catholic world in the seventeenth century.

The foregoing achievements of the Society by no means exhausted its activities, and we must say something here about its missionary undertakings properly so called. In Europe, notably in those parts overrun by the Protestant heresy, the work of the Jesuits was at many points crowned with success; [2] but we must not overlook the tremendous impetus given by them to the missions in pagan territory, the epic of St Francis Xavier,[3] and the exploits of so many Fathers from the Zambesi to Monomotapa, from Macao to Mexico, at the court of the Negus and among the slaves in Morocco.[4] We must likewise remember their creative role in the very different field of art. From 1568, when Vignola began the 'Gesù,' their famous church in Rome, their influence was so strong that the Society alone of the great Orders has given its name to a form of art, 'the Jesuit style,' [5] which continues to flourish. It may in fact be said that there is no department of human affairs (even politics, economics and finance) in which the Jesuits have failed to discover means for the advancement of God's glory.

Of all these means one characteristic is particularly striking: all are constructive, none is negative or polemical. They reflect the essence of St Ignatius's thought: that it was necessary, before and above every other task, to refashion the Christian man. This did not mean that the Jesuits would not later become involved, like the Dominicans, Capuchins and other Orders, in the rough and tumble of the counter-reformation, where they had many battles to fight. Their primary purpose however lay elsewhere: what they sought to do was to rebuild the very structure of Catholicism, its substance and its outlook; the rest would be a mere corollary. Nothing is more absurd than the oft-repeated assertion that 'the Society of Jesus was founded to extirpate heresy'—excepting perhaps the old cliché which links 'the Jesuits and the Inquisition' in a single formula of reprobation. On the contrary, the Society of Jesus kept strictly aloof from the Inquisition, even when the latter had been reorganized by Rome and made an important part of the ecclesiastical organism.[6] No one has ever ventured publicly to declare that St Ignatius was responsible for the death of any man, and he himself never prosecuted an adversary with a view to his execution by the secular arm. All the first Fathers were remarkable for their spirit of gentleness and charity, the spirit of true apostles, and not for that fanatical zeal which is attributed so unjustly to their Society. It was a

---

[1] 'In vast herds,' said a disgruntled Calvinist, for the sons of many non-Catholics also frequented them.
[2] On the work of St Peter Canisius in Germany and Poland see pp. 334–5.
[3] See Chapter IV, section 8.
[4] See p. 274.   [5] See p. 389.   [6] See p. 86.

Jesuit, St Peter Canisius, who coined the beautiful phrase 'our separated brethren,' to denote those who are not of the faith. In any case, until the death of Loyola, the Jesuits were very little concerned with polemics and the struggle against Protestantism; they intended to use other weapons in order to oppose and checkmate heresy.

13. EXPANSION OF THE SOCIETY AND DEATH OF ST IGNATIUS

When the saintly Cardinal Cervini was elected as Pope Marcellus II, in 1555,[1] one of the first things he did was to summon Ignatius of Loyola and ask him to appoint two Fathers who would live in the papal palace and act as his immediate advisers. 'Do you,' he said, 'muster troops and train them for the struggle; We will employ them.'

Those words are a perfect description of the part played by the Society from the day of its foundation, and which would soon become of capital importance in the history of the Church. With its strong organization, the spirit of discipline and enthusiasm which inspired its members, together with their moral, intellectual and spiritual excellence, it was a providential instrument which the Church could use to halt the advance of Protestantism and try to recover lost ground. The popes understood as much, and did their best to foster the growth of the young institute. The Bull *Regimini Militantis Ecclesiae*, while giving the Society canonical status, had confined the number of its members to sixty. Three years later (1543), Paul III's Bull *Injunctum nobis* suppressed this restrictive clause and allowed unlimited recruitment. Better still, in 1545, the same pontiff signed a brief exempting the Jesuits from episcopal jurisdiction, and empowering them to preach and confer all the sacraments wherever they might exercise their ministry, without having to ask the permission of parish priest or bishop. Julius III, one of those who had presided at Trent, had made friends with the Jesuit theologians [2] attending the Council. Immediately after his election he promulgated the Bull *Exposcit debitum*, confirming and 'renewing with added force' the privileges of the Society, pronouncing upon it a solemn panegyric, and formally declaring that it was placed 'under his immediate protection and that of the Apostolic See.' The election of Marcellus II, as we have just seen, ratified these measures.

Thus encouraged by the popes, and officially recognized as the spiritual army of Rome, the Society of Jesus was on the threshold of prodigious increase. Its expansion was exactly similar to that of the Mendicants at an earlier date, and perhaps even more impressive

---

[1] Unfortunately for the Church he died after a pontificate of only twenty-two days.
[2] Laynez, Le Jay, Salmeron and Canisius.

when we consider the difficulty of admission to its ranks and the meticulous training of its members. In 1540 there were ten Jesuits; in 1556, at the death of their Founder, they numbered 1,000 in 100 houses spread over twelve provinces. Forty years after their canonical establishment, twenty-one provinces included 5,000 members; a census taken in 1616 yielded 13,112 members, 436 houses and 37 provinces; while the second centenary of their foundation brought the membership to 22,000.[1]

There was immediately unleashed a veritable 'Jesuit offensive,' which had begun, it will be remembered, even before the Society existed as a canonical entity, and whose multiform and planetary character is something of a marvel. It seemed that the Jesuits wished to be everywhere and to have a hand in everything. Some of them were present at the Council of Trent, where their learning made a deep impression. Others served as legates at the court of Charles V, or as nuncios in Ireland and Scotland. When it became necessary to make a visitation of Corsica, where faith and morals were at a very low ebb, the duty was entrusted to a Jesuit. Meanwhile the Society's schools were multiplying, and Jesuit missionaries were at work in every quarter of the globe. One asks where they found sufficient men qualified to shoulder simultaneously so many different tasks; for others again were commissioned to revise the Bible, and to draw up the canons of Trent. Ignatius controlled the threads of all this huge tapestry from his office in Rome. In 1551, having finished work on the Constitutions, and believing his task fulfilled, he offered his resignation. But the Professed were unanimous in refusing to accept it; the chief was indispensable to the army. So he continued his labour to the end, writing innumerable letters to his subjects who were scattered over the face of the earth, as well as to correspondents in religious houses, to laymen, and even to the Emperor of Ethiopia.

Success of this kind was bound to have repercussions, and watchful jealousy reared its head. When the Theatine Giovanni Pietro Carafa succeeded Pope Marcellus II, Ignatius could not hope for the same benevolent interest as had been shown by his predecessor; the two men were at once too much alike in the inflexibility of their characters and too different in their manners. Thus Paul IV tried to impose traditional religious usages upon the Society, particularly the choral office. He also disliked the idea of such paramount authority at the head of an Order, and therefore suppressed the clause in the Constitutions which provided that the General should be elected for life. Ignatius, simple and modest as ever, submitted without a murmur to the papal decision:

---

[1] On 1st January 1954 they numbered 32,008, which makes them the second largest religious Order after the Franciscans (41,000), though the latter are divided into three branches. The Jesuits far outnumber the Dominicans (8,000).

he was entitled to remind himself that popes are mortal, and that what was done by one could be undone by another. This in fact is what actually happened on the accession of Pius IV. Moreover, in the closing months of his pontificate, the harsh Carafa showed signs of relenting, and even helped in the foundation of various Jesuit colleges, notably at Ingolstadt and Prague.

The Society met with resistance in many lands, especially in France. What, men asked, were these Spaniards, subjects of their enemy Charles V, doing in the kingdom of the fleur-de-lis? Would not the ultramontanism of the Professed, as evidenced by their fourth vow, tend to circumscribe the rights of the Gallican Church? Many bishops, particularly Eustache du Bellay of Paris, thought their privileges extravagant. Parlement and Sorbonne made themselves the spearhead of this opposition, and the first of these great corporations even refused to register the edict of Henri II authorizing the foundation of a Jesuit College in Paris. In spite of all the Society installed itself under the patronage of the Cardinal of Lorraine and Guillaume Duprat, Bishop of Clermont. The first Fathers arrived almost clandestinely, on the pretext of having come to study, and lodged in the house of their episcopal protector. Opposition gradually died down, so that they were able to make their projected foundations; but it was never fully appeased.[1]

More surprising was the resistance offered to the Society in Spain, the land of their origin. Whereas their success had been rapid and triumphant in Portugal, which Francis Xavier had reached in 1540, trial and tribulation awaited them in the most Catholic of all territories. These difficulties sprang from various causes, partly perhaps from the jealousy of the all-powerful Dominicans, who did not much care for the presence of such competent rivals on their home ground. Again, it may be that Charles V and Philip II, staunch Christians though they were in faith and utterance, mistrusted a body of religious who professed to serve none but the Pope. The fact that the Society was primarily Roman rather than Spanish may likewise have told against them. The result was something more than unfriendly manœuvring: there were acts of open hostility, such as the decree procured by the Dominicans from Philip II forbidding any Spaniard to study abroad— a direct blow at the Society. At Salamanca, the most eminent Dominican theologians, Vittoria and later Melchior Cano, his disciple, did not hesitate to attack the Ignatian spirituality on the grounds that it was tainted with mystical excess and even with illuminism. Nevertheless the Jesuits obtained a foothold in the land of St Ignatius: by 1554 there were three Spanish provinces (Aragon, Castile and Andalusia) with

[1] Henri IV drove them from the kingdom after the attempt on his life by Jean Chatel, because they had been more or less associated with the League. But he soon recalled them.

more than three hundred Fathers. The most striking feature of this achievement was the entry into the Society of Francis Borgia (1510–1572), Duke of Gandia, whom the *Exercises* had won for Christ and His new militia. He sought admission after the death of his beloved wife, and even before he had secured the future of his eight children.[1] In 1554 he was appointed 'commissary' of the three Spanish provinces, a position which he held for eleven years until his election as General.

As Ignatius looked into the measureless distances that now revealed themselves, what did he care for resistance and ill will? To attacks that were often furious he replied only with meekness and prayer, counselling his Fathers, if they met with opposition, 'to commit their adversaries to God, and do everything with a view to touching their hearts, not with fear of the contradictions or of the difficulties they might cause, but with charity.' His serenity was indeed admirable; but he knew that the work God had given him to do was now established on unshakable foundations. He could die, and those who succeeded him at the head of the Order would be able to follow his lessons and example, and to continue the forward march. He was in fact succeeded by a distinguished line of Generals, whose work was a splendid continuation of his own: Laynez, his companion; St Francis Borgia; the Belgian Mercurian; the Neapolitan Aquaviva, whose genius for organization gave the Jesuits an even stronger impetus.[2] If Ignatius had not been so profoundly humble he could have finished his life with this tribute to himself, which has been paid to him in our own day by a Protestant author: 'The Church is indebted to him for most of her victories and for the recovery of her vitality.' [3]

His end was marked by the quiet simplicity befitting one who, in the second week of the *Exercises*, recommends Christians 'always to think of themselves as if they were on the point of death.' He had long since made the 'necessary dispositions' and taken the 'necessary steps'; almost forty years ago he had made 'sound and wholesome choice.' On 1st July 1556 he fell sick; the physicians declared that his indisposition was not serious. Warned, it may be, by the Spirit of Light who had so often guided him, he replied gently that he was under no illusion and that he was going to die. At his bidding, his secretary Polanco left for Rome, to offer Paul IV a last greeting from his faithful son and to ask the papal blessing, That was on 30th July. A few hours later, on the morning of 31st, Ignatius of Loyola died peacefully, attended by only one of his Fathers. He had so loved solitude, and had

[1] The Pope granted a special dispensation enabling him to exercise his functions as viceroy during three years of his Jesuit scholasticate, so that he might make arrangements for the future of his family.

[2] It was he who published the educational principles of the Society in a work entitled *Ratio Studiorum*, which remained in use until the nineteenth century.

[3] G. Monod, Introduction to the French translation of Böhmer's work.

*C

spoken much of its spiritual benefits. At about the same time news
reached the Eternal City that far away, on the other side of the world
and looking towards China which he had longed to evangelize, Francis
Xavier also was dying. He too was alone. From the vow of Montmartre
to these solitary deaths, what a journey had been accomplished in the
space of twenty years![1]

13. The Papacy Intervenes

St Ignatius and his companions represent the high-water mark of that
tidal movement towards reform, which lifted up the Catholic soul and
drove it to confront the perils of the age. The experience of the Jesuits,
even more than that of other orders and congregations which came into
being or were reformed at about the same time, proved the existence of
a widespread and determined craving for personal perfection. It showed
likewise that this interior urge, so far from leading Christians to shut
themselves away behind the bastions of prayer, was preparing them to
take action in accordance with their faith, that is, to become effective
in the sphere of human contingency and human conflict. These profoundly mystical souls, like all the men of the Renaissance, considered
it their main business to live more intensely and for themselves. In
their view, however, living meant living in Christ; and because they
understood the demands made upon them by the charity of Christ,
instead of retiring to a monastic cell, after the example of Ignatius at
Manresa, they were resolved to carry their testimony into the world,
where the cause they held more dear than life was at stake. The necessary reform of institutions and morals could have had no better instruments than these men who had reformed themselves.

Moreover the very conditions in which this reawakening had come
about was a guarantee that any such reform would not deviate from the
straight and narrow path, that it would not end in one or other of those
anarchical movements which were becoming so numerous and which
pretended to rebuild the Church outside herself, in opposition to
herself. None of these Catholic reformers had dreamed of innovation,
but only of a return to the sources, of rediscovering a tradition more
alive in respect of its two main principles of progress and fidelity.
None of them, however clearly they might perceive the glaring defects
of Mother Church, had sought to remedy those defects by means of a
system proceeding from their own minds, but merely to lay firm hold
of eternal principles and apply them more effectively. Nor indeed had
any of them advocated a rupture with the ecclesiastical hierarchy, even
when that hierarchy was at its worst. Rejecting the dangerous pride that

[1] Beatified in 1609, Ignatius of Loyola was canonized by Gregory XV in 1622, together
with St Francis Xavier. See the final paragraph of Chapter V.

exalted men such as Luther and Calvin, they all submitted humbly to authority, especially to that of the Pope, who, being responsible to God for the Church, could alone take the initiative and render it effective.

All the prerequisites of a Catholic reformation were thus present. The men who would be its instruments were ready. The spiritual and moral climate demanded it. What more was required for its accomplishment? Something which had always been indispensable in matters of this kind: the intervention of supreme authority, that is, of the Papacy. Whenever the Church has had to pull herself together and lead the world back to the Gospel, the popes have always been, in short, the effective agents of reform. That was true in the sixth century under Gregory I, in the ninth under Nicholas I and later still in the eleventh and thirteenth under Gregory VII and Innocent III respectively. Great as were the saintly founders of religious Orders—Bernard, Norbert, Bruno, Francis of Assisi, Dominic and their like—they would never have managed to repair the Church but for the presence over them and at their side, throned in Peter's curule chair, of men invested by the Holy Ghost with infallible authority to recall Christians to their duty.

At the beginning of the sixteenth century, in a world seething with passion and aspiration, when Europe seemed tottering to its fall, the papal role appeared more important than it had ever been. Only the popes could undertake the work of reformation in all its fullness. Christendom had ceased to be; nationalism, growing everywhere, was turning its back more and more resolutely upon the ancient idea of Christian unity. Unless therefore personal initiative were taken in hand by Rome, it was powerless and might actually result in cleavages. There was no longer a lay sovereign capable (as Charlemagne, for example, had been) of controlling even the spiritual interests of the Church. The emperor was no more than a shadow. The popes alone survived.

So long as the Vicar of Christ hesitated to embrace the cause of reform, with the firm determination to crown it with success, nothing could be done; the broad stream of fervour and generosity then flowing through the Church would remain untapped. It is remarkable that all those who had occupied the Apostolic throne during the past hundred years or so had been fully aware of their primordial duty; even those whose mere presence in Rome seemed to demonstrate the necessity of reforming the Church, 'both in her head and in her members'; even those pontiffs whom we have seen caught up in the allurements of art, of politics, or of the flesh—all had spoken of performing that duty. One after another, to quote but a few examples, men had heard Nicholas V, supported by Nicholas of Cusa and John Capistran, declare himself about to correct the vices of the clergy; Pius II, terrified by the scourges threatening Christianity, drawing up a huge scheme of reform which began with Rome and the Curia; Paul II fulminating against simony and the laxity of religious houses; Sixtus IV proclaiming that monks should labour to sow the good grain of wisdom and uprightness in the souls of men; even Alexander VI himself, for a few fleeting months, summoning a commission of reform and directing it with noble ardour to prepare the cleansing Bull, *Flatus vocis*. None of these splendid projects got beyond the stage of design, of fine words or at the very most of tentative beginnings. True the Oecumenical Council of the Lateran (1512–17),[1] under the presidency of Julius II and then of Leo X, had promulgated some discerning observations on the evil of reserves and the accumulation of benefices, reminded cardinals of the duties of their state, and decreed wise measures on the subject of clerical morality; but its work had remained altogether incomplete, and its decisions were applied half-heartedly. The danger was clear for all to see. Leo X had rightly said 'that Christian truth was in peril, and that the hour had come to defend it'; only the courage and determination was lacking—above all, courage and determination on the part of Christ's Vicar to put in motion the machinery of reform where it was most indispensable, that is, in his own domain.

Nevertheless a wind of change was blowing. For what mysterious reason? Was the pressure exerted by the reawakened Christian soul upon the whole Church and even upon her leaders so powerful that it forced the new decision? Once again we can but remind ourselves of those secret intentions of Providence, whose ways are impenetrable by human reasoning. At long last the tiara was to be set upon the brow of popes not all of whom were saints, but who proved themselves more faithful to their vocation and lent a ready ear to the repeated summons of the universal Church. The reform which had appeared so hard to undertake would be carried through in the space of about twenty years, not without effort and serious difficulties, but without violent shocks or startling innovations, simply by means of Catholicism's return to her true principles. 'An empire is easily conserved by the same means which created it.' These profound words of Sallust must have been familiar to many in an age so enamoured of ancient literature. Let them only be applied to the Church, and her true countenance would reappear.

[1] See *The Protestant Reformation*, Chapter IV, p. 250.

CHAPTER II

THE COUNCIL OF TRENT AND THE WORK OF THE SAINTS

1. A CORPSE IN SHREDS

TOWARDS evening on Sunday, 5th May 1527, sentinels keeping watch on the walls of Rome suddenly beheld along the slopes of Monte Mario the gleaming weapons and breastplates of a large armed force, and heard menacing shouts borne on the gentle spring breeze. They were not surprised; the blow had been expected for at least a month. It was known that the imperial troops were marching against the city at the almost incredible speed of eighteen or twenty miles a day; but it remained to be seen whether they would dare attack and violate the capital of Christendom, where lay the bones of St Peter. Whatever happened the papal units, inefficiently commanded by Lorenzo de Ceri, would certainly not be a match for them. One of the most appalling tragedies in Christian history was about to be enacted.

The enemy were a mixed lot, including Spaniards, Italians and Germans—many Germans. The fifteen thousand lansquenets, Lutherans for the most part and with Frundsberg at their head, believed themselves engaged in a holy war, and were convinced that by over-throwing the Pope of Rome they would triumph over Antichrist. The rest, the great majority, were driven to fanaticism by less exalted motives: desire of pillage and an appetite for violence. Months had passed since these men last received any pay from their commander-in-chief, who, when they yelled 'Money! Money!' showed them the opulence of Italy by way of answer: 'If you have ever dreamed of pillaging a town and laying hold of its treasures, here now is one, the richest of them all, queen of the world.' The speaker was the Constable de Bourbon, a traitor to his king, a Frenchman in rebellion against France, who lent himself to the crime of sacrilege, in hope no doubt of winning for himself a principality.

The affair was not long delayed. Bourbon was killed during the assault by a bullet which Benvenuto Cellini used to boast of having fired; but that did not prevent the mercenaries infiltrating through the gardens, scaling the walls and smashing down the gates. The doom of Rome was settled in a few hours, and it was a dreadful doom. Unchecked, mutinous and obeying no one, the troops of the Catholic emperor Charles V gave themselves up to an orgy of bloodshed. None can tell whether the taciturn Hapsburg had willed this thing—or tolerated or suggested it. For seven days the city was delivered to sack, to rape, to pillage. 'Hell,' said one diplomat, 'is nothing to what happened then.' Convents were the theatres of revolting obscenities in which the nuns were involuntary actresses. Fathers were seen to stab their daughters rather than allow them to be taken by the soldiery. Palaces and churches were rifled, their contents broken or mutilated. Then it was the turn of the merchant classes, from whom parties of troops exacted enormous ransoms at dagger-point. Ridicule was added to cruelty. The aged Cardinal Araceli was paraded through the streets in a coffin; bishops and other prelates were dragged like slaves for sale in the common market; drunken lansquenets, arrayed in liturgical vestments, brawled in the taverns. The sack went on until there was nothing left to steal or to destroy, and until the insufferable stench of corpses called for police measures.

From the narrow windows of the castle of Sant' Angelo, where he had taken refuge, Pope Clement VII watched this nightmare spectacle. He had managed by sheer good luck to save himself; but he was a prisoner, and before long his jailer would arrive: Alarcon, the same who had kept watch upon François I at Madrid. It was not so much his own situation, however, that grieved the pontiff as the horror of the spectacle. Violence had been unleashed and seemed likely to continue indefinitely; it reached all the Papal States and the Kingdom of Naples. And so, turning to the man who, whether or not responsible for the tragedy, derived the benefit therefrom, Clement VII wrote to Charles V accepting the harsh conditions imposed upon him. He would surrender the States of the Church, he would pay a huge ransom, he would agree to everything provided the frenzy ceased: 'Dearly beloved son,' he cried, 'we have nothing before our eyes but a corpse in shreds. . . .'

If it be asked whether he himself did not bear some responsibility for this catastrophe, the answer must be yes undoubtedly—at the political level; his own policy had been simultaneously too deeply committed and too hesitant, too temporal and too lacking in energy. After Pavia, alarmed by the progress of Charles V, he had determined to rely upon François I, encouraging him to denounce the clauses of Madrid and assuring him in writing that 'treaties concluded through fear are not binding.' He had also allied himself with the League of Cognac, formed to drive the Spaniards from Italy. He had in short done everything to attract the thunderbolt, but without taking the steps necessary to avoid the danger. Supported half-heartedly by the King of France (who was more generous of kind words than of material reinforcements), and attacked in Rome itself by the Colonna clique, he —and the city with him—suffered the consequences of that Italian policy in which the popes had entangled the Holy See too deeply during the past hundred years.

But it is not only political responsibility that can be ascribed to Clement. The outrage committed upon Rome by Bourbon's *reiter* was symbolic: it reflected for all the world to see those numerous other affronts to which the Church and all Christendom had been subjected in recent times. The sky was dark in so many directions. In Germany the Lutheran heresy was prospering and had just brought about the bloody upheaval of the Peasants' War. In Switzerland a new reformer had appeared, Zwingli, who was even more radical than Luther. In England a royal passion, which was common gossip, would soon raise the problem of divorce, a very difficult question. In France suspect trends were discernible, as also in Bohemia, in Poland and everywhere. Finally, on the eastern frontiers the Turkish peril was more grave than ever: Hungary had lately been overwhelmed by the blows of Solyman at Mohacs, and it looked as though the Moslem corsairs would soon dominate the Mediterranean. Providence seemed filled with wrath against the Church. And why all this, why this crowning tragedy which had now drenched the Eternal City in blood? Many could find but one answer: chastisement from heaven.

The weakness, frivolity and even unworthiness of too many recent popes were openly declared to be the supernatural but decisive causes of those innumerable woes. What else but this weight of anger could be expected of God in return for the Papal Court, the Curia, and even the Sacred College packed by one pope after another with their unworthy nephews and contemptible parasites? Surely the sword of Divine Justice had been brought upon the Church by Alexander VI, prey to the temptations of the flesh; by Julius II, devoured by ambition and the will to power; by Leo X, who allowed himself to become intoxicated by the delights of art to the detriment of higher interests; in fact by all those pontiffs who had proved unequal to their duties. Many courageous voices had denounced the manifold stain that disfigured the Mystic Spouse, yet what had the popes done to wash it out? Charles V, with gloomy countenance and feigned distress, exclaimed: 'It all happened by the judgment of God rather than by my order'; and many minds were ready to accept this excuse. A lampoon went the rounds, written by some scribbler in the imperial pay, in which each one of the sufferings endured by Rome was represented as the punishment for a particular piece of wickedness. St Peter's turned into a stable—what a striking symbol of so many Roman souls in whom dwelt none but the vices! Sacred hosts profaned by the soldiery—what an image of the outrages perpetuated on the Sacrament by so many unworthy priests! There were some of the opinion that this pamphlet told the truth.

Poised thus on the slope, the Church seemed destined to slide into

the abyss. Could no one check her fall, seize hold of her and compel
her to climb back? After the death of Leo X there was reason to think
that one man might be capable of fulfilling this herculean task: Adrian
VI (1522-3), formerly tutor to Charles V, Adrian of Utrecht,[1] an
austere priest, rigid and of unassailable morals, whom the Conclave had
elected almost unwillingly as a result of one of those polite manœuvres
which sometimes determine the outcome of a scrutiny. On the morrow
of his coronation the brave Dutchman had undertaken the work of
reform. He was known to lead the most edifying life in his palace, dismissing suspect persons from his court, together with every element of
pomp. In a number of sternly worded allocutions he denounced
scandals and criticized the venality of justice, the corruption of officials
and the misconduct which was rife among the clergy. A few examples
had provided an effective lesson. His excellent intentions, however,
had not been supported by those qualities of prudence and sagacity
which the situation had required. To grapple with all scandals at once
was to invite unanimous opposition. Powerless to arrest the progress of
Lutheranism [2] any more than that of the Turks, who had just taken
Rhodes from the knights of Villiers de l' Isle-Adam, and equally powerless to halt the intrigues of Francis of Sicily, Adrian VI soon showed himself unable to discipline the pawnbrokers and profiteers. The cardinals
whom he had ordered to modify their ostentatious way of life, the
holders of benefices to whom he had forbidden the practice of accumulation, the *datarii* and other secretaries whom he had tried to prevent
from lining their pockets—everyone in fact, or nearly everyone, had
quickly agreed to treat him as a 'churl' and a 'Teutonic barbarian.'
Some unfortunate remarks of his, too, had caused scandal. Gazing, for
example, at the wonderful examples of ancient sculpture collected by
his predecessors, he had exclaimed: '*Proh! idola barbara.*' And then
inevitably, as we learn from a Venetian ambassador, because of his
origins he had come to be regarded 'not as the common father of the
Christian republic, but as an agent of the German Caesar.' Vast
unpopularity had ended by enveloping this good man who, immediately before his death, had murmured this avowal of disappointment:
'It is sad that there are some periods in which the most upright of men
is forced to succumb.'

Such then was the situation which confronted the Dutchman's
successor, Clement VII (1523-34), a very different man. Neither evil
intentions nor degrading passions had any place in the distinguished
mind of this humanist cardinal who had been trained to public life.
The very opposite is true. The first acts of his pontificate had made an

---

[1] Contrary to custom he retained his baptismal name on the apostolic throne. He was
incidentally the last non-Italian pope.
[2] The German princes were beginning to secularize bishoprics and abbeys.

excellent impression. He had sought advice from Sadolet and Giberti, the two leaders of the reforming movement; he had appointed a commission of cardinals to study the necessary measures; he had kept himself well informed on the affairs of Germany, and had sent his legate to try and settle matters. But this refined intellectual was devoid of character; it has even been said that he suffered 'from a sort of anaemia of the will.' Vacillating, irresolute, incapable of making up his mind and sticking to it, he was bound to appear as lacking in sincerity. Besides, he was a Medici—son of Julian who had been assassinated in the Pazzi conspiracy—and could not refrain from mingling the interests of his family with those of the Church, or in taking a hand in those Italian intrigues where Florentine birth was no guarantee of success.

And so his entire reign is one long story of hopeless confusion, and produced nothing but a succession of defeats. Reconciled with Charles V, who needed him in order to defend his aunt Catherine of Aragon against the machinations of Henry VIII, he set about persuading the emperor to re-establish a Medici at Florence. Next, seeing the increase of Spanish influence in Italy, he prepared a new series of alliances; having performed the solemn coronation of Charles V at Bologna, he approached François I and arranged to marry his niece Catherine to the future king Henri II. Wholly preoccupied with Italian politics and family concerns, he could not handle the real problems of the Church amid the hurly-burly of the great conflicts that were shaking Europe. In the affair of Henry VIII's divorce he has the credit of having stood firmly by his principles, but his manœuvring and hesitation contributed something to the Schism. In Germany, apart from addressing some strong language to Charles V, he allowed the imperial policy to tolerate the Lutheran advance for too long. As regards the Turks, the situation was absolutely catastrophic: Solyman occupied all Hungary, and laid siege to Vienna with 300,000 men. Gregorovius has called Clement VII 'the most unfortunate of popes'; but he himself bears a measure of responsibility for those misfortunes.

And what of reform? How had it been progressing in such circumstances? The commission of cardinals, after numerous sessions and many valuable reports, dispersed without having accomplished any of those things which had been expected of it. Faced henceforward with the Lutheran doctrines, Catholics were everywhere clamouring for measures that would put an end to scandals and rob the heretics of their arguments. Rome was silent. The most serious point was that an idea sprang up in various quarters according to which some power was needed in place of the Holy See, since the latter was incapable of taking the indispensable decisions. But *what* power? Pens in the service of Charles V declared unequivocally: 'If the emperor reforms the Church

—and everyone knows how important such reformation is—he will not only render service to God, but will also earn for himself the greatest glory that any prince has ever enjoyed.' The danger was not illusory. Charles V was haunted at this time by the desire to reconcile the adversaries and thereby restore peace to the Empire. Now if he were to decide to summon a council, what would the Pope do? When an imperial proposition to this effect was made in more explicit terms (1534) Clement VII had the strength to refuse. But what a nonsensical situation! The Vicar of Christ refusing to take steps demanded by the best minds in the Church, forbidding another to answer the appeal and yet doing nothing about it himself!

Was all lost then? Must men despair of the future of the Catholic Church? No reply was forthcoming from the hesitant Medici pope, from his lily-livered Curia, or even from the Germanic emperor whose good Christian intentions hardly concealed his very definite ambition. It was given by all those fervent souls who were even then making ready for the decisive awakening by their return to their true loyalties. It was during the pontificate of Clement VII, remember, and with his encouragement, that there began many of those individual enterprises which we have seen at work refashioning the army of the Church. Theatines, Capuchins, Barnabites, Somaschi; it was Clement's reign that witnessed the birth of these and numerous other orders, institutes and congregations whose activity would prove decisive. This was not the fruit of mere chance. A few weeks before Clement VII's death, on 25th September 1534, Ignatius of Loyola and his six companions had vowed (15th August) in the little semi-subterranean chapel on the hill of Montmartre to devote themselves body and soul to the Church. That Church appeared to have reached the nadir of her existence, but her recovery was at hand. The 'corpse in shreds' would soon come to life again.

2. POPE PAUL III (1534–49)

On 13th October 1534 Cardinal Alessandro Farnese was unanimously elected Pope, and took the name Paul III. He was certainly no saint. Farnese belonged to one of those powerful Italian clans which used to dispute among themselves for the tiara; and that is why thirteen years earlier, on the death of Leo X, his candidature, opposed by the Colonnas and Medicis together, had not succeeded.[1] Must we attribute his easy election to his age, to his sickly and infirm appearance? One can hardly believe, in any case, that it was due to his prestige. No doubt his way of life had been regular since his ordination to the priesthood in

[1] He obtained twenty-two votes in a scrutiny instead of the necessary twenty-four. It was thanks to those squabbles around the urn that Adrian VI was elected.

1519. But the Romans did not forget that he had been created cardinal by Alexander VI at a time when his sister, the beautiful Giulia Farnese, was believed to have refused the Borgia nothing, and on this account Alessandro had been nicknamed Cardinal Petticoat. They remembered also that in the course of a rather stormy career he had begotten three bastards, Pierluigi, Ranuccio and Constanza, whose legitimation by Julius II did not perhaps suffice to excuse their existence. Alessandro Farnese was from top to toe a man of the Renaissance—cultured, a patron of the arts and a lover of pomp—and would remain so in the chair of Peter. One day he would be heard to let fall some words that sound strange indeed on the lips of a pope. Referring to Benvenuto Cellini, who was guilty of many crimes: 'An artistic genius,' said Paul III, 'is above the laws of morality.' He would still be seen attending brilliant hunts, entertaining the women of his family at table, and giving noisy parties in his palace with female singers, dancing girls and buffoons. His enlightened taste moreover would lead him to have painted on the walls of the Vatican, and above all in the castle of Sant' Angelo, frescoes of a strongly pagan flavour. The inclinations of the new pope were only too well known. Besides, when he began his pontificate by raising two of his grandsons (modestly described as 'nephews') to the Sacred College—Alessandro Farnese, aged fourteen, and Ascanio Sforza, aged sixteen—those true Christians who longed with all their souls for the reform of the Church were stricken with grief and believed that everything would continue as before. But they were wrong.

Paul III would prove himself neither a Clement VII nor a Leo X nor a Borgia. The man whom we still see in his portrait by Titian [1] at the age of sixty-seven, bent, almost hump-backed, with long aristocratic nose and white beard, possessed a character of enormous strength together with the shrewdest intelligence. Violent, but able to control the irascible instincts which sometimes blazed in his piercing eyes, he had succeeded in remaining at court throughout six pontificates, and in holding the balance so evenly in his relations with France and the Empire that François I and Charles V both declared themselves pleased with his election. Where Adrian VI had exhibited so much clumsy haste, and where Clement VII had shown himself so unskilful a diplomat, a man as firm, subtle and worldly-wise as Pope Farnese would be able to work wonders, no matter how little he understood the significance of the immense drama in which Christianity was then engaged. Now in point of fact Paul III did understand it, and thanks to him the Church would take the decisive step that had been so long awaited.

[1] At present in the Museum at Naples. It shows Paul III between two of his grandsons, Cardinal Alessandro Farnese and Ottavio, Duke of Parma and Piacenza.

In the Bull which he later sent to the Council of Trent he gave a perfect summary of the situation as he found it on ascending the papal throne. 'In those days all was full of hatred and dissension. Princes were everywhere at loggerheads one with another, princes to whom God had entrusted government. The unity of the Christian name had been shattered by schism and heresy. The Turks were advancing on land and sea; Rhodes was lost, Hungary devastated, Italy, Austria and Slavonia threatened. The divine wrath lay heavy upon all us sinners'. This clear-headed man understood that it was time to take a stand against the threefold danger of the Turks, political dismemberment and religious dissolution. But he also detected something even more serious: that sickness which was ravaging the Christian soul, that universal treason which was calling down God's ire upon the Catholics. Cries of fury or of desolation were rising from all parts of Christendom, imploring him or commanding him to put an end to the tale of scandal. While crossing the bridge of Sant' Angelo he had heard the voice of a strange man named Franz Titelmans, a former teacher at the universities of Angers and Louvain who had abandoned all, students and professorial chairs, to come to Rome and make his solemn protestation: 'To hell with sinners! To hell with adulterers!' This great humanist of Louvain, a keen opponent of Erasmus, had surrendered his chair in 1535 in order to take the Capuchin habit at Rome, where he died in the odour of sanctity on 12th September 1537. The Flemish Capuchin's cry was no solitary voice in the desert. There were countless men and women begging the Pope, as the jurist Caccia de Novara puts it, to restore to the Church 'her evangelical nature,' to lead her back to the humility, purity and heroism of apostolic times. 'The supreme merit of Paul III is that he listened to this manifold voice, the voice of Christian conscience, and that he did its bidding according to his means.

It suddenly became clear that the wind of change was blowing. The tenderest spot when Alessandro Farnese assumed the tiara was England. Here the affair of the royal divorce had reached the point of rupture between Henry VIII and his Catholic subjects, that is to say the point of persecution. John Fisher and Thomas More had been arrested. Paul III threatened the Tudor with interdict. He wished to obtain the intervention of the Catholic rulers against the schismatic, and carried on prolonged negotiations with this end in view. Neither France nor the Empire cared to break with an intermittent but useful ally. Besides, to withdraw Andrea Doria's fleet from the Mediterranean and send it to fight in the Thames estuary was to leave the coasts of Italy and France exposed to the Turks. Paul III, however, stood his ground. Holding fast by principle, he acted with great vigour against Henry VIII, urging Reginald Pole to wage his campaign of protest against the faithless monarch, and no doubt having a hand in the rising of the North. In December 1538 he laid the kingdom under interdict and excommunicated the sovereign. Clement VII's policy of temporization and double dealing was a thing of the past. In France also, where the affair of the Placards had just broken out,[1] Paul III encouraged François I to employ severity; and he exhorted the Catholic princes of Germany to unite against the League of Smalkald, whose troops were defeated. Finally, in order to make it possible for the Catholic sovereigns to fight against heresy, and likewise in order to deprive the Turks of one of their trump cards in the shape of the French alliance, he managed, at the cost of immense diplomatic effort conducted with supreme skill, to reconcile François I and Charles V by the ten-year Truce of Nice (1538). The ground was now clear for the most important work of all.

Reform of the Church, the goal proclaimed by so many voices, was not in doubt; nor was the means of its accomplishment, a general council. Paul III agreed as to both, but he foresaw a danger. Might not an Assembly of the Church convoked by himself rise up against him, against his court and against the Curia which was wide open to criticism from so many points of view? The age of conciliar theories was comparatively recent, and it was necessary to avoid at any cost resuscitation of the conflict. The very stature to which the Papacy had attained during the past hundred years made him unwilling to put himself in tow of a council. The only thing to do then was to start by reforming the head of the Church, as Adrian VI had tried unsuccessfully to do; that is to say, he must first restore order in Rome and the papal *entourage*. That would be the first stage. Then would come the second, the meeting of the Council, which would now be easier to direct and to control. Finally there would be a third and much more remote stage, at which Paul III clearly foresaw the Papacy, reformed and purified, applying the conciliar decrees. The courageous pontiff who intended to undertake this enormous task would never come near to witnessing its completion, but he has the singular merit of having conceived it as a whole.

Paul III set to work in the early months of his pontificate. The consistories of October and November 1534 afforded him an opportunity of admonishing with firm moderation the cardinals who were present: their manner of life must be less ostentatious, they must keep an eye on their households; and they were requested to resume ecclesiastical dress, for which some of them affected great disdain. Two new Congregations were created and placed under the direction of cardinals whose reputation was irreproachable: one to supervise the conduct of the Roman clergy, the other to inquire into the administration of the Papal States. In this climate even the appointment of two 'nephews' to

[1] See *The Protestant Reformation*, Chapter VI, p. 380.

the Sacred College was more easily explicable; perhaps it was nothing less than a supreme act of cunning, for the two lads, having been raised to the purple, were afterwards replaced in their posts at the Apostolic Camera and Chancellery by vicars who gradually brought those two important services under the Pope's direct control.

Above all, however, the pontiff's purpose and the steps he meant to take towards its realization become manifest when we consider his appointments to the Sacred College from 1535 onwards. Excepting one—Jean du Bellay, Bishop of Paris, whose red hat was a mark of favour to the King of France—all those whom Paul III raised to the purple were convinced reformers, men of integrity and ardent soul—pillars in the future work of reconstruction, as was said of them by the Polish bishop Stanislaus Hosius (himself made cardinal in 1560). In order to judge this pope one cannot do better than take a look at the counsellors whom he chose. We need in fact only cite the names of these men if we would understand the significance of Paul III's choice: St John Fisher, a prisoner of Henry VIII, who would soon lay his head upon the block through loyalty to the Catholic faith; his friend Reginald Pole; the wise and peace-loving Sadolet; the energetic Giovanni Pietro Carafa, co-founder of the Theatines and afterwards Pope Paul IV; Michele Cervini, who was destined to precede the latter for a few days on the apostolic throne as Marcellus II. Among these batches of cardinals there were such great diplomats as Schomberg and Caracciolo, such eminent administrators as Guinucci, and such noted canonists as Simonetta. There were also some outstanding humanists, e.g. Aleandro and Gaspard Contarini; the latter was a layman but one of the leading protagonists of Catholic reform, and he was elevated straightway to the rank of cardinal. Paul III even thought of conferring the red hat upon Erasmus, but the aged scholar gracefully declined.

From this brilliant company the Pope then chose the members of a 'commission of reform,' whose business it was to study the problem as a whole and to propose solutions. At its head were Sadolet, Pole, Contarini and Carafa. The Bull *Sublimis Deus* gave it, in addition to unlimited rights of inquiry, powers of sanction and coercion that extended even to members of the Curia. These saintly commissioners were guaranteed the fullest liberty, which they did not fail to use; their report of January 1538 was a model indictment, perfectly objective but sparing no one, even in the papal household. The regulations attached to this report by way of conclusion were given the force of law. They laid down the moral and intellectual qualifications needed for admission to Holy Orders; they imposed upon all clerics, from the humblest curate to the most exalted member of the Sacred College, a manner of life suitable to the duties of their state; and they even concerned themselves with the maintenance of buildings intended for divine worship. But were these regulations enforced? Did not their very rigour place them in jeopardy? It is hard to say whether this internal reform was any more effective than that envisaged by the Lateran Council; history shows that abuses of long standing 'are proof against official remedies, and need to be dealt with in a new setting.' [1] But at all events they forestalled the criticism which some members of the Council might have directed against Rome, and their most relevant clauses were embodied in the decrees of Trent.

It was not, however, to the Commission *de emendanda* alone that Paul III entrusted this indispensable task. His energy and foresight were expressed in many other ways. It is hardly necessary to recall that he granted canonical recognition to the Society of Jesus in 1540, at a time when the Commission entertained some doubt as to this new enterprise; that he authorized the foundation of the Somaschi; that he encouraged the Barnabites and Theatines; and that it was due to him that the Ursulines became in 1544 the great teaching Order that we know today. Even in 1542, when the newly established institute of the Capuchins was faced with the grave crisis brought about by the apostasy of Bernardino Ochino, Paul III's indignation yielded to his understanding that it would be absurd to destroy so useful an instrument.

Two organisms of capital importance in the subsequent history of the Church likewise owed their existence to this far-sighted occupant of Peter's throne. One was the Inquisition, an old medieval institution which had fallen into virtual desuetude everywhere except in Spain, where it had been reorganized in 1478 and had become to all intents and purposes a weapon of kingly government. Everywhere in fact the struggle against heretical doctrine had been left in the hands of careless, dissolute, and even suspect ecclesiastical courts. On the advice of Carafa, and also perhaps of St Ignatius, Paul III resolved in 1542 to re-establish a Roman organism whose duty it would be to fight 'against all those who had departed from or who attacked the Catholic faith, and to unmask such persons as were suspected of heresy.' Accordingly the Bull *Licet ab initio* erected the 'Holy Office.' It consisted of six (later of ten) cardinals, twenty-seven counsellors and three theologians. Carafa himself was appointed president, a fact which indicated from the start that there would be no half-hearted measures. The tribunals of the Holy Office were entrusted once again to the Dominicans. Although the jurisdiction of the new Inquisition was not clearly stated it seemed to include the whole of Christendom. A new weapon had been forged for use in the conflicts that lay ahead.

[1] Thus Orestes Ferrara, in his splendid work *Le XVIe Siècle vu par les Ambassadeurs Vénitiens*, throws doubt upon the effectiveness of the regulations drawn up by the Commission *De Emendanda Ecclesia*.

Another innovation of Paul III was the Index. Fully aware of the part played by books in the propagation of heresy, he deployed his forces likewise in this field. He had invited Cardinals Contarini and Aleandro to write a work that would instruct preachers in the proper method of expounding Christian doctrine to the various classes of society. But it was necessary also to prevent the spread of false teaching. Lists (indexes) of harmful works were compiled in several dioceses, and in 1543 stern penalties, including fines and even banishment, were imposed on those who sold condemned books. Such was the origin of the Congregation of the Index, which received its official status in 1557 during the pontificate of Paul IV.

This vast and remarkable activity enabled Paul III to clear the first stage of his grand design. The ground had been prepared; the Holy See's authority could no longer be disputed; weapons and troops were at the Papacy's disposal for the completion of its task. It was now possible to embark upon the second stage by summoning a council. But in this matter words were easier than deeds.

3. The Difficulty of Summoning a Council

In order to assess the merit of Pope Paul III we must take account of the formidable obstacles which he had to surmount. Many interests were ready to combine against him. He encountered opposition first from his own *entourage*, among the officials of the Curia who had bought their places and were vexed when the news of an impending reform lowered the value of their acquisitions; among his advisers, who warned him that any interference with the system of annates, expectancies and other Roman privileges would ruin the Apostolic See; and even among very pious folk—of the type, for example, which frequented the Oratory of Divine Love—who insisted that he was putting the cart before the horse in seeking to bring about an official reform while the interior and only efficacious revolution had not yet borne its fruits.

Then he had to reckon with the Protestants, who could not be ignored even though they subsequently stood aside. They too were demanding a council: long ago, on 28th November 1518, Luther had declared his appeal to the Assembly of the Church against Rome's sentence of excommunication. But the council which they wanted was of a particular kind, in which their pastors would rank as equals of the bishops, in which the tradition of the Church (especially the Bulls and decretals of the popes) would have been regarded as null and void, the 'pure Gospel' being alone sufficient to solve all problems. The 'presbyterian' council was altogether unacceptable; meeting on those bases the assembly would have ended by throwing the whole Church into the Germanic chaos.

Could Paul hope for support among the temporal rulers? Certainly not from Henry VIII, erstwhile Defender of the Faith and now excommunicate. François I was playing a double game, loudly declaring himself a partisan of the council, but in fact alarmed by the prospect that the Gallican Church might be forced to relax its privileges; besides, he had allied himself with the Lutheran princes in the League of Smalkald. No, François would not readily dispatch his bishops to a council. As regards Charles V, his attitude was still more ambiguous. As King of Spain he was an eager reformer and in favour of a council; but as emperor he desired above all to reconcile his subjects, and therefore did not much like the idea of an assembly which would condemn Protestantism. Failing an imperial diet, which he would have preferred, he dreamed of a Germanic council in which his word would have been law, and upon which he would most probably have imposed a formula analogous to the subsequent Interim.[1]

We see then that Paul III had to steer St Peter's barque among some dangerous reefs. But that was not all. Suppose them safely negotiated and the council actually in session: one delicate and very serious question would have to be answered: in what spirit would the assembly go to work? For indeed among those reformers who were most sincerely anxious for the welfare of the Church there were two currents more or less antagonistic. Speaking comprehensively and in frankly anachronistic terms, we may say that there were 'modernists' and 'integrists.' On one side were the Christian humanists, friends and disciples of Erasmus. These included Sadolet, Reginald Pole, Contarini and other kindred spirits who, though determined on reform, laid emphasis upon the spiritual life, but favoured gentleness, temporization and conciliatory formulae in the dogmatic sphere. Some of them, e.g. Erasmus himself and the Dominican John Faber, extolled the idea that the decisions of the council, before being approved by the full assembly, should be submitted to a kind of 'superior council' of cognizances— i.e. to themselves. The other current ran in the direction of severity, of categorical measures, of the Inquisition and repression. At its head was Cardinal Carafa; and it was favoured by circumstances, for it is a constant of history that in moments of great peril the rigorists carry the day. Was not the Pope, in choosing one or other method, likely to alienate the rest of the assembly.' It is not difficult therefore to understand that, as he himself wrote, 'amid all that turbulence of heresy,

---

[1] See *The Protestant Reformation*, Chapter V, p. 388. Charles's principal counsellor, the Franche-Comtois Granvelle, was so much opposed to a council that he spread a rumour everywhere that the Pope himself was of the same opinion and 'dreaded it like fire.'

dispute and war, amid all those storms which were the most terrible that had ever threatened the barque of Peter,' Paul III experienced a cold sweat of anguish and begged the Lord to 'comfort him and arm his spirit with strength and constancy, his intellect with the gift of wisdom.'

The courageous pontiff would have singular need of constancy and strength, for it took him no less than nine years of uninterrupted effort to reach his goal. On 2nd June 1536, having sounded Charles V and having sent his nuncio Vergerio to seek approbation in Germany, he summoned a council to meet at Mantua in May 1537. In fact, however, no one was altogether willing to attend. François I was directing his ambassador, Guillaume du Bellay, to inform his Lutheran friends that they need have no fears, even while the diplomat's brother, Cardinal Jean du Bellay, was assuring Paul III that his sovereign was well disposed. Charles V, furious at the choice of an Italian city, where he would not speak as master, vociferated to such good effect that the Duke of Mantua, alarmed or pretending to be so, declared that he could not answer for the security of the members of the council. A large majority of the cardinals therefore decided to stay at home.

The Pope then altered his choice in favour of Vicenza and postponed the meeting to 1st May 1538. He was now more hopeful; the Truce of Nice was on the point of reconciling those two great enemies, the King of France and the Emperor Charles. But too many interests were still opposed to the meeting of the council. When the papal legates reached Vicenza they found a total of five bishops, who seemed very surprised to be there at all.

There followed a multitude of negotiations and conferences, in which the elector Joachim of Brandenburg and Ferdinand of Austria played a prominent part, with a view to eliminating the obstacles. There was much talk and much discussion, and Paul III realized that this policy of conferences was intended as nothing less than a substitute for the council; under pretext of reconciling Catholic and Protestant theologians (which in any case was impossible), the grave questions touching the reform of the Church and the problems of faith would be ignored. Charles V was clearly behind this manœuvre, which had been devised by Granvelle. Futile meetings were held [1] at Speyer, Worms and Ratisbon. It seemed that plans for a council were being deliberately set aside. Reacting firmly, however, Paul III again proposed that the assembly should take place. Vicenza was no longer available because the Venetians refused to make it so. What about Piacenza or Bologna or even Cambrai? Ferdinand of Austria suggested Trent, a small city in the Tyrol, Italian by race and language but subject to the emperor. Charles V could not but bow before a choice that seemed to flatter him,

[1] See *The Protestant Reformation*, section 'Lutheranism becomes a Political Force.'

and on 22nd May the tireless Pope once more convoked the council. But another three years would pass before it actually met.

War was resumed between François I and Charles V, and the former forbade his prelates to travel to the imperial city. As for the emperor, he protested to the Pope because the Bull of summons had included, immediately after his Imperial Majesty, among the 'principal upholders and supporters of the Christian name the contemptible King of France, an ally of the Turks.' So the question of a council had to be postponed until the Peace of Crespy-en-Valois had reconciled the adversaries (17th September 1544). Then, however, the aged Paul flung himself into the affair, feeling that now was his last chance. François I and Charles V were both pressed to agree; negotiations were opened even with the Turks, who, being preoccupied with the Persians, undertook not to molest northern Italy. The Bull *Laetare Jerusalem* (19th November) summoned the council for 15th March, Laetare Sunday— a symbolic coincidence.

Would things be any better this time? No. Once again the legates, Cardinals del Monte, Cervini and Pole, arrived to find such a small attendance that they hurried back to Rome and asked the Pope to postpone the meeting until December. The whole summer was needed in order to send nuncios to round up the members. The Pope's grandson, young Cardinal Farnese, made another call on Charles V, who seemed more favourably disposed. But the French and Spaniards argued that Trent was too far away; the English and Scandinavians had passed to schism or heresy; and of course no German Lutheran would agree to come. At long last, on 13th December 1545, in the choir of Trent cathedral, Cardinal del Monte was able to celebrate the Mass of the Holy Ghost and declare the first session of the Council open. There were four cardinals (including the legates), four archbishops, twenty-one bishops, five generals of orders, and some fifty theologians and canonists. The number was small, but at least its end had been attained in principle. As for practical results, they were not forthcoming for another eighteen years.

4. DIFFICULTIES AND VICISSITUDES OF THE COUNCIL OF TRENT

'We shall see the end of this Council in a few weeks,' wrote one Italian bishop on arrival in the little city of Trent with its crowded mass of prelates, definitors, consultors and secretaries. Was not everyone agreed on principles? In actual fact an endless succession of obstacles lay ahead. 'Christendom,' both as an ideal and as a reality, was dead; and even in the sphere of the most urgent spiritual questions all sorts of private interests, enmities and appetites were at loggerheads.

There was certainly no lack of goodwill or of a sense of responsibility. Any member of the Council might have uttered the brave words spoken by the Cardinal of Lorraine in one of the final sessions: 'Whom shall we accuse my fellow bishops? Whom shall we declare to be the authors of such great misfortune? Ourselves; we must admit that much, with shame and with repentance for our past lives. Storm and tempest have arisen on our account, my brethren, and because of this let us cast ourselves into the sea. Let judgment begin with the House of God; let those who bear the sacred instruments of the Lord be purged and reformed!' Among these new Jonases there was not one who was not determined to do what was right. But they were still men, and the cyclone which shook this vessel of the Church was so violent that none could immediately distinguish what course to take in order to round the cape.

Motives of conflict were only too numerous. Some arose from differences in character, inevitable in so large an assembly of men, and they led sometimes to farcical incidents. Some prelates hurled abuse at one of the legates disputing the nobility of his birth; a Neapolitan bishop, having been described by a Greek bishop as 'ignorant and perverse,' rushed at him, seized his beard and shook it so violently that he tore out a handful of hair. But behind such personal animosities there almost always lay national antagonisms. Among these princes of the Church there were very few who were able to forget their loyalty to some temporal prince and, while serving the supreme interests of Catholicism, to refrain from upholding those of their own countries. The haughty Spaniards posed as sole defenders of faith and morality, but were reminded of the fact that in Spain the Church was curiously subject to the civil power; and one day, when one of them was talking too loud he was interrupted with a shout: 'Are we at the Council of Toledo?' The French, whose doctrine was viewed by some with grave suspicion, made vigorous answer to their critics. A French bishop was interrupted during a discourse on the necessity of reforming the Curia with these sarcastic words: 'My, my, listen how well the cock crows!' To which he retorted: 'Yes, and at cock-crow St Peter roused himself and wept.' A tactful observation! As for the Italians, whenever there was an important vote to be taken, they profited by the comparative nearness of Trent to dispatch whole swarms of bishops; and this caused one member to observe: 'The Holy Spirit arrives in Rome's baggage.'

These clashes were not in themselves particularly serious, and the history of the Council is by no means reducible to incidents of this kind. A great majority of members, though of widely differing temperament, worked together in a noble cause, impelled by longing to do aright, by devotion to their lofty task and by the certainty that their labours were of paramount importance for the welfare of the Church.

Among the presiding legates, all passionately loyal to the Apostolic See, were del Monte, Crescenzi, Gonzaga, Morone, Cervini (afterwards Pope Marcellus II) and Reginald Pole, a man of truly oecumenical learning and judgment. The numerous theologians from various religious Orders, who drew up reports and prepared theses, included the Jesuits Le Jay, Laynez and Salmeron, the Augustinian Seripando, Musso, a Franciscan, and Bernardin of Asti, a Capuchin; Cano and Soto were two of the outstanding Dominican representatives. We can imagine them busy, not only at plenary sessions in the cathedral of St Vigilius, but also in working groups at the smaller church of S. Maria Maggiore, on various committees in the halls of the palace, or in convent cells where specialists wrote their refutation of heresies and drafted the decrees that would rebuild the Church.

If the Fathers of the Council had been left alone to look after the interests of the Church, without political obtrusion, their work might have been soon accomplished. The sovereigns, however, and one in particular, claimed the right to interfere in the business of the Assembly, and long made real progress impossible. Charles V was mainly responsible for these complications; extremely distrustful of the Papacy, which he always dreaded seeing predominant in Italy, he was equally anxious to avoid breaking with the German Protestants and thus prevent trouble in his dominions. He thought that the Council should be a friendly meeting-ground between Catholics and heretics, whereas the popes and the Church as a whole considered it rather as the occasion for a show-down which had become necessary even at the cost of rupture. These opposite views were long maintained, and in all sorts of circumstances. For example, it was asked whether definition of dogma or reform of discipline should be given priority. Charles V replied through his representatives: 'Discipline first,' in order to avoid irrevocable condemnation of the Lutheran theses. 'Dogma,' said the rigorist party who understood the menace of heresy; even Campeggio's suggested compromise, that the two matters be studied *pari passu*, gave rise to some heated debates. On the other hand, it is beyond doubt that in spite of their meritorious efforts to make the Council a success, several popes failed to take a firm stand apart from and above politics, and that all or nearly all laid themselves open to attack on the purely temporal plane. These facts explain the extraordinary duration of the Council of Trent, which was four times interrupted, suspended for nearly ten years, and did not reach its goal until the general situation freed Rome from political entanglement.

Meeting first, as we have seen, in December 1545, and relatively weak in numbers, the Fathers of the Council held eight sessions in a period of six months. Methods of procedure were carefully worked out so as to avoid recurrence of those demagogic tendencies which had appeared long ago at Basel and Constance. Strangely, though perhaps not altogether by chance, a plan was adopted similar to (and maybe as a reply to) that of the Confession of Augsburg, whereby some excellent results were obtained at the doctrinal level on the role of Holy Scripture as the rule of faith, on the doctrine of original sin, on justification and on the sacraments. A serious beginning was also made in the field of disciplinary reform by laying down the duties of bishops. But when Charles V learned the content of the dogmatic decrees, he gave vent to ominous rage, and ordered the Council to proceed no further on this road. It was a cruel setback. Notwithstanding the efforts of the cardinal-legate del Monte, many bishops felt a slackening of their zeal now that the emperor spoke so loud. At that moment too, about mid May, Trent and its guests found themselves in the grip of an epidemic, a sort of lethal influenza which was nicknamed 'lentil sickness' because the victim's skin was covered with tiny round disks. One, two, four, then ten, then twelve Fathers of the Council betook themselves to more salubrious neighbourhoods. The Council had to be transferred to Bologna (February 1548), where two insignificant sessions were attended by the Italians alone. The Imperial and Spanish members remained at Trent by order of Charles V, and there was nothing for it but to suspend the Council.

Just then, however, there occurred an unfortunate incident. Paul III, yielding once more to family feeling, had detached the duchies of Parma and Piacenza from the Papal States and conferred them on his own son, Pierluigi Farnese. Cardinal Gonzaga had protested. 'Marvellous!' he had declared in presence of the pontiff. 'A new prince springing up like a mushroom overnight!' The emperor also had been very displeased, and had retorted by appointing as Governor of the Milanese another Gonzaga, Ferrante, a bitter enemy of Pierluigi. Tension had grown throughout the years 1545 and 1546 until September in the latter year, when Pierluigi was assassinated. His body, riddled with dagger wounds, was thrown from a window of his castle, while Gonzaga hurried to occupy Piacenza in the name of His Imperial Majesty. Though he made a great show of innocence, Charles V was strongly suspected of complicity in this crime. Distraught and terribly worried that the event might herald another attack upon Italy in the manner of 1527, Paul III, while negotiating with the emperor to suspend the Council (17th September 1549), was actively preparing a Holy League against him with the support of France, Switzerland and many Italian cities; and he was even proposing to hurl the Turks against Vienna when he died, on 10th November 1549, at the age of eighty-two, having most gloriously laid the foundations of reform, but still far from having achieved his purpose and full of anxiety for the future.

There was indeed good cause for anxiety. The last months of the pontificate had witnessed Charles V take a step whose consequences none could foresee. Partly with authority from Rome, and partly on his own account, he had signed the *Interim* of Augsburg[1] on 15th May 1548, thus strengthening the Protestant hand by entitling married priests to continue their ministry and granting the laity communion in two kinds.[2] The future was undeniably obscure.

The danger of the situation was abundantly clear when the Conclave met to choose Paul's successor. The cardinals assembled late in November, but did not make up their minds to elect a pope until 8th February 1550. This Conclave, one of the longest in the history of the Church, was the scene of open conflict between the French and imperial factions, and could not reach a decision until the two young leaders of the opposing parties, Cardinal de Lorraine and Cardinal Farnese, reached agreement on a candidate.

The choice fell upon Cardinal del Monte, a former president of the Council. He was a man of personal respectability, although perhaps a little too much inclined towards earthly pleasures and works of art; and he was surrounded, like his predecessor, by greedy relations. In memory of Julius II, among whose domestic prelates he had been, he took the name Julius III (1550–5). This pope has been harshly judged; it has even been written that 'he said nothing and did nothing to reform the Church.' That is not true. Friend and confidant of Paul III, very well aware of the Farnese pontiff's grand designs, he was firmly resolved to resume the Council's mighty task, as all the members of the Conclave had sworn to do. But he was not a man of very strong character; besides, though still in his sixties, he was prematurely aged, suffered from gout and was scared of Charles V. It is therefore not surprising that he preferred negotiation to a fight. His nepotism also, if less scandalous than that of his predecessor, was none the less notorious; nor did the business of Parma and Piacenza, which continued to give trouble and even to provoke armed hostilities, allow him a free hand. His undeniable goodwill was seriously impeded.

On 1st December 1550 the Council was summoned to reassemble at Trent on 1st May following. The emperor, who had given his consent and promised to send his bishops, was in no particular hurry to help them on their way. As for the French, they had been forbidden by Henri II to leave the kingdom, first because war with Charles V was again on the point of breaking out, and secondly because relations between the Louvre and the Curia were so bad as to be on the verge of rupture. The ambassador Amyot informed the Pope that France, 'pure

---

[1] See *The Protestant Reformation*, Chapter VII, p. 504.
[2] Paul III's curious indulgence is again explained by nepotism; he had obtained consolatory favours for Ottavio Farnese, who had become the emperor's son-in-law.

from all heresy,' had no need of a General Council, and that she could quite well hold a national synod. Nevertheless a handful of bishops, meeting at Trent with the legate Crescenzi and Bishop Lippomano of Verona as presidents, did substantial work in the course of four sessions upon dogmatic decrees dealing with the sacraments. They were gradually joined by others, and even witnessed the arrival of a Protestant delegation, which they were obliged to admit upon the express demand of Charles V and which submitted two declarations of the German Lutheran faith.

Political factors once again intervened. Ottavio Farnese refused to surrender Parma to the emperor as the Pope had promised. He was supported by Henri II, who had been offended by the Holy See's policy in the matter of benefices, and who openly criticized Julius III and his Council. Turkish galleys, invited by the Most Christian King, were cruising off the shores of the Papal States; and but for the restraining hand of Cardinal de Lorraine, Henri might even have drifted into schism. His troops occupied Siena, which Montluc subsequently defended against the Imperialists with heroic vigour. The whole of Central Italy was prey to fire and sword, ravaged by the partisans of Ottavio Farnese, and behind it all the hand of Charles was evidently still at work. News suddenly reached the Council that Maurice of Saxony, in rebellion against the emperor, had just invaded Tyrol, had nearly succeeded in capturing his overlord at Innsbruck, and was preparing to march upon Trent. Confusion reigned, and on 28th April 1552 it was decided to adjourn the Assembly at once for two years.

At the end of that period Julius III had not the courage to resume his task. Disheartened by so much intrigue and opposition, increasingly sick and weary, he had taken refuge in the stately villa he had built outside the Porta del Popolo, and seemed no longer interested save in the beautiful gardens with which he had surrounded his new home. Only his silent and solitary death suggested that his conscience was not quite at ease. Many throughout the Christian world were beginning to ask themselves whether a council was really the best means of solving the Church's problems, whether such gatherings were not likely to produce an overdose of controversy, and whether an individual acting on his own might not achieve better results. This last idea was about to find its way into the mind of Pope Paul IV.

5. POPE PAUL IV

On Ascension Day (23rd May) 1555 the Church was thrilled by news of the papal election. The Conclave had chosen one who, by styling himself Paul IV, showed clearly that he meant to follow in the footsteps of Farnese. Another pope had just vanished from the scene,

Marcellus II (immediate successor of Julius III), of whom it has been said that 'he was shown rather than given to the Church.' This man of God, this living image of reform, was one who, as Cardinal Cervini, had presided over the Council. He had been taken seriously ill less than a fortnight after his election, and had died ten days later. Palestrina had not had time to complete the wonderful Mass he was writing for the coronation. The unexpected death of Marcellus, an active man still in his fifties, had given rise to anxiety in many minds; and that anxiety was not completely removed by the election of his successor. The Dean of the Sacred College would naturally be on the side of reform; but Marcellus II had hoped to accomplish the work in a spirit of peace and by gentler methods, thinking rather to appease than to condemn. Would the new successor of St Peter take the same line? He had been chosen by the Conclave for tactical reasons, in order to exclude both the Cardinal of Ferrara, who was too much involved in Italian politics, and Reginald Pole, who was suspected of intending to hurl the Church against the English monarchy. The new Pope was none other than the terrible Cardinal Carafa.

This grand old man remained as impetuous and imperious at the age of almost eighty years as he had been in the flower of his youth at Naples, where he had scoffed at the Spanish authorities even while he dreamed of restoring to the Church her sanctity. Slender, lean, taut and with glowing eyes, he was, says a contemporary, 'like an arrow, ever ready to strike home on its target.' His speech was said to be 'volcanic,' and his outbursts 'as unpredictable as those of Vesuvius.' The gentleness of his friend St Cajetan of Tiene, with whom he had founded the Theatine Order,[1] had not influenced him in the least. Being also intelligent, refined, learned in theology, deeply pious and of a retiring disposition, he undoubtedly possessed the highest virtues, although the violence of his temperament sometimes interfered with their rightful employment. His lofty notion of the dignity attaching to the Holy See, together with his personal pride, led him to a theocratic concept whose anachronism he does not appear to have understood: kings, emperors and peoples must kneel before the Pope; there must be no nations, only large groups absolutely subject to the Vicar of Christ. It was unfortunate that he lived in the sixteenth century and not in the days of Innocent III.

The brief pontificate of Paul IV (1555–9) therefore marked a pause in the labours of the Council; it was indeed more than a pause, it was a change of orientation. A man of his calibre would hardly be anxious to leave the taking of necessary decisions to an assembly not subject to his control. He would be able of his own accord to carry out the work of reform through the medium of arbitrary Bulls and decretals; this

[1] See Chapter I, p. 21.

D

empty theological chatter was utterly fruitless. Six days after his election he held his first consistory, but said nothing about the Council —although he, with his fellow conclavists, had sworn to resume it. The cardinals looked at one another: they had understood.

It cannot be denied that Paul IV's personal efforts at reform proceeded from the best of intentions and even produced some excellent results. A number of peremptory decrees recalled bishops to the duties of their state; forbade any dispensation from the rule that fixed the minimum age for their appointment; strictly forbade the alienation of ecclesiastical goods upon any pretext whatever; reorganized the principal Vatican offices, notably the Dataria, in order to prevent simony in that quarter; abandoned such revenues of the Apostolic See as might be thought open to question; and in short clearly demonstrated that a real change had been effected in the Church. Certain cardinals whom the Pope adjudged worldly heard themselves publicly rebuked; and he of Ferrara, the ostentatious Ippolito d'Este, was overtly distributing gold with a view to his future election when he received orders to quit the Papal States without delay.

This watchful solicitude was extended to as many areas as possible. A trustworthy cardinal was appointed for each country, whose duty it would be to keep the authorities informed of all papal directions. Bishops were given increased powers, together with detailed instructions for the supervision of their clergy. Superiors of congregations were firmly requested to put their houses in order, even if this necessitated calling in the secular arm.

One picturesque episode in this campaign is worth recording here. At Rome, as indeed in all the great cities of Christendom, there were large numbers of 'gyrovague' monks wandering about in defiance of the law of enclosure. Their lives were generally far from edifying, and a papal Bull ordered them to return to their monasteries or incur the penalty of excommunication. One month later the gates of the Eternal City were closed, and the pontifical police began hunting down their prey. Several hundred were rounded up, of whom two hundred were imprisoned or sent to the galleys. No pope had ever been known to employ measures of this kind.

Paul IV's chief instrument of reform, however, was the Inquisition, in charge of which Carafa had himself been placed at the time of its re-establishment by Paul III; and it was now 'the apple of his eye, the favourite of his heart.' The Venetian ambassador at Rome wrote: 'The Pope's violence is always great, but in the matter of the Inquisition it is really indescribable. On Thursday, the day appointed for its meetings, nothing on earth could prevent him from attending. I remember the day when the Spaniards occupied Anagni: all Rome was running to arms, trembling for its life and property; but Paul IV calmly went off to preside over the Holy Office, dealing point by point with the agenda, just as though there were no enemy at the gate.' Controlled thus by the Pope's iron hand, and entrusted by him to Ghislieri,[1] a Dominican prior no less rigid than himself, the Inquisition acquired formidable authority, receiving extraordinary and almost unlimited powers. It was ordered to prosecute even the semblance of heresy, 'in no case to employ gentleness,' never to hesitate in making an example even of the highest dignitaries. All suspects—pedlars of unorthodox books, Jews and Moors—were arrested and brought before the stern Dominican tribunals.

Reviving and giving legal form to another of Paul III's ideas, Carafa established the official catalogue of forbidden books, the Index (1558), which was soon afterwards entrusted to a special Roman Congregation. Sixty-one works came under the ban.

The Inquisition was quite impartial, and had no respect of persons. The Patriarch of Aquilea, for instance, had excused a Lenten preacher who had spoken too lightly of predestination. He was summoned to appear, and, though exonerated, lost the Red Hat he had been promised. Cardinal Morone, the famous diplomat, who ventured to remark that violence in the sphere of religion had never borne good fruit, was imprisoned in the castle of Sant' Angelo. Cardinal Pole, being guilty of the same offence, was deprived of his position as legate in England and summoned to Rome, whither his sovereign, Mary Tudor, wisely prevented him from travelling. Every Catholic State was requested to provide facilities for the Inquisition. France declined, but Spain, where it had long been powerful, joyfully agreed; and it was at this period that all suspected of Lutheranism, Erasmianism or Illuminism were subjected to the fiery persecution which has earned the Spanish Inquisition so vile a reputation. Beautiful writings, such as John of Avila's *Audi Filia*, were condemned. St Teresa herself fell under suspicion. Thousands, nay, tens of thousands of works were consigned to the flames. At the instigation of his fellow Dominican Melchior Cano, 'who could smell heresy at a distance of ten leagues,' Archbishop Carranza of Toledo was arrested because of a commentary on the catechism which had been declared suspect. This appalling reign of terror, though justified to some extent by the perilous situation in which the Church then stood, was surely going too far; such at least was the opinion expressed in many quarters.

Moreover Paul IV, an upright pope, determined to place the welfare of the Church above all temporal interests, became involved in political affairs of which the least that can be said is that they added nothing to his glory. A Neapolitan, whose family had suffered under Spanish rule, he detested everything to do with Spain, and was fond of saying that no

[1] Afterwards St Pius V.

such evil man as Charles V had been born on earth for a thousand years. Like Julius II, he dreamed of expelling the 'Barbarians' from Italy and of reconstituting the peninsula as a fourfold entity, with Venice, Naples and Milan unquestionably subject to the Apostolic See. Urged by his nephew, Carlo Carafa, and more or less supported by the King of France, he hurled his troops against Naples; but the Duke of Alba brushed aside the attack. Simultaneously the terrible defeat of France at Saint-Quentin (10th August 1557) obliged François de Guise to return in haste and oppose the invaders of his country. The collapse of the papal armies was complete. Rome was humiliated, and to crown her misfortunes the Tiber overflowed its banks to such a depth that it was possible to row a boat in the piazza of St Peter's. Amid this desolation Alba made his entry, coming with scornful humility to pay his respects to the common Father of the faithful.

The political sovereign of the Papal States had been taught a harsh lesson; but worse was to come, this time from the hand of Providence through the medium of Carlo Carafa, his much too well-beloved nephew, a young soldier of fortune whom he had raised to the Sacred College and appointed Secretary of State. Carlo was a man devoid of morality, who, though governor of the Milanese and general of the Empire, had defected to the French from the lowest motives of self-interest, and whose private life and intrigues were a permanent scandal. Paul IV, however, thought the world of him. Around this young adventurer a whole family clique, including the Duke of Palliano and the Marquis of Montebello, was busily engaged, while a network of dispensations and privileges brought in handsome profits. A day came at last when rumours of the scandal reached the pontiff's ears, perhaps through the good offices of a Florentine agent. The aged Pope was greatly upset and ordered Padre Isackino, a saintly Theatine, to investigate. His report was far from satisfactory, and Paul IV now showed admirable strength of soul. Mastering his grief he held a secret consistory (January 1559) at which he delivered an astonishing address. He admitted his fault in having trusted unworthy men, and announced that three of his nephews—Cardinal Carlo, Palliano and Montebello—were dismissed from all their ecclesiastical offices and banished from Rome. Young Cardinal Alphonso, who alone had done no wrong and therefore remained at his post, was forbidden ever again to speak of the exiles. Six cardinals vainly besought the Pope to mitigate the rigour of the sentence. Disconsolate as he was, he grimly refused to yield—'a splendid example,' says Massaretti, 'of honesty and true magnanimity.'

The old man had nevertheless been broken by this tragic event. While multiplying his own fasts and other penances, as if to expiate the fault which his conscience would not forgive, he redoubled his intransigence in the work of reform, hurling terrible invective at bishops who lived at Rome instead of residing in their dioceses, referring the slightest peccadillo [1] to the Inquisition, and having his police spy on the private morals of Rome, just as Calvin did at Geneva. He died a holy death on 18th August 1559, and that evening there was serious rioting by the Roman mob, which had lately honoured him with a statue for having reduced taxation. The Dominican convent and the offices of the Inquisition were sacked; heretic prisoners were freed; insult was heaped upon the dead Pope's memory, and the famous statue overturned.

In the church of the Minerva at Rome, above the heavy sarcophagus of marble framed in gold, the image of Pope Paul IV raises its right hand in everlasting benediction—or everlasting menace.

6. Pius IV Brings the Council to a Successful Conclusion

If one thought may be said to have been uppermost during the arduous Conclave which opened at the beginning of September 1559 and lasted for more than three months, it was determination not to subject the Church to another ruler as harsh and authoritarian as the dead Carafa. Except for this, however, the cardinals were in almost total disagreement. Divided as they were into three groups, 'Spanish,' 'French' and 'Carafist,' [2] they took a long time finding the candidate who would satisfy them all. As generally happens in such cases, they ended by choosing a 'back-bencher' of whom no one had hitherto spoken much good nor yet much evil, and who had never held very high office. This man was Cardinal Giovanni Angelo Medici, Archbishop of Ragusa and a native of Milan. His supporters claimed him to be descended from the illustrious Florentine family of that name, but the wags called him *Il Medichino*, 'the pocket Medici.' He belonged in fact to that middle-class society which had its sons educated at the best schools and was not averse from seeing them hold office in the Church.

Medici was a sexagenarian, of stoutish build, but vigorous, full of high spirits and astute simplicity. Panvinius, a witness of his election, has left this portrait which there is every reason to accept as truthful: 'Wide forehead, blue eyes, sideways glance, prominent red nose, scanty beard and fullness of figure. His features, and above all his gait, were somewhat lacking in dignity: a stoop and mincing steps invited laughter rather than respect.' With such characteristics he was obviously a very different man from his fiery predecessor; but it could at least be hoped that the well-known law of alternation, which

---

[1] e.g. violation of the Friday abstinence, which was punished with imprisonment.
[2] Constituting those who had been admitted to the Sacred College by Paul IV.

appeared to operate almost invariably in the field of papal elections, might produce a moral contrast no less profound than the physical dissimilarity which was plain for all to see. Modest, moderate, careful to break nothing and even to repair what had been broken, the new Pope took the auspicious name of Pius IV. His reign, which lasted until 1565, followed paths very different from those of his predecessor.

It was possible to breathe once more, but an all-important question remained: would he encourage the reform? If so would he straightway reassemble the Council? He had sworn in writing to do so at the Conclave, where he had given every sign of readiness to fulfil that undertaking. Not that he himself was altogether beyond reproach, for three illegimate children bore witness that he had paid handsome tribute to the disorderly spirit of the age. But when all was said and done, he had managed to preserve discretion; he had never caused scandal, and, as Panvinius notes with perhaps a touch of irony, 'he had distinguished himself by his bearing and reputation' in the various secondary posts which he had occupied. Sanctity then was not the principal characteristic of this man, to whom would belong the credit of having resumed and finally accomplished the indispensable work of reform, both with vigour and with greater ability than his forerunner. Here indeed we have one of the more surprising episodes in this amazing story: for the performance of so manifestly a providential task, God makes use of such instruments as Paul III, Paul IV and Pius IV.

The first acts of the new pontificate did not seem to indicate a firm resolve to break with the deplorable errors of that age. Many were sullied by the most obvious nepotism. Among the issue of his four brothers and five sisters Pius IV had many nephews, and this hungry horde descended upon him in full cry immediately after his coronation. But for all his apparent simple-mindedness, *Il Medichino* had a crafty eye and was no bad judge of men. Those of his nephews who came begging received offices and honours galore, but in such sort that they were kept at a safe distance from Rome and could exert no real influence. There lived at Milan another young nephew of the Pope, who asked for nothing. This was the son of his sister Margaret, wife of Ghiberto Borromeo; a brilliant student at the University of Pavia, he was also known to lead a blameless life amid the dissipations of his youthful contemporaries. Pius IV, with whom he was a great favourite, summoned him to Rome, and a few weeks later not only gave him the Red Hat but also appointed him Secretary of State. The fortunate lad was barely twenty-two years of age. Here indeed was an act of nepotism if ever there was one; but Heaven must have had a hand in this choice, and the Pope must have been a first-class judge of men, for the young cardinal turned out to be one of the greatest saints of the age, 'the

Pope's right eye' in the labour of reform. He is known to history as St Charles Borromeo.

With the aid of this peerless collaborator, whose temperament, though firm as a rock, bore no trace of violence, Pius IV was able to retain but at the same time to modify the system introduced by his predecessor. So far from suppressing the Inquisition, for which he had no liking, he was at pains to emphasize that in doctrinal matters its authority remained universal and absolute: it had the right, nay the duty, to proceed against anyone, even a bishop or a cardinal, who yielded to the lure of heresy. He was careful, however, to insist that it must not intrude elsewhere; simoniacs, blasphemers, ill-behaved clerics and sodomites were outside its jurisdiction. In several cases the new Pope inclined to mildness. For example, the unfortunate Bishop of Aquilea, who had been haled before the Inquisition for having merely excused a suspect preacher, was allowed to submit his writings for examination by a more lenient authority, and was completely exonerated. The terrible Index of Paul IV, so brutal that St Peter Canisius called it a 'stumbling-block,' was revised and curtailed. For instance, it no longer included the complete works of Erasmus, which had been condemned *in odium auctoris*; only certain treatises were expressly named. There was thus a change of climate; the aims of Paul IV were not abandoned, but the means thereto were altered.

In one case alone Pius IV showed himself implacable, almost to the point of ferocity. It was a mysterious business of nightmare quality, reminiscent of a Shakespearian tragedy—the affair of the Carafas. The late Pope's nephews had countless enemies, whom they had offended in the days of their power and who were determined on revenge: Colonna, Sforza, Gonzaga, Pallantieri and others. These men considered that Cardinal Carlo had escaped too easily from the punishment due to his scandalous conduct; besides, he had imprudently returned to Rome and was behaving with all his old swagger. A shocking piece of news made it possible to reopen the dossier. The Duke of Palliano, alias Giovanni Carafa, suspecting his wife Violaine of adultery, assumed judicial functions and accused her, together with her alleged accomplice, before a court presided over by himself and two of his relations. By means of torture he secured a full confession from the young man, whom he promptly stabbed with his own hand, leaving him dead with no fewer than twenty-seven gaping wounds. Then, with the approval of the unhappy woman's own brother, Violaine was declared an adulteress and, though seven months pregnant, suffered a hideous death by strangulation with a cord. The crime had been committed while Paul lay on his death-bed, leaving vacant the Apostolic See; but reports reached Rome, there were angry protests on all sides, and those who hated the Carafa clique immediately broke loose.

A formidable record was drawn up; it filled eight chests and constituted an overwhelming indictment of the family of Paul IV. Even young Cardinal Alphonso, by far the best of them, was charged with abuse of confidence and extortion. Arrested and tried by a consistory that knew no mercy, while Rome was put in a state of siege to avoid any possible demonstration, the Carafas were found guilty, despite the intervention of the King of Spain. The three murderers of Violaine were hanged, as was only right; so also was Cardinal Carlo, the justice of whose execution is open to doubt.[1] Alphonso alone was acquitted, but was ordered to take up residence in his diocese and not to leave it during the remainder of his life. As for the Duke of Montebello, another Carafa of ill repute, he managed to escape in time to avoid arrest. Was the inflexibility of Pius IV on this occasion due to pressure of public opinion? Or did he seek to prove that he had broken with the habits of his predecessor? Or again, was he reminding the clans, and even the cardinals, that in spite of his apparent good nature he was more than capable of wielding authority? It was at about this time that he made a quaint remark which caused much mirth in Italy: 'I have four great worries, all beginning with a C.' The four C's were Carafa, Colonna, Cardinals and Council.

The last of these worries was by no means the least. It had undoubtedly weighed upon the mind of Pius ever since he had assumed the tiara, and he was working patiently for the fulfilment of his plan. The personal initiative of Paul IV had evidently failed, and a return must be made to the Council. Those insurmountable difficulties which had prevented the success of the Council some fifteen years earlier had lately been removed. Charles V, who had retired to the monastery of Yuste in 1557, died there on 21st November 1558. His vast dominions were now shared between two empires, Spain under Philip II and Germany under Ferdinand, neither of whom dreamed of reviving the pretence of a Holy Roman and Germanic Empire. Henri II died in 1559, shortly before Paul IV. Since the disappearance of the two great adversaries the climate had improved, and with the return of political peace it had become easier to work for the reform of the Church.

Pius IV saw that the occasion was propitious. He acted accordingly and opened negotiations with the great rulers. Philip II was in principle very much on the side of reform, but he was thinking of marriage with the Protestant Elizabeth of England. Ferdinand, whom the Sovereign Pontiff hoped to win over by conferring upon him the imperial crown, showed himself less favourable to a council than to a series of simple 'conferences' at which his Catholic and Protestant subjects might in the end agree. Catherine dei Medici, regent of France,

---

[1] A revision of the case, ordered by St Pius V, proved that a number of documents produced against him at the trial were forgeries.

still preferred a policy of *rapprochement*, temporization and 'conferences'; the breakdown of the Conference of Poissy in August 1561, and the famous 'Massacre of Vassy' in the following year, had not wholly sufficed to convince her that chances of reaching agreement were remote. Difficulties notwithstanding, the Pope remained firm, and his Bull *Ad Ecclesiae Regimen* summoned members to Trent for Easter Sunday 1561. Complications did not cease for all that, and many months of involved negotiation were necessary before the Council could resume. Happily for Pius IV, he was aided in this most difficult task by a remarkable collaborator, who was perhaps the ablest diplomat of his time—Cardinal Morone, whom his terrible predecessor had flung into prison on suspicion of heresy, and whom the Roman lampoons treated as an 'enemy of the Blessed Virgin and the saints.' Formerly nuncio to Ferdinand, who called him his friend, Morone succeeded in persuading the emperor that his true interest lay in supporting the Council. At the same time Catherine dei Medici discovered that Protestantism in France might prove a very real threat to her power, while some judicious promises of gold helped the waverers to make up their minds.

That fair weather lay ahead became apparent as, week by week, the little Alpine city welcomed an increasing number of bishops, theologians and other dignitaries. Whereas the early sessions of the Council, long ago, had been attended by no more than sixty to eighty members, the final meetings took the votes of more than two hundred and fifty delegates in presence of a large audience. Titian's famous picture in the Louvre gives some idea of the grandeur of these plenary sessions. Seated before the altar of Santa Maria Maggiore, the four legates presided over a sea of white mitres watched by the accredited representatives of every Catholic nation. The streets, squares, palaces and convents, and even the humblest dwelling-houses, were literally packed.

Reassembled at last in January 1562 under the direction of Cardinals Ercole Gonzaga,[1] Stanislaus Hosius, Girolamo Seripando and Luigi Simonetta as legates, the Council set to work in good earnest, bent upon obtaining solid results with the least possible delay. Nine sessions were held in the space of three months; and although personal conflicts were not entirely absent, they were not envenomed by political differences, nor were they so bitter or so violent as before. There were a few awkward moments, as when Catherine dei Medici, furious at seeing the Council resolved to curtail princely privileges, ordered her ambassadors to leave Trent; but on the whole everything ran smoothly.

Most of the great dogmatic and disciplinary problems then facing the Church were studied one by one. The Eucharist, the Mass, the cult of saints and Purgatory were the subject of dogmatic decrees; others

[1] His place was afterwards taken by Morone.

regulated the residence of bishops, the morality of the clergy and the rights of princes. 'No Council in the history of the Church,' says Cardinal Hergenröther, 'has determined so many questions, established so many points of doctrine or made so many laws.' It was an immense achievement: after so much delay and opposition the Church managed to formulate with extraordinary vigour and absolute precision answers to the heretical theses as well as to the criticism directed against herself. Before long the Missal and Catechism, approved by the Council and compiled by some of its members, would disseminate this teaching among the great mass of the faithful. Before long the seminaries advocated by the Council would provide the Church with an altogether new type of clergy, ready for the labour of reconquest. And before long the Papacy—which, in spite of all its faults, must be credited, in the persons of Paul IV and Pius IV respectively, with having initiated the Council and brought it to a successful conclusion—would devote itself under St Pius V to the task of injecting the reform into the blood and marrow of the Church.

'I cannot describe,' wrote an eye-witness, Paleotti, 'the spiritual joy of all, their gratitude to God, their act of thanksgiving when the Council sat for the last time. I myself saw many of the most solemn prelates weep for joy, and those who had the very day before treated one another almost as strangers embrace with deep emotion. An astonishing outburst of cheers for the Pope marked this final gathering.' The date was 4th December 1563. The decrees were solemnly signed by four legates, three patriarchs, twenty-five archbishops, one hundred and sixty-nine bishops, seven abbots, seven Generals of Orders, ten episcopal procurators and the ambassadors of all the Catholic powers. Confined to his palace, old and sick, suffering from asthma and rheumatism, but receiving daily reports on the progress of the Council, Pius IV might well be proud to have been the instrument of this imposing and decisive work. Yet when his two intimate friends, Charles Borromeo and Philip Neri (both future saints), congratulated him upon his success, he replied simply: 'All was done by God's inspiration.'

7. THE COUNCIL OF TRENT AND THE DEFINITION OF DOGMA

A tree is judged by its fruit, and in order to appreciate the importance of Trent one need only consider its results. These are immeasurable, and such that no other council in the whole history of the Church has been of equal consequence. The decisions made in the course of its troubled sessions established the Catholic faith in such a way that it has never since been questioned. 'I ask you,' says Bossuet, 'to show me a single Catholic author, a single bishop, a single priest, a single man whatever he be, who thinks he can remain in the Catholic Church and say that he does not accept the faith of Trent, or that the faith of Trent is open to doubt. That will never be.' In this passage the great orator is referring exclusively to the doctrinal work of the Council, although its achievement in respect of morality and administration, if less conclusive,[1] was equally significant from an historical point of view. Whereas each of the dogmatic decrees included a 'canon,' i.e. a short clause anathematizing those who deny the doctrine set forth, the disciplinary decrees, whose purpose was to reform the Church, contained no censures. All, however, dogmatic and disciplinary alike, were adopted according to no predetermined plan or logical order, but with so broad a vision of the problems confronting Holy Church that together they fill fourteen quarto volumes of the official edition begun in 1901 and still incomplete.

The dogmatic work of the Council of Trent is a monument of wisdom and exactitude. The faith of the Church, based upon Scripture and Tradition, is formulated with a clarity, force and inclusiveness which she had never previously enjoyed. We feel the passage of a mighty wind; we observe at the same time and at every step the firmness of those theological notions which were the fruit of immense labour extending over more than a thousand years. Here is no system sprung, like the doctrines of Luther and Calvin, from a single brain; here indeed is expressed the collective conscience of the Church, not only at that date, but in the past and in the future. Catholicism was no longer destitute of theologians as in the early days of the Lutheran attack. A great majority of the Fathers of the Council were men of outstanding ability, well acquainted with theology, patristic, canon law and Scripture.[2] Above all, they 'felt with the Church' so deeply that they naturally followed the surest line of tradition even in matters upon which they were not thoroughly informed, and every detail of their conclusions is today in full accord with the demands of historical criticism. The *rota scripta*, reports drawn up by the consultors, amaze us with their erudition, and still provide ample material for dictionaries and handbooks of doctrinal history. It was not in vain that there had occurred half a century earlier that revival of theology which has been described as one of the glories of the Catholic Renascence.[3] As the Council set forth the dogmas of the Church, there hung over it a cloud

[1] On the dogmatic plane the decisions of the Council are binding on all Catholics: to reject them is heresy. In the field of discipline, on the other hand, he who disputes or refuses to subscribe them is rash or rebellious, even schismatic, but does not thereby put himself outside the Church.

[2] Less well with the history of dogma; but the reformers themselves were no better off in this respect.

[3] Fr. Cayré, *Manuel de Patrologie*.

of witnesses: Cajetan (1468–1534), the great Dominican cardinal and theologian of the Trinity, whom the Papacy had sent against Luther; [1] Ambrose Catharin (1487–1553), an authority on Grace; Francesco Vittoria, the renewer of Thomism; many controversialists who, from Johann Eck to John Fisher, from Clichtove to Tapper, had fought with such determination against heresy; and the splendid figure of St Ignatius who was represented there by several members of his Society. Among those present at the sessions, and playing a decisive part therein, were the Dominicans Melchior Cano and Dominic Soto, disciples of Vittoria, to whom modern theology is heavily indebted. It was the manifold effort of all these thinkers which ultimately led to the stupendous edifice of the 'canons.'

Here we must frankly acknowledge the historical (or dialectical) function of Protestantism in the evolution of these principles. The part played in the great debate by Luther, Calvin and the rest was exactly that recognized long since by St Paul, in a celebrated passage to the Corinthians, [2] as belonging to heretics. On the strictly spiritual plane the Catholic revival, as represented, for example, by Cajetan of Tiene, Zaccaria, Giberti and Ignatius of Loyola, owed nothing to anti-Protestant endeavours; but on the doctrinal level the blows delivered by the heretics led the Church to discern more clearly those points of her structure which were threatened and to reinforce them accordingly. Every one of the great Protestant theses was surveyed by the Council, which opposed to it the Catholic truth, especially the three fundamentals bearing upon revelation and the bases of doctrine, upon the rôle of faith, works and grace, and upon the sacraments with particular reference to the Eucharist.

Protestants claim that every Christian must discover Revelation in direct contact with God by means of the inspired Book, which is the expression of His Word. To read and meditate the Bible is sufficient to establish genuine Christianity solidly upon its bases; the teaching of the Church contributes nothing to knowledge of the truth. The Council replies that 'the teaching mission of the Church is to guard the perfect integrity of Holy Scripture and Tradition, [3] the two sources of our faith.' These twin sources are equally necessary to the life of the Church. The first of them is indicated with absolute precision: the Council establishes the Canon of Scripture [4] and declares that all the books which constitute the Bible were written 'at the dictation of

---

[1] See *The Protestant Reformation*, pp. 298–9.

[2] 'For there must also be heresies, that they also who are approved may be made manifest among you' (1 Cor. xi. 19).

[3] The Council always uses the plural 'traditions'; but it is now established custom to speak of 'Tradition,' a rather less comprehensive term than the former.

[4] This is the 'canon' followed in all Catholic Bibles. It makes no distinction between what we call the 'protocanonical' and 'deuterocanonical' books.

the Holy Spirit.' The text as at present approved is that of the Latin *Vulgate*, St Jerome's illustrious work, the definitive edition of which was begun immediately the Council ended and was published in 1592. No one, however, may interpret the sacred books in his own way; no one must 'in matters concerning faith and morals attribute to Scripture a meaning other than that which the Church has given and does give to it.' Tradition also is expressly attributed to 'the dictation of the Holy Spirit.' What then is Tradition? The Council does not define this word dogmatically; but its content is revealed by reference to the Fathers and Doctors, to the decrees of recognized councils, to papal decisions, and to the intentions and consent of the universal Church. Thus a communal notion is opposed to Protestant individualism, the principle of authority to anarchism. It is the Church that enables her children to derive from Holy Scripture whatever fruits they can expect therefrom; she it is who teaches them what they must believe and what not believe. A complete exposition of all this doctrine was provided by the *Catechism* of the Council of Trent, published in 1566.

There is another point, besides the sources of faith, at which Protestants diverge from traditional teaching; I mean the rôle of faith in man's supernatural destiny. Luther won many followers by his doctrine of justification by faith, even while Calvin preached the terrible thesis of predestination in the cathedral of St Peter at Geneva. Against these theories the Council took its stand, perfectly aware, however, that their success was due to certain deep-seated aspirations of the age, to an anxious search for the true laws of Christianity, to a hungry longing for salvation. It is remarkable that the Assembly of the Catholic Church, without yielding to the temptations of pagan humanism, remains infinitely closer than its adversaries to humanism properly so called. It does not despise man, it does not belittle him as do the vehement prophets of heresy; the decrees of the Council bear witness to that optimism which St Augustine, St Bernard and St Thomas have made part and parcel of Catholicism. Luther and Calvin place no confidence in man. The Council of Trent has such confidence, because man bears within himself an ineffable likeness, which no defilement can erase. This is not to say that he is unscathed; original sin is there sure enough, and is minutely defined in five canons. But, darkened as it is by sin, human nature is not irremediably affected. Reason and will are damaged, but it is not true that they are without clear-sightedness, integrity and energy. What God asks of man is that he should co-operate fully in the work of his salvation, certain meanwhile that his effort is vain without grace, but equally assured that grace will not be refused to him so long as he remains faithful. Works therefore are necessary; faith alone is not enough. A Christian guilty of mortal sin is deprived of grace and condemned, even though he believes. Considerable stress is laid upon this double rôle of faith and works in the decrees of the sixth session (thirty-three canons in sixteen chapters), which are due in large measure to the saintly Cardinal Cervini, afterwards Pope Marcellus II. Justification is not secured by faith alone, still less by Luther's 'conviction' of being justified. It requires human effort *as well as* the operation of God's mercy. Our Lord's sacrifice, the merits of God made Man, save each one of us from the consequence of sin, from the intolerable burden of his wretchedness; they touch the depth of his conscience, at the innermost point of his freedom, and lead him to the presence of eternal light. Man's free will is offset by the infinite goodness of God. It is of course, as the Council emphasizes, 'with fear and trembling' that man must work out his salvation; but it is not true to say that God, as a whimsical tyrant, calls some to heaven and dooms others to hell by virtue of an incomprehensible act of predestination. The central dogma of Catholicism is *not* the Fall, the terror of eternal chastisement consequent upon sin; it is the Redemption, the charity of our Lord Jesus Christ, His love of our unhappy race.

The sovereign favour of Christ is not limited to one period or to one set of circumstances; it is for ever active in the sacraments, where the ineffable operation of grace joins with the faith, the transport and the effort of a faithful soul to lead it to salvation. On this point also the Council takes a firm stand against the tenets of Protestantism. It imposes, under pain of anathema, belief in the seven traditional sacraments, upholding their divine origin upon the strength of Holy Scripture. It defines their essence and their mode of operation. The function of the sacraments is not, as Luther taught, to nourish faith; they are not, as Zwingli maintained, 'signs of Christianity'; they really contain the grace which they signify, and they confer it upon those who do not oppose it with evil dispositions. Baptism is indispensable to salvation; but it is false to maintain that salvation cannot be lost except by loss of faith, as if baptism itself exempted man from the duty of co-operation. Confirmation, rejected by heretics as 'injurious to the Holy Ghost,' is declared to be man's free and unqualified undertaking to play his bounden part in the work of salvation. Penance and Extreme Unction, condemned or misrepresented by the Protestants, who consider the essential of forgiveness to reside in the merit of Christ, are declared holy, sacred and necessary. In absolving the sins confessed by a penitent, the priest performs a supernatural 'judicial act' in the name of Christ, who has delegated His powers to him; and the act of contrition is an integral part of that self-conquest which is a *sine qua non* of salvation. Holy Orders, likewise rejected by the heretics, are vouched for with the utmost solemnity. Their scriptural origin is declared; the power of consecrating and offering the Body of Christ belongs exclusively to those who have been rightly ordained. Against those who uphold the theory that marriage is simply a contract, and who therefore maintain the validity of divorce, the Council firmly asserts marriage to be a sacrament, instituted by Christ Himself, who has willed that it shall be indissoluble. Finally, in the thirteenth, twenty-first and twenty-second sessions, the sacrament of the Eucharist was defined with such vigour and precision as had never yet been accorded it in any official document of the Church. Eight chapters and eleven canons are set against the multiple and contradictory interpretations of the reformers. They assert the *real* presence of Christ in the host, His *substantial* presence (not virtual, as Calvin said), and His *entire* presence under each species; and they teach *transubstantiation* as opposed to the Lutheran doctrine of impanation. In practice, for traditional reasons, communion in both kinds is reserved to priests. The Council emphasizes the moral and spiritual dispositions with which the faithful should receive the sacrament, having first confessed their sins in order to be in the state of grace. The Eucharist, however, is something more than a sacrament offered to men for their salvation; it is also and above all a sacrifice offered to God (which the Protestants unanimously refuse to admit), a sacrifice which re-enacts that of Calvary, and continually applies the merits thereof. The supernatural framework within which this sacrifice is offered is the Mass, whose central place in the work of redemption is declared.

Thus on all essential points of difference between Catholic tradition and heretical doctrine the Council speaks and resolutely determines what is to be believed. Its achievement is of capital importance, assuring to the Church stability of her foundations, removing revealed truth from the arena of debate, establishing rules which none henceforward can reject without thereby lapsing into error. It must also be observed that this immense doctrinal undertaking was not limited to urgent problems. In fact there was no current question, great or small, upon which the Assembly did not touch and provide a solution. The cult of saints, for example, was declared lawful within certain limits which would avoid abuses. As regards indulgences, they are linked with the power given by Christ to His Church to 'bind and loose'; they must never be abused, but are recognized as perfectly legitimate. On several other doctrinal points the Council avoided anything in the nature of dogmatic definition, but laid down certain principles which would guide the Church in subsequent decisions. Thus the first official statement of Our Lady's Immaculate Conception is contained in a decree of Trent, which formally declares her exempt from the otherwise universal taint of original sin.

8. The Council of Trent and the Reform of Discipline

By including all dogmas within an almost complete system the Council of Trent established the Catholic faith as an indivisible whole, against which heretical error would be powerless. But this all-important work could not endure so long as the human society entrusted with the deposit of faith remained open to attack at many points. Disciplinary reform was therefore a necessary appendage of the doctrinal task. Besides, the two elements frequently interlock. It is, for example, upon the theology of the Church conceived not only as the spiritual assembly of the elect, but also as a human society possessing its own laws, organization and hierarchy, that depend such decrees of the Council as are intended to clarify those laws, to substantiate that organization, and to place that hierarchy on more secure foundations. It was of course upon their own theology of the Church that Luther, Bucer and Calvin had relied in their assault upon Rome and her priesthood.

The most pressing need, after so many years of fruitless endeavour, was to eliminate certain deplorable customs which dishonoured the Church and justified the criticism directed against her. An impressive body of decrees, interweaving and completing one another, laid down rules governing the whole hierarchy of persons from the Supreme Pontiff to the least of the faithful. *In capite et in membris*: the words had been so often repeated; the necessary reform must operate both in the head and in the members.

Not much is said about the head; it is indeed one of the few points upon which the Council saw no need to define and expatiate. There is no decree relating to the Pope as others do to episcopal residence and the power of secular princes. There is mention of the Sovereign Pontiff in Session XXV, where it is said that 'nothing new in the Church can be decided without consulting him.' Infallibility, though put forward by the Jesuit theologians, was not included. On the other hand, the Pope is declared 'universal Pastor having full power to rule the universal Church.' This is repeated several times, and he is reminded in terms reminiscent of St Bernard's *De Consideratione* that he is 'bound by the sacred duties of his office to watch over the universal Church,' to extirpate abuses and to keep a watchful eye upon negligent pastors, 'because Jesus Christ will call him to account for those shepherds whose evil government has shed the blood of their flocks.' He is implored, in a pathetic adjuration, to choose as cardinals none but those worthy of their exalted dignity; and here no doubt is the reason for the Council's reserve in respect of the Papacy, whose past faults it wisely abstained from criticizing. Only let the Pope create good cardinals, selected from all parts of the Christian world, and there would be no more bad popes on the throne of Peter. Reform properly speaking takes place at a lower level.

The cardinals themselves were treated less gently. It is curious, and incidentally strong evidence of the freedom reigning in the Catholic Church, to find members of the Council—some of them bishops, others mere theologians—adopting a strongly critical attitude towards the Sacred College. The saintly Archbishop Bartholomew of Braga, for instance, threw this neat little dart at the *porporati*: 'It is my opinion that their illustrious Lordships are in sore need of illustrious reform.' The Council itself took this view; it bade the Princes of the Church to lead exemplary lives, to be frugal and to despise worldly vanities: 'Since their duty is to assist the Sovereign Pontiff in the government of Holy Church, it is only right and proper that they should possess such outstanding virtue and regulate their conduct in such a way as to serve as models for the rest of mankind.' That familiar figure of the dissolute cardinal, the red-hatted brigand, henceforward stood condemned.

The Council showed immense solicitude for every detail relative to the episcopal order, whose duties were the concern of no fewer than twelve sessions. They are the king-pin of the whole structure: *Ecclesia in episcopo*. The most important duty of which they are reminded is that of residence, to which the Council returns several times. Ancient penalties were revived and new ones enacted against those who neglect the souls committed to their care. A bishop must never be absent from his diocese for more than three months, never during Advent and Lent. The obligation of residence automatically prevented accumulation of benefices, which is forbidden by another decree; it was impossible to live at one and the same time at Mainz, Speyer, Trier and other places. Residing in his diocese the bishop would also be better able to fulfil the functions of his office. What were those functions? The Council enumerates them with rather more detail than method; but taken together its admonitions present a fine picture of the bishop: attentive to the needs of his clergy and flock, careful not to confer Holy Orders upon any but worthy subjects, visiting all the churches in his diocese at least once a year, preaching without fail every Sunday and feast day, keeping himself aloof from politics, financial interests and family ties. The type thus represented was a little too perfect to allow of its immediate realization; but it set an example which ultimately took effect, and continues to be a powerful influence.

The Council also devoted a good deal of attention to priests, and its work in this respect proved to be among the most fruitful of its undertakings. The ideal is similar to that proposed for bishops: 'Those who handle the Lord's vessels must be purified in order to serve as examples;

those who are to be initiated into the sacred ministry must be trained in the practice of every virtue.' The Council repeats itself in this key over and over again. The familiar figure of the worthy and venerable parish priest, living modestly in his presbytery, charitable to the unfortunate and devoted to his people, can be traced in the decrees of Trent. He will be unmarried; the Council absolutely refused to follow the Protestants on this point, imperial entreaties notwithstanding. He must, like his bishop, keep residence and preach, explaining to his flock the Holy Scriptures, the sacraments and the liturgy. Will he be capable of doing so? Indeed yes. For the Council, taking its cue from such contemporary educationists as the Jesuits and even Calvin, proposed the establishment of seminaries, schools for the training of young clerics. In these special colleges the future priest would receive solid intellectual grounding in the liberal arts; a religious education in Scripture, patristics, hagiography and everything necessary for the proper administration of the sacraments, particularly that of Penance; and a moral formation which would fit him for his lofty mission. Rich and poor alike were to be admitted to these colleges; the Council even shows some preference for the poor, and every bishop is urged to have a seminary in his diocese. All this was a splendid initiative of vital importance for the future of the Catholic Church.

As for the regular clergy, the Council did not overlook their need of improvement. In the time of Paul III the Commission of Reform had proposed a drastic remedy in the shape of suppression of all existing Orders. The Fathers of Trent did not accept this radical measure, for many definitors and counsellors were themselves religious. But they did create a repository of regulations binding upon the regulars: age and conditions of admission, material organization of convents, election of superiors, etc. Nothing was omitted from the code, strict application of which was entrusted to the bishops. The Council also attempted to put an end to the scandal of *commendam* by prohibiting the grant of abbeys to persons who were not regulars.

Thus the whole hierarchy was covered: the teaching Church and her clergy would have no excuse for misconduct. Moreover these 'moral' decrees properly so called were accompanied by others intended likewise to restore religion to its full dignity, to revive the deepest Christian loyalties in the field of worship, to safeguard the principles of unity and authority within the Church. The use of Latin, for example, the traditional language of the liturgy, was upheld against the heretics by the Council, which unanimously rejected that of vernacular,[1] and also upheld the custom of pronouncing in a low voice the most sacred words of the Mass, viz. part of the Canon and the formulae of Consecration. The vernacular however, is not forbidden in certain

[1] See a discussion of this question by A. Michel in *L'Ami du Clergé*, 15th January 1953.

well-defined cases, e.g. in private reading of the Bible, where its use is likely to be more profitable to the faithful. Strict rules are also laid down governing the duration of Mass as well as the respect and solemnity with which it must always be celebrated.

The Church, however, includes not only clerics; the mass of the faithful are of even greater importance, since it is in the last resort on their behalf and with a view to their salvation that all the foregoing measures are prescribed. The Council does not forget them, and the eighteenth session obliges them to hear Mass on Sundays and holidays of obligation. Other decrees forbid duelling and fix the minimum age for marriage. All the same, it is a little surprising that not one of the numerous sessions was devoted entirely to a portrayal of the true Christian layman, of the faithful Catholic inspired by the spirit of reform. This may be because the Catechism, which had been ordered by the Council and upon which a special commission was busily engaged, would provide the laity with all the necessary rules.

There remained one very serious problem, in one sense the most difficult if reform was to be achieved: how to prevent interference in ecclesiastical affairs by the secular rulers, who were in large part responsible for abuses. On this point the Council was visibly hesitant, and did not come to grips with it until the twenty-fifth session. It may have felt that its advice would fall on deaf ears, that its orders would prove ineffective. In the closing sessions there is a distinct advance towards freedom from secular interference, but some members were still too closely allied with the sovereigns. There was tremendous uproar when the project for 'reform of princes,' in forty-two chapters, was duly submitted to the ambassadors attending the Council. Those of France and Spain were for once in agreement, and joined forces in an indignant protest. The Fathers were not disheartened, and prepared a new scheme; but to everyone's amazement the Archbishop of Prague, acting in the emperor's name, demanded its withdrawal. After prolonged negotiations a number of decrees were passed forbidding princes to interfere in ecclesiastical matters, requiring them to apply the conciliar canons in their several States, and calling upon them to respect the rights and property of the Church.

These difficulties showed the Council, and indeed the Church as a whole, that one final problem had yet to be solved: the problem of enforcement. Decrees, canons and censures had been plentiful enough in the past: the last Council, some fifty years earlier, had paved the Lateran with good intentions; but what was left of them? 'Unarmed laws fall into contempt,' said Cardinal de Retz a hundred years later. The question now was whether Holy Church possessed weapons wherewith to enforce the wise laws she had just made. The Fathers of Trent were wide awake to the difficulty, and that is why, in submitting their decisions to Pope Pius IV,[1] they requested him to set up a 'Congregation of the Council,' whose duty it would be to carry out the decrees and, when necessary, decide the manner of their application.[2] But this was hardly sufficient. It was abundantly clear that such energetic measures of reform hurt too many interests, and not only those of secular princes. It was therefore necessary that the Council, itself the fruit of a great reawakening in the Christian soul, should extend its work by transmitting its own courageous spirit to the whole of Christendom. This was to be mainly the task of the saints; but it would also be necessary to establish an authority of sufficient dignity and strength to address appropriate language to vested interests. Italy, the Empire, Portugal and Poland were willing to 'welcome' the decrees as bidden; but who would overcome the hesitation of Spain, the touchiness of the Low Countries, the cantankerous Gallicanism of France? The Council had accomplished its task. It was now the turn of the popes; and Providence, which had enabled the Church to take the decisive step, willed that the pontiffs who took over from the Assembly should understand their duty and be qualified to fulfil it.

9. St Pius V

The pope upon whose shoulders was placed the formidable burden of proving to the world that the decisions of the Council of Trent were no mere *flatus vocis* turned out to be at once a man of consummate ability and a saint. At the first consistory after his election he delivered an allocution whose import was summed up in two sentences: 'We shall not paralyse the advance of heresy except by an operation proceeding from the heart of God. It is we, the light of the world, the salt of the earth, who must enlighten men's minds, enliven their hearts by the example of our holiness and our virtues.' He himself practised these principles in striking fashion. Rome soon learned that the new pontiff lived in a monastic cell, drinking only water, spending hours in prayer and meditation on the Passion of Christ, weeping prostrate before the Blessed Sacrament or reciting the decades of his Rosary. It soon became clear also that there would be no more splendid processions of lordly cardinals through the city streets, no more prelates driving in their carriages with pretty women. There was no longer talk of galas and scandalous feasts; on the contrary, charitable undertakings received generous donations and a new impetus was given to works of public utility. Admiration reached its zenith when the Vicar of Christ was seen going barefoot, carrying the monstrance or visiting the basilicas

---

[1] He ratified them by the Bull *Benedictus Dei* on 26th January 1564.

[2] Henceforward too anyone receiving an ecclesiastical benefice had to sign a formal declaration that he submitted to the decrees of the Council.

as a humble pilgrim. Such a thing had not been witnessed for centuries. The citizens were thrilled, and wished to erect a statue to this undoubtedly great pope, but he refused.

The new occupant of Peter's chair was a lean figure of a man, with heavily lined features, wide forehead and the prominent cheek-bones of a Ligurian peasant. His keen, deep-set eyes seemed fixed immovably on their appointed goal. Behind the heavy moustache and long white beard an unsmiling mouth proclaimed a will of iron, inflexible resolution. His effigy on the noble medallion struck in 1570 is vaguely reminiscent of Calvin. 'He is no laughing matter,' wrote a Venetian ambassador; and that was indeed the least that could be said. Does one laugh at the Inquisition, with which formidable institution he had identified himself? Michele Ghislieri had for many years, ever since he joined the Dominicans at the age of fourteen, lived so austere and devout a life that Cardinal Carafa took a liking to him, made him his associate in the direction of the Holy Office, and finally, when he became pope, appointed him head of that institution. Under Pius IV the Grand Inquisitor had dared to protest loudly against all misdeeds, even when the Pope himself was at fault. He was indignant, for example, at the elevation to the purple of a thirteen-year-old Medici, as well as of an Este who was no more than twenty-two; but his prestige was so high that no one had been able to bring him down. The laborious Conclave following the death of Pius IV hesitated for some time between the rather disturbing character of Morone, the scholarly but insignificant Sirlet, and the colourless Montepulciano. The electors ultimately agreed, though not without some trepidation, upon the Prefect of the Holy Office. Cardinal Charles Borromeo, a nephew of Pius IV, did much to further this triumphal choice, perceiving in Ghislieri the mark of the Holy Spirit. The new Pope assured those who trembled at seeing Carafa's heir, the Inquisition incarnate, upon the papal throne: 'I will act in such a way that Rome will regret my death more than my accession'; and he kept his word. When asked under what name he wished to rule, he showed himself to be without malice and anxious only to serve the Church. He would not take that of his master and model, Paul IV, but chose to be called after his immediate predecessor, whose work he was going to continue. He would be known as Pius V (1566–72).

The cause of reform was certainly in good hands. Immediately after his election he proceeded to carry out the disciplinary decrees of Trent. Bishops were forthwith ordered back to their dioceses under pain of imprisonment in the castle of Sant' Angelo. The canons of St Peter's were called to heel: their ancient privileges were no longer valid. The parish priests of the city were reproved for allowing their congregations to laugh and joke in church: they were informed that this must cease, and several of them were arrested. Ormaneto, a stern priest from Verona and formerly Vicar-General to St Charles Borromeo, was directed to reorganize the Curia upon strict principles. Simony, traffic in favours, nepotism, everything of the kind must be at once abolished —an undertaking rather too comprehensive to be of lasting effect. Some disgruntled voices were heard to complain that the Pope himself had set a poor example by appointing his nephew Michele Bonnelli cardinal secretary of state. True the young Dominican was no more than twenty-five years old; but his conduct was beyond criticism, and his uncle never overlooked his slightest fault. The cardinals created by Pius V were men of outstanding virtue—Souchier, abbot-general of the Cistercians, for example, and the saintly Burali. Other members of the Sacred College, together with the bishops, were visited with an unwelcome flood of reproach, admonition and more dangerous invective. A wind of austerity was beginning to blow through the Church; it had already reached gale force at Rome. Here the papal police swept the streets clean of prostitutes. Horse-races akin to the Sienese 'Palio' had long been staged in front of St Peter's; these were now banished to a remote quarter of the city, and soon became obsolete. The uncompromising pontiff would also have liked to suppress the Roman Carnival. Since this was impossible, short of provoking revolution, he instituted the Forty Hours' Prayer as atonement for the licentiousness of those days, and himself withdrew to Santa Sabina where he spent the time in penitential exercises. One of his most spectacular and most questionable acts was to clear the papal palaces of as many pagan nudities as he was able, a gesture of which the city of Rome took advantage by founding the Capitoline Museum.

Together with such coercive and punitive measures Pius V adopted others of a more constructive kind. Once again in obedience to the decrees of Trent, he concerned himself with the editing and publication of those books which the Council had held to be indispensable. It was not sufficient to exclude harmful works, which were named in the revised 'Index; he must give the faithful that wholesome nourishment for which their souls hungered. Accordingly there were published in succession four books that were to be absolutely fundamental: the *Catechism*, the *Breviary*, the *Missal* and the *Summa* of St Thomas Aquinas.

Preparation of the Catechism had been begun during the last weeks of the Council by a commission under the presidency of Cardinal Seripando. After the dissolution of the Assembly the work was continued by Cardinal Borromeo assisted by three Dominican theologians. It was not until September 1566 that the Catechism appeared, after five years of unremitting effort; but the result was a magnificent achievement, setting forth in precise terms all that a Catholic may and must believe as regards the Creed, the sacraments, Christian morality and the spiritual life. Quickly translated into all languages and distributed throughout the world, this compendious volume was destined to be the code and charter of Catholics, and it remains in constant use.

The Breviary, wherewith the clergy (and pious layfolk too) follow the 'canonical hours,' had existed for a very long time. The most popular version was known as that of the Minors and dated from 1277. It had received numerous additions in the course of centuries, and had become much too bulky. In the time of Leo X someone had conceived the unfortunate idea of introducing mythological hymns and other pretty things which were dear to the humanists [1] but far removed from true Christian tradition. Clement VII had set up a commission to correct these abuses, and the Spanish cardinal Quinones had compiled another breviary, called after Santa Croce, which had proved unsatisfactory. Pius IV established a commission for the reform of the Breviary in 1564, but little was accomplished. It was Pius V who took the business in hand with his accustomed energy; he entrusted it to a commission of cardinals, brought it to a successful conclusion, and finally (1568) published a new breviary that was shorter, more firmly centred on the principal office and relieved of many superfluous feasts. Only a very few Churches (e.g. Milan, Lyons and Toledo) refused to adopt it.[2]

Reform of the Breviary presupposed that of the Missal, which was carried out in the same spirit of uniformity. Hitherto the Western Church had celebrated Mass according to four rites: Roman, Milanese or Ambrosian, Gallican and Mozarabic. The commission of cardinals which had just remodelled the Breviary prepared a new missal; it was published in 1570 and eliminated the differences, which were considered unsuitable for public worship. Certain new features were also established, such as the *Introibo* and *Confiteor* at the beginning of Mass, the beautiful prayer *Suscipe Santa Trinitas* at the Offertory, and St John's prologue as the 'last gospel.' [3] Excepting some very small details to which a few Churches [4] and Orders [5] remained faithful, the Missal of St Pius V was adopted by the whole Catholic world, and remains in use almost unchanged today.

Lastly, there was a fourth publication, which, though perhaps less well known than the other three, exerted an enormous influence on the subsequent history of the Church. Pius V, himself a Dominican, had been familiar with St Thomas from youth upwards, and he considered

[1] Our Lady, for example, was described as 'blessed goddess' and the Trinity as 'threefold visage of Olympus'!
[2] See an article 'Les Réformes du Bréviaire au XVIe siècle: rôle de l'Espagne' in *L'Ami du Clergé*, 20th May 1954, p. 305.
[3] See Daniel-Rops, *Missa est.*
[4] e.g. Lyons and Milan.
[5] e.g. the Carthusians and Dominicans.

Aquinas's thought as the firmest possible foundation upon which to rebuild the Church, 'a solid barrier against the storm.' In 1567 he proclaimed St Thomas a Doctor of the Church, placing him alongside Ambrose, Augustine, Jerome and Gregory the Great. Next he instructed two theologians of his Order, Giustiniani and Manrique, to prepare from the Vatican manuscripts a definitive edition of the *Summa Theologica*, the cost of which he himself defrayed. The universities were directed to teach only Thomism, which was adopted soon afterwards by the Jesuits.

All this activity in the fields of doctrine and discipline was far from sufficient to occupy the days of Pius, who strove at every level for a return to Christian loyalties, for unity and for good government. Secular princes, without exception, were requested in no uncertain terms to further the designs of the Church by promoting reform among their subjects and by employing all their forces in the struggle against heresy. The Bull *In Coena Domini* reminded them of their duties. Not all submitted with an obedience proportionate to the Holy Father's urgency. But that lean old figure in the Vatican, never abandoning his principles, and despising the customary means of diplomacy, advanced at every point, speaking forthrightly, threatening whenever necessary, and supported by the incorruptible agents of the Inquisition.

Orthodoxy launched a huge offensive on so many fronts that we can scarcely grasp it as a whole. In Germany, the land *par excellence* of heresy, Maximilian II appeared to be making dangerous concessions; but he was checked by a threat of excommunication, just as the Diets of Augsburg (1566) and Speyer (1568) were about to place Catholics and Protestants on an equal footing. In England, where Elizabeth I was erecting her State Church, Pius V spoke up regardless of the fatal consequences that must and did ensue:[1] he excommunicated the heretical queen and released her subjects from their allegiance. The Duke of Alba, who was fighting the Protestants in the Low Countries, received encouragement and blessing.[2] In Poland the Pope did all he could to assist the efforts of King Sigismund II, who, despite the insecurity of his own position, was trying to bring back his country to the Roman faith. But when Queen Catherine Jagellon of Sweden, a faithful Catholic, agreed at the instance of her husband to communicate in both kinds, she quickly received a Bull of excommunication. It need hardly be said that reaction was more severe in a country where the pontiff's influence was capable of immediate exercise. The Italian princes, cowed or convinced, rallied to his side without a moment's delay. A few executions were sufficient to exclude any risk of Protestantism obtaining a hold upon Florence and Venice. At Mantua the Dominican Casanova made a sensational swoop, seized the Protestant

[1] See p. 204.   [2] See Chapter III, p. 188.

minister Celaria, and delivered him to the judges of the Inquisition, who burned him at the stake. The imperial ambassador protested, but was quickly snubbed by Pius V. In Spain an even warmer welcome awaited the radical measures recommended by the Pope. Philip II (1558–89), an austere and taciturn but earnest monarch, was by no means willing to submit without question to the least wish of Rome; but in this matter he adopted of his own accord a policy of repression. From the depths of the Escorial, where he spent his days between work and prayer, there issued a stream of Draconian orders for the hunting down of heresy, free-thinking and the faintest scent of Protestant sympathies.[1] The Inquisitors appointed by him displayed a sombre zeal. Prisons were crowded, and the smoke of many an *auto da fé* rose into the sky. Tons of books and hundreds of men perished in the flames. As for France, in the Machiavellian hands of Catherine dei Medici, she began by offering passive resistance, endeavouring to protect her suspect bishops (among them Cardinal de Châtillon) from the hammer-blows of Rome. But when the Parlement of Paris resolved to take arms against the Protestants, Pius V dispatched a strong contingent of reliable troops to assist in this holy task.[2] His ceaseless activity left nothing undone that might secure the triumph of Catholicism, and he actually thought of negotiating the conversion of Russia under Ivan the Terrible!

In the mind of this Pope, whose outlook was still so largely medieval, the policies of loyalty and Christianity were identical. To him, as Vicar of Christ and guardian of the deposit of faith, belonged the right and duty to teach men what Christianity required of them, to dispose of earthly crowns in the interests of the Church and her faith, to direct the necessary struggle everywhere. The climax of his vast activity, in which he seemed truly to be blessed by heaven, was the thrilling victory of Christendom over the Infidel, for which he was ultimately responsible. Profiting by the incompetence of the new sultan, Selim, unworthy son of Solyman the Magnificent, Pius V's anachronistic genius revived the idea of a crusade. Nuncios were sent to the various courts, and, wonderful to relate, obtained more than empty promises. The Pope himself provided money and ships. Commanded by Philip II's twenty-four-year-old half-brother Don Juan of Austria, who was assisted by an experienced Catalan seaman, Luis de Requescens, the international fleet of Christendom set sail against the Moslems. On 7th October 1571 Christ's warriors, chanting the psalms, gave battle in the Gulf of Lepanto. It was a terrible engagement, full of surprises and anxiety. Don Juan himself stood on the prow of his flagship, holding a crucifix. When evening fell over the glorious bay, the smoke of burning Turkish galleys spread a reek of timber and corpses. The entire enemy fleet had

[1] See Chapter III, p. 153.   [2] See p. 172.

been destroyed or captured, and aboard the *Marquesa* a wounded soldier named Miguel de Cervantes, whose arm had been shattered in the fight, joined in the *Te Deum*. When Pius V received the news he cried out in reference to the youthful victor: 'There was a man sent from God, whose name was John!' It seemed that the loss of Constantinople was avenged; and when the aged pontiff died (1st May 1572), this brilliant triumph appeared as the crown of all his efforts, the pledge of his permanent success.

The facts, however, were not quite so straightforward. Lepanto was indeed a glorious episode, but without a morrow. The manifold policies of Pius V were by no means fruitful of lasting results, and immediately after his death religious passions once again broke loose, more violent and confused than heretofore. Pius V was a very great pope, notwithstanding his unbridled precipitateness, and his enduring title to posterity's gratitude and admiration is summarized by Cardinal Grente in these words: 'The decisions of the Council of Trent would become reality; the ardent labours of Catholicism would receive fresh impetus.'[1] Nevertheless it has to be admitted that so enormous a task could scarcely have been fulfilled in a pontificate of only six years had there not existed at the same time a galaxy of saints who strove with all their might to reanimate, reorganize and invigorate the Catholic Church, men and women no less venerated [2] and perhaps better loved than Ghislieri: St Charles Borromeo, St Teresa of Avila, St John of the Cross and St Philip Neri.

10. Episcopal Reformers: St Charles Borromeo

The Council of Trent had laid down the necessary principles of Catholic reform. The Holy See, in the person of St Pius V, had shown its firm determination that they should not become a dead letter. But it was necessary to inject the new spirit deep into the Christian conscience, even in the remotest parishes.

Once again the honour and the burden of this undertaking lay first of all with the bishops, of whom the Council had drawn so noble a portrait in reminding them of their duties. Would they be capable of understanding what the Church required of them? One might expect that they would, especially when it was recalled [3] that godly men had effected wonderful transformations in many a diocese long before Rome took official charge of the reform. Their series had never been interrupted: the line had remained unbroken from early to late, from

---

[1] *Saint Pie V*, 1914, *ad fin.*

[2] Five hundred years had passed since a pope (Gregory VII) had been canonized in 1085. Four hundred more elapsed before the canonization of another (Pius X). Clement X, a Dominican, beatified Pius V in 1672; Clement XI canonized him in 1711.

[3] See Chapter I, section 3.

the precursors of reform to those who must execute its decrees.[1] The solicitude and courage exhibited by Giberti at Verona, by St Thomas of Villanova at Valencia, and even (with some mistakes) by Guillaume Briçonnet at Meaux, would be found no whit the less in numerous other prelates. Among them stands one particularly radiant figure: St Charles Borromeo (1538–83), Archbishop of Milan.

On 30th January 1560 Pope Pius IV had created three new cardinals. One of these was his nephew,[2] Carlo Borromeo, son of his sister Margarita. A few weeks later he appointed Carlo his Secretary of State, and subsequently poured out upon him a wealth of lordly titles: Archbishop of Milan; Protector of Portugal and Lower Germany; Legate at Bologna; Protector of the Carmelites, of the Canons of Coimbra, of all the Franciscans and of the Order of Christ; Archpriest of Santa Maria Maggiore and Grand Penitentiary. In addition, Borromeo received a host of rich benefices which brought him an income of more than 100,000,000 francs. The citizens of Rome, who delighted in treating all Vatican business with a measure of sarcasm, laughed heartily. They had seen a fair number of papal nephews loaded by their uncles with honours and prebends, without exactly benefiting the Church. Here was one more of them. The new pope would do no better than his predecessors.

The wits of the Piazza Navona were mistaken. The young cardinal, summoned at one stroke to such exalted responsibilities, was more than adequate to the burden. He was only twenty-two years old, but his experience of life, his wisdom and intelligence were far beyond what is normal in a youth who has scarcely emerged from adolescence. It might indeed have been asked whether he had ever been a child. At the age of five, little Carlettino's favourite game was to build altars and play at liturgical ceremonies. He received the tonsure when no more than eight years old, and at twelve became abbot of a monastery. In this last capacity he took so important a view of his office that he actually determined to reform his monks! During seven years at the University of Padua he distinguished himself by his inexhaustible charity towards misfortune of whatever kind, as well as by his gaiety and devotion to study. He was a tall, lean fellow, with a long aquiline nose and unattractive looks, but he gave an impression of calm inflexibility, of efficiency and cool courage. On the death of his elder brother he afforded striking proof of his vocation: instead of asking his uncle for permission to return to the world and take his place as head of the family,[3] he made haste to have himself ordained priest.

[1] Thus Ormaneto of Verona, trained in the school of Giberti, became Vicar-General to St Charles Borromeo.
[2] Another was a young Medici aged seventeen.
[3] Although a cardinal he was still only a subdeacon.

God had indeed marked Borromeo with His seal, and his austere manner of life quickly gave the lie to those who scoffed at his elevation as an act of nepotism. 'Of wealth,' said the preacher of his funeral oration, 'Charles possessed no more than a dog receives from its master: water, bread and straw.' He had no sooner taken residence with his uncle than he showed himself in his true light, and he would have been the same in whatever situation Providence might have chosen to place him. A tenacious worker, spending much time also in prayer and meditation according to the *Spiritual Exercises* of St Ignatius, his only recreations were an occasional hunting party to keep himself in form, and those little gatherings of a few friends for serious discussion, which he laughingly called his 'Vatican nights.' Was it possible then to be the Pope's nephew, Cardinal Secretary of State and holder of innumerable benefices, and yet to be a saint? The Roman people and the Curia yielded to the evidence. So did the Sacred College, which, having seen him at work as an administrator preparatory to and during the Council of Trent, thought for a moment of offering him the tiara on the death of his uncle, and followed his advice when he unexpectedly put forward the name of Cardinal Ghislieri. Charles Borromeo was now aged twenty-eight; he stood on the threshold of an astonishing career.

The Council had completed its work, a new pope had been elected, and the former Secretary of State considered that his principal duty now was to set an example by removing to the archdiocese of Milan in obedience to the decree of episcopal residence. It was an enormous province, covering not only the Milanese but also parts of Venetian territory and the Swiss Alps; no fewer than fifteen suffragans were subject to his jurisdiction. So long as important ecclesiastical business detained him in Rome or at Trent, he had been obliged to leave its government in the hands of Ormaneto, that virtuous and talented priest whom Pius V summoned to Rome in order to reform the Curia. The situation in the archdiocese of Milan was certainly deplorable. Its priests were devoid of zeal, and so ignorant that most of them could not pronounce the words of absolution in Latin; some of its empty churches were used as barns, while the monasteries were fallen so low that their parlours and refectories were the scene of balls, weddings and banquets. A formidable task confronted Charles Borromeo, and to it he devoted the remainder of his life.

He made his solemn entry into Milan on 23rd September 1565, and forthwith assembled a provincial council, which all his suffragans were ordered to attend for the purpose of enacting the decrees of Trent and receiving his instructions. Next he gathered around him all who seemed likely coadjutors: Jesuits, Theatines, Barnabites and clerics of the Oratory lately founded by St Philip Neri. A vast, centralized reform of administration restored order in eight hundred parishes. These were henceforward grouped in deaneries or *pieri* under *vicars forane*, subject to regular visitation by special inspectors and even by the archbishop himself. It was also arranged that provincial councils would meet at stated intervals to study problems common to all the dioceses, each of which was to hold an annual synod. Following the directions of Trent, large seminaries were established, among them the famous Collegio Borromeo at Pavia (whose noble porticoes still preserve the founder's memory), the Swiss College at Milan and the seminary at Ascona on Lago di Maggiore. Discipline was everywhere restored. Lax priests found themselves invited to make a 'pilgrimage' to the archiepiscopal residence, whence they were courteously but firmly conducted to a house of retreat, not to emerge until they had done penance and amended their lives. The monasteries too were brought back to better ways. There were to be no more ballrooms, no more junketings; and nuns received orders to cover their windows with grilles solid enough to keep the gallants out. One can hardly imagine a more rigorous application of the Tridentine decrees.

Knowing well the importance of his work, Borromeo preserved every one of his mandates and pastoral letters, every one of the ordinances resulting from the deliberations of his provincial councils. All this material was collected and published, thus providing reformers the world over with a detailed interpretation of the ideas of Trent. Valieri of Verona aptly described Charles Borromeo as 'the Doctor of Bishops.'

It would be idle to pretend that activity of this kind was to everybody's liking. When Charles Borromeo set out upon his chosen path he had enemies secret and avowed. The Spanish governors of Milan had too many personal or national interests in the affairs of the Church to accept without opposition the austere independence of the archbishop. His many conflicts with them went as far as excommunication, and Rome dismissed all appeals against his sentence. There were also the 'Humiliati,' a degenerate offshoot of what was in effect a Benedictine third order. These pseudo-monks numbered about two hundred; they had made huge profits from the wool trade, and lived in scandalous luxury. When Borromeo sought to curb their excesses they were so angry and made such an outcry that he was obliged to threaten them with severe penalties; one of their members, Farina, learning what was afoot, shot and slightly wounded the archbishop during Mass. Yet another source of opposition were the canons of La Scala, who claimed to possess some ancient privilege exempting them from visitation by their hierarchical superior. More secret but no less dangerous was a minor war which seems to have been waged by the Jesuits. It was not that they failed to agree upon ends and means, but they wished that the Society might benefit by their efforts and obtain for itself all the best subjects. Charles Borromeo, thinking of his own seminaries, could not allow this; while admiring the sons of St Ignatius, and helping them to erect colleges, it was no doubt in order to resist their pious encroachment that he founded the Oblates of St Ambrose, a kind of secular missionaries under his immediate control.

Such a man could not but make a deep impression by his wonderful determination, his sanctity and his example. The people, to whom he gave all his goods, held him in veneration. His hospitals and hospices were full. His Schools of Christian Doctrine gave religious instruction to thousands of children. He was even excused for having regulated the Carnival and forbidden masked fêtes. His influence extended far beyond his archdiocese, even to Lucerne, where his arrival seriously alarmed the Protestants of Switzerland; and to him the famous Golden League of the Catholic cantons, sometimes called the 'Borromean League,' owed its existence. His glory attained its zenith in 1576, when there broke out at Milan one of the most horrible plagues of the century. No one dared risk trying to relieve the sick, who were shut away in the lazar houses to die of cold and hunger as well as of the epidemic. Their archbishop, however, was not afraid to visit them, celebrate Mass for them and give them holy *viaticum*, meanwhile exhorting his clergy and people in letters of sublime charity to organize collective aid. He had sold all that belonged to him, including his furniture and bed-clothes. 'He has nothing left upon which to live,' said a contemporary, 'but it might be said that he raises the dead by his presence.'

Exhausted by all this incredible effort, Charles Borromeo died in 1584, at the age of forty-eight, leaving to the Church that model of a bishop which was later reproduced in St Francis of Sales, Cardinal Bérulle and many others. Three churches at Rome were dedicated to him, whereas St Francis of Assisi and St Dominic have only one each. 'It was a long time,' writes Fléchier, 'since the Church had beheld anything so great as a cardinal, an archbishop, a nephew of the Pope, descend from riches to become poorest of the poor in his diocese.' . .

What St Charles Borromeo did with such brilliance at Milan was accomplished on a more modest scale, but often with striking courage and enthusiasm, by many other bishops in all the four corners of Christendom. Certain of them were remembered with such affection by their people that in several dioceses these bishops of the Catholic Reformation are venerated somewhat after the manner of those who, amid the chaos of the 'Dark Ages,' were the self-appointed guardians of the city and defenders of the faith. Here we may recall the picturesque Archbishop of Braga, Bartholomew of the Martyrs, who had taken a notable part in the deliberations of Trent and who founded the first Portuguese seminary; Alessandro Sauli, apostle of Corsica, the heroic reformer of a people in sore need of reformation, and who even tried to abolish the 'vendetta'; Cardinal Hosius, Bishop of Chlom in Poland and of Ermeland, one of the presidents of the Council, who did much to bring his country back to Catholicism by means of his personal endeavour as well as by the catechism which he edited; and also Cardinal Lorraine, who, though his life had not always been exemplary before the Council, thereafter chose the road of reform and in 1567 founded at Rheims the first French seminary.[1] There were indeed many more: Paleotti at Bologna, Burali at Piacenza, Guerrero at Granada, Ribera at Valencia, Ludovico de Torres at Monreale and so on. Twenty years after the closing of the Council the Church possessed a body of first-rate bishops, prepared to hold the course set for her by the Fathers of Trent.

11. REFORM OF THE OLD ORDERS: ST TERESA AND ST JOHN OF THE CROSS

The same spirit of revival which had found its way into the religious congregations and institutes during the last half-century was henceforth greatly strengthened and increased under the official auspices and guidance of the Church. The old Orders, in competition with the more recent formations of clerks regular, perceived that nothing less than a determined effort of reform would enable them to survive. And so, while other foundations, e.g. the Oratory, continued to appear, the better elements of the older institutions pulled themselves together and gradually returned to their ancient discipline. This movement lasted far into the seventeenth century.

Among the Benedictines reform, as we have seen, had already made considerable headway at Bursfeld, Montserrat, Padua and Monte Cassino. It now won Germany under the leadership of Fulda, and Austria, where Abbot Gaspar Hoffman of Melte provided the necessary inspiration. In Lorraine, Didier de la Tour, a young monk of Saint-Vannes near Verdun, started a movement which was joined by forty abbeys. Many of these were in France, including Saint-Pierre at Jumièges; and in 1621 there sprang from this reformed branch the famous Congregation of Saint-Maur. Among the sons of St Bernard, the white-cowled Cistercians, the most important reform was that brought about in 1573 by Jean de la Barrière, commendatory abbot of Feuillant near Toulouse, who had been converted to the strict observance and imposed it on his monks. The 'Feuillants' became very numerous in France and Italy; their monastery at Paris, which became celebrated during the Revolution (for reasons far from religious) was founded in 1588. Reform of the Premonstratensians was accomplished

---

[1] He afterwards degenerated, so that his work must be considered rather as a false start.

almost simultaneously in Spain by Abbot Didace de Mendieta of
Trevino, and in Lorraine first by Daniel Picard, abbot of Sainte-Marie
au Bois, then by his successor Gervais de Laruelle. The congregation
of Lorraine favoured 'the ancient rigour' and lasted until the Revolution. Meanwhile, among other canons regular, those of the Augustinian
tradition, there began a notable movement led by St Peter Fourier
(1565–1640), which was to go far beyond the limits of a monastic
reform.[1] The Mendicants, who had for long, if somewhat sporadically,
set an example of return to good traditions, were everywhere in the
grip of reforming zeal. In Spain and Portugal the influence of St Peter
of Alcantara (1499–1562)—an ascetic who practised the most terrible
austerities, who was among the first to recognize the vocation of St
Teresa, and who died just as the Council drew to its close—exercised a
deep posthumous influence on the whole Franciscan Order. At about
the same time the Capuchins, now separated from the Observants and
formally recognized as 'true sons of St Francis,' underwent enormous
expansion, reaching a total of 18,000 members. One of the most active
and most efficient Orders of the time, they were joined by some
remarkable men with various titles to fame: St Felix of Cantalice, St
Laurence of Brindisi, St Felix of Sigmaringen, who was martyred by
the Calvinists, and Joseph Le Clerc du Tremblay, afterwards celebrated as Richelieu's 'Grey Eminence.' Nor did the reforming spirit
fail to penetrate even the Augustinians, who had been so severely tried
by the apostasy of Luther and many of his brethren. They made considerable advances in Spain through the influence of St Thomas of
Villanova, in Lorraine through that of François Hamel, while in
France, where they were known as 'Little Fathers,' they were extremely
popular. Thus a gigantic movement towards better things stirred the
old Orders during the half-century following the Council of Trent, a
movement in which the female branches also shared, and one of such
complexity that no adequate account of it can be given in two short
pages. Nowhere does it assume more impressive and more sublime
characteristics than in the ancient Order of Carmel, where there
appeared at this time two of the richest personalities that the Church
has ever produced: St Teresa of Avila and St John of the Cross.[2]

In the last days of August 1562, while the Fathers of Trent in their
twenty-second session were preparing to discuss the 'decree on the life
befitting clerics,' there took place in a little city of far-away Old Castile
an event of apparent insignificance, but one which was to become an
example and a symbol in the great work of Catholic reform. Huddled
inside her rust-red walls, swept in winter by the cold north winds of

[1] Chapter V, p. 370.
[2] They will be studied here only as reformers; for their mysticism see Chapter V,
pp. 356–9.

the high plateaus, with her network of narrow streets and irregular squares, Avila already contained so many convents, chapels and churches that the foundation of one more hardly called for comment. At angelus time it was by hundreds, and even thousands, that the celestial voice of bells bore over the sierra the multitudinous prayer of a people for whom their faith had ever been the most important business of life. Avila of the loyal, Avila of saints and knights, was one huge monastery. What difference could it make that the tolling of one more little bell would rise to the dark blue sky of Spain from the new convent of St Joseph situated in the northern and most populous quarter of the city?

In actual fact, however, this tiny convent [1] was intended by its foundress to be very different from the rest, especially from the great convent of the Incarnation with which everyone was familiar as a daily resort for gossip with the religious. In this new convent the walls were unplastered; a double grille of closely intersecting rods stretched right across the choir and completely hid the nuns. It was said that those who joined the community would never again emerge; that they would devote the whole of their days to prayer, fasting and the discipline; that they would wear habits of material so rough as to recall the camel-hair of the ancient hermits, and that they would go barefoot. 'Mitigation' of the primitive rule [2] had been accepted and confirmed by Pope Eugenius IV in 1482. Since then, the Carmelites thanked heaven, wiser practices had prevailed. Abstinence from meat had been reduced to three days a week; the uncouth habit had given place to broadcloth, which was better suited to the distinguished members of the Order; and as for solitude and silence, they had found a substitute in a pleasant régime of visits to the parlour, where the conversation of such godly persons could not but exert the best of influences upon their guests. The convents of women were specially devoted to this form of apostolate, and it sometimes happened that a pretty young Carmelite would carry her zeal so far as to prolong such a conversation far into the night, outside the enclosure. It was precisely against these usages and customs, to which no sensible person objected, that La Madre took her stand, and in leaving the Incarnation to found her shabby little monastery she was considered to be out of her wits. Her name was Teresa de Cepeda, she was of 'pure blood,' belonged to the ancient nobility and was at this time aged forty-seven.[3]

Seeing her twenty-five years earlier walking in the street, slender and

---

[1] The nuns' choir was only about ten yards long.

[2] It had been given about 1220 by the patriarch Albert of Jerusalem to the rugged solitaries who claimed to be heirs of the prophet Elias.

[3] One of twelve children, she was born in 1515, a few months before the accession of Charles V, on the threshold of that golden age of Spain to which she herself would contribute so much brilliance.

E

gracious, her figure neatly arrayed in velvet petticoat, swinging at every step an enormous skirt of orange taffeta striped with black, who could have foretold that the daughter of Don Alonso and Doña Beatrix de Ahumada would one day become the 'austere, fanatical reformer,' as she was later called by her erstwhile companions? Fanatical she most certainly was not, nor yet austere in the sense used by malicious tongues. This middle-aged spinster, a little stout, but with rosy cheeks, still youthful looks and plump red mouth, loved to sing and dance and laugh, and would often tell sanctimonious hypocrites that she 'disliked gloomy saints.' In her rather prominent dark eyes there shone by turns rapture and tenderness, a touch of merriment and high intelligence. Her father was a man of stern piety, and she had been inured from early youth to long periods of prayer, daily rosary, silence and compunction; but despite this harsh upbringing she had never lost her faith, her virtue or her happy disposition. In that strong soul of manly intellect and courage, but of feminine tact and intuition, grace had found a soil marvellously prepared for the accomplishment of God's work.

On 24th August 1562, when she founded her quaint little convent of St Joseph, Madre Teresa was obeying an order from on high. It would not be untrue to say that she had long lent a somewhat inattentive ear to the summons of her Lord; but we shall perhaps better represent the development in her of that sublime love which she would one day prefer before all else if we speak of the 'intermittent reactions of her heart.' An initial impulse had driven her to the cloister at the age of twenty; but the impulse had derived additional strength from the bitter ponderings of adolescence, which, having left the enchanted gardens of childhood, discovers life with its tares, suffering and misery, and asks whether all is not vanity of vanities. She had become a Carmelite as others contract a marriage of convenience, from disgust and uneasiness. All the same she was a faithful and even fervent Carmelite, as far as it was possible to be so in the company of one hundred and eighty more or less worldly religious. Her youthful decision, however, her 'determination' as she liked to call it, had linked her more closely than she suspected with her true destiny. Because she had 'great firmness and constancy in the pursuit,' even while continuing to live as a Carmelite of the 'mitigated' observance, with one foot in the convent and the other in the city, she had advanced along her road, nursing the most repugnant cases in the infirmary and spending long hours in prayer. She never allowed 'Christ with His Cross' to fall.

Then the great crisis had come upon her, a twin crisis of body and soul. During the years 1537 and 1538 she had been the victim of nervous disorders, fainting, vomiting and partial paralysis, symptoms in which the irreverence of modern psychiatry claims to recognize religious hysteria. Her condition was so grave that on one occasion she was thought to be dead, and came near to being laid in her coffin. These terrible sufferings passed away for the time being, only to be succeeded by another crisis which Teresa herself afterwards considered to have been even more serious. This was 'the period of infidelity.' For a long time she wearied of the choral office, prayed only with her lips, discussed embroidery with her sisters, and romances of chivalry with kindly folk who visited the parlour. Yet even while she did so she rebuked herself for her infidelity to what a silent voice in the depths of her heart repeatedly assured her to be the true Carmelite rule. In her wonderful autobiography she speaks of 'that soul which so often destroyed itself.' No, that soul was never destroyed, but it was gravely imperilled. In 1543 the cruel shock of her father's death had momentarily torn her from herself—'God's first knock upon the door.' The advice of a strict Dominican confessor had helped her to recover her balance, though not for long and quite inadequately. She was able once again to pray, but did not yet completely renounce the world: for ten more years she attempted to reconcile the irreconcilable and continued uncertain of herself.

God, however, lay in wait for her. One day in the year 1553 He struck and spoke. We must leave Teresa herself to describe the scene. As she was passing through the chapel she came face to face with a bust of the *Ecce Homo* which had recently been placed there. 'It was so striking a representation of Christ covered with wounds that at first glance I was overwhelmed with feeling for His sufferings on our behalf. My heart was shattered as I thought of my ingratitude for His wounds. I threw myself on my knees before Him, and begged Him to give me strength once and for all, that I might never again offend Him.' This was the decisive shock, the ray of light similar to that which long ago had stricken Saul on the road to Damascus. Having recovered possession of herself, clear-eyed now and resolute, Teresa the worldly Carmelite understood that she was henceforth 'Teresa of Jesus.' While her Jesuit confessors gave her firm guidance and restored her to full strength through the discipline of fervent communion, Christ Himself came upon the scene with slow mysterious tread. Strange phenomena occurred in her, around her and by her agency. A mystical link was forged between her and the God of ineffable espousals. She experienced such feverish ecstasies that she emerged from them haggard and speechless, but her countenance shone with unearthly radiance. Sometimes the nuns and other worshippers in the chapel of the Incarnation saw her raised several feet above the ground, although she clung with all her strength to the grille. Certain people were deeply troubled by these fantastic happenings, wondering whether they might not proceed from Hell. No, replied the visionary with her charming laugh, she 'cocked a snook at the demons.' That was also the opinion of two of the greatest saints then living, Peter of Alcantara and Francis Borgia, to whom the matter had been referred. Filled with such mystical graces as few in this world have known, walking firmly in the unitive way, Teresa of Jesus might have penetrated the realm of inconceivable happiness and forgotten the world. But no; the great ecstatic was a woman of flesh and blood, a true daughter of the Spanish highlands, filled with the sense of reality and well aware that she was called to something other than escape into the empyrean. Was it her astonishing combination of solid realism and spiritual energy that had caused the Sovereign Master to choose her from among all others? A day came when the Presence, who was her almost constant companion, showed her that she had been sent as a witness and a guide. In order to 'compensate' Our Lord for the sufferings which Luther and other heretics were causing Him, and for all wicked religious, she would found a convent of perpetual prayer and unrelenting penance, in accordance with those principles whose requirements had been stated in the *Book of the Institution of the First Monks* (1507). The example of the sublime Franciscan, Peter of Alcantara, had proved that such a life was by no means impossible. Thus was born Teresa's decision to found the convent of St Joseph of Avila, the first house of the Carmelite reform.

St Joseph's, a mustard grain, was the tiny seed of what was to become a mighty tree. In that small community,[1] robed with the white mantle of Our Lady, there was set on foot a spiritual venture whose riches would be discovered in the results that flowed from it. Teresa herself had already taken wings and learnt the royal flight of infinite space. What of the others? Must she 'drag these souls with a tow-rope' or handle them 'with great gentleness for their greater good'? This first convent at Avila, for which she felt a peculiar tenderness throughout the remainder of her life, was a testing ground where she learnt how to lead souls to a higher life by the right admixture of sweetness and compulsion. With what loving cogency she would address the sisters, begging them to 'yield entirely to the dramatic truth of the Incarnation, Passion and Redemption.' With what terror in her voice she would paint for them 'the world on fire,' Catholicism threatened both from within and from without. Teresa would have her daughters 'solitary, silent, disdainful of the body and its demands, but gay as children; humble, but never forgetting the dignity of their souls; submissive, but to the Holy Ghost; in love, but in love with Christ; stripped of everything, but queens of the world.'[2] This little convent was 'a heaven on earth if ever there was one'; it became the model for sixteen other houses of women founded by the indefatigable Teresa in a space of twenty years, not to mention those friaries which would follow her example.

---

[1] At the beginning it consisted of no more than five or six nuns.
[2] Marcelle Auclair, *Sainte Thérèse*, Paris, 1950.

Five years passed, five years of ripening in seclusion. Then Teresa, led through prayer into the region of activity, and free in the freedom of the Spirit, set out upon the appalling roads of Castile, which were quagmires in winter and carpets of dust in summer. For fifteen years she was continually on the move, herald of God's commandments, revolutionary of Christ, opposed to all the easy-going morality of her age, a permanent invalid who seemed to be made of iron, at once the victim of love and the shrewdest of organizers. The same soul whence sprang, with cries of exaltation and anguish, the burning pages of the *Interior Castle* and *Thoughts on the Canticle*, gave birth also to three concise codes: the *Constitutions*, the *Book of Foundations* and the *Visitation of Monasteries*. Both groups of works were written in the same cramped script, without punctuation and obviously thrown off in feverish haste. They form a singular blend of reason and passion, of austerity and childlike gaiety, of the most impetuous spiritual elation and the most down-to-earth realism, which is so characteristic of this extraordinary saint and which Bergson rightly advances as proof of those solid mundane qualities which are usually found in the great mystics.

The first man to understand Teresa, and to see at a glance what she could do for the Order, was Fr Rubeo, Prior-General of the Carmelites and a native of Ravenna, who happened to be making a visitation at Avila. Reform was already in progress elsewhere, notably at Brussels, where the example of St John Soreth survived, and at Venice, where the austere Audet had done good work. The measures proposed by this holy nun were therefore of sound lineage, and he gave her every encouragement. Duly authorized to found convents according to the strict rule (the original rule of Carmel) which she applied at St Joseph's, and even to establish monasteries of men if she was able to do so, Teresa set to work without delay. Her first campaign lasted from 1567 to 1571, during which period she made seven foundations, at Medina del Campo, Malagona, Valladolid, Toledo, Pastrana, Salamanca and Alba de Tormes. The heavenly Spouse gave visible aid to His beloved on earth, and her steps must have been guided by the angel who had long ago transfixed her heart with a fiery javelin. The proof is in her meeting at Medina with a man who was indeed sent by God and of whom she had need if her work for the male element of the Order was to be accomplished. This man is known to history as St John of the Cross.

A little slip of a fellow, agile, furtive and emaciated, he was not quite five feet tall; but you scarcely noticed the fact when you met the penetrating and almost unendurable gaze of those dark feverish eyes. Born in 1542, he was not yet twenty-five, and could have been Teresa's son; but young as he was, he had already led a hard life. His father was dead, 'abhorred' by his relations for having married a very poor girl, whom he had left with three infant boys. The widow Catalina worked at a hand-loom in order to support herself and her sons. Little Juan had had to make trial of various trades on the noisy fairground at Medina; but the pure race of the Spanish hidalgos was visible in his features and his conduct. His intelligence was as a flame of fire. At the time of his meeting with Teresa he had managed to study at the Jesuit college, earning his daily bread meanwhile as a hospital attendant. Then, at the age of twenty, he had joined the Carmelites and had been sent to do his theology at Salamanca. Turning his back, however, upon worldly ambition, despising the doctoral cap and ring, he had returned to his monastery with the intention of living that life of renunciation, the life of Carmel in days gone by, which was the centre of his dreams. If his superiors would not let him do so, he would join the Carthusians. Teresa and John were well suited to understand one another. The reformer, who possessed a marvellous gift of insight, and the enthusiastic little friar 'were in perfect accord from the very first words they exchanged.' Teresa invited the young man to put away all ideas of the Charterhouse and to collaborate in her great work. He was thrilled, but added with all the impetuosity of youth: 'On one condition—that I won't have to wait too long.'

There would be no waiting. John of St Mathias, as he was then called, donned the new habit of the Discalced Carmelites which Teresa herself had tailored: the tunic of rough serge, the scapular, the leather girdle three fingers wide and the white mantle of Our Lady. And now straightway to work! After the foundation of the first male Carmelite house, at Duruelo in 1568, monasteries of the reform quickly multiplied. The authority and fervour of the Discalced attracted many first-rate subjects, for the austere grandeur of the new Observance made a deep impression. Fray Juan himself, preaching by example and practising the most terrible asceticism, went so far beyond the requirements of the primitive Rule that on one occasion he scourged himself to blood for having taken a morsel of food before the community's dinner time, because he felt faint. The custom of Perpetual Adoration, introduced by him, spread throughout Spain. Thanks to the simultaneous and combined activity of these two fiery souls the reforming movement made triumphant progress. The convent of the Incarnation at Avila, which Teresa had left, witnessed her return as prioress by order of the Apostolic Visitor, together with her spiritual companion John, whom she brought as confessor. She was determined to reform the Incarnation, and by dint of patience, tact, charity and love she won admission for the new ideas. Having fulfilled that task, she embarked on her second campaign, in course of which she founded convents at Segovia, Beas, Seville and Caravanca, and once again drew to herself innumerable souls. It seemed that her efforts were irresistible.

Teresa had yet to discover one of the secret laws of Providence, that nothing durable is achieved in this world except through resistance and combat. She met this inevitable opposition for the first time at Seville, in the person of a shabby little nun who was green with envy and accused her of the most shameful conduct. The famous Jesuit Rodrigo Alvarez came down on Teresa's side; but the gale had been let loose, the decisive storm from which few can escape who are called to a great destiny. The ensuing struggle is known as the 'War of the Mitigated.' One can indeed understand those feeble religious, those pampered nuns, who thought they were doing no great wrong in offering a few sops to the world and yet were so fiercely castigated by the example (and sometimes by the speeches) of Teresa and her daughters, and even more fiercely by the voice of public opinion. It was all too easy to compare the heroic efforts of the Discalced with the easy-going routine of the Mitigated. Again, here were the apostolic visitors sent by Pius V to make known the decrees and wishes of Trent, overriding the General's instructions and lending full support to the reform. There were angry murmurings. A general chapter at Piacenza took steps to counter the 'excessives,' which shows how difficult it was for the Church, even under the ablest of popes, to give effect to the new spirit everywhere. When the nuns of the Incarnation assembled to elect a prioress, the voting was rigged and Teresa ousted in favour of a *mitigata*.[1] But her very fame protected her from serious hurt: King Philip II himself had made her acquaintance, while no less a person than the Grand Inquisitor, who had carefully examined her autobiography, professed to hold her in the greatest esteem. The enemy therefore rounded upon John, her friend and collaborator. He was seized by night, chained like a criminal and carried off to the house of the *mitigati* at Toledo, where he was doomed to long months of suffering. Every day, in the refectory, he was subjected to the discipline, each friar administering a stroke; and what strokes those were, accompanied with insult and mockery. Next they tried to seduce him: let him only renounce his follies, and he would be appointed prior somewhere. He refused, and more ill treatment followed. Was he not an *alumbrado*, one of those detestable Illuminati whom the Inquisition was hunting down? Calm, supernaturally calm in his dungeon, John employed his pen; and from that darkness leaped the flame of his *Spiritual Canticle*.[2] At length, after seven months of captivity, he managed to escape; and at the same time Teresa won a glorious victory. She had moved heaven and earth, petitioned the king, used every measure of diplomacy and caused Rome

---

[1] The fifty-five religious who had voted for Teresa were declared 'excommunicated and accursed.' The rest, by choice or compulsion, rallied to the cause of the 'Mitigated.'

[2] By a curious coincidence El Greco was then at Toledo painting his famous picture, *The Division of the Seamless Robe*.

to intervene. The Pope upheld the Discalced: his Brief of 1580 erected them into an autonomous province subject to the wide direction of the General of the Order.

It remained to be seen whether this victory was decisive. John, who since his imprisonment had adopted the name John of the Cross, might at one time have thought it was. He had been made prior of the beautiful Carmel at Granada; and there in his cell, from which he had a magnificent view of the Alhambra, the Generalife and the plain of the Genil, he wrote the *Ascent of Mount Carmel*, the *Dark Night* and the *Living Flame of Love*. The same might have been thought by Teresa, the last act of whose astonishing career closed with a scene of triumph. 'Old and weary, but always young in her desires,' she took the road more than ever 'God's wandering lady.' In spite of sickness, which was undermining her strength, and the exhaustion caused by her austerities; despite the hazards and perils of the way, she set out for a third time, travelling from city to city and founding convents at Villanova de la Xara, Palancia, Seria, Granada, Burgos. Seventeen houses of women and fifteen of men: what a noble harvest! The final picture of herself bequeathed to posterity is that of an aged nun, crouched beneath the awning of an uncomfortable wagon, wrapped in her great white mantle and with lowered veil, moving along the roads of Castile to the merry music of jangling mule-bells. One can name few examples of such sublime power used with such simplicity.

On 4th October 1582 her forces were spent, and she was obliged to halt at Alba de Tormes. It was the feast of St Francis, and Teresa had always loved the Poverello. Was he coming to gather her to heaven? She believed her work to be finished: the chapter at Alcala had approved the Constitutions of the reform, and everything seemed in good order. She herself could do no more. 'I have not a good bone left in me,' she would murmur; and then, carried along by that mysterious strength derived from the mystical marriage, she would add with a radiant smile: 'Now it is time to see one another, my love, my Lord.' She remained in full possession of her faculties to the very end, continuing to advise on the government of the house in which she lay and guiding its young steps. Her final moments were wonderfully peaceful; the old lady's wrinkles seemed to have disappeared, her countenance was pale, 'the colour of full moon,' but gave forth a certain luminosity. With her last breath she recited the psalm: 'Reject not, O Lord, a penitent heart. . . .' Of what need she repent after all her heroism and mortification? But in the eyes of the saints there is no limit to humility.

Left alone on earth, deprived of her support, Teresa's spiritual son John continued the task she had begun. So many and such terrible difficulties, however, beset his path that it seemed Providence intended to lead him to the pinnacle of sanctity by way of suffering. At that time the reformed Carmelites experienced a crisis similar to that through which the Franciscan Order passed on the morrow of the Poverello's death. Fr Nicholas Doria was a man of 'angular features, commanding look, devoid of feeling and possessed of iron determination.' [1] He belonged to the proud Genoese family which had produced the famous admiral Andrea Doria, and in temperament was utterly different from St John of the Cross. The age of the mystics was succeeded by that of the organizers. These were years of confused antagonism and of episodes that were often painful to a degree. The factions clashed at various points, both of course appealing to the lessons of 'good Mother Teresa.' She had always said that the mystical experience should find its fulfilment in apostolic endeavour, that the contemplative must not pray and practise mortification for himself alone. This, however, was not exactly Doria's view; he improved upon the asceticism of the primitive Rule and objected to the Carmelites taking up missionary work. Those who attempted to oppose this formidable man—he was known as the 'Lion of Carmel'—met with pitiless retribution, and hundreds of regulations were added to the articles of the Rule.

St John of the Cross obeyed in silence for some years. Then he expressed his disapproval, and the new heads of the Order directed their fury against him. Deprived of his dignities and offices, he was forced to retire to the desert of Peñuela, where he continued peacefully to lead that life in God which had always enabled him to endure earthly trials with equanimity. His mystical experience became still more exalted, still more intense, a continuous dialogue of his soul with Christ Himself. When it became clear that he was a very sick man at the end of his strength, with his feet and then a large part of his body covered with ulcers, he was carried to the convent of San Salvador at Ubeda, a bleak Moorish fortress scourged by the high winds of the plateaus. There he died in 1591, having passed so far beyond the regions of the world that he suffered neither in his poor body, which was devoured by ulcers, nor mentally at the sight of his work and that of Teresa thus undone.[2]

In fact, however, the crisis did not end, as it had done with the Franciscans, in permanent division among the Discalced Carmelites. In 1587 Sixtus V authorized them to have their Vicar General. In 1593 Clement VIII made them totally independent of the 'great Carmelites,' that is, of the Mitigated, and formed them into an autonomous congregation with its own General. In 1611 the Constitutions received their definitive form. This was a triumph for the spirit of St Teresa and St

[1] Fr Bruno, *St John of the Cross*, 1929.
[2] He was beatified in 1675, canonized in 1726, and in 1926 proclaimed a Doctor of the Universal Church. The canonization of St Teresa is described in the closing pages of this volume.

* E

John of the Cross, its lofty mystical demands and its apostolic realism. With Thomas of Jesus the Carmelites, who were primarily contemplatives, formally linked themselves to the ancient eremitical tradition, to the 'Holy Desert,' where it would be lawful for those who felt themselves called to the mixed life to work for the glory of God by preaching, works of charity and public worship, more or less as did the sons of St Francis.

The reform of Carmel quickly spread to large parts of the Christian world. It subsequently proved to have been one of the most important events in the history of the Church, and countless souls would drink at the well-springs reopened by the two great mystics. Today the Carmelites in their silent cloisters bear witness that the spirit of St Teresa and St John of the Cross is not dead, that God promised the two heroic founders a teeming progeny. It was their spirit which in recent times became incarnate among us in the sublime figure of St Thérèse of Lisieux.

12. St Philip Neri and the Foundation of the Oratory

The riches of the Catholic Reformation become evident when we consider that the Church produced in that single period saints so different as Pius V and Ignatius of Loyola, Francis Borgia and Cajetan of Tiene, Charles Borromeo and Teresa of Avila, not to mention Francis Xavier and Peter Canisius. We must emphasize and be grateful for these very differences, which appear in both character and conduct. It might seem at first glance that to reform the Church by recalling the Curia, the religious Orders, the secular clergy and the laity to the better observance of Gospel principles would be a humdrum business, carried out according to a given set of rules and with unvarying success. This idea is very far from the truth; all those leaders of the Catholic Reformation, in their united effort to advance God's cause, show differences amounting sometimes almost to contraries. No two of them, whether popes, bishops, abbots or religious founders, were hewn to the same pattern.

Such is the liberty of God's children, and of that liberty no saint in all the history of the Church has given more striking testimony than St Philip Neri (1515–95), founder of the Oratory. About 1590 you might have seen in the streets of Rome an odd-looking fellow with bald head, bushy beard and tall ungainly body. Gesticulating wildly, he would talk and laugh with anyone he happened to meet. The least one can say is that he showed no trace of affectation. He enjoyed nothing so much as dropping a witty remark, a popular joke and even raising a laugh against himself. You might have said he was determined you should not take him seriously; but it is just this kind of humility, this mingling of ease and playfulness, which appeals to men. If rebuked for his shabby clothes, he would appear next day clad in the richest furs, and walk more solemnly than a cardinal in procession. If applauded at the end of a spiritual discourse, he would act the clown, tottering down the altar steps like a drunkard, and then break into a fantastic dance. His disciples were vastly entertained. They seemed to delight in his broad humour, and scarcely a day passed without their beloved Pepo doing one of these turns of which he alone knew the secret; but a close look made it clear that each conveyed a lesson. Here are two overdressed young dandies following in the train of his companions: as they pass the gallows on the Ponte Sant' Angelo the saint grasps them by the shoulders and invites them to step up amid loud jeers from the crowd. Here is a solemn citizen who has never learnt that heavenly joy is also human simplicity: the saint hands him a little dog and orders him to carry it for several hours. One day a pretty girl joined his circle out of mere curiosity. Philip clapped his spectacles on her nose and burst into peals of laughter. 'Come, you dunce, you great fathead, you brute-beast!' he would roar at someone whom he had caught in the act of sinning, at the same time pulling the man's ear, his beard or his jacket. But all was done with such simplicity that no one except a fool would dream of showing resentment. His 'continual hilarity of mind' was infectious, and his humour, which he scarcely ever put aside, lay on the borderline of tenderness and irony, of moral counsel and facetiousness, just at that point where Christian liberty finds vent in joy.

At the same time, however, this curious and in many ways alarming individual possessed a soul of spotless purity. He was also a very great mystic and Heaven loaded him with visible graces and charismata. It was said that Christ Our Lord had hallowed him in a mysterious encounter, of which Philip never spoke but which was unquestionably a determining influence in his life. The story goes that at that moment his fleshly heart became too small to contain the ocean of his super-natural love, that it swelled and swelled until the curvature of his ribs increased to make room for the dilated organ.[1] We are told also that when he prayed he belonged no more to this earth, that he escaped into heaven whither he stretched his thin and almost transparent hands. In the sick-room, one of his most favoured spots, it was plain that God used him to effect miraculous cures. In the chapel where he said Mass, what were those cries, those songs and mysterious dialogues, which lasted for hours at a time? Scarcely a marvel has been left unrelated of him. He had only to look at a cardinal to know whether his purple

---

[1] An autopsy performed after his death showed that his heart was in fact abnormlly large, and ribs raised. Aneurism, anatomists will say.

would one day turn white, his red hat become a triple crown. His
penitents had no need to recite their sins, for the saint, like the Curé
d'Ars nearly three hundred years later, could read their hearts better
than could they themselves. If anyone ventured to ask him 'How do
you know, Father, that I have committed this fault?' he would burst
out laughing and reply: 'By the colour of your skin.'

Such was Philip, a saint far removed from the new model created by
St Ignatius. He was born into a family of poor shopkeepers at Florence
in 1515, the fateful year in which St Teresa first saw the light of day,
and his sweet ways won for him in early childhood the nickname *Pepo
buono*, 'good little Philip.' Towards the end of his sixteenth year he
was sent to learn the secrets of business with one of his uncles, but
suddenly enlisted in the service of Christ. For years he lived in
wretched conditions, sleeping in churches or their porches, carrying his
food in the hood of his cloak. At the same time he took a share in the
lay apostolate, a rather hirsute messenger of the Word, member of
a class inconceivable today, but common enough at that time. He
preached in the open air to eager groups in all parts of Rome, even in
the most disreputable quarters, and effected some astonishing conversions. He was often seen in the catacombs praying before the tomb
of some martyr, and regularly made the pilgrimage to the 'seven
churches,' the most famous and most venerable basilicas in the Eternal
City. The Brotherhood of Charity, whose members were drawn from
all classes of society, had no more devoted servant than this odd layman
whose lips were filled with God.

A small nucleus of the faithful gathered gradually around him as if by
chance. They were recruited among those whom he had challenged in
the streets with his famous cry: 'Ah, brother, is it today that we're
going to do good?' For reasons which are not very clear, and under
influences no less obscure, he agreed to become a priest, although he
seems never to have taken a regular theological course. Theologians
and theology, however, are not indispensable to the working of God's
Spirit, and it was most certainly that Spirit which spoke through
Philip's mouth.

In the little church of S. Girolamo della Carità, or rather in the
crypt of that church, he used to receive his friends, who met together
as fervent souls in quest of truth and virtue. This little group was
known as the Oratory,[1] one of the most singular institutions (at least in
its beginnings) ever recognized by the Catholic Church. With characteristic spontaneity Philip gave rise to a new method of spiritual
exercises entirely different from that of St Ignatius. A free verbal commentary, it was called *Oratorio*, and gave its name to one of the most

---

[1] The name had been applied somewhat earlier to other small bodies of a like sort, from
which it must be carefully distinguished. (See p. 6.)

beautiful forms of religious music. One of the brethren began by reading a passage from some edifying book. Another explained and commented upon this text. A third asked questions, put forward objections and elucidated such points as were still obscure. But one must never remain too long upon the dizzy heights of speculation; so another member would narrate an episode of ecclesiastical history, while another recalled day by day the events of Our Lord's life. Philip presided; at every stage he would interject some remark or observation, and it was always he who rounded off the discussion. After this the meeting broke up, hurried down the steps of the church and started in procession through the streets. Then they all went to pray in the catacombs, or perhaps from St Peter's to St John Lateran, from San Lorenzo to the basilica of Santa Croce, which preserves the memory of the crusaders. As they walked they sang with alternate voice those splendid antiphons which had lately been set to glorious music by a brilliant composer named Palestrina.

It is quite certain that Philip had at this time no idea whatever of founding an Order. He would have been astonished to learn that he was in fact doing so; he would doubtless have answered with a smile that there were quite enough Orders as it was: all those ancient bodies which were in process of reform and all those which had been established during the past thirty years—Theatines, Barnabites, Somaschi and the Oblates of St Charles Borromeo, not to mention the most active of all, the Jesuits, whose new General, Francis Borgia, was leading them to glory. There were also numerous Orders of women. What need then of yet another congregation? This, however, is exactly what resulted from his anarchical exertions. A brotherhood was created from the many princes and religious, artisans and aristocrats, who took part in the daily *Oratorio*. Some of them, in their various ways, contributed work of prime importance to its foundation. Among these were the little Florentine tailor Parigi, who served Philip for thirty years at San Girolamo; Cacciaguerra, an ex-merchant, who became a lofty mystic; the elegant Tarugi, a papal chamberlain, whose grand velvet suits rubbed shoulders quite happily with the fustian of his brethren; and Baronio, a homely student from the Abruzzi, who was afterwards celebrated as the great historian Cardinal Baronius. The Oratory now began to hold its meetings in the larger church of Santa Maria in Valicella. Crowds were attending the exercises, and the Florentines invited their fellow countryman to take charge of the church and parish of St John which they maintained at Rome. But the nucleus from which all this proceeded was very small, perhaps no more than fifteen members. Later they were obliged to dissolve and give more regular shape to the movement, which would otherwise have run into trouble. During the last years of his pontificate, indeed, Paul IV expressed his disapproval, and even Pius V let it be seen that he did not altogether trust them.

Thus, in spite of Philip's hesitation and resistance, the Oratory came into being, and groups were established at such places as Naples, Milan, Lucca, Fermo and Bologna. At Naples the institution was well organized, at Lucca and Fermo hardly at all; in no case was there more than the slenderest link with that of Rome. Nor was it until 1575, by express order of the Pope, that Philip allowed his free movement to become a congregation. The new congregation, however, was unique: clerics and pious laymen were to pray and work in common, subject to a very simple rule which imposed no external discipline or strict regulations. It was to be a republic controlled by Love, wholly different from the Society of Jesus. The one and only tie acknowledged and proclaimed was 'that born of mutual affection and daily intercourse'; and when Philip was asked what was the sum total of his Rule, he answered quite simply, grave yet smiling: 'Nothing but charity.'

Nevertheless this first Oratory, whimsical and unorganized though it was, exerted considerable influence and produced many men who distinguished themselves in the great struggles of that age. The idea was of such spiritual strength that it became even more widespread than did the institution properly so called. In France, during the next century, Cardinal de Bérulle used it to found an Order somewhat different in appearance, though in spirit fairly close to that of the sublime vagabond of the Roman streets, whose initial impulse passed later still to the Oratory of Gratry.[1] In his own day and country Philip's example took effect among the clergy. To his 'school of sanctity and Christian gaiety' the priests of Italy were to owe those most attractive characteristics of simplicity and graciousness which we find among them even today.

The holy founder himself, confined to his room by sickness and old age, died in a manner worthy of his life. Having obtained the privilege of saying Mass at home, even in private, he took advantage of it to spend several hours in offering the Holy Sacrifice. Feeble and emaciated, resembling a fine candle or a sheet of old parchment, he continued until the last a victim of the same joyous fever, the same supernatural flame. To everyone who came to see him he would repeat the precept he had made his own since adolescence: 'Live in God and die to self.' He was now an octogenarian, but the doctors solemnly assured him that he was in perfect health and would live to be ninety. Philip,

---

[1] Other congregations of clerks regular came into being at this time: the Clerks Regular of the Mother of God, founded at Lucca by St John Leonardi for preaching and the struggle against Protestantism; the Clerks Regular of the Pious Schools, founded at Rome by the Spaniard St Joseph Calasanctius mainly for the rescue of abandoned and delinquent children. The example of St Philip Neri's Oratory was later imitated by St Francis of Sales, St Vincent de Paul and others.

however, by way of a final jest, decided to give them all the slip. Only a few beheld his passing: a pale hand was raised in blessing, a light murmur hovered on his lips and God's fool slept in Christ (1595).

13. A New Church or a New Look?

When we consider the history of the Church at that decisive turning point in the sixteenth century, we cannot but fix an admiring gaze upon the popes who summoned the Council and gave effect to its decrees, upon the Fathers responsible for those decrees, upon the bishops who applied them throughout the Catholic world, and upon all those saints, both men and women, who expended whole treasuries of courage and faith in the reform of ecclesiastical institutions and of souls. The results of their manifold effort were immense, and we continue to profit by them. They are summarized as follows by a 'neutral' historian: [1] 'The work of unification was at the same time a work of purification and rejuvenation. There was indeed, in 1563, a new Catholic Church, more sure of her dogma, more worthy to govern souls, more conscious of her function and of her duties.'

We may, however, question the accuracy of this phrase, 'a new Catholic Church.' It deserves careful consideration, because such expressions are common and are used even among Catholics. The question is, whether the religion of Trent is identical with that of the medieval period and with that of the early Christian ages. Here is an example of the kind of thing one meets in the writings of authoritative commentators: 'Since times had changed, the popes, bishops and theologians who led the resistance to the new men and their ideas were obliged to establish a new religion in the shape of Tridentine Catholicism, which we have by no means defined until we have done something more than study its dogmas.' [2] In some Protestant circles, too, it is commonly maintained that Protestantism alone brought about a return to genuine Christianity, to the pure evangelism of the primitive Church, and that Tridentine Catholicism is a fabrication, half Italian and half Spanish, far removed from the true faith.

This interpretation of events is equally untrue in respect of both Catholicism and Protestantism. The equation 'Reform = Return to the primitive Church' is the expression of a myth propagated by the enemies of traditional Christianity but contradicted by historical facts. '"Reform" and "Primitive Church" are convenient terms wherewith to hide from their own eyes the rashness of their secret desires. What

---

[1] H. Hauser, *La Prépondérance espagnole*, p. 7, being vol. ix of the series *Peuples et civilisations*.

[2] L. Febvre: 'Une question mal posée: Les origines de la Réforme française et le problème général des causes de la Réforme' in *La Revue historique*, clxi, 1929, p. 76.

they really wanted was not restoration but innovation.'[1] As had already been observed,[2] the objective judgment of history considers the 'Protestant Reformation' as a revolution cutting short the development of Christianity. No less objectively, the Catholic Reformation can be traced back in unbroken line to Christian origins, both as regards the manner of its operation and in respect of the principles to which it adhered. Bossuet proved as much in his penetrating reply to a letter addressed to him by Leibniz, in which that great philosopher explained the Protestant objections to the Council of Trent.[3] His arguments remain valid.

There is no measure adopted by the Council, or by the popes of that time, whose origin cannot be detected in the earlier principles and organization of the Church. There is no article of faith proclaimed by the Assembly which is not solidly based upon Scripture and Tradition. Nor are those articles in fact so very numerous as they may seem; they are all reducible to five or six central notions. 'If the Church was obliged to multiply them,' says Bossuet, 'it was because those whom she condemned by their means had stirred a proportionate amount of mud.' It is also true that at some points the decrees of Trent appear to go beyond what had hitherto been taught. But it has always been agreed in the Church that she has an unquestionable right and duty, as the depository of faith, to make ever more explicit what is implicit in Revelation. That has been the essential function of the Councils ever since Nicaea, which might with as much justice be accused of having 'innovated' upon the letter of the Gospels. It is quite natural that a religion which is to endure and develop through the centuries should not remain imprisoned within the limited framework of its origins. 'A growing tree is never the same, and yet it is always the same.'[4] The changes brought about by Trent did not constitute a 'new religion'; they were necessary steps taken to preserve the old. It is precisely this balance between absolute fidelity to revealed truth and the evolution of formulae and customs dictated by the passage of time that has characterized the Catholic and Roman Church throughout her history. Therein lies the full significance of what she understands by Tradition.

We are not dealing then with 'a new religion.' But is it possible to maintain that on the morrow of the Council of Trent the Catholic Church was exactly such as she had been in the age of the cathedrals and crusades? Certainly not. New features appeared, others became less

[1] Ibid., p. 60.
[2] See above, p. 1 et seq.
[3] The letter and the reply are printed in Lachat's edition of Bossuet's *Works*, vol. xviii, pp. 198–210.
[4] L. Cristiani, *L'Église à l'époque du concile de Trente*, 1948, being vol. xvii of Fliche and Martin's *Histoire de l'église*.

marked, while others again completely vanished. A new spirit emerged, of which it has been rightly said that 'we have by no means defined it until we have done something more than study its dogmas'; a spirit whose elements it is not easy to determine—inviolability of principles, increased sense of unity, strengthening of discipline—but which borrowed ideas from the circumstances attending its emergence, and which, as it penetrated human groups and their mental habits, took on a variety of colours while remaining substantially the same. The spirit of the Council of Trent is found in devotional practices as well as in architectural forms, in the liturgy as well as in music.

One more phenomenon is likewise familiar to history. The Christian religion, though permanent and faithful to itself in the unchanging certitude of Revelation, assumes manifestly different aspects as it makes its way during the course of centuries into the most varied forms of society. The Church of the 'Dark Ages' is not in all respects identical with that of the Roman Empire under Constantine any more than with that of Byzantium; and the Church of St Bernard and St Louis appears in many ways original. Similarly today the Church in the United States, while holding the same dogmas and subject to the infallible authority of the Pope, wears a look very different from that of the Church in France, in Italy or in Spain. Because she is human as well as divine, the Church inscribes her destiny in the register of history, of geography and of sociology. Thus her one and only self reveals a variety of facets; and it was just such a new look that she presented on the morrow of Trent.

We must now review the fundamental characteristics of the Tridentine spirit, in order to obtain a proper idea of this 'new look.' Undoubtedly the most striking feature is that the dogmas of the Church, being now clearly defined, are found to be more solid and inviolable. The indignant Leibniz, in his letter to Bossuet, is fully aware of this fact: 'Henceforward one cannot without heresy call in question the authenticity of a single book or any part of Holy Scripture; one can no longer doubt that justification is effected by an inherent quality, or that the justifying end is distinct from confidence in divine mercy; or that there are seven sacraments; or that the Body and Blood of Christ are present in the Eucharist together with His divinity; or the matter, form and minister of the sacraments, or the indissolubility of marriage.' He was perfectly correct, and herein is the primary contribution of the decrees of Trent, whose effects would be transmitted to the faithful by way of the Catechism and Missal. From now onwards it would be impossible to dispute and call into doubt truths upon which the Church had pronounced judgment in the most solemn and definitive terms. Those truths had been too fiercely assailed to allow of their being left without a protective wall. The Tridentine Church is first and foremost *orthodox*, concerned above all with the security of doctrine and loyalty to dogmas; and this characteristic has remained prominent ever since.

Here is a second and no less striking feature: the Church's new look represents a religion infinitely more worthy, more grave and at the same time more mystical, seeking to satisfy the anxious pursuit of souls hungry for the Absolute. I say first more worthy; this is an aspect to which we, the heirs of Trent, are so accustomed that we find it almost impossible to imagine a Church which allowed dogs to disport themselves in buildings dedicated for public worship, and permitted gentlemen to go there 'carrying their hawks, like half-witted buffoons,' joking at the tops of their voices during holy Mass. It is likewise impossible for us to understand those entertainments, held even in the sacred edifice as well as in the streets, at which clerics joined the common folk in every kind of tomfoolery. The Council put an end to all this kind of behaviour, which had been common enough as late as 1540.

The very type of the Christian was henceforward changed. Reception of the sacraments and more frequent communion transformed the better sort of men. Faith at this period was perhaps no greater nor more ardent than in the Middle Ages, but it tended to give daily life a more deeply religious rhythm.[1] Morality also benefited, although its progress, particularly in the domain of sex, was rather slow. A wave of mysticism, however, caught up the loftiest and most ardent souls, whom we find in the Oratories of St Philip Neri no less than in the austere Carmelite houses of Spain; and that wave continued to roll throughout the following century. A regenerate clergy also made its appearance. It was better trained, thanks to the seminaries, and the great majority was free from those shortcomings for which it had been erstwhile and justly criticized.[2] At the head of this clergy we see the gradual disappearance of pleasure-seeking, political or warlike popes, giving place to wise and respectable pontiffs, many of whom were prudent administrators or fervent mystics.

We come lastly to the third feature of the 'new look.' It was around a regenerate Papacy that the Catholic world became more strongly unified. The Church of the Council of Trent is a more centralized Church, more highly organized than in the Middle Ages. The prestige of the 'Bishop of the Universal Church,' having grown considerably

---

[1] Certainly among the spiritual *élite*. As regards others, was there not a risk that this grave and solemn countenance of religion might separate religion itself from the rest of life? Was it not the origin of the modern divorce between the two halves of man's existence, between the fulfilment of his duty to God and everything else, in which God scarcely features at all?

[2] Ecclesiastical dress underwent a change. It differed increasingly from secular costume and black, which had been approved by St Charles Borromeo, became the fashion.

since the happy ending of the Schism and the conciliar crisis, emerged still greater from this half-century during which the Papacy had both directed and approved the Council's work. To the democratic and anarchical tendencies of Protestantism there was opposed a monarchical system, which continued to increase until its coronation three hundred years later with the dogma of Papal Infallibility. Ever more widely recognized as supreme head of the hierarchy, the Pope came also to be looked upon as competent to exercise control over all that the Church thinks, believes, wills and does. Moreover he now had at his free disposal the Society of Jesus, a body comparable to a regiment of picked troops. Discussion as to the principle of authority became steadily less frequent. The principle of unity was still a matter of doubt; but while some Catholics long continued to protest against 'ultramontanism,' the ultimate acceptance (explicit or tacit) by all States of the Tridentine decrees and papal decisions proved that the authority of the Holy See was no longer in question. The Council of Trent abruptly halted an evident inclination on the part of monarchs to establish national Churches; and although this tendency might still give rise to such crises as that of Gallicanism in the seventeenth century, those responsible never had the least intention of destroying Christian unity.

But admiration for the results obtained in the Tridentine period must not blind us to certain shadows in the portrait as a whole. The Church's new look included some less attractive features to which attention has been rightly drawn by adversaries of the Council and its work; these, however, have not escaped the notice of sound historians on the Catholic side.[1] In so far as it was a genuine return to life-giving sources, an act of heroic obedience to the demands of faith, the Catholic Reformation is beyond disparagement. But it was accomplished in an atmosphere of often tragic strife, for the Church had forcibly to defend herself against the theories and encroachments of heretics. The result was a certain hardening, an inevitable rigidity, even a certain narrowness; and in so far as the Tridentine reform was obliged to become a 'counter-reformation' it developed characteristics which we cannot overlook if the truth is to be told.

The Church of the 'new look' was a fighting Church. The Fathers of Trent alone pronounced more condemnations than all previous councils together; they could not have done otherwise when confronted with a swarm of propositions hostile to her teaching, and when they saw the advance against Mother Church of adversaries who, under pretext of strengthening her walls, would have irretrievably destroyed her. All the same, Trent most certainly hallowed a final breach with the Protestants. As things stood when the Council ended its work, this

---

[1] See, for example, G. Bardy, 'L'Église catholique, moyen âge et temps modernes' in *Année théologique*, 1949, fasc. iv, a model of intelligence and probity.

rupture was not only desirable: it was quite indispensable. Protestant-ism was no longer an affair of wavering on the part of Luther, or of tentative agreement on that of Melanchthon; Calvinism had forged a block of steel which was nothing less than a well-organized counter-Church. Invitations to discuss points of difference were bound to prove illusory and deceptive, so that the only possible reply was a categorical 'Non possumus.' This was clearly understood by those theologians of the Council, particularly the Jesuits, who had laboured to prevent any sort of compromise; and the same fact explains the attitude of Laynez, second General of the Society, at the Conference of Poissy, where he seems to have done all he could to make a settlement impossible. Many historians have blamed the Church of Trent for this 'intransigence.' But the charge is of its very nature mere 'lay' or 'Protestant' reaction; the Church, as guardian of Christ's deposit, could have no truck with error. Neither the Fathers of the Council nor the popes, however well disposed they might have been, could have recognized the character of truth in the vagaries of Luther, Zwingli, Henry VIII and Calvin. A Catholic, if he desires to remain an orthodox Catholic, is bound in conscience unreservedly to subscribe the anathemas of Trent. It remains, however, none the less true, on the historical as distinct from the theological plane, that this hardening and stiffening, concomitant with a similar process in the Protestant camp, did much to involve the whole of Christendom in the bloody discords which marked the end of the sixteenth century, and from which the Church of Christ as a whole would emerge exhausted, and maybe for ever mutilated.

Within the closed circle of Catholicism also we discover certain features which appear to have altered the ancient visage of the Church. 'Because they were fighting a heresy, the Sovereign Pontiffs and the Fathers of the Council gave their definitions such heavy outlines that one can easily lose sight of those positive riches with which they were not called upon to deal. Formulae devised for the condemnation of error are always partial, throwing light upon only one aspect of the truth; but we must not forget that revealed truth is richer and more fruitful than can be expressed by definitions. The unhappy crisis of the sixteenth century led the Catholic Church, or at least a fair number of her theologians, to thrust into the background some essential factors of her doctrine and life. The thesis of justification by faith is affirmed by St Paul, repeated by St Augustine and taught by the councils of Milevis and Orange.'[1] It may therefore be asked whether the anathemas, indispensable though they most assuredly were, did not result in a narrowing of Christian thought.

Some critics have detected the same phenomenon in the composition of the Catholic community. It is quite certain that a greater degree of

[1] G. Bardy, loc. cit.

unity and more centralization were necessary if anarchy was to be avoided; but Protestants have argued that the result was a kind of militarism, a system of absolute uniformity, and that the Church has been impoverished by the disappearance of that astonishing diversity which is so noticeable, for example, in St Jerome's violent clash with St John Chrysostom. The criticism is hardly justified. One need only consider such exact contemporaries as St Philip Neri and St John of the Cross, or their immediate junior St Francis of Sales, to see that differences of character and vocation were by no means impossible within the strict hierarchical setting which had now become the rule. Besides, the very succession of popes and the diversity of their characters ensured an opportunity for discussion, arbitration and improvement.

More evident is another feature which cannot fail to impress the historian. 'In order effectively to oppose the Protestant doctrines concerning the invisible character of the spiritual Church, emphasis was laid almost exclusively upon the visible Church regarded as an institution, a system of government, an organism. The tract *De Ecclesia* developed along these lines, in the margin as it were of theology properly so called, one party viewing it as a thesis of Apologetics, the other as a part of Canon Law. . . . They ended by virtually forgetting the interior aspect of the life of the Church as Mystical Body of the Saviour and habitual dispenser of Grace'; [1] and it is one of Pope Pius XII's most outstanding titles to fame that he stressed the need for a theology of the Mystical Body, without which Catholics become mere members of a society and, eventually, of a party. Nevertheless it cannot be denied that the Council of Trent, by placing so much emphasis upon the visible Church, did much to give her the characteristics of a social force, characteristics which the triumphs of a renascent art, under papal direction, endowed with such imposing (though sometimes disconcerting) magnificence. Of the two inseparable elements which constitute the divine majesty of Christ, it is His Glory rather than His Cross that seems in profane eyes to be exalted by the Tridentine Church. True Catholics alone know that the one implies the other, and even the marbles of St Peter's somehow reflect the presence of Him who is God of the poor in spirit.

Such then is the 'new look' presented to history by the Church. When the Council ended, and when Pius V died, the terrible crisis which had shaken the Christian world for half a century was far from ended: it had still to reach its bloody culmination, but at least the barque of Peter had been secured against shipwreck. Catholicism had confronted heresy. By reforming herself she deprived her adversaries of their most powerful means of propaganda, and defined her teaching with such force and clarity that souls in quest of the Absolute would no

[1] G. Bardy, *loc. cit.*

longer need to ask Luther and Calvin for the fulfilment of their ancient hopes, but would obtain it through St Teresa or St John of the Cross. She also managed to graft into her own thought whatever was acceptable in humanism, all the creative intellect which that movement had given to the world; and she had revealed that living synthesis through the medium of her saints—through Ignatius of Loyola, for instance, as she would do later through St Francis of Sales. Meanwhile, as if to compensate for the losses of people and territories inflicted upon her by Protestantism, she sent other saints in the wake of Francis Xavier[1] to win for her a world. Indeed the Tridentine Church with her new look is no less great, no less admirable, than her predecessors. She had cleared a decisive stage on the dark and difficult road by which redeemed humanity has striven for nearly two thousand years towards the light.

14. In the Mirror of Art

The new countenance of Holy Church is so reflected in the mirror of art that the spirit of the Council of Trent is perhaps nowhere so fully manifested as in the achievements of architecture, painting, sculpture and music which flowered in its climate.[2] These were very numerous in the half-century between the death of Leo X (1522) and that of Pius V (1572), during which the Tridentine reform took shape in men's mind, found expression in the conciliar canons, and at length began to pass into the manners and institutions of society. For while that reform was a movement towards austerity it was by no means systematically hostile to the arts. Exactly the opposite is true. Against the Protestant iconoclasts, who rejected painted and sculptured images, and would have nothing but bare walls in their temples, the Church encouraged veneration of artistic works which allow the faithful to strengthen their belief with beautiful forms; she continued more than ever to regard the splendour of her churches as glorifying the majesty of God. In all countries where Protestantism had failed to obtain a hold, and especially in Italy, which was almost wholly free of the taint, art continued to live the same intense life it had enjoyed in the preceding era, and the Church to fulfil her ancient role of patron and protectress.

Of the eight popes who occupied the throne of Peter during those fifty years, only one, Adrian VI of Utrecht, showed himself indifferent to the arts, except to despise and condemn the masterpieces of antiquity

---

[1] See Chapter IV,

[2] Before dealing with this subject we must pay tribute to Émile Mâle, who has shed so much light upon its every facet. To follow the chapters of his great work, L'Art religieux après le concile de Trente (1932), is to understand completely the spirit of the Council of Trent.

as pagan idols. But Clement VII, during whose pontificate the sack of Rome seemed to destroy the creative urge, took the first opportunity to do all he could to revive the tradition of his predecessors. He summoned Michelangelo to begin work in the Sistine Chapel, and took a close interest in the building of Saint-Louis-des-Français, the first window of which he had long ago erected as Cardinal Giulio dei Medici. Paul III, who first convoked the Council, was a man of encyclopaedic mind and an exquisite connoisseur. Responsible for many artistic undertakings, he built the Porta Santo Spirito and the celebrated Palazzo Farnese, the young Sangallo's masterpiece which was completed by Michelangelo. He also constructed the Pauline Chapel and Sala Regale, in the Vatican, and did much to advance the work at St Peter's. Julius III concentrated almost exclusively upon his delightful Villa del Monte; but Palestrina's masterpiece, the *Coronation Mass*, is associated with the name of Marcellus II. Paul IV continued work on St Peter's, encouraged his niece to build the Roman College and also the Annunziata, the apse of which was afterwards richly decorated by Zuccari. He was able to recognize in Michelangelo's 'Last Judgment' his own solemn and tragic faith. Pius IV, under whom the Council ended its labours, ranks as a patron with Julius II and Leo X. He laid out the Piazza of St Peter's, created the famous Casino Medici in the Vatican gardens, rebuilt the precincts of the Sacred Palace, completed the ceiling of St John Lateran, erected the Porta Pia and the Porta del Popolo (near which latter he built a charming villa), and had Michelangelo build the ingenious and imposing church of Santa Maria degli Angeli in the Baths of Diocletian. Other work was done by his order at Ancona, Ostia and Civitavecchia, and it was also he who assured the triumph of Oratorio. The austere St Pius V gave more attention to works of public utility than to works of art properly so called. It is none the less to his credit that he did not impede what had already been begun, and even encouraged the widespread movement which, on the morrow of Trent, caused many bishops and all the religious Orders to restore their churches or build new ones.

Nothing is more false than to imagine a sort of hiatus between the popes of the Renaissance and those of the Tridentine era. What those of the fifteenth century had commenced was carried on by their successors in the sixteenth—in a different spirit, no doubt, but with the same determination. There is no more remarkable proof of this statement than the history of St Peter's, of that stupendous building site the opening of which in 1499 marked the beginning of the 'High Renaissance,' and which never closed during a period of one hundred and fifty years, notwithstanding storm and stress in the shape of war, revolt, intrigue and human weakness. Bramante, who conceived the brilliant project, had long been dead; Raphael, his successor in charge of operations, had followed him too soon into the grave, as also had his two assistants Fra Giocondo and Giulio Sangallo. Immediately after young Antonio Sangallo had taken his place, work was completely suspended by the terrible disaster of 1527. But the task was resumed as quickly as possible: once again hundreds and hundreds of workmen took over the site; once again marble and other precious materials were brought from far and wide. In 1546 Michelangelo took charge of the gigantic work so well suited to his colossal genius, and returned to Bramante's plan for a Greek cross.[1] But he decided to substitute for the cupola which was to have been modelled upon that of the Pantheon, another and even more wonderful structure inspired by Brunelleschi; and he laboured until death to realize this titanic dream which was to figure forth the greatness and incomparable majesty of the Church. The amazing history of St Peter's is a concrete sign of the determination of Catholicism to declare itself and triumph.

It must, however, be added that this loyalty to art, of which the Tridentine Church afforded such striking proofs, went hand in hand with a profound modification of her attitude towards the very significance of art. The great humanist and patron popes had thought of it as an end in itself, destined to lend surpassing radiance to the Church and particularly to the Holy See, without trying to place it at the service of faith. The result was a large measure of ambiguity and some questionable complacency, from which even the Tridentine popes were not altogether free. Many of the works of art produced between 1522 and 1572 were secular and profane, sometimes in the least agreeable sense of this word. Certain frescoes painted in the Vatican and the Castle of Sant' Angelo for Paul III were curiously pagan in tone; and the enormous sums spent by Pius IV on his 'Casino' are no less surprising. It remained to be seen whether art, under ecclesiastical patronage, would remain outside the great current which was urging it to renew and purify itself. Here also the Spirit of the Council played a part.

In the twenty-fifth and final session it was decreed that 'the Holy Council forbids the placing in churches of any image which is inspired by an erroneous dogma and might lead the simple astray. It wishes that all impurity be avoided, that images be not given suggestive charm; and it forbids the erection anywhere, even in churches not subject to visitation by the Ordinary, of any unusual image unless first approved by the bishop.' These words represented a new attitude of the Church towards religious iconography, which was to be pruned, corrected and purified from a moral as well as from a dogmatic point of view. Such was the negative aspect of the Council's aesthetic work; but before long, as fruit of the same spirit which animated the Assembly, a

[1] This was subsequently abandoned by Maderno. See the beginning of Chapter V.

positive operation was set on foot tending to transmit that spirit to the realm of art, an operation whose principles were formulated by Molanus in his Latin treatise on *Painters and Sacred Images* (1570).

The first sign of the existence of a new spirit was a wave of modesty. In 1558, during the lifetime of Michelangelo, Paul IV anticipated the conciliar decisions by giving orders that the nudities of the Sistine Chapel must be covered, an undertaking completed by St Pius V. Later, under Clement VIII, it was nearly decided to *erase* all 'scandalous' frescoes. The action of Paul IV was generally approved; St Charles Borromeo followed his example wherever possible, and Bellarmine subsequently boasted of having extracted a promise from an artist friend never to paint a nude. Some bishops were even more zealous, destroying all pictures and statues which they considered immodest. The eviction of pagan statues from the Vatican Palace by Pius V was yet another manifestation of the same spirit; and this campaign of prudery was afterwards carried to such lengths that Pope Innocent X had a charming new-born Infant Jesus, by Guercino, covered with a shirt! [1]

The same attempt to correct ancient manners was pursued in all directions. It was not only nude figures that were banished from the churches, but also those of 'useless' persons and 'trifling' episodes, all those curiosities in fact which lent a frequently charming but none the less unchristian picturesqueness to the works of the Renaissance. Paolo Veronese was actually summoned from Venice to appear before the Holy Office on a charge of having introduced into a 'Last Supper' figures unworthy of so grave a subject. He could only reply that he put them there to fill gaps in the canvas and 'do good'; upon which he was ordered to retouch his picture within three months. Naturally enough everything suggestive of doctrinal error was ruthlessly condemned. In the years immediately following the Council religious censorship objected even to the apocryphal traditions, of which medieval painters had made frequent use. Some artists met with disapproval for having shown the Blessed Virgin swooning at the foot of the Cross, whereas the Gospel says that she was standing: *Stabat.* Later on a more generous attitude was adopted; but the Apocrypha had become a dead letter, and would be ignored altogether by modern artists.

A still more considerable effort on the positive side corresponded to this negative aspect. The Church of the Council of Trent, seeing the possibilities of art in the field of apologetics, resolved to employ it as a weapon against heresy and as material in the rebuilding of Christianity; and this resumption of art by the Church is one of the outstanding

[1] Note, however, that this modesty extended only to works placed in churches. Pagan decorations, though often very free, were still accepted in private residences, even those belonging to the popes, e.g. the Palazzo Farnese,

events of the age.[1] Whereas the Renaissance, particularly in the fifteenth century, had marked the zenith of creative individualism, the period following the Council corresponded to the flowering of a Catholic art with new and well-established characteristics, which most certainly found inspiration as well as hostility among the theologians.

This profound transformation of artistic ideals was facilitated by the fact that artists themselves were affected by the impulse of contemporary trends; an increasing number were believers. Towards the end of his life Michelangelo, under the influence of his saintly friend Vittoria Colonna and that of the Society of Jesus, whose spirit and methods he greatly admired, behaved in all respects as a Christian, grave and austere, filled with anguish at the thought of death and judgment. 'Now I realize,' he exclaimed, 'how mistaken was the passionate illusion that made me look upon art as a sovereign idol. . . .' The type of dilettante and pleasure-seeking artist so familiar to the Renaissance, working with equal enthusiasm and equal talent both in the religious and in the pagan sphere, vanished almost completely. It gave place to a very different type, whose members believed and practised the Catholic faith, sometimes with conspicuous piety. Among these was Guercino, who heard Mass each morning and went to pray in church every evening; Bernini, who communicated twice a week and made an annual retreat; and the devout but sugary Carlo Dolci, who made a vow never to paint a figure which could not lead souls to devotion.

'Since art had become a form of doctrine, the artist also came to consider that the subject of his pictures was an essential part thereof.' In the Renaissance period the theme of a work was often a mere pretext for the joyful play of shape and colour. But from now onwards, and with growing importance throughout the seventeenth century, what mattered was the truth which an artist sought to express, or rather that which his theological advisers asked him to express. So it was that after the Council of Trent art took its place in the battlefield, where its protagonists devoted themselves to exalting all that Protestantism condemned: 'The cult of Our Lady, the primacy of St Peter, belief in the sacraments, in the efficacy of prayers for the dead and of good works, the veneration of images and relics—all these dogmas or ancient traditions were defended by art in alliance with the Church.' The subjects represented during a period of more than one hundred years bear the stamp of this apologetic and combative purpose.

---

[1] On this point especially the labours of Émile Mâle have thrown entirely new light. In the Introduction to his great book he admitted with splendid humility how much his thought had been modified in this respect. At the end of *Art religieux à la fin du moyen âge* he had written: 'Henceforward there would still be Christian artists, but no more Christian art.' Later studies caused him to change his mind. In all works of art produced after the Council of Trent, which he had tended to despise, his genius and patience discovered a symbolism and an apologetic in harmony with the preoccupations of that time.

Art, however, took its cue not only from the thought and activity of the Tridentine Church, but also from her climate. Catholicism as regenerated by the Council was a solemn and moving religion, in which the faithful soul was invited, e.g. by the *Exercises* of St Ignatius, to meditate the Passion of Christ and to think of life in terms of death. Art likewise assumed this character. During the Renaissance Christian art had been free to exalt the joy of living. But this new art looked farther back to the late Middle Ages, so pregnant with anguish and with terror; it no longer gave expression to repose in God, but to the terrible adventure [1] of seeking for the Absolute as experienced by the great sixteenth-century mystics. Artists no longer conjured up the beauty of creation, but the tragedy of man doomed to death by sin; and some of them, e.g. Valdès Leal of Seville, carried this tendency to the point of the macabre. Funereal pomp, so dear to the Jesuits, and catafalques carved in stone were other indications of the same outlook. The masterpiece of this period [2] is the 'Last Judgment' in the Sistine Chapel, Michelangelo's last great undertaking. Begun on the morrow of the sack of Rome, in the gloomy atmosphere of that appalling tragedy, and completed just as the master's interior development drew level with the spirit of Trent, it is a prodigious achievement, almost inaccessible to our human sensibility. We find in it no trace of open air or countryside to refresh the eye or give the heart repose; all is bathed in an atmosphere of molten lead and vertigo, a perfect reminder of that unimaginable 'day of wrath' spoken of by the *Dies irae*, when time and space will collapse into the abyss, and when the human race, herded as in the fresco beneath the uplifted hand of its Eternal Judge, will cower in terror on the frontiers of despair.

But the reaction of a believing soul to sin and punishment were not the sole preoccupation of Tridentine art, which strove at the same time to express the glory of the Church in her new-found strength and certitude. This purpose is evident henceforth in every field, in architecture as well as in painting and sculpture. The Annunciation, Transfiguration, Ascension and Assumption, all those themes in fact which show Earth supernaturally linked to Heaven, were represented time and again in the glory of cloud and nimbus, but soon also against the magnificent spread of gold and purple hangings, symbolic of the Church Triumphant. Architecture was similarly affected. Abandoning the regular harmonies of the Renaissance (themselves copied from antiquity), flat ceilings and painted decoration, as well as the play of light and shadow so dear to the Gothic builders, it adopted a new type

[1] Note, however, that St John of the Cross repeatedly describes it as a *happy* adventure: *dichosa ventura.*

[2] Perhaps we should say one of the masterpieces, remembering the cruel 'Deposition from the Cross.'

of church whose model was the famous Gesù at Rome, which Vignola began for the Jesuits in 1568. The type of religious edifice adopted by the Counter-Reformation, and carried to all four quarters of the world by the Society of Jesus, is as far removed as it is possible to be from the Protestant temple. Among its features are a proud façade, rising tier upon tier and seemingly alien from what lies behind; purely ornamental pediments broken by statues and turrets; a nave with cylindrical vaulting and bordered by independent side chapels; and a monumental dome above the transept crossing. It is in fact a building devoid of mystery, containing so much coloured marble, stucco and gold ornament that it suggests a palace drawing-room [1] rather than the house of a lowly God.

It is difficult to say what influence these ideas exerted upon Christian art from an aesthetic point of view. For the period of their introduction followed the disappearance of the sublime architects of the High Renaissance, who were succeeded by men of great talent that sometimes amounted to brilliance, but who no longer possessed the creative power of their forerunners. The geniuses who were later inspired by the Tridentine spirit in countries beyond the Alps were either as yet unborn or had scarcely begun their work: in 1572 El Greco was twenty-five years old, and Rubens had not seen the light of day. Michelangelo alone of the race of Titans survived at Rome until 1564. In no technique do we find men of equal stature with their predecessors: Brunelleschi, Bramante and Michelangelo were unmatched by Vignola, 'the modern Vitruvius,' by Vasari,[2] or even by Palladio (1518–80), to whom Vicenza owes its beauty and Venice the church of San Giorgio. In sculpture neither the clever and somewhat boastful Benvenuto Cellini (1500–71), who was far removed from the spirit of the Catholic Reformation and spent most of his working life in France, nor Sansovino (1485–1570), who made the bronze doors for St Mark's at Venice, could show anything to rival the masterpieces of Donatello and Verrocchio, let alone the 'Moses' and 'Slaves' of Michelangelo. In painting Primaticcio (1504–70), with his firm talent, happy, smiling and equal to every task imposed upon him by the King of France, could not be considered the equal of the great masters.

To this slackening as it were of creative intensity there is only one exception: Venice. In that opulent city, queen of the Adriatic, lady paramount of Cyprus, and conqueror of Lepanto, who knew not that

---

[1] This impression, however, which makes the Jesuit churches look like secular monuments, must not cause us to forget that these 'boudoirs of God' were designed with a view to religious functions. They were meant to enable all the faithful to see the altar and follow the Holy Sacrifice, whereas the old Gothic rood-screens hid the altar from the congregation.

[2] He built the Palazzo Uffizi at Florence, but is better known as the author of *Lives of the Painters, Sculptors and Architects*.

she was already in decline and was intoxicated with her own splendour, three men continued on a level with the masters of the golden age. Titian, who died in 1576, reached the age of ninety-nine without losing anything of his power or fervour; he seemed rather to have derived from his length of years a sovereign serenity which perfected the richness of his gifts. His often refractory pupil Tintoretto (1516–94), son of a dyer named Robuski, was a genius at once popular and aristocratic, eager to cover enormous surfaces.[1] His tireless and cunning hand decorated churches and palaces, as well as producing a whole series of retables. Paolo Cagliari of Verona, better known as Veronese (1528–1588), used delicate and splendid colours to depict blazing sun, luminous tresses and golden breast-plates. To him fell the honour of painting, in the Doge's Palace, the most glorious scene in the history of his country; and this picture, 'The Triumph of Venice,' would alone suffice to show posterity the magnificence of the Serenissima.

All three of these masters entered the service of the Tridentine Church, though it would be too much to claim that they did so altogether without mental reservation and regret. There are still pagan and Renaissance elements in their work, where Sacred Love, as in Titian's famous picture, is not seldom opposed by Profane Love. The conciliar canon, one feels, did little to inspire Tintoretto's dazzling 'Susanna,' in which the bather and her bracelets are well calculated to tempt the hungry old men lying in wait for her; and, to choose but one of many beautiful forms, Veronese's 'Judith' is little more than a gorgeous Venetian courtesan. Nevertheless there are whole stretches of their work in which these illustrious masters of the city of the Doges are completely in accordance with current religious trends, celebrating Holy Church in her new-found glory, indicating the return to Scripture which was so characteristic of that age, expressing the gravity of faith and the depth of the Christian drama. Titian's 'Entombment,' Veronese's 'Calvary' and Tintoretto's fifty pictures in the Scuola di San Marco (among them a striking 'Ecce Homo') bear witness to the deepening of the Christian spirit in these men's souls; just as their portraits, e.g. Titian's famous 'Paul III with his Nephews,' and their vast biblical scenes, e.g. Veronese's 'Marriage at Cana,' proclaim the solemn pride then experienced by the Church, the majesty of the popes, and the splendour of reawakened tradition.

Unfortunately the whole artistic achievement resulting from the Council of Trent was destined not to remain at this high level. Like all great creative movements, the Renaissance had hatched its own perils. The most serious of these was mannerism. Talent sought to discover the secrets of genius, and, as always happens in such cases, found only recipes. Systematic consideration of genius and its methods led to some

---

[1] His 'Paradise' is the largest known picture.

curious excesses. The awful God of Michelangelo, having been copied over and over again by Guido Reni and Domenichino, became in due course a commonplace, just as Leonardo's Christ and Raphael's Madonnas became more and more insipid until we reach Guido's Jesus and Dolci's sentimental Virgins. The disciplinary rigour of the Council of Trent, by imposing upon artists imperious moral criteria, subject-matter, and sometimes even models, produced the same sort of result, a pious conformism from which religious art would not always benefit. It cannot be doubted that here we have one of the least happy results of the Tridentine achievement. It contributed in large measure to the success of a 'sacred art' in which neither the great creators of the Renaissance nor the romanesque and gothic sculpturs and masons could any longer have recognized themselves.

But despite mannerism, which was the logical outcome of lessons learned from genius, and despite the sumptuous, vain-glorious and purposely theatrical features of Tridentine art, there was still a chance of improvement. The possession of superior and almost excessive technical means, the love of rich materials, the mystical glow resulting from the experience of the great ecstatics, and a certain mysterious madness which so often seizes decadent arts as if to lead them back to the innocence of their origins—all these factors combined to create a new style which would flower from 1570 onwards and produce some most alluring masterpieces. I refer of course to Baroque, the unexpected but none the less legitimate heir of the austere reformers of Trent.[1]

The visual arts were not the only ones to profit by the solicitude of the Council. Music also was reformed, nor had it, as had painting and sculpture, to await inspiration.[2] At the close of the Middle Ages religious music, like everything else, was in a sorry plight. Gregorian chant, which the Church had made peculiarly her own, was hopelessly decadent. Since the coming of *ars nova*, in the early fourteenth century, its grave homophony had been ousted by a polyphony which, though sometimes attractive, was often full of eccentric ingenuities and laden with secular, not to say vulgar, elements. Liturgical melodies served merely as themes for the rivalry of contrapuntists; and as for the liturgical text, it was very difficult to understand one word. The twenty-third session of the Council determined to abolish these vagaries. It decreed that young clerics must be taught Gregorian chant,

---

[1] Baroque will be studied in the last chapter of this volume, p. 387.

[2] The spirit of the Council of Trent hardly appears in secular literature; theology, mysticism and spiritual writings properly so called seem to have monopolized all the talents. The true literary masterpieces of this period are the works of St Teresa and St John of the Cross. Tasso's *Jerusalem Delivered*, with its brilliant setting, its picturesque episodes and its constant praise of Christian courage, corresponds in a way to the spirit that led to the victory of Lepanto; but its mediocre sentiments and its suspicious episodes leave one with the general impression of a religious veneer rather than a true religion.

and that the accompaniment must be kept clear of anything unseemly or lascivious; the music known as 'measured' or 'figured,' i.e. which was written with notes instead of the strokes used for plainsong, was just tolerated on condition that it did not interfere with the wording of the liturgy. Was this then the death of sacred polyphony? No; for it met with several great masters who thought of their art in terms of the new regulations and caused it to blossom as never before.

The first of these masters was Costanzo Festa (*ob.* 1545), whose *Te Deum* is still in the repertory of the Sistine Choir. Next came Giovanni Animuccia (*ob.* 1571), whose *Magnificat*, hymns and motets, while remaining polyphonic, were in full accord with the new spirit; he also composed for the Oratory of St Philip Neri those first little musical dramas of narrative songs from which Oratorio afterwards developed. But the real leader of this reform was Giovanni Pierluigi Palestrina (1526–94), formerly choir-master at Palestrina. When the bishop of that diocese became Pope Julius III, he brought Giovanni Pierluigi to Rome, and there the young musician's bewitching and abundant genius proved to the most supercilious reformers that consonant harmony, perfection in counterpoint and the ablest use of polyphony could go hand in hand with the most genuinely religious aspirations. Himself a sincere believer and a disciple of St Philip Neri, for whose Oratory he too composed 'oratorios,' he was wellnigh bound to write music of calm faith and ecstatic purity. The works of this angel of song include ninety-three Masses (of which *Papae Marcelli* is the most celebrated), six hundred motets, forty-two psalms and innumerable *ricercari*, not to mention a host of secular pieces, while his *Stabat Mater* is even today upon the lips of every Catholic. His influence still remains decisive, for he accomplished a permanent revolution in the world of music. His pupil and rival, Tomas Luis de Vittoria (1540–1611), was a Spaniard living in Rome. He was of a more mystical turn of mind than Palestrina, and his works reflect the markedly Spanish characteristics of St Teresa; but already during the lifetime of his master he was employing the latter's technique to such an extent that he was nicknamed Palestrina's 'swan'—or 'ape' by some malicious tongues.

At Rome there is one day in every year upon which the spirit of the Tridentine Church seems to make its presence felt. This day is Good Friday, when we have only to attend the ceremonies in order to find ourselves swept right back into that atmosphere of splendour and anguish, of mystical elation and reborn dignity breathed by the Church in those years of the sixteenth century during which the great task was completed. On that holiest of commemorations the Pope himself comes to celebrate the liturgical rites in the Sistine Chapel. The cringing figures of Michelangelo's 'Last Judgment' seem to have been placed there expressly to remind him of life's tragedy. But if he raises his eyes he beholds upon the ceiling, where prophets and sibyls mount pensive guard, the gesture of sovereign love whereby with outstretched hand the Almighty everlastingly gives man his being. That is the place, beneath the silent gaze of that attentive throng, in which to hear the sublime music of Palestrina's *Stabat Mater* and *Improperia* [1] soaring to the vault on voices so pure that they might belong to Cherubim and Archangels. It is then and there, as the august celebrant unveils the Cross, that the significance of the whole historic drama is suddenly revealed. Prostrate in his person before the instrument of suffering and shame, the whole Church feels herself exalted, delivered from the faults, the weakness and the misery of all those human individuals of which she is composed. Prostrate likewise, the Christian soul realizes that she is destined to a future of light and glory, because she has again renewed her loyalty to the message entrusted to her by God and sealed with His Most Precious Blood.

[1] Both the exclusive property of the Sistine Choir, which supplies the music on these occasions.

CHAPTER III

THE RENDING OF CHRISTIAN EUROPE

1. THE AGE OF FANATICISM

ON ONE of the many occasions when St Teresa of Avila was explaining to her nuns the meaning of that prayer which asks the Lord to 'have pity on those who have no pity on themselves,' she cried out: 'My God, the world is in flames.' It was true. During the last third of the sixteenth century the entire world, or at least the whole of Christendom, fell victim to fire and sword. Some kingdoms found themselves engulfed in civil war; in others terror alone had been able to establish an often precarious peace; and there was once more bloody conflict between States. Men were everywhere burned at the stake, hanged, quartered or beheaded, and all without a qualm of conscience. That impassioned century would have considered itself untrue to its vocation if the closing years had made way for mercy. Fanaticism triumphed; cruelty reigned.

Painful as it may be to a follower of the God of Love, one thing is beyond question: responsibility for this manifold tragedy must be attributed to religion. In this respect, of course, religion was faithless to the teaching of its Founder; but it had been established thus in the great majority of consciences by fifteen hundred years of strife, political contamination and ineradicable prejudice. If we are to understand the men of that period we must not judge them by our standards of 'liberalism' and 'tolerance'; we must, in Vacandard's phrase, make for ourselves 'an ancestral soul.' And this is not perhaps so difficult when we think of the depths of horror to which other fanaticisms have led in quite recent times, fanaticisms which, with their domineering social and political interests, jeopardize the whole future of man, the very meaning of life. In the sixteenth century discussion centred not upon the 'death of God,' but upon the manner of interpreting Christian revelation; the debate, however, was no less acrimonious.

The problem of heresy, and of the attitude to be adopted towards heretics, had confronted the Church right from her beginnings; it was already a well-worn topic in St Augustine's day. But it had never received definitive and permanent solution. Throughout the Christian centuries some had advocated gentleness while others favoured coercion. The Church, through her Fathers and theologians, upholds *in principle* the dictum of St Bernard that 'faith is a work of persuasion, not of force; but *in fact* many of her sons, and even of her rulers, have acted just as if belief could be imposed by violence. There is even an appalling decretal of Innocent III which orders the withholding of medical attention from a sick man unless he consents to receive the sacraments, even if it involves the patient's death. Surely it is lawful to take counter-measures against those who not only reject the faith, but by degrading and perverting it lead souls into error. The Bishop of Hippo had already allowed them as a kind of prophylactic. In an age like the sixteenth century, when the terrible crisis of western society endangered the very conception of the world and of man, it was surely natural that believers should uphold the legitimacy of measures which, by demolishing adverse doctrines, would ensure the triumph of their own views. To leave a man free to choose his faith would have seemed a betrayal of those principles which were dearer than life itself; and *neither camp* would tolerate such treason.

I say 'neither camp,' because nothing would be more unjust than to saddle the Catholic Church alone with responsibility for a disaster that involved the Christian world in an orgy of bloodshed. Fanaticism was no one's monopoly. There are many documents to show that Protestants indulged the same cruel intransigence as their opponents, taking their stand upon those very principles by virtue of which their brethren perished at the stake. It was Luther who wrote: 'If we have the power we must not tolerate contrary doctrines in the State; and to avoid greater evils those who do not believe must be forced to attend sermons, to hear the Decalogue explained and to obey at least externally.' These were most moderate requirements; his henchman, the gentle Melanchthon, wished 'the civil authority to employ the sword against abettors of new doctrines.' The two Wittenbergers had in mind such men as Hoffman, Thomas Münzer and other Anabaptists; but these arch-heretics themselves thought no differently upon this point. 'A man deprived of God has no right to live, for he is an obstacle to pious souls,' said Thomas Münzer, in whose own case the precept was to be literally applied.[1] We know what John of Leyden did, once he had established the 'Kingdom of Zion' at Münster.[2] Zwingli, another of Luther's rivals, fully agreed with him in this respect, declaring that 'it is the Lord who has commanded "Slay the wicked one who is in your midst."' From Calvin, naturally, one could compile a rich anthology of fanatical maxims. The whole of his *Defensio Fidei*, written after the death of Servetus, repeats as a sort of *leit-motif* that 'it is lawful to punish heretics, and their execution is perfectly in order.' This theme was obligingly taken up by his successor Theodore Beza: 'To pretend that one must not punish heretics is equivalent to saying that one

---

[1] See *The Protestant Reformation*, Chapter V, p. 313.
[2] *Ibid.*, p. 349–50.

should not punish parricides and matricides.' We might indeed fill page after page with a monotonous series of such excerpts, but Beza himself provides the conclusion of all these maxims: 'What is liberty of conscience? A diabolical dogma.' [1]

It is to the honour of humanity that there were exceptions to this apparent unanimity in fanaticism. There was one man who even attempted with uncommon heroism to stem the current. In 1554 Sebastian Castellion, whom Calvin had driven from Geneva,[2] wrote a treatise to prove that Scripture provides no justification whatever for the execution of heretics. From the religious standpoint, he explained, there are two kinds of heretics: heretics in conduct, whom we ought to amend by instruction and the example of an upright life; and heretics in opinion, whom it is impossible to judge since their crime is committed deep down in the heart, beyond the estimation of man. Here are some words of his which show him to have been far in advance of his time, and suggest that he may have been satisfying a taste for paradox: 'Having often sought to learn what a heretic is, I have discovered only that we consider as heretics all those who do not agree with our opinion.' Elsewhere again he says: 'You do not prove your faith by burning heretics, but by dying for it'—a wonderfully penetrating observation, as true to-day as when first uttered.

Here and there throughout Christian Europe, especially in humanist circles, there were men who thought just what Castellion had so aptly expressed in words, and some of them had the courage to say so. Such were the 'Meaux Group,' 'those men infatuated with hope, who knew not how to hate.' Such was the great Sir Thomas More, who would one day give his life for the true faith, but who wrote in *Utopia*: 'Every man has the right to confess the religion of his choice, and to try to convert his neighbour by force of reasoning as well as by his friendly behaviour. But he must refrain from any show of aggressiveness towards the opinions of other people and from supporting his arguments by recourse to violence.' Such also were Erasmus, Rabelais and many others in every country and of every obedience, whether Protestant or Catholic, who together formed the embryo of a 'third party.' Its success would be long delayed, but its sporadic existence during the whole period of the drama was consoling, more especially as these moderates were also good Christians (Catholic or Protestant as the case might be). Their tolerance must not be confused with the scepticism of, say, Jean Bodin, forerunner of Bayle and Voltaire, who

---

[1] Fanaticism was not peculiar to the West. In Russia the theologian Joseph of Volokolamsk, opposing the theories of Nil Sorsky, exclaims: 'To kill a heretic with one's own hand and to kill him through prayer by converting him are one and the same thing. Besides, death is redemptive of heretics themselves: it diminishes their responsibility before God.'

[2] See *The Protestant Reformation*, Chapter VI, p. 4 7.

advocated a natural religion having in his eyes all the appearance of Positivism. So serene an attitude, however, was out of harmony with an age that was passing through a grave crisis of conscience and regarded unbelief as even more unthinkable than reprehensible. Those who appealed to it were denounced, censured and vilified in both camps,[1] and their influence was for a very long time almost negligible. Men could not turn to them until at length Christendom, exhausted and weary of carnage, realized that the probable end of internecine warfare was mutual destruction. The Edict of Nantes would have to await the passing of another thirty years.

We know that the bloody storm, 'the hideous carnage' which Etasmus prophesied, had begun to rage long before the 1560's; why then, one may ask, did it now assume a fresh degree of violence? For two reasons, one of which was due to the religious situation itself. At the time of Calvin's death and the closing of the Council of Trent, a certain inflexibility becomes apparent on both sides. Neither the rigid system of Geneva nor that of Trent allowed room for mediation or temporization. The combatants were both encased in steel. The second reason was largely political. Powerful interests of an altogether temporal nature were everywhere at work: the German princes took their stand henceforward on the famous principle *Cujus regio, hujus religio*; the French monarchs were disquieted by the sight of their kingdom threatened with cleavage; the French nobility were determined to control the State; and the Dutch bourgeoisie were exasperated with Spanish officialdom. Religious liberty, 'that strange and ridiculous thing,' as one contemporary German chronicler described it, was all the more inacceptable because it led to a kind of permanent conspiracy against the security of States, a conspiracy in which revolutionaries at home were supported by foreign powers. Elevated thus to the height of a major conflict, in which factions, governments and whole peoples were opposed, the religious problem sought solution in bloodshed, the horror of which was aggravated by the almost unlimited means at its disposal.

2. CATHOLICISM AND POLITICS: SPAIN UNDER PHILIP II

Philip II (1556–98) occupied the throne of Spain during the second half of a century that witnessed his country's highest achievements. He is a man of mystery, haloed in glory yet bearing the unmistakable impress of defeat. The fact that he represented a complete fusion of the religious and the political order, in which the latter received from the former not only its principles, but also its means of action, makes it

[1] Calvin treated Castellion as 'a poisonous beast.'

hard to speak dispassionately of a man who, even in his own lifetime, was the object of contradictory but always violent judgments. He was called by some 'the Demon of the South,' by others 'the Wise King'; but neither term is exactly true, let alone both combined. That slender figure with its lanky limbs, uneasy countenance and hesitant imitation of a smile, as Titian painted him at the age of twenty-five, carried upon his shoulders the weight of a vast empire for forty years and without a moment's weakness. What was his aim? To what did he aspire? Why did he thrice commit himself to enterprises whose possible rewards were never equal to the risks involved? Was it through pride, through fanaticism, through lack of intelligence? Who can tell? No one has ever penetrated the secret of those sea-green, inexpressive eyes, of those immobile features, of that pale face which masked a Fleming become Spaniard to the very marrow of his bones. It may be that his terrible self-discipline represented a half-conscious determination to resist the forces of mental disintegration bequeathed to him by his unfortunate grandmother Juana.

His personality is reflected in the Escorial, that prodigious monument which he built in the rocky chaos of the Sierra Guadarrama,[1] three thousand feet above sea level, amid the slag of abandoned iron-works. It was a fortress, palace, convent, ministry and mausoleum all in one; planned in the form of an instrument of torture, erected to commemorate a military victory, and placed under the protection of a martyr.[2] There, in complete solitude, he strove day after day to handle the threads of that enormous skein whereby his power encircled the globe. In his austere ante-rooms, with their whitewashed walls and high, uncomfortable wooden seats, crowds awaited audience: ambassadors, prelates, conquistadors on leave and famous generals. The yellow gleam of candles lit up long, stern faces reminiscent of Greco's portraits, the white habits of Inquisitors, starched ruffs and black velvet doublets. No one spoke, unless in a whisper. On the other side of the royal door, which was padded with armorial upholstery, the puny little man sat working twelve hours a day, attending in person to the smallest details, examining every file, filling reams of paper with his fine handwriting, never stopping except at the canonical hours, when he took his breviary and prayed. The instrument that served his principles (or his dreams) was quite stupendous. On the abdication of Charles V, Philip inherited only one-half of his father's dominions; but that half sufficed to make him the most powerful sovereign of his time, ruling Spain, the Milanese, the Kingdom of Naples, Sicily,

[1] About twenty-four miles from Madrid, an artificial capital which he created for no other reason than his dislike of the ancient cities of glory and revolution.

[2] Philip II built the Escorial in memory of the victory of Saint-Quentin on the feast of St Lawrence (10th August 1557). Its shape is that of a grid, upon which the saint suffered martyrdom.

Sardinia, the Burgundian realm of Franche-Comté, Artois and the Low Countries, together with those immense and still almost unknown territories which Pizarro and other brilliant adventurers had added to his crown. A fine empire, to be sure, for a prince of twenty-five! Although he had mortgaged part of his revenues against sums advanced by the German banks, he was also by far the richest of kings—thanks to the galleons from America. His military strength was likewise unsurpassed: no fewer than 150,000 men (a huge force at that date) were in his service, commanded by such illustrious leaders as the Duke of Alba, Don Juan of Austria and Alessandro Farnese; while 'their lordships' of the *infanteria*, recruited from among the nobility, already claimed to be 'invincible.' Had he an idea of the lethal germs hidden in the womb of his glorious empire? Did he realize that the tide of gold and silver [1] flooding Spain was disorganizing the economy, accustoming men to idleness, and thus breeding a nation of hidalgos, priests and beggars; that the Spanish countryside was becoming depopulated; that his commerce was gradually passing into foreign hands; that Flanders fretted beneath the yoke of occupation; and that England, which was then discovering the Ocean, might set up as a rival to his vast Atlantic ambitions? Undoubtedly not. One needs to be more than a scrupulous administrator to fathom the drift of historical events.

The reign of Philip II was indeed the 'golden age' of Spain, which not only benefited from a long and as yet intact accumulation of power, riches and strength, but revealed a wealth of creative force in every sphere. Castilian was beginning to dominate the whole kingdom and far beyond, the tongue whose 'splendours, majesty and wonderful stateliness' Francisco de Medina declared 'worthy to be carried to the most distant provinces in the folds of victorious banners.' Miguel de Cervantes (1547–1616), who had lost an arm at Lepanto and lived in direst poverty, was preparing his masterpiece, *Don Quixote*, in which he combined the lessons of the Middle Ages with the essence of the Renaissance to exalt, even to the point of absurdity, his people's love of glory and independence. Lope de Vega and Guilhen de Castro were rebuilding the foundations of drama; while their contemporary Vittoria, a musician of consummate skill and strong emotion, came forward as the rival of Palestrina and competed with him even in Rome.[2] It was also at this time that the pictorial genius of Spain became conscious of itself and blossomed everywhere, at Valencia no less than in Catalunya and Castile. Pedro Berruguete adapted the style of Michelangelo to the old polychrome sculpture, and many foreigners sought work on the royal building sites. Meanwhile Toledo was the home of Dominikos

---

[1] The silver mines of Potosi were discovered in 1543, and the process of treating raw silver with mercury was first used in 1554; hence the enormous influx of this metal.

[2] See p. 147.

Theotokopoulos, 'El Greco' (1547–1614), heir of Byzantium and
Venice, whose incomparable eye penetrated as none before or since the
mystical and impassioned soul of Spain, and whose supreme technique
has embodied it for ever in those intense yet secret portraits.

Above all, the reign of Philip II was the age of St Teresa and St John
of the Cross; and if the monarch had had to choose from all the manifold splendour of his kingdom, he would without doubt have chosen
the last—the splendour of the saints. At that astonishing scene of
abdication in the great hall of the palace at Brussels, Charles V had
passed on his burden with these final words: 'My son, preserve the
Catholic faith in all its purity.' And Philip had replied: 'Father, I will
do so.' Throughout his reign he endeavoured, sometimes with excessive zeal, to fulfil this undertaking. How could he have betrayed his
oath? The faith was part and parcel of himself; it impregnated his whole
existence. Every day he spent hours in prayer, and confessed frequently; he declared that he could not live without the Blessed Sacrament close to his room; and his reading, apart from official papers, was
confined almost exclusively to the mystics, especially John of Ávila and
Teresa. Just before he died in atrocious agony, he spoke these words of
sublime conviction: 'My sins cause me more pain than do my sores.'
One might indeed ask what exactly was the nature of that sombre,
anxious and (to use an anachronism) somewhat Jansenistic faith, which
seems to have lacked mercy, the flower of spiritual refinement. But
there can be no doubt whatever that his faith governed his life, bidding
him serve God and defend His Church. Was it impossible for the
interests of God and of the Church to be identical with those of the
Spanish crown? That is the crucial question.

'I would give a hundred lives and my kingdom rather than have
heretics as subjects.' These words of Philip II were spoken in all
sincerity; but in carrying out this resolve with implacable severity he
appears at the same time to have followed the pattern of centralization
and unification initiated by his ancestors Ferdinand and Isabella. In his
hands the Inquisition was more than ever before an instrument of
religious, political, administrative and even financial domination. A
Venetian ambassador wrote: 'It is fair to say that the real master of the
Holy Office is the king. He personally appoints the Inquisitors. He
uses this tribunal to control his subjects, and to chastise them with his
characteristic secrecy and severity. The Inquisition and the Royal
Council are always in step and constantly assist one another.' Here
indeed the confusion of religion and politics attained its zenith; every
enemy of the king was looked upon as an enemy of the faith; and was
treated as such. The outrageous methods often employed by the
inquisitorial courts—calumny, uncorroborated accusations, false testimony, torture—were placed at the service of the State, so that the

entire kingdom groaned beneath the weight of dictatorial terror. No one would have dared defy the all-powerful Office. It is here in Spain, during the reign of Philip II, that we must gaze upon the traditional image of the Church, which has ever since been exploited to her disadvantage: the doleful procession of condemned, clad in the *sanbenito* and accompanied by troops of priests, soldiers and monks; the *auto-da fé*, where they receive sentence; the crowds abjectly eager to come and witness the spectacle; and lastly a column of smoke curling skyward, spreading far and wide the reek of charred human flesh. . . . Now which is it that bears responsibility in the royal conscience for this horror, faith or temporal policy? The two together, inseparably.

Two classes of subjects were the victims of these terrible methods of government, both considered as enemies of the faith and therefore as rebels. First we have the Moriscos, former Moslems who had been forcibly converted, 'Christians in theory, Moors in fact,' most of them hard-working peasants and absolutely peaceful. It was the Inquisitors Pedro Guerrero and Diego de Espiñoza who 'charged the royal conscience' with the duty of obliging these people to renounce their secret beliefs. Villages were raided, adults imprisoned, children kidnapped; the persecution went forward with implacable brutality. Revolt flared up, led by a descendant of the Ommayads, and the whole country from Almeria to Malaga, together with a wide area around Granada, was put to fire and sword. Merciless retaliation followed under the leadership of Don Juan and his Neapolitan troops. After four years of savage fighting thousands of Moriscos fled to Africa, abandoning their lands which Spanish agriculture never managed completely to recover until quite recent times. Such was the first stage on the road to unity of faith.

Another stage was cleared simultaneously and still more rapidly. The number of Protestants in Spain was insignificant, a few hundred perhaps; but the very existence of such heretics would not allow the king a wink of sleep. He was scarcely seated upon the throne when he organized the struggle against these vile hotbeds of iniquity, and also incidentally against the remnants of Illuminism and Erasmianism. The Grand Inquisitor, Fernando Valdès, very skilfully dispatched his agents to spy in suspect quarters, after which a number of arrests were made. Seville and Valladolid, the main heretical centres, suffered severely. Five great *autos-da-fé* during the years 1559 and 1560 practically annihilated such elements of Lutheranism, Erasmianism and Calvinism as the peninsula had harboured. On the day of his arrival in Spain, Philip II had been required by the Grand Inquisitor to uphold the faith and to entrust the Holy Office with that task. He had sworn upon the naked sword to do so, and no oath was ever more strictly observed. At one *auto-da-fé* an Italian captain on his way to the stake called out to the king: 'How can you, a gentleman, allow another gentleman to perish at the hands of these monks?' Raising his voice for once, Philip replied: 'If my son were as perverse as you I would myself bring wood for the stake that was to burn him.'

It might be possible to destroy by fire the small Protestant groups in Spain; but the same means were not so easily employed in those possessions of the Crown where heresy was already entrenched. It was while attempting to apply them in the Low Countries that Philip II suffered one of the major setbacks of his reign: the revolt of the 'Beggars,' the exhausting struggle against the insurgents, and the final secession of the United Provinces. Catholic dictatorship and the methods of force could make no headway against the Dutch Calvinists and their determination to be free.

It is not only in home affairs that we can detect Philip II's constant identification of his personal interests with those of the religion he claimed to defend. His foreign policy affords no less striking examples. The evidence suggests that religious conviction was not invariably the primary source of his imperialism; all the same, it was so closely bound up with his temporal planning that it is almost impossible to discern where ambition and pride began, and where the designs of faith ceased to operate. Considered as a whole, his reign appears to have been a multiple endeavour to protect the interests of Catholicism and the authority of the Church in every field of European politics; nor indeed have historians hesitated to represent it as such. But this familiar portrait of Philip as champion of the faith requires a good deal of retouching.

After his victory over the French at Saint-Quentin, he found another adversary in Pope Paul IV,[1] who was thoroughly alarmed by the rapid spread of Spanish power in Italy; and the 'Catholic king' promptly hurled Alba's mercenaries against the holy capital of the Church. What was the policy he recommended in England as husband of Mary Tudor? High-handed restoration of the faith, the same policy of repression as he applied in his own country? By no means. He favoured temporization, perhaps in order to keep England in a state of weakness that would be profitable to his own interests. During the negotiations at Cateau-Cambrésis, when there was question of a Franco-Spanish offensive against the Protestants of Germany or Geneva, Philip II showed much less enthusiasm than Henri II. He did not finally set himself up as the champion of intransigence until he realized that by doing so he would become leader of the Catholic world. Thus it was largely his vigorous efforts that ensured the successful issue of the Council under Pius IV; but at Trent his enormous delegation, consisting of more than two hundred prelates and ambassadors, so often

---

[1] See Chapter II, section 5.

gave an impression of serving the interests of Spain, rather than those of the Church, that they were several times openly rebuked.

From this Catholic imperialism Philip II did not always obtain the happiest results. On one occasion indeed the whole world beheld him lead the arms of Christendom to victory. This was at the battle of Lepanto (1571), where his fleet, blessed by Pope Pius V, escorted by the prayers of all Catholics, and commanded by his own illegitimate half-brother Don Juan of Austria, sank three hundred of Sultan Selim III's vessels, thus showing Islam that any attempt to invade the western Mediterranean was doomed to failure.

The *Te Deum*, however, which the ascetic and imperturbable monarch icily intoned when he received the glorious news, was to be the last of his career as champion of the faith. For this magnificent picture is offset by another of a very different kind, in which we see Philip's ambition disappointed and the failure of his schemes for the restoration of Catholicism. A second enterprise upon the waters ended in disaster. It is doubtful whether his declaration of war against Elizabeth of England was dictated solely by the Catholic cause. There were many political and economic factors, both in the Low Countries and on the high seas, to account for mutual hostility; the bleeding head of Mary Stuart was a mere pretext. The huge Spanish expedition included 130 ships carrying 2,700 cannon, 10,000 sailors and 19,000 troops, while an army of 30,000 men was concentrated in Flanders; and it seemed certain that this mighty host would repeat against heretical England the victorious operation conducted seventeen years earlier against the Turk. But Providence decided otherwise, and we know what became of the 'Invincible Armada' (1588), buffeted by storm, pursued by the English fireships, scattered along the coasts of Scotland and driven on the rocks. Sixty-five ships lost and 20,000 dead: such was the debit of that enormous crusade in which too many altogether temporal interests were at play.

In France the 'Catholic' policy of Philip II had no more success, though it suffered no comparable disaster. We may doubt whether it was in the single and unselfish hope of rendering France true to her ancient loyalties that he set out to profit by the bloody crisis in which the kingdom of the Valois was then struggling, that he sided with the rigorists so as to exert influence by their means in the royal counsels, that he perhaps even incited the Massacre of St Bartholomew, and that he assisted the League with money and with men. Coligny spoke the truth when he taunted his adversaries with 'having in their bellies the red cross of Spain.' The interlocking of political and religious interests was never so apparent as in these complex and tragic affairs, and the underlying motive of the ambitious Spaniard was certainly to have his own daughter Isabella ruling in the Louvre. The result was disappointing. It is beyond question that the appearance of Spanish troops in the streets of Paris helped not a little to provoke the national upheaval which enabled Henri IV to establish himself firmly on the throne of France. Even French Catholics could not welcome the indiscreet hand of a foreigner meddling, upon pretext of faith, in the affairs of their country.[1]

In the end how futile Philip's 'Catholic policy' appears. He left his kingdom weaker than when he received it, exhausted by so many colossal undertakings, ruined by bankruptcy, unable to prevent English corsairs from insulting Cadiz, and already on the downward path that would reach its lowest point in the seventeenth century. As regards the Catholic cause, Spanish arms had led it to victory neither in the Low Countries nor in England nor in France; it won the day in Spain only by means of the *auto-da-fé* and blood-stained repression. Must it then stand condemned? In the secret places of the human heart the most upright intentions can mingle, almost unconsciously, with so many selfish motives; and it is very probable that that ascetic prince, whose strongest wish was unquestionably to be a saint, remained sincerely convinced that in following his own interests he was defending also those of his faith, those of the Church and those of humanity. Such is the conviction (or the pretext) of all despots. In this case it may in fact have been true; for as Joseph de Maistre observed long ago, 'of all European countries, that which shed least blood was the kingdom of Philip II, the Spain of Catholic authoritarianism.' The Inquisition in the Hispanic peninsula certainly claimed far fewer victims than the wars of religion in France and Germany or than the tribunals of Henry VIII, Edward VI, Mary Tudor and Elizabeth in England. It was perhaps part of the cruel genius of that age to make evil means serve the very best of causes.

3. THIRTY-SIX YEARS OF HORROR IN FRANCE

On 1st March 1562 the bloody affray of Vassy [2] set in motion that drama which every intelligent Frenchman had known to be inevitable ever since matters of religion had tended to become political affairs and the two Churches had organized themselves into opposing factions. The method of temporization tried by the diplomatic Catherine dei Medici, acting as regent for young Charles IX (1560–74), had failed completely. The Conference of Poissy had proved fruitless. Twenty-eight Protestants had been killed in a barn in Champagne, and a

[1] No religious pretext was invoked to justify the most fruitful imperialist measure of Philip II's reign. The annexation of Portugal took place in 1580 after her heroic King Sebastian, Philip's nephew through his mother, had been killed during a glorious but foolhardy crusade in Morocco. Portugal remained Spanish until 1641.

[2] See *The Protestant Reformation*, Chapter VII, p. 514.

hundred wounded had only just escaped death. In various parts of France there were spontaneous and savage outbreaks of violence: at Tours two hundred Calvinists were drowned; at Sens their temple was destroyed, and in the ensuing riot both Huguenots and Catholics went 'to revictual the fishes of the Yonne.' The tragedy was beginning, and was destined to last for thirty-six years.

Two parties were at loggerheads. The nobles were adhering to the Reformation in ever-increasing numbers, some through conviction, others for the more or less conscious purpose of recovering for their caste that authority which the monarchy had been steadily under-mining during the past hundred years. The Bourbons and Chatillons could not leave the profit of this undertaking to the Guises; in going over to the heretical camp they took with them, willy-nilly, whole villages of their tenants, and thus obtained troops. The Catholics, however, seeing power in the hands of an unreliable Italian woman and a frail little king, turned to the strong men who seemed capable of defending their faith with more courage. In fact Michel de Castelnau's *Mémoires* show clearly that from about 1560 bishops, priests and preachers looked upon the royal authority as no longer sufficient to guarantee the rights and fortunes of Catholicism. All the makings of a civil war were combined, including the vague feeling of anger which was noticeable throughout a kingdom which was severely shaken by economic difficulties resulting in rising prices, and in which the ter-mination of hostilities with Austria by the Treaty of Cateau-Cambrésis had thrown officers and men out of work. If one side were to begin the conflict the whole kingdom would quickly be alight. It was the Protestants, fearful for their safety, who took this responsibility.[1] Among them were honest Coligny and ambitious Condé, who were followed before long by a whole section of the aristocracy. Most of their pastors, even those who, like François Morel and Antoine de la Roche-Chandieu, belonged to the aristocracy, tried to prevent armed insurrection, but were overruled by their troops. Christ of the Gospels gave place to Ronsard's 'Christ under arms.'

What a strange spectacle of paradox is France in the second half of the sixteenth century, running with blood yet glittering with art, with gold and beauty. For we cannot forget, while narrating the various episodes of this tragedy, that they are exactly contemporary with the fertile period during which, as we learn from historians of art and

---

[1] Not without anxiety and hesitation. Agrippa d'Aubigné's *Histoire universelle* describes the pathetic scene when Admiral Coligny's wife urged him to take arms in defence of his co-religionists. She persuaded him only by declaring that on Judgment Day she would bear witness against him unless he did his duty. Lucien Remier in particular has asked whether that was not a grave mistake, whether the Protestants would not have done better to temporize all they could while continuing their propaganda, so as not to give the superior Catholic forces an opportunity to crush them.

literature, the High Renaissance reached its full development in France. Just when the hideous conflict was beginning there rose from the ground those delightful buildings whose architecture combines in single harmony the French tradition with the tradition of antiquity from beyond the Alps. Everywhere illustrious painters were at work, covering great stretches of canvas or expressing every slightest detail in the most wonderful portraits. Musicians also were busy revising the fundamentals of their art. Nor perhaps has France ever witnessed such an outpouring of prose, and especially of verse, as at this time when her language, 'protected and ennobled' by the hand of inspiration, became fully conscious of its excellence. This literary activity plays a part in the politico-religious drama, sometimes merely by way of narrative, as, for example, the *Commentaires* of Montluc and Castelnau's *Mémoires*. Sometimes, however, it enters directly into the struggle, so that we have a Protestant literature, which, from Agrippa d'Aubigné to the anonymous authors of popular laments, occupies a place in the struggles of the Reformation. But alongside this 'literature on active service' there developed another and far richer type, whose outlook was more agreeable, hedonistic, and even pagan. The same is true of art, where the most important work seems designed both to make room for and to celebrate the joy of living, even in that unhappy age. The sculpture of Ligier Richier (1500–67) [1] may be held to reflect the atmosphere of his time, but it may equally be considered as re-echoing the anguish of the fifteenth century.

The Wars of Religion did not prevent the erection of such masterpieces as the châteaux at Chambord, Amboise, Azay-le-Rideau, Écouen, Dampierre, Valençay and many others, all of which were visited in turn by the kings and their courts. Pierre Lescot (1510–71) built the Louvre; Philibert Delorme rivalled him with the Château d'Anet; the brilliant and mysterious chisel of Jean Goujon (1515–63) intuitively rediscovered the beauty of ancient works of art; and Germain Pilon (1535–90) moved during an eventful life from firm and serene realism to the tomb of Chancellor Birague with the joyous grace of its nymphs whom he called virtues. Bernard Palissy (1510–90), with face scorched at the mouth of his furnace, but with soul on fire despite his many sufferings, gave a new dignity to ceramics; while Léonard Limosin (1505–77) opened up fresh fields to the art of enamelling. Primaticcio (1504–70) completed those enormous sculptural decorations which made Fontainebleau the centre of a school, and Benvenuto Cellini laboured with incomparable skill. It is hard to say whether Jean Clouet or his son François penetrated more deeply, with unerring assurance, into the thoughts and feelings of those whose features they have immortalized. This was also the period when Palestrina's master

[1] Particularly the tomb of René de Chalons at Bar-le-Duc, where a magnificent skeleton brandishes its heart.

Goudimel (1510–72), Roland de Lassus with his delightful motets, and Antoine de Baif (1532–89) were preparing new perspectives for music. What shall we say of literature? Ronsard (1524–85), Remi Belleau and Noël du Fail survived Joachim du Bellay (1522–60) to witness the Massacre of St Bartholomew. The *Discours des misères de ce temps* shows that not all were indifferent to the anguish of their country. It is amid the noise of gunfire that we hear a gentle voice sing ' *Mignonne, allons voir si la rose . . .*' to the music of Jehan Chardavoine. This was the tune whistled by Henri de Guise as he strode across the courtyard of the château at Blois to meet his assassins. The great wisdom of La Boétie (1530–63) and of Montaigne (1533–92) was in large measure a reaction against the blood-stained follies of their time.

In order to appreciate the vitality of sixteenth-century France we need only point to the extraordinary fact that she was quickly revived by a few years of prudence and good order once the crisis had passed. It was because she felt young and vigorous that she lashed herself with such fury and seemed to place so small a value upon life. None of the generals who led her opposing armies was more than twenty-five years old, an age at which men loved fighting for its own sake, but were no less fond of magnificent velvet doublets, impeccable ruffs, elegant embossed breastplates and plumed caps. They danced and killed and died. Ladies of quality wore the *vertugarde*, but that was a poor defence of somewhat easy virtue. The pitiless conflict had its festive side: opera, for example, reached France, with the *Ballet Comique de la Reine*, only a few weeks before the assassination of Henri III.

It is against this variegated background of France with all her brilliance, pleasure-seeking yet productive of so much beauty, that we must visualize the monstrous stains of massacre committed in the name of Faith. Never in all her history, except perhaps during the Revolutionary terror, has that nation, which claims to be so wise and moderate, provided such an example of unrestrained violence and inhuman ferocity. We find assassination, murder of the wounded, massacre of whole populations after the capture of a city, and the same contempt of human life, aggravated of course by a common fanaticism but no more frenzied on one side than the other. 'It would be impossible to recount the barbarous cruelties perpetrated by each of the opposing factions,' says the jurist Pasquier,[1] an impartial witness and tolerant Catholic. 'Where the Huguenot is master he destroys all the images, demolishes the sepulchres and funeral monuments, carries off all sacred property. The Catholic, in retaliation, kills, murders, drowns all those whom he knows to belong to this sect, and gluts the rivers with their bodies.' The *Commentaires* of Montluc, Marshal of France and illustrious veteran of the Italian wars, coldly recite the numerous executions of

[1] *Recherches de la France* (1560).

Calvinists for which he was responsible in Guienne. 'It was possible thus to tell where I had passed, for the remains of those whom I had hanged were to be seen suspended from the wayside trees.' And he adds this practical observation: 'One man hanged was more frightening than a hundred in action.' Having learned that the inhabitants of Terraube, near Lectoure in Gers, were sheltering heretics, he sent a company with orders to 'dispatch everyone they found there.' His orders were faithfully carried out; and when all were dead their corpses were thrown into the city well, 'which was very deep, but was so full that one could touch them with the hand.' Here are the gallant butcher's concluding words: 'It was a very good riddance of very wicked fellows.' In the south-east, however, a Calvinist leader, Baron des Adrets, committed such horrors that Coligny described him as a 'mad beast.' Having taken Montbrison, he forced the defenders to throw themselves from the walls on to the raised pikes of his soldiers. Castelnau informs us that at Mornas, near Orange, 'when some of those who were flung from the windows tried clinging to the bars, the baron most inhumanly had their fingers cut off.' But after he had quarrelled with the Calvinists and became reconciled with the court, his earlier conduct did not prevent him receiving the Collar of St Michael and from calmly declaring that he had never acted except by way of reprisal or intimidation.

The population of France, however, did not consist entirely of unbridled brutes [1] devoid of all but pitiless ambition. The very Catholics who formed the armies of these bloodthirsty captains used to crowd the churches and remain to pray long after Mass, for fervour was never more keen. Their Protestant adversaries, too, would sing in all purity of heart their affecting psalms of love and mercy. But antagonism had become so strong as to expel every humane feeling. We learn from La Noüe that before joining battle on the plain of Dreux, in the first great fratricidal combat, 'everyone present stood firm, revolving in his mind that the men whom he saw coming against him were neither Spaniards, nor Englishmen, nor Italians, but Frenchmen, nay even the bravest of Frenchmen, among whom were some of his own companions, friends and relations, and that within an hour they would have to kill one another—a thought which inspired them with some degree of horror, but without diminishing their courage.' These last five words perhaps supply the key to those souls; they were not without feeling, but believed they must be ruthless in the name of Christ.

[1] Montaigne relates that Montluc himself, 'having lost his son, a gallant nobleman and one of great promise, who died in the island of Madeira, mentioned particularly among other regrets, how bitterly grieved he felt at never having written to him, and at having, as a result of paternal coldness and reserve, lost the advantage of knowing and appreciating his son, and also of assuring him of the great good will he bore him and the high opinion he entertained of his virtue.' So this ferocious man had a heart accessible to feeling.

Such was the climate of what the seventeenth century called 'the Wars of Religion' in order to discredit the faith which had caused such crime and misery. Contemporaries spoke simply of 'the troubles.' On the religious plane they were among the worst manifestations of the great upheaval into which the Protestant revolt had precipitated the Church of Christ. On the political plane they were one of the major episodes in the development of monarchical dictatorship. It is usual to reckon eight of these wars between 1562 and 1593; but in reality there was a single conflict lasting for nearly thirty years, though interrupted by periods of truce. The whole of France was involved; there was fighting almost everywhere. The principal encounters took place in Normandy, where English reinforcements might be landed; but the two sides clashed also in the region of the middle Loire, in those radiant provinces where the Valois trailed their courts from one château to another, where Condé dreamed of carving for himself a State within the State to serve as a base for his offensives, with Orleans as capital— Orleans, beneath whose walls François de Guise was shot down by Poltrot de Méré. Nor was the south-west spared. Here the Protestants were able to conduct some dangerous operations, being securely established from Saintonge to Languedoc and Béarn, and also in the remote districts of the Rhône and the Alps, which were less accessible to central authority than were the plains. Nevertheless, however appalling may be the spectacle of a whole kingdom drenched in blood, we must not, when speaking of the 'Wars of Religion,' imagine large-scale operations employing huge armies like those of today. There were few great battles. At Dreux, on 19th November 1562, neither side had more than 12,000 men; at Jarnac, Condé charged with 300 cavalry to rescue Coligny; at Montcour, on 15th October 1569, the Catholics numbered 24,000 against some 20,000 Protestants. As the years went by it became increasingly difficult to pay mercenaries, operations were reduced to a succession of local episodes, and the forces engaged dwindled accordingly. This war, with its classic eightfold division, cannot be understood in terms of highly organized strategical manœuvres. One would need rather to follow its course province by province, city by city, and even village by village; to imagine a fanatical clique at work in such-and-such a town, or the passage of an armed band bent on murder, loot and rape; to think of a more or less general reign of terror causing intermittent but none the less atrocious suffering. Perhaps the nearest modern parallel is to be found in the Spanish Civil War of 1936–9.

A final complication, just as in the last named conflict, took the form of foreign intervention, the machinery of which is perfectly described by Michel de l'Hôpital in an address to the States-General: 'We see that an Englishman and a Frenchman whose religion is the same have more affection and friendship for one another than two [French] citizens who belong to the same city and are subject to the same over-lord, but who adhere to different religions.' Both sides then sought victory in reliance upon foreign powers. The Catholics relied upon Spain, with whom they maintained such close relations that the Spanish ambassador in his secret correspondence referred to Cardinal de Lorraine [1] simply as 'el amigo.' The Protestants looked to Protestant England. An atmosphere seeming to our eyes very much like treason hung over all these military operations, in which Frenchmen sacrificed the interests of France to their fanaticism. The Reformers actually delivered Le Havre to the English, while the Catholics went so far as to admit Spanish troops into Paris; and very few were shocked by such proceedings. Thus throughout those thirty blood-stained years inter-national politics were bound up with home affairs. With a view to securing power for his daughter Isabella, Philip II endeavoured to obtain control of France, playing a subtle game by assisting the Protestants and humouring the Valois. All this foreign intervention balanced the contending forces, and thereby did much to prolong the fratricidal strife in which neither adversary was strong enough to administer a decisive blow, but in which the fury of both sides ended by turning a beautiful kingdom into what Pasquier called the 'Corpse of France.'

4. CATHERINE AND COLIGNY: ST BARTHOLOMEW

The Wars of Religion, like a tragedy on the stage, consist of three main acts, during each of which some outstanding personality played the leading part. The drama was eventually terminated by Henri IV, when France, exhausted and sick of so much bloodshed, became once more accessible to reason. The central and culminating act was domi-nated by Henri III, a vacillating prince, torn this way and that, inspired by sombre passion and ungoverned instinct. The principal character of the first act was Catherine dei Medici, whose portraits declare the enigma of her personality. Balzac describes the 'secretive, unhealthy face nestling in its white ruff, with forehead bulging beneath the tip of a gloomy veil, and large round eyes, dark and prominent—the mask of an abbess, withdrawn and emaciated, wary and inquisitive.' Although she was alert and energetic, fond of riding, feasts and buffoonery, there was another side of her nature in harmony with the widow's weeds she never laid aside: like her fellow countryman Machiavelli, she was obsessed with a sombre passion for intrigue and lacked the slightest trace of moral principles. Nor was this true only in the realm of politics. We know for what purposes she employed the charming bevy of

[1] Nephew of the man who founded the seminary at Rheims, of which place, however, he was archbishop, as his uncle had been.

her maids of honour; these poor little pawns on the queen's chess-board were trained to servile obedience by every possible means, including the roughest chastisement, which Her Majesty administered in person. From the religious standpoint she practised a kind of indifference, superior alike to dogma and to jurisdiction. Thus she wrote a most curious letter to Pope Pius IV, suggesting that he reduce religion to a few elementary precepts (those of the Decalogue), which would enable all men to consider themselves Christians adhering to a single faith. In dealing with opposite factions such a woman would certainly never indulge a spirit of religious fanaticism; her sole ambition would be to command and to defend by every means at her disposal the throne entrusted to her care. She would pursue that policy not only with her accustomed cynicism, but also with natural dignity, practical intelligence and undeniable ability.

The intention of Catherine dei Medici was certainly to maintain the royal prestige above internal disorders, and she managed to do so for about ten years. When death rid her, almost at a single stroke, of Antoine de Bourbon, François de Guise and Maréchal de Saint-André, she imposed the first 'religious peace,' the Edict of Amboise (March 1563), which gave France four years of peace; and she took advantage of this lull to mount an expedition which recovered Le Havre from the English. Then, during the years 1564 and 1565, by way of diverting the French in accordance with the advice of François I, she staged a slow and magnificent journey through the provinces in order to show her people young Charles IX, who, having attained his thirteenth year, had just been declared of age.

This truce, however, was most precarious. Condé and Coligny suspected the good faith of the Queen-Mother; they feared that Pope Pius V was urging her to adopt repressive measures, and that Philip II had made her certain promises with the same end in view. Though defeated at Dreux, the Protestants by no means considered themselves crushed. As for Catherine, she seemed to dread a decisive Catholic victory, which would have delivered her into the hands of the Catholic reformers. At all events she granted the heretics freedom of worship in the suburbs of such towns as were subject to the jurisdiction of a bailiff or were the residences of those having a right to administer justice within the limits of their estates; and this privilege was later extended to all places (Paris alone excepted) where Protestants delivered sermons in public. Montluc, aware of her purpose, exclaimed in fury: 'We win by force of arms, but the Protestants win with their damned writings!'

Hostilities were resumed in 1567 and 1568; Montmorency was killed in battle at Saint-Denis while trying to deliver Paris from blockade by Condé. The Calvinists were beaten at Jarnac and Montcour, but

Coligny stood firm and regained the advantage. This alternation of success was so favourable to the queen's interests that she could not but encourage it. Officially she was angered beyond measure by an insolent attempt of the Huguenots to kidnap the king at Monceaux; but she was at the same time negotiating a marriage between her daughter Marguerite de Valois and young King Henri of Navarre, who had become leader of the Calvinist party at the age of fifteen.

At this period also the star of Gaspard de Coligny (1517–72) was in the ascendant. 'He was looked upon,' says Brantôme, 'as a distinguished nobleman, a wise, mature and upright man, a shrewd politician, a bold critic, a sound judge of opportunity, loving honour and virtue.' It was with regret and, as we have seen, after much hesitation that he agreed to take part in civil war, and he often used to tell his companions 'that there was nothing on earth he detested so much.' He was a handsome man of serious aspect, with bright blue eyes and face that betokened energy. As good a Frenchman as he was a fervent Protestant, he desired above all things the prosperity of his country. 'It is indeed true,' says Brantôme again, 'that he was very ambitious on behalf of his king, yearning and striving to make him great.'

Summoned to court by Charles IX in 1571, Admiral Coligny at once became an influential member of the Royal Council, and promised the young monarch great things. He considered it a matter of vital importance to renew the traditional anti-Spanish policy and to form a grand alliance with England, the Lutheran princes of Germany, the Tuscan Medicis, the Swiss cantons and the Turks. The Low Countries had just rebelled; it was time 'to throw war from within to without'; Huguenot volunteers under La Noüe were even then helping Louis of Nassau to occupy Mons and Valenciennes. The Huguenot nobility, which had assembled in Paris for the wedding of Henri de Navarre (18th August 1572), seemed suddenly to have the upper hand.

Catherine was not at all pleased. She would not agree to be supplanted in the guardianship of her son. She was also aware of the difficulties confronting the proposed foreign alliance. Elizabeth was not disposed to commit herself; the Lutheran princes felt no sympathy for the Dutch Calvinists; the Turks had recently been overwhelmed at Lepanto; and an army of reinforcements under Genlis had been annihilated before reaching Mons. The admiral's cold and haughty airs at length exasperated the queen. She accordingly laid her plans in conjunction with François de Guise's son Henri (1550–88), a good-looking lad of twenty-one, strongly ambitious and ruthlessly enterprising, who saw in an ulta-Catholic policy the supreme opportunity of his career. Philip II likewise encouraged her schemes. And so, on 22nd August, four days after the royal wedding, a man named Maurevert, who belonged to the Guise faction, hid himself in a house at the corner of the Rue des Fossés-Saint-Germain and the Rue des Poulies, and fired on Coligny as he came out of the Louvre. One of the admiral's fingers was severed, another shot ripped open his left arm; but he was still alive, and he knew who had armed the assassin.

Charles IX was beside himself with rage: 'Am I never to have a moment's peace? Trouble, trouble, always fresh trouble!' He called on the wounded man and assured him he would avenge the crime 'in a frightful manner.' That evening Catherine pestered him, as she well knew how, to tell her what the admiral had said to him in secret. Charles was then twenty-two years old, but in the presence of his mother he was still a little boy. Coligny, he said, had advised him to rule by himself. Catherine panicked. Surely all these Huguenot nobles who had come to Paris for the wedding were preparing to get rid of her; Coligny would undoubtedly sway the feeble mind of her child; the first shot had misfired, she would have to begin again and cut down all the leaders of the Reformation. Such was the advice given her by a number of persons, among them perhaps the Spanish ambassador and certainly the young firebrand Guise. This appalling crime, undoubtedly the most terrible ever perpetrated in the name of Faith, would prove after all to be nothing but the desperate expedient of a great ambition brought to bay.

On the evening of the 23rd August Catherine visited her son and spent two hours representing to him the peril of his crown, the danger threatening his brothers, the hand of England secretly at work in the affairs of France. Motherly, provocative and imperious by turns, she inflamed the young man's sickly sensibility to such an extent that he completely lost his head. One after another the most trusted of his counsellors threw their weight into the balance: Birague, the Italian Gonzaga, Duc de Nevers, Maréchal Tavannes and the Chevalier d'Angoulême—all insisted that France was again on the threshold of civil war. Then, in a moment of blind fury bordering upon insanity, he gave the celebrated order: 'Kill the lot! Not one must live to reproach me.' Plans for the massacre were settled at dead of night. Guise took charge. It was decided that only Condé and Navarre would be granted their lives, because of the royal blood in their veins. Operations were to begin at dawn on 24th August, conducted by the city militia and the Swiss Guard. At the last moment the royal family, seized with dread, tried to suspend the whole business; but it was too late: the tocsin was already sounding from Saint-Germain-l'Auxerrois. Dawn was breaking over Paris, the dawn of a heinous day: it was the feast of St Bartholomew, apostle and martyr.

Henri de Guise went straight to Coligny's residence, where the door was forced and the guards jostled aside. The admiral, awakened by the noise, appeared in his dressing-gown. A Czech mercenary, one John

Yanowitz called Besme, demanded: 'Are you the admiral?' 'I am,' he replied, then added: 'Would to God I had been killed by a man instead of a menial.' He was struck in the stomach and then stabbed, but he continued to breathe. Down in the street Guise was shouting at the assassins to make haste, and they threw the dying man from a window. Henri recognized him, spurned him with his foot and went off without another word. The head of the Grand Admiral of France was cut off for dispatch to Rome; his body was carried to the gallows at Monfaucon like that of a condemned criminal. There followed an orgy of murder, a contagion, as it were, of blood. It had been intended that only the leaders should be killed, but there were in fact more than two thousand victims. The populace awoke and joined in the game: innumerable Protestants were dragged from their beds and butchered or drowned by frenzied termagants and half-wits. There was slaughter in the corridors of the Louvre, and even in the young Queen of Navarre's bedchamber, where her squire, the Vicomte de Léron, was discovered hiding under the bed. Condé and Navarre, summoned to the king's presence, were offered 'Mass, death or the Bastille.' They abjured. On the afternoon of the 24th, Charles IX gave instructions that the carnage—and the looting, which was also in full swing—must cease. But his order went unheeded, and it was not until the 27th that the besotted people quietened down. In the provinces, Meaux, Orleans, Rouen, Troyes, Toulouse and Lyons imitated Paris; but the Catholic governors of Dauphiné, Burgundy and Auvergne managed to prevent a repetition of such scenes within their territories. It is not known exactly how many victims there were in the whole of France; estimates vary between eight and thirty thousand. Among these were the great humanist Ramus and the musician Goudimel. Michel de l'Hôpital, who lay sick at Vignay, was forgotten, but he died of grief a few months later. Charles IX, alternately frozen with horror and drunk with blood, never forgot those abominations for which he had been responsible; they proved too much for his mental equilibrium.

International repercussions were considerable. 'What a crushing blow for us!' exclaimed William the Silent, leader of the rebels in the Netherlands. As for Philip II, the Massacre of St Bartholomew was one of the great joys of his life. What was the Pope's attitude? It has been severely criticized, but always on a superficial basis. St Pius V had certainly urged Catherine for a long time to 'the complete extermination of heretics,' as appears from a letter of 1569. What he desired, however, was open warfare, not collective butchery. His successor, Gregory XIII, shared his views, and when he heard that the French Court was planning the assassination of Coligny and Condé he expressed his disapproval in no uncertain terms. He was likewise furiously indignant when he learned that Cardinal de Lorraine had entered the Vatican in company with Maurevert, who had fired on the admiral. 'The man's a murderer,' he cried. The Papacy therefore bore no responsibility whatever, directly or indirectly, for the Massacre of St Bartholomew. But Gregory XIII, deceived by tendentious reports reaching him from Paris, thought that the news referred to some great battle lately won, and this misunderstanding caused him to exclaim that the information was 'more welcome than fifty victories of Lepanto'— an exaggeration in true southern style. He then proceeded to have a commemorative medal struck, and directed Vasari to immortalize this latest triumph of the Church on the walls of the Sacred Palace.[1]

At home the Massacre of St Bartholomew resulted in a very grave turn of events, for the French reform underwent yet another transformation. It had been, as Léonard aptly remarks, 'an opinion, then a Church, then a political party in arms'; now it became in Michelet's phrase, 'a Protestant republic,' a counter-state. When the nobility adopted it they were thinking almost exclusively of their religious liberties; many were now dead, and five hundred and twenty-seven of them had abjured, together with Condé and Henri de Navarre. The terrified middle class fled to Geneva or London. But in the market towns and countryside the cause was taken up anew by the common people, headed by the small landowners of Béarn, Languedoc and Rouergue. With Nîmes, Montauban, Sancerre and La Rochelle as its key points, the 'Protestant Republic' took shape, assisted in large measure by the old communal traditions of the South. In December 1574 an Assembly at Millau drafted the constitution for this scattered and fluctuating State; its articles provided for a military structure, the creation of elective consuls and the levying of troops. The Calvinist democracy poured out a stream of tracts and lampoons denouncing the rule of the assassins. While one of these pamphlets ridiculed the *Life, Actions and Misdeeds of Catherine dei Medici*, Theodore Beza's *Rights of Magistrates over their Subjects*, Hotman's *Franco-Gallia* and the anonymous *Vindiciae contra Tyrranos* [2] were laying the juridical bases of an insurrection, developing (a century in advance of their time) the theory of Social Contract, and demanding convocation of the Estates-General to appoint a new king. Montluc says that this propaganda spread throughout France, that the Calvinist peasantry was everywhere proclaiming themselves, the sovereign people, to be the rightful rulers of France. The situation which Catherine had foolishly hoped to improve by means of an abominable massacre had greatly deteriorated.

Charles IX was dying, ravaged with tuberculosis, worn out with the

---

[1] Gregory has been bitterly censured for this mistake. See Vacandard, 'Les Papes et la Saint-Barthélemy' in *Études de critique et d'histoire religieuse*, vol. i, p. 221; K. Remier, 'Les Événements de Rome et la préméditation du Massacre' in *Rome au XVIe Siècle*, p. 529, 1913.

[2] Attributed to Duplessis-Mornay or Languet.

pleasures of love, awakened by hideous nightmares in which he beheld his former friends covered with blood and bitterly reproaching him. He rendered up his soul on 30th May 1574, weighing with terror the consequences of his act, the curse called down upon his kingdom by the blood which he had shed, the curse of which Agrippa d'Aubigné would one day write:

> '*Cités ivres de sang et de sang altérés,*
> *Vous sentirez de Dieu l'épouvantable main.*
> *Vos terres seront fer et votre ciel d'airain . . .*'

5. HENRI III AND THE HOLY LEAGUE

When he learned of his brother's death, Catherine's third and favourite son Henri, whom she had made King of Poland, left Cracow in secret and hurried to occupy the throne of France. He was twenty-three years old, 'a tall, thin and slightly stooping figure, who looked down at one without affectation, with a majestic grace and at the same time much ease and much reserve. Though his intelligence was of a high order, he suffered from periodical failures of will-power, which made him seem indifferent to public affairs, whereas in fact he had them much at heart. Like Charles VII, he sometimes lacked firmness until the moment when he needed it for everyone's sake. He was as frivolous in the small things of life as he was grave in matters of state, and his extravagance, his whims and fads, which were sometimes carried to absurd lengths, would disconcert and then exasperate men whose good opinion was often kept alive by nothing else but his talents as an orator and statesman.' [1] He was thus a highly complex personality, passing from the most scandalous masquerades to the most exaggerated forms of devotion,[2] surrounding himself with undesirable favourites, yet marrying for love and adoring his wife. Indeed he was the first king of France to receive from his subjects the official style of 'Majesty', and he fully deserved it. But was he equal to the terrible responsibilities which circumstances placed upon his shoulders?

The reign of Henri III (1574–89) was the period of France's worst ordeal, fifteen dreadful years of unrelenting civil war and large-scale foreign intervention. Three factions henceforth divided the kingdom: (1) The Protestants, organized as the Calvinist Union, a 'State within the State' as Richelieu later described it. (2) The violent Catholic group, exalted by what they regarded as their victory and resolved to impose their ideas by every possible means. (3) A third party, for which

---

[1] Duc de Mirepoix: *Guerres de Religion.*
[2] On one occasion, at Lyons, he took part in a procession stripped to the waist and taking the discipline.

it was not difficult to discover antecedents, if only in the ideas of Michel de l'Hôpital,[1] but which became an actuality through force of circumstances, detestation of bloodshed and instinctive common sense. The members of this last association were known as 'politicals' or 'malcontents,' two words that indicated clearly both their feelings and their programme. Governors who had refused to authorize the massacres, Catholics horrified by so much bloodshed, moderate Huguenots who saw that in the long run war would be fatal to their doctrines, and recent converts—all desired national reconciliation and peaceful tolerance. Their leaders were Henri Montmorency, Governor Damville of Languedoc and François, Duc d'Alençon.[2]

Very soon after that tragic night in August 1572, the Protestants had restored their fortunes, thanks to the new party and to the indomitable resistance of La Rochelle and Sancerre. Henri III, hoping to soothe everyone and urged thereto by Catherine dei Medici, granted the Peace of Beaulieu (May 1576). The reformed worship was permitted everywhere, except at Paris; eight strongholds were conceded as the regular arsenals of a faction that could henceforward regard itself as legally mobilized for war; free access was allowed to all the frontiers; while in the Parlements mixed tribunals were created to try cases in which Protestants were involved. The Crown was thus recognizing 'a State within the State.'

Now those Catholics who had chosen the way of violence could not agree to a measure which appeared as an act of surrender by the king, and their retaliation took shape in an organization intended to oppose the Protestant union. Armed confederations had come into being here and there during the first years of the 'troubles'; but on the morrow of the Peace of Beaulieu, when Condé was appointed governor of Picardy, and Navarre governor of Guienne, the cry went up of 'Treason!' At Péronne, d'Humières called upon the Catholics to form 'a holy Christian union' which should prevent Condé taking possession of his province, and 'restore the holy service of God and obedience to His Majesty the King.' Thus was born the League. The same course was followed in Languedoc, Champagne, Nivernais and Burgundy. Paris, ardently attached to Roman orthodoxy and responsible for the extent of the massacres, responded to the fanatical appeal of monks and parish priests who went about stirring up the mob. In this way there arose a second 'State within the State,' led by a man of implacable audacity, Henri de Guise, nicknamed *Le Balafré* (the Scarred) because of a wound lately received at the battle of Dormans. The party's aims,

---

[1] e.g. 'Gentleness will do more good than violence.'

[2] D'Alençon's connection with the party was unfortunate. Youngest brother of the king, dissatisfied with his lot and ready for anything, he was a mischief-maker whose ambition was not always of service to this noble cause.

hastily set out by the Jesuits, were comprised in four words: 'Full reinstatement of Catholicism.' Loyalty to the king was earnestly proclaimed; but there was also talk of summoning the States-General in the event of the sovereign failing to carry out the suggested programme. To make assurance doubly sure Guise had the genealogists prepare a family tree showing his descent from Charlemagne! Meanwhile Philip II's emissaries were promising the League subsidies and reinforcements.

The position of Henri III was thus extremely serious. Was he fully aware of the fact? History has discarded the traditional picture of a painted puppet, interested only in lapdogs and mummery. The king was far from a nonentity; he was indeed the first of the Capetians who conceived the idea of a general code [1] to reorganize the French economy by bringing all trades within the guild system. But in those critical days the realm of the fleurs-de-lis needed at its head someone very different from this scion of an ancient and doomed race.

Confronted with the League, Henri could think of nothing better to do than to declare himself its leader and, after another passage of arms, to issue the Edict of Poitiers (October 1577) restricting the benefits conferred upon the Huguenots in the previous year. Having made these concessions he ordered the League to dissolve, imagining rather naïvely that the two sides would thus be rendered powerless. He was sincerely anxious to restore his country to peace and order, as well as to revive the prestige of his crown; and it was at this time that he instituted the Order of the Holy Ghost, whose members would swear obedience to himself. In the domain of foreign politics he played a subtle game, allowing his young brother François to intervene in the Low Countries against Spain, but not preventing many others of his nobles from associating their names with the grand project of a crusade against Elizabeth of England, which a group of enthusiastic Jesuits was attempting to organize. This seesaw policy, however, was doomed to failure. Among the Leaguers, Henri de Guise would never willingly step down among the rank and file; nor had the Protestants any intention of renouncing the advantages they already enjoyed, particularly as the Calvinist Union now possessed a first-class military leader in the person of Henri de Navarre who had returned to heresy and fled from Paris.

A new and indecisive period of hostilities seemed to promise some kind of understanding when the question of succession once again fanned the embers into flame. Henri III had no children, and appeared to be impotent. His heir, the turbulent François, died on 19th June 1584, after a tubercular haemorrhage, and the right of succession passed by virtue of the Salic Law to Henri de Bourbon, 'King of Navarre,' who was accordingly recognized by Henri III. Indignation

[1] The 360 articles of the Grand Ordinance of Blois.

ran high among the Catholics: was it possible, they asked, that a traitorous renegade should occupy the throne of St Louis? It was an alarming situation, which the heir apparent took care not to exploit for the time being. Remaining at Nérac, where he competed with his wife 'Queen Margot' in gallant escapades, he had the good sense, says d'Aubigné, 'to hide behind himself.' But his mere existence was enough to exasperate the feelings of others.

The League reappeared spontaneously and in several parts of the kingdom, even before the three Guises (Henri *le Balafré*, the cardinal and Charles, Duc de Mayenne) had returned to the scene. A great majority of those Catholics who had defended their faith for so many years thought it inconceivable that a Huguenot should become King of France. There was, of course, the Salic Law, but above it there was this more fundamental law: 'Jesus Christ, King of France, with His lieutenant there administering justice, and always a Christian.' Such was the spontaneous reaction of the people, who instinctively upheld this principle before all political interests. At Paris the League's propaganda won over the middle class, the Parlement, the legal fraternity, the butchers' guild and the small tradesmen. Châlons-sur-Marne, Dijon, Mâcon and other places were secured by various members of the nobility in preparation for the coming struggle. Henri de Guise sent word to Philip II, who promised a monthly subsidy of 50,000 crowns. An idea began to take shape that in the event of the king's death the Catholics would recognize as sovereign the aged Cardinal de Bourbon, uncle of Henri de Navarre; and Pope Sixtus V signed a Bull declaring the Béarnais incapable of succeeding to the throne of France. Civil war was impending, and would be more savagely contested than ever before. The North, the East, the West and nearly all the large cities took arms against 'those who were trying to subvert the Catholic religion and the State.' Cardinal de Lorraine himself called upon the king to summon the States-General.

Henri III was in a fix. The Duc d'Épernon undertook a fruitless mission to beg Henri de Navarre to return to the bosom of the Church; the heir apparent, as usual, would give no more than vague promises and assurances of loyalty. The Catholic protest now became an ultimatum. In July 1585 the king allowed his mother to sign the Treaty of Nemours: Protestant worship was forbidden, its adherents were commanded to abjure within six months under pain of exile and Navarre lost his right to the crown. The League had triumphed. This was the signal for what is usually called 'the eighth War of Religion,' the longest [1] and the most violent. Foreign intervention became more and more active, so that the unity of France had never been in such peril since the days of the Armagnacs and Burgundians.

[1] It lasted for eight years.

The popularity of Henri de Guise steadily increased. 'France,' wrote a contemporary, 'is crazy about that man; "in love with him" would be an understatement.' While Henri de Navarre, who controlled the south-west, was crushing the Duc de Joyeuse (one of the king's favourites) at Coutras, Guise won two small engagements in Champagne, which clever propaganda represented as major victories achieved by the 'new Maccabeus.' The League gradually enlarged its authority to include three-quarters of the kingdom. It drew up a programme intended to link the reformed French clergy with Rome, to restore to the nobility and towns their privileges and immunities, and to support Philip II's great expedition against England. Henri III found himself completely outstripped by events. Through Montaigne he kept in contact with Navarre. It was Guise whom he mistrusted most, and when the latter sent word that he was on his way to Paris, the king forbade him to enter the city. Guise, however, ignored the royal interdiction and was rapturously acclaimed. Was he going to depose his sovereign? Rumour said as much, and it was also whispered that Henri III, who had just brought troops into the capital, was preparing to arrest and perhaps to assassinate his rival. On 12th May 1588, the 'Day of Barricades,' there was a sudden outbreak of rioting, during which sixty of the king's soldiers were killed; and only the authority of Guise was capable of ending it.

Henri III was furious, and fled to Chartres. There he played a redoubtable game with masterly cunning. He pretended to grant his fortunate rival everything required. Guise was appointed lieutenant-general of the realm. In the States-General, which met at Blois in October 1588, he showed himself conciliatory towards the demands of the League and even went beyond them. Publish the decrees of the Council of Trent? Certainly. Include the banishment of heretics among the fundamental laws? With pleasure. He was not unaware, however, that the young fools of Guise's *entourage*, particularly his sister Catherine, Duchesse de Montpensier, were in the habit of showing their visitors the scissors they would use to tonsure the king as if he were some common Merovingian idler; and he secretly prepared to take revenge.

On Saturday, 23rd December, two days before Christmas, the Duke was summoned to His Majesty's apartment. Eight noblemen were there, all staunch supporters of the king. Guise entered and bowed. The eight stood up as if to show their respect—then set to work. Stabbed in front and from behind, his loins pierced by their swords, Guise called in vain for help. Being a man of unusual strength, he was able, on the very threshold of death, to drag the whole gang of assassins as far as the royal bed, where he collapsed. Next day Cardinal de Lorraine was murdered and Cardinal de Bourbon thrown into prison.

'Now I'm king!' cried Henri III. 'I'm determined no longer to tolerate insult or injury.'

Events followed with pitiless logic. Paris revolted and set up a General Council to co-ordinate Catholic action; almost every city hurried to join the League; the Duc de Mayenne was appointed 'Lieutenant-General of the State and Crown of France'; the king and Henri de Navarre were reconciled; and the Pope summoned Henri III to Rome, to answer for the murder of Cardinal de Lorraine. The aged Catherine had died, broken-hearted, in January. Henri III, though denounced as 'perjurer, abettor of heresy and sacrilegious assassin,' faced the storm with a courage remarkable in one so effeminate. Allied with the Protestants of Navarre, he went and besieged his capital with thirty thousand men, firmly resolved to have nothing more to do with the League.

But one dagger attracts another. Paris under blockade was in the grip of wild excitement. Furious sermons, pamphlets and pictures exhibited in the streets as well as in the churches raised public imagination to white heat. Many good people sincerely believed that both Henri III and Henri de Navarre, if victorious, would employ the same violent methods as Elizabeth of England in dealing with her Catholic subjects. The idea of necessary regicide came to dominate men's minds. A young Jacobin friar aged twenty-two, one Jacques Clément, an uncouth fellow of peasant stock and low intelligence, decided to make himself the instrument of divine justice. Having prayed, fasted and, as he said, been encouraged by mystical visions, he entered the royal camp at Saint-Cloud on 1st August 1589, obtained audience of Henri III on pretext of having secrets to deliver, and forthwith plunged a large kitchen knife into his belly. Then, with arms crossed, he waited to be cut down by the guards. Before dying the king had time to bless his successor, who had ridden at full speed from Meudon.

6. HENRI IV THE PEACEMAKER

A new reign was beginning, destined to be one of the most glorious in French history (1589–1610); but it was beginning amid the worst possible confusion. D'Aubigné, an eye-witness, has left us an account of the agitation reigning at Saint-Cloud, where the late king's body lay in state, watched by two friars of the Order of Minims. Great lords clapped on their hats, or flung them to ground exclaiming angrily: 'Better a thousand deaths than a Huguenot king.' The princes and high officers of State recognized Henri de Navarre as King of France, but he could not be unaware of the difficulties confronting him. On the other hand he was never one to despair.

Henri IV: no king of France has bequeathed to the national conscience a memory of greater friendliness and forbearance. Nevertheless he had many defects: he was 'a creature of foreign race, very firm as a soldier, but in all else changeable as water'; an inconstant lover, an unfaithful friend; a braggart and more prodigal of compliments than of gold; quick to forget favours no less than injuries. Though not, as Shakespeare says, 'lying water,' he was the very opposite of a reliable man. All the same, those virtues which he did possess were solid: a profound understanding of men and events, patience and courage, the rare gift of being able to choose the right man for the right place, and inexhaustible common sense. Opposed to stern measures, and giving his orders the appearance of requests, he desired, says Pasquier, 'in the handling of affairs of State to be trusted absolutely.' This whole complex web of merit and demerit, together with his straightforward and familiar ways, his slightly contemptuous good nature, his easy benevolence, his bravery, his confidence in himself and in his star, made him the kind of hero in whom the French delight. None could resist his ingratiating manners, his keen glance, his caressing voice, his tears, his witticisms or his laughter. All these qualities were so many trump cards in his hand, and he knew how to play them.

Henri took in the situation at a glance. The League held Paris, the larger towns and some of the provinces. Cardinal de Bourbon, who had lain in prison since the murder of Guise, had been proclaimed king as Charles X by the Duc de Mayenne. The Protestants were urging the new monarch not to exchange their proven loyalty for the inconstant backing of sworn enemies. The 'politicals' were reminding him that, as head of a confessional minority, he could not rule over a people the majority of whom were still attached to the Roman Church. Henri IV, uplifted by the conviction of his legitimacy, 'pale with anger and fear,' as d'Aubigné relates, protested against 'the violence with which he was assailed at the moment of his accession . . . with which he was bidden to strip his heart and soul upon entering the regal state.' Nevertheless, albeit he had declared, with his invaluable gift for striking phrases, that he had on his side 'all those among the Catholics who loved France and honour' and that 'he was king of the brave and would not be abandoned except by cowards,' he understood that he must return to the faith of his ancestors if he wished to reign.

On 4th August he announced that he would uphold 'the Catholic, Apostolic and Roman religion in all its fullness, without any innovation or change,' and that 'he was ready and desired nothing more than to be instructed in the said religion by a good, lawful and free general council of the nation.' He was not the sceptic that some of his more intemperate remarks might lead us to suppose; but recent history and his experience as a leader had shown him a sufficient intermingling of temporal and religious loyalties to convince him that God knows His own beneath ritual and even doctrinal differences, so that salvation is to be had in either confession. Moreover he possessed so lofty a notion of monarchy, so keen a sense of France's needs, that he would not hesitate to sacrifice his own scruples.

For the moment, however, since half the troops investing Paris had deserted, the only solution was to withdraw into Normandy and thus maintain contact with England. Mayenne followed in pursuit, but was defeated in two bitter engagements. The first of these (September 1589) took place at Arques, near Dieppe; the second (March 1590) at Ivry, near Evreux, where, with his tremendous charges—the *panache blanc* of Ivry—Henry IV won his unshakable reputation as a dauntless and irresistible commander. But, while making his provisional capital at Tours, the cunning Béarnais knew well that so long as his present circumstances continued a change of faith would be barren of results, appearing simply as a desperate manœuvre. Patiently therefore he laid plans for his attack.

It was because the question of Henri's personal religion was far less important than the extreme danger of France that the lawful king, awaited by the nation and helped by a good sense that taught him the necessary steps, triumphed over the worst difficulties. Spain hoped to attract France into her orbit. Philip II therefore, abandoning the reconquest of the northern Low Countries, ordered his best general, Alessandro Farnese, to relieve Paris, which had lain under siege since the battle of Ivry, and to throw a garrison into the city; and, since the Catholic candidate 'Charles X' was at the point of death, he tried to have his daughter Isabella Clara Eugenia [1] recognized as Queen of France. In promising dismemberment of the kingdom he was acting in concert with other pretenders. Among these was Charles Emmanuel, Duke of Savoy, a nephew of Henri III, who took possession of Aix and Marseilles; Charles III, Duke of Lorraine, son-in-law of Henri II, who laid claim to the eastern districts; and the Duc de Mercœur, a cadet of the house of Lorraine, who roused Brittany and placed Spanish garrisons on the northern coast of the peninsula. Surely the nation would react to these treasonable proceedings.

The thirty thousand fanatics who organized armed processions in Paris, and supported the terrorist government of the representatives of the 'sixteen quarters,' offered no resistance; but the middle class and particularly the better members of the Parlement, being more or less Gallican, objected to the thunderbolts launched by the Holy See against a man whom the Salic Law had brought to the throne of France, and wished for an understanding with the Béarnais. As the insurrectionary committee at Paris hanged the first president and some counsellors of

[1] She was granddaughter of Henri II through her mother, Elizabeth de Valois.

the Parlement, Mayenne was obliged to execute four members of the municipality which sided with the League. But all this led nowhere.

Henri IV, 'a king without a crown, a general without money, a husband without a wife,' then understood that it was wrong to disappoint the secret hopes of those who awaited him. The League held its States-General at the beginning of 1593, and the presence of the Duke of Feria, ambassador extraordinary of Philip II, showed that the choice of Isabella would undoubtedly be proposed. Henri forthwith suggested a conference of reconciliation, and delegates met at Suresnes on 5th May. Renaud de Beaune, Archbishop of Bourges, supported the principle of monarchical legitimacy, to which Pierre d'Espinac opposed the necessity of a Catholic sovereign. Then, on 17th, Beaune announced that the king would embrace Catholicism.

Abundant contemporary evidence reveals the psychology of Henri IV in those decisive hours. Events were crowding upon him. He would have preferred to make himself master of Paris before changing his religion, but there was no hope of that; any further delay would be disastrous. There was no mincing of words by politicians on either side. 'Take your choice,' said the Marquis d'O, a Catholic; 'either satisfy your Gascon prophets by returning to evil ways and leaving us to do the best we can to protect ourselves, or else conquer the League, which fears from you nothing so much as your conversion . . . and thereby become within a month absolute King of France, gaining more in an hour at Mass than you will do by twenty victories in the field or twenty years of labour and peril.'

His friend Rosny, afterwards Duc de Sully, re-echoes much the same feeling on the Huguenot side: 'You will never obtain complete possession and peaceful enjoyment of your kingdom except in one of two ways. The first of these is force of arms, which will necessitate the use of strong decisions, severity, harshness and violence—all of which are contrary to your temperament and inclination. It will also necessitate your having to endure countless difficulties, fatigues, pains, vexations, dangers and toils; you will have to be continually in the saddle, wearing helmet and breastplate, grasping pistol and sword. Even worse, you will have to bid farewell to repose, pleasures, pastimes, love-making, mistresses, games, dogs, birds and buildings; for you will escape from such troubles only at the price of many towns captured, many battles fought, signal victories won and much shedding of blood. The second way is to fall in with the wishes of the majority of your subjects as regards religion. If you do that, you will not meet with so much embarrassment, so many anxieties and hazards in *this* world. I don't know so much about the next. . . . You will not expect me as a Protestant to advise you to hear Mass; but I will go so far as to say that by doing so you will employ the quickest and easiest means of over-throwing every monopoly and of bringing all malicious designs to nothing. . . .'

The famous sally, 'Paris is worth a Mass,' is no doubt apocryphal; but it does express one of the causes of Henri's inevitable choice. Nevertheless he looked deeper into the political setting. Thus, when Pastor La Faye endeavoured to hold him back, he appealed to the national interest. 'If I followed your advice,' he answered, 'there would soon be neither king nor kingdom in France.' In order to sway the man as distinct from the politician, Gabrielle d'Estrées added her entreaties. Was she then, as the irreconcilable d'Aubigné maintains, 'the final instrument which did more than all the rest'? The intransigent Catholics scoffed at her behaviour. She owed them a grudge. 'When the hope of attaining royal status by matrimony was strengthened in the mind of this lady,' says the Calvinist historian, 'and when she was made to understand that all the ministers together could not dissolve the first marriage and that only the Pope was able to strike such a blow, she was strongly encouraged by those who boast of having changed their minds after a careful scrutiny of the earlier view; and thereafter she took advantage of her great beauty and every convenient hour of the day and night to discuss the benefits of a change.' Besides, had not Henri been promising for the last four years to receive instruction? Surrounded by Huguenot ministers, who were unwilling to let him go and whom he overwhelmed with fine promises, as well as by prelates who vowed their skilful and meritorious services, he had come to the conclusion that 'the difference between the two religions was not great, except for the animosity of their preachers, and that one day his authority would be able to resolve it.'

He therefore convoked a meeting of some twenty bishops, theologians and parish priests at Mantes. Then, on 23rd July, at Saint-Denis, he heard 'an account of all the main controversial topics of the age.' This conference lasted five hours, and Henri listened attentively. When the subject of Purgatory was raised he could not help interrupting: 'Now there the Church has a splendid source of income!' But when they came to discuss the reality of Christ's presence in the Eucharist he assured them: 'I have no doubt of it, for I have always believed as much.' The account of his conversion which he gave to the first presidents of the Parlements of Paris and Rouen was so tactfully worded as to reconcile his own goodwill with reasons of State and the operation of Divine Grace. 'He assured us,' notes Claude Groulart of Rouen, 'that ever since God called him to the crown his whole desire had been to seek the means of his salvation, which he valued above all worldly goods, and had prayed the Divine Majesty to open the road for him, but especially during the last few days since he came to realize that his Catholic subjects desired it; that he had put himself into the

hands of some theologians, and had derived so much profit from conferring with them that he had been induced and had at length determined to profess the Catholic religion; and that although he had in his
early years been brought up in the contrary profession and confirmed
therein, he was nevertheless beginning, by the grace of the Holy Spirit,
to appreciate the arguments which had been urged upon him.'

He was not, however, aware of the consequences of his act. While
foreseeing the loss of some support, he did not weigh the corresponding
advantages; and it is in the light of this ignorance that we must understand the well-authenticated words scribbled in a note to Gabrielle
d'Estrées: 'I shall make the perilous leap on Sunday.' On 25th July
1593 an enormous crowd, inquisitive but well behaved, filled Saint-
Denis. Henri IV entered the famous abbey, where the Archbishop of
Bourges awaited him at the bottom of the nave. 'Who are you?' 'I
am the king.' 'What do you ask?' 'I ask to be received into the bosom
of the Catholic, Apostolic and Roman Church.' 'Do you wish it?'
'Yes, I wish and desire it.' He read his profession of faith, signed and
returned it to the archbishop, and received absolution. Then he disappeared behind the altar to make his confession while the *Te Deum*
pealed forth; after which he heard Mass and communicated.

Military operations were suspended for three months. The good folk
of Paris would flock together on the look-out for His Majesty, whom
they wildly acclaimed. He was winning men's hearts. A pamphlet had
been circulating clandestinely since the beginning of spring; it was the
work of a group of poets and parliamentarians, and had appeared first
at Tours under the title *Menippean Satire*. By ridiculing the League
States, Mayenne, the intransigent monks, the legate and the Spanish
ambassador, it hastened the dissolution of the League. Since Rheims
was held by a friend of the Guises, Henri IV had himself crowned at
Chartres on 27th February 1594; he also touched for the king's evil,
for he was now monarch by holy unction. He was able to enter Paris on
22nd March and to watch, from a house near the Porte Saint-Denis, the
departure of the Spanish troops. Pope Clement VIII, disillusioned by
the poor results of Philip II's diplomacy, advised also by several
enlightened Jesuits and by his confessor St Philip Neri, who threatened
to refuse him absolution unless he recognized Henri, showed himself
more tractable. On 17th September 1595, after the Abbé d'Ossat and
Bishop du Perron of Evreux had acknowledged on behalf of their
sovereign the invalidity of the absolution at Saint-Denis and had
promised publication of the Tridentine decrees in France, he granted
the official pardon of the Church.

Henri IV had won the day, but this did not mean that he had overcome every trace of malice, which was never fully disarmed. Shortly
before his conversion a soldier of the League, at the instigation of two

G

Jesuits, had formed a plan to assassinate him, but had been caught and broken on the wheel. A few days after the ceremony at Saint-Denis, one Chatel, a pupil of the same Jesuits, also tried to kill him, but only cut his lip. Chatel was quartered, one of the Fathers was hanged and the Society was expelled from France. The king of tolerance was destined to live beneath the constant threat of murderers lurking in the shadows, even to the day of Ravaillac's knife.

Meanwhile the situation was completely reversed. Henri was now the lawful sovereign, and he profited by the invaluable support of those who longed for an end to this era of misery and slaughter, the support of the whole French people who were prepared to love him from the moment of his reconciliation with the Church. It must not be imagined, on the other hand, that all difficulties were annulled by a single act. The League had been so powerful, Spain had been so deeply involved, and the king was so short of military and financial resources, that it was impossible to hope for the immediate and undisputed submission and pacification of the country. Burgundy under Mayenne, Picardy under the Duc d'Aumale and Brittany under Mercœur—all stood as bastions of resistance. But Henri was equal to the situation. By means of a loud and commanding voice offset by a skilful mask of affability, by distribution of offices and confirmation of privileges, by recourse to arms and still more frequent use of money as a timely bait,[1] and by constant activity in every field, he managed within four years to rally the whole of France. Under the auspices of the papal nuncio, who was anxious to effect a reconciliation between the two principal Catholic states, the Treaty of Vervins (2nd May 1598) put an end to the Spanish war; its articles were similar to the conditions of peace laid down at Cateau-Cambrésis forty years earlier.

The attempt to solve the religious problem by warfare had miscarried, and the status of French Protestants had still to be decided. Their numbers had been reduced and most of the leaders had disappeared; but their communities, encouraged by the pastors, co-ordinated by periodical assemblies and hardened by suffering, had become one of the irreducible elements of national life. The king's relations with his former co-religionists were strained. The Edict of Poitiers had been revived in 1591, and Henri wished to preserve and guarantee its essential provisions. When negotiations with Spain drew to a close, the Protestants understood that they could do nothing but accept another edict, which was accordingly signed at Nantes on 13th April 1598.

This celebrated document contained ninety-two main articles and fifty-six articles of application. Defining the religious rights of the reformers, it granted them unlimited freedom of conscience, but it

[1] In order, as he subsequently declared, 'to buy his kingdom rather than conquer it.'

restricted their liberty of worship to the places authorized at Poitiers in 1577 and to those localities where it was practised in 1597. It likewise forbade all Protestant ceremonies in Paris, in the episcopal cities within a radius of five leagues therefrom, in the royal residences and in the armies. The Huguenot minority was allowed full civic rights and admission to all offices, as well as to the universities and hospitals; and with a view to the impartial administration of justice, tribunals composed of members belonging to both confessions and known as *chambres mi-parties*, were set up at Paris, Grenoble, Castres and Nérac.

Such was the 'general, clear and absolute law' which is still its maker's chief title to glory. The Edict of Nantes has often been described as 'a milestone in the world's history.' Whereas in Germany, Spain and England governments imposed a single faith upon their subjects, France was the first to adopt religious liberty. We must not, however, exaggerate the importance of a measure which was accepted by Frenchmen for very different reasons—political discretion or (as in the case of Sully) indifference to Churches and ecclesiastical loyalties far more often than respect for the spiritual freedom of souls. Henri IV had a hard struggle to secure registration of the Edict by the Parlements. 'You still have something Spanish in your bellies,' he told the counsellors of Toulouse. There was the same sort of resistance on the Protestant side, and the king was obliged to add two warrants. By the first of these he undertook to defray the expenses of the reformed worship; by the second he allowed the Huguenots an eight-year tenure of one hundred 'strong places,' whose garrisons he himself would pay. It would be anachronistic to represent this edict of pacification as welcomed with unanimous cries of joy. We must not forget that when he read its text Pope Clement VIII exclaimed: 'This crucifies me!' and that he added some words very similar to those once heard on the lips of Calvin and Theodore Beza: 'Liberty of conscience for each and every one is the worst thing in the world.' Such were the ideas of the age.

France emerged from the terrible ordeal ravaged and drenched in blood, her land lying fallow, her peasants starving and ready to revolt, her commerce ruined. She needed, as King Henri said, 'to recover breath.' The Catholic Church was in a way victorious, because the sovereign, in order to establish his authority, had been forced to submit to her; but the separation of so many of her sons remained an open wound in her side. This work of plain common sense and sound policy, so far in advance of contemporary feeling, might have proved dangerous and short-lived, but for the appearance of a king who took a completely fresh view of the religious problem. Unity of faith was declared in the preamble of the edict to be the supreme advantage; circumstances alone had inspired common-sense arrangements, which would henceforward be the rule.

7. Three Protestant Victories: The United Provinces of the Netherlands

Protestantism in France had won no victory; it had merely obtained *de facto* recognition. At the same time, however, it was able to celebrate its triumph in three countries: England, Scotland and those northern provinces of the Low Countries which belonged to but were lost by Spain. In this last region events ran parallel to and continually interlocked with those of the religious crisis in France. By unsettling the richest area of the Spanish domains they gave the French monarchy a chance to strike at its rival in the Escorial. Coligny, as we have seen, dreamed of reconciling the French people and leading them to war against Philip II; François, Duc d'Alençon, twice employed his turbulent energy in hopes of carving for himself a Flemish principality; and Henri IV would place his own diplomacy at the service of the revolted provinces, in order to secure recognition of their independence. Conversely Spanish troops operating in the Netherlands were often sent to France for the purpose of assisting the League. But to anyone concerned with the Church's history during this cruel period the revolt of the future 'United Provinces' is of enormous interest on its own account. It shows how religious passion, by crystallizing political and economic discontent, made a small people fully conscious of itself and fashioned gangs of raging rebels into citizens of a lasting state. Without Calvinism the republic born at the mouths of the Rhine and the Meuse could never have seen the light of day, or at any rate could not have been such as it was. The story offers a striking example of the mutual influence of politics and religion which characterizes this stage of historical evolution in the late sixteenth century.

Among the territories of the great dukes of Burgundy, which passed by inheritance to the Hapsburg descendants of Charles the Bold, were seventeen provinces stretching from Artois to Friesland. The whole area, being damp and constantly liable to inundation by the rivers and the sea, was known as the 'Low Countries' (Netherlands). When Charles V divided his vast dominions he included it in the empire of his son Philip, thus linking its destiny with that of Spain. It was one of the most fertile and most industrious regions in the whole of Christendom. Its extraordinarily dense population was already well acquainted with the methods of intensive cultivation, and reared a fine breed of cattle on the *polders*,[1] while the towns and villages alike were noted for their manufactures of woollen goods and linen. Whereas the ancient metropolis of Bruges was in decline, the warehouses of Antwerp, Middelburg and Amsterdam were crammed with spices from the Indies

[1] Farmland reclaimed from the sea.

as well as with the products of Mexico and the Antilles, which they redistributed throughout the whole of Europe. The economic crisis, through which the western world was passing at that time, was felt less severely in the Low Countries than at Augsburg, Genoa or Lyons, and the Antwerp exchange dominated the international market.

The advent of riches had helped to make this small region one of the most prolific centres of art in Europe. During the past hundred years five generations of great painters had poured out a succession of masterpieces: Van Eyck, Rogier Van der Weyden and Thierry Bouts, Hans Memling (1433–94), Gerard David, and finally Quentin Matsys (1466–1538), whose sensitive brush seems to foreshadow Rubens. In the mid sixteenth century we have Peter Brueghel the Elder (1545–69). Heir of the fantastic and occasionally satanic Hieronymus Bosch (1450–1516), he devoted his entire genius to the amusement of his contemporaries, but he managed also to reflect his country's ordeal in the terrible 'Mad Margot.' In every thriving city nobles and merchants built themselves the most luxurious mansions, smelling of wax, spices and strong beer; and the walls of these houses were decorated with magnificent tapestries for which Van Orley (1495–1533) and his pupils drew the cartoons.

This ostentatious wealth, however, went hand in hand with grave social problems. The great landowners made fortunes by the sale of corn and cattle, while too many peasants found it difficult to pay their rents; middle-class business men, rolling in money, controlled both the marketing of essential goods and the labour market, while a wretched and rapidly increasing proletariat crowded the industrial towns. If the Spanish government had had the sense to leave the higher grades of native society in possession of their traditional liberties and privileges, it might have stood apart from and thereby avoided the consequences of this division between the classes. Charles V had taken care to do that, for he understood his beloved Flanders. But Philip II, who wished to be exclusively Spanish, and who never left his Castilian palaces after 1559, was not interested in the Low Countries except in so far as they were useful to his foreign policy and his exchequer. Refusing to tolerate any limitation of his own power, and wishing to exercise universal control even at a distance of 1,750 miles, he intended to hold the seventeen provinces in tutelage. From 1558 onwards he avoided summoning the States-General, which were entitled to discuss any increase of taxes and to defend local exemptions. He entrusted the government of the Low Countries to his sister, Margaret of Parma, and Cardinal Granvelle, an ambitious upstart from Franche-Comté; but he allowed them to do no more than carry out his orders, and the imposition of heavy taxes exasperated the middle classes. The nobility, who played a predominant part in the States-General, and had grown up in the public service, remained essentially loyalist; but they could not endure this humiliating constraint. The situation quickly became tense, particularly as men of all degrees—the middle classes, who feared for their freedom of initiative; the aristocrats, who demanded respect for their ancient autonomy; and the workers, who were in the throes of rebellious ferment—were largely won over to Protestantism and strongly opposed the religious restrictions introduced by the absolutism of the Escorial.

About 1560 the provinces as a whole had been affected by Protestant propaganda: conversions had been made first among the proletariat, then among the middle classes, the nobility and the higher ranks of the army. Confiscation, fines, banishment, and even a few executions (e.g. at Tournai), had all alike failed to damp the ardour of those preachers who had hurried from Geneva, Alsace, France, Germany and England, or who, like the Walloon Guy de Bray, had received their training at home. Hundreds and sometimes thousands of the faithful, many of them carrying arms, attended meetings which assembled in the open air, outside the city walls, because the houses were now too small to hold them. They were perfectly aware that Philip II, the champion of European Catholicism, had determined upon a systematic offensive against heresy. He had in fact persuaded the Pope to create fourteen new bishoprics, which were formed from the territories previously included in the enormous and unwieldy dioceses of Utrecht, Tournai, Cambrai and Arras; their purpose was to ensure a stricter supervision under the supreme control of Granvelle, who had been promoted Archbishop of Malines. At Douai he founded a university where missionaries were trained by the Jesuits, and he increased the powers and authority of the Inquisition.

Resistance began with the nobility, who withstood the Spaniard's disregard of their political privileges no less than his religious oppression. The heads of the Burgundian Order of the Golden Fleece consulted together at their regular meetings, where three men soon took the lead: the Count of Horn, the Count of Egmont and, above all, William of Nassau, Prince of Orange on the Lower Rhône, who had large possessions in Brabant and Luxembourg. They asked for the withdrawal of Spanish troops; they demanded the recall of Granvelle, whom they held responsible for the detested methods of government; and, in order to strengthen their hand, they refused to sit henceforward in the Council of State. Granvelle was dismissed in January 1564, but no other changes followed. Egmont then visited Madrid, but in vain: by letters dated 'from the Wood of Segovia' on 17th October 1565, Philip ordered that the pursuit of heresy be continued without restraint.

Tension increased. English competition was causing difficulties in the textile industry, and employers were turning away labour; the harvest had been bad, and Denmark was no longer exporting grain to balance the scarcity; prices were rising and poverty was rife. Gangs of unemployed assembled in the city squares, while vagrants roamed the countryside. The Calvinist message had found its most enthusiastic welcome among these unfortunates, who were scandalized by the Church's wealth and by Spanish egoism; it was estimated that 90 per cent of workers in the serge factory at Hondschoote had been converted. The thousands who had emigrated and found work abroad, especially in England under a far-sighted government, inflamed the wrath of their brethren at home. In the demand for liberty, in its various shapes and forms, the claim to religious freedom was overwhelmingly the strongest.

Those members of the gentry and middle classes who had adhered to Protestantism realized that circumstances favoured a coalition of the entire Flemish and Burgundian 'fatherland,' which would reprobate any and every form of oppression. Nine of them, among whom were Jean and Philippe Marnix de Sainte-Aldegonde and Gilles de Clerq, a barrister from Tournai, drew up a 'compromise,' which, having set forth the rights of the people and nobility of the Low Countries, demanded convocation of the States-General, withdrawal of the 'placards' against heresy and suspension of the Inquisition. This document was handed round, and was signed within a period of eight weeks by two thousand Catholic, Calvinist and Erasmian aristocrats, some of them prelates of the Church. On 2nd April 1566 two hundred noblemen, who had adopted the wallet and bowl as tokens of their sympathy with the poor, presented it to the regent Margaret. She was deeply moved and burst into tears. 'Beggars, madam,' cried one of her counsellors; 'are you frightened of these beggars?' The petitioners adopted the word and made it a title of glory: beggars in the cause of religion or beggars in the cause of civil rights, they stood together like the Huguenots of France, and marched forward on the road of insurrection.

About 10th August, first at Hondschoote and Armentières, then throughout the country, mobs of destitute and frenzied people hurled themselves upon the churches, breaking the statues, shattering the retables, pillaging the treasuries and profaning the Sacred Host. The local authorities found themselves suddenly overwhelmed; the nobility made no effort to interfere; and William of Orange allowed the iconoclasts to ravage the sanctuaries of Antwerp for four days before assigning three of the city's churches for Protestant worship. The fires of revolution blazed for nearly a fortnight. On 23rd August the helpless regent agreed that preaching of the reformed faith should be lawful wherever it had hitherto taken place, and freedom of worship was introduced at Tournai, Antwerp, Ghent, Oudenarde and Ypres. The first temples were hastily erected, and synods met at various places.

The Calvinists, however, made a grave mistake in abusing their success and showing the same intolerance which they themselves had deplored. The fury of the iconoclasts was causing terror, and Margaret rallied the higher nobility for the purpose of restoring order. Egmont, a Catholic, pacified Flanders; and the government, which had raised a few troops, recovered control of the situation between December 1566 and May 1567. Antwerp and Valenciennes were subdued; and William of Orange, who had behaved with such restraint as to incur both the wrath of Spain and the mistrust of the fanatical pastors, fled to Germany. The regent considered it was now time to summon the States-General and also to abolish the Inquisition, which, as an Italian writer said, had fewer than twenty partisans out of a population of ten millions.

It is hard to say whether this policy of moderation could have prevented the explosion. In any case there was no time in which to apply it; for at this juncture Philip II sent someone else to Brussels. Ferdinand Alvarez de Toledo, Duke of Alba (1508–82), whose name is everlastingly identified with the bloody drama of the Low Countries, was one of the greatest of Spanish commanders, a man of steel, capable of cold cruelty and utterly implacable. Twenty years earlier he had defeated the Protestants at Mühlberg; and now (July 1567), at the head of twenty thousand soldiers, he moved from northern Italy along the French frontiers by way of Savoy, Franche-Comté, Lorraine and Luxembourg, bringing horror to the Netherlands. Margaret, abandoning all hope, resigned. Alba set up a 'Council for the Suppression of Disorders,' whose 1,800 sentences of death soon caused it to be named the 'Council of Blood.' He had the Counts of Egmont and Horn, heads of the lawful Catholic resistance, publicly executed at Brussels on 5th June 1568; he forbade emigration, foreign studies and communication with the rebels; and his police kept an eye on printers and publishers. Furthermore, since he had need of money, he imposed crushing taxes on the seventeen provinces without consulting their States-General. Bishops and preachers protested in vain. Pius V described him as the new Gideon and ordered a statue of the duke trampling underfoot the enemies of religion.

Meanwhile William of Orange (1533–84), who had withdrawn to his German estates in Nassau, was preparing to resume the struggle. He was a man of action, but also of powerful intellect; cold and tenacious (whence his famous cognomen 'the Silent'), he knew how to be generous and win his way into the people's hearts. Trained for high office in the public services of Charles V, endowed with tireless energy and indomitable courage, he seemed the perfect model of a leader. He began by interesting the Emperor Maximilian in a region which, until quite recently, had formed part of the 'imperial circle of Burgundy,'

and suggested that he should take up the matter with Madrid. Philip II
shed tears of sorrow and vexation. William knew that the German
princes were prepared to take a chance and sell their mercenaries. He
made an initial descent upon Friesland in 1569, but the attempt was
premature. Joined as he was in friendship with Coligny, he hoped
above all for the intervention of France.

The arrival of new elements upon the scene restarted the movement
in the Low Countries themselves. Opposition had at first been mainly
Brabantine and Flemish; now it was inspired for the most part by men
of the North, rugged sailors of Zeeland, Holland and Friesland, bold
and indomitable, realistic enthusiasts. These 'beggars of the sea'
included first the herring fishers and whalers, then those small shipowners at Amsterdam, Rotterdam and Dordrecht, whose busy trade as
carriers in the Baltic and North Sea was causing anxiety at Antwerp,
and lastly the shrewd cultivators of the polders and peat-bogs. Calvinism was admirably suited to engage their sympathies with its austere
and exalting spirit, its practical morality, its simplicity of worship; and
they adopted it.

When we recall that it was the northern half of the seventeen
provinces that was finally wrenched from Spain and formed into a
Protestant state, we cannot but appreciate the decisive part played by
those sailors, graziers and tradesmen of Holland, Zeeland and Friesland. Avoiding official enrolment by flight in their heavy boats, they
scoured the sea from the Gironde estuary to the Danish straits, established a base at Dover with the consent of Elizabeth, made a surprise
attack on their enemy's coast, pillaged churches and hunted down
monks and priests, whom they forced to attend their sermons. Alba's
reprisals could not reach them. On the night of 31st March–1st April
1572 they occupied the stronghold of Brielle at the mouth of the River
Meuse, and this was the signal for a general rising of the North. In
Zeeland Louis of Nassau, who had armed his boats at La Rochelle,
seized Flushing; the cities of Holland, Gelderland, Utrecht and Friesland expelled the Spanish garrisons; William of Orange assumed
leadership of the revolt, and the Estates of Holland proclaimed him
'Stathouder,' i.e. 'Lieutenant of the Commonwealth.' Philippe Marnix
de Sainte-Aldegonde introduced his Song of the Beggars, in praise of
the leader who 'remained faithful to the fatherland . . . braving the
pride and combat of the tyrant.' The South, more firmly controlled by
the Spanish forces, remained cautious; but Mons and Valenciennes
were seized with the help of French Huguenots.

This offensive was brought to a sudden and unexpected halt when
the Massacre of St Bartholomew left the Protestants of the Low
Countries to work out their own salvation. Alba retook the cities he
had lost, and massacred the defenders of Haarlem who had resisted him

* G

for six months. But William of Orange, having fallen back upon Holland and Zeeland, captured Antwerp, fortified himself by breaching the dikes, and prevented the Spanish fleet from approaching his islands and seaboard. Philip II, realizing at length that force was of no avail, decided to recall the terrible governor, who left behind him a fearsome memory, and who, as the Bishop of Namur confessed, had certainly 'done more harm to religion in seven or eight years than Luther, Calvin and all their henchmen.'

Don Luis de Requescens, who succeeded Alba, offered the royal pardon to all. Too late: William was no longer prepared to accept it. Divorced from a Saxon princess, he was on the point of marrying Charlotte de Bourbon-Montpensier, unfrocked abbess of Jouarre, and had openly embraced Calvinism. He knew that he could depend upon his co-religionists in Holland and Zeeland; though only a minority, they were violent men, denouncing the Catholics as traitors, agents of Spanish imperialism, and inspiring whole populations at once with terror and fanaticism. He rejected the offer of negotiations suggested by the Pope to the Escorial; he wanted no more provinces administering their affairs through their assemblies and existing as autonomous units within the framework of a great constitutional monarchy. No, he dreamed of an independent state.

Requescens therefore resumed the offensive and besieged Leyden; but William had the dikes broken, so that boats were able to sail across the flooded plain and revictual the place. Inflamed by this success, he endowed the great manufacturing city with a university which became the principal intellectual centre of reform in the northern Low Countries. In April 1576 Holland and Zeeland united under the prince's authority, banished 'all forms of worship contrary to the Gospel,' and called upon the other provinces to defend political and religious liberties. Their answer was the Pacification of Ghent.

Requescens had just died, and government was in the hands of a Council of State all of whose members, except one, were natives of the Low Countries. The Spanish garrisons mutinied for pay: at Antwerp, on a day of 'fury,' they sacked the warehouses and rounded up the leading citizens. Accordingly representatives of all the provincial assemblies met at Ghent on 8th November 1576 and reached an agreement, whereby they undertook to drive out the Spaniards, to suppress existing measures against heresy and to allow each province the choice of its religion. Was William then on the threshold of victory? Were the seventeen provinces going to repudiate all ties with the Escorial and accept the system of religious equality favoured by the duke? A few years sufficed to consummate the rupture between North and South, dedicating the former to independence and Protestantism, the latter to a Spanish and Catholic destiny.

Notwithstanding their anxiety to defend their political privileges, events had shown that the southern provinces, where the Catholic counter-reformation was thoroughly well organized, remained as a whole true to their ancient faith. They could not but view with alarm those advantages which the emboldened Calvinists derived from the Pacification. In Gelderland, where the number of Protestants was small, William's brother, John of Nassau, introduced preachers of the reformed religion together with a body of reliable troops, and made such changes among the magistrates that Catholic worship was no longer celebrated in certain towns. At Antwerp the burgomaster and colonel-commandant, Philippe Marnix de Sainte-Aldegonde, expelled the Jesuits and Franciscans. At Ghent William of La Khétulle arrested the bishops of Bruges and Ypres; his successor, John of Hembyze, tolerated the sack of monasteries, the confiscation of their goods and the execution of their monks. At Brussels the churches and convents were laid waste. William of Orange exerted himself to establish a legal religious system in place of violence, and proposed that every form of worship should be lawful in any city where it was desired by one hundred households. But he spoke to deaf ears, and was even denounced by his fanatical co-religionists. In 1577 the states, persuaded thereto by the Catholics of the South, had promised 'on their conscience, before God and men, to preserve and maintain in all things and everywhere' the Roman religion; yet the following year witnessed a veritable hecatomb of priests in the South. Calvinist fanaticism was aggravating the situation from day to day.

On 6th January 1579, at Arras, the French-speaking districts of Artois, Hainaut, Lille, Douai and Orchies united to uphold Catholicism. Alessandro Farnese, son of Margaret of Parma, a brilliant strategist and subtle diplomat, realized that it was worth while making indispensable concessions in order to purchase the reconciliation of these confederates with Spain. And so, on 17th May, he concluded peace with them, proclaiming an amnesty, confirming the privileges of cities and provinces, excluding foreigners from the Council of State, restoring to the States-General their right to approve taxation and authorize the introduction of reinforcements, but officially recognizing only the Catholic religion.

The answer was not long delayed. On 23rd January, at Utrecht, the provinces of Holland, Zeeland, Utrecht, Gelderland, Groningen, Overyssel and Friesland replied to the Union of Arras by banding together in rejection of all foreign sovereignty. William of Orange beheld this partition with sorrow and dismay; but since he had not been able to prevent it, he did the next best thing by devoting all his energies to liberating the confederates of Utrecht from the Spanish menace. The Escorial denounced him as a public malefactor, and a price was put upon his head. With the proud words 'I will uphold' he signed the Apologia written to justify his conduct by the French pastor Loyseleur de Villiers.

On 24th July 1581 the northern states of La Haye proclaimed the deposition of Philip II. A new state was born, but its existence was precarious. Farnese undertook a systematic reconquest; capturing the rebel cities one after another, he had the good sense to guarantee their administrative autonomy, and although he deprived Protestant worship of all freedom, its initiates were not disturbed so long as they abstained from any form of proselytism. In 1584 he retook Ypres, Bruges, Cambrai and Ghent; in 1585 Brussels and Antwerp. On 10th July 1584 William of Orange was assassinated by Balthazar Gérard of Franche-Comté. 'God have pity on this unhappy people' were his dying words.

The young republic was saved by the barrier of its rivers, by the English alliance, by the defeat of the Armada, by the order given to Farnese to strip the Low Countries of Spanish troops so as to help the Leaguers in France, by the death of that great captain, by the victory of Henri IV, by raids upon the Spanish settlements by seamen from Holland and Friesland, by the prosperity of Amsterdam and by the skill of Maurice of Nassau, son of William the Silent. In 1598 the situation was such as it had been twelve years earlier: the southern provinces, corresponding more or less to modern Belgium, had been recovered by Spain and by a rejuvenated and conquering Catholic Church. The United Provinces of the North, firmly rooted in Calvinism and hostility to the Hapsburgs, combining the intransigence and courage of their statesmen with the practical sense of their merchants, had shown that the little confederation had a soul.

Nevertheless Philip II hoped, before he died, to reunite the Low Countries. On 6th May 1598 he decided to entrust them to an autonomous government directed by the Archduke Albert, youngest son of the Emperor Maximilian II, and by his daughter, the Infanta Isabella Clara Eugenia, whom he had lately dreamed of making Queen of France. He was greatly mistaken if he believed that the northern provinces would be willing to submerge themselves in the old unity. They felt themselves completely estranged from those regions which had retained their loyalty to the monarchy and which, tutored by the Jesuits, dominated spiritually by the universities of Douai and Louvain, and superintended by a nuncio of the Holy See, left staunch Protestants no remedy but exile; they paid no attention to measures taken by the King of Spain. Military operations, which had been suspended on the left bank of the Meuse, were resumed in 1600; but there was no question of political conflict. The archdukes, on behalf of the Escorial, were endeavouring to bring back rebellious subjects to their obedience, while the latter struggled for recognition of their independence. There could be no more serious thought of extirpating heresy from the northern regions, where it had triumphed, and it is remarkable that the Act of May 1598 contained no religious clause.

Maurice of Nassau, using Ostend as his base, sought to occupy the Flemish littoral as far as Dunkirk. The Catholic peasants rose against him; he ventured as far as the Yser, but had to withdraw. The Spaniards then laid siege to Ostend: Ambrogio Spinola, a Genoese, invested the town with great skill, and forced it to capitulate on 3rd September 1604. This success, however, bore no fruit. The Spanish infantry was the best in Europe; but it was irregularly paid and was consequently no docile instrument. The northern Calvinists exploited their maritime advantages by establishing themselves in the Malay Archipelago and the Moluccas, destroying Spanish fleets before Malacca and off Gibraltar, and intercepting the American convoys near the Azores.

The war was terminated by an international congress. Towards the end of 1606 negotiations were opened at La Haye. Side by side with delegates from the Provinces, from the Union of Utrecht, from the archdukes and from King Philip III, sat the envoys of France, England and the German princes. The Papacy refused to be represented. The twelve-year truce signed on 8th April 1609, thanks to the good offices of Henri IV's ambassadors, recognized the seven United Provinces as a free State and agreed that they should have the right to trade wherever possible, that is to say, even in the Spanish colonies. Nothing, however, was said about the confessional question, which had been the crucial point of the whole struggle. The Catholic sovereign's plenipotentiaries implicity accepted Calvinism as the official religion of the new republic. As at Augsburg in 1555, the Hapsburgs surrendered to the Reformation territories which they had been unable to keep for that Church whose defender they had so proudly claimed to be.

8. THREE PROTESTANT VICTORIES: SCOTLAND AND JOHN KNOX

While the revolt led by William of Orange was preparing the victory of Calvinism in the Low Countries a second and equally fanatical rebellion was establishing (apparently once for all) the most rigorous form of Protestantism in another land. In Scotland, under the bewitching but feeble sceptre of Mary Stuart (1542–68), two attempted reforms had failed to eradicate the grave defects of a decadent Catholic Church, which now proved itself no match for well-organized propaganda. Brutal reaction, such as that which sent George Wishart to the stake in 1546, had done nothing but exasperate men's minds. Retaliation had been swift, for Cardinal Beaton was assassinated only three months later. Ten years afterwards there took place the trial of Walter Milne, an old priest of eighty years, who had apostatized and married. In the course of these sensational proceedings the accused pronounced an unprecedented indictment of Catholicism, and the Catholic members of the court were unable to silence him. Milne was burned; his execution made an unfortunate impression, but was far from stemming the flow of heretical propaganda. One individual needed only to rally the partisans and lead them into battle, and the Catholic defences would collapse like a house of cards.

That individual was John Knox (1505–72),[1] a bold violent man possessed of a seductive eloquence. This bearded prophet, with his prominent cheek-bones and hard, cold gaze, was the very archetype of fanatical demagogue; his portraits remind one of Michelangelo's 'Moses.' Originally a priest, he had abandoned the ancient faith, rather as Luther had done, and perhaps under the influence of his works, but mainly as a result of studying St Augustine. Wishart, to whom he was deeply attached, finally won him over to heresy. A leading member of the plot which ended in the murder of Beaton, he sought refuge with his fellow conspirators in the citadel of St Andrews. There he was taken prisoner by the queen's French guard, and he rowed for some time in the galleys of Henri II, until Somerset obtained his release. Cranmer welcomed him to England with transports of joy, and even offered him a bishopric. When he refused, the archbishop appointed him chaplain to Edward VI, and Knox's influence did much to lead the king towards heresy. On the accession of Mary Tudor he was obliged to flee from London and took refuge in Geneva. There, for five years (1554–9), he lived under the shadow of Calvin, translating the Bible into Scottish and writing his famous pamphlet *Against the Monstrous Regiment of Women*, which was aimed at Mary Stuart and her mother the queen-regent, Marie de Guise-Lorraine, but which also grievously offended Elizabeth. From the shores of Lake Leman he wrote countless letters explaining to the nobility of his country how they would profit by seizure of ecclesiastical goods, and assuring the Catholic middle classes that a clergy so degenerate as theirs had no right to continue as their leaders. At his suggestion a group of Protestant lords, headed by the Earl of Moray, an illegitimate half-brother of the queen, formed the 'Congregation of Christ' with a view to destroying 'the Congregation of Satan and Idolatry.' One of their emissaries travelled to Geneva and urged Knox to come and take spiritual charge of the party. He agreed, and landed in Scotland on 2nd May 1559.

Events now moved swiftly. Amid the indifference and inertia of the Catholic authorities Knox stirred great crowds with his inflammatory

[1] See *The Protestant Reformation*, Chapter VI, end of section 'The Triumph of "God's Steward".'

speeches. At Perth, on 11th May, some religious houses were attacked
and pillaged, statues broken and sacred vessels profaned. A month later
it was the turn of Scone Abbey, where the kings of Scotland had been
crowned, and then the friaries at Stirling. Tension rose. In the Parliament of 1560 both Lords and Commons publicly denounced the
Catholic priests as 'thieves, murderers, perverters of wives and
daughters, adulterers and, in brief, abominable folk.' The 'Scottish
Confession' drawn up by Knox was then adopted. Based on the
doctrine of Calvin, it voiced a dreary view of sinful man condemned
by his sin to the 'dungeon of absolute darkness, where the worm will
not die nor the fire be extinguished'; a proud and sombre morality;
desire for an austere cult stripped of the Mass and the whole liturgy;
and, of course, refusal to recognize the authority of the 'Bishop of
Rome' in any shape or form. These innovations took effect with
astonishing rapidity in the realm of a queen who strove to be in all
things a true Catholic and whose husband was King of France.

As a legislator and organizer Knox was even more talented than his
master Calvin, and he established his Church without delay. Its charter
was his implacable *Book of Discipline*. Carrying to their extreme the
ideas of Geneva, the Scottish Church, known to history as 'Presbyterian,' abolished every trace of a hierarchy and entrusted the administration of its communities to democratically elected ministers, elders
and deacons. It impressed upon its members a system of morality no
less rigid than that prevailing at Geneva: control of private life, State
education of children, public penance, etc. The social character of this
régime is remarkable in that it sought completely to ignore class distinctions, threatened with 'heavy and terrible judgments of God' the
rich, the self-satisfied and buyers of ecclesiastical goods, and recommended all 'to have a great regard for the poor brethren who dig and
manure the soil.' Thus was born an egalitarian theocracy which was
destined to exert a profound influence upon the Scottish people and
pave the way for those seventeenth-century 'Covenanters' who fought
with such determination against James Stuart.

What did the Catholic authorities do? Very little; and that little
bore no fruit. After the death of her young spouse François II (1560),
Mary left the smiling land of France with a heavy heart, and returned
to her cold, crabbed Scotland in 1561. Presbyterianism had just been
established there, and Knox invited her to embrace the heresy. Now
this charming girl was somewhat light-headed, impulsive and sensual;
she was moreover a woman to her finger-tips, and made frequent use
of the right to change her mind, which is recognized as a privilege of the
'weaker sex.' But it is to her credit that she would not yield when
pressed to make the decisive choice. The Pope had given her the
Golden Rose, an honour reserved for loyal servants of the Church;

Catholic she had been born, and Catholic she intended to remain. She declined to ratify the Acts of Parliament and continued to hear Mass.

She might have won this final round had she not allowed her feminine instincts to take precedence of her duties as sovereign. Amid the storm unleashed by the preachers she felt terribly alone, and looked around for some support. Wisely rejecting Leicester, the former favourite of her cousin Elizabeth, she thought to find a guide, philosopher and friend in her own cousin Henry Darnley, a handsome young man and not without charm. The choice was fatal. While Knox thundered from the pulpit against 'Ahab and Jezebel,' the poor queen found herself caught in that inexorable machinery of intrigue and treason which would lead her straight to disaster. Darnley was both cruel and contemptible, but he was also ambitious. Furious at being excluded from a share in the prerogatives of the crown, he made himself odious to Mary, who committed an egregious mistake by taking as her too intimate adviser a little Italian musician named Rizzio, who had come over with the Duke of Savoy. The Scottish nobles, and Darnley in particular, resolved to get rid of the upstart, whom they assassinated as he hid in the queen's skirts. A few months later Mary gave birth to a son, the future James VI (James I of England), whom evil tongues declared to be Rizzio's offspring. What happened then? No one exactly knows; the 'secret of Mary Stuart,' a favourite theme of many dramatists, has never been pierced. Feeling her position untenable, and loathing Darnley, she committed a third and even worse mistake: partly of her own free will and partly under duress, she placed herself in the power of the Earl of Bothwell, whom all Scotland utterly despised. Some weeks later Darnley's country residence was blown up at dead of night, and his body was discovered in the flower-beds. Bothwell's guilt seemed undeniable, and three months afterwards Mary wedded the assassin.

Even in the mid sixteenth century such conduct was likely to cause scandal; adultery and felony together provoked rebellion. Abandoned by all her friends, by the Pope, by Spain and by France, Mary found herself pursued as though by a pack of wild hounds. She was taken prisoner at Carberry Hill and carried captive to Edinburgh, where the populace greeted her with murderous yells and disgusting obscenities. Forced to abdicate in favour of her son,[1] she managed to escape, but not to regain her throne. She rode southward at full speed, believing that her one hope lay in an appeal for refuge to the Queen of England. . . . But that queen was Elizabeth.[2]

---

[1] James being then only thirteen months old, Moray was appointed regent.

[2] The fall of Mary Start marked the final establishment in Scotland of the Presbyterian Church, whose rigid and democratic features became more pronounced during the ensuing years. James made futile attempts to establish Anglicanism there, and Scotland remains Presbyterian to this day.

9. THREE PROTESTANT VICTORIES: ELIZABETH AND ANGLICANISM

Elizabeth: 'The woman without men'; 'The cruel executioner of Mary Stuart'; 'The great lady of Protestantism.' In these three phrases some ingenuous historians have thought to describe a queen who is from many points of view mysterious and whose very greatness is enveloped in a halo of uncertainty and contradiction. But no such formulae can summarize that long reign (1558–1603), a reign so powerful and impassioned, so full of events, achievements and personalities, a reign no less important for England than that of Philip II for Spain or that of Louis XIV for France. The English people have reason to see in their 'Elizabethan age' a fruitful and decisive period during which their national genius became conscious of itself in every sphere wherein it was destined to attain the heights of glory. Upon the stage, alike in palaces and public theatres, the greatest of all dramatists, William Shakespeare (1564–1616), added to the patrimony of mankind those imperishable masterpieces that are *Hamlet, Macbeth* and *King Lear*. Among his rivals, though not his equals, were such men as Marlowe, Thomas Dekker, Ben Jonson and Webster. At sea the British flag was beginning to command respect all over the world, flying at the mastheads of Drake and Cavendish, borne to far distant lands by Chancellor, Hawkins and Walter Ralegh. In the heart of the City of London, Thomas Gresham founded the Royal Exchange, and the Thames warehouses received from every quarter of the globe products obtained in remote Hesperides by the Levant Company (1581) and the East India Company (1600). English wool, vying with that of Flanders, was winning a reputation in every European market. And England's tiny corvettes were more than a match for the proud convoys from Spanish America. A splendid picture indeed; nor, twenty years after the death of Elizabeth, 'greatest of the English,' did Purchas exaggerate when he paid her this tribute: 'Thou hast taken from England her crutches; thou hast taught her not only to stand erect and without help, but also to support her friends.'

A close study of this reign will show beyond a possibility of doubt that Queen Elizabeth was not so much obeying the dictates of a carefully arranged programme, or predetermined plan, as following the course of circumstances and her own keen sense of England's need. This is clear, if only from the caution with which she meddled in the affairs of France and the Low Countries, never committing herself too deeply, and supporting one side while negotiating surreptitiously with the other. But prudence, far-sightedness and political sagacity are priceless gifts and rare in a woman, particularly when she is, as was Elizabeth, young, pretty and inclined to coquetry.

She was twenty-five years of age when she succeeded to the throne on the death of her half-sister, the Catholic Mary Tudor (17th November 1558). Although she had waited for the crown with alternating hope and despair, humiliation and tranquillity, she received the news of her accession with true English phlegm, quoting from the Psalmist: 'This is the work of the Lord, and it is wonderful in mine eyes.' Daughter of the charming Anne Boleyn, she was English to the marrow, with light auburn hair, fine milk-white skin, rather large greenish-blue eyes and bright red lips. Slim and supple, despite the ruffs and billowing skirts dictated by contemporary fashion, she had perhaps less beauty in the strict sense than grace and glamour, a glamour which reflected the majesty of the Tudors but bore no trace of that arrogance and stiffness which Mary had unfortunately inherited from a Spanish mother. The English people at once took her to its heart, for the trials of her youth recalled the vicissitudes of the nation's history. Premature experience of men and events; perfect self-control, which sometimes led to stark imposture; unlimited egoism, together with a cold passion for power—all these qualities, served by peerless intelligence, helped to form an exceptional personality. She had been well educated in the humanist tradition: she knew both Greek and Latin, spoke fluent French and Italian, and was interested in everything pertaining to intellectual, economic and political affairs. These are manly attributes, and she would have been no woman had not evasiveness, inconsistency and a vacillating temper counterbalanced her enormous capacity for work and her meticulous attention to details. She would have been no Renaissance princess, no daughter of Henry VIII, had she not loved dancing, pageantry, jewels and sumptuous materials. Her character was indeed complex, and was rendered even more so by a physical infirmity which prevented her from bearing children, not to mention certain habits to which she is said to have been introduced at the age of fifteen by Thomas Seymour, second husband of her father's widow Catherine Parr. Elizabeth never gave to any man the status of husband and partner in her closely guarded royal prerogatives; but she often employed coquetry as a political instrument, and chose temporary favourites with an abandon that was no doubt little more than cunning.

To be queen meant more to this woman than did anything else; she had the most exalted idea of her sovereignty. The Tudors bequeathed to her a system of government which tended to centralize, to dominate Parliament, which was summoned as infrequently as possible, and to keep a tight rein upon the courts and the civil service. Elizabeth's ambitious temperament accorded so well with these trends that she could not but attempt to hasten their fulfilment. On the other hand she was too clever to risk failure by appearing to flout the nation's love for its time-honoured customs and institutions. Her genius made her alive to the reactions of her subjects and enabled her to keep in touch with them. Accordingly, though she had declared in 1569 that after holding three Parliaments in eleven years she would never summon another, she did not hesitate to convoke six more when her foreign policy required heavy subsidies. And even while asserting in private that princes are answerable to none but God, she showed herself ever ready to flatter the common people with a few well-chosen words. 'God save Your Grace,' the crowds would cry as her carriage passed. 'God save my people,' she would answer with her most winning smile. Dutifully served by her great minister William Cecil, afterwards Baron Burghley, in whose judgment she had unwavering confidence, Elizabeth was able to give the Crown a degree of authority and influence which it had never before enjoyed. And that power, sugared with kind words, concessions and a wealth of cunning, was accepted without demur.

Religion, in the eyes of such a ruler, was nothing more than a means of government. Her mother's marriage had led her father to break with Rome. Brought up outside the Catholic tradition, she had learned to detest the Papacy, but had acquired a taste for liturgical pomp. In order to save her life, she had been obliged to pass from Henrician 'orthodoxy' to the Calvinism of Edward VI, and thence to the 'papist' Mass; and these manœuvres, together with her intellectual training, had made her somewhat sceptical in matters of doctrine. Besides, she experienced no spiritual qualms. She thought that it was right to invoke God in order to secure obedience to earthly monarchs, and that the Church's hold upon the people was useful to the State. Meanwhile ceremonial splendour satisfied her love of display and ostentation. She considered as treason the loyalty of Catholics to a foreign pope, but she disliked the Calvinist suppression of the hierarchy and liturgical magnificence. As for such controversial matters as justification, predestination and the significance of the Eucharist, they were a little beyond her understanding.

All this led her to re-establish the hybrid system adopted by her father, a system in which she saw the sovereign's authority over the English Church as the most important element. Nevertheless she was obliged to take account of what had happened since 1547: Catholicism, which had been restored by Mary Tudor, was still practised by a majority of her people; it was also defended by the House of Lords, wherein sat the spiritual peers. Calvinism, however, which had been introduced under Edward VI, had made great progress among the middle classes and prosperous tenant-farmers of the south-east; the House of Commons too was inclined that way. Elizabeth therefore steered a middle course, and gradually, with matchless skill, erected official Anglicanism on firm foundations.

She manifested that skill in the very first acts of her reign. She promised to make short work of 'any attempt to violate, alter or change any order or custom at present established in the realm,' and had herself crowned according to the ancient rite; but she forbade the elevation of the host during the coronation Mass, and allowed the epistle, gospel and ten commandments to be read in English.[1] She avoided adding to her royal title that of 'Supreme Head of the Church of England,' but she substituted the word *etcaetera*, which anyone might interpret as he pleased. In actual fact, however, she had secretly approved the 'project for a change of religion,' which had been submitted to her by Cecil and squared so well with her own most cherished desires; nor did she hide from those who enjoyed her confidence that some measure of force would be necessary in order to silence both Catholics and Calvinists.

In March 1559, despite a resolution by Convocation in favour of the Roman Mass, papal supremacy and the authority of the Church in matters of faith, Parliament re-enacted the law of royal supremacy. Elizabeth availed herself of this opportunity to allow communion in both kinds; but, feeling there was something offensive in the title 'Head of the Church' when applied to a woman, she asked to be styled 'Supreme Governor of the Church of England.'[2] In April, notwithstanding a speech by the Bishop of Chester, who vindicated point by point the orthodox conception of the Eucharist, the Act of Uniformity (passed by a majority of three votes) brought back the Prayer Book of 1552, omitting, however, the 'black rubric' which directed the faithful to receive the Lord's Supper standing, expressing no view as to the Real Presence, and removing from the litany a clause which read: 'From the tyranny of the Bishop of Rome and all his abominable atrocities, O Lord deliver us.'

This fraudulent game was played with the utmost skill, but it failed to win the clergy's submission. Here Elizabeth encountered an unexpected difficulty. All the bishops, excepting only Llandaff, declined to swear obedience to the Act of Supremacy, and were consequently

---

[1] This Mass was celebrated by the dean of the chapels royal, because no bishop would agree to omit the elevation. According to ancient custom the queen could have demanded communion in both kinds, but she did not communicate at all. Soon afterwards (February 1559) she broke off relations with the Holy See.

[2] Elizabeth, as head of the Church of England, treated her clergy with a high-handedness that was often quite entertaining. One bishop tried to prevent her giving certain ecclesiastical property to a member of her council. 'Proud prelate,' wrote the queen, 'remember what you were before I made you what you are. Unless you obey my request immediately, by God! I shall unfrock you.' On another occasion, in St Paul's Cathedral, when the preacher was expressing views which displeased her, she called to him from her seat: 'Enough! That is quite enough on that score; get back to your text, Mr Dean!' Checked thus in his stride, and unable to continue, the unhappy orator came down from the pulpit.

deposed. But among the lower clergy, which numbered about ten thousand priests, not one in ten refused the oath. Fear of the royal commissioners who visited each parish in turn, failure to understand the gravity of what they were required to do and sheer indifference— all these factors no doubt helped to endow Elizabeth's Church for the time being with an inferior body of men, among whom strength of character was hardly the most distinguished virtue. In the first place there was a shortage of leaders. The chapter of Canterbury was looking for an archbishop; the queen proposed Parker, who had been deprived of his benefices under Mary and was living in the country with a wife and children. Now custom required four bishops for the consecration of a metropolitan; but all the bishoprics except one were vacant, so the queen chose four prelates who had already been consecrated and appointed them to dioceses. On 17th December 1559, at Lambeth Palace, these four imposed hands upon Parker, ordained him priest and consecrated him according to the Ordinal of Edward VI, which a special decree of the queen had included in the Act of Uniformity. During the succeeding months Parker himself consecrated thirteen bishops, many of whom were drawn from the universities. Elizabeth and Cecil sought out brilliant students, to whose ambitions they threw open the finest of careers. Thus in 1564 they noticed at Oxford one Tobie Matthew, a young man of twenty-two, whom they made in turn a canon, president of St John's College, dean of Christ Church, vice-chancellor of the university, Bishop of Durham and Archbishop of York. Matthew married a widow, herself the daughter of a bishop, stepdaughter of an archbishop and niece of four other bishops! He delivered nearly two thousand sermons and was tremendously successful. Nevertheless not all these chosen few were destined to give Her Majesty unqualified satisfaction; for on the same visit to Oxford she noticed another promising youth, whose name was Edmund Campion.[1]

The gaps in the lower clergy were quickly filled. Clerics were created by the score, Parker ordaining as many as 150 in a single day! He can scarcely have had much doubt as to their worth, for most of them were ignorant dolts, half of whom had taken wives. But all vacancies were filled, the loyalty of their occupants to the official Reformation was assured and nothing else mattered.[2] It was now possible to enter upon

[1] On Edmund Campion and his martyrdom see Chapter V, section 5.
[2] It is from Parker that the whole Anglican clergy derives; the validity of his orders raises a problem of capital significance, for it affects every ordination since conferred in the Church of England. The controversy lasted three centuries: Catholics maintained that ordination according to the rite of Edward VI could not be valid 'from defect of intention and insufficiency of the words used by the Anglican heretics,' as was said in the answer to a question submitted by the Curia by an Anglican bishop, John Clement Gordon (1704). The result was that no one had been validly ordained in the Church of England since 1559. This fact was repeated by Leo XIII in the Bull *Apostolicae Curae* (15th September 1896): 'In conformity with all the decrees of Our predecessors relating to the same

another stage. In 1563 Convocation presented the Elizabethan Church with its creed, having revised the forty-two articles of 1552 and reduced them to thirty-nine. These Thirty-nine Articles, which are the basis of Anglicanism, declare that Scripture is the one and only source of faith; that the Roman Church has erred in its teaching on Purgatory, indulgences, relics and the worship of images, which contradicts the word of God; that Jesus instituted only two sacraments: Baptism and the Lord's Supper; that Masses, inasmuch as they add nothing to the Redeemer's sacrifice, are falsehoods and deceits; and that priests are entitled to marry. The twenty-eighth article states that, for those who communicate with faith, the bread is a participation in the body of Christ and the wine a participation in His blood, but that 'transubstantiation cannot be proved from Scripture; it is in fact altogether repugnant to the sense thereof; it destroys the nature of a sacrament and opens the door to superstition.' Care was taken as always not to elucidate this delicate question.

A great majority of the people accepted without demur the new religious recantation, and this was only natural. A man of fifty had been offered in turn Catholicism, Henricianism, Calvinism and again Catholicism. A man of twenty-five had learned in childhood to abhor the Bishop of Rome as an avaricious foreigner; at the age of eighteen he had had to revere him as a father; and now he was suspected of treason if he listened to him. It was too much for the ordinary run of mortals. Was it not, after all, sufficient that there remained two truths: on one hand the Gospel, the good news of man's redemption from sin, and on the other obedience to the sovereign? It was for the latter to choose between one confession and the next, and her commands would be obeyed. The Venetian ambassador wrote, perhaps rather too severely: 'The English follow the example and submit to the authority of the ruler in all matters; they esteem religion only in so far as it allows them to fulfil the duties of a subject towards his prince, living as he lives, believing as he believes and, in a word, doing whatever he bids them do. This people would adapt itself to any religion.' Cardinal Bentivoglio [1] estimated that four-fifths of the nation would become Catholic once again if Catholicism were legally re-established, but were at the same time incapable of revolting against an heretical government.

The principle *Cujus regio, hujus religio* was supreme in England no less than in Germany or Spain. To be more exact, its acceptance was made possible by various happenings which shook the English throne,

---

matter, fully confirming and renewing them by Our authority, We do of Our own purpose and certain knowledge pronounce and declare that ordinations according to the Anglican rite have been and are absolutely null and void.'

[1] His view is supported by the Anglican historian Burnet.

and in which religion and politics were closely linked. With a wonderful sense of expediency Elizabeth twice seized an opportunity of turning to her own advantage events which seemed for a moment to endanger her; and by doing so she managed finally to detach her people from Rome and Catholicism,[1] and to impose the belief, which endured almost as an obsession with the English until quite recent years, that membership of the Church of England was a sign of loyalty and the surest warrant of patriotism.

The first shock originated in Ireland, which was attached to the Crown by a personal and feudal link. English colonists had settled only in the east, in a district known as the Pale; the rest of the country looked with distrust upon this handful of intruders. Henry VIII, as we have seen,[2] had managed to force the Act of Supremacy upon the Irish Parliament, but outside the Pale neither Henricianism nor Protestantism had been able to exert the slightest influence. Religious houses continued to flourish, while the mass of the old Celtic people loved their priests, venerated the saints and were interested only in disputes between the clans. At the head of the O'Neills was Shane O'Neill, a vigorous and energetic character. With great skill he won the confidence of Elizabeth, in order to strengthen his influence, and then proceeded to rally all the queen's Irish enemies, perhaps with a view to severing the English connection. The year was 1565, and Pope Pius IV shared the universal sense of well-being engendered by the Council of Trent, whose labours had just been brought to a successful close. He thought it would be useful to make Ireland a stronghold of Catholic orthodoxy on the flank of faithless England. The Irish Jesuit David Wolfe landed at Cork, gathered a body of missionaries in the south of the island, and won back for Catholicism the few upper-class families which had gone over to schism in the hope of confiscating ecclesiastical property. Elizabeth's retort was prompt and severe. Ruthless armies were let loose in the island; and as they advanced, massacring bishops and priests, pillaging monasteries and convents, an Anglican clergy was introduced, to whom their property was transferred. After this reign of terror the queen imposed upon unhappy Ireland a legal system involving such complete subjection of one people by another as had never been known to history. The Irish nation, deprived of its most elementary rights, was literally enslaved; and its attempts to rebel, though backed by Spain, provoked reprisals which only increased its suffering. The period was one of blood and mourning for the ancient land of St Patrick, but an age likewise of glory; for despite the most

---

[1] The 'protestantization' of the country was in other respects very slow. Some estimates limit the number of sincere converts to 1 per cent of the population.

[2] See *The Protestant Reformation*, Chapter VII, section 'Calvinism Mounts its Attack' *ad fin.*

terrible persecution the Irish kept intact their faith, which was henceforward their pride, their hope and their consolation in misfortune.

The same interlocking of religion and politics is manifest in the
affairs of Scotland,[1] to which Elizabeth could not remain indifferent.
Her character being what it was, she was certainly not inclined to
recognize the revolt of a people against its sovereign. Knox's Calvinism
too disgusted this pleasure-loving and disillusioned humanist. But
troublesome political events occurred to influence her feelings, which,
in the case of Mary Stuart, were not sentiments of unalloyed tenderness
and pity. Although perhaps unconsciously, Elizabeth detested many
things about her pretty cousin, who was her junior by nine years: the
delicate charm of that beautiful oval face with its gentle, melancholy
eyes; her elegant bearing (Mary was taller than Elizabeth); her uncon-
strained and spiritual refinement. A fit of burning jealousy had once
wrung from her this frank admission: 'She is lightened of a fair son,
and I am but a barren stock.' Besides, the Stuart descendant of King
Henry VII would be her heir—Mary, a papist and friend of the Pope of
Rome. So when the poor storm-tossed bird came to seek refuge in
England, Cecil found it easy to persuade the queen that her very
presence was a danger and that she must be caged.

The disastrous incidence of politics furnished Elizabeth with an
opportunity to get rid of her rival. The fair prisoner became a nucleus
of opposition to the dictatorial and heretical policies of the queen. The
northern counties would not relinquish their feudal exclusiveness or
their Catholic fervour, and they harboured refugee priests from
Scotland. The great landowners rebelled and marched on York, a red
cross stitched to their garments and the Five Wounds embroidered on
their banners. At Durham they tore up the English Bible and Prayer
Book. They declared (too loudly) that, having won the day, they
would enthrone Mary Stuart, who would marry Thomas Howard,
Duke of Norfolk. But Philip II failed to support them, and they were
crushed.[2]

It was about this time that William Allen opened a college at Douai,
in the Spanish Netherlands, for the training of English missionaries
who would ultimately return to their own country. About this time
also Pius V excommunicated Elizabeth, and John Felton, who had
dared to publish the Bull in London, cried upon the scaffold that the
queen's deposition would ensure the salvation of the realm. Since
revolt, disobedience and subversion appeared to be synonymous with
Catholicism, repression seemed perfectly legitimate, and it claimed

[1] See section 8 above.
[2] Philip's attitude towards the Anglican schism was curious. He pretended not to understand the significance of the events of 1559, and defended Elizabeth before the Roman
Court! In 1560 he intrigued to prevent the Pope sending a nuncio to England in order to
investigate the situation.

eight hundred victims. By means of the Pacification of Perth, Elizabeth hurriedly secured the victory in Scotland of a democratic Protestantism which at rock-bottom she detested, and she sent reinforcements to the new regent Morton. Then she set about acquiring an even stronger hold upon the religious beliefs of her own subjects.

Before 1570 the English laws were fairly moderate. A priest convicted of having celebrated Mass, whether in public or in private, was liable, on the first occasion, to suspension from his benefice and six months' imprisonment; on the second to permanent removal from office; and on the third to imprisonment for life. The person who had arranged the gathering was fined. In order to incur the capital sentence it was necessary twice to refuse the oath acknowledging the queen's spiritual supremacy. After 1570, however, every gesture of Catholicism, even the very suspicion thereof, was regarded as high treason and punishable by death; woe to anyone who brought into the country a document emanating from Rome, to the priest who absolved a subject of the queen, and to the penitent who received his absolution. Anyone refusing to attend the parish church was fined £20 a month, instead of one shilling as hitherto, which meant the speedy ruin of his family. As from 1580 profession of Catholicism was taxed at an annual rate of £240. Adherence to the ancient faith severed a man from the community of his fellow countrymen.

Nevertheless, after 1574, priests arrived from the Continent; though hunted down by professional informers, they visited the indomitable little flock, strengthening them in their determination to have no truck with heresy, but exhorting them at the same time to remain loyal to the temporal head of the kingdom. One of these priests, the Jesuit Edmund Campion, hurled defiance at 'the right honourable Lords of the Privy Council' in order to 'sound a spiritual alarm against the shameful vices and haughty ignorance' which were leading astray so many of his compatriots; and he entrusted to the clandestine press his 'ten reasons for making known the confidence with which he offered to defend the faith in open debate with his adversaries.' To Elizabeth herself he addressed an appeal begging her to follow the example of her ancestors and the heroes of Christendom; and it was for her that he prayed on the scaffold: 'Your queen is my queen, to whom I wish a long, peaceful reign with every manner of prosperity.'

But public opinion as a whole was deaf to the protestations of one hundred and forty-seven martyred priests. Following the arrest of an accomplice and the discovery of some correspondence, the public was shocked to learn of the activities of Parsons and Crichton. The foolhardy intrigues of these two Jesuits were said to involve the papal nuncio, the Spanish ambassador, the former Catholic Archbishop of Canterbury, some English noblemen and the Guises in a plot which, had it succeeded, would have dethroned Elizabeth, got rid of James VI and made Mary Stuart queen of both realms. England shuddered when her privateers told how those of them who fell into Spanish hands were dragged before the Inquisition and suffered the fate reserved for heretics; and fury knew no bounds when it was learned that some criminals had wished to make an attempt on the queen's life. Dynastic prestige, the liberties of England and the Anglican confession were all fused into one, just as, on the other side, were the rancour of the last English feudal lords, the efforts of the missionaries sent from Douai by the Society of Jesus, the ambitions of Philip II and the cause of the Roman Church. This is the climate to which we must return in order to pass an equitable judgment on the tragic end of Mary Stuart.

Throughout her imprisonment, which lasted for nearly twenty years, Mary had never been able to resist the lure of a rather childish taste for conspiracy. Most threads of the complicated and sometimes ridiculous intrigues woven against Elizabeth passed through that lonely room where the beautiful but slowly ageing captive produced little bits of needlework for her jailer. Elizabeth had one weapon at hand for use against her: her share in the murder of Darnley was sufficient to have the adulteress sent to the scaffold by an impartial court. None can tell whether the 'Casket Letters' produced in evidence against Mary Stuart were genuine or forged; nor is it possible to say exactly what part the captive played at the time of a certain conspiracy organized by a party of young fools, in which she was implicated by an *agent provocateur*. At all events Walsingham persuaded Elizabeth that it was time to strike. Tried and unanimously condemned at Fotheringhay (1587), Mary was not executed at once, as the Commons demanded. For reasons that are very obscure, Elizabeth hesitated for three months. When told of the execution [1] she feigned grief and indignation; but she herself had arranged some of the details. The fact was that Mary's removal from the scene had become necessary; it was part of a larger political scheme of repression and 'protestantization.'

Parliament enacted that any subject of the Crown who had been ordained abroad by papal authority, and who remained for more than forty days within the realm, would be adjudged guilty of treason. The whole of England felt itself in mortal danger, menaced by terrible foes. Pondering her weakness in presence of the tentacles that were reaching out to seize her, Elizabeth cast prudence and half-measures to the wind. Accepting the advice of her headstrong Secretary of State, Walsingham, she sent the Earl of Leicester with six thousand men to support William of Orange, welcomed the envoys of Henri de Navarre, negotiated with the Calvinist princes of Germany and allied herself with Scotland in order to protect the Reformation in the island. When

---

[1] A hideous affair: three strokes were necessary before the head fell.

Drake burned the Spanish vessels before Cadiz; when the great Armada, which had made London tremble, had been dispersed by cannon, fireships and storm; when, in short, the project of invasion collapsed, it was not only Elizabeth and her kingdom who celebrated their deliverance, but European Protestantism, of which she had become a kind of symbol.

The Anglican Church had now taken its place among the hallowed institutions of England. Respect for it was the criterion of a loyal subject. But to feel satisfied with her authority and the conduct of her affairs, to be contented with her ambiguous formulae as a sound preparation for eternal life, was quite another matter. And just as she appeared to be winning all along the line Elizabeth came up against fresh difficulties. Hatred of Rome was not sufficient by itself to foster spiritual life. Foxe's *Book of Martyrs* rubbed shoulders in the library with collections of sermons, manuals of piety and the Holy Bible. Since the death of Mary Tudor, Protestant missionaries had returned bringing with them 'purified' doctrine, the egalitarian spirit of Geneva, and ready to follow the example of Hooper who, in 1551, just as he was offered the See of Gloucester, declared the ritual of consecration to be idolatrous. In Scotland they found autonomous communities, governed by their Elders and electing their ministers. They spurned priestly vestments as the 'livery of Antichrist,' and would have no organs, stained glass or impressive and complicated liturgy. With bitter wrath they denounced the higher clergy who accumulated benefices, gave parties and frequented the court. In 1564 Archbishop Parker had reprimanded all pastors who were making themselves conspicuous by the adoption of simplified rites; in the diocese of London 37 per cent of incumbents refused to mend their ways. Moreover, on the outskirts of the Established Church there were a number of intransigents who thought that they alone practised the pure Gospel. These 'Puritans' or 'Nonconformists' were aflame with religious austerity, contemptuous of 'the Devil's bishops' and of the parish priests, 'ignorant as asses and foul as pigs.' The humanist Cartwright gathered around himself the partisans of an egalitarian 'Presbyterian' Church, and a few Anabaptists dreamed of purifying the whole of society. The House of Commons was not without hope of injecting this spirit into the official doctrine and ritual practices, while the new primate, Grindal, refused to ban those meetings at which pastors and people, following the Calvinist example, used to read and expound the Scriptures for one another's benefit.

Elizabeth was not disposed to tolerate the movement. She considered that a reform designed by the Lower House of her Parliament to abolish the hierarchy, set religion on a popular basis and deprive it of its pomp was contrary to her royal prerogative and to the grandeur from which she regarded that prerogative as inseparable. She replied to evangelical passion with political argument, in accordance with the habit which, throughout her life, expressed her inmost feelings. She found an advocate in Whitgift, Archbishop of Canterbury, her 'black husband'; and for him, in 1585, she created a high commission of forty-eight members, a regular Inquisition which could impose the oath and keep an eye on all printing houses. Between those two piers of Anglicanism, the principle of uniformity and the queen's supremacy, there was no room for dissidence; to cut adrift from them was to commit the religious crime of heresy or the political crime of republicanism.

In 1588, soon after the defeat of the Armada, appeared the first pamphlet signed 'Martin Marprelate.' Under this suggestive pseudonym two young intellectuals, John Penry and Job Throgmorton, availed themselves of a printer's obliging audacity to publish some truculent invective against the official clergy. Here was something to interest the populace, something that overleapt at a single bound the narrow circle of the theologians. All was laid bare: the avarice, luxury, gluttony and folly of the 'henchmen of Beelzebub.' Against this was set the picture of an austere Church, egalitarian and undefiled, for which the Puritans yearned. Martin Marprelate made fools of the police, published letter after letter, was silent for a little, then handed over the pen to his son. The government now enlisted the services of John Lyly: his *Euphues* employed Marprelate's own weapons—abuse, calumny, caricature, anger—and the laughter was shared by both sides. At last the comedy was ended. Penry fled to Scotland, and came back only to be hanged; Throgmorton disappeared, and Cartwright was thrown into prison. It was said that Calvinist seed would never fertilize the official Church, and that England would be torn between second-rate governmental conformism and an ardent but suspect Puritanism.

It was certainly not in Elizabeth's nature to worry about this contradiction and to suffer in consequence of this new crisis in the drama of Protestantism. She was growing old, haloed with pride and glory. Nicholas Hilliard's portrait in the National Gallery shows the queen as she appeared in the last years of her life: cheeks plastered with make-up to hide the wrinkles; bald cranium concealed beneath a wig 'of colour never known to nature'; garments covered with pearls, diamonds, gold and silver spangles, and a whole apparatus of majesty in keeping with the quasi-Byzantine caesaropapism of her reign. At the age of sixty-six she would still dance the coranto—then fall exhausted on her cushions. And Essex, the spoiled child whom she had sent to the block for treason, was not the last of her favourites. Behold a painted idol at once grotesque, terrible and magnificent, but one which was, in her own words, a true figure of 'the instrument chosen by God to uphold

His truth and His glory, and to defend the kingdom against the people, dishonour, tyranny and servitude.' Yes, all that was true: Elizabeth had arrayed her country in the armour of Anglicanism and made it one of the citadels of heresy and schism; but she had also made England something of which she herself was the perfect incarnation—a new power in Europe.[1]

10. Situation of Protestantism on the Threshold of the Seventeenth Century

As the sixteenth century, an age of fire and blood, drew towards its close, the third generation of actors in that long drama was departing from the stage of history. After that of the revolutionaries, after that of the preservers, professors and church-builders, there had arisen a generation of politicians, for whom religious fanaticism had been a weapon in the service of purely temporal interests. One after another they entered into a peace more final than that of their precarious agreements. Philip II died in 1598, and five years later Elizabeth followed him to the tomb. Sixteen years had passed since William the Silent was struck down by an assassin in 1584, and Ravaillac's knife had only ten years to wait before being raised against Henri IV. On the threshold of the French *Grand Siècle* the world was in a state of flux; new groups were emerging, and there was some alteration in the balance of forces. What now was the position of those Christians who, at Luther's call, had risen against the ancient Church and agreed to separate from her?

One fact thrusts itself upon our notice and is made plain by a glance at the map. Christian Europe was divided into two enemy blocs. Beyond the ancient *limes*, built by Rome to stem the barbarian tide, Lutheranism was triumphant, excepting only in the Catholic enclave of Westphalia and in Poland, which had lately returned to the faith. West of this line, Catholicism and Calvinism, both aspiring to universalism, shared the government of souls. It was indeed a most lamentable situation, for it perpetuated that cleavage of Christendom which we have seen gradually widening since the fourteenth century. The baptised no longer had a sense of their brotherhood, despite the liberal efforts of a few rare souls, who, like St Peter Canisius, were determined to see in their enemies none but 'separated brethren.' Could it at least be said that a point of equilibrium had been reached at which the hostile forces would be powerless against one another, and the minds of men turn to thoughts of peace? Alas, no. On the threshold of the seventeenth century, in many parts of Europe, it was clear that the gravest problem

---

[1] She died in January 1603, refusing to call a doctor, her forehead against the wall, alone and sullen, in despair at having at the last to recognize James VI, a Stuart and son of her old enemy, as heir.

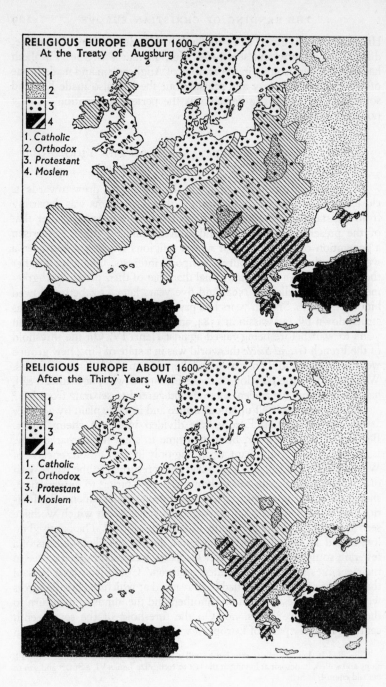

RELIGIOUS EUROPE ABOUT 1600
At the Treaty of Augsburg

1
2
3
4

1. Catholic
2. Orthodox
3. Protestant
4. Moslem

RELIGIOUS EUROPE ABOUT 1600
After the Thirty Years War

1
2
3
4

1. Catholic
2. Orthodox
3. Protestant
4. Moslem

had received no final solution. This was true particularly of Germany, of the Low Countries and of France, the future battlefields. The situation was rendered even more explosive by the crystallization elsewhere of units, both Catholic and Protestant, which seemed to be training champions for the struggle that lay ahead. Generally speaking, the North was Protestant and the southern peninsulas were Catholic. In the drama that was about to open, religion played a part that became more and more closely identified with that of politics.

In the North then four States had witnessed the triumph of the Reformation; Protestantism in one form or another had been made the official religion and imposed upon the minds of men. Inevitably therefore the whole Protestant policy rested upon these solid bases. Denmark occupied a strong strategic position, dominating Norway, southern Sweden and Holstein, of which last her king was duke; she was also the watchful guardian of the Straits, able to lay heavy customs duties on all trade between the North Sea and the Baltic. She had been Lutheran since the conversion (from motives of self-interest) of her king Christian III, and showed herself under Christian IV ready and anxious to intervene in German territories on behalf of the Reformation. In Sweden the adoption of Lutheranism by Gustavus Vasa was accompanied by the formation of a strong independent monarchy. Her choice had been vainly disputed when the Holy See and the Society of Jesus tried to convert John III, and while Sigismund Vasa wore the elective crown of Poland together with his own. In 1603 the old quarrels with Denmark were terminated, and the country was taken in hand by the towering figure of Gustavus Adolphus (1611–32), a military genius and brilliant organizer. Devoting his revenues from iron and copper mines to the creation of a modern army, and his forests to the construction of a fleet, this energetic and enterprising man was destined, in the political and religious conflicts of his age, to become the flaming sword of the Protestant faith to which he was passionately devoted. The triumph of John Knox and the fall of Mary Stuart had made Scotland a bastion of Puritanism. That dour, hardworking and humourless people had found its true soul in the most austere and most coercive brand of Calvinism; and it became, under the leadership of its assemblies of elders, its ministers and its deacons, a kind of spiritual barracks whence the Protestant camp obtained its finest troops. This fact was all the more serious because the little Nordic kingdom, once the traditional friend of France, would no longer play its former part as a counterpoise against England.

In England itself the situation of 'Anglican' Protestantism as imposed by Elizabeth was established once for all by her successor, of whom the Papacy entertained great hopes when he first assumed the crown bequeathed by the last Tudor. James I (1603–25) was James VI of

Scotland, son of the unfortunate Mary, and there was some idea that he would prove himself loyal to the faith of his fathers. Such, however, was not the case. This strange individual with his bandy legs and tongue too big for his mouth, with his dirty hands and shabby clothes, this relentless babbler whose heady theological discourses sent his visitors to sleep, had the same exalted and imperious sense of royal power as had his predecessor. He had written two treatises to show that kings, being chosen by God, possess all the rights, and their subjects only the duty to obey. He was more than ready to accept and to maintain the splendid heritage transmitted by Elizabeth: a Church dependent on the sovereign alone, thirty-nine articles defining its faith, an official prayer-book, and ecclesiastical commissions to superintend both the written and the spoken word. Anti-democratic in Scotland, where the Presbyterian system disgusted him, but where he was unable to make his views prevail over the opinions of his uncouth subjects, he made up for it in England, where he was more Anglican than anyone. He offered to abolish the fines to which Catholics were liable, but on condition that they ceased altogether from proselytism and recognized his authority instead of the Pope's. This was unacceptable, and some Catholics saw no hope except in conspiracy and regicide. Led by Guy Fawkes, a brave soldier who had learned the sapper's art while serving in the Low Countries, they planned to blow up the House of Lords while the king was present, and believed that their subsequent insurrection would be facilitated by the inertia of the mob. But an accomplice revealed the secret; Fawkes and his associates were taken and executed. The Jesuits, who were falsely suspected of having encouraged their designs, were hunted down, and their Provincial, Fr Henry Garnet, was put to death. The Gunpowder Plot (5th November 1605) provoked such horror, and so aggravated public opinion against the 'papists,' that it finally extinguished the last hopes of the Catholics in England. The sternest reprisals seemed justified. Henceforward all Catholics were required to take the oath of allegiance, implying recognition of the king's complete independence in relation to the Holy See. Pope Paul V forbade them to do so, and persecution was resumed; but it was not so bloody as in the days of Elizabeth, because James I preferred to inflict fines which would replenish his coffers, and only twenty-four priests perished during his reign. But all adherents of Rome were dispossessed of a third of their incomes, deprived of the administration of property belonging to their children who were minors, and barred from the legal and medical professions. Mary Stuart's son had become by force of circumstances one of the champions of Protestantism; he allied himself with the United Provinces, intervened in Germany and married his daughter to the Protestant Prince Palatine.

Between these four States where national Churches had adopted the Reformation, and the Mediterranean peninsulas which formed the bastions of Catholicism, the whole of central Europe was in an ambiguous and most disturbing situation. It had formed the background of long, complicated wars which had given rise to so much rancour and involved so many interests that there could not but be fires still glowing beneath the ashes. The confessional struggles had been more or less terminated by religious 'peaces' that were in fact no more than compromises. Each of the antagonists continued to hope for complete victory, and these settlements were essentially no more than political manœuvres. The Church would not agree to a division of the faithful, to a recognition of heresy; she had temporarily withdrawn from the field, but was ready to resume the struggle as soon as possible. On the other side the partisans of the 'pure Gospel' had been forced to accept the limitation of their work and worship to prescribed areas, but they were everywhere endeavouring to gain ground, to make conversions and to place their members in key positions. The age of fanaticism was by no means ended.

Two 'solutions' had been found: partition and compromise. In Germany the Peace of Augsburg (1555) decided that each principality should choose between Rome and Wittenberg, each prince obliging his subjects to follow his own practice; but this ruling left in suspense the case of Calvinism, which was again not recognized by the twelve-year truce signed in 1609. In the Low Countries, while the South under Spanish control preserved its Catholic faith, the United Provinces of the North obtained recognition of their Calvinism, together with that of their political independence. In Switzerland, though without the machinery of official negotiation, the same partition had been effected: some cantons had been won for Calvinism, others remained faithful to the Pope. At a lower geographical and political level similar arrangements repeated the dismemberment of Christian Europe among Churches equally official and equally intolerant.

In France, Poland and Bohemia the violent conflicts had been terminated in another way. Three official enactments had established a *modus vivendi* of mutual respect and understanding. The most famous was the Edict of Nantes; two others had likewise proclaimed freedom of conscience, regulated Protestant worship side by side with the Catholic religion, and conferred upon all subjects alike an equality of rights. The first of these two enactments, the Convention of Warsaw, was passed by the Diet in 1573, on the morrow of the Massacre of St Bartholomew. It declared perpetual peace between adherents of the various confessions. The second was the Letter of Majesty (1609), wrung by his Czech subjects from the Emperor Rudolf II (1576–1611). That whimsical Hapsburg, preoccupied with his art collections and with astrology, was recognized for some years as champion of the Counter-Reformation, but was ultimately relieved of the imperial government by his brother Mathias (1612–19). Driven by the latter from his hereditary dominions of Austria, Hungary and Moravia, he found himself confined to Prague and Bohemia, where, ruined and despondent, he accepted the compromise forced upon him by a revolt of the Hussites.

But what were all these settlements worth? Who considered them final and was prepared to respect them unreservedly? In Bohemia the Protestants wished to enlarge their authority, and their desire for religious expansion ran parallel with their resolve to obtain political independence. In Poland the secular nobility had signed the Convention of Warsaw, but all the bishops except one had refused to do so. Very soon therefore it became necessary to make concessions to the Protestants. In Bohemia Rudolf had granted them the right to elect a special Diet and to employ 'defenders' who would negotiate in the event of conflict with the Catholics. In France one calls to mind the 'places of security' and Protestant assemblies allowed by Henri IV. In Poland, where a majority of the population had remained profoundly Catholic, nothing more than a change of sovereign was needed to reopen the question.[1] Whether dictated by the self-interest of princes, provinces and cantons, or bearing witness to an unusual readiness to admit the idea of tolerance, these solutions were simply the fruit of circumstances, the equilibrium of uncertain forces. The plain fact was that Christian Europe had been rent asunder: the very idea, holy and legitimate as it was, that Christ's tunic should not be left in shreds prevented reconciliation, forgiveness of the recent past and the pacification of souls. Here indeed was a terrible dilemma.

Here we must observe that during the period in question a few men, whose thought was as liberal as it was utopian, conceived ideas of international union, with a view to reviving the ancient unity of the baptized in a form adapted to modern conditions. Hopes of this kind had been entertained since the fourteenth century,[2] when Pierre Dubois dreamed of 'a federation of Christian States' as part of his great project for a crusade. About 1460 George Podiebrad, King of Bohemia, had cherished another scheme, amounting to nothing less than a 'League of Nations,' where every State would have been represented in a council for world government. From notions such as these descended, in the early seventeenth century, the famous 'grand design' which Sully afterwards attributed to Henri IV, but which seems to have been merely the dream of an aged recluse bored with his solitary existence. His 'Most Christian Republic' was to consist of fifteen major powers:

[1] See Chapter V, p. 336.
[2] See *The Protestant Reformation*, Chapter II, section 'The Nostalgia of Christendom'.

the Holy See, the German Empire, France, Spain, England, Hungary, Bohemia, Poland, Denmark, Sweden, Savoy, a Lombard kingdom, the Seigniory of Venice, the Italian republic, the Low Countries and Switzerland. The very idea of supposing these fifteen States to possess equal power must be considered as belonging to the domain of pure imagination, unless we attribute it to a somewhat alarming *furor rationalis*. According to this project the Most Christian Republic would have to agree upon a single profession of faith or, if that were impossible, to allow princes and peoples to choose one of three recognized forms—Catholicism, Calvinism and Lutheranism. A 'Most Christian Council' was to direct the Confederacy, having at its disposal an army whose organization Sully describes in great detail.[1] All these noble aspirations were illusory; none of them ever bore fruit, but they have continued to haunt the minds of men as testimony of our craving for the unity that is gone beyond recall.

Unity was indeed a thing of the past. The temporary peace was becoming daily more questionable at the beginning of the new century during which the modern world would finally emerge in its true shape. Protestantism, to which Sully so naïvely assigned two-fifths of the European States, was beginning to find itself more and more on the defensive. The peaceful counter-attack led by Catholic missionaries was already under way.[2] There was no longer a hope for the Reformation in Poland. In Styria, where the 'College of Wisdom and Piety' at Gratz had laboured devotedly for the cause, and where as many as two hundred churches had been built, the ceaseless activity of the Jesuits and of the local princes was winning almost the whole country from the Protestants. In Italy the germs of heresy had been virtually annihilated. Even in Germany there were ominous signs that the Peace of Augsburg was in danger. In 1583, when the archbishop-elector of Cologne went over to Lutheranism and thereby raised the number of Protestant voices in the electoral college to four among seven, the Catholic princes combined to support the rival prelate nominated by Gregory XIII, and a Spanish expedition sent from the Low Countries helped him to win the day. At Strasbourg a Lorrainer had forestalled a Brandenburger in the episcopal see. Then, in 1606, tension was increased by the affair of Donauwörth. Most of the population of this small free city on the Danube were Protestants, though encircled by

---

[1] A little later Cruci proposed another system, an Assembly of Nations, based on liberty of conscience and with headquarters at Venice, while Pannonius of Belgrade revived the idea of a crusade (see Bernard Voyenne, *Petite Histoire de l'idée européenne*). It should be observed that at about the same time a more realistic effort was undertaken by a number of jurists, who sought to establish a 'Law of Nations.' Chief among them was the Spanish Jesuit Suarez and the great Dutch professor Hugo van Groot, known as Grotius. Their aim was to infuse Christian principles into international institutions.

[2] See Chapter V, section 5.

the Catholic territories of Maximilian of Bavaria. Trouble broke out during a procession when the 'papists' were stoned and driven back into their church. By way of punishing the guilty, Maximilian sent troops into the town—and would not withdraw them. The heretical churches were closed, their pastors reduced to silence and the Jesuits installed in the city. Feeling ran high in the Protestant camp.

As a result of this episode a solution was found to the problem of German Calvinism, which had hitherto been a source of endless complication. In the dominions of the Elector Palatine, in the duchy of Zweibrücken, in Hesse-Cassel, and even in Bremen, Calvinism inspired the most vigorous Protestant thought in Germany, far more vigorous than the Lutheran Churches with their narrow exclusiveness and lack of vitality. Yet Calvinism had been ignored by the edict of 1555, and the rivalry between the Palatine house and that of Saxony had transformed doctrinal differences into open hostility. The affair of Donauwörth showed all Protestants that they were in danger. On 16th May 1608 there was signed the constitutive act known as the Evangelical Union, whereby a majority of the Protestant principalities and cities, both Calvinist and Lutheran, were reconciled for a period of six years under the presidency of the Elector Palatine Frederick IV. The signatories promised mutual aid in case of emergency, and agreed to vote alike in the Imperial Diet. Only the elector of Saxony, an uncompromising Lutheran, refused to join the Union.

The Catholics hit back. At the instigation of Maximilian, Duke of Bavaria, a Holy League was established to include all the small Catholic States of southern Germany under the three ecclesiastical electors.[1] Its declared purpose was to prevent the Protestants from making any further progress and to deprive them of those territories which they had occupied since the Peace of Augsburg. It intervened for the first time to secure the succession of a Catholic ruler in Cleves and Juliers. As this small mosaic of petty Rhineland States on the borders of the United Provinces seemed likely to fall into the hands of Protestant princes, the elector of Brandenburg and the prince of Neuburg, the Holy League stepped in and the emperor Rudolf II placed these territories under sequestration.

The Peace of Augsburg was evidently doomed. The two camps assembled, marked out their positions, sought alliances and levied troops. Henri IV clandestinely supported the Union; the emperor sided with the League. Baron de Tilly, one of the most brilliant and experienced generals of the age, took command of the Catholic forces, and a new war of religion would certainly have broken out in 1610, had not the assassination of Henri IV temporarily paralysed the French monarchy. But the government at Paris would take the earliest

[1] The archbishops of Trier, Mainz and Cologne.

opportunity to work for the overthrow of the Hapsburgs; the settlement of political and religious scores had merely been postponed.

The spark destined to fire the powder was struck in Bohemia. Treaties of partition and acts of compromise could no longer restrain Christians who had now become mortal foes. Mathias, who in 1611 had secured his election as King of Bohemia in place of the weakling emperor Rudolf, allowed the Catholic members of his *entourage* to deny the Czechs those rights which had been granted them by the Letter of Majesty. Still worse, in 1617 Ferdinand of Styria, a staunch adherent of the Roman cause, received the crown of St Wenceslaus. He created a Regency of Bohemia, which was entrusted to ten lieutenants, all of them hostile to the concessions of 1609. Two Protestant churches had been built on ecclesiastical estates among the mountains. Their existence was not provided for in the Letter of Majesty, so by order of the Archbishop of Prague one of them was demolished and the other closed. The ten 'defenders of the faith,' led by the Count of Thurn, combined to resist the closing of this edifice. They decided to petition the emperor and ask him to respect the terms of the Letter of Majesty. On 23rd May 1618 the conspirators entered the Hradshin (the royal palace at Prague), where a meeting of the Regency was in progress. Their intention was to 'follow the example of their ancestors' [1] by flinging the government from the windows. They were particularly anxious to get rid of two individuals, President Slavata and Baron Martinitz, who were believed to have inspired the anti-Protestant measures. After an hour of uproar and confusion, these two officials and a secretary named Fabricius were in fact thrown down from a height of ninety feet. But not one of them was killed; the heaps of old paper and other filth with which the moat was carpeted softened their fall. The second Defenestration of Prague was, however, the signal for armed conflict. The Protestants set up the insurrectionary government of the 'Thirty Directors,' whose first act was to proclaim the deposition of Ferdinand and his replacement by Frederick, the Elector Palatine.

Germany was straightway involved: nothing could henceforward reconcile Ferdinand II and Frederick. The fiery emperor was determined not to be evicted without a struggle, while the Elector Palatine, a fearless soldier, was convinced that a glorious future lay before him. The anti-Hapsburg rebellion immediately spread to Hungary, where a Calvinist-inspired Church included a large section of the people. In 1619 Gabor Bethlen, a Transylvanian nobleman, semi-barbarian but afire with religious ardour, made himself master of the greater part of the kingdom which had not been overrun by the Turks. He had himself elected 'Prince of Hungary,' rallied to the cause of Frederick and

[1] For the first 'Defenestration of Prague' see *The Protestant Reformation*, p. 164.

marched on Vienna. Thus began the new conflagration known to history as the Thirty Years War. In 1620 the Protestants of Mansfeld were crushed by Tilly at the White Mountain, and a terrible persecution fell upon Bohemia. Once again the religious drama, complicated by political factors, was about to engulf Western Christendom in seas of blood.[1]

Simultaneously another dispute arose between the seven Calvinist United Provinces of the Netherlands and the southern Catholic provinces. The matter at issue was one that had been supposedly settled by the partition of territory between the rival faiths. The twelve-year truce was drawing to a close, and the archduke Albert, who was governing at Brussels, and whose Belgian subjects had again become staunch Catholics, thought the time had come to launch an offensive against the North and give the death-blow to heresy. His view was shared by Olivarès, the all-powerful minister of young Philip IV, who ascended the throne of Spain 1621. Among the Calvinists, Maurice of Nassau, Stathouder of six of the seven provinces, was thinking of renewing the struggle. He hoped to found a kingdom for the benefit of his family, and he was supported by the nobility, the working class and the most hot-headed among the pastors. The merchant class of Holland and Zeeland, who had no share in government, were far from dismayed by the prospect of an armed conflict which would enable them to enlarge their colonial interest to the detriment of Spain and Portugal. Consequently when the truce expired in August 1621 the two sides agreed on one point: recourse to arms.

As for France, to whom Henri IV had hoped to restore peace, she was equally unsettled. Despite the Edict of Nantes and its supplementary guarantees, the Protestants felt no more secure than their brethren in Bohemia. Gone was the hope they had cherished towards the middle of the sixteenth century of rallying the kingdom to themselves. If the Edict of Nantes had rewarded the tenacity of forty years, it had nevertheless condemned the Huguenots to be for ever a minority, protected by civil and military rights, but restricted in their religious activities. At this date, instead of the 2,150 communities which had existed in 1561, a royal census counted only 951 churches (257 of them manorial chapels) served by 700 ministers and 400 students in divinity awaiting ordination, and frequented by 274,000 families (1,250,000 souls), among which were 2,468 noble houses. Although it is true that the regulations of the Edict enabled these numbers to increase by a third during the first twenty years of the seventeenth century, the Protestants never represented more than a tenth of the whole population of France. The map of 'secure places' showed that Protestantism had assumed a distinctively regional character. In the north and centre

[1] The Thirty Years War will be studied in vol. vi of the present series.

it led a scattered existence, tending to gather in the region of the Loire, on the southern and eastern slopes of the Massif Central, in Poitou, Saintonge, Aunis, Guienne, Béarn, Languedoc and the Rhône corridor. It appeared in fact to avoid the centralizing influence of the capital. Yet even in that neighbourhood the pastors had care of between twenty thousand and thirty thousand of the faithful.[1]

True the Edict of 1598 had been sealed with the green wax used for irrevocable documents; but the Protestants were fully conscious of its precarious nature, as well as of the fact that it was an unprecedented gesture on the part of a monarchy inclined to absolutism. After the death of Henri IV, and in spite of the Edict's confirmation by the regent Marie dei Medici, they were worried by the change in foreign policy, and feared that the government, having fallen into incompetent hands, might be controlled by ecclesiastical circles devoted to ultra-montanist ideas. Under pretext of renewing the mandate of their representatives with the Crown, they obtained leave to hold their General Assembly at Saumur in the spring of 1611. The 'cautious,' led by the aged Duplessis-Mornay, believed that the better elements of their party were to be found among senior civil servants, magistrates, lawyers, engineers, merchants and manufacturers, whom Henri IV had trusted and who still occupied high positions. They therefore advocated strict loyalty. But the 'Constant' or 'Ambitious,' with Henri de Rohan at their head, wanted additional guarantees that would place them in a state of immediate readiness for war; and although the nobility played a less prominent part than hitherto in the life of the communities, this second view prevailed. The Assembly of Saumur asked the king to repair the defences of the 'places of security' and to pay the full wages of their garrisons. When the government refused, the party was thoroughly reorganized: the religious structure was preserved, grouping churches managed by their consistories into districts administered by 'conferences,' and these districts into sixteen provinces under provincial synods. The whole edifice was completed by the national synod and the general council of Churches; the territory was divided into eight circles, each with its assembly and all subject to a General Assembly. Thus was established, in the most alarming fashion, a 'State within the State.' Its capital was La Rochelle, whose army was the garrisons of the forts, whose navy was the local fleet and whose ambassadors were the two deputies at the French Court. The home policy of these representatives was to defend the letter of the Edict at all costs; as for foreign relations, they could look for support to the German princes, to the United Provinces and to England.

During 1619 Béarn was occupied by royal troops, in order to secure

[1] Their church was situated first at Ablon, and was then transferred to Charenton.

the complete re-establishment of Catholic worship and oblige the Huguenot nobility to restore to the bishops of Lescar and Oloron the ecclesiastical property which Henri IV had deemed wise to leave in their hands. At Christmas 1620 the General Assembly of La Rochelle once again took up arms, and there were small-scale military operations on the coast of Charente and in the neighbourhood of Montauban. Such a policy, which was in fact akin to insurrection, might succeed as long as the government was weak and in uncertain hands. There was no great danger in opposing the regent Marie dei Medici, a dull, egoistic and indolent Italian, or her favourite Concini, an adventurer whom she had created Maréchal d'Ancre. It was also possible to profit by the fruitless agitation of the States-General in 1614, and, after Concini's assassination (1617), to defy the authority of Luynes, who was deeply embroiled with the rebellious nobles. The situation, however, was completely reversed with the coming of Richelieu, a man of iron, convinced that the king should be master in his own house. There was some hardening of royal policy even before the cardinal's official introduction to the Council. In October 1622 the Peace of Montpellier reduced the number of Protestant strongholds. A cunning distribution of pensions and honours won over a few great Huguenot lords such as Rohan, Soubise and La Force. The time was fast approaching when the French monarchy, guided by Richelieu and fighting for its life against Hapsburg domination, would no longer tolerate a Protestant republic within the realm. In 1622 war was raging in France as in Bohemia, Germany, Hungary and the Low Countries. The place which the Reformation had carved for itself in the world was once more at stake. The Christian world was rent asunder, and rivers of blood would again flow from the open wound.

11. PROTESTANT SECTS AND DISSENSIONS

It was not only the cleavage between Catholics and Protestants that brought about such disastrous consequences. There was apparent within the Reformation itself a process which had begun in the early days of the religious revolution, and would gather impetus with the years. It is the nature of a heretic, explains Bossuet,[1] 'that is to say, of one who holds exceptional views, to cling to his own ideas; it is the nature of a Catholic . . . to prefer the common belief of the whole Church to his own opinions.' Unlike Catholicism, which knows itself to be the one true and unalterable faith, the Protestants, each man for himself, followed the inspiration of his own thought in order to interpret the message and revelation of Christ. Liberation from ecclesiastical

[1] *Histoire des variations des églises protestantes.*

tutelage had therefore given free rein to religious individualism. 'There is constant change in heresies,' says Bossuet again, and history bears out his words. The phenomenon of sectarianism, so characteristic of Protestantism today,[1] was everywhere manifest as early as the sixteenth century; and the internal history of the reform is the history of that strange proliferation.

During Luther's own lifetime there were already noticeable trends far removed from his teaching. Alarmed by the excesses he had seen run riot in Germany, the prophet of Wittenberg had invited the princes to enforce an external discipline which the small regional Churches had transformed into intellectual conformity. Bucer had conceived and Calvin organized an ecclesiastical edifice buttressed by a new dogmatic orthodoxy; but it was risky to attempt to stabilize the Reformation by such means, which were so clearly opposed to its spirit. Diversity was its natural law, a logical result of the principle of free inquiry. Thanks to their personal prestige, the great founders had been able to maintain a semblance of unity. Once they were dead, and had been succeeded by men who were often second rate, even that semblance began to fade. Notwithstanding the repeated use of the phrase by Catholic historians, Wittenberg was never 'the Lutheran Rome.' Geneva had been a model, a nursery of pastors, but never an undisputed mistress of thought; it was now no more than the chief town of a Swiss canton.

Here we need only recall the many deviations and variations which Luther had been obliged to resist, in order to preserve what he considered the purity of his faith. First against Karlstadt, then against Zwingli, Bucer, Oeclampadius, and even his beloved friend Melanchthon, he had had to defend his eucharistic theories; and this 'sacramental' dispute had caused him much distress.[2] Against John Agricola, his colleague at Wittenberg, he had had to wage an acrimonious controversy, in which he called his opponent an 'antinomian' (adversary of the Law), accused him of wishing to undermine the whole field of morality, and finally drove him into exile. Then he had witnessed a clash between the two wings of his own adherents, in which Melanchthon and the partisans of moderation were accused by Mathias Flacius and his more violent followers of culpable indifference,[3] of laxity, and even of popery. He had also been obliged to contend with Osiander, a professor at Königsberg, who, alarmed by the moral consequences of Luther's teaching on justification, had put forward his own more nearly Catholic doctrine, according to which it is not faith alone that saves, but faith together with human effort to merit the grace of God. This last

---

[1] There are at present in the United States 263 'religious denominations' proceeding more or less directly from the Protestant Reformation.

[2] See *The Protestant Reformation*, Chapter V.

[3] In Greek *adiaphora*, whence the name given to this controversy.

quarrel assumed an aspect of sombre violence, for Albert of Prussia sided with Osiander and expelled his opponent. But when Albert died a strong reaction set in; it lasted for many years and involved the death of one of Osiander's followers. In 1567 the doctrine itself was jointly condemned by the Lutheran Churches. It is not difficult to appreciate the anguish felt by Luther himself in face of these unhappy disputes, an anguish which he at length confided to his dear Master Philip in these words: 'How many different teachers will the next generation follow? Confusion will attain its zenith.' [1]

With the disappearance of Luther confusion became indeed worse confounded. Justification by faith and the doctrine of the Eucharist were stumbling blocks upon which Lutheranism repeatedly came to grief. What part exactly did the will play in the work of salvation? None at all, said some: 'Man is an inert log' in the hands of God. Others, however, would not accept this view; they claimed to associate the human with the divine will—a doctrine known as synergy. The result was a furious duel between rival theologians and moralists; it lasted for twenty years (1555–75), during which Melanchthon, Pfeffinger and Flacius Illyricus denounced one another as 'renegades' and 'mamelukes.' The Duke of Saxony at length intervened and ended this debate by imprisoning the synergists; but it was immediately resumed over the question of original sin. The 'substantialists' maintained that sin had affected human nature so deeply as to become its substance, while the 'accidentalists' allowed that this wound had not penetrated to the creature's inmost being. Furthermore, at about the same time, Melanchthon himself was suspected of secretly adhering to the doctrines of Geneva. This 'cryptocalvinism' expanded after his death (1560), under the influence of his son-in-law Gaspard Peucer; it caused violent repercussions during a period of thirty years, and the princes were hostile to Master Philip's disciples, whom they regarded as pernicious democrats. What chaos! An attempt was made to impose the Formula of Concord [2] on all German Lutherans, but in vain; unanimous agreement could never have been reached.

The wranglings we have just described all took place within the general framework of Lutheranism as taught at Wittenberg. But it is possible to detect many other forces at work, impelling men to break away more or less completely from the established Churches, and to found little Churches and pet religions of their own. Among these people were the 'Schwenkfeldians,' [3] named after their founder, one Schwenkfeld of Silesia, who, though encouraged by his sovereign the

---

[1] See *The Protestant Reformation*, Chapter V, p. 353.

[2] Drafted at Torgau in 1576, it was revised and recast at Bergen in the following year.

[3] These remote descendants of the Docetists continue to exist in Silesia and the United States.

Duke of Leignitz, was quickly shown the door by the reformers of Strasbourg. According to him the whole universe was a mystical vision, including the Incarnation; Christ's body was not of flesh, but a 'precious substance.' There were also the disciples of Weigel, a Saxon. This man, a devoted admirer of Tauler, Suso and Meister Eckhardt, taught a kind of theosophical pantheism, according to which man, a creature of God, finds the whole of revelation and his principles of conduct in the interior light shed within himself by pure love. Yet again there were the 'Familists' or 'Children of Love,' founded by Heinrich Niklaes of Münster. Their teaching was in some sense a fore-shadowing of quietism, and they spread to England and the Low Countries. On the threshold of the seventeenth century this strongly mystical nonconformity, as opposed to the caesaropapism of Lutheran princes and the pharisaism of official Churches, became incarnate in Jacob Böhme (1575–1624), a man of great intellectual refinement but full of common candour, a 'barbarian of genius' in whom blew the wind of the Spirit and of poetry. Böhme was a humble shoemaker of Alt-Seidenberg, but his true life passed in a succession of ecstasies. Wandering in search of the *magnum mysterium*, but obsessed with burning evangelical faith to which he gave utterance in his *Road to Christ*, he was persecuted as a heretic by the Lutherans, driven from one city to another, yet continuing to write those strange, vivid and obscure pages, which exerted a profound influence on German romanticism and still have their admirers.

More dangerous than these gentle, mystical dreamers were the doctrinaires who denied the existence of the Holy Trinity. At first these 'antitrinitarians' or 'unitarians' consisted only of small groups, maintaining contact with one another but in no way organized. Michael Servetus, whose execution in 1553 had marked the triumph of Calvin at Geneva, was one of them; so was Valentine Gentilis, beheaded at Berne in 1566, and Sylvanus, who was executed at Heidelberg in 1572. The established errors were mere chaff to these more radical heretics. The movement assumed greater significance with the appearance of the Sozzini, uncle and nephew. Lelio Sozzini (1525–62), a Sienese of noble family and a jurist by profession, had made a critical study of the Bible on his own, and had explained to those who specialized in Holy Scripture that he could find no evidence in the sacred text for a trinity of Persons in one God or for the doctrine of predestination. Bullinger and Melanchthon had sharply rebuked him; Calvin had seen fit to publish a stern warning against him. The Italian had therefore kept his ideas to himself, revealing them only to a few select circles. But his nephew Fausto (1539–1604), who was equally fond of bold theories, obtained possession of his unpublished writings, had them printed, and expounded them. The Trinity, he argued, is incompatible with the unity of God, which is so strongly emphasized in both Testaments. Christ is no more than a creature—infinitely perfect it is true, and one whose pre-eminent virtues caused him to be carried up to heaven, but nevertheless a man like all others; for the co-existence in a single being of the divine nature and a human nature is contrary to reason, and attributes to God a pure absurdity. Finally, he added, the imputation of Adam's sin to all his descendants is an insult to God's justice and goodness. Thus was born Socinianism. Fausto Sozzini left for Transylvania in reply to an invitation from John Blandrata, who was tired of seeking a straight way among all the currents of the Reformation. Thence he travelled to Poland (1579), which was at that time, under the régime established by the Convention of Warsaw, a refuge for all heresies; and here he found small groups of adherents who were anathema to both the Lutherans and the Calvinists. Accordingly, within a very short time, the turbulent Sienese had formed a Socinian Church whose teaching was fundamentally opposed to the Protestant beliefs. These 'Polish Brethren' were supported by the nobility, especially in Little Poland; they became organized, with their own pastors and assemblies; and they even had their own catechism, known as the catechism of Rakov, which was published in Polish during the year 1624 and immediately translated into English, Dutch, German and Latin. Curiously enough the Catholic authorities took very little notice of this last word in heresy, doubtless because the Socinians embarrassed the Lutheran and Calvinist Churches, and because they were not the object of any serious public protest. The sect recruited members in England, Switzerland, the Rhine Palatinate and Transylvania. It continues to flourish.

Armed, like Sozzini, with scriptural authority, Theodore Coonhert rose to attack the doctrine of predestination. With Sebastian Castellion, he maintained that God, being infinitely good, cannot but will the final happiness of His creatures, and he denounced the 'falsehoods' of Calvin. Controversy over such matters assumed an unwonted degree of violence in the Low Countries, where Calvinism had just supplanted Lutheranism. 'God,' declared some, 'has from eternity predestined the elect to heaven and the damned to hell.' 'Not at all,' answered their opponents; 'predestination is linked with charity, that is to say, with the good or bad use made of grace by man's free will.' There they were then: 'Supralapsarians' on one side, 'Infralapsarians' on the other.[1] The dispute was transformed into a pitched battle when two professors of Leyden University, Arminius and Gomar, entered the lists, each belonging to one of the two camps. Arminius, a pupil of Theodore Beza at Geneva, had undertaken to refute the Infralapsarians; but he had been converted to their beliefs, and had established them on firm

[1] *Supra*, before; *lapsus*, fall; *infra*, after.

theological foundations. The great merchant families of Holland had welcomed a doctrine infinitely more humane than the intransigence of Calvinism. Gomar, on the other hand, defended strict Genevan orthodoxy against these 'evangelicals' or 'libertines.' So long as the war of independence lasted the adversaries were obliged to restrain their ardour; but as soon as the twelve-year truce had been signed they were at one another's throats, and some well-defined political and economic interests were immediately involved in this theological dispute. The wealthy merchants, backed by the Grand Pensionary of Holland, Oldenbarneveldt, esteemed a religion which clearly distinguished between the spiritual domain and that of business, thus enabling them to make large fortunes with a good conscience, and which was also supported by the persuasive arguments of Grotius. Intransigence, however, represented by small tradesmen, artisans and the poor, wanted religion to dominate the whole of civil life and tried to protect the honest folk of the Low Countries against the spirit of lucre. The entire country was soon divided between these two parties. In the first public disputation (1608) Arminius was declared the winner. But this victory did not put an end to the conflict any more than did his death in the following year; his disciples continued to propagate his ideas with even greater determination, and their activities gave rise to so much unrest that Maurice of Nassau intervened. As he depended on the favour of the masses, he had Oldenbarneveldt tried and condemned: the State Church and princely absolutism had every reason to be on good terms. In 1619 a synod was held at Dordrecht, attended by delegates from France, England, Scotland, Switzerland, the Palatinate and Brandenburg.[1] This Assembly, which might be described as a timid Protestant imitation of the Council of Trent, rejected all liberal interpretation of the fundamental theses of Protestantism. Taking its stand on the rigorous 'Netherlands Confession,' it declared the Arminians to be heretics and dismissed their preachers, eighty of whom were banished. In 1625, however, on the death of Maurice of Nassau, these exiles returned and were granted not only freedom of worship, but also (except at Dordrecht) the right to build churches, which have survived until the present day.

Thus political considerations, which had occupied so important a place in the origins of Protestantism under its several forms, were likewise influential in its development. Nowhere was this fact so plain as in England. If the ecclesiastical framework modelled upon that of Geneva aroused criticism on the part of those who looked for revelation of the Truth only to their own enlightened conscience, all the more inevitably was the Anglican Church, which had retained so much 'popish' organization and liturgical pomp, assailed by wrathful

[1] The Lutherans of Germany and the Scandinavians refused to appear.

adherents of 'interior' religion. The movement began during Elizabeth's reign and was followed by many pastors. On the accession of James I a petition was presented, demanding (i) that each minister be allowed to choose whether or not he would wear the surplice, and (ii) the removal of all traces of superstition, e.g. genuflexion, bowing the head at the name of Jesus, and even the wedding ring. None, however, sought abolition of the episcopal hierarchy and the adoption of a Presbyterian Church. Others, the more radical Independents, abhorred the idea of an official Church. Lastly there were some Anabaptists, known as Mennonites, who completely abandoned the idea of revolutionary upheaval, and expected an inward light to direct their conduct.

All these currents proceeded from the single trend towards the purification of religion. The Puritans, for example, were distinguished by their detestation of personal adornment, of the theatre and of sexual aberration; they lived, as it were, on familiar terms with the bibical patriarchs, prophets and psalmists. James I was not one to approve of such views. He had forced a hierarchy on the Presbyterian communities of Scotland, and he was certainly not going to suppress the English episcopate. At the Hampton Court Conference he declared: 'If you want a Presbyterian Church you will find it as hard to reconcile such a thing with monarchy as to reconcile the Devil with God . . . Jack, Will and Tom will proceed to criticize my actions . . . I conclude then: no bishops, no king. If that is all your party has to say I will force you to conform or drive you from the country.' Convocation made sure that parochial clergy adhered to each of the Thirty-nine Articles, to the Prayer Book, to the liturgy and to the hierarchical constitution; it pronounced excommunication, ordered the episcopalian oath to be taken in the universities and obliged three hundred ministers to reign.

These harsh measures, reduced to the dimensions of a particular Church, seemed absurd, especially as they were applied in the name of a dynasty which, unlike the Tudors, had not succeeded in winning favour with the people. In vain Ben Jonson's *Alchemist* ridiculed the Baptists: the vitality of English Protestantism was to be found not among the official Anglican clergy, but among the puritanical sects, which continued to multiply and whose religious doctrines were closely linked with political creeds. Such were the Congregationalists, whose organization rested on a number of small groups claiming the total separation of Church and State; suppression of the hierarchy; and, for the more perfect establishment of God's kingdom, a diminution of pastoral authority so as to make each of the faithful a kind of priest participating in the sacerdotal order. Later, from these puritanical circles—Independent, Congregationalist, Baptist—arose Henry Robinson's theories on Liberty of Conscience and those of the Levellers, which led to revolutionary evangelicalism.

This sectarian ferment was destined to play an important part in the political history of England during the seventeenth century, and not only in that of England or even of Western Europe. For the persecution of nonconformity by James I resulted in events of untold consequence. Rather than remain in the kingdom and await a change of which there was as yet no sign, dissenters began to leave the country. Many of them settled in the United Provinces, but a few ventured farther afield. There were thirty-five who, after residing first at Amsterdam and then at Leyden, agreed with other English *émigrés* to ask the Virginia Company for a grant of land in its American territories. Their ship, the *Mayflower*, with 102 passengers on board, was driven by storm far north of Virginia, to a point near Cape Cod, on the coast of a humid region which they soon afterwards named New England. On 21st December the thirty-five 'Pilgrim Fathers' founded the colony of Plymouth, modelled upon biblical society, the plan of which was set out in a pact or 'Covenant.' There they welcomed all who, for reasons often anything but religious, landed on those shores. Within a few years the population of Plymouth was increased by three hundred, and other communities were established. In 1630 John Endicott founded Boston and brought into being the colony of Massachusetts, germ of what is now the United States of America. During the past hundred years, thanks to Spanish and Portuguese voyages of discovery, Catholics had extended the reign of their faith over new worlds.[1] Protestantism was now opening up an immense field to the conquering enthusiasm of her sons. This, however, was the work of nonconformists, who, once again and in striking fashion, gave proof that the essence and dynamism of the Reformation were perpetuated in the 'variations' paradoxically condemned by those Churches which had destroyed the unity of medieval Catholicism. Such was the remarkable and, on the whole, tragic career of those Churches which had been thrown up by the religious revolution. They were driven of their very nature to divide and subdivide *ad infinitum*, to oppose one another and to fight one another, by virtue of the very principle of freedom which remained their best chance of survival. It is when we contemplate the spectacle presented by these offshoots of the Protestant reform that we realize the profound truth of some words written by a devout Huguenot, Charlotte de Laval. In a letter to her husband, Admiral de Coligny, she described her co-religionists as 'members torn from the body of Christ.'

[1] See next chapter.

12. PROTESTANT EUROPE

In the year 1600 the Reformation was again on the defensive at many points; it seemed to lack harmony, to be devoid of unity and cohesion. Nevertheless it had achieved one impressive result: in the world of spiritual forces, as in that of material civilization, Protestantism had won for itself a position which, though it might be restricted, could never be destroyed. It had set its seal upon the conscience of mankind: because of it human character and institutions, art and literature, even costume and the manner of living, had become more austere than hitherto. There was now a Protestant Europe very different from, but existing alongside and sometimes interwoven with, Catholic Europe. It continues in our midst.

In every country where it existed Protestantism was no longer what it had been three-quarters of a century earlier, an episodical movement, without deep roots in the hearts of men, isolated from ancient loyalties. Since then a tradition had been created. The articles of faith were now enriched with the memory of heroes who had perished in their defence. The first edition of John Crespin's *History of the Martyrs* appeared as early as 1554; its perusal, declared Matthieu Lelièvre, is sufficient to inject 'a little iron into the blood.' By 1579 this work had reached its fifth and much enlarged edition. The reformed communities were thrilled when they read of the splendid deeds accomplished by women whose courage rivalled that of their menfolk, and who fought like lionesses for the Protestant cause: the Dame de Miraumont, who for so many years wore a breastplate and wielded a sword; Juliette Couillard of Saint-Lô, who had resisted Matignon's troops; Marguerite d'Ailly, who in her husband's absence had successfully defended their castle at Châtillon; or the unknown girl nicknamed 'Colte Rouge,' who had performed prodigies of valour on the high plateaus of La Mure in order to check the soldiers of Mayenne. Popular ballads had glorified these noble figures long before the fanciful and startling realism of Agrippa d'Aubigné had raised to epic dignity the seven songs of his *Tragiques*, that haunting picture of the greatness and sufferings of the Huguenots. Similar foundations for new loyalties had been laid wherever the Reformation had obtained a foothold. John Foxe gave the Anglican Church its patent of nobility in his *Acts and Monuments* (1563). Buchanan and Knox told how Scotland was converted to the 'pure Gospel.' For the seven United Provinces, as for the reformed Christians of Scandinavia, Hungary and Bohemia, the contest for the new faith was inseparable from the struggle for political freedom, both of which were indissolubly linked in song and story. Throughout Germany, Lutheranism had given the peoples a national consciousness for which they had long been searching, and the theses of Wittenberg buttressed the political régime. Meanwhile the Massacre of St Bartholomew, by driving from France such men as Hotman, Doneau and Scaliger, made scholarship the common property of Europe.

During the best part of a century three successive generations had received a religious upbringing which exerted strong influence upon society and created a new type of man and woman. The fundamental tenets of Protestantism in all its forms were, first, fidelity to the sole authority of Scripture and a haughty refusal to recognize that of priests; second, a conviction that in the mind of each and every man the Holy Spirit, as the *Christian Institution* had declared, reveals the truth 'by means of a sense no less clear and infallible than are black and white in showing the colour of objects'; third, the certitude that sinful man, alone and desolate, stands face to face with inconceivable Omnipotence. And these tenets forged characters at once proud before men and humble before God, unyielding in the field of morality, inflexible in their principles, falling short of the ideal through narrowness of mind and sectarianism, yet not without greatness. Florimond de Rémond, first Catholic historian of the Protestant heresies, draws this picture of their adherents: 'They were the sworn enemies of luxury, debauchery and frivolity, which were all too fashionable among Catholics. At their assemblies and dinners, instead of music and dancing, they read from the Bible, which always lay on the table, and sang spiritual songs, particularly the psalms at larger gatherings. The women, with their modest dress and deportment, appeared in public like doleful Eves or penitent Magdalens, as Tertullian described the females of his day. Their menfolk too had changed, and seemed as though possessed by the Holy Spirit.' These words, though tinged with sarcasm, are substantially and in general accurate. One need only stand before the anonymous triple portrait of the brothers Châtillon-Coligny, in the museum at La Haye, to see what the new faith could give to those who embraced it without reservation.

Protestantism, however, did more than mould the individual: it merged with some forms of society and with some important aspects of civilization. A number of historians have praised or criticized the Reformation as the origin of modern capitalism, of democracy, and even of socialism and communism. In such matters we must tread warily, remembering Pascal's observation: 'All things are causative and caused, connecting and connected.' It is perhaps untrue to say that the Reformation and the new economic and political forms are related as cause and effect; but it is certain that there is some link between them, as if the Protestants instinctively followed certain contemporary trends which they felt deep within themselves.

'The Reformation,' wrote Karl Marx, 'was the daughter of that new economy, the capitalist economy, which arose at that time and quickly overran the world.' Weber and Troeltsch consider it not as the daughter, but as the mother, of capitalism. The truth is, no doubt, that it was both. Protestantism was born in a particular intellectual, moral, social and political climate, where the capitalist economy was developing simultaneously; there was a sort of kinship between them. Whereas the Catholic ideal, even when in fact betrayed, urged men to despise the goods of this world, what do we read in Calvin? 'Riches do not come to men on account of their virtue, wisdom or labour, but by the sole favour of God. . . . Riches are not to be condemned in themselves, as some fools imagine. . . . It is even a great blasphemy against God to reprobate riches in this way. The angels bore Lazarus to Abraham's bosom. And who was Abraham? A man rich in cattle, money, kindred and everything.' Here we are obviously in a climate very different from that of Franciscanism. Commercial profit considered as a divine blessing and a sign of duty done is an expression of middle-class mentality. That mentality originated in the sixteenth century; it was encountered by Protestantism, and from her received the mark of justification.

Protestantism also encountered another trend, this time political, which led to modern democracy. Calvin's view of ecclesiastical and social organization was as follows: 'Civil liberty is a peculiar token of God,' and 'an election is a sacred act.' Protestantism offered its support to the forces that were beginning to take their stand against royal absolutism. It was the Protestants who later represented the spirit and the hazards of freedom in opposition to the centralizing policy of Richelieu. It is not quite so certain, however, that true liberty dwelt in the Protestant camp, and that true democracy resulted from Protestantism. Merejkovsky assures us that 'Rousseau sprang from Calvin, and Robespierre also'; but what a strange notion of his neighbour's freedom was displayed by Robespierre! At the end of his great work, *The Political Thought of Calvin*, M. E. Chenevière states that 'there is no spiritual kinship between the Reformation and modern democracy.' This is surely an exaggeration. Protestantism manifested some of the elements which later developed into modern democracy; it was not the *parent* of that democracy, but it did to some extent give the institution shape and colour.

As for social influences, those which we detect in the reformed doctrine are equally complex and debatable. We may well smile at the assertion that 'every great undertaking directed against the moral and social scourges that afflict mankind has been the work of Protestants; Catholicism has done no more than plagiarize and copy what Protestantism has inaugurated.' [1] The truth is not nearly so simple. The

[1] *Journal de Genève*, June 1930; quoted by Pastor Jean Saussure in *A l'Étude de Calvin* and by Pastor Caldesaigues in *Calvin et la réforme en France*.

spirit of the Reformation revealed itself as a social influence in two somewhat contradictory ways. On the one hand there undoubtedly was in Calvin's Geneva, as in many reformed communities, a genuine social spirit, which took the form of charitable works and mutual assistance. But in some other places where the Reformation had triumphed—notably in Puritan England, and even more so in Scotland —there was a measure of contempt for the poor, poverty being the manifest wages of sin; so that vagrancy and begging were even condemned as criminal activities. This twofold attitude was that of an age which had a deeper sense of human personality, but an age in which money also had a very real place. Nor, it would seem, is such an attitude entirely a thing of the past.

Protestant man and Protestant society expressed themselves henceforward in very distinctive forms of art and literature. Chateaubriand, in his *Essay on English Literature*, says that 'the Reformation clipped the wings of genius and made it walk.' His words have been repeated parrot-fashion by many Catholics, but they are completely unjustified. The tree of Protestantism put forth those fruitful branches whose names are Marot, d'Aubigné, Dürer, Jean Goujon, Bernard Palissy and Goudimel, not to mention Bach and Rembrandt at a later date. Fairness obliges us to acknowledge that the Reformation set its seal upon the productions of the mind; it did not destroy them.

With the advance of Protestant thought a literary heritage accumulated in the works of theologians, scholars and controversialists. Luther's translation of the Bible into High German was a very great literary achievement, so great that, in spite of grievous political divisions, it impressed itself upon the Germanic world, giving it a language and a soul. Hans Sachs, the cobbler-poet of Nuremberg, exalted 'the nightingale of Wittenberg.' In France Protestant literature took an important step forward in those scholarly circles where the Reformation had received an immediate welcome. The printer Robert Estienne, his son Henri the Hellenist, Ramus who re-established the cult of Plato against Aristotle, and the learned Casaubon were all members of the new camp.[1] The Huguenots evolved a brand of humanism which was not exclusively devoted to the worship of ancient writers, as was the case in Italy, but associated therewith a veneration of the Bible. It was heedful of new ideas and scientific discoveries; and it expressed itself, with Maurice Scève and others, in a scientific poesy which, though too often abstruse, was never indifferent, excepting perhaps in the delightful prose poems of that brilliant surgeon Ambroise Paré (1517–90). Familiarity with the Holy Scriptures gave Protestant literature its accent, and often its subject-matter as in the

---

[1] Guillaume Budé himself was not professedly Protestant. But his widow and children were and they settled at Geneva.

sacred dramas of du Bartas (1544–90), Theodore Beza, Desmasures
and Antoine Tiron. The influence of the *Christian Institution* and its
stately language was also noticeable. History took its place in Protestant
works with de Serre and d'Aubigné; with the memorialists La Place,
Regnier de la Planche and La Roche-Chandieu; and, of course, with
Crespon and Beza. Pedagogy had a master in the Genevan Pierre
Viret (1511–71). All this material has been described as a literature of
intellectual warfare, militant and apologetic. True, but Frenchmen
should never forget that it gave them poets who were masters of
rhythm, of exquisite wording and of a sonority that still has power to
move. Clément Marot (1496–1544) and Marguerite de Navarre both
drank at the springs of the Reformation, of which their poems enshrine
the memory. Jean Tagaut, Simon Goulart, Samuel du Lis, Bernard de
Montméja and Philippe de Pas are other names that deserve better than
to be damned with the faint praise of an anthology. Agrippa d'Aubigné
(1552–1630) surpasses them all by the diversity of his gifts, his truly
universal mind, his mystical imagination, his power of creation and
synthesis. He will be badly misjudged by anyone who thinks of him
only as the austere poet of the Reformation. His was the beautiful line
'*Une rose d'automne est plus qu'une autre exquise.*' Such was the wealth of
Protestant literature in France. Elsewhere, though with less profusion,
the same kind of thing is discovered wherever Protestantism had taken
hold, driven by the same wind of Scripture, spurred by the same
militant ardour. In England, before Milton breathed all his faith into
Paradise Lost,[1] Lyly had sung of that 'God who is the English God,'
and Sidney had given his life on the battlefield in fulfilment of a poetic
pledge to strive for a victory of the forces of light over the dark Catholic
powers of Rome and Spain.

   In many places and in many ways the faith born of Luther and
Calvin found expression through the pen; so it did in the domain of
art, which is even more surprising. The reformers condemned the
plastic arts as manifestations of human sensuality or as evidence of
grave doctrinal errors. Their ideal was a temple devoid of ornament,
without statues or pictures, where no image would distract worshippers from meditation upon the stern realities of faith. This outlook was
none the less able to command an austere world of art, which might, by
some stretch of imagination, be likened to that created by the Cistercians under the influence of St Bernard's aesthetic principles.[2] The
Reformation thus effected a complete break with the Renaissance, in
particular with the sensuality of the Italian Renaissance whose influence
was very slight in Protestant localities. Instead of theatrical pomp,
wherewith the exuberance of Italian Baroque and the Flemish school

---

[1] Milton was fourteen in 1622, and was already thinking of poetry.
[2] Léon Wenzélius: *L'Esthétique de Calvin.*

was decorating many churches at the beginning of the seventeenth century, it preferred strict accuracy, close observation, half-tints, portraiture and landscape, in which the painters of Holland, home *par excellence* of Calvinism, excelled.

Protestantism then did not give birth to a religious art properly so called, but it did exert a marked influence through its interior operation on men's souls. Calvin was not merely an iconoclast, as some have represented him. He declared the arts to be 'vain and superfluous if they are not orientated to the Word and the Spirit.' But if an artist allowed his whole life to be governed by the Word and the Spirit, he would surely produce works that would reflect his faith. If the Reformation did not provide artists with subject-matter and opportunity it certainly transformed their outlook, and in such a way that there was a real resemblance between them despite differences of technique and national character. It is in this sense that we can speak of Protestant art, an expression of the new Christian soul fashioned by Protestantism.[1]

The drama of the early years, the great searching of mind and heart such as Martin Luther had endured, was depicted by Albrecht Dürer (1471–1528) with a rich but obscure symbolism which tried to penetrate beyond the mysterious phases of this world and discover man face to face with his uncertain destiny. The secret of such men as Luther and Melanchthon, engaged in the terrible adventure of breaking with the past, but retaining their pungent and pugnacious enthusiasm, was revealed in vivid and noble portraits by Lucas Cranach (1472–1553). Less refined, but equally penetrating, was the art of Nicolas Neufchâtel, Zwingli's accredited portraitist; and from the likenesses of Calvin [2] there flames forth all that was most austere, excessive, nay inhuman, in his teaching. Very few of those who held the reformed faith were able to avoid the hard aesthetic discipline of Protestant art. Among them perhaps was Jean Goujon, who seems to have kept his art separate from his faith, and to have been so attached to the traditions of antiquity that his exquisite skill could not bear witness to the faith which he himself had chosen. Another was Hans Holbein the Younger, the direct heir of Italy and her splendours rather than a spiritual son of the Reformation. It was mainly in Holland that the influence of Protestant thought, combined with a marvellous technique (partly borrowed from the Italians but transfigured in the national climate), gave birth to its greatest masterpieces. On the threshold of the

---

[1] Strohl, in his *Luther*, suggested some degree of Lutheran influence on Michelangelo's work in the Sistine Chapel, perhaps through the intermediary of small 'protestantizing' circles in the household of Vittoria Colonna. According to him the image of God sitting in judgment, and the finger of God symbolizing the Creator's power, are related to certain themes of the Reformation; but he recognizes also that they derive ultimately from St Augustine.

[2] Curiously enough the best are by anonymous painters.

seventeenth century Frans Hals (*c.* 1580–1666) probed deep into the soul of those middle-class folk who did battle with such determination for their freedom and their faith. Meanwhile, in a mill near Leyden, there was born Harmens van Ryn Rembrandt (1606–69).

The Protestant soul, however, expressed itself much more effectively in music than in the plastic arts. Music occupied a prominent place from the very start of the Reformation, sharing in the development of its doctrine and in the growth of its Churches. The use of music as a means of action was one of Martin Luther's most ingenious ideas; he employed it in conjunction with vernacular, the language best suited to show his 'dear German people' the hidden forces that dwelt within them. All the reformers followed his example; the Protestant Churches sought to imbue Christians with a sense of community and brotherhood; so choral song appeared to them as a heaven-sent gift, uniting in anonymous concord the exaltation of each and all. Protestant music rejected the organ and relied upon the human voice, which alone was able to proclaim repentance and faith, the sinner's shame and the believer's joy, untainted by the suspect charms of instrumental accompaniment. For a hundred years this sacred music of the Reformation had been linked with its history, its tragedies and its hopes. The Calvinist martyrs of France had gone to the stake singing psalms translated or composed by Theodore Beza and Clément Marot, and set to four-part harmony by Philippe Jambe de Fer and, above all, by Goudimel. The *Wilhelmuslied* had been continuously associated with the struggle of the United Provinces for independence. In the work of propaganda, the canticle, the psalm and the chorale, using sound as the most perfect of international languages, had played exactly the same part as had been long ago assigned by St Ambrose to the Latin hymn. They had evangelized the people in homely fashion, without having to depend upon melodic accents and embellishments borrowed from profane music. Then, little by little, a more studied form emerged from these manifestations of popular and collective piety. The chorale profited more and more by highly finished polyphonic performances, and a wealth of immense talent was brought to the new-born Churches by several great musicians. Chief among these were Hans von Hassler, Eccard, Vulpius, Proctarius and Luys Bourgeois, all of whom had early been converted to the reformed faith. Goudimel (1510–72) surpassed them all: Goudimel, the illustrious victim of the Massacre of St Bartholomew, who was the master of Palestrina.

Thus a new society, severed from its ancient roots, with its own traditions, manners and ways of self-expression, had been established on the soil of ancient Europe, side by side with Catholic society, its mortal enemy. Such was the result of so many mistakes (of which neither side had a monopoly), of so much mutual misunderstanding, of so much violence and injustice. By the end of the sixteenth century the scandalous division of Churches had taken on a character that seemed irrevocable. Christ had given His Church unity as its peculiar sign: 'That they may be one, as Thou, Father, and I are One.' Christian unity, a reflection of the Trinity, was to be the mark of those whose duty it was to pass on His message to posterity throughout the ages. Considered as a whole, all the baptized were responsible for this act of treason, of unpardonable infidelity to the bidding of their Master. Three hundred and fifty years have not healed this gaping wound; they have driven it yet deeper and rendered it more painful. No believer can conclude this tragic page in the story of Christ's Church without a sense of anguish and repentance.

13. Moscow: the 'Third Rome'

Dismemberment of the West was not the only violation of Christian unity. Beyond that half of Europe where Catholics and Protestants treated their brethren in Christ as foes, there existed another region which must not be forgotten; it had been separated from Western Christendom both by the schism of 1054 and by the Turkish invasion. Rooted in the proud conviction that it alone was the incarnation of true Christianity, of *Orthodoxy*, it had, during the sixteenth century, given new expression to its ancient certitudes, and felt itself called to a high destiny.

It had evidently not seen this opportunity among the Churches subject to the Turkish yoke. Their history had followed its course, quiet and uneventful; the fall of Constantinople had not altered the position of her patriarchs as much as might have been expected. The latter were no doubt continually in danger from intrigue and liable to be assassinated; but this was nothing new, and it was not the work of their conquerors. They had been clever enough to reach an understanding with the sultans, who had recognized their jurisdiction over all Orthodox Christians, thus giving them more authority than they had ever before enjoyed. They were at one with their Moslem masters in their furious hatred of the Latins as well as in their determination to check the missionary efforts undertaken by the Jesuits at the end of the sixteenth century.[1] Residing now in the Phanar quarter, they extended their authority from the Danube to the island of Crete and from Dalmatia to the Persian frontier. The other patriarchates, once independent, more and more often received their titulars from the patriarchs of Constantinople. This was particularly the case with Antioch. Here Constantinople had long made a practice of establishing its own

[1] See Chapter V, p. 270.

creatures in order to prevent a movement towards reunion which had originated there. The titulars of Jerusalem, all of them Greeks, were seldom in residence; they preferred life in the capital. The same was true of Alexandria, but in this case by order of the Sultan, who left a mere archimandrite at the head of a patriarchate that was now utterly decadent. Constantinople exercised a like sway over the monastic republic of Mount Athos, where the proportion of Greek houses steadily increased; over the unfortunate inhabitants of Cyprus, who, having gladly welcomed the Turks in 1571 because of their hatred towards the Latins, revolted against the oppressive tutelage of Constantinople and suffered prolonged chastisement; over Bulgaria, where the patriarchate of Okhrida was created for Greeks; over Rumania, where Greek became the liturgical language; and lastly over Georgia, which remained completely docile. The only resistance to this heavy-handed centralization came from Serbia. Here the mountaineers of Tcherna Gora combined against the patriarchate of Ipek, which had been revived in 1557 by the Grand Vizier Mehemed Sokolovich, a Serbian renegade, on behalf of his brother Macarius. The remote and almost inaccessible diocese of Sinai, huddled around the celebrated monastery of St Catherine, was recognized as independent in 1575 and managed to remain so. As for the small heretical groups which survived in several places, they all led a precarious existence, suspected by the Turks, denounced by the orthodox Greeks and often prey to internal dissension. They included monophysite Armenians, who had for a time returned to the Roman obedience but afterwards resumed their doctrines and their jealousies; the Jacobites of Smyrna, who had as many as three jurisdictions; the Nestorians, who had been driven from Central Asia by the onslaught of Tamerlane, had taken refuge in Mesopotamia, and were similarly divided among three rival patriarchates; and lastly the monophysite Copts of Egypt, who were subject to innumerable vexations and hopelessly decadent. This disunion and subjugation of oriental Christendom would present a sorry spectacle but for the fact that in nearly all the Churches mentioned above there appeared from time to time a few outstanding personalities who in spite of everything preserved faith and hope in an age of servitude. It was not, however, to Constantinople that these loyal Christians looked for light, but to a far-off city which had lately established itself as a religious capital—Moscow.

Moscow . . . Since the beginning of the fifteenth century that name, hitherto obscure, had shone with unwonted brilliance in the immensity of Russia, whose soul it was destined to create. Long, long ago [1] Alexander Nevsky, saint of the Church and hero of his fatherland, had

---

[1] See *The Protestant Reformation*, Chapter II, section 'Russia Emerges as Byzantium's Heir'.

halted the Swedes and Teutonic Knights (1240) and thereby given his tiny principality its chance. His descendants, like the Capetians, were regular 'collectors of territory'; they had continued and enlarged his work, profiting by the weakness of the Mongol overlords, the Khans of Kipchak, to intrigue, to cringe, to betray, to strike and eventually to grow in prestige and strength. In 1380 the raids of Tamerlane had enabled them to defeat the occupying power at the battle of Kulikovo. Moscow was no longer a village gathered around the Kremlin, the laughing-stock of Kiev and Novgorod; she was now a capital with walls of brick and many venerable churches, a city where her princes had managed with consummate skill to lure and settle the Patriarch of All the Russias (1326). As a political and religious centre she had become during the fifteenth century fully conscious of the destiny that lay before her; she had made Muscovy a new State of some consequence in Europe and one of the heads of Christendom.

Russian historians tell us that the first of her Grand Princes to leave his mark upon the future was Ivan III the Great (1462–1505), and they are right. This iron despot, this diplomat of feline cunning, who was a match for Louis XI of France, placed Muscovy fair and square upon the map of history. As he set the crown upon his head he cried: 'All Russian soil belonging to our ancestors from the remotest times constitutes our patrimony.' Yaroslav and Rostov, a part of Riazan, the whole of Tver and the anarchical republic of Novgorod came beneath his sceptre; and he even had the audacity to wrest some territory from the powerful kingdom of Lithuania and Poland. Then the khan of the Golden Horde, attempting to revive a lapsed tradition, demanded tribute. Ivan refused, and his troops, massed behind the Ugra, for several days defied the Mongol, who dared not attack. At home he reduced the turbulent boyars almost to the rank of common soldiers, confiscated the lands of malcontents, and, with Greek and Venetian help, built up a diplomatic service, a small standing army and a force of artillery. Moscow bristled with cathedrals and palaces that sparkled with gold and brilliant colouring. Thanks indeed to Ivan the principality had assumed the leadership of Russia, and his name was respected throughout the East.

By one timely gesture he acquired the halo of immortal prestige. After the fall of Constantinople, where Constantine XI, last of the Palaeologi, died sword in hand, the nephews and nieces of the Basileus took refuge with Pope Pius II; Paul II and Sixtus IV continued to guarantee their safety. Among them was a girl of shrewd and impulsive mind, enormously fat and in search of a husband. Ivan asked for her hand, and the Pope agreed, hoping no doubt that so excellent a Catholic would help towards reunion of the Churches (1472). He was quickly doomed to disappointment. Zoë altered her name to Sophia, and as soon as she arrived in Russia, amid the acclamations of her people, she was found to be more Orthodox than anyone else, and the unfortunate cardinal-legate Bonumbre cut a sorry figure. Sophia obtained a good deal of political influence, and she helped to stir Ivan's hatred of the Moslems who had dethroned the house of Palaeologus. Heir hence-forward of the Byzantine emperors,[1] the ruler of Moscow appeared as head of Orthodox Christendom, the flaming sword that would resume the crusade against the infidel, and protector of the Church as he had been of the Byzantine Basileis.

This necessary union of civil and ecclesiastical power, which Ivan had discovered in the tradition of the Palaeologi, had long prevailed in Russia also. While she was fighting for her life against the Moslems and the Latin West her Church had embodied the national soul, to which her martyrs had borne witness. St Alexis was the companion and counsellor of the Muscovite princes, and St Sergius of Radom sent his soldier-monks to fight the Tartars on the field of Kulikovo. The Byzantine heritage, which had been descended more or less to Russia and was now officially received as Sophia's dowry, transferred to Moscow the essential factors of caesaropapism adapted to the Russian style.

While Ivan III donned the imperial insignia, took the two-headed eagle as his arms, and adopted the ostentatious and complicated cere-monial formerly used at Blachernae; and while hired flatterers built up a whole cycle of legend to tell how the Emperor Comnenus sent the crown and golden epaulettes of Constantine IX Monomachus to the grand prince Vladimir, a group of theologians propounded the doctrine of the 'Third Rome.' 'Two Romes have fallen; Moscow is the third Rome, and there will never be a fourth.' Such was the theory, grandiose indeed and well fitted to exalt the Russian soul, which was set out by the metropolitan Zozimus in his *New Easter Canon*, by the pious monk Philotheus of the convent of Eleazar at Pskov, and by the great ascetic Joseph Volotskoy whose writings were very widely read. The disap-pearance of Byzantium did not mean annihilation of the Orthodox Empire. It did not follow that because the amphora was broken the contents had evaporated. 'The Lord may have allowed the Infidel to triumph over the Greeks, but He would never allow the true faith to be utterly destroyed or subdued by the Latins and the Ismaelites. The true faith is eternal; it will disappear only on the day when all things are consummated. But since the world continued to exist for the time being, the broken amphora had to be replaced with a new amphora, so that the living water of faith which it contained might henceforth be preserved from taint. This new amphora was Moscow, the Third Rome.' [2]

Such a doctrine of course was welcomed by Ivan III and by all his

---

[1] Venice was first to recognize him as such.   [2] Brian-Chaninov.

successors who laboured so resolutely for the splendour of Moscow. Theologians of the Third Rome had taken over the Byzantine doctrine and thereby justified the omnipotence of the Autocrat. 'The Czar,' wrote Joseph Volotskoy, 'is by nature similar to other men, but in power he resembles God. He is God's vicar on earth, supreme head of the State and of the Church.' That was the principle which governed internal policy, and it was no less favourable to the Muscovites in the domain of foreign relations. Heir through Byzantium of universal empire, heir of Constantine and of all those Basileis who had fought with such determination for the faith, Moscow could lawfully claim leadership of the Orthodox East against two ancient enemies, the infidel Turk and the heretical Latin. *Fiat Russia orbis!*

The descendants of Ivan III were fully conscious of the implications flowing from this doctrine, particularly his grandson Ivan IV (1533–1584), aptly surnamed 'the Terrible.' This curious individual was a mass of contradiction. Ferocious tyrant and morbid executioner though he was, he was nevertheless deeply versed in Scripture and the Fathers, as well as in literature both ancient and modern; he was also interested in the arts and even composed music. A debauchee long abandoned to sensuality and drink, he would nevertheless quite suddenly, as it were, rise above himself and with the lucidity of genius make the very decisions of which the interests of his throne stood in most urgent need. He was at once a Mongol, a Renaissance prince, a perverted aesthete and a Byzantine autocrat. When he decided to marry he sent for a thousand 'fiancées' selected from the most beautiful girls in Russia, and threw one of them his handkerchief, as was done in a Turkish harem; yet he would engage in learned conversation upon moral and mystical theology with the heads of his Church. This alarming man was the exact contemporary (and in various respects the equal) of Michelangelo, Calvin, Ignatius of Loyola, Cortez, Pizarro and many other outstanding figures. He continued his grandfather's work at every level. By continually increasing his armed strength, and hurling his forces beyond the hitherto narrow limits of the principality of Moscow, Ivan the Terrible advanced in every direction and absorbed the last independent States of the Russian plain—Riazan, Kazan, Astrakhan. He founded many new cities, among them Ufa, Samara, Saratov, Briansk, Voronesh, and even Archangel in the far north. He pushed across the Urals into Siberia, and ended by ruling an empire which extended from the White Sea to the Caspian, from Lithuania to the Yenisei. At home he made enormous strides towards despotic centralization, state-socialism and police organization. The first ministries and the first nucleus of a standing army date from this period. A special class of six thousand men known as the Oprichnina, who combined the duties of bodyguard, police, senior civil servants and courtiers, rode all over

Russia with a dog's head and a broom hanging from their saddles, and were the instruments of a frightful but none the less efficient government. The reign of Ivan IV was as great as it was terrible.

In 1547 he officially adopted the title of *tsar* or *czar* (Caesar). This was intended to manifest his increase of power. It was already employed in Muscovite diplomacy, it had been used by Maximilian and the Doge of Venice as a mark of respect towards his father, and had even appeared on coinage; but it was not as yet in common use. Monastic scribes too prepared a fantastic genealogy linking Ivan and his ancestors with the Emperor Augustus! In 1561 the Patriarch Joseph of Constantinople, happy to be able to give the Orthodox Church this political and sentimental advantage, recognized and confirmed the monarch as 'Tsar and Grand Prince, Autocrat of Great Russia.' The magnificent ceremonial of Ivan's consecration proclaimed his glory; so did the youthful power of a crown which was now hallowed by Holy Church herself.

This did not mean, however, that relations were always good between the Church and the despot. It must be acknowledged, to the honour of the Russian clergy, that some of its members dared to protest against Ivan's abominable cruelty. The saintly Prior Philip of Solwotzk, who for thirty years had been the wonder of Russia on account of his fervour and austerity, was advanced to the metropolitan see of Moscow; but having spoken his mind in no uncertain terms, he was deposed, imprisoned in the convent of Tver, and then strangled by order of the sovereign. More fortunate was Nicholas, one of the *yurodivye*, whose ascetic life compelled admiration; he called the Czar a 'cannibal' to his face without being immediately cut down. But such cases were exceptional: by and large the vassalization of the Church, her complete subjection to the secular power, continued uninterruptedly through the reign of Ivan the Terrible. Besides, was he not the living embodiment of divine authority delegated upon earth?

The Byzantine character of Russia was still further accentuated by her ritual, liturgy, costumes and architecture; all of these were inherited by the Third Rome from the Second, together with some Asiatic and Tartar elements. The Czar, whose ceremonial robes were exact copies of priestly vestments, was henceforward the real head of the Church, overshadowing the metropolitan, presiding over synods by his deputies and interfering as he pleased in religious affairs. The territorial expansion of Moscow had all the outward likeness of a crusade, which the Church could only applaud. On one occasion, for a few months, the Orthodox faithful might have been disturbed by the attitude of their Caesar-Pope. He went so far as to say that he would make overtures to Rome, negotiate with the Pope and agree to union of the Churches. But this was just a manœuvre in the best Asiatic style, intended merely to secure the services of the legate Possevino in negotiating a necessary peace with Poland. Once that peace was signed he dismissed the Jesuit and reverted to his normal policy. The alliance of throne and altar, or rather the fusion of the two powers, was so valuable to Ivan IV that he could never seriously have contemplated renouncing it.

Another step in the same direction was taken during the next reign. Once the tyrant was dead,[1] *de facto* power and then the throne itself passed into the hands of an ambitious boyar, a member of the Oprichnina, a man of luminous intelligence but tigerish ferocity: Boris Godounov, whom Moussorgsky's opera has made famous. Acting first in the name of his guileless brother-in-law Czar Fyodor, and then as sole master (1578–1605), he set himself to continue the work of Ivan IV both as regards home policies and territorial expansion, fortifying the Don-Terek line and preparing for the annexation of Georgia. In 1588 the Patriarch Jeremiah of Constantinople visited Moscow to ask for support and solicit alms. Boris Godounov seized this opportunity. Harassed by the court and deluded with promises, the poor petitioner agreed to an unconscionable decision which was in fact far beyond his power: he raised Moscow to the status of an independent patriarchate and appointed to this newly created see one Job, a creature of Godounov. Russian gold, cleverly distributed, dispelled the qualms of conscience expressed by a Greek council held at Constantinople. This was an event of capital importance: it made the Russian Church autocephalous, the equal of Byzantium and other glorious patriarchal sees and the true leader of Orthodoxy against Rome. It need hardly be said that, though loaded with temporal favours, possessing enormous estates [2] and governing thousands of serfs, the patriarchs remained none the less mere creatures of the Tsar, subject to his every whim, backing his policies and turning a blind eye to the vices of drunkenness, idleness and cupidity that were becoming ever more deeply rooted among the clergy and the people.

For Russian Christianity in general revealed (and far more blatantly) the same blemishes as had disfigured the Western Church previous to its reform by the Council of Trent. The morals of the clergy were at a very low ebb. Parish priests, most of whom came of peasant families, were treated by the landowners almost as peasants themselves; and they were almost as ignorant and given to drink as the common herd of moujiks. The monasteries as a whole were completely decadent, even those which had profited long ago by the reform of St Sergius and which preserved the memory of a fervent past. Ignorance was rife; apart from the New Testament, monks were too often acquainted with

---

[1] The manner of Ivan's death was horrible: his flesh began to decompose while he was still alive.

[2] At this time the Church held about one-third of the country.

nothing but scraps of the Old and extracts from the Fathers contained in such anthologies as *The Pearl*, *The Emerald* and *The Golden Wave*. There was no solid system of dogmatic theology, despite the endeavours of Joseph of Volokolamsk, and almost no religious literature excepting hagiography which was full of legend. When the community of Solovsky decided to write the lives of their holy founders, Zosimus and Sabentius, they found only one Serbian monk capable of doing the work correctly.

All this did not mean that there were no exceptions, no bright spots in an otherwise gloomy picture. Like the West at its worst moments of degradation, Holy Russia could still show a few personalities who saved the honour of the Church and of the faith. Such were Maximus the Greek, a former monk of Mount Athos, who took an active part in the struggle against the 'judaizers' and the *strigolniki*;[1] Joseph of Volokolamsk, whose *Illumination* was the earliest Russian venture into theology; the metropolitan Macarius, whose enormous hagiographical collection, entitled *Great Readings*, has remained popular ever since. All these men represent a considerable intellectual revival. The Council of One Hundred Chapters busied itself with laying down the principles of a timely sacerdotal reform, but those principles were scarcely applied. A few monastic circles had produced souls of sublime spiritual grandeur. In the depths of forests beyond the Volga holy ascetics, of whom St Nil Sorsky is most notable, protested against the way men of God forgot their vows of poverty and engaged in worldly affairs. In many places also the *startzy* practised a contemplative asceticism which made a deep impression on the people. St Philip of Solwotzk, the heroic metropolitan who fell victim to the rage of Ivan the Terrible, was remembered for his charity and compassion. And almost everywhere one met those *yurodivye*, those 'fools of Christ,' a kind of biblical prophet, who, despising money and ease as well as bodily cleanliness, dared to proclaim the truth of God to all and sundry, great and small, rich and poor, and to lash them with bitter reproaches. At Moscow the magnificent church built by Ivan IV still enshrines the memory of their most illustrious member, Vassili the Blessed. These were noble exceptions, but exceptions none the less, serving to emphasize the mediocrity that prevailed among the ranks of the clergy. As for the people themselves, provided they attended the offices, no one took offence if they wallowed dead-drunk in the mud or were quick to draw their daggers in a quarrel. Men, after all, were poor sinners whom God always pardoned if they had humble hearts! The Church, which guaranteed their orthodoxy, promised to all her faithful salvation in return for their submission—a characteristic feature of the Russian mentality even today.

[1] See *The Protestant Reformation*, Chapter VII, section 'In the East the Greek and Russian Churches Reject Protestantism Absolutely'.

Thus did Moscow, the 'Third Rome,' capital of the true faith and substitute of Constantinople as head of the eastern Church, assure its unity. Like Catholicism, and like it heir of the Roman Empire, Russian Orthodoxy offered in this massive and monarchical unity a striking contrast to the dismemberment of the Protestant Churches. But the great difference between the Russian Church and that of Rome was that the latter was universal and the former imperial. Catholicism was open to all men, without distinction of nationality or race. Orthodoxy, on the other hand, being more and more closely identified with Moscow, had the empire as its framework; it was universalist as the empire itself, that is to say, as the empire's political ambitions. There emerged a kind of Russian messianism, whose fundamental tenet was that Holy Russia, the Third Rome, was sole witness and herald of genuine Christianity, and that by aspiring to universal dominion she was serving the interests of God. Between the Catholic Church and a Church which took this view of its mission there was a great gulf fixed, such as had never existed between Rome and Byzantium.

The events which marked the beginning of the seventeenth century managed to translate this division into explicit terms. Boris Godounov, in the closing years of his reign, faced the challenge of an enigmatic adventurer pretending to be the czarevich Dimitri who had been assassinated by his order. Then, after Boris's death and the murder of this first 'false Dimitri' in a riot, there appeared a second, who was certainly an impostor. He was recognized by the other's widow and supported by an uprising of the masses. This dreadful state of affairs continued until March 1613, when a national coalition brought to the throne Michael Romanov, a young nobleman fifteen years of age, whose father was a churchman and related to the family of the earlier sovereigns. This was the 'Time of Dissensions,' of which Russian historians speak with nothing but shame and sorrow.

Now during the whole of this unhappy period religious and political affairs were interlocked. In order to obtain subsidies and troops from Poland the first 'false Dimitri' became a Catholic, married a Catholic and assured the nuncio that when he became czar he would bring back his Church to union with Rome. This betrayal of the national ideal was largely responsible for the public wrath unleashed against him, which ended in a scene of butchery. His body was forced piecemeal into the mouth of a cannon and literally vaporized. Soon afterwards the Poles, taking advantage of the anarchy reigning at Moscow, advanced as far as the capital and secured the election of Ladislaus, a young prince of their own race and religion. It was against this intrusion of the Polish Catholics that the national and religious conscience of Russia eventually turned. The Church played a leading part in this episode; Russian minds and hearts were uplifted by the sight of the Patriarch

Hermogenes urging them into the struggle with fiery appeal and roaring encouragement in face of the Polish charge, as also by that of the monastery of St Sergius resisting the enemy as though it were a fortress. Although it started at Nijni Novgorod at the instigation of one Minim, a butcher, and was then supported by Prince Pojarsky's troops, the movement of national liberation had also the character of an upsurge of loyalty to the Orthodox faith and Holy Russia.

Hatred of the Latins as aggressors, usurpers and heretics would henceforth be one of the fundamental articles of the Russian creed. It was in terms of these disastrous images that the people nurtured by the Orthodox Church would henceforth think of Rome, her dogmas and her customs; and many legends, of which there are traces even in Dostoyevsky, would represent her as first of the Powers of Darkness, tool of Satan. In the East, as in the West, the sixteenth century closed with the dreadful scene of Christendom in shreds and of permanent rupture. Would the Seamless Garment ever regain its unity?

CHAPTER IV

DE PROPAGANDA FIDE

1. CATHOLICISM ATTAINS WORLD STATURE

ON 3rd December 1552 a Catholic priest lay dying on a little island off the Chinese coast in solitude and dereliction, his body exhausted, his soul filled with grief. His name was Francis Xavier, and he belonged to that first party of Christ's soldiers whence arose the Society of Jesus, which was in the forefront of battle then as it is today. If this man had been asked why he had come to die there, at the other end of the world, and what was the meaning of his hidden sacrifice, he would no doubt have answered quite simply with these words from the Gospel: 'Go ye and teach all nations.' *All* nations. Our Lord's message was not intended exclusively for westerners, or even for those whose skin is white; it is addressed, *without exception*, to everyone upon earth who has a soul created in the resemblance of God and redeemed by the shedding of blood on Calvary. Such was the motive of St Francis Xavier. Such also was the motive which, at the same time, among unknown peoples and in far-off savage lands, was driving so many other men, adventurers of Christ, to run the same risks and to bear the same message to the world, a message in testimony of which many of them laid down their lives.

Here we have one of the most astonishing and most admirable features of the Church's history in this age of the Renaissance and the Reformation. Though unable to deny that at least one-third of her ancient home had collapsed, Mother Church would not allow herself to become exclusively preoccupied with the tasks of reconstruction and defence. She did more than strive to purify herself in the waters of Trent, more even than strive to nurture sanctity within her own bosom. Though still shaken by the religious revolution, she stood erect and faced the world; conscious as never before of her doctrine of expansion, she sent the best of her sons to lay new foundations. What she had now lost in Europe she would recover elsewhere, all over the world, in a future for which she had already started to prepare.

The idea of the mission, as we now understand the word, originated early in the thirteenth century, in the soul of St Francis of Assisi.[1] Since the crusade had ended in failure Francis wished to see it replaced

---

[1] See *Cathedral and Crusade*, Chapter XII, sections 4-6.

with the true tradition of Christ's conquerors, witnesses unarmed but with hearts full of love; and he himself set an example in that voyage to Egypt, where he made so deep an impression on the Sultan. His spiritual sons took up his idea, some of them trying to give it doctrinal standing, others putting it into practice. Not many years passed before the young Order of Minors had its martyrs, fallen to baptize the soil of Africa with their blood. The whole thirteenth century was a time of wonderful missionary endeavour, even in the heart of Asia, in the territories of the Great Khan and the Chinese emperor. In 1307 John of Monte-Corvino was made Archbishop of Pekin; a little later Odoric of Pordenone did good work in Persia, Ceylon, Java and China.

Another of these Franciscans was the mysterious and fascinating Raymond Lull, *Doctor Illuminatus*, an enthusiastic inquirer into the secrets of the 'great art,' but also a profound theorist of the missionary idea and an eminent teacher in the first missionary college, who received the crown of martyrdom after an adventurous and dangerous life. Dominicans also, faithful to the admonitions of St Thomas Aquinas, shouldered the great evangelical task. Persia and Armenia witnessed their white-robed members installed at the head of newly founded dioceses, and Fr Jourdain de Sévérac was appointed Bishop of Gulam in India.

During the second half of the fourteenth and most of the fifteenth century this magnificent progress was interrupted. By a remarkable coincidence numerous events both in Europe and in Asia combined to halt Christian expansion. The East suddenly awoke and assumed a hostile attitude. The Turks embarked upon their great military enterprises without provoking much reaction in the Christian camp: Bajazet's victory over the Hungarians at Nicopolis in 1396, and the fall of Constantinople itself in 1453, caused less of a stir (and less missionary effort in consequence) than did the catastrophe of Manzikert in 1071. Control of the Mediterranean passed into Ottoman hands without any counter-attack by the West. In remotest Asia the Mongol dynasty of Yuan, which had welcomed the Christians to China, collapsed in 1368 owing to the nationalist revolution of the Mings. A wave of xenophobia engulfed yellow Christendom, and it is not known whether the last Archbishop of Pekin, William of Prato, who was appointed by Urban V in 1370, ever managed to reach his post. Christians of China took refuge in the mountains, where they lost contact with the priesthood; their religion gradually languished, and by the time Fr Ricci found small groups of them in the sixteenth century, all they retained of their former faith was the custom of making the sign of the Cross over their food.

While missionary journeys were rendered impossible by these two series of events, Western Europe had foundered in chaos. The Hundred

Years War, the anarchical state of Italy, the Exile of Avignon, the Great Schism and the conciliar crisis were all destined to dry up the missionary source. At such a time the popes could not undertake the work of evangelization ordained by Christ. They were too busy defending their rights, their immediate interests and their very existence; and when they returned to Rome, as Erasmus mockingly observed, 'they left that work to St Peter and St Paul, who had the time, and kept for themselves the display and the pleasures.' We can hardly be surprised that in such conditions previous gains were everywhere lost. All the seed sown during the past hundred years was now represented by a few poor Catholic groups in the Indies, Persia, and Armenia; in Palestine by the gallant Franciscans who had had custody of the Holy Place since 1342; in Moslem Africa by the heroic efforts of Trinitarians and Brothers of Mercy among the slaves and captives, and even by those of certain captives themselves.[1]

The situation was completely different towards the end of the fifteenth century and throughout the sixteenth. Inertia and insolvency gave place to a wonderful upsurge of enthusiasm, which produced some impressive results. It seems that conscience was awakening in the bosom of the Church, forcing her to come to grips with her apostolic duties. Why was this? No doubt there were purely temporal reasons; the 'great discoveries' were enlarging the world, opening up ocean routes and new fields for the apostolate of would-be missionaries. The Spaniards and Portuguese, whose sailors and merchants were winning overseas empires, had so lively a faith that they could not help associating the Gospel cause with their material ambitions. Later the missions were hampered by political rivalry between the nations of Europe, by jealous mistrust of the Portuguese, and also by the piracy of Protestant adventurers from England and the Low Countries; but there can be no doubt that they derived much benefit at this early stage from their political links. Political considerations alone, however, do not explain their revival.

Here is an extraordinary fact, which throws further light upon the significance of that great spiritual crisis which marked the sixteenth century. During this decisive period the Catholic soul deepened its foundations and recovered its old loyalties which had been forgotten or betrayed. At the same time, while thus engaged, it experienced once more the apostolic urge which is part and parcel of the faith. The same impulse which carried St Philip Neri, St Ignatius of Loyola and St Teresa to the highest spiritual peaks, drove courageous hearts across the world, bearing the message of salvation to all mankind. The story

---

[1] Among those many unfortunates who bore witness to their faith in the prisons of Islam was Blessed Antoine Neyrot, a Dominican. Having apostatized while a slave at Tunis, he repented and suffered martyrdom in 1460.

of the missions is one with that of the Catholic Reformation, of
ecclesiastical reorganization and of mystical expansion; it is their logical
consequence and even, in a sense, their consecration.

It is noteworthy that Protestantism revealed no such missionary
impetus. One might have expected that those young Churches, born
of religious revolution, would have sought to bring their principles to
the non-Christian. But this was not so; Protestant leaders even showed
themselves hostile to any form of evangelization. Luther explicitly
declared that 'the other sheep' mentioned in the parable of the Good
Shepherd had long been in the fold, and that it was vain to seek them
far afield; the true mission must be conducted within a paganized
Church which needed to be brought back to Christianity. Moreover,
according to the doctrine of predestination, were not pagans, Turks
and Jews in their present state by God's will? Why oppose that will?
Calvin thought no differently. According to him zeal should not lead
us to canvass the intentions of Providence; we must, 'in order to
employ ourselves in God's service, wait for the door to be opened by
His hands.' It is not surprising that with such an outlook the various
brands of Protestantism had practically no missionaries nor a missionary doctrine.[1]

The Catholic attitude was quite different. All those who remained
faithful to the Roman Church, even those who criticized her severely,
took quite another view of their duty towards the pagans. Christian
humanists, in whom the sense of universalism was doubly rooted, felt a
powerful incentive to support the missions. 'How vast remains the
field where the Gospel seed has never been sown,' wrote Erasmus;
'travellers tell of distant lands, of gold and precious stones, but it
would be a greater triumph to bring them the wisdom of Christ, more
precious than gold, and the pearl of the Gospel which is worth all the
riches of the earth. Up then, you heroic leaders of the army of Jesus
Christ!' he cried with unaccustomed warmth. 'Put on the helmet of
salvation, the breastplate of piety; take the shield of faith and the sword
of the Spirit which is the word of God. And clad thus in mystical
armour, go forth to preach the Gospel of peace.'

Many men responded to such noble exhortations. A regular doctrine
of the missions was elaborated in a series of books, which, though of
unequal value, were all inspired by the same apostolic spirit. In 1516 a

---

[1] There were a few rare exceptions. These included some Calvinists who were brought
to Brazil by Villegagnon in 1556, but soon lost heart; Adrian Saravia, a professor of
Leyden, who expounded the duty of apostleship in a treatise which was opposed by
Theodore Beza; Pater (again at Leyden), Justus Heurnius who declared that 'the colonies
have not been given to the Dutch to be exploited, but in order to receive from them the
word of God.' In 1662, at Middelburg, appeared William Trelink's pamphlet *Ecce Homo*,
which favoured the missionary idea, and Anthony Walaens drew up plans for a Protestant
missionary training school. All these, however, were furtive trends.

treatise by the Dominican Isidore de Isolanis joyfully claimed for 'the Empire of the Church Militant' the whole world, even the remotest islands. In 1532 the *Epitome* of Nicholas Herborn, a Franciscan, explained the methods to be used for the conversion of pagans. Somewhat later, and for many years, the teaching of that great master of Salamanca, Francisco de Vittoria, advocated peaceful evangelization instead of conquest by violence. In 1574 appeared the Franciscan Focher's *Itinerarium*, a manual for missionaries, which was followed ten years later by Luis de Granada's splendid treatise on *The Reasons for Catechesis of the Indians*. By the end of the sixteenth century the Church possessed regular missionary compendia, thanks mainly to the Jesuits, who had engaged in this great adventure almost from their foundation. Fr Acosta's *How to Procure Faith for the Indians* (1584) had a large circulation; but the Carmelite Prior of Brussels, Thomas of Jesus, also wrote his *Stimulus Missionum* (1610) and his bulky treatise *For Procuring Salvation for all Nations*. These works were part of a widespread intellectual effort which placed missionary work on secure foundations and, above all, prevented it from becoming, as it might otherwise have done, dependent on the secular powers. Gradually there emerged the idea that Rome should have control of the missions as of all else in the Church. Once the dignity and authority of the Holy See had been restored through the united efforts of the Council of Trent and several popes, this idea would naturally take concrete shape and produce the famous Congregation *De Propaganda Fide*, for Propagation of the Faith.[1]

This work in the sphere of doctrine would have been useless but for the labours of many brave men who simultaneously translated theory into practice. Thus was written during the sixteenth century—an amazing century so rich in contrasts—one of the finest chapters in the history of the Church, the beginning of the missions in their present-day form. Catholicism attained world stature amid countless exciting, heroic and often bloody adventures.

2. THE WORLD ENLARGED AND THE NEW EMPIRES

The world had indeed grown greater. The end of the fifteenth century was marked by that prodigious expansion of knowledge, both theoretical and practical, which is denoted by a celebrated phrase: the Great Maritime Discoveries. Curiosity in matters of geography was not lacking in the Middle Ages, as is shown by the success of Marco Polo's

---

[1] 'Congregation' has virtually the same meaning as 'ministry' in secular governments (see pp. 328–9). Note that at the date of its foundation Propaganda had two simultaneous ends in view: evangelization of the pagans and the recovery of Christians who had fallen into heresy or schism. The means employed would vary according to circumstances, but were substantially the same, obeying the same principles and the same loyalties.

Book of Marvels. But here again the influence of decadent scholasticism was unfortunate. Armchair geographers, disdaining to acquire first-hand information and relying upon Scripture and the Fathers, as well as on Pliny the Elder and Solinus, peopled the unknown continents with long-eared, one-eyed monsters; they also imagined the earth to be a disk, with the Holy Sepulchre as its centre and surrounded by the river Ocean. At the beginning of the fifteenth century, however, some more intelligent minds, applying themselves to the ancient texts and the accounts of early travellers, began to destroy the accepted notions. Cardinal Pierre d'Ailly's *Description of the World* (1410), which was Christopher Columbus's bedside book, recognized the sphericity of the earth, and concluded with Aristotle, Seneca and Pliny that it would be possible to reach the eastern coast of India by sailing westward from Spain across the vasty deep. The Arabians, far in advance of Europe, had already acquired extensive geographical knowledge: their *portulans* [1] were surprisingly accurate, and the West began to study them towards the end of the fourteenth century.

At the same time, since maritime trade was barred from the Near East by the Turkish advance, the French, Catalans and Genoese were obliged to seek new markets elsewhere, particularly on the Atlantic coasts of Africa whence they imported ivory and gold; and this meant an increased interest in long-distance voyages. In 1402 the Norman Jean de Béthencourt settled in the Canary Islands and proclaimed himself king. The miseries and vicissitudes of the Hundred Years War prevented this embryo of a French colonial empire from developing and bearing fruit; but a Portuguese prince, contemplating the results of earlier enterprises, dreamed of undertaking similar expeditions and even (like Pharaoh Neco) of sending a fleet to circumnavigate Africa. He is known to history as Henry the Navigator.

Scientific progress eventually made navigation easier, or, to be more exact, a little less arduous. In place of the unreliable *calamites* and *marinettes* imported from China or copied from Chinese models, in which a magnetized needle placed on an oil-borne straw pointed approximately to the north, an Italian named Flavio Gioia substituted the compass. Here the needle was mounted on a pivot and revolved over a compass-card in a small box; it was a far more dependable instrument. The astrolabe, an Arabian invention, made it possible to determine the height of the pole-star above the horizon; while the so-called Alphonsine astronomical tables, drawn up by order of the learned Alfonso X of Castile, simplified the calculation of longitude. Galleys and *nefs*, the old medieval craft,[2] were replaced by vessels superior in

---

[1] Books containing descriptions of seaports, and showing currents and tides.—Tr.
[2] The galley was too low in the water for ocean voyages; the *nef* had plenty of free-board, but was heavy and much too slow.

size, shape and safety. First there was the three-masted caravel about ninety feet in length and with five sails. Later came the carrack; its equipment was continually improved, and it steadily increased in size until it reached a displacement of between 1,500 and 2,000 tons. Finally gunpowder, henceforward in common use, enabled mariners to venture with more courage than hitherto into regions so full of monsters, beasts and fearsome men.

The means of setting out to conquer the world were therefore much improved. Motives for doing so were not lacking, though they were a curious medley of immediate material interests and the queerest dreams. Men longed to reach the fabulous lands where spices grew, and to bring back pepper, nutmeg, cloves, cinnamon and ginger, all of which could be sold at enormous profit. They yearned likewise for Marco Polo's 'Cipangu,' where the very roofs and floors were made of gold. Yes, but they wished also to establish brotherly relations with 'Prester John,' the mysterious Christian prince whose name was on everyone's lips, but whose kingdom none could exactly locate; or even to set on foot a kind of global strategy which would enable them to take Islam in the rear, by way of India, and recover the Holy Places. All these purposes jostled one another in minds which the new intellectual climate of the Renaissance would shortly imbue with a more disinterested love of knowledge and with less empirical methods.

Scientific curiosity, commercial ambitions, vague plans for evangelization and crusade, many dreams: all these elements were present in the soul of a prince whom the famous portrait by Nuno Gonsalvez at Lisbon shows us with grave and meditative gaze, eyes of a poet and mystic set in the craggy features of a *condottiere*. Henry the Navigator (1394–1460) was indeed the man who launched his country (and the whole world after her) upon discovery of the globe. In his palace-laboratory at Sagres,[1] where he settled at the age of twenty and passed the remainder of his life, he assembled a library of maps, books of voyages and learned works. As head of what might almost be described as a school of navigation, astronomy and geography, he sent out each year an expedition for both commerce and discovery, the tradition of which Portugal continued to preserve long after his death.

Here now are the principal stages of Portuguese exploration: 1415, capture of Ceuta, which secured the sea routes; 1416, arrival at Cape Bogador; 1419, first vines planted at Madeira. Twenty-five years of effort, groping, fear; then, in 1445, it was Cape Verde. The Order of Christ, heir of the Templars, spent themselves in men and money on behalf of these great enterprises. The equator was reached in 1471. Henry was dead, but his spirit survived, and King John II followed in his footsteps. In 1487, while one of his officers, Peter of Covilham,

[1] Close to the sheer cliffs of Cape St Vincent, the most westerly point of Europe.

started via Egypt in search of the kingdom of Prester John, Bartholomew Diaz, with great daring and at enormous risk, reached the most
southerly point of Africa, the 'Cape of Storms,' to which his sovereign
gave the more auspicious name of 'Good Hope.' Glorious achievements! In that hostile continent the Portuguese under Diego Cão
actually penetrated as far as Timbuktu and the Congo valley. The great
difficulty of navigating south of the equator without a view of the
polar star was overcome by a German astronomer, Martin Behaim,
whom King John had summoned to Lisbon. In the last years of the
fifteenth century (1497-9) a stupendous expedition led by Vasco da
Gama seemed to fulfil the most ambitious of all dreams: it doubled the
Cape, reached India by a hitherto unknown route, returned in triumph
and disembarked with an immense quantity of gold and precious
stones.

While Portugal, a small country then at the height of her destiny,
was engaged in these splendid undertakings a competitor rose at her
side—Spain. Some years had yet to pass before another field of discovery became part of the Spanish Empire, for it was John II who was
first approached by a Genoese adventurer. This man, son of a weaver
but well married at Lisbon, proposed sailing due west, towards the
mysterious land of 'Antilia' which certain maps showed as lying close
to Asia, and thus opening a new route to India. But the Italian was
asking, in addition to three caravels, a patent of nobility, the hereditary
title of Grand Admiral, viceroyalty of the conquered lands and 10 per
cent of all future trade with the newly discovered territories. The King
of Portugal refused; and thus it was that Christopher Columbus (1451-
1506) passed into the service of Spain under Ferdinand and Isabella,
who, after much hesitation and bargaining, ended six years of negotiation by granting him almost everything he asked. Money supplied by
the brothers Pinzon, shipowners, together with sums allotted by the
Catholic sovereigns, enabled the great expedition to set sail. Its story is
well known: the first voyage of three caravels, the long months of
wandering on the lone Atlantic, the commander's unshakable determination and invincible hope; then, on 12th October 1492, a victorious
cry from the look-out: 'Land! Land!' and a new continent, identified
for another fifteen years with Asia, swinging above man's horizon.

Spanish settlement in these unknown territories, which were further
enlarged by three other voyages of Columbus (1493, 1498, 1502),
raised a juridical problem. The Portuguese claimed to have received
from Pope Martin in 1430 a Bull granting them sovereignty over all
lands yet to be discovered, a privilege which had certainly been confirmed by the Bull *Deum diversas* of Nicholas V in 1452. Calixtus III
and Paul III had done likewise. But Spain, having obtained a foothold
in the New World, disputed this monopoly and appealed to Alexander

VI against the decisions of his predecessors. Alexander studied the question with great care, and very wisely chose partition. The Bull of 1493 cut the world in two along a meridian passing one hundred miles from the Azores; Spain was to have everything west of this line, Portugal everything to the east. A year later the Portuguese Cabral, driven by a storm, discovered Brazil; negotiations were resumed, and it was eventually decided to move the famous 'Line of Pope Alexander' two hundred and seventy miles westward. The Treaty of Tordesillas (1494) avoided what would otherwise have been the first example of colonial rivalry. The Spaniards and Portuguese were dividing the whole world between themselves before they had discovered it!

The impulse had been given. In every country bordering the Ocean there awoke a feverish longing for the wide open spaces and an appetite for the fabulous riches to be won. John and Sebastian Cabot, Venetian seamen in the service of England, discovered Newfoundland (1497) and Labrador (1498), believing to the end that they had reached Asia. About the same time, however, another Italian, Amerigo Vespucci, took part in three expeditions to these mysterious 'Indies' (1497–1504); he was a better observer, and concluded that a new world had been found. Four years later (1508) tribute was paid to his sagacity by Canon Waldseemüller, in whose *Universal Cosmography* the new continent was called after him 'America.' The country proved to be quite different from what had been hitherto supposed. Cortereal visited the region now called Canada, but was disappointed: where were the gold and spices of these frozen lands? In 1513 Balboa crossed the Isthmus of Panama, and was the first European to set eyes on the Pacific Ocean. Who would be the first to sail around this globe, of the shape of which there could no longer be the slightest doubt? It was to be Magellan, another brilliant Portuguese, at that time in the service of Spain. And so the years 1519–22 witnessed that bold expedition which set out to tear from Earth her last remaining secrets. After countless perils, at the mercy of trade winds or dead calms, after the murder of their chief in a remote island of the Philippines, eighteen out of three hundred men returned. They had circumnavigated the world, and their leader Del Cano was presented by Charles V with a golden globe upon which were engraved the words: '*Tu primus me circumdedisti.*'

The age of discovery was by no means ended. Soldiers, merchants and miners landed in the new countries hard upon the heels of sailors and adventurers. The discoverers had merely opened up a way for the conquistadors, and violence was let loose with a ferocity born of avarice. Delivered by Albuquerque from the combined menace of Arabs and Venetians, little Portugal, like the ancient Phoenicians, found herself at the head of an enormous maritime empire, visible heir

* I

of the Dravidian and Javanese thalassocracies in the Indian Ocean, whence flowed to her a tide of untold wealth. Muscat and Ormuz on the Persian Gulf, Goa and Diu in India, then Ceylon, Malacca, Sumatra and the Moluccas—all those key-points which England subsequently discovered and occupied were Portuguese bases in the mid sixteenth century. Ships from Lisbon and Oporto reached Canton, Formosa and Japan. Westward, Madeira, the Azores, Concepcion and St Helena guarded the route followed by the banner of five escutcheons while Brazil gradually became Portuguese. This glorious page of history and adventure was given literary form by Camoens, whose *Lusiads* have immortalized the maritime genius of his people. But that page was destined to be brief. The Portuguese coastal settlements were soon easy prey to Dutch and English rapacity, while Portugal herself, ruined by excessive luxury and demoralized by slavery, lapsed into decadence. Of all her vast empire there at length remained nothing but a few shreds (among them Brazil), whose temporary subjection to Spain (1580–1646) did not succeed in taking them from the heirs of Henry the Navigator.

The Spanish Empire was much more secure. At the time of Columbus's first voyage, Ferdinand of Aragon founded the House of Traffic at Seville, to exploit the wealth of newly discovered territories, and the Council of the Indies was soon appointed to control these distant lands. San Domingo, Cuba and Jamaica were the first to be exploited. Charles V gave full support to the programme of conquest, which yielded quick results. Year after year during the great Hapsburg's reign his dominions were enlarged by men of steel. Sailing from Havana with eleven ships and seven hundred men, Fernando Cortez took possession of Mexico (1519–22). Ten years later (1532–5) a band of adventurers led by Pizarro and Almagro overran Peru. In sweat and blood—even the blood of whites, for they too were sometimes at loggerheads with one another—a gigantic empire was built, over which floated the banner of Spain. Venezuela (1520–40), Yucatan (1527–47), Colombia (1538), Chile (1540), and later on Paraguay and Argentina, represent the several chapters of a history which, because of the circumstances in which it was written, we cannot wholeheartedly admire. For while they mercilessly oppressed the natives, while they destroyed not only the harsh government of the Aztecs in Mexico, but also the paternalistic and communal tutelage of the Inca emperors in Peru, the conquistadors were establishing, by massacre and violence or imposture, their own rule over peoples who were terrified by their horses and their firearms.

In the middle of the sixteenth century, with the sole exception of Brazil, the entire continent from Mexico to the Straits of Magellan was in the hands of the Spaniards. A much more solid implantation in newly won territories than that of the Portuguese assured infinitely greater security to their dominions. A whole administration of viceroys and captains-general exercised power in the sovereign's name; and fleets of galleons, based on the Canaries, Bermuda and the Antilles, could cross the ocean in safety to unload their cargoes of gold, precious stones and spices in the ports of Spain. These riches were dangerous: having accustomed the Spanish people to idleness, they would sap its energy and facilitate its decline. For the present, however, that is to say throughout the sixteenth century, they made the crown of Madrid the richest in the world, and its king the most powerful in Europe. From a political and a human point of view, the birth of the Spanish Empire was one of the major events in the history of this period.

3. THE CROSS IN THE NEW WORLD

What did the future hold in store for Christian faith in those territories newly opened to white men? In appearance discovery and evangelization were inseparable. When Diego Cão reached the mouth of the Congo in 1482 he set up a 'padrao,' a column bearing the arms of Portugal and surmounted by a cross; and when Christopher Columbus landed at Guanahani, which he called San Salvador in honour of Christ the Saviour, his first care likewise was to erect a cross. The natives were deeply impressed by the sight of the conquistadors kneeling around the altar for the first Mass celebrated in Hispaniola. 'The monarchs of Castile,' Columbus told them, 'have sent us not to subjugate you, but to teach you the true religion.' That was true. One need only peruse the *Testament of Isabella* to be convinced of the fully Christian intention of the *descobredores*: 'In asking Pope Alexander VI to grant us ownership of half the islands and mainland of the Ocean,' wrote the Catholic queen, 'our definite purpose was to use all our efforts to induce the peoples of those new lands to embrace our holy religion, to send them priests, monks, prelates and other learned and God-fearing men who would educate them in the truths of faith, and to give them the manners and customs of Christian life.' She even besought her heirs never 'to allow the Indians to suffer any harm either in their persons or in their goods, but to see that they were well and suitably treated.' Excellent principles, which alas were imperfectly applied.

The real problem which the colonists would have to face was this: what should be their attitude towards the natives? As to the imperious duty of planting the Cross in all conquered territories, there was complete agreement among the Spaniards and Portuguese, both peoples of ardent faith and age-long Christian traditions. But the medieval notion of the pagan as akin to a brute beast and fit to be reduced to slavery continued to have many supporters; it also found favour with those

who saw foreign conquest merely as a financially rewarding undertaking. Not all accepted the sound doctrine, put forward by St
Thomas in *De Veritate*, concerning 'the revelation granted by God,
through interior inspiration, to pagans who follow natural reason in the
pursuit of good and avoidance of evil,' and concerning 'the necessity of
sending them reliable preachers, as Peter was sent to the centurion
Cornelius.' The medieval view was responsible for Nicholas V's
atrocious Brief, published in 1452 but fortunately annulled in the
following year, whereby the Pope authorized the Portuguese to reduce
the natives of newly discovered lands to slavery.[1] But St Thomas's
teaching inspired the heroism, the spirit of sacrifice and the inexhaustible charity of those missionaries who laboured to bring the
Gospel to ignorant souls. The history of the missions from their very
commencement, and for many years afterwards, was that of a conflict
between these two attitudes; nor is it certain that that conflict is not still
in progress.

Almost from the beginning of the great voyages, therefore, missionaries embarked for unknown lands. It is one of Alexander VI's good
points that he recommended the sovereigns of Portugal and Spain to
see that all such expeditions were accompanied by witnesses of God.
Borgia will have at least that to his credit on Judgment Day. Very soon
no caravel put to sea without its cargo of missionaries. Some of them,
especially in the early days, belonged to the secular clergy, but the most
active teams were furnished mainly by religious Orders: at first by the
Franciscans and Dominicans, each of whom discovered in their traditions the duty of evangelization and some illustrious examples; later
and above all by the Jesuits, whose arrival we shall presently see to have
been decisive. Of course not all of these hundreds of men were saints; [2]
some were overwhelmed by the climate or gave way under torture.
But on the whole there were very few failures; a vast majority of these
adventurers of God proved wonderfully faithful to their vocation of
heroism and charity.

Missionary work encountered many obstacles. Material difficulties

---

[1] This document is one of the most deplorable in the whole history of the Church.
See *L'Ami du clergé*, 12th March 1953. On 16th June 1452 Pope Nicholas V issued a
Brief (*Divino Amore communiti*) in favour of King Alfonso of Portugal. It said: 'The
kingdoms, duchies, counties, principalities and other dominions, lands, places and camps
in possession of the aforesaid Saracens, pagans, infidels and enemies of Christ. . . . By
Apostolic authority We confer upon you the full and free faculty to invade, conquer,
occupy and subjugate them, and to *reduce the inhabitants to perpetual servitude*.' But in
1453 the Brief *Romanus Pontifex*, stating that many of these infidels had been converted to
Catholicism, laid down that none might keep *the baptized in slavery*. Calixtus III, and after
him Sixtus IV, excommunicated those who enslaved converted natives.
[2] Secular priests and monks were occasionally sent to the Indies as punishment for some
offence, which certainly did not make them ideal apostles. Fr Tillisch, a German Jesuit,
relates that he witnessed the arrival on board a caravel of a whole group of such clerics,
chained together in pairs.

were numerous and not seldom formidable. At that date travel by sea was by no means as safe and comfortable as it is today; the most 'modern' vessels involved their passengers in terrible ordeals and often in strange adventures. What a splendid sight must have been the annual departure of the Indies fleet from Lisbon on 25th March, feast of the Annunciation, as the magnificent procession wound its way along the Tagus, amid songs, cheers and pealing bells, to the Tower of Belem (on that occasion luxuriant as a tropical forest), off which the caravels lay at anchor. Soon those beautiful ships, the wind swelling their sails, were gliding downstream accompanied by salvoes from all the guns of the fortress and of other craft stationed in the roads. But for those on board the picture left much to be desired. In those puny vessels,[1] even in those of 1,000 tons displacement, space was so limited that there was hardly room to move. Cargo of all sorts filled every nook and corner, together with food supplies for the long voyage. Soldiers, sailors and poorer passengers were crowded on deck, freezing or roasting according to time and place. For the rich there were tiny cabins, measuring about $6\frac{1}{2}$ feet by $4\frac{1}{2}$ feet, into which four, six or even eight persons were tightly packed. Add to that discomfort the ever-present bane of sea-sickness, and one obtains some idea of what life was like in these boxes during heavy weather as hundreds of men made sacrifice to angry Neptune. Missionaries were usually treated as privileged persons and occupied cabins; but they had to supply their own food, do their own cooking (the ship's provisions were intended only for the crew [2]) and wash their own linen—menial tasks in which a nobleman was once surprised to find St Francis Xavier engaged.

That lasted for months and even years on end. It sometimes happened that dead calm or adverse winds made the voyage impossible; passengers bound for Brazil might find themselves in Africa. When studying the missionary life we have to take account of the enormous amount of time and energy lost as a result of travelling. It usually took three years to reach Japan. In many cases the journey was never completed, for besides discomfort there were serious dangers to be faced. The ships themselves, being too heavy and massive, were not always a match for the sea, and powerful waves beating against their wooden sides quickly broke them up. In a storm the masts sometimes collapsed, rudders were carried away and the vessel was driven ashore like a drifting log. The Cape of Good Hope soon became famous for its many wrecks. Epidemics, which wrought havoc among those dense masses of humanity, were another grave danger. Yellow fever and cholera, not to

[1] St Francis Xavier's caravel scarcely exceeded one hundred tons, less than a modern French pinnace.
[2] The Indies fleet had abandoned the medieval custom of employing a *cargator*, an official who used to look after the feeding of passengers.

mention scurvy, were rife; and the phrase 'region of death' was applied to the belt of equatorial calms, where sailors and passengers shivered with fever in the sweltering and humid heat. By the time they reached journey's end—Goa, for example, an important cross-roads on the oriental routes—the missionaries were generally so exhausted that they were stretcher cases and had to remain for months in hospital. Camoens spoke the truth when he praised the apostles of Christ for having 'despised the most terrible dangers to carry the torch of truth.'

It might have been some consolation if the missionaries on landing had found an easy situation and ready means of accomplishing their task. But communications were abnormally difficult in those vast territories—e.g. Mexico, seven times the size of Spain—which were often mountainous and where there were only imperfect trackways; the sixteenth-century evangelist seldom had the benefit of anything nearly so convenient as the old Roman roads. Moreover in many regions the population was little disposed to welcome the Christians, particularly in Moslem countries, where hatred of the 'roumi' was easily roused, and in China, where the xenophobia of the Mings lasted for a long time. In America disproportion of armaments gave the Spaniards irresistible superiority over the natives, upon whom they were thus able to impose their faith; but the old religions of the Aztecs, Toltecs and Quechuas were so deeply rooted in the hearts of those peoples that they long survived the introduction of the Gospel, and still continue to exist in a number of strange forms.

But the worst difficulties encountered by Christianity were due to the very men who paved the way for the missionaries and enabled them to proceed with their work: conquistadors, sailors, soldiers and criminal adventurers. Not that these brave fellows were hostile to religion. Quite the contrary. 'Friends,' said Fernando Cortez to his troops in an order of the day, 'let us follow the Cross, and, if we have faith, by that sign we shall conquer.' But the Church, as we know, had not always reason to be proud of these rough soldiers who claimed to conquer by the sign of the Cross. Many a viceroy, captain-general and high official considered the missionaries as a class of superior employees whose business it was to spread the Word among these subjugated peoples and thus to ensure among them good order and a friendly spirit. Some even looked upon them as commercial agents. 'Pepper and souls' was a common saying in the Indies. It need hardly be added that there was nothing of the sacristan or choir-boy about these men, who sailed to the farthest corners of the world in face of such appalling hazards. All or most of them were thirsty for gold, proud and immensely ambitious, if not sadistic lovers of violence and bloodshed. They may have been, as Cortez told the Aztec Montezuma, quite sincerely 'horrified at the thought of so many pagan souls, who,

because they knew not Christ, would soon find themselves in hell';
but this did not for a moment prevent them from burning the live
bodies of those same pagans in order to obtain possession of their
wealth. 'The torments inflicted upon us,' said one wretched Indian
under torture, 'are much worse than any that could be devised by all
the devils in hell.' And though the reports of Bartholomew de las
Casas may exaggerate Spanish atrocities, such facts as he relates appear
to be true: children butchered or impaled on swords for fun, prisoners
used to feed mastiffs. Even without such horrors the system of
encomiendas and *repartimientes*, whereby native villages were forced to
work for the benefit of a few Spaniards, was in fact nothing less than
abominable slavery. This was the kind of situation that confronted
missionaries in many places, especially in America. To accept these
cruelties, or even the mere régime, was to betray the Gospel; to oppose
them was to incur the hostility of soldiers, administrators, settlers and
even perhaps the government at home.

It is in these very difficult and dangerous circumstances that we have
to picture the missionaries setting out to win the world for God and
sowing the message of love at the cost of their own lives. Whatever
may have been the crimes and errors committed by Catholics during
this period of blood and glory, the mere presence among them of
missionaries suffices to give their undertaking a truly Christian flavour.
Compare the rapid fusion of European Catholics and native converts,
which was so characteristic of Latin America, with the total disappearance of the Redskins under Anglo-Saxon and Protestant rule in
North America. Many place-names still commemorate the inauguration
of those missions and the great Catholic achievements to which they
gave rise: São Tomé, Trinidad, San Salvador, Vera Cruz, Santa Fé,
San Domingo, San Francisco, etc. Such names are no vain testimony,
but the sign of a living and lasting reality.

4. IN THE LUSITANIAN 'PATRONATE'

Nowhere was colonization more closely identified with the apostolate than in territories occupied by the Portuguese. The system known
to history as 'patronate' had originated with the popes themselves.
Although we do not possess the Bull which Henry the Navigator
always claimed to have received in 1430, the two documents signed by
Nicholas V in 1452 and 1453 leave no room for doubt. The lands
already discovered or to be discovered would be 'clearly recognized as
belonging to King Alfonso and his successors in perpetuity'; but the
Catholic sovereigns of Portugal pledged themselves 'in all places,
islands and territories, already acquired or to be acquired, to build all
churches, monasteries and other pious foundations, as well as to send

out all secular priests who might volunteer and those belonging to the
Mendicant Orders appointed by their superiors.' To the religious
authorities thus established in the new empire the Holy See granted the
most extensive powers for the administration of the sacraments, but it
was clearly specified that the rights and duties of the colonial Churches
were closely linked with the authority of the monarch at Lisbon. The
Portuguese kings were thus the canonical 'patrons' of those Churches,
and all of them were fully alive to their responsibilities. All of them,
especially Emmanuel the Fortunate and John III, personally directed
the sending of missionaries to the new lands, and were jealous of their
privilege in this matter. For nearly two hundred years almost every
missionary destined for the East or West Indies sailed from the estuary
of the Tagus. Even the birth of the Spanish Empire and the partition
of Alexander VI did not end this pretention or this *de facto* primacy, to
which the kings of Spain claimed to have succeeded when they temporarily conquered Portugal.

The early achievements of the Portuguese missions were not in fact
particularly outstanding. It was not really until the arrival of the
Jesuits, who were invited by John III in 1542, that the apostolate was
given systematic shape and took firm root as a fully organized institution in the various countries. Meanwhile, however, the work of evangelization got off to a flying start in Africa. In 1484, following Cão's
expedition, a party of Franciscans landed in the Congo, and obtained
some encouraging results. Five years later they converted a local chief.
Then, shortly afterwards, the native king himself was touched by
grace and received at baptism the name of John, for the King of
Portugal was his godfather. Eight of his successors were Christians.
His son, called Alfonso, proved himself a sort of African Clovis, urging
his people to conversion, asking for more priests (who were not always
equal to their task) and protesting with Christian generosity against
the shameful traffic in black slaves which was then developing with
America. Alfonso conceived an idea far in advance of his time. Finding
that many missionaries quickly succumbed to the climate, he thought of
creating a native clergy. Accordingly he sent one of his sons, Henry, to
Lisbon, to be instructed and ordained priest. Now King Emmanuel
took a liking to the young man, who was indeed highly intelligent and
extremely handsome; and as he happened to be sending an embassy to
Leo X, to do solemn homage for his overseas empire, he entrusted its
leadership to the young Negro, who was incidentally a good Latinist,
and asked the Pope to grant him episcopal consecration. The humanist
Leo was curious and amused; he let five years pass while Henry completed his studies, but at the end of that time (1518) he proceeded without hesitation to make him Bishop of Utica *in partibus infidelium*, the
first black bishop, at the head of vast Congolese territories whether

baptized or yet to be baptized. Good King Alfonso, his father, continued throughout his life to do battle for the faith against paganism and witchcraft, which earned him a fine letter of congratulation from Pope Paul III. But alas, these first fruits were not destined to be followed by permanent harvests. The black prince-bishop Henry had no successor of his own race. The bishopric of São Tomé erected in the island of that name, with jurisdiction over Guinea and the Congo, was ephemeral. The native clergy consisted of a mere handful of men. As for the white missionaries, those who did not die of fever quickly deteriorated and set a far from edifying example. Henceforward, while India and America drained all the live forces of Portugal, the whites resident in black Africa were interested in nothing but the slave trade. The prestige of Catholicism was so seriously affected that after the death of Alfonso, heartbroken on account of this decadence, his successor Diogo expelled all missionaries. Even the Jesuits failed to revive the Congolese mission; though not completely abandoned, it vegetated, and did not really regain its vigour until the nineteenth century.

In Brazil evangelization began immediately after Cabral's discovery of that country; it was a task to which the Franciscans dedicated themselves with great earnestness, but somewhat sporadically and almost at random. For this, however, the size of the country was in part responsible. At various points along the coast they established small Christian settlements, where there soon became manifest that tendency to cross-breeding between whites and natives which was afterwards characteristic of Portuguese colonization. Marriages between Christians and Indian girls were usually fortunate in their results. One instance is found in the charming story of Catherine Paragassu, known as Catherine of Brazil, whose memory is still associated with the foundation of Bahia. Daughter of a small local chieftain, she was married according to native rites to a shipwrecked Portuguese, who took her to Europe. Landing at Saint-Malo, she became friendly with the wife of Jacques Cartier, the explorer, and received baptism. After reaching Paris she fell sick (1528), and had a vision of Our Lady, who bade her return and carry the Gospel to her own country. This she did, and throughout a virtuous life, which was prolonged to the age of eighty, she laboured unceasingly to obtain priests, build churches and multiply works of charity, planting the Cross firmly on the shores of the 'Bay of All Saints.' [1] Those small Portuguese settlements, however, did not begin to grow until the dispatch of government officials from Lisbon and, above all, of the first Jesuit team by Fr Laynez in 1549.

The Franciscans had long been hard at work in the East Indies, and

[1] See Olga Obry, *Catherine du Brésil* (Paris), 1954, which offers a lifelike if slightly romantic portrait of this curious woman.

some of them had actually suffered martyrdom. The arrival of the Portuguese on the coasts of the vast peninsula gave a new impulse to what was left of their missions, and from the beginning of the sixteenth century there were fairly prosperous churches at Cochin, Calicut, Cranganor and Goa; particularly at Goa, which was the post of transhipment on voyages to all Portuguese bases in the Indian Ocean, as well as to China, Zanzibar and Macao. It was also at Goa that the Franciscan John of Albuquerque created an Indian diocese, the first and for a long time the only one in the Far East. But conversion of the natives was at first a very slow business. This was due mainly to the bad example set by the colonists. Most of the latter were a pack of scoundrels, adventurers without faith or law; the richest kept harems and slaves, upon whom they lavished more floggings than religious instruction. Disheartened and disgusted, the Franciscan missionaries felt powerless to alter this frightful situation; besides, they themselves were more or less contaminated. They certainly baptized a few natives, but—their methods! A catechumen was asked not 'Do you wish to be baptized?' but 'Do you wish to enter the caste of *Prangui*?'—that is, of the Portuguese. Such contempt of their ancient traditions was bound to alienate the Brahmins, just as violence repelled the common people. There were some grounds for fearing that the Church in India would suffer the same fate as in the Congo. Then a loud voice was heard denouncing these vagaries, branding those Catholics who beat their slaves 'and counted each blow upon their rosaries,' the voice of the greatest apostle of that age. Whatever faults may have been committed in the Portuguese mission fields, this much, if nothing else, stands to the undying credit of Lisbon: it was King John III who summoned St Francis Xavier to his aid and sent him to the East aboard one of his caravels.

5. AMERICA OF THE CONQUISTADORS: BARTHOLOMEW DE LAS CASAS

When Spain entered the great colonial competition she did so with the same intentions as Portugal—to evangelize as well as occupy and exploit. Moreover the Bulls of partition signed by Alexander VI, while granting her the same privileges, imposed the same apostolic obligations. Even the Treaty of Lerida (1529), which was negotiated directly between the two powers in order to avoid conflict, and without consulting the Holy See, made reference to the duty. A juridical fiction? No, a sacred purpose: temporal sovereignty undertook to justify itself by its work in the service of faith.

Thus the very first voyages of discovery were accompanied by missionaries. On his second expedition (1493) Christopher Columbus took with him a party of monks and priests led by Dom Bernard Boyl, a Benedictine of Montserrat; on the third (1498) he was accompanied by Franciscans. In 1494 the first church in the New World was built on the island of Hispaniola (now Haiti—San Domingo). The impetus once given did not cease. All existing Orders from now onwards appointed some of their members for apostolic work. There were Benedictines, Cistercians, Carmelites, Augustinians, Mercedarians, Jeronymites; and at first a good deal of courage was wasted, because they were unable to work out an overall scheme for concerted action. Progress began about 1510, when the Franciscans and Dominicans each assumed responsibility for definite areas and definite tasks.

A rudimentary system of administration came into being, and showed itself in characteristically Spanish form by the establishment of a hierarchy. The Spaniards had hardly explored the territory where they proposed to exercise their apostolate when they asked and obtained from Rome the creation of dioceses. In the Antilles that of San Domingo was erected in 1511, followed soon afterwards by Concepcion de la Vega and San Juan in Puerto Rico. On the mainland the diocese of Darien in Panama was formed in 1513; then in quick succession came Mexico, Santa Fé, Lima, Bogotá and Caracas, each at the head of an archdiocese covering an enormous area. Canonically the new creations were dependent on the Holy See, but in 1520 the title 'Patriarch of the West Indies'[1] was conferred upon the chaplain-general of the Spanish Army, a title which, though honorary, was capable of more ambitious claims.

Despite this grand theoretical framework, the earliest attempts at evangelization were scattered and sometimes rather peculiar. We find conquistadors, quite happily and without the least preparation, baptizing every tribe along their route, so hastily indeed that their chaplains were often obliged to restrain their enthusiasm. We read in the memoirs of Bernard Diaz, Cortez's lieutenant, the advice given him on this point by Friar Bartholomew of Almeda: 'It is not a good thing to make Christians by force, better to let these folk acquire some knowledge of our holy religion.' Mere accident occasionally enabled native peoples to become acquainted with Christianity, and even to adopt it, before the arrival of any missionary and sometimes with extraordinary results. In Cuba, for example, a worthy sailor, illiterate but full of faith, was entertained by the *cacique* of a tribe, and he spoke so effectively about the Blessed Virgin that those excellent savages erected a church and altar to the Mother of Christ; but since the theological learning of their visitor was limited, they knew no better than to stand before the altar repeating over and over again: 'Ave Maria! Ave Maria!' and nothing more. From 1521 onwards the Papacy took increasing interest

[1] It is still borne by the Archbishop of Toledo.

in this work, and the Franciscans joined the Dominicans in a concerted effort. First Leo X and then Adrian VI, at the request of Charles V, gave the two great Mendicant Orders 'authorizations' in the nature of privileges and recommendations.

Evangelization was now intensified. All regions to which the conquistadors and their troops penetrated witnessed the arrival of Christ's spokesmen at their side, and among these missionary teams were numerous men of great merit, outstanding virtue, and even sanctity. In the Antilles two Dominicans, Peter of Cordova and Antony of Montesinos, founded the first house of their Order in the New World at San Domingo; Hispaniola, 'the island of St Dominic,' became the starting-point of missions to the mainland. Penetration was rapid in Mexico, where brown and white robes worked together. Credit for this belongs to the Franciscan Martin of Valencia, who, as apostolic legate, presided over the first Mexican synod (1524); to his colleague Juan de Zamarraga, the noble Bishop of Mexico; and also to Bartholomew de las Casas, most celebrated of the Dominicans, whose influence was to be felt far beyond the limits of the Aztec Empire. In New Granada (modern Colombia) the whole apostolate was dominated by the splendid figure of the Dominican St Louis Bertrand. A soul of sublime magnanimity, he was favoured with the gift of tongues, worked numerous miracles, witnessed the fulfilment of his prophecies, and by his own efforts won more than 150,000 natives for Christ. It was also the Dominicans who built the first church in Peru (1532), and subsequently converted the temple of the sun at Cuzcoa into a cathedral. At Lima, under their auspices and in the Third Order of St Dominic, there blossomed a wonderful but short-lived flower of sweetness, humility and charity, St Rose of Lima (1587–1607), so good to the natives, so generous in attending to their bodily and spiritual needs. Peru in fact became a centre of evangelization, with its famous university of Lima, a model of organization which produced St Alfonso Turibe, the 'Borromeo of America' who was for a long time at its head.

From north to south of the enormous continent missionaries were at work, not always with success, but doing their best everywhere. In Ecuador, where the savage Jivaros offered fierce resistance, Christianity took root thanks to the Dominican Alfonso de Montenegro: and in that young Church there soon unfolded another exquisite flower, the 'Lily of Quito,' Blessed Marianne of Paredès. In Chile, where again the implantation of Christianity was fraught with difficulty, and where several missionaries suffered martyrdom at the hands of the terrible Arauncanos, the faith eventually triumphed. In Paraguay and Uruguay all attempts failed until the arrival of the Jesuits. The last region to be won for Christianity was Argentina. Here, at the beginning of the eighteenth century, you might have seen a man go by 'barefooted and

without provisions, carrying his portable altar, a small violin, a few
books and a large crucifix' [1]—St Francis of Solano, a charming
personality, very much like his spiritual father Il Poverello. He used to
go from village to village, first playing a few simple tunes, then talking
to the Indians in their own language and thus taming 'the birds and
even the inhabitants.'

The missionaries wisely devoted themselves to the twofold task of
furthering instruction and instituting relief work. Four hundred
monasteries, countless churches—built in that curiously attractive
style in which the traditions of old Spain quickly combined with local
influences—universities, seminaries, schools, hospitals and hospices
bear eloquent testimony of results achieved by those hundreds of
Franciscans and Dominicans thanks to whom Latin America attained
and still occupies so important a place in the Catholic world.

But it was in Latin America also that there arose in its gravest form
the problem of relations between missionaries and colonists, between
the principles of the Gospel and those of colonization. Unlike the
Portuguese, who confined themselves to establishing rich coastal
trading stations, the Spaniards quickly resolved to build for themselves
an empire and to install themselves securely in the new territories. As
early as 1499 Christopher Columbus, in founding the system of
encomiendas, had shown his intention of settling colonists by placing
Indian labour at their disposal. The result was a form of native serfdom,
which was recognized by Spanish law as a survival of Roman institutions. The Church found herself unable to prevent this practice, but
from the very start she endeavoured everywhere 'to improve the condition of slaves and to protect them; she enfranchised large numbers
and saved many men from servitude.' [2] For their part, and under
ecclesiastical influence, the kings of Castile steadily refused to recognize
the legality of what was in effect nothing other than slavery, and
repeatedly declared that the Indians must be treated as free men. The
facts, however, were unfortunately quite different. For reasons that are
easy to understand, the colonists continued to enlarge the bonds of
slavery and to render them still more severe. Men were needed to till
the soil, to work the mines and to carry heavy loads along interminable
tracks in blazing heat or drenching rain. And what was the result?
First and foremost a terrible mortality among the natives, and this,
together with senseless slaughter and atrocious cruelty, soon decimated
entire populations. Within half a century the native populations
declined at an almost incredible rate. In Cuba twenty years saw numbers fall from 50,000 to 14,000, in San Domingo from 100,000 to
15,000, while in some parts of Mexico there was total annihilation. It is

[1] Georges Goyau.
[2] This tribute was paid by the great jurist G. Scelle in his *Histoire de la traite négrière*.

hard to understand how civilized men, and Christians at that, could have committed (or permitted) such heinous crimes.

It is to the credit of Holy Church that some at least of her children did not resign themselves to this situation. While many priests and even bishops were in league with the exploiters, and therefore refused to denounce these abominations, some had the rare courage to protest. Among them was Fr de Montesinos, one of whose sermons was the origin of a glorious destiny, the vocation of Bartholomew de las Casas. Another was Peter of Ghent, in whose veins flowed Hapsburg blood. Having reached the Indies, he sacrificed the brilliant future assured by his family ties, and devoted himself as a simple Franciscan lay-brother to the defence and education of the Indians. Juan de Zammaraga was another nobleman attracted to this yet more noble cause. Bernard de Sahagun arrived in Mexico at the age of thirty, and lived there until his death sixty-one years later; he published the first useful encyclopaedia of Mexican civilization and strove to make the catechism familiar to the beloved faithful of his diocese. Toribio de Paredès, surnamed 'the Poor' by the poor, was the first historian of the 'Indians of New Spain'; his was a truly Franciscan soul, overflowing with brotherly love for the victims of colonization. But none of their voices had such range and power as that of Bartholomew de las Casas (1474–1566).

One Sunday in the year 1510 this tall, slim young man with a slight stoop watched Fr de Montesinos mount the pulpit in the church of San Domingo. He had no idea, of course, that the Dominican's voice would be for him the voice of Christ, and that he would leave the building a new man. But so it was. He the son of a man who had sailed with Columbus, he the youthful and ambitious adventurer, had never given a thought to such things as the friar had uttered. Yet now, quite suddenly, he was convinced to the very depths of his soul: he and his fellows were betraying Christ, their baptismal vows and the mission itself; the Spanish sovereigns had agreed to undertake on the Pope's behalf the evangelization of the New World. Appalled, he straightway turned his back upon the past and altered his destiny without a moment's hesitation.

There was a grave shortage of priests in America; in less than two years he had been ordained, and immediately went into action. Now it was his turn to proclaim the message of Fr de Montesinos, to denounce inhuman masters and needless cruelty. As rector of Zanguarama, the poorest parish in Cuba, he devoted himself heart and soul to the work of which he had dreamed; but he also found time to accompany the stern conquistadors Narvaez and Velasquez in hope of being able to restrain their cruel impetuosity. In order to strengthen his hand he joined the Dominicans, and before long all those vast territories which were in process of becoming the Spanish colonies in America heard tell that this austere monk, who ate like the humblest slave, was indeed a witness of God.

That, however, did not please everyone. Bartholomew's criticisms and indictments upset the men of property, who arranged to silence him at the earliest opportunity. Such an occasion seemed to present itself when the community of Vera Paz, which he had founded, was attacked by the ferocious tribes of the neighbourhood. Priests were massacred, and this was held to justify the terrible reprisals which followed. But no, the missionary would not acknowledge defeat. He spoke up even more loudly than before. And since his voice was likely to be drowned in the colony by those of powerful interests (some of them episcopal), he decided to go to Spain and speak to the king himself.

He undertook voyage after voyage and all sorts of difficult manœuvres in order to reach the sovereign's presence, despite the many obstacles placed in his way. One colonial governor had a brother who was a minister; General So-and-so was cousin to a bishop, while many smart prelates had invested money in the American enterprise, and naturally hoped it would pay dividends. Nothing, however, could stop that dauntless man, conquistador turned advocate of Christ. Charles V himself was impressed; he realized what was at stake, and promulgated the decrees suggested by Bartholomew de las Casas. There was to be no more slavery, no more excessive requisitions, no more *encomiendas*. But alas, Madrid was a long way away, and powerful executioners were on the spot.

This heroic struggle lasted for the remainder of Bartholomew's life; nothing could make him yield, neither the attacks of hired theologians who were set upon him like a pack of hounds nor even the menaces of the Inquisition. He seemed to live only for his Indians, his beloved Indians, whose sufferings lay heavy on his mind; so much so that in a moment of blindness he gave his assent to the abominable means chosen by the colonists to make good their lack of man-power—the trade in African Negroes, whom the worst Portuguese dealers landed in shiploads on the coasts of America and sold as slaves to the colonists.

He was then seventy years old. Embarking once again, he returned to his Indian friends, armed this time by the king with those 'New Laws' which were supposed to put an end to the scandal. Charles, as token of his admiration, had wished to confer upon him the archbishopric of Cuzco in Peru; but that was too much, too rich, for the 'Father of the Indians,' the Dominican of the disinherited; he would accept only the diocese of Chiapas, hidden among the mountains of Guatemala. But he did not stay there for long. From all quarters he received the same news: the royal decrees remained a dead letter. There was no abatement of those crimes which he had denounced in his lately published and controversial book, *A Very Brief Account oj the Destruction of the Indians*. Was it to last for ever? Were fifteen million corpses, as he reckoned, not enough? With the approval of the Archbishop of Seville, Sepulveda was able to denounce him as a half-witted revolutionary and professional trouble-maker; but Bartholomew listened only to his conscience. Finally, in order to compel conquerors and colonists alike to respect the principles of the Gospel, he ordered all confessors within his jurisdiction to refuse absolution to anyone who had behaved cruelly to the natives or had acquired riches by robbery and violence. This man of God shrank from no means that might help to achieve his purpose.

When he died, at the age of ninety-two, even the remotest Indian villages held funeral ceremonies and long bewailed their father. Modern historians of Spain and her colonies have severely criticized the testimony of Bartholomew de las Casas. Some have declared that he multiplied by at least one hundred the actual number of those who perished at the hands of the conquistadors; he has been denounced as a bad Spaniard, a disparager of his country and of the effort (in many respects praiseworthy) made by his compatriots to open up the new lands to civilization and Christianity. But even if he did exaggerate; even if, as is probable, Bartholomew de las Casas was more the friend of social justice than of historical truth, he is still one of the most admirable, one of the most exemplary and one of the noblest figures ever produced by Spain. He dared to challenge iniquity and scandal, and such men, even though mistaken upon certain points of detail, are champions of the cause for which Christ died.

What were the results of that immense effort accomplished by missionaries during the first half-century following the conquest? As far as numbers are concerned it is hard to say, because figures vary from one witness to another. Some have felt justified in declaring that by about 1540 Latin America contained ten million Christians. At all events a great deal had been done to place the Church upon secure foundations in these new lands, with her governmental system, her buildings, her institutions and her principles. Was she in fact a Church adapted to the needs of the peoples whom she had converted? Was she not rather a sort of annexe to the Spanish Church, which had simply been transported overseas with her hierarchy, her methods, her psychology and even her imagination? This question is difficult to answer. South American Catholicism has always retained a character markedly Spanish, but, as one of its historians has said,[1] 'tropicalized,' imbued with the violence and luxuriance peculiar to the country and the peoples of the *gana*. Neither the Dominicans nor the Franciscans—not even the best of them, such as Las Casas—had any clear notion of a

---

[1] Juan B. Teran: *La Naissance de l'Amérique espagnole*, Paris, 1930.

properly indigenous Church, adapted to the deepest instincts of those people, part and parcel of themselves. Only the Jesuits, who came somewhat later, were able to envisage some such enterprise. The notion of a missionary Catholicism, varied in its outward appearance and sociological elements, as well as oecumenical in its principles and organization, is a modern idea of quite recent origin.

Nevertheless the Christian faith soon showed itself to be deep-rooted and effective among these masses of native converts, producing more than one splendid example of belief. The boy Cristobal, son of an Indian and scarcely fourteen years old, was killed by his own father in 1527, because he had asked for baptism. Then there was the half-caste Bro. Martin de Porrès (1579–1659), son of a Spanish father and an Indian mother. A Dominican lay-brother skilled in medicine and pharmacy, he always refused to become a priest, so that he might stay closer to the outcasts of a race to which he felt that he belonged.[1] It was also to a very humble native peasant, Juan surnamed Diego, that the Blessed Virgin appeared several times in 1531, as if to show God's tenderness towards these vanquished and oppressed peoples who were none the less called by faith to a new life—Our Lady of Guadalupe, patroness of what was once America of the conquistadors but now America of the baptized.

6. THE GREAT JESUIT RELIEF

The entry of the Jesuits upon the scene gave the apostolate a fresh impetus, so strong that in many areas the mission itself seemed to be identical with the Society of Jesus. From the very birth of his institute St Ignatius had intended it for missionary work; he had inspired his companions at Montmartre with the idea of setting out for the Holy Land and labouring for the spiritual reconquest of the East. Later, because of insuperable difficulties and at the express wish of the Pope, they had turned their steps in other directions. But Paul III's Bull *Regimini*, which recognized the Society, obliged the Jesuits to go without excuse or delay wherever the Sovereign Pontiff might choose to send them, 'whether among the Turks or among other infidels, no matter where, even to that region known as India.' Besides, their own Constitutions said: 'It is part of our vocation to travel about the world, to live in any country where it is possible to enhance the glory of God and save souls.' The young foundation still numbered a mere handful of men when it answered an appeal from John III of Portugal and detached two of its members for missionary work, which was to become one of the most prominent features of its activity.

[1] See his Life by Claire Huchet-Bishop, Paris, 1954.

Jesuits quickly made their appearance in all four quarters of the globe. The Society, as has often been remarked, already seemed to enjoy a certain gift of ubiquity, enabling it from its earliest days to undertake simultaneously every task to which it was invited, as if its ranks were sufficiently numerous to furnish an unlimited supply of qualified men. Their achievements constitute, as it were, a glorious and mighty volume in the history of the Church; some of its chapters are not nearly as familiar as they deserve to be, but none is lacking either in excitement or in spiritual significance. It is impossible to elucidate the whole of their multifarious activity. In 1548 Portugal sent a Jesuit mission to Ceuta and Tetuan. Following in the footsteps of the heroic and saintly Fr Contreras, its purpose was to ensure a regular body of chaplains among Christian captives in Africa and to try to ransom them. Some of its members bore names now illustrious in the annals of the Society: Fr J. Nunes Barreto, whom we shall meet again in Ethiopia, and Fr Luis Gonsalvez, who was destined to play an outstanding part along with St Ignatius and afterwards at the Portuguese court. Another Jesuit was the Belgian Fr Clénard, whose desire to convert the Moslems led him to seek intimate acquaintance with their religious and scientific books. For this purpose he went to live in Morocco, at Fez, and his body now lies in the church of the Alhambra, a former mosque. Jesuit also were the missionary groups sent by the popes on several occasions to Constantinople. There, despite the policy of the sultans, which fluctuated between benevolence and persecution, they managed to open schools and even to preach, which more than once brought them into conflict with the schismatic Greeks.

The foregoing are little-known episodes, but indicative, among many others, of the diversity of undertakings conducted by the Society. At many points it seemed to set itself the duty of relieving earlier evangelists who had either grown tired or had laboured with indifferent success. Such was the case of St Francis Xavier in the Indies, though his activity, as we shall see, went far beyond the limited task of relieving others. Their efforts were not everywhere crowned with triumph. In the Congo, for example, Frs Souveral and Sylveira obtained only trifling results; but at least they paved the way for the creation in the Negro world of new dioceses in Angola and San Salvador. On the east coast, in Mozambique, the Jesuits met with worse failure: their attempt to establish themselves at Quilimani, Chinde and Sena resulted in the martyrdom of their little bands, who were the victims of Moslem fanaticism.

In America, on the other hand, Jesuit intervention was often decisive. To begin with, at any rate, they did not try to compete with the Dominicans and Franciscans in districts where those ancient Orders had been successful. Instead they placed their indefatigable energy and superb organization at the service of the apostolate in countries where the missions appeared to be doing little or to lack co-ordination. This was so in Brazil, where the Franciscans had obtained none but meagre and scattered results. Six Fathers arrived there in 1549, with Fr Nobrega as their superior; having settled not far from where Catherine of Brazil had begun her work, they learned the language of the country, took a keen interest in the material conditions of native life and soon converted several hundreds. Five years later there were five new Jesuit stations, one of which, São Paulo, was destined to a great career, and it was not long before Fr Jose d'Achieta composed those vernacular hymns which are still sung in Brazilian churches. The incompetence of the first bishop, who reached Bahia in 1552,[1] temporarily jeopardized the results already achieved, but it did not altogether destroy them. On the threshold of the seventeenth century Fr Antonio Vieira, the apostle of Rio de Janeiro, began his work of evangelization in the towns and countryside, and he was so zealous in defence of the natives against the rapacity of certain colonists that he found himself in trouble with the Inquisition.

It was chiefly in Paraguay and Uruguay that the Jesuit missions proved themselves most original and most effective. In these countries the Franciscans had had very little success: the Guaranis remained faithful to their customs and ancestral ideas. The Bishop of Tucuman, Francisco Victoria, therefore determined to seek help from the Society. Three Jesuits arrived in 1558 and were joined soon afterwards by several more of their brethren. They also, to begin with, obtained negligible and disappointing results. Seeking to know why, they came to the conclusion that there were two great obstacles hindering the progress of evangelization: first, the natives were nomads, lazy and hard to reach; second, they detested the Spanish colonists who pillaged their goods and stole their wives. It was therefore necessary, if possible, to separate them from the Spaniards and to settle them in territories where they would learn to work. This was a revival and adaptation of an old missionary idea familiar in the Dark Ages: to Christianize you must first civilize. The Jesuits accordingly set to work with this new outlook, persuading a number of Guaranis to allow themselves to be 'reduced' to civilization.

Thus, at the end of the sixteenth century, there was inaugurated and tested a system known in history as 'reductions.' King Philip III of Spain was convinced of its excellence. Some thirty districts ('reductions'), containing about 120,000 natives, were organized as regular Jesuit fiefs, the Fathers assuming responsibility for direction, administration, supervision, military defence, control of production and exchange, and of course religious instruction. The life of the Guaranis

[1] He was later devoured by cannibals.

was transformed. They learned to build houses, to cultivate the soil and to handle weapons. A truly communal régime was established, under which every man possessed only his house and his fields, but was secured by collective ownership against the risks of scarcity or enforced idleness. A daily distribution was made to each family in order to avoid waste, for the Indians were most improvident. Everyone did his turn of work on 'God's domain,' an estate intended to supply the Fathers' own needs and to cover the cost of public worship and assistance. It is pleasant to recall that the Jesuits, finding that their natives had a strong liking for music, gave a prominent place to concerts and community singing in their missionary work. This curious practice, which helped to create the 'legend of the kindly savage,' lasted until the suppression of the Society in 1768; it is one of the most astonishing proofs of a limitless faculty of adaptation among the sons of St Ignatius for the greater glory of God.[1]

But it was not only to the Indians that the Jesuits brought the word of God with so much courage and understanding. One of the most splendid jewels in their crown is the fact that they did not forget the wretched human cattle who were rounded up in Africa by pitiless traders and shipped across the Atlantic in frightful conditions, dying by thousands or suffering a fate worse than death.

One Father in particular devoted himself to the care of these unfortunates: St Peter Claver (1580–1654), son of Catalonian peasants, who joined the Society and was sent to Colombia. Settling at Cartagena, the great missionary showed himself a true friend and protector of the Negroes; he met them on arrival, cared for the sick and wounded, accompanied them to the plantations and squalid huts where the colonists herded them together, and never ceased for thirty-nine years to convert, baptize and love them. Nothing was able to turn St Peter Claver from his apostolate, neither the wrath and counter-attacks of the whites, nor even the occasional obtuseness of his own poor charges, some of whom detested him because of the mere colour of his skin. No missionary has ever possessed a soul more gentle and fraternal, more enlightened or more tender, than did this son of Loyola.

7. JESUITS IN THE REALM OF PRESTER JOHN

Among the numerous adventures experienced by the Society of Jesus during the first half-century of its existence, one of the strangest and most lively took place in the most mysterious country of that time, the famous 'Realm of Prester John.' Throughout the Middle Ages there had been talk of this fabulous personage, who was said to be

[1] It was from this practice that the dramatist Hochwälder borrowed the theme of his beautiful play *On Earth as in Heaven*.

descended from Solomon and the Queen of Sheba. According to tradition he dwelt with unimaginable pomp in his capital, Hulna, served by seven kings at a table of gold and amethyst, reigning over an empire of seventy-two monarchies, officially styled 'King of Kings of the Three Indies, of the Pygmies, Amazons, Cynocephali and Horned Cocles.' The only trouble was that no one knew the exact whereabouts of this empire, which Marco Polo, William of Plan-Carpin and Rubrouk had tried to discover in the heart of Asia. About 1230, however, an Ethiopian abbot and his community, living on the Mount of Olives in Palestine, declared themselves to be subjects of Prester John; and from that time it was generally considered that the mysterious kingdom was none other than Abyssinia, the mountainous region of Ethiopia which for hundreds of years had been the home of Monophysite Christians.[1]

At the end of the fifteenth century contact was established between the Negus [2] and the West. In mortal peril from the Moslem tide, Ethiopia turned to the Latin Christians, since those of the East were now powerless to assist her. In 1481 an embassy reached Jerusalem, appealing for help to the Franciscans of the Holy Land. Upon their advice it travelled to Rome, and a legation under Friar John Baptist of Imola was sent to assure the Negus of the Holy Father's sympathy. Not long afterwards a Portuguese expedition landed in Abyssinia, where some of them remained to support the local Christians in their struggle with Islam. The Moslem threat became more serious during the reign of the Negus David, Lebna Denghel (1507–40), and Portuguese assistance, friendly and generous though it was, appeared insufficient. The Negus appealed once again to Rome, and a number of delegations passed between Ethiopia and Italy; they were partly diplomatic and partly religious, for the Negus had let it be known that he was prepared to re-enter the fold of the Catholic Church.

Then a ludicrous incident occurred. David's successor, Claudius Asnaf Sagad (1540–59), wrote to King John III of Portugal asking him whether he could throw some light on the case of a man who was claiming to be Roman Catholic Patriarch of Ethiopia, but of whom he had good reason to be suspicious. The man in question was John Bermudez, a Portuguese settler, an aspiring adventurer whose ignorance was matched by a sense of his own importance. This fellow had played a trick that was common enough, but easy to pull off in an age of slow communications: having presented himself in the West as Patriarch of Ethiopia, he returned to Abyssinia and assured the Negus, without producing a scrap of evidence, that the title had been conferred upon him by Pope Paul III in private audience.

[1] See *The Church of the Apostles and Martyrs* and *The Church in the Dark Ages* (Indexes).
[2] This was the secular title of the mythical Prester John.

The episode had an unexpected result. The King of Portugal asked the Jesuits to investigate the whole affair. St Ignatius agreed to do so and ordered a careful inquiry to be made; he even interrogated several members of the Council of Trent, and received from Fr Salmeron a detailed report which proved Bermudez to be an impostor. But the hoax had drawn the Society's attention to Ethiopia and the opportunities for evangelization which they might find there. The position of the Negus being more than ever endangered, both by the Moslems and by his own vassals, small Portuguese commandos were sent to reinforce him. St Ignatius determined to seize this opportunity and launch a fully organized mission. Fr Gonzalo Rodriguez was sent out alone to have a look at the country and study the general situation; then, in 1555, Pope Julius III officially appointed three Fathers to go and establish a Catholic hierarchy in Ethiopia. Fr Nunes Barreto, formerly prison chaplain at Tetuan, received the title of Patriarch; Fr Andrea d'Oviedo, the great mystic who had received the secret vows of Duke Francis Borgia, and Fr Melchior Carneiro were to be his coadjutors. Before they left to carry out this difficult undertaking, St Ignatius gave his sons meticulous and remarkably pertinent instructions, which were destined to serve as the guiding principles of many subsequent missionaries. He advised them to adapt themselves as far as possible to the customs of those whom they hoped to convert, to take with them books and scientific instruments, and to make a point of rendering the Ethiopians all those services which the higher standards of European civilization enabled them to provide. This was exactly the method employed in China, fifty years later and with such great success, by Fr Matteo Ricci.

As things turned out this first Jesuit mission accomplished very little. The Patriarch Nunes Barreto was prevented by sickness from joining the group, so that the actual leader was Fr Oviedo, who fell foul of the royal household, of the Monophysite clergy, and even of certain European merchants. At his first meeting with the Negus he was completely disillusioned. His patriarchal title, inherited on the death of his superior, sounded most impressive; but he was really nothing more than a poor, ragged priest in a miserable village called Tigre, digging his own garden to supply his modest wants, yet radiantly happy in that oppressive solitude. A party of Jesuits sent from Goa to relieve him had been captured by Arab pirates. Father Carneiro was no more successful. Worse, however, was to come: an unco-operative Negus was succeeded by Adamas Sagad, a former Moslem, who showed himself openly hostile. Persecution followed; Oviedo was arrested and held in custody until the tyrant's death (1563). But the aged Father, who had been joined by a few younger men, proudly and heroically declined to follow the advice of Pope Pius V to quit that ungrateful land. He died in 1577, still loyal to the mission entrusted to him by St Ignatius.

The Society of Jesus was determined to persevere, whether or not Oviedo's tenacity bore fruit. The situation was grave: the Turks controlled the Red Sea, thus blocking the route to Ethiopia, which was itself in the throes of a ten-year dynastic crisis. Despite these obstacles a fresh team of Jesuits set out in 1589. It consisted of two men, each remarkable in a different way. One, Fr Antonio de Monserrate, had long resided at the Great Mogul's court and was well acquainted with Moslem customs; the other, Fr Pedro Paez, was fluent in the dialects of Ethiopia—Gheez, the liturgical language, and Amharic, the language of common speech. The new Negus, Susnejos Seltan Sagad (1607–32), was seriously alarmed by the Ottoman advance, and realized that nothing but Western support could save him. He consulted Fr Paez, who advised him to write a letter to the Sovereign Pontiff saying that he wished to be instructed in the Roman faith; and some time later (1613) he formally notified the new Patriarch, Fr Mendez, that he accepted Catholicism.

There followed a wonderful period of intense and successful apostolic activity. Travelling continually over hill and dale, delighting his audiences with his knowledge of their tongue, and at the same time exploring Ethiopia [1] and writing his *History*, Fr Paez obtained an impressive number of conversions. Not every stage of the enterprise, however, was quite so simple. Fr Abraham de Georgiis, a Lebanese Maronite who had been sent to help Paez, disguised himself as an Armenian merchant; but despite his dress and swarthy Levantine complexion, he was spotted by the Turkish coastal police and beheaded. Yet it really seemed that the whole of Ethiopia was on the point of re-entering the Catholic fold, and Pope Urban VIII was already singing a Hosanna.

The battle, which had started so well, was lost through the fault of the new Patriarch, Fr Alfonso Mendez, one of the very few Jesuits of that period (and perhaps of all time) who proved themselves incompetent. Fr Paez, worn out before his time, [2] beheld with dismay the peril threatening his work as his new superior demanded written forms of abjuration from the Negus's relations and from all the great vassals, as well as taking steps to abolish the traditional liturgy and reorganize the Jacobite clergy. Mendez was in fact running directly counter to the wise methods advised by St Ignatius; and when he decided to forbid circumcision and the observance of the Sabbath (two practices observed by the Ethiopians from time immemorial) indignation knew no bounds. The Negus endeavoured to support him,

---

[1] He was the first European to see the sources of the Blue Nile.
[2] He died in 1622 at the age of forty.

but succeeded only in precipitating a revolution against himself. A few years later his successor expelled the Jesuits and closed his empire to all Western missionaries. The Catholic cause had come to grief in the realm of Prester John.

8. A Sublime Pioneer: St Francis Xavier

The missionary vocation, which had summoned Jesuits to every part of the world since the very foundation of the Society, was assumed in all its plenitude of purpose and self-sacrifice by a man whose name became symbolic. When he was ordered to the East, he replied in four short words: '*Pues sus! Heme acqui!*' ('Forward! Here I am!'). No religious has ever repeated them, in equal circumstances, with so much joy. And which of them, striving and suffering in distant lands 'for the greater glory of God,' would not henceforward carry in his heart the memory of that stupendous person who in the space of ten years travelled more than 62,000 miles, from whose hand the baptismal water flowed upon the brows of many thousands, who planted the Cross where it had never yet been seen, and to whom Christ granted the supreme grace of dying in His service stripped of all earthly things? It may be that some of his miracles, prophecies and other extraordinary gifts are legendary; indeed twenty-five years after his death the Society ordered a strict investigation in order to distinguish truth from error. But what is most certainly *not* mere invention is his boundless activity, his inexhaustible charity and that burning fever, as it were, for the salvation of souls; in a word, his brilliant understanding of what the apostolate requires. There was not in his time, nor has there been from that day to this, a missionary who did not feel himself in some sense a disciple and debtor of St Francis Xavier (1506–52).

King John III of Portugal, ever in search of good apostolic workers for his empire overseas, had heard tell of a young religious foundation which was said to be achieving great things, and he asked Pope Paul III to give him some of its members. That was early in 1540. Francis was in Rome. The founder, St Ignatius, at once agreed without stopping to ask himself whether the departure of two or three would not leave a disastrous gap in the narrow ranks of his little band. A Jesuit does not evade an order from the Pope. The first man selected fell sick, so the leader chose another—and what another! His dearest friend perhaps, one of the companions of his early years, his spiritual brother. To part now was to part for ever, and both knew it. 'To see one another again face to face, to hold one another once more in fond embrace, that is for a future life,' wrote Francis some time later to his superior. But what did it matter, since the Master willed it so? On 7th April 1541, aboard the flagship *Santiago*, whose large square sails marked with a scarlet cross were leading the annual Portuguese flotilla to the East Indies, Francis, accompanied by two of his brethren, set out upon an enterprise he would never abandon until he breathed his last. He was then thirty-five years old.

He owed his vocation, nay his salvation, to one who had shown him Asia as the field of his apostolic labours. If the 'martinet' Iñigo, the beggar of Mont Sainte-Geneviève, had not come to share the room he then occupied with Pierre Le Fèvre at the College of St Barnabas, it is doubtful whether Francis would have overcome the worldly ambitions then besetting him, whether his dreams would have become dreams of God. To him, as to his comrades and so many others, the Basque's *Spiritual Exercises* revealed the straight road that leads to Christ. On that bright morning of 15th August 1534, when with his five compaions he signed the vow of Ignatius on the hill of Montmartre, his life took a new direction, or, rather, discovered its true destiny. The King of Portugal's appeal and this journey into unknown worlds merely provided him with an opportunity to accomplish what he had undertaken once for all to do: to serve God without dispute, without hesitation, without regret, until the very end.[1]

As he embarked for the Indies, wearing the long soutane and square cap, Francis was a fine figure of a man; nobility was stamped upon his features. In his veins ran the ardent blood of the Jassu, lords of Xavier, who had fought in many a battle for their Navarrese overlords against Castile. Of middle height and very well proportioned, with eyes set straight in pleasant features, he was attractive at first sight, and the warmth of his speech alone was sufficient to convince. But beneath these luminous externals there were also many mysteries, and even contradictions. A proud man vanquished, an ambitious man who had placed his desires at the service of a sublime cause? Yes, most certainly; all his life long there would be found in his taste for adventure the impetuosity of his youth, and in his natural authority his old liking for domination. For the rest he seldom gave utterance to his thoughts, writing hardly at all (only thirty-seven of his letters have survived) and never speaking either of himself or of his interior struggles: a secret man, who has remained such in the eyes of history. It is easy to recall the stages of his life, but far less so to follow, in the apostle's conquest of the world, God's conquest of the apostle. Only by watching him at work, by measuring the extent of his charity and heroism, can we guess that an ineffable union with Christ must have lain at the root of his adventurous life. Francis Xavier ranks alongside Bernard of Clairvaux, Joan of Arc, Louis IX of France and Teresa of Avila, all of whom considered temporal work as the living expression and projection of an interior and invisible experience.

[1] See Chapter I, section 10.

K

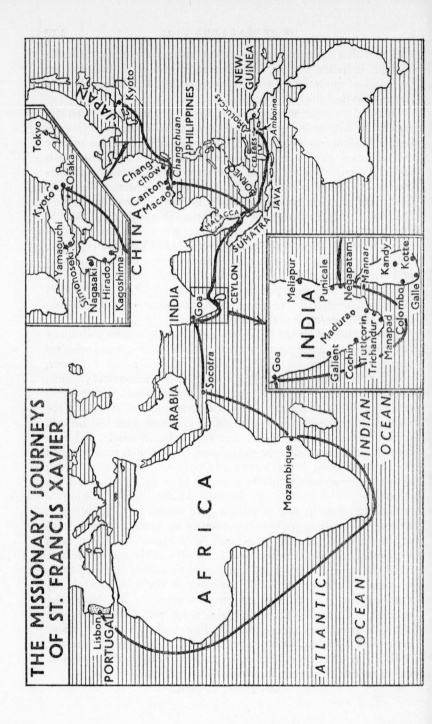

THE MISSIONARY JOURNEYS
OF ST. FRANCIS XAVIER

He soon had occasion to begin his apostolate aboard the very ship that was carrying him to the East. The voyage was appalling; in normal circumstances it took six months to travel from Lisbon to Goa, but the *Santiago* took thirteen. The tireless missionary pursued his task of kindliness and consolation among the little mass of humanity— emigrants, Ethiopian slaves and crew—huddled between decks and exasperated with one another's company day after day. Thanks to him there were fewer brawls, blows and blasphemies on that voyage than was usual. He preached on deck, he preached to the slaves; and when he landed at Goa in May 1542 he was already looked upon as a man of God.

Officially he arrived as apostolic nuncio, accompanying the viceroy and armed with full powers. A remarkable nuncio forsooth, who disdained pomp and ceremony, knelt humbly before the Franciscan archbishop, John of Albuquerque, and went to lodge in the hospital, caring for the sick and even lepers. He quickly became well known among the poorest inhabitants of Goa. When he walked through the streets, ringing a little hand-bell, people crowded round, eager to hear him. There was a striking contrast between this man of God and too many members of the Portuguese clergy resident in the city, who were hand in glove with the colonists and traders, and hardly troubled to evangelize the native masses. It was with those very natives that Francis was chiefly concerned. Not that he made no effort to improve the conquerors; but from now until the end of his life he was deeply afflicted by the sight of Catholics behaving so cruelly, so unjustly and so dishonestly; by the knowledge that masters flogged their slaves, that clever and shameless swindlers obtained ivory and precious stones from the Hindus in exchange for worthless materials and hideous trinkets. He wrote frequently to the king at Lisbon, protesting against such methods, but it is doubtful whether those letters ever reached His Majesty.

Then, leaving Goa and its European playboys, he set off on the great hunt for souls. His nunciature gave him authority over almost the whole of Asia, at least from Ormuz to the Pacific Ocean. Having made a start, he seldom again paused. The remainder of his life was spent, as it were, in the grip of traveller's fever, journeying continually by land or sea, halting just long enough to sow the Gospel grain and see it sprout. It was indeed a superhuman task performed in burning heat or the heavy monsoon rains, along roads that were rivers of mud or carpets of dust, or in the hold of a storm-tossed vessel. His health rapidly deteriorated, but not his faith or his enthusiasm. If the population of a native village, to whom he had done his best with the aid of an interpreter to explain the rudiments of Christianity, asked for baptism, he felt all his efforts well rewarded.

As a fisher of men he drew his miraculous draughts from among the

lonely, the despised, the pariahs. Among the high castes little or no
headway was made; to the Brahmins and great lords the very idea of
Christian brotherhood was an object of contempt. But the apostle had
a good deal of success with the unfortunate husbandmen of the plains
and the pearl-fishers on the coast, especially among the Paravers around
Cape Comorin. These people had already been given the rudiments of
faith, which were now only vague memories and paltry rites; Francis
rekindled these dying embers of Christianity and conferred baptism
upon thousands. Not every stage of his apostolate, indeed, was quite so
easy. For example, he sent one of his disciples to Manar, intending no
doubt to make the island, once converted, a stepping-stone to Ceylon;
but the sudden rage of a petty Moslem despot caused a massacre. The
blood of martyrs, however, has always been the seed of Christianity.
Sorrowful, but by no means discouraged, the missionary resumed his
task. On the coast of Travancore he did good work among the 'Christians of St Thomas'; [1] he performed wonders among the pagans, ten
thousand of whom were said to have been baptized in a few weeks.
Surely this was Heaven's best answer, the true sign. Within a period of
thirty days Francis converted more Hindus than all his Portuguese
predecessors had done in thirty years.

This rapid apostolate, whose extent has sometimes been disputed,
reminds us of the great missions of the Dark Ages conducted by such
men as St Martin, St Boniface, St Amand, St Columbanus and St Gall,
when whole tribes received baptism without possessing theological
knowledge proportionate to their goodwill. It seems more than
probable that St Francis Xavier's panegyrists have exaggerated his
apostolic achievements. One says he baptized 400,000 souls; another
puts the figure at over a million—329 a day! But the apostle himself
informs us that he several times effected mass conversions and administered the sacrament to entire villages at a single ceremony; he even
states that on some occasions his arm was weary. Do such methods
entitle us to regard him as a rash adventurer, a record-holder in non-
stop baptism? We have no right to judge so extraordinary a man and
his work according to the standards of our discretion and our narrow
human wisdom. What knowledge of Christianity, it may be asked, had
those converts who had merely been affused with holy water and to
whom the missionary, ignorant of the language, could say nothing
directly? He himself supplies the answer in a noble letter: 'The
important things of life need no interpreters.' His real instruments were
charity, brotherly compassion, the mercy of Christ in action. What he
revealed by this frenzied religious propaganda (as some might call it)
was the heart-rending conviction that all the peoples of Asia had been
entrusted to him, and that he must succour them quickly before the

[1] See *The Church in the Dark Ages*, p. 370.

powers of Hell could establish dominion over them. He voiced this anguish in the splendid 'Prayer for the Conversion of Infidels,' which he wrote at Goa just before re-embarking for more distant lands and which may be taken as a summary of his thought.

Farther, still farther, to win souls, ever more souls! Following the Coromandel coast northward, Francis reached Meliapur in 1545, expecting to find other remnants of the 'Christians of St Thomas.' Thence he journeyed to Malaysia, where there were still some Portuguese settlements. He called at Malacca; spent two years of constant travel among the islands of Sunda and the archipelago of Molucca; interrupted his voyage at Amboine, in order to combat the 'excessive carnality' which reigned in those voluptuous regions; and spent some time among the fiercest tribes of Keram and the island of More, resisting every onslaught of fatigue, every disappointment and every temptation to despair. In December 1547 he returned to Malacca, the crossroads of all the Far Eastern routes, and there God's will was made known to him again.

This time Providence revealed itself in the shape of a little man with olive skin and narrow eyes, wearing a brown tunic and carrying a lacquer-sheathed sword such as was never seen in that part of the world. He was accompanied by a Portuguese who was known to Francis, and who told him that this strange little fellow had travelled hundreds of leagues by land and sea for the express purpose of meeting the missionary. He was a Japanese, one Hashiro, whose name Dom Alvarez rendered as 'Angiro' when introducing him to Francis. Between the two men there was immediately established complete confidence and affection. Baptized as Paul of Santa Fé, the Japanese had only one idea—to take the saint back to Japan and thus bring about the conversion of his fellow countrymen. All that he told Francis Xavier seemed to the latter pregnant with possibility. And so, returning with his disciple to Goa, he set aside a wealth of good advice to the contrary and made careful preparations for the stupendous undertaking which was to end by his planting the Cross in the Empire of the Rising Sun.

The voyage, made during the summer of 1549, was fraught with danger and discomfort. The Chinese junk chartered by the missionary was a mere hulk, and all the prayers recited, all the sticks of incense burned before the idol in its niche on the forecastle, did not prevent a typhoon from battering the frail craft and nearly sinking her. Despite those pious offerings, also, there was sickness among passengers and crew, and the skipper's daughter was swept overboard by a wave. At length they reached Japan and landed at Kagoshima, Angiro's home. The ruler, a certain Prince Satsuma—'the duke,' Francis calls him— gave them a kindly welcome, and some converts were made. But these auspicious beginnings did not last very long. Japan was at that time in the throes of feudal anarchy, under the purely nominal authority of an indolent Mikado. The Shoguns—they may be compared to the ancient Merovingian mayors of the palace—governed exclusively in their own interests, while the great vassals in the provinces did exactly as they pleased. The disorder was such that the Buddhist monasteries were turned into fortresses, as a necessary measure of self-defence; but they were also the strongholds of brigand chiefs. A humble missionary might go unnoticed amid this chaos, but it was unlikely that he would accomplish very much.

St Francis Xavier did not abandon hope. Having learnt Japanese he agreed to take part in a series of public debates with the bonzes, hoping that if he convinced them the rest of the people would follow. The first of these discussions was cut short; exposition of the Christian theology made the Buddhists laugh; but when they realized that the foreigner was gaining some influence with the people, the priests obtained from the local *da'imo* an order depriving him of civil rights. This was a good excuse for yet another journey. The missionary had heard of Miako (modern Kyoto) a city of ninety thousand houses, capital of the Mikado and an intellectual centre where nearly four thousand students attended five universities. Landing therefore on the largest island of the archipelago he set out for his destination. It was winter, a winter whose severity he had not foreseen. Weeks of suffering followed, from snow and ice and biting winds; at every halting-place there were poor lodgings and often mockery or a shower of stones hurled by children. And all for—what? A twofold disappointment: half ruined by civil war, the wonderful city was now an abode of misery; while the Mikado, suspicious on account of their shabby appearance, would not receive the heralds of Christ.

Fortunately—the episode is delightful, worthy of the *Golden Legend* —Francis had brought in his baggage a few smart European suits and some valuable presents: a clock, a sort of clavecin or cithern, a handsome arquebus, telescopes and mirrors. Thus transformed into an ambassador of the King of Portugal, he looked more presentable, and was received by a member of the aristocracy. For several months it seemed that his mission was going to be fruitful; here there was no longer question of mass conversions, but of a slow and lasting conquest of souls, some five or six hundred baptisms. The most sensational conquest was that of 'Laurenço,' the half-blind wandering minstrel, who was famous throughout Japan and who afterwards became the first Jesuit of the yellow race. The highest hopes seemed justified when Francis received a letter from St Ignatius appointing him Provincial of the East Indies; he had to quit the land of islands and return to Goa, leaving behind him a young and growing Church.

He brought back, however, from Japan, apart from these encouraging memories, a new and grand idea. He had repeatedly heard tell of China as the motherland of civilization, a beacon illuminating all the Far East. To China therefore he must carry the Gospel, so that it might radiate thence over the whole of Asia. But his first task was to deal with the Society's affairs at Goa. In place of an inefficient Superior of the Seminary he appointed Fr Barzée, who had done great work at Ormuz; then he bequeathed to the Fathers as his spiritual testament a body of decisive instructions, which revealed his uncompromising devotion to humility, abnegation and sacrifice. Those duties were quickly performed, and he once more put to sea.

Humility, abnegation, sacrifice—no words could better describe the spirit of this final stage. The gateway to China was Canton, where the Portuguese had a trading post. How to get there? Once more to Malacca; once again to board a miserable hulk bearing the proud name of *Santa Croce*; and once again to face the perils of the sea, whether from pirates or from sickness. This latter proved to be the worst. Just as his ship arrived at the island of Chang-chuen-shan, within sight of China, a malignant fever struck down the apostle. He had to be carried ashore in agony, grievously disappointed that he was not able to receive the answer to his request for permission to land at Canton, but still hoping against hope to penetrate China and win souls. At Chang-chuen-shan, on the very threshold of the Promised Land, he died (Saturday, 3rd December 1552), in a wretched thatched hovel, attended by a Hindu deacon and a young Chinese cleric, the future Fr Antonio de Santa Fé, to whom we owe the account of his noble end. The apostle's last words were not understood by his Chinese disciple, for in his delirium the dying man spoke Basque, the language of his childhood; but he was heard to repeat several times the name of Jesus.

St Francis Xavier's lonely death was not that of the vanquished. Lying there on the threshold of a continent he would never reach, where he would never sow the seed of Christ, he would certainly not have said that all his work had been in vain. It would clearly be an exaggeration to call his achievement an unqualified success; subsequent events showed it to have been in large measure ephemeral.[1] On the other hand we must realize that one man, almost single-handed, confronting the immensity of Asia and the solid ranks of Buddhism, could not in the space of ten years have obtained a lasting success. The real function of St Francis Xavier was that of a pioneer, a conqueror, a sublime precursor. He himself knew that such was his vocation when he wrote: 'I pray God to give me the grace to open the way for others, even though I myself accomplish nothing.'

[1] Less than thirty years after his death the Christian communities he had founded in India were in serious jeopardy, and those in the Moluccas had relapsed into paganism.

'A missionary is not a man who can call a halt, any more than is a sower. An apostolate that ceases to progress can no longer be called missionary.' [1] Pius XII described the missionary's duty as follows: 'He must extend the kingdom of the Divine Redeemer even to the most distant and unknown dwelling, even to the most distant and unknown of men.' [2] And the same Pope paid a splendid tribute to the rôle assumed by Francis in these words: 'Cautious planning . . . would never have had the effect of that great flame of love which devoured him in a few years and which shines for ever on the shores of the Far East.' [3]

9. PERSECUTION AND MARTYRDOM IN THE 'FLOURISHING GARDEN OF GOD'

The history of the missions in Asia during the two hundred years after the death of St Francis Xavier is simply that of the flowering and then the destruction of his work. When quitting Japan in 1551 he left behind a single Father, Cosimo de Torres, but also some firmly established Christian centres. Provided reinforcements were made available, there was every possibility that these centres would soon increase. One Jesuit priest and two lay-brothers were sent in the following year, and they set to work without delay. When Fr Nunes Barreto [4] visited the young Japanese Churches in 1556, he wrote a report paying tribute to the results already obtained by the great apostle and his immediate successors. Was this only because the political situation was at that time highly favourable, the general anarchy causing the *da'imos* to rely upon the Portuguese for help against the princes of Hondo? Or was there some mysterious link between the Christian religion and the Japanese people with their profound moral sense, their great dignity and their exquisite delicacy? Whatever the answer, progress was rapid. A nobleman writing from the island of Sanga in 1558 expressed surprise that a faith 'contrary to the laws, customs and notions of Japan' should make so strong an appeal to so many of his compatriots. Despite obstacles with which for many years the ocean and its typhoons constantly harassed all the missionaries sent out from Goa,[5] the grain scattered by St Francis Xavier did not cease to germinate. Among the most outstanding leaders of this early apostolate was Laurenço, the wandering minstrel whom Francis had admitted to the Society. By means of his

[1] Mgr Chappoulie, *Rome et les missions d'Indochine au XVIIᵉ Siècle*, Paris, 1943.
[2] *Evangelii Praecones*, 1951.
[3] Speech to the Superior Council of Pontifical Missionary Works, 28th August 1952.
[4] Formerly Patriarch of Ethiopia; he was St Francis Xavier's second successor as Provincial of the East Indies.
[5] Fr Vilhana was drowned with four other Jesuits in a shipwreck off Macao.

songs and his personal charm he won for the Christians, at any rate for a time, the goodwill of Nobunaga, the most powerful member of the nobility, to whom everyone kowtowed.

Fifteen years after the departure of St Francis Xavier the number of Japanese Christians reached, according to the most reliable estimates, the astonishing figure of 150,000. Fr Luis Froes, who arrived in 1563, founded Christian communities at Omura, Sakai and Nagasaki, which last became the most active centre of the Japanese Church. He wisely laid stress upon every feature of Christianity which might remind the Japanese of their ancestral customs (e.g. ceremonies in honour of the dead), and we still possess his moving account of a Japanese 'Holy Week.' The conversion of four bonzes was a bright feather in the Society's cap. Moreover Nobunaga, who became master of Japan after a tragic crisis involving the assassination of the Shogun, hated the Buddhist monks and encouraged the Jesuits. Nor did his fall and death by hara-kiri long impede the success of the white missionaries.

This was the zenith of Catholicism in the Empire of the Rising Sun, 'the age of the greatness of the Southern Barbarians,' as a contemporary Buddhist romance describes it. Landing in 1579 under the leadership of Fr Valignani, an energetic and capable Italian, fourteen Jesuits divided the islands into missionary sectors and were brilliantly successful at almost every point. More than three hundred churches were built in less than thirty years; the number of baptized was approaching 200,000, and the Father Visitor spoke enthusiastically of Japan as the 'flourishing garden of God.' When he left for the Indies he took with him a delegation of four young Japanese Christians of the highest nobility, proposing to send them as ambassadors of the Church in Japan to the King of Portugal and the Pope. The four youths were away from home for five long years, and they had some thrilling experiences: Philip II received them with great pomp, they were welcomed by Gregory XIII, and they attended the coronation of Sixtus V. Everywhere they gave evidence of their perfect manners, and when they returned to Japan they told their fellow countrymen of the wonderful things they had seen in Europe. Three of them became Jesuits, one of whom, Julian Nakaura, died a martyr's death.

But amid all this happiness the Japanese Church soon met with misfortune. To begin with, the progress of Protestantism in Europe and the growth of Dutch and English sea-power had one deplorable result: ships carrying missionaries were often intercepted by their European enemies. Again, the political situation in Japan itself continued unsettled, with serious consequences for the Church. The first alarm was sounded in 1587, when the Taikosama, 'supreme ruler,' [1] having dethroned the benevolent Nobunaga, promulgated anti-Catholic

---

[1] So he styled himself, though he was nothing but a common bandit chief.

* K

decrees, simply because two Christian girls had refused to enter his seraglio. The Jesuits lay low until the storm had passed, and then came out of hiding. At this time there were 134 of them ministering to 300,000 souls. At their request the first Japanese bishopric was created in 1592, and now the hurricane broke loose.

Its causes were various and complex. Some can be traced to the internal affairs of Japan. The Taikosama Hidyeshi must have noticed the increasing influence of Christianity, and he was doubtless alarmed thereby; fifty thousand baptisms in five years might well give him food for thought. Again, Fr Coelho, the Provincial, was surely at fault in asking him to intervene against one of his vassals, an apostate Catholic. But above all, Hidyeshi's destruction of the feudal regime, and his efforts to create a unified and centralized state, led him inevitably to adopt a policy of more or less anti-foreign nationalism. This movement became more noticeable under his successor Ieyasu, who founded the powerful Shogun dynasty of Tokugawa.

There were nevertheless other causes for the catastrophe that was about to overwhelm Christian Japan, and responsibility for them lay with the Catholics, and even to some extent with the Jesuits themselves. The extraordinary success of the Japanese mission inspired other religious Orders with an ambition to go and win their laurels there, especially the Spanish Cordeliers in the Philippines. Quite rightly, and not only in the interests of their own Society, the Jesuits objected that the introduction of different clothing, different customs and even a slightly different theological approach was likely to upset the Japanese neophytes, and in 1585 they obtained from Gregory XIII a Bull which guaranteed them a monopoly of missions to Japan. But the Mendicants, driven, one likes to think, by a lofty if untimely evangelical zeal, would not rest until they had persuaded Clement VIII to revoke the Bull (1600) and allow them to preach in Japan. Bishop Cerqueira protested to Philip III, but in vain.

If only these newcomers had imitated the wisdom of the Jesuits; if only they had behaved with moderation and discretion. But no, they conducted themselves with the same arrogance that too many of their brethren were showing in America. Closely allied with the Portuguese traders, they appeared to the Japanese as what in fact they were—foreigners—whereas the Jesuits had enabled them practically to forget that they too were of another race. A single incident sufficed to unleash the fury of the Taikosama. In 1596 a Spanish captain, whose ship had been driven ashore on the coast, objected to the confiscation of his cargo, which was common practice in Japan. The Spaniard, however, blustered; he was stupid enough to tell the Japanese officials that the King of Spain would come and avenge this insult, that he would conquer Japan as he had conquered America, and that the missionaries were there to prepare for his arrival. It would have been a near-miracle if the Taikosama had not reacted to such provocation.

But the persecution was destined to have more disastrous consequences than it might otherwise have had, because the Jesuits, instead of admitting Japanese Catholics to the priesthood, kept them at arm's length for many years,[1] fearing that the new converts had insufficient theological training. They thought also that the Japanese Catholics, most of whom were very poor, would not be able to make proper provision for their priests. Furthermore the Spanish and Portuguese authorities considered that the creation of a native clergy would contradict the famous Bulls which entrusted their respective sovereigns with the duty and privilege of evangelization; so much so that when Blessed Sotelo, a Franciscan, obtained from Pope Paul V the promise that he would create a Japanese national bishopric, King Philip III had him expelled from his dominions and even imprisoned for a time at Manila. The Japanese Church, forced to remain a mere 'mission' church, would share the lot of its European missionaries; once they had been driven out, she would not be able to struggle on alone.

An initial persecution, then, broke out in 1596; it was relatively moderate in the sense that it did not aim systematically at the destruction of Christianity. Nevertheless it had its victims. Six Franciscans and twenty neophytes, including six Jesuit lay-brothers, were arrested, taken to Nagasaki, tried and condemned. They were crucified on 5th February 1597; among them were an old man and three children aged between eleven and thirteen, whose sublime deaths were worthy (though historically true in every detail) of those martyrs of the Golden Legend who sang amid their torments. However, this first blood-bath did nothing to prevent the growth of the Japanese Church. On the contrary: haloed thus with boundless veneration, of which there is evidence in a collective letter to the Holy See asking for the immediate canonization of the twenty-six crucified, the martyrs preached by the example of their deaths. Between 1598 and 1612 there were more than 100,000 new conversions: the Japanese Church had reached the number of half a million souls.

The second persecution cut down this young Christian tree and long continued to ravage the 'flourishing garden of God.' It began with an ignoble gesture on the part of some Dutch and English Protestants. Prompted by commercial rivalry, they approached the Shogun and told him that the Spanish and Portuguese Catholics were ready to revolt, that the Catholic sovereigns of Europe were going to land on his islands and attack him. The terrified Ieyasu promulgated in 1614 a decree banishing all missionaries, condemning the religion of the 'Southern Barbarians' and ordering the destruction of their churches.

[1] The first ordination of a Japanese took place in 1601.

More than one hundred Jesuits were conducted to Manila or Macao, and duly warned that if they returned they would be put to death without hope of mercy. A close watch was kept upon all ports. As for the Japanese Catholics, they found themselves subjected first to innumerable vexations, and then to downright ill treatment. Despite the heroic efforts of a handful of Jesuits and Franciscans who dared to remain secretly in Japan, or who returned there from exile, the Catholic communities were severed from their clergy and no longer had much chance of survival. In 1623 began the terrible persecution by the Shogun Yemitsu, a worthy rival in Christian history of Decius and Diocletian.[1] Victims were racked, roasted over slow fires, drowned in dung-water; there were astonishing acts of heroism, but also a number of defections, and some fled. Forty years later the Catholic Church in Japan was dead, and the only westerners admitted to the Empire of the Rising Sun were Dutch Protestant traders, and even they were obliged to trample on the cross before they were allowed to land.

Perhaps the most fundamental reason for this catastrophe is to be found in the choice of a wrong method. Christianity, a religion of foreigners, an imported religion, had not been able to take sufficiently deep root in the 'flourishing garden'; it had failed, as St Paul would have said, because it had been unable to make itself 'Japanese among the Japanese.' This error at least was not committed in China and India.

10. CHRIST ENTERS CATHAY WITH 'LI-MA-TEU'

In the year 1583 there landed at Macao two handsome Italian Jesuits who had been appointed by their superiors to the Chinese mission: Fr Michele Ruggieri, a Sicilian who had already made brief visits to those parts, and Fr Matteo Ricci. Macao was at that time the only Christian base in (or rather at the gates of) the Middle Kingdom, and so it was known as 'the city of the Holy Name of God.' And although the trading station was commonly regarded by the Chinese as a 'canker in the side of the August Empire,' the avarice of the mandarins at Canton had maintained the Portuguese in this small and easily isolated peninsula, where the courteous Chinese officials did not disdain to profit by the trade with Europe carried on at this free port. It was thirty years since St Francis Xavier had died on the little island of Chang-chuen-shan, at the mouth of the Canton River, which every missionary saluted with a fervent prayer as his ship sailed by. China was not much more open to the Gospel than it had been in the days when the holy pioneer had beheld it with his dying eyes, so near yet inaccessible. Nevertheless a few brave missionaries had set foot there. In 1555, while

---

[1] This persecution will be studied in the next volume of the present series.

on his way to Japan, the Father Visitor, Nunes Barreto, made two short stays of a month each; and in the following year a Dominican, Fr Gaspar de Cruz, was able to walk freely in the neighbourhood of Canton without being molested. When Fr Valignani was appointed Visitor-General for the Indies, in 1573, he decided to make Macao the permanent centre of missionary operations in China and to send there Fr Matteo Ricci, who had been the most distinguished of his pupils when he was prefect of the Society's college at Rome.

To penetrate the heart of China was considered in those days as the most perilous of undertakings. Very little was known about Central Asia at all, and the existence of the Himalaya was scarcely more than a rumour. There was even a geographical mystery about China itself: was it 'Cathay' of which Marco Polo had written in his *Book of Marvels*? Was 'the country of the Seres' really the land of silk visited by the Venetian traveller? And could it be reached by way of the Continent? St Francis Xavier had thought so; he had even written to St Ignatius, shortly before starting on his last journey, that he proposed to return directly from China to Europe via the Holy Sepulchre. It need hardly be said that the West was no less ignorant of the customs, literature and religion of China than of its geography. True there were books on these subjects, many of them translated from the Arabic, but very few Europeans thought of studying them.

It is to the unique credit of Fr Matteo Ricci (1552–1610) that, from the day of his appointment to the Chinese mission, he prepared scientifically for his apostolate with all the resources of a peerless intelligence. Ricci, son of well-to-do parents, was born at Macerata in the March of Ancona; he entered the Society of Jesus at the age of nineteen and quickly gave evidence of his encyclopaedic mind, typical of a Renaissance humanist. He was brilliant alike in ancient literature, in philosophy and in theology, but also in mathematics, cosmography and astronomy, all of which attainments, as we shall see, were to stand him in good stead. He went to the Indies in 1578 as professor first at the college at Goa and then at Cochin; and when he learned that his former teacher, now his superior, was thinking of sending him to China, he learned in the short space of one year to speak Chinese fluently and even to make a little headway with Chinese script. With his grave, handsome countenance, the long beard which he allowed to grow and his air of utmost reserve, he had already been taken for an Oriental; and, for good measure, his southern Italian complexion was not exactly one of roses and lilies.

Matteo Ricci knew China before he landed there. He had studied its philosophies, its classics and its religions. He knew that the Chinese held their country to be 'the head, or rather the very body of the world,' and that it would not be inopportune to flatter this pride. He was aware that the scholar caste wielded a good deal of influence, and therefore concluded that they were the people whom he must first approach, in order, if possible, to win their confidence. Never has a missionary plan been so carefully thought out as the strategy of this subtle and learned Jesuit. Making their residence at Chow-Kow, Ruggieri and Ricci spent some time cautiously observing local conditions and preparing their future action, without seeking to begin a premature apostolate. Fr Ricci was a skilled painter: his pictures soon won him the esteem of connoisseurs and scholars. So while Fr Ruggieri returned to Europe, in order to explain the situation in China to the Holy See and the Society, Fr Ricci continued his preparatory work, first at Chow-Kow, then at Nankin and finally at Pekin.

He was now well acquainted with China and the Chinese, especially with Chinese scholars. Studying the various religions practised in that country, he made a clear distinction between *Taoism*, an amalgam of polytheistic superstitions, *Buddhism*, agnostic and also somewhat corrupt, and *Confucianism*, a philosophy of morals rather than a religious doctrine; and he realized that all the intellectual *élite* was Confucian. Turning his back therefore upon Taoism and Buddhism, he lost no occasion of showing the Confucianists that Christianity was very much like their own teaching, and emphasized with great skill the points of resemblance. The technique was not new: the Fathers of the Church had done the same with Greek philosophy, and St Thomas Aquinas with Aristotle. Where there was a gap the able Jesuit filled it of his own accord. For example, as the word 'God' did not exist in Chinese, Ricci allowed that 'Lord of Heaven' or 'Sovereign Lord' perfectly expressed the idea. As for the Chinese ritual of kowtow and incensation, it was child's play to incorporate them with Christianity. Thus converts had no need, upon receiving baptism, to break with their immemorial customs. Chinese scholars, too, gladly associated with this eloquent and cultured man who taught them so many wonderful things without interfering with their way of life. They gave him (and it was a high honour) a literary name in their own caste—'Li-ma-teu,' a phonetic translation of his Christian name.

But what astonished the intellectuals more than anything else were the scientific instruments brought by the Jesuits, which were quite unknown in China: watches with their mysterious tick-tick, the astrolabe, the compass and the prism, which, by breaking up the solar light, seemed an absolute prodigy. Ricci's copy of *Theatrum Mundi*, a map by the Fleming Ortelius, dumbfounded all who beheld it; so much so that the Emperor San-li himself desired to make the acquaintance of these learned foreigners and summoned them to the Forbidden City. Fr Ricci and his helpers presented themselves to him dressed in the silken robes of a mandarin, which they had adopted several years earlier; they used their Chinese literary names, and behaved with all the elaborate ceremonial of Chinese courtesy. No fewer than half a dozen visits of four or five hours each were needed to exhaust the emperor's curiosity and that of his *entourage*. The Son of Heaven was enchanted: he had the use of the various instruments explained to him, and when he saw the map he asked Fr Ricci to make him a copy. But the Jesuit, with infinite tact, did far more than simply carry out the order. A former pupil of Fr Clavius, he knew enough of geography and cosmography to make with his own hands a new planisphere upon which the Chinese Empire, as was right and proper, occupied the centre and thereby appeared larger even than it was. The delivery of this map was considered so important that it was officially recorded in the annals of the Ming dynasty. The enraptured emperor directed that copies of the masterpiece should be made for all parts of his vast dominions, and he gave the Jesuit, his new Ptolemy, who of course had had this very end in view, permission to preach freely wherever he chose.

Such was the admirable result of a missionary method which, it must be said, was not to everyone's liking. Incidentally, in the course of his labours Fr Ricci had come to the definite conclusion that China was identical with 'Cathay' and 'the country of the Seres.' The Society, however, wishing to make assurance doubly sure, ordered one of its coadjutors, Bro. Bento de Goes, a Portuguese from the Azores who had had a somewhat stormy past, to undertake the journey. Disguised as a merchant, he travelled in about four and a half years from Goa to Suchow, where he died exhausted in the arms of a Christian who had been sent by Fr Ricci to meet him. The mystery of Cathay had been solved at last.

As for the strictly apostolic results of Fr Ricci's work, they may appear at first sight as out of proportion with the enormous sum of intellect and effort expended. When he died, on 14th May 1610 (the date of Henri IV's assassination in Paris), the number of Chinese converts did not exceed 2,500. Nevertheless nearly all of them belonged to the *élite* of China. There was 'Doctor Li,' for example, the leading mathematician of his country, who translated Aristotle; there were also a number of high officials, and even a future viceroy. It was clearly a very small flock that had assembled under the direction of the Jesuit mathematician and cartographer; but the door was henceforth open, through which the missionaries would be able to pass on their way into the enormous empire. The method inaugurated by 'Li-ma-teu' had proved so satisfactory that it was employed by very many Jesuits, and for nearly a century Jesuits were found at the court of Pekin acting as the emperor's official mathematicians and astronomers. About 1650 there were estimated to be about 150,000 Catholics in China, and the

Holy See was thinking of elevating Pekin to the dignity of a patriarchate, which would have included two or three archbishoprics and a dozen bishoprics. A splendid posthumous reward for the brilliant missionary, who, by showing the Son of Heaven the stars through his small telescope, succeeded in opening to Christ the most inaccessible country of that time.[1]

11. 'A Brahmin among the Brahmins': Fr de Nobili

If there was one country where missionaries had made the mistake of trying to impose the framework and methods of European Catholicism upon native converts, that country was India. St Francis Xavier worked hard to tear the missions from lamentable practices which caused the native mind to identify missionary work with European conquest. In poorer districts and among the lower orders of society he achieved the results we know; but it is doubtful, to say the least, whether he himself appreciated the importance of the caste system and understood the impossibility of ignoring it. On the other hand his constant journeying allowed him no time in which to study the dialects and civilization of India. In 1548 he had certainly ordered the compilation of a Tamil dictionary and grammar; but the job was bungled, and the translators were guilty of some appalling and occasionally amusing howlers. For instance, they translated 'Mass' as 'Misel,' which in Tamil means 'moustache.'

Consequently in the second half of the sixteenth century the only parts of India that had been seriously affected by the Gospel were the coasts of Cape Comorin, Travancore, Coromandel and the island of Ceylon, which together included some 300,000 Christians. The archbishopric of Goa, with its suffragan bishoprics of Meliapur and Cranganor (not to mention Macao in China), presented a handsome façade behind which there was little spiritual reality—dioceses administered on European lines, and more Portuguese than Hindu. In 1599, however, Catholicism won a notable success: the 200,000 descendants of the 'Christians of St Thomas' in the region of Cochin, who were subject to the heretical and schismatic Jacobite patriarch of Mesopotamia, but who retained vivid memories of a visit paid to them by St Francis Xavier, determined to submit to the Holy See. Unfortunately they were soon led to regret their decision by the stupidity of a few Western missionaries who wished forcibly to latinize the age-old Syro-Chaldaic rite, and to forbid them to pray in the popular tongue of

---

[1] Unfortunately, about fifty years later the Quarrel of Rites broke out. It was started by the Dominicans, and had some deplorable results. Fr Ricci's idea of 'baptizing' Chinese ways and customs was held to be unacceptable. See the next volume of this series.

Malabar. The resulting tension produced a new schism of 1633.[1] The whole affair was only too indicative of a widespread and vexatious spirit.

In 1610 this state of mind was judged by a missionary as follows: 'One great mistake committed by the Portuguese was to accept and appropriate to themselves the name *prangui* (applied to them by the Hindus), and even to describe Christianity as the religion of the *pranguis*, as is seen in their catechism. It is said there that "to practise the Christian religion is to live as a *prangui*." Hence the presumption in that country that Christianity was exclusively the religion of the *pranguis*, and that the crucifix was their peculiar sign. Such mistakes made it for ever impossible to preach the holy Gospel among those peoples.'

These forthright words were penned by an Italian Jesuit, Fr Roberto de Nobili (1577–1656). Grand-nephew of Pope Julius III, nephew of Cardinal de Nobili and of Cardinal Bellarmine, and son of the lord of Montepulciano in Tuscany, he was in the fullest meaning of the term an aristocrat; and when he introduced himself as a European 'rajah' he was not lying. Entering the Society of Jesus, he felt at once a strong attraction towards the Indies, and his mind was haunted by the example of St Francis Xavier. He therefore begged to be assigned to the mission, and in 1604 his request was granted. He landed at Goa, was attached for some time to the college of Cochin, then sent to the Fishery coast, and finally, in 1606, was given a post at Madura, farther inland.

Here the apostolate had achieved little or nothing. At the very most an occasional native was baptized *in articulo mortis*. The head of the mission, Fr Fernandez, was undoubtedly a holy man, but his enthusiasm had led nowhere. Fr de Nobili took stock of the situation and saw why. Fernandez, poor fellow, was living as a *prangui*, overlooking the social and religious organization which was much more rigid at Madura than on the coast. The Brahmins despised him for his readiness to mix with pariahs, while the common people looked upon him as a barbarian because he ate butcher's meat and drank intoxicating liquor. For these reasons the *prangui's* apostolic labours had inevitably failed.

Father de Nobili saw at once that, if he were going to succeed where his predecessor had experienced nothing but disappointment, he would have to introduce a completely new method of approach. Since it was evident that the high castes controlled public opinion, they were the people with whom he must deal first. The only thing to do was to follow Fr Ricci's example in China and make himself one of them, 'a Brahmin among the Brahmins.' Passing immediately from theory to practice, he assumed the yellow linen robe of the *sannyási* or 'ascetics' who were greatly respected. Like them he wore the toque turban-wise,

[1] Part of the Syro-Malabar Church became Catholic once again in 1930.

a red veil passed behind the head and gathered over the shoulders to the left arm. On his breast he hung the Brahmin *poûnoûl*, a cord of five strands, three gold and two silver, from which he hung a cross. He also adopted the wooden-soled sandals with a peg between the great and second toes; nor did he fail, when appearing in public, to carry the staff and leather pouch used by persons of his class for the reception of offerings. His lodging was the traditional hermit's hut of the *sannyâsi*, with whom he completely identified himself.

Before long everyone in Madura was talking about the Roman rajah who had become an ascetic, who ate no flesh-meat, drank no wine, lived only on vegetables and was never seen to speak with an 'untouchable' pariah. He was soon an object of curiosity, esteem and fellow feeling. He had made a close study of India, her peoples and her languages; he was fluent in Tamil, the popular dialect, but was also a master of Sanskrit. His knowledge of the Hindu Scriptures was so great that the most learned Brahmins came to talk with him, amazed to hear their sacred texts quoted from memory. Eventually they went so far as to ask him, a European, to enlighten them upon certain points of their own doctrines. Fr de Nobili discovered in the *Vedas* a tradition which he afterwards put to good use. It was related that once upon a time men had four ways of attaining to truth and salvation, but because of their wickedness the fourth and surest had been lost. Just as long ago St Paul had told the Athenians that their 'unknown god' was none other than Christ, so now Fr de Nobili explained to the Brahmins that Christianity was the lost way. So persuasively did he argue that in 1609 seventy of them were converted, and their example was followed not only at Madura, but also in Mysore and the Carnatic. These neophytes were convinced that by becoming Christians they were in no way breaking with their old faith and ancestral customs, and the Jesuit naturally allowed them to retain every one of their traditions that he did not consider idolatrous or superstitious.

This skilful method was not approved by all the Christians; Fr Fernandez in particular regarded it as a disavowal of his own, and also as an insult to national pride. In condemning 'pranguism,' as he did so freely, Fr de Nobili seemed to wish to expel the Portuguese from those districts where they had been authorized to preach the Gospel. Accused before the Father Visitor, the Italian Jesuit defended himself in a long and vigorous memorial, which we still possess and which is one of the most lucid expositions of missiology ever written. He shows that his technique was exactly such as the Church had always found successful, such as Pope St Gregory I had long ago advised when sending his missionaries to England. Reviewing the objections lodged against him —dressing in Hindu fashion, agreeing to take ritual baths, burning sandalwood and wearing the Brahmin cord—he proved that they were

absurd. As regards his rule that none but high-caste catechumens might
enter his Church, he explained that he had been led to make it by his
converts themselves, who would infallibly have been kept away by the
mere presence of pariahs. Despite this energetic defence, Fr Fernandez
succeeded in having his colleague's methods condemned by the
Inquisition at Goa. But de Nobili did not lose heart; he appealed to a
superior tribunal of the Inquisition at Lisbon, which upheld him in a
judgment that was confirmed in the most explicit manner by Gregory
XV. The affair of the 'Malabar Rites,' as it was called, had thus been
settled; but it was subsequently revived, and was one of the decisive
arguments used against the Society of Jesus in the eighteenth century.
Rome decided only that there were henceforth to be two classes of
missionaries: one, the Brahminical, for the high castes, and another,
known as *pandaras*, for the pariahs.

When he died (1656) at the College of San Thome, after an apostolate of nearly fifty years, Fr de Nobili left prosperous missions with
100,000 Christians at Madura, Trichinopoly and Selam. Missionaries of
today rightly look upon him as a precursor.

12. NON-JESUIT MISSIONS: CARMELITES IN PERSIA

Although the Jesuits undoubtedly occupied first place in the great
missionary struggle from about 1550, they were not the only partici-
pants. Several branches of the Franciscans were distinguished by their
zeal, particularly the Cordeliers, Capuchins and Recollects. The
Dominicans, whose courageous efforts had been responsible for many
foundations in Latin America, continued their work there and attacked
at other points as well. Among new Orders, the Discalced Carmelites
showed the greatest enterprise in this field, though not without internal
difficulties. The Spanish branch, led by the celebrated Fr Nicholas
Doria, the Genoese adversary of St John of the Cross,[1] declared its
hostility to the missionary ideal, whereas the Italian branch, faithful to
the teaching of Fr Jerome Garcia, warmly supported that ideal. The
Italians ultimately imposed their views, and the Carmelites, cross in
hand, played an important part in the conquest of the pagan world.
Between 1550 and 1622 [2] there were very numerous missions scattered
up and down the world. Their fortunes varied, and since it is impossible
to deal with them all here we will select three examples.

In the heart of the Pacific Ocean lay a vast archipelago called the
Philippine Islands in honour of the Infante Philip. Discovered by

[1] See Chapter II, p. 125.
[2] For the importance of this date, see the final sections of this and the following
chapter.

Magellan in 1521, it was partially occupied in 1542 by order of Charles V, who was thereby enabled to say that the sun never set upon his empire. When the Infante came to the Spanish throne as King Philip II, he interested himself in that far-off domain, and sent missionaries 'to win the natives of those countries to a knowledge of our holy Catholic faith and to enlarge the patrimony of the royal crown of Castile,' another example of the combination of spiritual and temporal interests. In 1565, when the Basque Miguel Lopez de Legaspi took up residence in the islands, he had strict instructions to protect and help the Augustinians, who had recently begun to prepare the ground for their apostolate. Twelve years later, in 1577, the Franciscans arrived and set vigorously to work. The city of Manila was founded in the island of Luzon and soon became the Catholic capital of the Pacific. The natives, most of whom were well disposed and docile, gladly accepted baptism; and a kind of census in 1591 showed that there were 667,000 catechumens. Meanwhile the Dominicans appeared on the scene, and they too exerted the utmost zeal, founding the University of St Thomas Aquinas. In 1579 Manila was created a bishopric, and they obtained the see for one of their brethren, Fr Dominic Salazar, who was moreover a remarkable man. Black Friars did not hesitate to venture into the most remote and unfriendly islands, and thus it was that Frs Alfonso, Garcia and Onufrio suffered martyrdom at New Segovia. On the eve of the seventeenth century the Philippines constituted a bastion of Catholicism—a rather peculiar brand of Catholicism, it is true, mingled with Hispanism and Polynesian undercurrents, but none the less active. Manila, which was raised to the dignity of an archbishopric in 1595, had suffragan bishops thousands of miles away, and from its quays missionaries sailed in turn not only to evangelize Japan (with consequences we have already noticed), but also to plant the Cross in the Celebes and the Moluccas.

Christianity was brought to Java by Franciscans in 1584. Having learned, as a result no doubt of Jesuit reconnaissance, that there were still some pagan kingdoms in the islands of Sunda, they wisely considered that it would be easier to make conversions in regions as yet untouched by Islam. They actually managed to secure a foothold in one of those petty kingdoms in the north of Java, among a savage people who practised cannibalism; and there they founded a Church which can be said to have been far in advance of its time. This bold undertaking, however, did not last long; the conquest of the small Catholic zone by the Moslems about 1600 destroyed the diminutive outpost of Christianity.

But the most wonderful adventure was certainly that of a group of Carmelites who were sent by the Holy See to the Shah of Persia's court at the very beginning of the seventeenth century. Shah Abbas

(1557–1628) is rightly considered by historians of Iran as one of her most illustrious princes. He was an intelligent and energetic man, but no humanitarian scruples were allowed to impede his government. When he tried a criminal case he was surrounded by twelve executioners, a whole pack of mastiffs and a tiger, these creatures being intended for the carrying out of his sentence. Abbas, however, loathed the Turks, who were his neighbours and the hereditary enemies of his race. Persia, of course, was Shiite, and therefore in orthodox Moslem eyes heretical and doomed to Allah's chastisement. But the Shah, who was considered by his fanatical soldier-monks as the 'Mahdi,' the last Imam, was at this time much stronger than the Sultan, whom he had lately defeated in battle. Two Christian provinces, Georgia and Armenia, had fallen into his hands. Shah Abbas, a clever statesman, realized that in dealing with an enemy like the Turk he would have to practise the policy of encirclement. Accordingly he entered into negotiations with the West through the agency of Portuguese missionaries at Ormuz and Goa. He also welcomed two astonishing English adventurers, the brothers Shirley (they remind one of T. E. Lawrence), and asked them to modernize his empire on European lines. In 1600 he decided to send an embassy to the Pope; it was led by one of the Shirleys and a high official of the Persian Court, who carried a personal letter inviting His Holiness to make an alliance with the Shah, in order to crush 'that monstrous lion, that bloodthirsty beast, the Turk, and smash his teeth once for all.'

The Pope at that time was Clement VIII,[1] and the Shah's request found him well disposed. The Portuguese Jesuit Francisco da Costa had just informed him that the sovereign of Persia was extremely favourable to the Christians, because of his hatred of the Turks; and the idea of a crusade that would outflank the Sultan appealed to Clement no less than did the hope of being able to plant Christianity in Iran. He therefore replied to the imperial letter with a flowery missive, referring to the Sultan in the same terms as Abbas himself had borrowed from the bestiary, and he sent da Costa with another Jesuit to carry it to Ispahan. So much for the diplomatic half of the programme; what was to be done in the matter of evangelization? At that time the courts of Spain and Portugal were at loggerheads with Rome over the question of who should control the missions,[2] and the Pope was becoming more and more convinced that, in order to derive the fullest benefit from the apostolate, he ought to withdraw it from the political authority of the Portuguese-Hispanic patronate and take it into his own hands, an idea which resulted somewhat later in the establishment of the Congregation of Propaganda. Learning that the Archbishop of Goa, by order of the viceroy, had sent a small delegation of Augustinian monks

[1] See chapter V, p. 321.　　　　[2] See section 15 of the present chapter.

to the Shah, Clement looked about for another Order that would agree
to go to Persia in *his* name.

Now just at that crucial moment he was approached by a party of
Discalced Carmelites from the province of Naples, a young Spaniard
and three Italians, who suggested in a long and well-argued memorandum that they should go to the Holy Land and found a Carmel in
that country where the Order had long ago originated. On the first
page of the memorandum Clement VIII wrote with his own hand: *In
Persidem*; and when he received the would-be missionaries in audience
he told them he considered it more important that, instead of going to
be butchered in Palestine, a team from their Order should start out for
Persia. In memory of the Apostles who, according to tradition, had
been the first to set foot on Persian soil, he named one of the two
leaders of the delegation Paul-Simon and the other John-Thaddeus,
and he entrusted them with a second letter to the Shah.

The Carmelites then embarked on an undertaking so fraught with
adventure and excitement that one could easily make it the subject of a
most thrilling romance. It might indeed be said that every circumstance
combined against the good friars to make their task more difficult and
their journey more arduous. They set out from Bohemia, where they
were man-handled by Protestants, who wished to make sure that their
cowls did not conceal diabolical horns. This kind of treatment continued until they reached the Russian frontier, where they found themselves involved in the political crisis that followed the mysterious
disappearance of little Dmitri, son of Ivan IV, and the accession to
power of Boris Godounov.[1] Protected by the Poles, and suspected on
that account of being secret agents of the 'false Dmitri,' that enigmatic
personage who claimed to be the rightful czar, and who moreover had
become a Catholic, the Carmelites were detained for more than a year
on the Russo-Polish frontier. And other snares awaited them in the
empire of the czars. Russia was then in a state of complete anarchy:
a second 'false Dmitri' had appeared, and no one knew who was the
master. Billeted at Tsaritsin throughout an atrocious winter, during
which two of them died of scurvy, they wondered if they would ever
reach the promised land of Persia towards which imperious papal
Briefs continued to direct their steps. At long last a change in the
policies of Moscow cleared their road. The Jesuit Francisco da Costa,
returning from his embassy by way of the Volga, assured them that at
Ispahan they would enjoy such success as would compensate for all
their sufferings. Travelling onward through Astrakhan, Frs Paul-
Simon, John-Thaddeus and Vincent of St Francis reached the Caspian,
three years after leaving the Eternal City.

Journey's end was paradise compared with its beginning. Escorted

[1] See Chapter III, section 13.

by the younger Shirley, introduced by him to Shah Abbas, and received more kindly than they had dared hope by the Portuguese Augustinian emissaries of the Archbishop of Goa, they obtained an immediate audience with the emperor and handed him the pontifical letter. Their arrival was timely: the Shah was again on the worst of terms with the Sultan, whose ambassador he had recently sent home after cutting off his beard and wrapping it up in a parcel as a pleasant gift to the enemy! Among the presents brought from Rome was a statue of St Michael trampling on the dragon; the Shah was delighted and declared that he saw it as an omen of the fate awaiting the Turk. Sumptuous presents were offered to the Carmelites, who distributed them among the poor and the soldiery. A comfortable house was put at their disposal, where they were able to live as a community, open a chapel and say Mass. In February 1608 the sacred rite of the Catholics was publicly celebrated for the first time in the Iranian capital, and the Carmelites were well rewarded for all they had endured.

Shah Abbas was sometimes vexed at finding the West so slow to 'smash the teeth' of the Turkish lion; but despite the difficulties resulting from his occasional ill humour they managed to form a regular congregation, even converting the Shah's beautiful niece Sampsonia and the Anglican Shirley. While Fr Paul-Simon returned to Italy to inform the Holy See of what had been accomplished, the others were joined by a few reinforcements and continued their work, enjoying friendly relations both with the Uniate Armenian Christians and those separated from Rome. A new Carmelite house was established at Ormuz, far from Ispahan; and as Shah Abbas lay dying, Bishop Antonio de Gouvea of Cyrene arrived in Persia to organize these young Catholic Churches. Such were the beginnings of a mission which continues to flourish in the land of jasmine and roses.

13. End of the Hispano-Portuguese Monopoly and Missionary Awakening of France

And now what of France, the 'eldest daughter of the Church'? It must be confessed that in the missionary field, as in several others, she had as yet shown no initiative. No French names had so far occurred among those of the great adventurers of Christ. The wars in Italy exhausted the energies of the kingdom; then she found herself entangled in the grave crisis of the Wars of Religion, during which French Catholics were more concerned with defending themselves against their separated brethren than with marching in a body to win territory and souls for Christ. Besides, if France had wished to send any of her sons to evangelize the world she would have been prevented by the

clauses of Alexander VI's celebrated partition, as well as by the omni-
potent patronate of Portugal and Spain, both of which countries were
soon united under one sceptre. 'In the Indies,' Philip II abruptly
declared, 'political and religious power both belong to me.' He had not
the slightest intention of renouncing either, nor even of sharing with
other countries his rights and privileges as evangelizer-in-chief of pagan
lands. Madrid and Lisbon were particularly mistrustful of the French,
who were frequently their political enemies and always suspect as to
doctrine. There is extant a complete list of the Jesuits sent from
Lisbon to China down to the year 1655: it includes three Frenchmen
out of a total of one hundred Fathers.

Would the Spanish and Portuguese monopoly last? Officially it
would endure for a great while to come: not until the Spanish colonies
won their independence in the nineteenth century did the Pope decide
to send them a Vicar Apostolic or even a representative of Propaganda,
let alone a nuncio. In fact, however, the Holy See had long since begun
to break the famous monopoly: in 1573, for example, by the appointment of an Italian Jesuit, Fr Valignani, as Visitor-General of the Indies;
by encouraging the dispatch to Japan, China and India of many Italian
Fathers, such as Ricci, Ruggieri and Nobili; and also by taking direct
initiative in the sending out of such missions as those of the Carmelites
to Persia. The opposition of the Papacy, after St Francis Borgia's death,
to the election of any Spaniard as General of the Jesuits had the same
end (among others) in view—to loosen the peninsula's stranglehold
upon missionary work. Very soon the reawakening of France would
prove the most serious blow to that monopoly.

When François I read Alexander's Bull carving up the planet he was
beside himself with rage. 'The sun shines for me as well as for them!'
he shouted; 'I should like very much to see the clause in Adam's will
that excludes me from a share of the world!' But because of the struggle
he was obliged to wage against Charles V there was little he could do.
This does not mean that France had no hand whatever in the great
work of spreading Christianity. She played her part, but in a rather
peculiar manner, upon which there was a considerable difference of
opinion at the time. I am referring here to the alliance concluded
between the Most Christian Monarchy and the Turks, an alliance whose
consequences, even on the religious plane, were far from negligible.

The prestige of France had remained very high in the Levant. St
Louis had left there an imperishable memory; Philippe le Hardi and
Charles VI had maintained contact with the rulers of the Near East.
Again, Jacques Cœur, for obviously commercial reasons, had sent his
own nephew to the Sultan of Egypt. The younger man had availed
himself of this opportunity to secure certain privileges for pilgrims to
the Holy Land, and diplomatic documents were duly signed, making

France protectress of Christians in Palestine. Under François I the general attitude became a major issue of foreign policy: surely an understanding with the Turks would checkmate his most dangerous enemy, the Austrian. Solyman's attack on Vienna probably saved France, notwithstanding the protests of those who, in all parts of Christendom, looked upon the alliance as a downright scandal. It must be acknowledged that relations between the Louvre and the Sublime Porte were remarkably courteous and refined. We have, for instance, the letter addressed by the Sultan to François while the latter was held prisoner at Madrid and abandoned by all: it expresses the utmost friendliness in a most charming style. And François I, as a good Catholic, profited by these warm-hearted relations to obtain from his Turkish allies guarantees for all Christians in their dominions.

From 1534, when the first 'capitulation' [1] was signed, we can say that the King of France exercised a veritable patronage over the Holy Places. Thanks to the treaty, Christians were able to restore their churches and occupy the sanctuaries 'where they were allowed complete freedom to perform the ceremonies of their religion.' Article VI protected Christians living in the Turkish Empire, e.g. the Greeks; it guaranteed them religious freedom and guaranteed that they would never be forcibly converted to Islam. One very shrewd clause (Article XI) provided that the Holy See might be a co-signatory of the treaty; the French diplomats were clever enough to guess that the Papacy would one day be confronted with the arrogant Hispano-Lusitanian monopoly, and might then be glad to have a friend in the government at Paris.

Such an act shows well enough that France was by no means uninterested in religious problems or in the spread of the faith. As protectress of oriental Christians and of the Holy Places, she would for centuries exercise in the Near East a profound influence, against which other powers would strive in vain. The Levant was henceforward the happy hunting ground of French missionaries, especially when the battle of Lepanto crystallized Moslem hatred of Spain, Genoa and Venice, and thereby gave France a monopoly for many years of trade with Turkey, Palestine and Egypt. However debatable from the Catholic standpoint, this alliance of France with the Turks did produce results that were beneficial to the interests of the faith.

But Frenchmen were soon at work in important missionary lands other than the Near East. France at first took little or no part in the great voyages of discovery; only one French name is memorable among the early explorers: Jean de Béthencourt, in the Canaries. By founding Le Havre as an 'ocean port' on the Atlantic, François I

---

[1] i.e. despite the unpleasant overtones of the word, the first Franco-Turkish treaty negotiated and signed by the ambassador Jean de la Forest.

showed his resolve to have a share in the partition of the world; and he ordered his grand admiral, Philippe de Chabot, to fit out expeditions 'for the purpose of seeking a passage from Europe to China and of occupying new and fertile territory.' In 1524, when the sailors of Jean Ango, a shipowner of Dieppe, and the crews sailing under the French flag with Verazzano reached the coasts of North America and reconnoitred the waters of Hudson's Bay, a new chapter was opened in the history of white colonization. To this a splendid page was added ten years later (1534) by Jacques Cartier, who started from Saint-Malo in search of a route to the Indies [1] (forty years after Christopher Columbus) and landed in Terre-Neuve (modern Newfoundland). This was an important episode in the history of evangelization; for the French ships carried missionaries, and Cartier's first act on going ashore was to plant crosses marked with the fleur-de-lis and to have Masses celebrated. The Catholics of France would soon display in Canada their apostolic vigour and their faith.

At the turn of the seventeenth century the Spaniards and Portuguese were no longer the only peoples concerned with the missions. In France also small groups of pioneers were longing for the great adventure. They read the letters of St Francis Xavier, Fr Acosta's *Natural and Moral History of the Indies* and Fr Maffei's *History of the Indies*, all in French translations, while the *Indian Letters* published by the Society of Jesus from 1578 onwards had subscribers in Paris. There were missionary enthusiasts in the royal household, among them the famous Fr Coton, confessor to Henri IV. Moreover a diplomatic move of the very first importance had recently opened up the world to French missionaries. The Treaty of Vervins (1598) contained a secret clause explicitly contradicting the Bull of Alexander VI and giving France a free hand in all colonial settlements 'north of the tropic of Cancer and east of the meridian of the island of Hierro, to be called henceforth the Line of Friendship.' And, like the Crowns of Spain and Portugal not long ago, the French Crown meant to be loyal to its Christian vocation and to associate the work of evangelization with that of overseas expansion. In 1615 the publicist Montchrétien, having spoken in his *Treatise on Political Economy* about the material advantages of colonial enterprise, went on to say that France, 'to whom still belongs supremacy in literature and arms, art and civilization, and true Christianity also, whatever others might claim, should dedicate herself to the sublime task of making God's name known among the many barbarian peoples devoid of all culture, who call to us, who stretch out their arms to us, begging us by holy teaching and good example to set them in the way of salvation.' This was a magnificent programme, which teams of

[1] Rabelais, who went in person to Saint-Malo to gather evidence from Cartier, shows us Pantagruel also seeking the same route.

Frenchmen were already labouring hard to fulfil in the distant lands of America.

14. THE DIFFICULT BEGINNINGS OF FRENCH CANADA

The first French missionary in North America was not a priest but a layman: Jacques Cartier himself. That great sailor had apostolic as well as commercial designs, and when he set foot in the new country he immediately gathered the savages around a thirty-foot cross and preached the Christian faith. To begin with, of course, he used signs, pointing to the cross and then to the sky, at which, he tells us, his audience was 'much amazed.' Next year, having managed to teach two natives the rudiments of French, he undertook with the aid of these interpreters a missionary campaign in a district where now stands the city of Quebec. The result was so encouraging that on the occasion of his third voyage he decided to take with him six priests or religious; and in this he was warmly supported by François I, who was delighted with the prospect of a new French and Catholic empire. The material riches it had been hoped to find proved non-existent; pieces of quartz or glittering mica-schist had been mistaken for precious stones, and there was a proverbial phrase current in Paris: 'false as a Canadian diamond.' Ten years after Jacques Cartier's landing there was no longer a Frenchman or a Catholic on the shores of this new world. But the splendid dream had by no means utterly vanished from the minds of men; it was kept alive by the many marvels related in the reports of various travellers. Half a century later other daring souls, full of faith, would try to make that dream a spiritual as well as a material reality.

Once again the pioneer was a layman. Marc Lescarbot, an advocate of the Parlement, was interested in all theological problems. He had translated Baronius and St Charles Borromeo, drawn up a plan for reunion of the Churches, and devoted much thought to other religious matters. If the expression 'to teach one's grandmother to suck eggs' had not existed in French, it would certainly have had to be invented for him. An ardent supporter of the missions, in whose service he wielded an indefatigable pen, he addressed to the clergy and bishops solemn adjurations in both prose and verse, imploring them to take some interest. He himself awaited only an opportunity to set them an example. At the beginning of the seventeenth century, after the Treaty of Vervins, a Picard nobleman, one Jean Poutrincourt, having obtained the king's licence to trade in furs with the lieutenant of North America, established a small factory on the peninsula of Acadie (modern Nova Scotia), where he founded Port-Royal. He had wanted to take a few priests, but none would agree to risk the adventure. 'I myself will go,' declared Lescarbot; 'are not all Christians priests?' Had he not read that in ancient times the laity had the right to carry on their persons the sacred bread of the Eucharist and to distribute it themselves? The religious authorities did not agree, and the Society of Jesus had him informed that they were prepared to send one of their own Fathers. But Lescarbot did not like the Jesuits, and he replied that the ship already carried her full complement. So he set sail, self-appointed chaplain to the expedition.

Arrived at Port-Royal he proceeded to preach every Sunday—'sometimes oddly,' according to eye-witnesses—teaching the colonists

'not to live like beasts, but to set the savages a good example.' At the same time he was collecting material for his great *History of New France* (1609), in which he expounded a complete plan of systematic colonization and apostolate in the newly discovered territory. But truth obliges us to say that his efforts to convert the natives bore no fruit at all.[1]

Since his lay apostolate had not succeeded as he had hoped, he was obliged to fall back on the idea of an appeal for priests. Once again the Jesuits offered themselves, and once again Lescarbot judged them too heavy to be put aboard. Eventually he found a brave priest of the diocese of Langres, Josse Fléché, who agreed to make the journey; and this worthy man succeeded in baptizing twenty-one natives, among them an aged chief known as 'Sagamo Membertou,' who had known Jacques Cartier. It was all very satisfactory, and Lescarbot undertook

[1] The map shows the present-day boundary of the 'United States' as a geographical aid; needless to say, the term is an anachronism.

to proclaim the triumph in Paris by publishing a report on the *Conversion of Savages*.

Meanwhile Henri IV had become interested in the affair. As early as 1607 he had looked forward to sending Jesuits to Acadie, and had allocated 2,000 livres a year for the support of their mission. After his death his widow Marie dei Medici resumed the idea; being a clear-headed woman, not much inclined to be led astray by Lescarbot's statistics, she ordered her husband's plan to be carried out and arranged for two Fathers of the Society to be sent to America. Lescarbot, however, was still at daggers drawn with the sons of St Ignatius, and in agreement with the Huguenot capitalists of Dieppe, who were financing Poutrincourts' venture, he tried to prevent them from sailing. This matter reached the ears of Mme de Guercheville, one of Her Majesty's ladies in waiting. She was renowned at court for the manner in which she had rejected the advances of the king, who had acknowledged his defeat and praised the firmness of her refusal. The good lady was a great friend of the Jesuits, and she determined to force the hand of rascally unbelievers who were preventing the Society from going where its duty called.

This was quickly done, for Mme de Guercheville was powerful; so quickly in fact that those responsible committed a serious indiscretion. The two Jesuits were registered simply and solely as shareholders in the financial undertaking which controlled Poutrincourt's operations. The enemies of the Jesuits never forgot this move, and the great Arnauld himself, at the time of the Jansenist quarrels, used the contract of 1611 to show that the Jesuits sought nothing from the missions but monetary gain.

Anyway, the two Jesuits departed: Fr Biard, a scholar, and Fr Ennemond Massé, a stern ascetic. As soon as they landed in Acadie they set about evangelizing the Souriquois and Echemins of French Bay. Their initial inquiries into the results obtained by Josse Fléché were far from satisfactory. The new Christians imagined that in accepting baptism they had 'become Normans'; they knew nothing about Christ, and proudly introduced to the Jesuits the six or seven wives which every one of them possessed. The Fathers therefore decided to baptize none but the better instructed. This resolution infuriated the civil authorities, who looked for a steady flow of converts; but the two priests continued to do their best, learning the native dialects, compiling a native catechism, and founding a new missionary centre at Saint-Sauveur on the other side of French Bay. Fr Biard sent an optimistic report to Paris, and Mme de Guercheville invested large sums in the peninsula, which was clearly destined to become another Catholic France.

But alas, not far from there some English Protestants had settled in

Virginia. In July 1613 a Welsh adventurer named Argall swept down upon the small French establishments, sacked them and took the Jesuits prisoner. He repeatedly threatened to hang them, but finally allowed them to return to France, content with having destroyed their work. For the time being nothing remained of this Acadian venture but a splendid and tragic memory, which Fr Biard extolled in his report of 1615, and which Fr Massé, now minister of the celebrated Collège de la Flèche, made dear to his pupils who sat enthralled as he told them the story. If a new generation were one day to follow in the footsteps of the first pioneers the efforts of the latter would not have been in vain.

At about the same time, but farther inland, along the banks of that wonderful river soon to be called the St Lawrence, other missions had been at work and had even, so it appeared, been crowned with some success. The man whose name remains principally associated with Christian origins in Canada properly so called was Samuel de Champlain (1567–1635). He too was a layman, but he had nothing in common with the fiery, quick-tempered and blundering Lescarbot. Champlain, an intelligent, brave but level-headed man, began in 1603 his exploration of the banks of the great river, following it upstream as far as he was able, in constant hope of discovering a route to China. Aboard his vessels he maintained strict discipline, and did all he could to see that the crews behaved like Christians; nor did he hesitate, as if he himself were a priest, to deliver pious addresses to his soldiers and sailors. He too regarded colonization and the apostolate as inseparable. During the summer of 1603 he explored the regions of Quebec, Trois-Rivières and Grand Sault, as well as the island later called Montreal, explaining to the natives the mystery of the Holy Trinity by showing them the confluence at Trois-Rivières.

Champlain's grand idea, which afterwards bore good fruit, was to people the new territories with French folk who would cultivate the soil, breed families and gradually absorb the natives at the same time as converting them. The monastic agriculturists and teachers of the Dark Ages would certainly have approved this programme. It did not appeal much to the trading class, who preferred to sell alcohol and trumpery goods to the savages rather than to settle down as French peasantry. But Champlain stood his ground: coming and going, crossing the ocean several times, he gradually interested a number of important peoples in his project, which began to materialize.

In 1614 he entered into correspondence with the Recollects, a reformed branch of the Franciscans which had returned to the strict observance; [1] and they, as faithful heirs of the Poverello, father of the modern missions, at once agreed to send a few of their brethren to Canada. The House of Clergy, which met for the States-General in that

[1] See Chapter II.

year, voted 1,500 livres to finance an expedition of four friars; and
Champlain, in order to place his undertakings on solid bases, formed
the 'Company of Associates,' a body of merchants at Rennes and
Saint-Malo.

Accordingly four Recollects, Frs Jamet, Dolleau, Le Caron and
Duplessis, set sail in the spring of 1615. The least we can say is that
their first experience of Canada was by no means encouraging. At
Tadoussac, a port of call, they were obliged to attend a cannibal feast
at which a party of Montagnais Redskins flayed and roasted two
prisoners from a neighbouring tribe. The good friars decided it was
high time to preach the charity of Christ in those parts. Setting to work
there and then, they erected a chapel dedicated to the Immaculate Conception alongside the poor huts of which Quebec then consisted, and
celebrated Mass on the site of what is now Montreal. Then they continued their journey upstream, exploring and baptizing, as far as the
Great Lakes. Their success varied a great deal among the numerous and
very different Indian tribes. They could do little with those eternal
nomads, the Montagnais and Algonquins; but the settled and peace-
loving Hurons were more amenable, and at the end of a year Fr
Le Caron succeeded in compiling a Huron dictionary. These were
years of heroic effort, during which the missionaries penetrated to
unknown regions, carrying the canoe on their backs from lake to
lake, eating horrible messes of Indian corn and water, tearing their
feet on jagged rocks, and assailed night after night by crane-flies and
mosquitoes.

They became more than ever convinced that immigrants must be
brought from France, as many as could be persuaded to come. The
Company of Associates did not share their views: the process would
be costly and would show no immediate returns. But neither Champlain nor the Recollects lost heart. Looking into the future they could
already see the emergence of a new race born of marriages between
Frenchmen and native women. They even envisaged—much in advance
of their time, as things turned out—the foundation of a seminary for
the natives, which would train a Redskin clergy destined to evangelize
their race. Appearances suggested, and it was even stated openly by
some Huron chiefs, that the tribe had no objection to a French population in its territory. In 1619 the construction of the seminary of St
Charles at Quebec, a well-built house thirty-four feet long, proved the
success of French Catholic enterprise, and the future seemed very
bright.

Just then, however, difficulties began. In France the Company of
Associates tried to get rid of Champlain and was suppressed by the
government. But its successor was worse, controlled by fanatical
Protestants who were unwilling to send out more priests and opposed

the idea of immigration. The little colony on the banks of the St Lawrence was indignant and sent Fr Baillif to present a list of grievances to
the king. This curious document clearly stated that the heretics were
supplying the savages with guns and ammunition, 'encouraging them
to massacre the French.' It also requested the dispatch of a garrison of
fifty men, funds necessary for building a fort, and, once again, immigrants to settle on Canadian soil. Thanks to the courage and determination of the Recollects—there were only six of them—small missionary
centres were established at Tadoussac and Trois-Rivières. Not long
afterwards at Trois-Rivières, one fine morning in 1624, Champlain
and his missionaries welcomed two hundred Hurons, Iroquois and
Nipissings, who came to celebrate their Christian brotherhood with a
long and friendly banquet, amid a great heap of spoils won in the chase.
It seemed then that all initial difficulties had been overcome, that evangelization could go ahead without fear of the future.

In fact, however, the Catholic community in Canada was doomed,
as was Acadie a little later, to undergo a terrible ordeal.[1] One sad day
in 1628 an English squadron commanded by the brothers Kirk, but
piloted by a French Huguenot, sailed up the St Lawrence, attacking
and destroying one after another the ill-defended settlements of New
France, Quebec included. The missionaries were driven out, the
catechumens dispersed. This tragedy appeared to have annulled the
difficult and heroic beginnings of the French apostolate in America,
but the ordeal proved to be shortlived. Four years later, when Anglo-
French hostilities ended, the work of colonization and evangelization
was resumed, and with the Jesuit missions a decisive stage began in the
history of French-Catholic Canada.[2]

15. THE HOLY SEE TAKES CONTROL OF THE MISSIONS:
THE CONGREGATION OF PROPAGANDA

In this first chapter of modern missionary history, colonial expansion
and religious apostolate are found closely linked, in Canada as in Latin

---

[1] As the present volume ends at the year 1622, the sequel to these events will be studied
in the next.

[2] In 1612 a similar scheme of French immigration and Catholic mission was tried in
Brazil under the direction of two Capuchin priests, Claude d'Abbeville and Yves d'Evreux.
They landed at the mouth of the Amazon among tribes whom they called 'Topinambos.'
First results were encouraging, but the Portuguese governor of Pernambuco was resolved
to destroy the French enclave. Portugal having been under Spanish rule since 1580, the
political alliance with Madrid, sealed by the marriage of Louis XIII with Anne of Austria,
caused France to abandon this diminutive and far-off settlement. Friars and colonists
re-embarked, taking with them to Paris six charming Topinambos who were solemnly
received by the king and in whose honour a *Te Deum* was sung in Notre Dame. All that
remains of this short-lived enterprise in Brazil is the name of St Louis, after whom the
Capuchins named their house and which is still borne by the city built over its site, São
Luiz de Maranhao.

America, in India as in Africa. Nor was this association particularly happy, and in the early years of the seventeenth century an idea was gaining ground that the whole system ought to be changed. This Hispano-Portuguese patronate had been useful at the start, but now it was less help than hindrance. Japanese Catholics had suffered because they were believed to be agents of a foreign power, whereas in China and India excellent results had been obtained by missionaries who were free from State control. All this evidence was conclusive. It was surely time for the Pope himself, whose authority had been greatly increased by the Catholic revival, to take over the missions, to provide for their administration at the highest level, to emphasize their exclusively spiritual character and at the same time to liberate them from any sort of dependence upon the civil power.

This view had already been in the air for a number of years. It was put forward about 1560 by Jean de Vendeville, a Belgian of high intelligence and remarkable courage, whose fellow countrymen became so passionately interested in the missions, and proved themselves such dedicated workers, that St Francis Xavier wrote to St Ignatius: '*Da mihi Belgas.*' Vendeville, a professor of law at Louvain, was, like so many of the best spirits of his age, an ardent devotee of the apostolate, as indeed of every cause involving the honour of God and the future of the faith. He had helped to found the celebrated college at Douai, where priests for the English mission continued to be trained until the eighteenth century. This layman, so concerned for the interests of Holy Church and living like a saint, spent his time preparing a vast plan for a worldwide apostolate, which would be under the sole direction of the Papacy and whose organization he described in great detail. His central idea, borrowed perhaps from Raymond Lull or from his own compatriot Fr Clénard, the apostle of Islam, was to create special seminaries for training competent missionaries. Throughout his life he explained his plans to one pope after another, supporting them with an inexhaustible flow of scriptural, theological and historical argument. Left a widower in 1580, Vendeville sought Holy Orders, and seven years later his outstanding virtues won for him the See of Tournai. As a bishop he continued even more vigorously and with increased authority to defend his ideas, in which he managed to interest St Charles Borromeo, St Robert Bellarmine and the future Cardinal Allen. Pius V, Gregory XIII and Sixtus V all gave him a sympathetic hearing; and when Gregory XIV was elected Vendeville wrote him a letter of congratulation in which he spoke once more of his grand design.

The wise delay which always governs the conduct of the Apostolic See did not allow him to witness the triumph of his plan; the Bishop of Tournai died in 1592 without having had that joy, but he had at least set the idea on foot and had even watched it make some progress. For

L

in 1568 Pope Pius V, moved by the spirited plea of the Louvain professor and further convinced by the Jesuit General, St Francis Borgia, set up a commission of cardinals with a view to creating a pontifical institute for the training and dispatch of missionaries; but this commission got no further than reports and theoretical discussion. Gregory XIII retained it, entrusting it particularly with the apostolate in the North and the Levant, and thereby showing that in his view (which eventually prevailed) missionary work in pagan lands and that of reconquering the territories lost to Protestantism should not be separated. Gregory's commission concerned itself mainly with the question of attaching oriental Christians more closely to the Roman hierarchy; it considered the foundation of oriental seminaries and publication of the Catechism in various languages. Clement VIII retained the commission for the North and the Levant, but he created in addition (1599) a more extensive body, a preliminary sketch as it were of the future Congregation of Propaganda, under the presidency of Cardinal Santorio. Among the distinguished members of the new organism were Baronius, Bellarmine and Antoniano; their duty was to vitalize and control the apostolate in every part of the world. This general secretariat worked for two years, dealing with India, the Philippines and Mexico, settling certain disputes between the Franciscans and the Jesuits, and laying down a number of wise regulations for the future of the missions. Then, for some unknown reason, it ceased to function; but it had pointed the way.

The cause found its next great advocate in Thomas of Jesus, a Carmelite of persuasive eloquence. He was a true descendant of Fr Jerome Garcia, who had committed the reformed Order to apostolic work against the wishes of Fr Doria, and thanks to whom Carmelite missionaries, heirs of St Teresa of Avila, had found their way to the Congo, to America and to Persia. Andalusian by birth, but living in Belgium as his second home, Fr Thomas of Jesus had studied the ideas of Vendeville. He examined them thoroughly, developed them, and finally published in 1613 a massive Latin treatise on *How to Bring Salvation to all Nations*. The work was prophetic; it surveyed and expounded in detail everything that subsequently dictated the Church's apostolic methods for two hundred years down to our own day. One chapter was actually entitled 'The Institution of a congregation *De Propaganda Fide*.' The Carmelite advocated the setting up of a committee of cardinals which would meet at regular intervals to study problems relating to the apostolate. It was to be divided into five subcommittees, each assisted by a permanent secretariat, one for each part of the world. Dependent on this Congregation there were to be special seminaries—one for each nation it was hoped, but at all events one for each Catholic group—and also one for the training of clergy destined for each particular country. This brilliant man likewise provided for a seminary intended to link the Orientals with Rome, another to send missionaries to Russia, another to study Islam and others again to work among the Protestants. Fr Thomas's ideas quickly spread to all circles interested in these problems, and they won the enthusiastic support of two influential figures: Fr Dominic of Jesus and Mary, a future general of the Carmelites, who had been secretary to Santorio's commission, and the Capuchin Fr Jerome Narni, who was at that time the leading preacher at the Papal Court. The battle was as good as won.

When Cardinal Ludovici became Pope as Gregory XV he was known to favour these ideas. Because of the Roman policy of centralization, resulting from the Council of Trent and the Catholic Reformation, it was natural and inevitable that the missions should be taken over by the Sovereign Pontiff. The Congregation of Propaganda was instituted on 6th January 1622. It held its first official meeting on 14th January, under the presidency of the Pope himself, with thirteen cardinals, two prelates and a secretary. The Carmelite Fr Dominic of Jesus and Mary was soon afterwards co-opted, a distinction which he most richly deserved. Then, in June, the Bull *Inscrutabili divinae* gave the new institution its canonical bases and at the same time prescribed its duties. The task of the members of the Congregation was clearly defined: 'They are to discern and discuss the problems as a whole and each particular matter affecting the propagation of the faith throughout the world and keep Us informed thereof; they are to supervise all missions sent out to preach the Gospel and Catholic doctrine.' To make use of all existing missionary elements and to create new ones; to appoint bishops or vicars apostolic; to divide the world among the various religious Orders so as to avoid friction, and employ them in the best way possible; to determine the aims of missionary enterprise: such was, and is, the vast programme of the Congregation of Propaganda. Five years later Fr Thomas's other dream was realized by the foundation of the College of Propaganda. This was effected with the help of Vivès, minister at Rome of the Archduchess Isabella, Spanish regent in Belgium. A new page was opening in the history not only of the missions, but of the Church. By thus assuming official responsibility for Catholic expansion throughout the world, the Papacy showed itself faithful to its apostolic calling, to the order given long ago by Christ to His disciples. The year 1622 marks a new awareness of an everlasting duty. The character of the Church as we see her today owes much to that decision which had been prepared for by so many efforts and so much sacrifice.

CHAPTER V

THE NEW FACE OF THE CHURCH

1. St Peter's

DURING THE year 1612 the numerous Roman idlers who used to watch the building of St Peter's had great news to tell their fellow citizens: the basilica was nearly completed. It was known that fresh impetus had been given to the project six years earlier when Maderno was entrusted with its supervision and decided to lengthen one arm of the original Greek cross so as to make the edifice Latin and Roman even in its ground plan. Thousands of people hurried across the Tiber to admire the masterpiece, about which some did not feel altogether happy. Everyone agreed that Michelangelo's dome was a brilliant piece of work, surmounting the huge drum with such purity and grace. But was the façade in harmony with the general lay-out of the structure? The Corinthian columns, it was said, were too high; the horizontal line of the attic broke the upward surge of the whole; and what about that array of thirteen gigantic statues outlined against the sky? No matter: it was almost miraculous that the vast undertaking should have reached its term, that the largest church in the world should be standing there over the Apostle's tomb, that the sacred ensign crowning the dome should rise so far into the Roman sky. It seemed quite natural, too, that the proud Borghese pope, Paul V, to whom belonged the merit of completing the work, should wish to immortalize his name and that of his family in an inscription below the pediment.

As a matter of fact the basilica of St Peter was not yet quite finished; it did not yet look as it does today. The world would have to wait until 1626 before it was opened for public worship. The interior was still in the hands of innumerable decorators who could be seen at work everywhere, especially inside the dome, where they were setting in mosaic a quotation from the Gospel in gigantic letters. Outside, the piazza of St Peter's was nothing but a vast builder's yard. The obelisk, however, was already in place, that obelisk which was brought from Egypt by Caligula and which Sixtus V had excavated from a heap of ruins and erected as the pedestal for a cross containing relics; but it was not yet enclosed by those two arms of stone with which Bernini, forty years later, would lock it in a stupendous embrace. If much remained to be done, that was nothing by comparison with what had been accomplished. The basilica of the Apostle stood there in all the youthful brilliance of its marbles and its gold, enormous, inescapable, a tangible sign of the Church's victory and her visible affirmation.

Thus was closed a splendid chapter in the history of art, which was likewise a chapter of Christian history. For one hundred and fifty years the site of St Peter's had been at once the radiant crucible of the arts and the most striking indication of the Church's vitality. Five generations had succeeded one another there, and the most famous names of Italian splendour were associated with it: Bramante, Raphael, Michelangelo. . . . Above all Michelangelo, whose godlike hands had thrown into space that cupola which was the envy of Florence and eclipsed the memory of Brunelleschi. The aged master did not live to see his work completed; others had continued if not equalled it: Vignola and Ligorrio, Della Porta and Fontana, and lastly Maderno, who, though lacking genius, possessed tenacity. Inconceivable riches of intelligence, labour and money had been spent upon this monument in which the Church sought to express her truth, her strength and the firmness of her foundations. There it stood, ready to weather the centuries, to offer future generations an image of incomparable majesty.

Incomparable majesty: those are indeed the words that spring to a man's mind when he gazes on St Peter's, as he crosses the gentle incline of the piazza, climbs the steps and at length passes beneath the colossal portico into that sombrely shining nave at the far end of which there falls a shaft of light directly on to the spot where lies the first pope, the martyred Apostle. Is it only because this is the most enormous church in Christendom, with an area of more than 15,000 square yards and nearly 500 feet long—because, as the inscriptions on the pavement remind us, it could contain any other in the world? Is it because every detail—statues, pictures, inscriptions, mosaics—is conceived on a superhuman scale? These material facts do not account for the impression which escapes no one, an impression which all the words expressing size, strength and power can only partially convey. Something is present there which the various artists all experienced and which they rendered into concrete terms: the grandeur, the might, the majesty of the Catholic Apostolic and Roman Church founded upon a divine promise, the pledge of a Word that shall not pass away.

St Peter's has often been described as 'cold'; some have criticized the lengthening of that arm, which makes the nave a sort of long tunnel devoid of charm; others think the pillars too massive [1] and dislike the heavy monuments above which they tower. We may even admit that a great majority of the 'works of art' placed there during the last three hundred years are ugly or insipid. But what really matters is the *general* effect conveyed by this stupendous edifice, which is revealed as the manifest centre of the Christian world, unshakable and indestructible—

[1] They measure more than 210 ft round.

because the Church is built upon a Rock, and the Rock lies there, the aged Apostle to whom Christ Himself gave this nickname.

Such as it is, St Peter's is a perfect image of the Church on the morrow of Trent, seated secure upon her principles, embattled with her dogmas and decrees; that Church which had lately fought such stern battles and was now rejoicing in the full flush of her victory. The great basilica, with its pillars and its walls like bastions, is indeed the symbol of that spiritual fortress which Catholics had managed to defend and to preserve. Its size and strength proclaim the faith re-affirmed by Trent in all its amplitude, the faith whose every element has been scrutinized by theologians; they proclaim a resolution never to compromise upon essentials, the determination of Catholic society never again to allow itself to be broken up by heresy, but to form within the framework of a re-created discipline one body and one soul.

This is the explanation of those vast empty spaces which astound the solitary visitor as he walks on and on through the nave, feeling so puny and so lost. St Peter's is essentially the basilica of the visible Church, of that human society as it emerged from the Tridentine decrees. Its true significance is apparent only on great ceremonial occasions, when the immense vessel is full to overflowing with a human tide, when the light from thousands of lamps is reflected from marble surfaces, when a whole people is indeed a single soul, a single surge, a single love. It is the evening of Maundy Thursday: the Cardinal Arch-priest at the head of a long line of clergy in dalmatics, and dignitaries in gorgeous robes, moves to the papal altar, which he bathes with fine wine and then dries with long plumes of white feathers. After that the crowd kneels in silence to receive the blessing given high up on the balcony of Veronica with authentic relics of the Passion. Magnificent also are the ceremonies of canonization, when the Vicar of Christ, speaking in the name of the Holy Spirit, raises a human soul to the altars of the Church. It was for such occasions that St Peter's was built, for those great days when, sailing above a roaring sea of men, there appears one upon whom repose the certitudes of Catholicism— the pontiff himself, carried in the *sedia gestatoria*, his head slightly bowed beneath the weight of the tiara, his hand raised to right and left in benediction.

For if the basilica of St Peter is the abode of the visible Church, it is so only by virtue of him who bears responsibility for that Church *hic et nunc*, directing her and leading her to God. Everything here is intended to remind us of the bond which links his power with that of its sacred origins. On the façade there is a bas-relief which shows Our Lord giving the keys to Peter. In the immense vestibule there is another, in which Christ is saying to His apostle: 'Feed my sheep.'

On the pediment of the central doorway is Giotto's mosaic (badly restored), the *Navicella*, showing Jesus in the height of the storm helping Peter to walk upon the waters. Peter is present everywhere. His is the ancient bronze statue whose foot has been worn away by the kisses of innumerable pilgrims; on great ceremonial occasions it is crowned with a tiara and vested in a rose-coloured cope. He is the hero of many scenes from the Gospels or Apocrypha, painted or sculptured: he cures the sick with his shadow, crushes Simon Magus, heals the lame man at the Porta Speciosa, baptizes his jailers in the Mamertine prison, and finally dies upon a cross like his Master—but head downwards, from humility. Why such insistence? Doubtless because the basilica is dedicated to his glorious memory; but also because the glory of Peter, the primacy of Peter, is likewise that of the man who is his direct heir, his successor, the Vicar of Christ. 'St Peter's Chair' was an object of veneration (especially after the feast was restored in 1518) long before Bernini set it high up in that flamboyant reliquary, where it can no longer be seen. The significance of all this is explained by the giant inscription around the inside of the dome: 'Thou art Peter, and upon this Rock I will build my Church. . . .' Here is the answer to Protestant theories, an affirmation in stone of undisputed power.

Such is the most striking aspect of St Peter's, whereby it corresponds to many features in the new face of the Church,[1] of a Church which had survived a terrible ordeal and felt herself more than ever firmly established. It is evident that of the two immediate and inseparable factors of Christianity, God's glory and the Cross of Christ, St Peter's, like the whole Tridentine Church, emphasizes the first rather than the second. Nor is it forbidden to prefer other houses of prayer erected by other hands and appealing more to human sensibility. In the nave at Chartres or the lower church at Assisi a more interior voice speaks more readily to the soul; the religious spirit which finds expression there is not that of the theologians and organizers, but of the mystics and the saints.

This, however, does not mean to say that the Apostle's basilica is totally devoid of that other (and indeed more essential) Christian reality, which is not completely hidden by its great bulk and its heaped-up riches. Stand back and look at St Peter's from a little farther away, from the terraces of the Pincio, for example, or from the height of Monte Mario, and you perceive that other reality, which imposes itself upon the mind. At evening above all, when the liquid splendour of the setting sun pours itself in gold and fire above the roofs of the city, the enormous edifice assumes a strange and wholly interior charm. It might be said at such an hour to be rediscovering its own mystery; its atmosphere of resolution and command is then transformed into a mystic flight, a song of love. All else is forgotten; only the dome

[1] See Chapter II, section 13.

remains with its sweeping curves, whose skyward ascent is so clearly spiritual. You feel it to be deeply rooted in the ground, in that city whose russet and white expanses surround it on all sides, in those long centuries of faith of which it is the crown. But at the same time it draws the gaze irresistibly upward and beyond itself, a visible link between man and the supernatural powers to which he has entrusted his salvation.

In this way the basilica of St Peter expresses more profoundly than may appear at first sight the Church's work in the age of the Council of Trent, a work which was not only one of reorganization, of recasting institutions and formal discipline, but also and even more essentially one of interior reawakening and regeneration through sanctity. What it recalls to the faithful Christian is that the Church, his Church, is not a merely human society established on firm foundations by patient effort, but a work of love, a permanent creation of intelligence fertilized by the Word. The wonderful harmony of Michelangelo's dome is that of Catholic wisdom, which managed to shed the excesses of Renaissance humanism while integrating all that was best and most valuable therein, yesterday with St Ignatius and tomorrow with St Francis of Sales. Its flight is that of the great mystics, of St Cajetan, St Teresa, St Philip Neri and St John of the Cross. Its radiance is that of the missionaries who sailed to the uttermost boundaries of earth, carrying everywhere the truth which is light. The visible rests on the invisible, says Keats, and no great effort is required to understand the truth of this assertion when we gaze upon St Peter's.

Indeed the invisible is present there, to be seen and to be touched, especially since recent excavations have shown that the basilica covers the site of a very ancient cemetery where martyrs' tombs have been discovered.[1] The symbolism is inescapable: this earthly church, whose nave is filled by huge crowds on great festivals, is but the image and the promise here below of a supernatural society of souls united throughout the ages by the same love. The basilica reminds us of this most beautiful perhaps of all Christian dogmas. Kneeling at the balustrade which surrounds the opening through which is seen the 'confession' of St Peter,[2] how easy it is to experience that consoling truth, to feel ourselves not only a member of a human organization, but brethren of the holy martyrs, sharing with them the message of Christ in the communion of saints. When in 1594 Clement VIII built the monumental altar which we see today over the Apostle's resting-place, that altar at

---

[1] In the midst of a pagan necropolis the recent excavations have brought to light some Christian tombs, and also a raised monument dating from the middle of the second century. This latter commemorates St Peter, and probably stands over the grave in which his remains were laid after his execution.

[2] So called by the medieval pilgrims, because it was the spot upon which St Peter 'confessed' his faith by martyrdom.

which only the Pope celebrates Mass, he did not destroy the old medieval altar erected by Calixtus II early in the twelfth century. He ordered it to be encased in the new masonry. Now an official document, dating from 1123 and reporting the construction of Calixtus's altar, states that it was built so as to cover a third and still more ancient one, which bore 'on the side facing the apse the seal of St Sylvester.'[1] Herein is a profound symbol, whereby the Tridentine Church declared that while presenting a new face to the world, adapted to contemporary needs and conditions, she was always essentially the same, one with the Church of Apostles and Martyrs, with that of the Dark Ages and with that of the Cathedrals and Crusades, a Church ever new, ever faithful and eternal. At the same time she proclaimed that the splendid edifice built to show forth her glory was founded upon the invisible but unforgettable presence of all those Christians whose labours, prayers and hidden sacrifices during a period of eleven centuries had enabled her to live and to increase.

2. THE POPES OF THE CATHOLIC RESTORATION

The completion of the basilica which provided such a magnificent ending to a great period in the history of the Church, that of the Renaissance and Reformation, also marked the beginning of the seventeenth century, during which Catholicism, with characteristics somewhat different from those of the past, experienced a new and wonderful expansion. What was the appearance of the Church at this date, when she stood at two generations' remove from the Council of Trent and was herself making ready to bring forth the Church of 'Classical' times?

Fifty years had passed since the death of St Pius V (1572), that great pope who had taken over the Tridentine achievement, determined to make it the flesh and blood of Catholicism.[2] History does not regard this half-century as one of those robust and significant periods during which a great idea predominates and seems, while subordinating events to itself, to give them a unity and simplicity which may, however, give rise to many illusions. The hideous results of the dismemberment of the Christian world continued to unfold;[3] but meanwhile, in other fields that were all her own, the Church tenaciously pursued the task undertaken by those whose courage, intelligence and sanctity enabled her to escape from the forces of dissolution and death. Her predecessors

---

[1] The excavations have shown how these altars were encased one inside the other. Over the Constantinian monument was laid a first altar, probably in the time of St Gregory the Great. This was enclosed in the one consecrated by Calixtus in 1123, which underlies that of Clement VIII.

[2] See Chapter II, page 110.   [3] See Chapter III.

had bequeathed to her a twofold duty. On the one hand she had to complete the work of defending and affirming Catholic doctrine, to strengthen the Christian citadel, to counter-attack wherever possible, and to establish institutions so firm that nothing would be able to shake them. On the other hand she had at the same time to perpetuate and develop still further the recent spiritual awakening which had not only uplifted men's souls, but had urged and almost compelled the official Church to carry out the long-awaited reform; she had to see that the leaven remained active in the lump, and give to the salt of the earth its fullest flavour. It was along these lines that the Church had laboured for fifty years, a period of steady endurance and unbroken effort, which can be described by a single word—a period of *restoration*. Outwardly it is not quite so impressive as the two preceding periods, but it is of capital importance. There was effected a slow synthesis which would give life to the future.

This half-century then was dominated by the decisions of Trent, as well as by the spirit of the Council with all its admirable qualities and all the subtle danger that it bore within itself.[1] We first notice a change of climate in the Church when considering her leaders, the Vicars of Christ. From 1572 to the brief pontificate of Gregory XV (1621-3) nine popes succeeded one another on the apostolic throne. They were not saints like their glorious predecessor Pius V; some of them even found it difficult to avoid the lure of politics and to give themselves wholly to the task of restoration. All, however, possessed a keen sense of their duties; and every one of them—at any rate of those to whom Providence allowed sufficient time in which to accomplish anything— did his best to continue the indispensable work summarized above.

When the Dominican pope was succeeded by Cardinal Buoncompagni, men wondered whether this thirteenth Gregory would remind them otherwise than by his name of the great reformer who had been the seventh. A peaceable septuagenarian, a learned jurist and a good priest, against whom no one had had anything to say (at any rate since his ordination), he was known to have enjoyed the close friendship of Pius IV. But would he be worthy of Pius V? He was indeed. Gregory XIII (1572-85) proved himself, to the astonishment of many, an inspiring leader and a true restorer. His name is still associated with the reform of the calendar, which he undertook for the strictly logical purpose of completing that of the missal and the breviary, and of bringing the civil into line with the liturgical year.[2] He also invited

[1] On the spirit of the Council of Trent, see Chapter II, section 13.
[2] The primary motive was to make the date of Easter coincide with the March full moon, in accordance with the decision of Nicaea (325). There was no longer any such coincidence. The Julian calendar, which had been in use since 46 B.C., fixed the year at 365¼ days, which gave a leap year every four years. The astronomical year in fact consists of 365 days, 5 hours and 48 minutes. The result was an increasing difference which by the

Cardinal Sirleti to revise the Martyrology, and published the great compendium of canon law prepared by Pius V.

But it was not only on the intellectual plane that Gregory XIII left his mark; he did much good work in the creation and development of seminaries. He gave new life, for example, to the Roman and German colleges founded by St Ignatius. He made the German College a nursery of priests well trained for missionary work in Germany, where St Peter Canisius had lately paved the way; while the Roman College (the college of all nations) was transformed by him into the celebrated Gregorian University, whither he summoned the most eminent teachers and which has produced hundreds of bishops, scores of cardinals and thousands of preachers and missionaries. He even added a Hungarian College and a Maronite College, and gave fresh vigour to the Venerabile.

The Catholic restoration thus found a first-rate craftsman in the Pope, who appeared so easy-going but could take a strong line when necessary. His choice of bishops was in every case excellent; he left them in no doubt as to the obligation of residence; and he even went so far as to deprive some cardinals of titles whose tenure they did nothing to justify. He lent his wholehearted support to the policy of maintaining permanent nunciatures, which enabled the Sovereign Pontiff to be present, as it were, in all the principal courts of Europe. Nor are his merits invalidated by his frequent mistakes in the purely political sphere, as, for instance, his view of the Massacre of St Bartholomew as a pious victory; his failure to rally the Catholic word against the Turks or against Elizabeth of England; his rather brutal attempts to recover some ecclesiastical property, which precipitated serious trouble in Rome and the neighbourhood; or, lastly, the fact that he died a very sad man. The tribute paid to him by the Romans, who erected a statue to him at the church of Aracoeli, is unanimously considered to have been well deserved.

Such was not the reputation earned by his successor, whose fine statue on the Capitol was overthrown by an infuriated mob immediately after his death. This angry deed was unjust, for Sixtus V (1585–1590) was a great pope, energetic and enterprising; and though far

---

end of the sixteenth century amounted to ten days. Several Councils (and one session of Trent in particular) had expressed a wish to end this anomaly. The solution was found by the Calabrian astronomer Luigi Lulio: ten days would be subtracted from the current year, and a recurrence of the error would be avoided by providing that henceforward out of four secular years (e.g. 1700, 1800, 1900, 2000) only one should be a leap year, that namely whose first three figures were divisible by 4 (thus 1800 was and 2000 will be).

The Gregorian calendar came into force in 1582 by an Apostolic Constitution; so the day after 4th October 1582 was 15th October. The Protestants rejected the reform as 'emanating from Antichrist,' and did not adopt it until the eighteenth century; the Greek Orthodox Church has never adopted it. (Russia adopted it only in 1918, but certain Russian Churches in exile remain faithful to the old Julian calendar.)

removed from the spirit of gentleness, at the time of his unanimous election he was the centre of universal hope. This eloquent and learned Franciscan, whose sermons had once been the delight of St Ignatius and St Philip Neri, was a legendary figure. He was the son of poor peasants in the March of Ancona, and it was said that at the age of twelve he had lived as a swineherd. He had climbed every rung of the ecclesiastical ladder, and none withheld admiration for his outstanding gifts. Very soon, however, his temperament began to earn him less goodwill. Abrupt, pugnacious and possessed of a character that would allow no form of compromise, he ended by disdaining the most necessary prudence.

Nevertheless his energy served him well as it served the Church. From the moment of his accession he was determined to make an end of those brigand lords whose sinister exploits were alarming central Italy. The Piccolomini, the Orsini and others were brought to heel, and Cardinal Colonna swept the Roman Campagna with such vigour that people said there were more heads exposed on the Ponte Sant' Angelo than melons in the market. The finances of the Church were placed once more on a sound footing by methods no less drastic of their kind. But he undoubtedly went too far. When the papal police applied the same stern measures to moral faults, to adultery and prostitution, to theft and to the slightest misdemeanours, there were angry murmurs in Rome, and the tyrannical pontiff was bitterly lampooned. To quieten their crying children mothers used to say: 'Hush! Here comes Sixtus.' And a story went the rounds that St Peter himself had fled from the city, frightened of being hanged for having cut off Malchus's ear. Moreover the pontiff's violence achieved very little: in the international field he obtained few if any results. The excommunication of Henri III was a futile measure, and in dealing with Henri de Navarre Sixtus showed himself hesitant and circumspect. The 'Invincible Armada,' which he had encouraged Philip II to launch against Elizabeth of England, perished in an unprecedented disaster, and the crusade of which he dreamed never took place.

And yet this pope, notwithstanding his many faults, accomplished in five years a work that still endures. He completed not only (1) the dome of St Peter's, upon which he set more than six hundred labourers to work and ordered them to finish it within twenty-two months, but also (2) an edition of the Bible, the so-called Sixtine Vulgate,[1] which was based upon the Greek Septuagint and which was to be the basis of all subsequent editions of Holy Scripture once Clement VIII had corrected the errors caused by undue haste. Finally, and above all, (3) it was he who systematized the papal administration which was

[1] See p. 341.

hence-forward divided into major departments still called 'Roman Congregations.' [1] These three achievements surely do lasting honour to the name of Sixtus V; he is an impressive figure in the line of popes who, as heirs of Trent, shouldered the task of restoration.

After him the Papacy was accidentally eclipsed by the deaths of three successive popes who had no time in which to act: Urban VII after a reign of thirteen days, Gregory XIV after ten months, and Innocent IX after two months. The second of these was just able to intervene in the affairs of France by supporting the League against Henri IV, whom he excommunicated. But the great series of restorer-popes recommenced with Clement VIII (1592-1605). Cardinal Aldobrandini was a model of piety, confessing every evening, fasting and mortifying himself like a monk, and entertaining the poor at his table. But he was also a man of action, a vigorous organizer and a worthy heir of St Pius V. Under him reform made progress in every field. His promotions to the Sacred College were magnificent: Baronius, Bellarmine, Ossat, Du Perron and Tolet. Admirable too were the careful methods he employed upon new editions of the Missal, the Breviary, the Index and the *Pontificale*. He likewise ordered a revision of the Sixtine Vulgate, and the form which he thus gave it remains the official text of the Catholic Bible. This truly spiritual pope protected and encouraged all that could render the inner life of the Church more active and more holy. It was during his pontificate that St Philip Neri carried out his fruitful apostolate in Rome; that St Francis of Sales won back Chablais from the Protestants and was rewarded with a bishopric; that St Joseph Calasanctius founded the Congregation of Pious Schools. And when the 'Molinist' dispute between the Jesuits and Dominicans threatened to sow discord, Clement VIII stepped in as arbitrator and prevented a grave crisis.

This man of God would not yield to the violent transports which did so much harm to the work of Sixtus V. The Church during his pontificate did not show that harsh and grisly face with which some have reproached him. He it was who held out a helping hand to draw Henri IV back to the shores of Holy Church: at the request of Cardinals Ossat and Du Perron he sent Cardinal Alessandro dei Medici as his legate and agreed to absolve the Bearnais from censure.[2] He even tried to restore England to Catholicism, and it was also he who by his wise discretion prevented the rivalry of the French and Spanish factions at Rome from turning into open antagonism. Clement VIII was a great pope, typical of that age of slow but steady work in the cause of restoration; and the acclamation of three million pilgrims who visited Rome for the Jubilee in 1600 was not misdirected.

[1] See section 4 of the present chapter.
[2] This event is commemorated by a column near Santa Maria Maggiore at Rome.

This moderate and wise pope was succeeded [1] by Paul V (1605–21), a man of very different character. The well-known and fairly constant law of alternation took effect; for Borghese was a strong man, an experienced jurist and a born leader, but also a hard man, violent and dictatorial, of a type not unlike that of Sixtus V. Though renowned for his piety and irreproachable morals, he might have done better with more charity and moderation, and perhaps also with less love of pomp and less prodigality towards his nephews. Yet even his faults managed somehow to serve the Church, since it was he who entrusted Maderno with the completion of St Peter's and got him to accomplish the task in six years. His sternness, however, did not always produce such favourable results. The execution of Piccinardari, a pamphleteer accused of high treason against the memory of Clement VIII, may have strengthened his authority; but the trial of Galileo [2] disturbed the minds of many intelligent men, and earned for Paul V a reputation for obscurantism that has detracted somewhat from the glory of the Church. His foreign policy was no more fortunate. The Venetian affair [3] showed that papal authority could be successfully defied; in England the condemnation of the oath of allegiance did nothing but intensify the persecution of those faithful to Rome; [4] neither did all Catholics look with an approving eye upon the Pope's encouragement of the emperor to crush his Bohemian subjects, nor upon the solemn procession with which he celebrated the victory of the White Mountain.[5]

However, as regards the great work of restoration Paul V was worthy of his predecessors, from whose policies he never deviated. All clerics without exception were sternly bidden to keep residence; the bishops themselves, even if they were cardinals, received orders to choose between their dioceses (with their revenues) and domicile in Rome. Strict injunctions were transmitted to parish priests throughout Christendom to devote the utmost care to their sermons and to instruct their flocks. Missionaries were everywhere encouraged, and in order to improve their training a chair of Arabic was established, theoretically at least, in all universities. This pope, who canonized St Charles Borromeo and St Frances of Rome, who beatified Ignatius of Loyola, Thomas of Villanova, Francis Xavier and Teresa of Avila, and who did much to

---

[1] After the twenty-seven-days pontificate of Leo XI, formerly Alessandro dei Medici, the 'Cardinal of Florence,' who had so skilfully negotiated the abjuration of Henri IV, and who would have been, had he lived, Clement's worthy continuator. Two notable episodes occurred during Clement's reign: that of Giordano Bruno, whose condemnation, as we shall see, was perfectly justified; and that of the Cenci, son, wife and daughter of a Roman patrician of cross-grained character, who had been assassinated by his exasperated family. The sentence of death passed upon the criminals was considered too severe by the Roman people, especially in the case of Beatrice Cenci, of whose guilt there was some doubt.

[2] See p. 351.   [3] See p. 326.
[4] See p. 212.   [5] See p. 218.

help the Oratorians, as well as approving the Piarists and Visitandines, was certainly faithful to the spirit engendered by the Council of Trent.

A little more moderation would have made Paul V's reign of sixteen years a very great pontificate. That of Gregory XV (1621–3), who followed him, was too brief to shed great splendour on the closing years of this period, just as the new century assumed its final character; but it was not altogether unproductive. The aged pontiff, so frail in appearance and always in ill health, was none the less animated by the same spirit of the Catholic reform and restoration. As well as possessing high spiritual qualities he was a cultured man, and his keen political intelligence was put to good use by a well-chosen *entourage* under the young cardinal-nephew Ludovisi. In twenty-nine months a surprising amount of work was accomplished in every field.

The diplomacy of Gregory XV was no less fortunate in its results than were his administrative decisions and his dogmatic decrees. He succeeded in holding the balance between the Empire and France; his skill won for the Catholics a seat in the electoral college, where the Protestants numbered only two out of seven. Marie dei Medici, grateful for the red hat bestowed on her young chaplain Armand de Richelieu and for the elevation of the See of Paris to metropolitan rank,[1] was on the best of terms with the Papacy, and the French Crown protected Christians in the East. It was Gregory XV who laid down the rules still in force at papal elections. It was he who understood the necessity for the Holy See to take control of missionary activities throughout the world, and who for that purpose created the Congregation of Propaganda.[2] He likewise successfully defended the Jesuits, his former teachers, against the attacks of their enemies, and gave them a fresh impulse which endowed their colleges and their missions with new vigour; but it was no less to him that the Benedictines of Saint-Maur owed their expansion. And the fourfold canonization in 1622 [3] proclaimed to all the world the sanctity of the Church, her radiant joy, the strength of her progress and the supernatural effectiveness of her mystical contact with God. Lastly it was Gregory XV who stimulated Catholic piety with some of its most popular devotions. Among these latter was the Immaculate Conception; he did not dogmatically define it, but he forbade its denial. With Gregory XV there ended a half-century of patient toil, thanks to which the spirit of the Council permeated the whole Church and prepared her for the tasks and difficulties that lay ahead.

[1] Hitherto it had been a suffragan of Sena.
[2] See Chapter IV, section 15.
[3] See the concluding pages of this volume.

3. GREATNESS AND PERILS OF THE VICAR OF CHRIST

The most striking feature then of the Church's new look is the dignity and greatness of the Papacy, which is far removed from the degrading atmosphere that too often hung about Peter's throne during the previous century. The popes indeed had human faults, some of them very considerable faults; but those cannot prejudice the respect due to them in their sacred character, and Savonarola himself could scarcely have reproached them. Of the nine pontiffs who succeeded one another after the death of Pius V none laid himself open to criticism. This is true even of Gregory XIII, for it has never been proved that his son was not the offspring of a perfectly legitimate marriage contracted before he received Holy Orders. Everything was not as yet perfect at the Vatican Court; but if nepotism, which had done so much harm, had not completely disappeared, we can at least say that it no longer possessed the scandalous character which we saw in the days of Innocent VIII or Borgia. True, Gregory XIII appointed his son Giacomo governor of the castle of Sant' Angelo, but the young man's conduct was exemplary. Clement VIII's nephew Cardinal Aldobrandini was invested with the purple at the age of twenty-two, but he was discreetly left in the shade. More reprehensible was the foolish prodigality of Paul V towards his nephews, but they themselves gave no cause for complaint; and as for young Ludovisi, whose uncle Gregory XV made him a cardinal at the age of twenty-five, he proved himself an invaluable collaborator, no less intelligent than energetic. Finally, the example of St Charles Borromeo showed that it was possible to be a pope's nephew, to be raised by him to the highest dignities, and yet to remain a true servant of God and of the Church.

The popes were thus respected; [1] some were haloed with gratitude and even with affection. There was a general feeling of thankfulness to all of them, even to those whose methods were sometimes harsh, for having laboured resolutely to restore order in the Papal States, for having expelled the unruly elements, for having suppressed the quarrels of the clans and for having restored financial security. Many of them were linked with the ancient tradition of papal charity, devoted to their people and anxious to relieve the sufferings of the lowly. Gregory XIII, for example, is known to have distributed 2,000,000 écus in thirteen years to poor students, and to have obliged the great lords to give back to the peasants those lands of which they had illegally

---

[1] Even in Rome their authority was no longer contested; the factions had been brought to heel.

deprived them. Urban VII found time during the thirteen days of his brief pontificate to take two measures: he ordered a list to be prepared of all the city's paupers, with a view to helping them, and he also paid the pawnbrokers all sums advanced by them to the poorest folk, who were thus enabled to regain possession of their pledges. Paul V himself established public granaries for the distribution of supplies to the unfortunate in times of want, and he also did much to help the peasant farmers.

The radiance of this restored and reinvigorated Papacy spread far and wide, assisted by the institution of Roman Congregations, which freed it from the meddlesome tutelage of ruling families. The creation of nunciatures also contributed to that influence. The manner in which the various States ultimately, though not always with good grace, accepted the decrees of Trent is significant. A less important but equally revealing fact is the adoption of the Gregorian calendar by the entire Catholic world. After 1622 the Congregation of Propaganda became one of the chief means whereby the Papacy made its authority felt, because the apostolate in every land was now directly subject to the Pope; but, as we have seen, its birth had been preceded by a long, slow period of ripening.

But this undeniable increase of power and prestige does not represent the whole picture. The centralization of the Church, in her services as well as in principle, which was one of the consequences of Trent, was not everywhere accomplished without resistance. Succeeding popes managed to secure it by a skilful use of gentleness and diplomacy, but such means were not in the character of every one of them; the way of stern authority was preferred to peaceful methods by Sixtus V and Paul V. This abrupt, violently dogmatic aspect of the Tridentine Church is particularly noticeable in certain pontiffs who were too prone to the exercise of dictatorial powers; they show us a Church bristling with defences and prompt to condemn. Herein surely lay danger for Catholicism; the age of theocratic pretensions was long past, and the West had no desire to see it return. The forces of the modern world had become conscious of themselves, and those who served them did so with the passion of youth. The seed of future conflict had been sown.

I say *future* conflict, but already certain episodes had the character of disquieting symptoms. The Papacy, once more strong and respected, naturally wished to pose as arbiter of the Catholic world. This is particularly true of Sixtus V, who desired to make Rome a sort of world capital whither ceaseless pilgrimages would bring millions of the faithful from every quarter of the globe, even from America, to venerate the Vicar of Christ and hear his admonitions. On several occasions, if at a more modest level, the Papacy did play the part of arbiter with complete success. In 1598 Clement VIII prepared the Peace of Vervins between France and Spain; in 1601 he patiently negotiated the Treaty of Lyons between France and Savoy. Likewise, in 1621, the indefatigable Gregory XV prevented the outbreak of hostilities between France and Austria over the high Alpine valley of Valteline, and paved the way for an agreement.

It was unlikely that the new Europe of absolute monarchies, nationalistic feelings and centralized States would be prepared to recognize the Vicar of Christ as arbitrator. Now that Christendom had been permanently dismembered, too many peoples stood shoulder to shoulder around their respective dynasties, and were aware of what made them unique, irreplaceable—in short, nations. It was already clear that papal authority, which, in the name of the spiritual principles of Christianity, should exercise control over the internal affairs of human groups as well as over their mutual relations, would meet with stout resistance.

Even in Spain, that most Catholic of countries, the heirs of Ferdinand and Isabella, tending though they did to identify the Church's interests with their own, seldom submitted to papal authority unless its decisions were of use to themselves. In 1580, when young King Sebastian of Portugal vanished during a rash but heroic crusade in Morocco, Gregory XIII was unable to prevent the master of the Escorial from laying hands upon the little neighbouring realm. Under Sixtus V there was almost uninterrupted tension between Madrid and Rome, between two equally authoritarian régimes. When it was proposed to absolve Henri IV, the wrath of Spain was such that the Most Catholic King's ambassador spoke of challenging Cardinal Aldobrandini to a duel. During the reign of Philip III the situation was unaltered: the governors of Milan and Naples were constantly lending money to the Pope's representatives, the bishops. One of the reasons that decided Gregory XV in 1621 to decree that papal elections should in future be by secret scrutiny and a two-thirds majority was undoubtedly his wish to free them from the undue influence which the Spanish monarchy thought it had a right to exercise in the deliberations of the Conclave.

The curious history of the Venetian Schism (1605–7) is yet another example of the spirit of insubordination towards the Holy See. Venice had long disregarded the rights of the Church. Sixtus IV and Julius II had both been at loggerheads with the proud republic; the Bulls of St Pius V, the decrees applying the decisions of Trent and the excommunication of Henri IV had all been treated as so many scraps of paper by the doges. Under Paul V the situation deteriorated when two ecclesiastics were arrested on a criminal charge in defiance of canonical privilege. The Pope, fretting and fuming, demanded the prisoners' release; then he excommunicated Doge Leonardo and the whole Venetian Senate, who replied by requiring all priests to take an oath of allegiance to themselves and by expelling the recalcitrant members of religious Orders. At this juncture Paoli Sarpi, a misguided but immensely learned friar who had been appointed official theologian to the Serenissima, published his *Treatise on the Interdict*, a satire purporting to question the authority of the popes. He also began his famous *History of the Council of Trent* (published in London, 1619), a skilfully biased work expressly designed to show that the Council had never recognized the authority claimed by the Pope. Nor was the episode a mere petty squabble; for when Paul V attempted to crush Venice, he found her fiercely upheld by the dukes of Savoy, Medina and Urbino, by the Protestants of England, the Low Countries and Germany, and also by the French Gallicans. Only the astute diplomacy of Henri IV and his ambassador, Cardinal de Joyeuse, managed to terminate this affair.

But France herself was not much inclined to accept without reservation the Pope's authority apart from religious questions strictly so-called. When Sixtus V supported the League the French clergy as a whole were far from approving his action, and the Parlement protested vigorously. The kingdom was riddled with Gallicanism, that leaven of national independence, compounded from a whole mass of traditions, practices and doctrines of great antiquity. Political Gallicanism recognized the Pope as having none but spiritual rights; ecclesiastical Gallicanism, though less extreme, was strongly attached to the customs and prerogatives of the French Church. It is not impossible that this outlook was inspired by some measure of secular influence. The doctrine of the divine right of kings, fervently expounded by Guy Coquille, by André Duchesne and, above all, by Loyseau, allowed the Pope no more than a secondary rôle in the transmission of power. If, it was argued, the king 'holds his crown from God alone, there is no power whatever upon earth, temporal *or spiritual*, that can have any authority over the realm.' So said the Fundamental Law presented to the States-General in 1614. A fresh pretext for the miniature war declared upon the Jesuits in 1594, and lasting until 1625, was found in Châtel's attempt (1596) upon the life of Henri IV, who ordered the expulsion of the Society, and yet another, after its recall (1603), in Ravaillac's regicide, wherein many claimed to detect the hand of the Fathers. The truth is that the Jesuits were hated for quite different reasons. These extremely able religious, who had a finger in every pie— one of them, Fr Coton, had succeeded in having himself appointed confessor to the king—were looked upon as nothing but agents of ultramontanism, of papal interference, of the Roman stranglehold upon France. The pamphlets and declarations of such eminent jurists as

Louis Servin, Étienne Pasquier and Antoine Arnauld [1] left no doubt upon this point.[2]

Such were the omens revealed by history. The Pope continued to be respected in his sacred capacity and listened to in the spiritual domain; but from the time of Gregory XV's successor, Urban VIII, it was perfectly clear that he would have to renounce all claims to govern the world. A revolution was in progress, whose outcome, as we know, was far from unhappy for the Church. In the long run, in our own day, a Papacy completely disengaged from politics has proved to be far more influential and of far greater stature; but three centuries and still more serious crises had still to be weathered before that result was achieved.

4. NEW INSTITUTIONS AND CAPITAL DECISIONS

The memory of those fifty years of patient effort is embodied in the institutions of the Church. During that time organisms were created which continue to play a leading rôle even today, and major decisions were taken which have never been reversed.

First among these innovations we must note the establishment of Roman Congregations by Sixtus V. The Bull *Immensa aeterni Dei* (1587) reorganized, systematized and gave increased efficiency to the entire Curia. The idea was not new, for Pius IV and Pius V had long since perceived the advantage of entrusting a committee of cardinals with the general direction of a whole sector of administration. Developed and multiplied, the Congregations [3] became more or less the equivalent of ministries in a modern State; but since the Church exercises her authority both on the temporal and on the spiritual plane, she has 'temporal ministries' as well as 'spiritual ministries,' each with its particular duties. To the first category belonged the Congregations of Abundance, charged with the Roman food supply; of the Fleet; of Roads and Aqueducts; of the 'Signature of Grace,' for the examination of all derogations from strict justice; and of the Vatican Press, to supervise purity of doctrine and the correction of texts as well as to control the operations of the Pontifical Printing Office. The second category was larger and more important. To the celebrated Congregation of the Inquisition or Holy Office, vigilant guardian of orthodoxy, and that of the Council, charged with carrying out the decrees of Trent, there were added many others: of Bishops, of Rites, etc.—a total of fifteen Congregations upon which depends the functioning of the

[1] Ancestor of the celebrated Jansenist whom we shall meet again in the history of Port-Royal.

[2] The problem of Gallicanism will be studied more thoroughly in the next volume of the present series.

[3] They were also known at that time as Dicasteries.

Church and which take cognizance of all matters formerly dealt with in Consistory. The principal benefits derived by the Church from the reform of Sixtus V were more seriousness, more thoroughness, more discretion; and that reform is particularly remarkable because, at the date in question, ministries and secretariats of lay States were far from having attained such logical precision.

One year earlier (1586), by the Bull *Postquam verus ille*, the same pope organized the Sacred College according to a system which has endured ever since.[1] The number of cardinals was fixed at seventy, a mystical number, being that of the elders who attended Moses, that of the disciples chosen by Christ and that of the translators of the Greek Bible (Septuagint). These high dignitaries, true pillars of the Church, are divided into three classes, not according to the power of orders, but according to the ecclesiastical title assigned to each at the time of his promotion: six cardinal-bishops, fifty cardinal-priests and fourteen cardinal-deacons. The same Bull laid down exact rules for their selection: they were to be chosen from the most worthy men of every country in the Christian world; they must have received minor orders, and have worn the tonsure and ecclesiastical dress for at least a year.[2] These were wise provisions, to which the popes submitted neither at once nor without exceptions, and even Sixtus V himself occasionally departed from his own rules; but they established a principle and prepared for the future.

The primary duty of the cardinals is to choose the successor of St Peter. This all-important act had long since been the object of careful regulation. The famous decree of Nicholas II, in 1059, withdrew the election from the interference of temporal princes and entrusted it to the seven cardinal-bishops, but added that it must be approved by the clergy and people of Rome and confirmed by the emperor. In 1189 the Third Lateran Council abolished this threefold operation, and decided that if the cardinals failed to agree unanimously in favour of any candidate, no one might be held to have been elected except by a majority of two-thirds. Gregory XV, who had had a very sound legal training and was anxious to exclude all undue influence of the secular powers in the choice of future popes, determined to revise the rules governing the Conclave. This he did by the Constitution *Aeterni Patris* of 1621, supplemented in the following year by the Constitution *Decet Romanum pontificem*, both of which, except for a few details, are still in force. Three methods of choice are permissible. Sometimes an irresistible current, the inspiration of the Holy Ghost, is directed to one man,

[1] Except that Pope John XXIII has considerably increased the number of cardinals and reserves the right to appoint as many as he may see fit.—Tr.

[2] Today, in point of fact, nearly all the cardinals are bishops, and the present code of canon law provides that all must be priests. But a bishop who is created cardinal is not necessarily a cardinal-bishop; he may also be appointed to either of the two other classes.

and the choice must then be unanimous; it is known as election by
'acclamation' or 'adoration.' Secondly, it may happen that the cardinals, unable to agree, appoint arbitrators from among themselves;
here again the choice must be unanimous and is called election by
'compromise.' Finally—and this is the most usual method—the
election takes place by scrutiny. In order to avoid intrigue and col-
lusion, to which secret voting is always liable, every elector must
write his name on his voting-paper, together with that of the candidate
he chooses. A two-thirds majority is required.

Elected thus with every possible precaution, and assisted in his work
by improved administrative bodies, the Pope has at his disposal yet
another means of action in the form of nunciatures. These appear first,
though very few in number, at the beginning of the sixteenth century.
Hitherto the Sovereign Pontiff's representatives had been legates.
Some of these were *legati nati*, residing in a particular country,
occupying episcopal sees by way of special privilege, and serving as
permanent deputies of the common father; among the holders of this
proud title were the archbishops of Bourges, Toledo, Canterbury and
Mainz. Others were *legati missi*, who were neither more nor less than
ambassadors at the courts of certain sovereigns, but usually in a more
or less temporary capacity. Others again were *legati a latere*, that is to
say, selected from the Pope's *entourage* and appointed for a particular
mission, a delicate piece of negotiation (e.g. that of the Cardinal of
Florence at the time of Henri IV's abjuration) or a great ceremony.
From the end of the sixteenth century the title *legatus natus* became
merely honorific, the rôle of *legati missi* became more important, while
the missions entrusted to *legati a latere* diminished in number and were
limited to definite occasions. Following the growing practice of all
major States,[1] the Papacy was henceforward represented by apostolic
nuncios wherever their presence seemed useful. Nunciatures were
opened all along the religious frontier which, alas, separated Catholicism from heresy: at Gratz in 1573, at Lucerne in 1579, at Cologne in
1580, at Brussels in 1606. There were others, of course, in all the great
Catholic capitals, but also in every place where religion was at stake:
at Warsaw, for example (1605), and even at Moscow, where the popes
wished to be represented. It must be added that the choice of these
nuncios was on the whole extremely good: Commendone at Cologne,
Bonhomini at Lucerne, Possevino in Russia and Sweden—all laboured
with devotion and intelligence under conditions that were often very
difficult.

Thus at the end of this long period, reaching from 1350 to the
threshold of the seventeenth century, the Papacy, after surviving so

---

[1] The Republic of Venice had long set an example with its corps of extremely able
ambassadors.

many and such grave crises, is found to be more securely established and more influential. Nevertheless one black spot remained. The Holy See was as yet far from exercising full control of the episcopate; in other words, it could not reach the faithful except through the agency of men who were not always reliable. The Consistorial Congregation had indeed been created to make preliminary inquiry into the qualifications of intended bishops and the translation of existing diocesans to other Sees; but its work, though theoretically indispensable, was often in practice more diligent than effective. Pragmatic sanctions and concordats too frequently enabled temporal sovereigns to impose upon the Church a man whom she herself would have preferred not to see at the head of a diocese. If the Pope consecrated the new bishop, policy and diplomacy had many means of bringing him to heel. Unless and until the Papacy won for itself the sole right of appointing shepherds of the flock, a grave problem remained to be solved.

5. In Quest of the Lost Sheep

However strong and powerful the Church might appear in the persons of her rulers, there was no doubt that she had suffered heavy losses, and the question was whether those losses could be made good. One need only glance at the religious map of Europe [1] to understand the magnitude of the disaster. The whole of northern Germany, a part of Switzerland, the Low Countries, Scandinavia, England and Scotland had seceded. It was a painful thought that those millions of baptized Christians were now separated from the flock. Holy Church was therefore obliged to face the fact that the extent of her territory and the numbers of her faithful had been sadly diminished; and she was well aware that she had not yet won their equivalent in those new Christian lands which her missionaries were labouring to establish from Mexico to Argentina. Nor can anyone who does not confine himself to a quantitative estimate of results avoid one further and perhaps more distressing observation: those Christian peoples who had alienated themselves from the Church had served her in the past as life-giving elements that were altogether irreplaceable. The Anglo-Saxon and Germanic Catholics had added their less rational impulse to the great systems of moral theology and canon law erected by the Latins. Surely the Church could not reconcile herself to the perpetual loss of the countries that had given birth to Suso, Ruysbroek, Tauler, Eckhart, Richard Rolle, the author of the 'Cloud,' and Juliana of Norwich—countries too that were still capable of producing abundant harvests of mysticism.

[1] See above, page 210.

No indeed, she would not submit to so terrible an amputation; never for an instant did she abandon hope, or cease to be tormented with anguish for the lost sheep. 'Rome is not worn out in her old age,' declared Bossuet in his sermon on unity, and his words have not died upon the wind; 'night and day she never ceases to call to the peoples who have gone farthest astray, inviting them to the banquet where all is made one.' That line on the map which separates the zone of Catholic loyalty from the zone of heresy has never been considered by the Church as henceforth unalterable. Moreover at the beginning of the seventeenth century there were unequivocal signs that the battle was not lost. Among them were the Catholic recovery in France, Hungary and Poland, and that kind of fermentation which appeared in Germany and which in fact precipitated the bloody crisis of the Thirty Years War. This attempt to regain souls and territory forms a splendid chapter of Catholic history. Thousands of men had no other ambition than to visit the land of heresy, there to manifest the presence of the Church and preach her message, even at the peril of their lives. Regenerate Catholicism quite naturally placed herself on a missionary footing, just as the early Church had done.

At the head of this enterprise, from its very beginning, stood the Society of Jesus. As we have already pointed out, the struggle against Protestantism was not the primary objective of St Ignatius; but in swearing to go wherever the Pope might send him, 'whether among the Turks or among other infidels,' a Jesuit undertook to go likewise among the unbelievers of Europe. This design assumed added importance under the second General, Laynez. The Jesuits, as experts in the field of education, soon undertook to train men specially for the fight against Protestantism on its own ground. The celebrated College of Douai, founded by William (afterwards Cardinal) Allen, sent to England missionaries whose ultimate goal was martyrdom. For Germany the same was done by the German College, to which Chemnitz has paid this tribute: 'If the Jesuits had done nothing but found the college at Rome they would deserve to be regarded as the most dangerous enemies of Lutheranism.' They did not confine themselves to that. Far from it. From their three citadels at Cologne, Vienna and Ingolstadt they mounted one offensive after another against the whole of Central Europe, and even as far afield as Poland and Scandinavia. True the Society's work in certain countries, notably in France, was open to criticism on account of its marked political bias, but in many other sectors its efforts were sublime and achieved magnificent results.

It was perhaps in England that the most glorious chapter of this story came to be written. During Elizabeth's reign of terror many Jesuits volunteered for the task of bringing back their brethren to Catholicism, or, if they were unsuccessful, of fertilizing their native soil with their own blood. Proclaiming themselves loyal subjects of their sovereign, and refusing to have anything to do with policies that fomented absurd plots, they sought only to pray, to bear testimony, to speak. 'We have made a pact,' wrote one of them, Blessed Edmund Campion, in a letter to the queen, 'all we Jesuits of the world, whose increase will survive all the machinations of England; we have made a pact, I say, to carry the cross, that cross which you lay upon us, and never to despair of your conversion. There will always be one of us to taste the joys of your gibbet at Tyburn, to endure the agonies of your tortures or to die in your jails. For thus the faith was planted, and thus it will be re-established.'

This prodigious undertaking of 'God's guerrillas' was full of dramatic episodes. One of the missionaries, John Gerard, has left an account of it in his autobiography, which is among the most impressive documents of that age, strangely similar to some we read today. Landing in secret, journeying continually, hunted by the police, obliged to disguise themselves in order to escape detection, lodging with a few old parish priests whom the authorities had forgotten, these adventurers of Christ showed a degree of courage that links them directly with the evangelizers of the first centuries. If they were captured they were generally doomed to an appalling fate. Tortured for days on end, exhausted and broken, they were first hanged, and then, while semi-conscious but still alive, they were turned over to a butcher who cut open their bellies and tore out their entrails. Thus perished at Tyburn Blessed Edmund Campion (1540-81), whose proud declaration is quoted above. A former Cambridge student of brilliant promise and looked upon with favour by the queen, he declined to accept the splendid career offered him in the Anglican Church, preferring to remain loyal to the faith of his fathers. What were the fruits of so much effort and sacrifice? At first sight, very meagre. England did not return to Catholicism; the criminal folly of the Gunpowder Plot (1605) infuriated public opinion, and Catholicism was long silenced in the homeland of St Thomas à Becket and St Thomas More. Yet, as we can now see, it continued secretly to flower in England; and who knows whether one day, in Tertullian's immortal words, the blood of the English martyrs will not prove to have been the seed of faith?

Circumstances were less dramatic in Germany, Poland and Central Europe; but the work of reconquest was even more energetic, and on the morrow of the Council the Papacy became interested in the task. Pius V sent his legate Commendone to Cologne in order to secure recognition for the decrees of Trent. Later the nuncios Portia and Ninguarda strove patiently at Salzburg and Ratisbon to establish bases from which Catholicism would subsequently launch its attack on heretical territories. Faithful rulers played their part by supporting these endeavours. Among them were Albert V of Bavaria, his son William V (husband of the pious Renée de Lorraine), the Archduke Ferdinand in Tyrol and, despite some nervous hesitation, even the Emperor Rudolf II. Above all, here as elsewhere, the Society of Jesus was in the forefront of battle, training in its colleges at Rome the future apostles of Germany, and founding numerous schools [1] and seminaries in the very heart of Protestant countries.

This immense undertaking was headed by a man of outstanding ability: St Peter Canisius (1521-97).[2] He was a Dutchman, son of a wealthy middle-class family at Nijmegen, a man of vigorous yet peaceable character and possessed of marvellous charity. When quite young and uncertain what to do with his life he heard an ineffable voice calling to him: 'Go and preach the Gospel to every creature.' At that time he was a student at Louvain, but he resolved then and there to serve God by giving himself to others. A meeting at Mainz with Pierre Le Fèvre, one of the first companions of St Ignatius, confirmed him in his choice, and the great founder, a connoisseur of men, forthwith esteemed and loved him.

For thirty years Peter Canisius never ceased to proclaim the Gospel and bear witness to its message. Germany, which he knew well, filled him with anguish, but at the same time with hope. He never despaired. 'I will not break the bended reed,' saith the Eternal, 'nor quench the smoking wick.' Firmly believing this divine promise he strove with all his might to straighten the near-broken reed and to rekindle the flame. He did not conceal his violent indignation against those who accepted the dreadful situation, who 'snore during the storm'; but he was never violent towards those who had been misled by wicked shepherds and wandered far from the Lord's flock. 'Let us confine ourselves,' he used to say, 'to expounding Catholic doctrine; we shall obtain far greater and better results than by force and polemics.' He called the heretics, whom so many Catholics doomed to hell, 'my separated brethren.'

During those thirty years of apostolic work he was successively professor at Ingolstadt and provincial of Upper Germania. For thirty years he travelled ceaselessly about Germany and its border States, founding colleges at Prague, Freiburg-im-Breisgau, Munich, Dillingen and many other places. Wherever he went he conversed, made contacts and persuaded. It was Peter Canisius who accompanied and advised the nuncios sent by the Holy See to the hostile Rhineland. It was he who compiled the summary of Catholic doctrine needed by the common people in order to reply to Lutheran libels; and he performed the task so well that even today, on the Continent, someone will ask a child 'Do

[1] Those at Vienna and Ingolstadt had already been founded during the lifetime of St Ignatius.
[2] His paternal name was Hond, which he latinized.

you know your Canisius?' instead of 'Do you know your catechism?' On another and more lofty plane, in concert with Bellarmine, he refuted the slanderous theories of the heretics concerning the Pope and the Church. Some of the conversions he made caused a tremendous stir, as in the case of two women who were members of the great banking family Fugger. In order to measure the extent of his success one need only consider the detestation in which he was held by Protestants. 'That fellow Canisius is a cynic,' exclaimed the gentle Melanchthon, and Wigand declared that 'that dog tears our holy scriptures to pieces.' The play on words was easy, but their wrath was an avowal.

The impetus given by Canisius and the Jesuits was felt indeed throughout large sectors of the Germanic world. Districts which had seemed to hesitate between heresy and Catholicism were strengthened in their loyalty to Rome. Princes who had been educated at Jesuit colleges worked hard on behalf of the Catholic restoration. Among them was Ferdinand of Austria, who checked the advance of Protestantism in the region of Gratz, forced the nobility of Styria, Carinthia and Carniola to submit, and applied, as was his right, the famous principle *cujus regio, hujus religio*. Others were William V of Bavaria and his son Maximilian, who, with the eager encouragement of Clement VIII, made their kingdom a strong bastion of the Catholic faith, which it has ever since remained. Meanwhile such ecclesiastical princes as the abbot of Fulda, the electors of Trier and Mainz, and the Archbishop of Wurzburg took courage and imposed strict obedience upon all. Meanwhile also in the Rhineland, where the situation had long been confused, the election of Ernest of Bavaria to the See of Cologne, of Cardinal Charles de Lorraine to that of Strasbourg,[1] and the recovery of Aix-la-Chapelle by the Archbishop of Liège, returned to or preserved for Catholicism those three important cities. At the outbreak of the Thirty Years War (1618), which called so many things in question, the situation in the Germanic world was nothing like it had been about 1530, when the whole Empire seemed on the point of becoming Lutheran.

In Central Europe results were perhaps not everywhere quite so satisfactory. In Bohemia, for example, a similar effort was made by Ferdinand I with the help of the Jesuits, and Peter Canisius went there in person. But the weakness of Maximilian II made it impossible to consolidate such successes as were achieved, and the blundering violence of Rudolf II ruined everything. The Czech quadrilateral, torn between opposing forces, was in fact the starting-point of the last of the great religious conflicts, the Thirty Years War.[2]

[1] With residence at Molsheim. It was not until the reign of Louis XIV that Strasbourg Cathedral became once more the scene of Catholic worship.
[2] See Chapter III, section 10.

The situation was even more complex in Hungary, that unhappy land cut into three fragments by the disaster of Mohacz and subsequent troubles. In the zone occupied by the Turks and subject to terrible oppression, Catholicism was the national faith; it was the Catholic clergy who kept alive the national feeling, who mingled with their pious hymns other songs bewailing the disgrace of servitude and lamenting that Buda had become a stronghold of Islam. In Transylvania, where reigned the widow Zapolya and then her son Sigismund, there was utter confusion. Four creeds were at loggerheads—Catholicism, Lutheranism, Calvinism and Orthodoxy—and the rulers who succeeded one another at the head of that little State, whether zealous Catholics such as the Bathorys or such liberal Protestants as Bethlen Gabor, could scarcely unravel the tangled skein. In imperial Hungary, on the other hand, the situation was quickly transformed in favour of Catholicism. Melius, 'the pope of Debreczen,' and his Lutheran confession were stoutly opposed, from 1565 onwards, by a group of Jesuits who had established themselves at Tyrgau. Elsewhere the 'Hungarian Church' lost some ground to Calvinism. The activity of Ferdinand II made possible a Roman counter-attack in which two great noblemen played leading parts. Both Nicholas Esterhazy, a layman, and Peter Pazmany, who had joined the Jesuits, led the anti-Protestant struggle with wisdom and energy that may be compared with those of St Francis of Sales. Twenty years later, in 1648, new prospects opened for Hungary, and the crown of St Stephen was ready to assume the fresh responsibilities imposed upon it by centuries of Catholic loyalty.

Poland, however, was undoubtedly the scene of the most impressive recovery. During the reign of Sigismund II (1548–72) it looked as though the Protestant Reformation, led by John Laski and the powerful Radziwill family, would win the day. This did not happen. The situation was restored by the courage of a few bishops, particularly Stanislaus (afterwards Cardinal) Hosius of Cholm, in Ermland; by the brilliant labours of St Peter Canisius in extraordinarily difficult circumstances; and by the skilful diplomatic intervention of the nuncio Commendone. The rest was achieved by the unshakable loyalty of the *chlopi* (Polish peasants) to their ancient faith. Little by little heresy gave ground. After a brief occupation of the throne by Henri de Valois (later Henri III of France), Henry Bathory (1576–86), a Transylvanian prince and an ardent Catholic, set about the work of restoration. He wasted no time in sending for the Jesuits, who founded many colleges, notably at Riga and Polotsk. Peter Skarga, the 'Bossuet of Poland,' undertook numerous missionary journeys and public disputations, as well as publishing his *Lives of the Saints* which was enormously popular among the lower classes. Sigismund III (1587–1632), a former pupil of the Society and a spiritual son of the famous Jesuit

Warszewicki, had almost completed this work as the sixteenth century drew to its close. Poland returned once for all to the faith that had always been part and parcel of her being and of her life.

There were even better things in store, for Poland, having become once again a Catholic bastion, devoted herself to an important missionary enterprise. She had numerous relations with Sweden, dynastic and otherwise, and thither she now sent Fr Warszewicki in an effort to convert King John III, husband of the Polish Catholic Catherine Jagellon. After much negotiation the hoped-for result appeared almost certain, and the nuncio Possevino, an earnest apostle no less than a clever diplomat, managed to obtain the sovereign's abjuration. This triumph, however, was ephemeral. On the death of John III (1592) the throne was seized by his brother Charles IX, a fanatical partisan of the Confession of Augsburg, who ignored the prior right of his nephew Sigismund III of Poland. Even so the Jesuits did not abandon hope; they maintained a house of the Society at Stockholm, and also founded a special institute at Brannsberg in order to train missionaries destined for Sweden, Finland and Russia.

Yes, Russia too was in the thoughts of Holy Church; the separated Orthodox brethren were not forgotten in her quest for the lost sheep. Sigismund III cherished such a dream in 1605, during the interregnum which followed the extinction of Ivan the Terrible's dynasty.[1] He hoped not only to place a garrison in the Kremlin, but also to plant the Roman faith throughout the empire of the czars. But he failed, and the accession of the Romanoffs in 1613 put an end for ever to that dream.

Nevertheless a more lasting result was obtained elsewhere. In 1595 the Jesuits, taking advantage of some patient labour on the part of Possevino and Skarga, accomplished an extraordinary feat by converting the Ruthenians, a people subject to Byzantine jurisdiction, accepting Byzantine doctrine and practising the Byzantine liturgy. They dwelt in the territories of Poland and Lithuania, and it was desirable to prevent them from looking towards Moscow. This union was made possible by the wise moderation of Clement VIII, who allowed the Ruthenians to retain their traditional rites, and did not oblige them to adopt the Gregorian calendar. There were violent repercussions, and the Orthodox caused ceaseless trouble. In Kiev Cathedral, for instance, a fanatic attacked the uniate metropolitan Pociej with an axe, cutting off two of his fingers; and St Josaphat Kuntsewycz, the great apostle of Ruthenia, suffered martyrdom in 1623. Directed, however, by a man of unflagging energy, Archbishop Rouski of Polotsk, a former Basilian monk, the uniate episcopate resisted every assault. Ruthenia is still faithful to Rome; not even Communism will subdue her.

[1] See Chapter III, section 13.

All these episodes are signal marks of vitality, a manifold and wonderful proof of indestructible hope. The sheep had strayed, but were not for ever lost; the Church did not renounce them. And now, far away from Ruthenia and Hungary, we may for a moment lift the veil upon a small Savoyard canton in the year 1594–5. Here a young priest, the provost of Annecy, was hard at work. He had determined to wrest Chablais from the Calvinists—Chablais with its 25,000 inhabitants of whom but little more than a hundred were Catholics—and he accomplished what he had set out to do, thanks to his level-headed courage and abiding gentleness. His name? St Francis of Sales. So long as he lives we shall meet him again at every crossroads of the Church's journey.

6. DEFENCE OF THE FAITH: BELLARMINE AND BARONIUS

The Church then was not indifferent and resigned in face of Protestantism and its impressive achievements. She did not shut herself up in the fortress of dogma and disciplinary canons built by the Council of Trent, though it must be admitted that her first care henceforward was her own defence. Never before had she been obliged to meet an attack that threatened her very existence and that of the faith whereby she lives. She was still a besieged city, courageously sending out the best of her troops to recover lost ground; but she had also to think of repelling the enemy's assaults. We must not overlook these facts if we wish to understand some of the steps we shall see her take, certain of her judgments in the field of ideas. Even during their own lifetimes Luther, Calvin and other reformers found themselves and their theories assailed by opponents who, though formidable, were never their equals. But the situation had now altered. There were theologians and exegetes qualified to deal with Protestant attacks; the counter-offensive of Catholic orthodoxy was conducted no less vigorously at the intellectual than at the military level.

The Protestants had made clever use of the printing press, and their numerous publications had done much to help the rapid spread of their theories. Their pamphlets and treatises circulated everywhere, sometimes bearing the forged names of Catholic writers and doing a great deal of harm. At the time when the Council of Trent was completing its labours they were making use of a monumental work known as the *Centuries of Magdeburg*, which might be described as a sort of anti-Catholic *Summa*. Its author, Flacius Illyricus, while expounding the whole range of Lutheran doctrine, pretended to explain the history of the world as the infernal game of Antichrist, i.e. of the Pope. Among numerous unspeakable insults—'lewd pot-belly' and 'sack of infamy' were the most polite expressions—this pamphleteer collected together

all the arguments against Rome and her pontiffs. Historical events skilfully marshalled, such as the episode of Frederick Barbarossa's humiliation before Alexander III at Legnano,[1] enabled him to present the
Pope as the worst of tyrants. A number of puerile stories were also
given credit and found their way into print, including the notorious
and ridiculous legend of Pope Joan.[2] According to the *Centuries*, of
course, murder was the favourite activity of the Roman pontiffs. One
of them is accused of having employed either the famous 'Italian sauce'
or 'Venetian soup' to poison no fewer than six of his immediate
predecessors! The *Centuries* was so successful that it was imitated by
other compilers. The *Catalogue of Witnesses of the Truth*, for example,
tells us that the heads of six thousand immolated children were found
in a certain convent of nuns! Finally, the *Stupenda Jesuitica* represents
the whole Society as a gang of professional murderers and debauchees
of more than Herculean prowess! These deplorable works could not
be left unanswered, and two Catholic names became illustrious in the
process: Bellarmine and Baronius.

St Robert Bellarmine (1542–1621) was a young Jesuit at Louvain
when the *Centuries* appeared. He conceived the idea, which was
approved by his superiors, of preparing a general refutation of heretical
theses, in order, as he said, 'to provide an arsenal for those whom the
Church will send out to fight the powers of hell.' Such was the origin

---

[1] See *Cathedral and Crusade*, pp. 193–4.

[2] The story of Pope Joan has been told by the enemies of the Church with many
variations. The substance of it is as follows. A young woman (variously described as
German, English and Thessalian) named Gilberte, or Agnes, or Glaucia, was in the habit
of dressing like a man. While visiting Rome she made a deep impression by her learning
and refinement, and obtained ecclesiastical preferment. Elevated to the Sacred College,
she was ultimately elected pope at a date which varies in the 'authorities' from 855 to
1100! She is supposed to have reigned for two years, and then, while taking a walk near
the Colosseum, to have been seized with the pains of childbirth.... According to some she
died giving birth to a son; others say she was tied to a wild horse's tail and her body torn
to shreds on the stones—a true Merovingian penalty! This absurd fable appeared during
the thirteenth century, inspired perhaps by certain vehement critics of the popes, who may
have used some such words as 'These popes are nothing but silly women!' On the other
hand, we may have here a distant memory of that period during the tenth century when
women more than once secured the Apostolic throne for their favourite candidates. In
that case Pope Joan was none other than Marosia (see her name in the Index to *The Church
in the Dark Ages*). Here, however, is another curious explanation. There existed at Rome a
pagan statue bearing the inscription *P. Pat. Pat. P.P.P.*, meaning *Publius* (or some other
praenomen) *pater patrum* (title of the priests of Mithra), *propria pecunia posuit*. The
Romans, always waggish, read it thus: *Petre, pater patrum, papessa prodito partum*.
Finally, there is an unseemly rider to this absurd story. It was said that every pope, on
his election, had to allow the cardinals to verify that he was really a man, in order to avoid
a second Pope Joan! As a matter of fact, this latter allegation originated in a curious
ceremony which was not abolished until after the reign of Leo X. After the proclamation
of his election, the new pope was carried by two cardinals on a porphyry chair while
the choir sang these words from the psalms: *Suscitans a terra inopem et de stercore erigens
pauperem*. The lewd imagination of the populace took the porphyry chair for a commode
.... For an excellent discussion of the whole legend see Vacandard: *Études de critique et
d'histoire religieuse*, vol. iv, p. 15 ff.

of the *Controversies*, an enormous Latin treatise that was quickly translated into several languages. Point by point, and with unusual objectivity, Bellarmine sets out the doctrines of Luther, Calvin and others, to which he then opposes the true Catholic faith. The idea was born of genius, and it would put into the hands of preachers and teachers the arguments best adapted to refute the assertions and theses of their adversaries, without indulging in the scurrilous polemic to which the *Centuries* too frequently descended. Bellarmine took account of everything advanced by heterodoxy against Christ, the Church, Grace, the liturgy, the sacraments and so forth. Appointed 'Professor of Controversy' at the Gregorian University, and then, despite his humble protest, Archbishop of Capua and cardinal, the great Jesuit spent the rest of his life training hundreds of students for the intellectual struggle, and invigorating the Roman Congregations—including that of Propaganda, of which he was one of the original members. He did not disdain a reply even to the absurd fables of the *Centuries*, such as that of Pope Joan. Bellarmine was deservedly canonized by Pius XI in 1923 and declared Doctor of the Church by the same pope in 1931. Few men did more than he to furnish Catholics with the armour of light which they required.[1]

Caesar Baronius (1538–1607), another cardinal,[2] was an Oratorian, a spiritual son of St Philip Neri, who suggested to him the plan of refuting Protestant claims in the historical field. His *Ecclesiastical Annals*, dealing with the Christian past, endeavouring to fix the exact dates of all the most important events, and supporting every statement with documents of indisputable authenticity, constitute a monumental work, which took its author thirty years to compile and for which historians should be grateful. Absolutely honest as he was, this precursor of critical history thought that one rendered 'more service to the Church by quietly burying facts that purported to enhance her glory but were not well founded than by repeating falsehoods'; and his researches among the Vatican archives were much in advance of the methods of his age. Baronius may have been mistaken on a number of points, but his truthfulness was exemplary; his work also, like that of Bellarmine, provided Catholics with a complete arsenal of arguments and refutations.

---

[1] It is amusing to recall that this future Doctor of the Church was nearly condemned by the Holy Office and his work placed on the Index. Sixtus V was indignant because Bellarmine had dared to write that 'the pope is not sovereign of the world in temporal affairs.' The cardinals appointed to try the case were sensible enough to prolong it until the death of the irascible pontiff.

[2] He too had trouble, not with the Index, but with some ferocious theologians who found fault with his work.

7. DEFENCE OF THE FAITH: THE POSITIVE EFFORT OF THEOLOGIANS

We turn now to the positive aspect of these controversial labours, which, though originally intended to ward off Protestant attacks, ended by endowing the Church with some impressive monuments. This aspect is found in many other fields. During the half-century following the Council of Trent a great effort was made to establish the doctrinal bases of Catholicism upon new and more solid foundations, and not to allow the enemy an exclusive prerogative of knowing the Bible perfectly and claiming to possess a lucid system of theology.

There existed an enormous mass of doctrinal material in the Canons of Trent, a veritable mine upon which generations of Christians might draw, as indeed they have continued to draw down to our own day. The official catechism of the Council, as well as those of Canisius and his imitators, circulated its teaching among the faithful. The missal, the breviary, the martyrology, all the fundamental books of Christian thought and piety, were revised. Nor did the effort cease there; to it belongs the scriptural achievement of Sixtus V, which, though it bears the mark of undue haste, was useful all the same. The Pope was a keen student of sacred history and exegesis, and immediately after his accession to the papal throne he announced (among many other fine projects) his determination to give the Catholic Church a Bible that would vie successfully with those of the Protestants. The idea was not altogether new, for Sirleti (or Sirlet), an eminent linguist, had been working for some time on a critical edition of the Gospels, and the Dominican John Henten was preparing a Latin Bible at Louvain. The dictatorial pontiff acted without delay: he ordered the Cassinese Benedictines to revise the Septuagint, had the text of the Gospels checked against the best known manuscripts, and took steps for the production of the 'Sixtine Vulgate,' whose purpose was nothing less than to supplant the version of St Jerome. The exegetes received orders to refer all difficult points to the Pope himself, who was quite convinced that the Holy Ghost guided him even in matters of textual criticism. The result was debatable and at once became the object of much adverse comment. Scholars did not hesitate to criticize the omissions, additions and textual inaccuracies. Bellarmine himself was furious. The Church, however, was not ashamed to admit the damage done by such excessive haste. Very soon after the death of Sixtus, Clement VIII determined to have the work revised, and a new text was established by a learned committee. The Sixto-Clementine Bible appeared in 1592, preceded by an entertaining preface in which, beneath a wealth of pontifical euphemism, it is possible to detect a gentle irony directed at

M

the misfortunes of the earlier version, but in which also just tribute is paid to one whose energy planned and accomplished a formidable undertaking. This Bible itself is not perfect; but it provides a satisfactory text, of which the Church has no reason to feel ashamed and upon which her theologians can safely rely.

There was now indeed an ample supply of theologians—too many, some have thought. Gone were the days when Catholicism had no champions to defend her against the arguments of Luther, Calvin and Zwingli. She had called in her apologists to study the truths that had been disputed and to establish them upon more secure foundations. The vast spiritual tide that flowed during the sixteenth century, producing an army of saints and the reform or foundation of religious Orders, was not without its effect upon the current interest in theological problems. Rivalry between the various Orders as well as between theologians of differing tendencies helped to enrich men's knowledge in this domain. Apart from established principles and defined dogma the Church wisely allowed a wide field for free discussion, and this clash of ideas was fruitful. The Molinist dispute, for example, clarified many points regarding subjects of the first importance.

Theology then flourished in many centres. Paris was no longer its capital, although her teachers included Maldonatus, a man of great reputation. Since the first half of the sixteenth century Spain had been in the forefront of liturgical revival with Francisco de Vittoria (1480–1546), a prolific commentator on the *Summa* of St Thomas Aquinas, and the entire School of Salamanca which included Melchior Cano, Domenico Soto and Bartholomeo de Medina. Now she enlarged her scope with Dominic Bañez (1528–1604), another Friar Preacher and an opponent of the Jesuits. Coimbra, the active university centre of Portugal, was the Society's theological fortress. Pedro de Fonesca taught there, as also for a time did his pupil Molina (1556–1600), before he went to lend his authority to the development of the newly founded University of Evora. Another professor at Coimbra, for more than twenty years, was Francisco Suarez (1548–1617), in whom it was said that 'one hears the whole school'. Louvain, whose university attracted thousands of pupils, was also one of the chief centres of theological studies: the generation of Pighi, Clichtoven and Latomus Masson was followed by that of Ruard Tapper, who attended the Council of Trent, of the alarming Baius and of his resolute adversary the Jesuit Lessius. Rome assumed importance when the Roman College became the Gregorian University: the Society's most brilliant masters, Toletus and Ledesma, Suarez and Bellarmine, occupied its chairs.

Theology thus revivified took on some new characteristics. Medieval theologians had been mainly *speculative*, seeking, in reliance upon ideas, abstract reasoning and philosophy, to expound and penetrate religious truths. We have seen to what decadence and mere verbalism that kind of approach too often led, and the attacks of Occamism had shaken the ancient edifice of scholasticism. Henceforward the best minds turned to *positive* theology. St Ignatius recommended it to his disciples, as Melchior Cano had done before him. The Protestants maintained that Scripture was the sole foundation of faith, and that the Catholic Church had perverted authentic Christian doctrine. Their opponents based their case upon the Bible and the Fathers, as well as upon tradition; and this new method, more firmly grounded in concrete reality, led to a reform of speculative theology. Methods themselves were likewise improved: the various sacred sciences—exegesis, patrology, ecclesiastical history and the history of dogma—were more clearly distinguished from one another. At the same time *moral* theology, which applies divine principles to the conduct of life, developed and became more practical.[1] The reforming tendencies of the age brought the problems to which they had given rise into the full light of day. It need hardly be added that under the influence of humanism theology conceived a sudden longing to shed her shabby old clothes, the rags of scholasticism at which Erasmus and Rabelais had jeered. Francisco Vittoria had led the way, and Melchior Cano's Latin claimed to be as pure and elegant as that of Cicero. Not all theologians, however, chose this happy road; dispute led some of them to multiply precisions, distinctions and subdivisions, with the result that they evolved a jargon little better than that of the scholastics. But this does not alter the fact that a real advance had been made in the direction of clarity, an advance which made the characteristics of the new theology those of the modern world. In a word Theology became the ally of Apologetics; it too played its part in the defence of the Church and in the work of reconquest and evangelization. The corner-stone of this entire theological edifice in course of construction was the *Summa* of St Thomas Aquinas. The *Sentences* of Peter Lombard were finally dethroned. The *Summa* became the classical text-book used in all universities—even at Louvain, where Augustinianism had been so strong, but where the Angelic Doctor triumphed in 1596. The Fathers of Trent had recourse time and again to the *Summa* in order to resolve difficult problems. St Pius V personally supervised the monumental edition of St Thomas's works and declared him a Doctor of the Church, to rank with St Ambrose, St Augustine, St Jerome and St Gregory. Ignatius of Loyola recommended his sons to follow the Thomist line in all questions of speculative theology, 'as the surest and most commonly received doctrine.' And in 1598, when some members of the

---

[1] Too practical, and even facile, according to the opponents of casuistry, the method then in fashion.

Society hesitated to accept this advice, the General, Fr Aquaviva, at the formal request of Pope Clement VIII, enacted the *Ratio Studiorum* which officially subjected the Society to Thomism. This was perhaps a little excessive. So much water had flowed beneath the bridge during the course of time that the arch erected by Aquinas, however firm, could not but have suffered damage. Protestantism raised problems that St Thomas could hardly have foreseen. Humanism had exerted its influence, as also had Occamian nominalism. The most celebrated Catholic theologian at the beginning of the seventeenth century was Francisco Suarez, the master of Coimbra, whom Paul V called *Doctor eximius ac pius*. Although he was officially a Thomist, his philosophy steers a middle course between that of St Thomas and that of Duns Scotus and Occam; in theology he tends to simplify Thomism, to render it more accessible, more striking, more modern and human, in accordance with contemporary needs.

Here beyond any doubt is the most original characteristic of all the new theology, which is more and more concerned with man. It might well be said that the centre of interest has shifted from the divine to the human—not perhaps without some danger. Under the influence of humanism and Protestantism, or, more generally, of the climate of that period, the predominant figure in religious questions is man, his striving towards God, his destiny and the drama of his salvation. After all, it was necessary to answer the heretics on points of such capital significance. The problem of Grace, in particular, is one of those which Catholic theologians approached with more care—and indeed with more passionate earnestness than ever before.

Luther, an Augustinian monk, had been condemned; but Augustinianism continued to water vast areas of the Catholic soul. Louvain, despite its official Thomism, remained largely faithful to the older teaching. Michel de Bay, called Baius (1513–89), professor and afterwards chancellor of Louvain, taught a doctrine in which he attempted to reconcile theses very much akin to Lutheranism with the precepts of the Church. Condemned by St Pius V, he humbly submitted, but his ideas survived. Many believed that justification by faith and some form of predestination were discoverable in the writings of St Augustine. A certain Bishop of Ypres, who had made a profound study of Baius and pondered long upon these things, wrote a book which appeared posthumously in 1640. His name was Cornelius Jansen.

But the most famous controversy on the subject of Grace, before Jansenism, centred upon what is known as Molinism. The Pope officially put an end to it in 1607, by imposing silence on the adversaries; but smoke still rises from the hot ashes. The battle was fought in two countries, Spain and the Netherlands, but theologians from all parts of the world (and even some Roman Congregations) took part in the affair. Two main armies were opposed: the Jesuits under Molina, whose work on *Free Will and the Gifts of Grace* (Lisbon, 1588) caused a great sensation, and the Dominicans under Bañez, Thomas de Lemos and Didace Alvarez. The fundamental idea of the Jesuit theologians, which they took from St Ignatius's seventeenth rule of orthodoxy, was that 'one must not insist too much upon the all-powerful efficacy of Grace, for fear of spreading in men's hearts the error which denies free will,' and of thereby discouraging man from making any effort to master himself. According to Fr Fonseca we have to recognize in God a 'mean knowledge,' which enables us to leave man the freedom of his actions and good works, but also to recognize the sovereign rôle of the operation of Divine Grace. That was the attitude of a Society dedicated to the apostolate, to the perfecting of the individual; it is an apologetic theology. The Thomists replied that there are two kinds of Grace: 'sufficient' Grace, which every man possesses, but which gives only the *power* to do good acts, without leading forcibly thereto; and 'efficacious' Grace, which alone imposes itself on the feeble will of man, and is a free and gratuitous gift of God. Twenty years of squabbling were not sufficient to consume the resources of the two camps, let alone to bring about agreement. It may be that no synthesis is possible between Molinism, which appears to give man too prominent a part, and Thomism, which centres all upon God. It is doubtless enough, as Bossuet says, to 'keep a firm hold on both ends of the chain,' which is in fact the advice given by St Francis of Sales in rather different terms. These fierce combats, however, whose details are beyond the patience of even the most earnest layman of today, do at least show the ardour with which the new theology applied itself to problems resulting from the Reformation and sought to discover sound Catholic solutions.

8. MORE INSIDIOUS DANGERS

Meanwhile, however, there were shadows in this otherwise splendid scene. Protestantism was not the only danger to Catholic faith; more insidious perils existed likewise, less obvious, but perhaps more grave in a sense, than could have been discerned even in the better aspect of Molinism. The general mentality of the age born of the Renaissance presupposed a shift from God to man in the whole interpretation of the world. Man tended to become the measure of all things. An anthropocentric apologetic was in harmony, perhaps unconscious harmony, with the whole contemporary outlook. This outlook was radically altering the view of man's relations with God, tending to give man a *natural* as distinct from a *supernatural* end, and to make him independent of God. At the beginning of the seventeenth century there were indubitable signs of this new trend, and they were destined to become more pronounced.

As we have seen,[1] irreligion properly so called had been a rare phenomenon, a passing phase in the lives of a few isolated individuals without real influence, most of whom were not fully aware of their own audacity and usually remained sincere Christians. Such men as Pozzi, Lorenzo Valla, Leonardo Bruni and Filelfe, at the beginning of the Italian Renaissance, were anticlericals rather than true agnostics; the daring spirits of the Roman Academy, who, like Pomponnazzi, denied the soul's immortality to the bitter end, were few and far between. Étienne Dolet, an atheist and a ferocious enemy of Catholic dogmas, was an exception among French humanists; even Rabelais, whose banter infuriated the devout, was certainly no resolute unbeliever. But during the last quarter of the sixteenth century and the first of the seventeenth, we observe some disquieting symptoms: certain tendencies are discovered to be hatching the ideas of modern civilization more than a hundred years before the Age of Enlightenment—radical atheism, 'the death of God' as Nietzsche called it, and the catastrophic substitution of the human in place of the divine.

First among these warning signs was the emergence of Scientism, a doctrine initially vague and ill defined, but one that later became more explicit. According to this theory, science, which had opened to man an immense field of knowledge and activity, would develop into a system accounting for every aspect of existence. No one denied that scientism greatly improved its methods. Following in the footsteps of Leonardo da Vinci (1452–1519), its brilliant precursor, it relied henceforward upon the real, the concrete; it sought to understand phenomena and their causes through experiment alone, not through the verbal procedure of the Averroist and Aristotelian schoolmen. In 1618 an obscure professor at Caen exclaimed: 'As if the authority of a single man, who bases his doctrine upon no observation or mathematical demonstration, can serve as an article of faith!' Thus the *Accademia dei Lincei*, founded at Florence in 1609 and named after the lynx with its piercing eyes, had no other purpose than to see clearly and not to be deceived, even by dogmas. In 1621 the Lord Chancellor of England, Francis Bacon (1561–1626), was found guilty of bribery and dismissed from all his offices; but all thinking men were influenced by the method propounded in his *Dignity and Progress of the Sciences* (1605) and *Novum Organum* (1620). Scientific progress indeed tended henceforward to eclipse speculation; and this tendency led in turn to the divorce of science from theology. 'The Bible says one thing but our eyes have seen another; gloss the Bible as much as you please but the facts of

[1] *The Protestant Reformation*, Chapter IV, pp. 196–7; Chapter VI, p. 368.

experience are irrefutable.' Those words were uttered not by a man of the twentieth century, but by Galileo.

Besides, the results of these methods were enormously impressive. Science made wonderful advances in every field. The most ignorant are aware of its geographical achievements: new worlds opened up to man, to his knowledge and to his appetites. The results in other branches of research may be less familiar and more debatable, but they were none the less solid. William Harvey (1578–1658) followed up the ideas of poor Michael Servetus and enunciated the revolutionary theory of the circulation of the blood. In astronomy the Dane Tycho Brahé (1546–1601) made numerous observations; Kepler (1571–1631) formulated the laws governing the heavenly bodies; while Galileo (1564–1642), the spiritual heir of Copernicus, developed the theories of his predecessor and presented them as a system of the world in his *Nuntius Sidereus* (1610) and *History and Demonstration of Solar Phenomena* (1613). The logarithmic tables published by John Napier (1550–1617) revolutionized mathematical calculation. One might continue almost indefinitely enumerating the gifts added by that half-century to human intelligence and its powers of world conquest. But the intoxicating fumes of knowledge rose to the brains of men less wise. They fuddled the gyrovague Dominican Giordano Bruno (1548–1600), whose *Banquet of Ashes* and *Auction of the Triumphant Beast* are mere anti-religious pamphlets parading in the robes of science. They likewise inebriated another errant Dominican, Tommaso Campanella (1568–1639), who was prevented from devoting himself to similar and dangerous follies by twenty years of imprisonment in the dungeons of the Holy Office at Rome and those of the Spaniards at Naples. He it was who wrote a defence of emancipated thought which is at the same time a confession of intellectual vertigo: 'Christians discovered the printing press, Columbus a new world, Galileo new stars. . . . Add the use of cannon, of the compass, of windmills, of firearms and of other wonderful inventions. The thinkers of yesterday were children compared with ourselves. We are free.' There you have the very essence of scientism. The satanic insurrection is near, the revolt of intelligence against faith.

Not all the great minds of that age were potential scientists; many even distrusted these bold assertions about the solar system and the circulation of the blood. They preferred the soft pillow of doubt and the old maxim 'What Know I?' which enabled them to take part in every quest while eschewing its rewards, to taste the joys of learning while avoiding the constraint of certitudes. Were these amiable sceptics then more faithful to Christianity? No. Their influence moved in the same direction and threatened the very bases of Christian faith. Their bent is personified in a single name: Michel Eyquem, seigneur de Montaigne (1533–92).

At the age of twenty-six Montaigne, already disgusted with the ostentation and ambitions of the world, withdrew to his peaceful estate amid the hills of Dordogne. There, in his beloved tower, guardian of his tranquillity, he never ceased to meditate upon men, institutions and manners, but mainly upon a subject that interested him above all else—himself. It is even more astonishing that when the magistrates of Bordeaux invited him to take office as mayor of their city, he carried out his duties with the utmost diligence without having to interrupt what he considered his primary task in life, the contemplation and analysis of his own thoughts. This introspective study is contained in a single book, the *Essays*, which first appeared in 1580, but which he continually revised and republished in one edition after another. It is indeed a unique book; his contemporaries doted upon it, and it remained the most popular French work far into the seventeenth century, not so much because it came from the pen of a very great writer as because a living presence is seen and felt in its pages. When we take a close look at the *Essays*, their straightforwardness may perhaps seem slightly artificial. But what ease and gracefulness are in that 'short and succinct mode of speech,' that daring yet elegant phraseology, that style at once intentionally extravagant yet so carefully designed, that harmony between lofty speculation, exact observation and uninhibited mirth, which last is characteristic of the Gascons. 'What delightful company he makes,' said Mme de Sévigné. Yes indeed, but wait a little. This nobleman who feared nothing so much as pedantry, and would have laughed at finding himself ranked with the philosophers, was a past master of the art of slipping into his delighted reader's mind a moral precept and even (though sometimes perhaps unwittingly) a metaphysical belief. Many educated Frenchmen in time to come would have their thinking shaped by the *Essays*.

And what of the doctrines that found favour with him? To begin with, 'doctrines' is much too solemn a word for those sparkling pieces. Only by force of reading and rereading, of comparison and deduction, can we draw out the threads of his tangled and shifting thought. The lesson is factual rather than theoretical, but it is quite easily learnt. How is Montaigne to be classed? First perhaps and essentially as a Stoic like his great friend La Boétie (1530–63), who taught him the ancient serenity, the 'soul's contentment,' and to 'bind himself' in order to attain to the ideal. The first book of the *Essays* is completely dominated by such thoughts as 'Well, when death itself comes . . .' In the presence of life, in the presence of pain, in the presence even of death, he must face facts and be truly a man. That precept is not without value at a time of tragic chaos when everyone feels his life to be in danger. The same sort of neo-Stoicism is found in Justus Lipsius (1547–1606), a professor at Louvain, in Guillaume du Vair, author of the *Holy Philosophy*, and in Pierre Charron, the good Vicar-General who tried after a fashion to harmonize Seneca with the Gospel. This emphasis on man's free will is altogether different from the Luthero-Calvinist doctrine of the servile will; but for all that it is hardly Catholic.

The second striking feature of Montaigne is his extreme mistrust of human reason, which he considered arrogant and stupid. How powerless is reason in presence of the many mysteries that surround it! At the most it can argue 'backwards to the infinite.' 'The bane of man is his belief that he knows.' Here appears the motto 'What Know I?' that key-word of all inquiry, that answer to all questions. 'It is through the medium of our ignorance rather than of our knowledge that we are learned.' Blessed ignorance: it saves us from all anxiety. Is that a Christian state of mind? Since Montaigne, as we shall see, remained formally and by numerous declarations a Catholic, the only solution was fideism. Reason on one side, faith on the other, ignorance between the two. This would have enraged St Thomas Aquinas.

Surely we have here, at rock-bottom, a certain epicureanism of the intelligence. Voluntary ignorance: how restful and consoling! It is on a par moreover with another sort of epicureanism, far more practical and immediate, of which Montaigne makes no secret. 'My intention is to spend what remains of my life pleasantly and not laboriously. . . .' An excellent principle! So too: 'I seize even the very slightest occasion of pleasure that I can find.' *Carpe diem* has never been accepted as an article of the Gospel, and if the command 'Deny thyself' has any meaning at all, it is certainly not that of the *Essays*. The morality of their recipe for happiness never rises above ground level. Anyone who wishes to judge how far it has led men away from Christianity need only consider its extension into our own times. Neo-Stoicism then is crowned with an agreeable hedonism and systematic doubt. This was something altogether new.

Nevertheless Montaigne by no means believed himself estranged from Catholicism. He made a pilgrimage to Rome and kissed the Pope's shoe, and another to Loreto, where he offered Our Lady a fine picture showing himself and family on their knees. Time and again in the *Essays* he affirms his faith. He surrenders blindly to the *magisterium* of the Church as to 'the authority of the sacrosanct will of God.' And pious Catholics are delighted to hear him say: 'Let us no longer dispute our motives of faith; reason has gone bankrupt.' Yes, but take a closer look at the work as a whole and you will find that the gentle irony of that magic pen disturbs the very foundations of Christianity. Neo-Stoicism is nothing but unconscious Pelagianism, which entrusts to man alone the determination of his ultimate fate, as if original sin had not wounded his nature and his will. Fr Pierre Garasse, the Jesuit,

* M

rightly observes: 'Softly, as if with a silken cord, he strangles the sentiment of religion.' 'Christian scepticism,' of which La Mothe le Vayer speaks, separates reason from faith, and thereby leaves faith dangerously exposed to the dictates of feeling, to conclusions which have no support. It is La Mothe also, a worthy disciple of Montaigne, who says: 'To seek for philosophy in theology is like looking for the living among the dead.' And as for Montaigne's epicureanism, we need hardly repeat that from a practical point of view it is poles apart from Christianity; we must conclude that it deliberately sets aside Grace and appeals exclusively to nature.

Briefly Montaigne gets rid of the divine in three ways. He thus appears as a highly significant witness to a whole current of thought, which is henceforth of the greatest importance. By about 1640 the leading French writers—Corneille, Descartes and Guez de Balzac— were all permeated in various ways with the spirit of Montaigne. In the words of his commentator P. Villey he 'acclimatized pagan morality in France'; and not morality alone, but pagan thought, pagan psychology and pagan metaphysics also. His doctrine, once it had become current coin, was one of the most dangerous channels of irreligion.

Nor was this circulation of Montaigne's doctrine long delayed. The stream of atheistic agnosticism, of which Dolet had at first been almost the sole representative, began to swell. Ponthus de Tyard and Guy de Bruès made it their own; Jacques Tabureau, in his *Dialogues No Less Profitable than Humorous*, let loose a flood of scepticism reminiscent of Lucian. The influence of the Paduans, which reached Paris with Vicomercato, had the same sort of effect. Montaigne provided these 'libertines,' as they were called, with arguments, justifications and claims to respectability, although he himself had detested such displays of impiety and vice. About 1620 the momentum began to increase. 'Libertinism' had as its high priests Vanini, an unfrocked Carmelite who dared to write that Jesus Christ was an impostor and that His miracles were mere sleight of hand; Théophile de Viau, a complete cynic, oscillating between Protestantism and Catholicism as his own interests dictated, and proclaiming more openly even than Montaigne the law of sovereign pleasure:

> On ne saurait dompter la passion humaine;
> Contre amour la raison est importune et vaine.[1]

The most serious thing was that these libertines were not isolated individuals. They had powerful friends at court and in the city, among whom were Bellegarde, Bassompierre, the Duchesse de Chevreuse, Saint-Amant and Boisrobert. It may well be that that generation was

---

[1] It is impossible to subdue human passion; against love reason is troublesome and vain.

ultimately responsible for the intellectual revolution of the eighteenth century, one hundred and fifty years later.

What steps did the Church take when confronted with such grave perils? In the most flagrant cases of impiety and atheism she was still too strong not to react by way of violence and the argument of authority. At such times she wore a grim and threatening look, as indeed she was obliged to do amid the terrible dangers that beset her; at such times the Inquisition struck. Giordano Bruno, who foolishly allowed himself to be arrested at Venice, was condemned and burned in the Campo dei Fiori at Rome (1600) for his heretical views on Transubstantiation and the Trinity, as well as for his theory of a plurality of worlds. Campanella just managed to escape with his life; after spending twenty-seven years in prison he died peacefully in the convent of Rue Saint-Honoré at Paris. Galileo was denounced to the Holy Office and condemned in 1616, less no doubt on account of his strictly scientific ideas than because of the tenacity with which he applied them to Scripture. His submission saved him from the worst, but did not protect him from a second trial in 1633.[1] Vanini had his tongue torn out by the executioner and was burned alive. Théophile de Viau was thrown into prison when the government of Louis XIII, by request of the Church, decided to inflict severe penalties on atheists and blasphemers (1617).

These, however, were particularly flagrant instances, which could not possibly have escaped the Church's notice unless she had been altogether blind. Where the process was more insidious, because more carefully concealed, she did not perhaps fully realize the danger. For example, when Montaigne, with every show of the greatest respect, submitted his writings to ecclesiastical censorship, the Church behaved with extreme indulgence, leaving to his conscience alone the duty of 'patching up' whatever he thought needed alteration. Some saw more clearly. As early as about 1570 Guy de la Borderie vigorously denounced the libertines and their dangerous activities.[2] And during the 1620's Fr Mersenne furbished the arms he was to use in an enormous treatise (1623-5) 'against the atheists, deists, libertines and sceptics,' in which he asserted that Paris alone contained fifty thousand [3] of the tribe. Bold spirits, however, were not brought to heel by pious tirades, nor by the diatribes of Fr Garasse, which were often scurrilous.[4] Catholic apologetics were not yet equal to the situation; but a time was coming when the Church would take stock of this new danger, when Pascal, reproving Montaigne, would say 'Yes, reason is stupid; well

[1] The affair of Galileo will be studied more fully in the next volume.
[2] The Protestant Henri Estienne did likewise.
[3] This figure is most probably an exaggeration.
[4] Garasse had none of the traditional spirit and style of the Society.

then, trust yourself to God,' and oppose to the 'proud diabolism' of the libertines the arguments of a faith supported by genius. St Francis of Sales had already devised a method for including the new tendencies, daughters of the old humanism, in the framework of Christian certitudes. He also wrote these words which condemn the whole current of neo-Stoicism, epicureanism and scepticism: 'It is a great folly to pretend to be wise with an impossible wisdom.'

9. In the Depths of the Christian Soul

We must not, however, exaggerate. The danger of irreligion was as yet very slight. Christian life, whose standards were at a very low ebb when the Protestant revolution began, did not cease to manifest itself in the second half of the sixteenth century; after the Council of Trent indeed it enjoyed a period of wonderful vitality, which continued throughout the great 'classical' era. This vitality was revealed not only in the practice and devotions of the people, but also in the secret life of the mystics, in those wholly interior experiences which the finest treatises cannot perfectly describe. Here and there the eternal dialogue of the soul with God was carried on more fervently than ever before.

One outstanding sign of the Church's vitality at this period was the abundance, one might almost say profusion, of her saints. Their reappearance on the stage of Christian history—a history which has never been aught but theirs, the history of the saints—marked the advent of reform. Men such as Cajetan of Tiene, Ignatius of Loyola and Antony Zaccaria compelled the official Church to pull herself together; it was they who created the climate in which the Council of Trent was able to fulfil its task. Later, when the Council had passed its decrees, other saints—Pius V and Charles Borromeo, for example— gave effect to those decisions, while Philip Neri helped to make them part and parcel of Christian life. The species of great and radiant personalities was by no means extinct. Drawn from all classes of society, they were of all ages and of every kind, for there are many ways to sanctity. Most celebrated and most representative of the bishops, naturally, was St Francis of Sales; many priests too would labour to give back to their order its greatness and prestige. We see the work of St Peter Fourier, and soon afterwards 'Monsieur Vincent' began his noble quest of souls and human suffering. Founders of new religious Orders dedicated themselves to the demands of inexhaustible charity: St Camillus of Lellis, St Caesar de Bus, St Joseph Calasanctius, St Jeanne Lestonnac. Then there were great missionary saints, rivals of St Francis Xavier: Louis Bertrand, Peter Claver, Francis of Solano. All Catholicism, high and low, rich and poor, produced these splendid figures. St Francis Borgia, General of the Society of Jesus, was among the highest dignitaries of Spain, and St Aloysius Gonzaga belonged to a princely family. But St Germaine, the charming 'violet of Pibrac' whose death was haloed in glory and miracle, was a poor farm-girl; St Fidelis of Sigmaringen was an ordinary member of the middle classes, as was the humble Capuchin St Lawrence of Brindisi. There were contemplative as well as active saints. During her lifetime very few people ever heard of St Catherine dei Ricci, the Dominican mystic of Florence, or of St Mary Magdalen dei Pazzi, whose letters hardly got beyond the enclosure of her convent; and few read the spiritual writings of St Alfonso Rodriguez,[1] the great Majorcan contemplative, until after his death. Yet they too bore witness in their seclusion. If we were obliged to single out a few of the most attractive faces in that mighty host, we might perhaps choose an exquisite triad of adolescents, in whom faith and the grace of youth combined to achieve marvellous results: Stanislaus Kostka, John Berchmans and Aloysius Gonzaga, the last of whom died at the age of twenty-three, victim of his own devotion to the sick in time of plague.

The presence of saints is always the clearest proof of Christian vitality in any society and in any age. This particular period, which produced so many, cannot have been unbelieving. There is abundant evidence of intense faith in every land. Take France alone. When the Cardinal of Florence (afterwards Pope Leo XI) visited that country as legate *a latere* in 1596 to arrange Henri IV's reconciliation with the Holy See, he was pleased to discover that the French 'feel great affection for their churches; in spite of so many invasions and changes of religion, they have preserved many such things as silver crosses, reliquaries and ornaments of worship.' He was surprised to find small children able to recite the *Pater, Ave* and *Credo* without a mistake, and he came to the conclusion that in town and village alike there were many persons 'of good life and so zealous for the Catholic faith that they put monks and priests to shame.' 'On the feast of Corpus Christi I celebrated Mass [at Grenoble],' he adds, 'and, at the request of the bishop and people, carried the Blessed Sacrament in procession amid scenes of such devotion on the part of the faithful that it was a wonderful thing to see.' [2] At Paris, during the Wars of Religion, churches were full to overflowing, and had to remain open all day in order to accommodate the faithful who came to implore God's mercy. The same is true of Germany. We need only look upon the magnificent cathedrals, abbeys and episcopal palaces of the Baroque period, which lend so joyous a note to German Catholicism, and those innumerable and picturesque country churches, to see at once that the people who built

---

[1] He must not be confused with Fr Alfonso Rodriguez, author of a famous spiritual book still popular with novices of the Society.

[2] *Lettres du Cardinal de Florence sur Henri IV et la France*, Paris, 1955.

them possessed a strong and lively faith. As for Italy one has but to open the monumental *Storia di Roma* [1] to find countless small indications of a piety that expressed itself readily in laughter and song, groans and tears, as it stirred itself to confident familiarity with the Madonna and its favourite saints. The piety of the Italian people remains unchanged today.

That piety was nourished by the sacraments, which the decrees of Trent had defined in solemn terms. There was no more doubt as to Christ's presence in the sacred Host. The Mass, whose liturgy had been fixed by the missal of St Pius V, was attended with a respect and veneration that it had by no means always enjoyed in times gone by. Although there was as yet no firmly established custom, daily Mass became the general rule in most dioceses, as a result of Jesuit and Oratorian influence. Frequent communion, which the influence of the mystics and the *Imitation* had tended to popularize towards the end of the fifteenth century, was advocated by the Council of Trent and became widespread; and it was not uncommon to see numbers of the faithful communicate whenever they heard Mass. The Council had prescribed monthly communion for religious houses; but all those touched by the spirit of reform invariably communicated weekly. Some spiritual directors even advised *daily* communion, a practice of which many theologians disapproved. It was at about this time that Italy adopted 'solemn first communion' of children, a custom introduced to France by St Vincent de Paul and the Lazarists.

All the ancient forms of devotion took on a new lease of life. Pilgrimages were more fashionable than ever. Between 1593 and 1612 more than twenty thousand Christians went each year to the Holy Land, despite innumerable difficulties on the way. Countless visitors were drawn to the Virgin of Trois-Épis, in Alsace, and to Our Lady's House, which was believed to have been carried by angels to Loreto. The Magdalen of Vézelay became once more a favourite, as did Mont Saint-Michel. In jubilee years gigantic crowds flocked to Rome: three million in 1600. But there were also some new devotions, which remain popular today. In 1527 Antoine de Grenoble founded a small confraternity which met four times a year to pray for forty hours continuously. Ten years later the city of Milan was threatened by plague, and the Capuchin Giuseppe da Fermo persuaded the magistrates to adopt this pious custom. Many great saints, among them Ignatius of Loyola, Philip Neri and Charles Borromeo, welcomed it with such enthusiasm that St Pius V and then Clement VIII introduced it at Rome, appointing the Forty Hours Adoration for the days immediately preceding Shrove Tuesday, in order to make reparation for the excesses of the

[1] Or the engaging work of M. Romani, *Pellegrini e Viaggiatori nell' economia di Roma del XIV al XV secolo*, Milan, 1948.

Carnival. It was adopted in 1615 by the diocese of Paris, whose example was quickly followed by the whole of France. St Anthony Zaccaria was the first to conceive the idea of Perpetual Adoration; his purpose was to form a 'guard of honour' for the Blessed Sacrament, which was to be exposed in all the churches of a town, one after another in continual succession, so that Jesus the Victim might never be forgotten by men. Paul IV was delighted with this scheme, which was introduced at Paris by Fr Auger, a Jesuit, in 1575; Spain also adopted the practice, adding a month of solemn processions in honour of the Blessed Sacrament.

Devotion to the Sacred Heart was formally proclaimed a little later, thanks to the efforts of the Carmelites of Liège and St John Eudes; but it was already practised by Peter Canisius, Peter of Alcantara, John of Avila, Luis of Granada, the great Teresa, Catherine dei Ricci, Magdalen dei Pazzi, Alfonso Rodriguez, Francis of Sales and Bérulle. What peace and happiness, to take refuge in that Side pierced by the lance, in that Heart which beat only for the sake of men! Cult of the Blessed Virgin, which was already widespread in the preceding age, and which was rendered even more popular by insulting Protestant attacks, enjoyed unparalleled increase; all the great spiritual figures of the age, from Philip Neri to Francis of Sales and Bérulle, were devoted to Our Lady. Theologians were more and more agreed upon the Immaculate Conception, and three successive popes—St Pius V in 1570, Paul V in 1616, Gregory XV in 1622—formally declared it unlawful to maintain that Mary was subject to the taint of original sin. In 1616–17 Seville, anticipating the official Church by nearly one hundred years, established a magnificent feast of the *Purissima*.[1] It was natural to associate St Joseph with the God Man, whose early years on earth he protected, and with the chaste spouse whom he loved. Accordingly Gregory XV, looking back to Gerson and the Council of Constance, decided in 1621 to give him a special feast (19th March) binding upon the universal Church; and it was to St Joseph that the first missionaries on North American soil dedicated Canada.

This religious ferment and renewed ardour were symptomatic of a slow and highly significant evolution which began towards the end of the sixteenth century, but which was accelerated by the terrible crisis suffered by the Christian world. After the break-up of medieval Christendom the Church lost much of her power over society and the temporal world; but she came more and more to be seen for what she is in fact, for what she had never ceased fundamentally to be since her earliest days—a school of sanctity. It was in the secret realm of souls that Christianity tended to operate with increasing energy. There was no doubt a danger that Catholics might dig a ditch between their

[1] See J. F. Bonnefoy, O.F.M., *Quand Séville fêtait la Purissima*, Nicolet (Canada) 1954.

day-to-day activities and the spiritual life, that they might limit themselves to the private practice of religion, without troubling to apply the Gospel precepts in their dealings with others. Unfortunately this danger was destined to grow with the passage of time. On the other hand that evolution was responsible for an undeniable religious elevation, a more pure fervour in many souls, a refinement and deepening, as it were, of faith.

To this the spiritual masters of the Renaissance contributed a great deal. The improvements they effected in methods of piety, as well as in the exposition of the highest branches of knowledge, played a decisive part in the interior transformation of souls. The first whom it is fair to mention was the anonymous author who had long ago committed all that is purest and most vital in Christian experience to the pages of a book that is the most touching and most simple of any we possess: *The Imitation of Jesus Christ*. Its profound influence continued to be felt: edition followed edition; it was translated into every language, and it has been responsible for forming generations of Catholics.[1]

In the sixteenth century all was animation. Spiritual life manifested itself with unprecedented variety and fecundity, expressed by men of genius whose writings gave to countless souls a new meaning of life. First and foremost surely stands the work of St Ignatius; for the Society of Jesus succeeded in establishing itself all over the world. Innumerable fervent Catholics would henceforward practise the *Spiritual Exercises*[2] in one form or another, and not only among religious. The spirituality of St Ignatius was perfectly adapted to the needs of men living in an age which laid great stress upon human liberty, but which had learned in the struggle against heresy to understand more fully the weakness of fallen nature. Its teaching is fundamentally ascetic, and is far more precise than anything previously accomplished; Christians who followed it would be firmly grounded and reliable. But it is also a mystical doctrine, even though we do not find there a direct initiation into the ways and graces of mysticism; for it tends to lead man irresistibly to a state of perfection impossible except in so far as it accorded with a divine resemblance, in sovereign submission to 'the greater glory of God.'

From Spain there flowed over the world a current of mysticism so exacting and so lofty that it seems at first glance to be necessarily reserved for pure contemplatives, for devotees of prayer and asceticism. Nevertheless it found its way into many lay circles. Philip II was not the only one who nourished his soul upon the words of St Teresa; and when the *Spiritual Canticle* was published, more than twenty years after its author's death, the burning words of that wonderful poem

---

[1] See *The Protestant Reformation*, Chapter III.
[2] See Chapter I, pp. 32–36.

inflamed countless hearts. The river of fire had its sources in the works of three remarkable men who had described their own experiences: the *Audi Filia* of Blessed John of Avila; the two complementary volumes of Luis of Granada, *A Book of Prayer and Meditation* and *The Sinner's Guide*; and St Peter of Alcantara's monumental *Treatise*. But the flood was swollen by many lesser streams—Archbishop Bartholomew of Braga and St Thomas of Villanova, to name only two. With the appearance in all their glory of two brighter flames, the river overflowed its banks as if to set the world alight with love.

While St Teresa of Avila [1] pursued the cycle of her adventurous and fruitful existence, while convents sprang up beneath her hands throughout the length and breadth of Spain, she found time to write of her inmost experience in terms whose force and exactness have never since been surpassed. Her *Autobiography* (c. 1569), *The Way of Perfection* (1570), and above all the *Interior Castle* (1577), form a complete and strictly logical method of prayer, which, if correctly followed, will cause the soul to be truly inhabited by God, substantially associated with ineffable splendour. First, prayer and self-renunciation. The foundress was too skilled in the guidance of her daughters not to teach them that asceticism is the necessary basis of all spiritual effort: they must practise the three virtues of charity, humility and detachment; above all, they must pray. Then the soul can begin its journey to the light of God. She will become acquainted in the first place with the states of active prayer: 'recollection,' where she waits in expectation; 'quietude,' a sweet and profound peace, where the spiritual forces are refreshed; and 'sleep of the faculties.' Thus detached from self and open to the divine wind, she will next rise flight by flight to passive and unitive prayer, where the will is seized and the understanding wholly directed to the passionate search for God; then to 'intimate union,' where the Lord begins to treat her with familiarity, causing her to suspect and to desire what He still has in store for her; and finally to 'transfiguring union,' perfect divine friendship, in which 'the soul or rather the spirit of the soul becomes, or so it seems, one thing with God.' Teresa's analysis is logical, unassailable, but in no way didactic and abstract. For the whole mystical adventure is conveyed in terms of a poetry that might almost be described as oriental. The myth of the Interior Castle with its seven mansions is accompanied by numerous striking, alluring and enchanting comparisons, while the ultimate attainment, the ineffable union, is described in phrases so pure, so adequate and so beautiful that we seem to feel God, to see Him and to touch Him, so far as is possible with our poor earthly means. An irresistible yearning carries her towards that state where all will be

[1] On the life and reforming work of St Teresa and St John of the Cross see Chapter II, pp. 115–25.

known, where God Himself will be apprehended by the liberated soul, a yearning so powerful that life itself becomes a burden. It is then that there springs to the mystic's lips the celebrated and unforgettable cry: 'I die because I do not die!'

With Teresa's disciple and friend, St John of the Cross, there is less logic and precision in the analysis of states of prayer, but what soaring strength! He was a poetic genius, one of the greatest lyric poets ever born of the white race. *The Ascent of Mount Carmel* and *The Dark Night* (1579–83), *The Living Flame of Love* and the *Spiritual Canticle* (c. 1584–5), are four jewels in the treasury of the Christian West. Only pronounce the titles and the purest song rises in the secret places of the soul, while the astonished mind gazes upon the noble images of night and flame, with which each of these strange treatises is woven, as it were, from end to end. John's purpose is not that of Teresa. She was addressing herself to nuns, many of whom were starting out on the road to sanctity; he was talking to souls already far advanced in virtue, to whom he wished to offer the means of reaching higher mystical summits. At first, ignoring the 'purgative way' which is that of beginners, and saying only little about the 'illuminative way,' where even advanced souls have not yet attained to union, he takes his stand on the highest peak of exigency, in that 'unitive way,' whose other name is contemplation, where a man possesses at once 'a general and affectionate attention to God' and 'a general and affectionate knowledge of God.' At that supreme stage what adventures still await the soul! She must first plunge into the 'active night,' where she ends by stripping herself of all that attaches her to earth—appetites of the senses, appetites of the mind. Thus she truly enters into contemplation. Then, however, she feels herself cast into another death, a 'dark night,' more dense, the 'passive night' where, in solitude and anguish, fearing herself abandoned, she awaits the Coming. . . . She thought she had reached the summit of the mountain, but 'on the mountain nothing!' Let her not despair: God is there, present in that absence.

> How well I know the fountain's rushing flow
> Although by night . . .

In that night absolute light will dawn, the flame—

> O flame of love so living,
> How tenderly you force
> To my soul's inmost core your fiery probe!
> Since now you've no misgiving,
> End it, pursue your course
> And for our sweet encounter tear the robe![1]

[1] Both the above are qoted from *The Poems of St John of the Cross* translated by Roy Campbell, by kind permission of The Harrill Press Ltd and Pantheon Books Inc.

Here then is the summit, the highest crest. The body is nothing but an inert mass; the spirit nothing but that flame which burns within it. This is the moment of total union, of spiritual espousals. In scholastic terminology one would say 'transforming union'; but we are dealing in fact with a state so exalting, so inconceivable, that it will not fit into any category, and words fail. 'I see clearly that I cannot utter it and that the thing would appear less if I did utter it.' Did not St Paul himself admit that what he had seen in the highest spheres could not be uttered with earthly words? Up there, in silence and a flash of fire, the little Carmelite's experience was fulfilled; but those who have followed him have perhaps tasted, in a manner beyond their own comprehension, some of the joy which will be that of the saints in Paradise.

Such experiences were not uncommon during the sixteenth century, though none perhaps equalled that of St Teresa and St John of the Cross. We must not overlook the fact that in many parts of the Christian world other mystical souls followed similar paths—from St Cajetan and St Philip Neri to St Catherine dei Ricci, or the astonishing St Mary Magdalen dei Pazzi (1566–1667) who confessed: 'I no longer know whether I am alive or dead, out of my body or within it. . . .' These Italians are singled out because Italy also had its mystical school, directed more towards action perhaps than was the Spanish, and more closely associated with contemporary problems. Catherine and Mary Magdalen wrote to popes and cardinals, begging them to continue boldly with the task of reform and purification upon which they had embarked. From one such lofty experience the Theatine Fr Lorenzo Scupoli (1530–1610) derived the material not of a speculative work, but of a practical treatise—one might almost call it a handbook—in which he made available to all Catholics the methods of prayer. I refer, of course, to the famous *Spiritual Combat*, which St Francis of Sales made his own bedside book.

This again is characteristic of the age. We have seen [1] that there existed two centuries earlier an intense mystical current whose principal representatives were the Brethren of the Common Life, the disciples of Ruysbroeck and the author (or authors) of the *Imitation*. But that *devotio moderna* often appeared to isolate itself from the harsh and dangerous world of men. Should mystics hide themselves away in the cloister and follow all by themselves the arduous road that leads to heaven? The prodigious success of the *Imitation* (written in a monastery no doubt) had shown to what extent souls were hungry for such teaching. Then suddenly the impulse of holiness, of which the Council of Trent was the culminating point, tended to make spiritual life more intense, nearer to the daily round. Hence the Oratories of Divine Love, the retreats given by Recollects and Jesuits. The foundations were laid

[1] See *The Protestant Reformation*, Chapter III.

of a spiritual school intended fully to satisfy Christian needs, a school so simple and accessible that everyone, no matter how little advanced in the way of light, could hope to practise its precepts. At the same time this new school took to itself all the knowledge of man that two centuries of effort had been able to acquire, in order to link it with the faith. The first man to effect this decisive synthesis of 'devout humanism' and mystical wisdom was St Francis of Sales. Close behind him march the troops of that 'mystical invasion' so dear to Henri Bremond, the powerful cohorts of the 'French school' [1] which was to be the glory of the 'Classical age.' The highest religious idealism wedded to the humble routine of daily life; faith enlightening all branches of knowledge, but absorbing them all; it seemed that this hope was about to be fulfilled, a hope which had stirred mankind since the Renaissance, but which, through failure to recognize itself in time, had caused so many tragedies. Two centuries of effort are summed up in some words of Cardinal de Bérulle, which give the answer to many errors: 'What is man? A nothing capable of God.'

10. REFORM MUST ALWAYS BEGIN ANEW

The spectacle afforded by the mystics, and even by a whole people sincerely Christian, must not lead us to undue optimism. We must not think of the entire Church, towards the end of the sixteenth century, as a society of saints and devout persons unanimously resolved to obey the precepts of the Council of Trent and to live according to the Catechism. It was too much to expect that a few decrees would suffice to put an end to vagaries that had lasted for two hundred years. It was wonderful enough that a handful of determined men and women had been able to impose upon the official Church the reformation they desired, and that the Papacy, in complete agreement with their view, had undertaken to make that reformation a universal reality. It would have been foolish to hope that forty or fifty years would suffice to win such general acceptance of a few sound principles that there would be no exceptions. Round about 1600 the situation in many countries seemed not very different from what it had been in 1500. Numerous facts, taken in isolation, would almost entitle us to say that no serious result had yet been obtained, and that the age-old law of evil, which for ever drags the souls of the baptized (and their Church) towards the abyss, was then at work as busily as ever. To say so, however, would be inaccurate. It is certain that the Catholic people as a whole had made genuine progress, that the clergy had improved and that the majority of religious Orders were in excellent condition. But it remains none the less true that there were many deplorable exceptions, so numerous

[1] It will be studied in the next volume of this series.

indeed in certain sectors that one might think they were the rule. We need not dwell long upon this monotonous picture, for it shows us nothing new; the symptoms were exactly the same as those of long ago.

There were still too many bishops, provided with sees for quite uncanonical reasons, who did not observe the law of residence, whose interest in their dioceses was purely financial, and who were politicians and courtiers rather than priests.[1] In reports sent to Rome during his legation in 1596 the Cardinal of Florence, while marvelling at the faith of the French people who 'filled the churches for the divine offices, and attach great importance to indulgences, blessed medals and the *Agnus Dei*,' often had hard things to say about the French episcopate as a whole, whom he found to be 'lacking in diligence and negligent.' One bishop, he says, was never in his diocese; another exploited his flock in an odious manner; and yet another was reputed to 'lead a licentious life.' 'I do not wish to expatiate,' he adds, 'on the abuses relating to ecclesiastical benefices; I should have too much to say.' True he goes on to admit frankly that 'the churches are not in the bad state of repair one might have expected as a result of these disadvantages'! His observations were made thirty years after the closing of the Council, but one does not receive the impression that things were any better at the end of yet another thirty years. Bérulle, though moderate in his judgments, appears by all the evidence to have thought likewise, and notes 'the little power our French bishops have over the secular ecclesiastics . . .' Were things any better elsewhere? Certainly not in Germany. 'The great danger,' wrote Cardinal Otto Truchsess to Gregory XIII, 'is the damage done by the too frequent backsliding of bishops, who, defying the Holy See and setting themselves up as sovereign rulers, confound the temporal with the spiritual just as they please, and have no respect for God or man.' The typical Germanic bishop, brutal and almost military, had by no means disappeared. So long as episcopal appointments were not subject to strict control by the Holy See such irregularities would continue.

The secular clergy still showed, in too large measure, the defects which we discovered in their ranks on the eve of the Protestant revolution. The senior members, in close contact with the bishops, gladly followed their bad example. There were frequent complaints, especially in Germany, of young noblemen promoted to canonries, who gave no time to study or to their duties, and a current proverb said: 'The vicars go to church for the canons, but the canons will go to hell for the vicars.' Cardinal Truchsess again draws attention to innumerable parish priests 'guilty of criminal acts, living in concubinage, drunkards, tainted with simony, apostates.' The Cardinal of Florence is no more

---

[1] Note, however, that their moral behaviour was generally far less reprehensible than erstwhile.

indulgent regarding the situation he found in France. He emphasized especially the penury of the priests and their bad training. Thus the old faults which had done so much harm to the Church were still there: an intake of second-rate priests, ignorance, questionable behaviour and even worse. Thirty years later, about 1620, Vincent de Paul was horrified by what he saw in the neighbourhood of Châtillon in Dombes, and pronounced this terrible judgment: 'The Church of God has no worse enemies than priests who live as most priests live today.'

Were the regulars any better? Some were, but the majority, it seems, were not. Let us take another look at the reports of Cardinal dei Medici. 'The religious Orders have almost abandoned the straight road. Their members are dissolute, ignorant, ill mannered, mean, dirty and lazy. The rule is completely ignored, except among the Carthusians. . . .' Nuns were for the most part in a very poor way. 'They do not observe the law of enclosure, they spend months at a time with their relations and they wear lascivious clothes. From the appointment of abbesses for life, and the fact that they hold titular abbacies, there results an infinity of evils: simony, violence, favouritism and so forth. Nuns pass from one convent to another, young girls are created abbesses, others take possession by force.' In Germany the legates Ninguardia and Portia had much the same tale to tell: some abbeys had no novitiate; they were the refuge of undesirables; their occupants were sunk in laxity and indiscipline, 'no longer religious,' says Dom Poulet, 'but thelemites.' These observations were made in 1590, but let us now return to France. In 1602 when the future Angélique Arnauld [1] arrived at Port-Royal she found a community that was indeed benighted. It had heard only seven or eight sermons in forty years; the nuns' confessor, a Bernardine, could not translate the *Pater*; the library contained only one book, a breviary; and life flowed by in masquerades and joyous feasting. Port-Royal, however, was a spectacle of high morality compared with the abbey of Maubuisson, near Pontoise. Here the abbess, Angélique d'Estrées, eager no doubt to surpass the gallant records of her sister Gabrielle, titular mistress of King Henri, gave birth to no fewer than twelve children, each of whom she brought up according to the father's social standing. Someone may ask at this point: What about the reform? It was effective in various religious houses, but by no means in all. It even became a cause of enfeeblement among the Orders, for there was usually a great deal of hostility between the 'reformed' and the 'relaxed.'

It need scarcely be said that the Christian laity revealed, in addition to the happy symptoms already pointed out, many less edifying characteristics. True, as G. Thibon has aptly remarked, if they had as a whole no more *moral sense* than their counterparts in the twentieth

---

[1] She was then hardly twelve years old.

century, they had *morals*, a healthy and stable public spirit, submitting in principle to an ideal of faith and Christian morality. These bases, however, were themselves undermined. Certain areas were threatened with nothing less than 'dechristianization.' They returned to a state of something like savagery; it was currently said in Italy that 'the Abruzzi, Apulia and Calabria are the Italian Indies.' In countries that appeared to remain more solidly Catholic, behaviour was, generally speaking, far removed from the Ten Commandments and the precepts of the Gospel. We need only read the memoirs of the reigns of Henri IV and Louis XIII to see with what cynicism the self-styled governing classes scorned the laws of religion and morality: brawling, duelling, abduction and bribery were all rife at Court, among the nobility and even among schoolboys. It was hardly to be expected that things would be any better among the common people. Disorder was everywhere, the fruit of too many years of violence and anarchy. Italy and Germany present the same spectacle.

One outstanding symptom of this disorder was the continued prominence of superstition in all its forms; it even appeared to have made progress. Witchcraft spread alarmingly, together with all the varieties of magic. Somewhat later than the period with which we are here concerned, M. Olier found in the neighbourhood of Saint-Sulpice an altar of Beelzebub, intended for the celebration of black masses. Trials for witchcraft were numerous, despite the protests of theologians such as Pierre de Valence, Jean Weyer, Cornelius Loos and 'Leon d'Alexis,' who was none other than the young Abbé de Bérulle.

It was indeed an afflicting spectacle, but one that should not surprise us. The reconquest of a society by principles cannot be accomplished in the twinkling of an eye; it is a task requiring long effort and meticulous patience. During the fifty years following the Council of Trent progress was made: an auspicious evolution is noticeable, which is very difficult to grasp in all its details, but which we shall be able to appreciate in its results. Here and there, by a process that varied according to time and place, the idea of reform gained ground. Above all, its means of action began to impose themselves on men's minds. Side by side with some disturbing symptoms there existed many favourable signs. On the threshold of the seventeenth century it was not unreasonable to hope that the battle in which the Church was then engaged might be won.

11. An Ideal for Clergy: Bérulle

If one of these good omens had to be chosen as the most decisive, that one would be no doubt the increasingly strong assertion of an idea for the clergy. It is upon them that the whole Church ultimately rests. Let the priests become once more worthy of their vocation, let them be more carefully selected, better trained, better instructed, let their conduct make them living examples, and they will reanimate the whole mass of Christians. Blanc de Saint-Bonnet's saying was more than ever true: 'A holy clergy makes a virtuous people. . . .'

Now it was just this renewal of the clergy that was taking place. We have already shown that even at the worst of times there were fortunate exceptions. Now the exceptions were tending to become the rule, or at any rate were regarded by the Christian conscience as the norm. The efforts of the saints and the regulations of Trent bore fruit. Progress was obvious from top to bottom of the scale of duties and titles.

The standards of the Sacred College were raised considerably. The cardinals were completely worthy of the high responsibilities conferred by the purple. Bellarmine, Baronius, Du Perron and D'Ossat were among them; so was Alessandro dei Medici of Florence, whose reports we have cited, whom Clement VIII hoped would succeed him and who was in fact for a short while Pope Leo XI; so also was Pierre de Bérulle, who washed his own plate as usual on the day that he learned he was to receive the Red Hat.

The same process is observable in the episcopate. There had always been reforming bishops whose lives were an example to their brethren; the memory of Giberti and St Charles Borromeo was still alive; and the number was increasing, *even in countries where the appointment of bishops was absolutely dependent upon the will of the sovereign.* In France, for example, the case of Henri IV is particularly significant. At the Assembly of the Clergy in 1605 he was able proudly to proclaim: 'As for elections, you see what I have done. I am glad to find those whom I have nominated different from those in the past.' And this was very near to the truth. He did of course nominate a few undesirables, e.g. his bastard brother Charles de Bourbon to Rouen, and to Rheims the young Cardinal de Lorraine who succeeded him in the favour of Charlotte des Essarts. But generally speaking his selection was good: Camus for Bellay, Fenouillet for Montpellier; for Embrun, Honoré de Laurens, who restored a situation gravely compromised by his unworthy predecessor; François de la Guesle for Tours, and for Venice, Pierre du Vair who consistently refused to leave his poor diocese. Henri IV even wished to make bishops of Fr Coton and Bérulle, both of whom declined, and to raise St Francis of Sales to the archiepiscopal See of Paris. His goodwill went so far as to allow the Pope to set aside names submitted for his approval. After his death the government continued this policy; the appointment of Armand du Plessis de Richelieu as Bishop of Luçon, 'the most bedraggled of French dioceses,' was no bad choice.

The phenomenon was general. In Germany too the raising of episcopal standards was due to secular princes—Albert V and William V of Bavaria, the Archduke Ferdinand, and even Rudolf—and to the influence of young noblemen educated at the German College, who gradually replaced illiterate canons in the cathedral chapters and second-rate bishops in the episcopal sees. The dioceses of Augsburg, Wurzburg, Mainz, Speyer, Paderborn, Breslau, Olmuz and Trier were thus firmly governed by men devoted to sound if sometimes harsh ideas.[1]

In drawing attention to the influence of the German College, we have recognized the importance of those institutions which the Church soon created in large numbers for the training of her priests. The Council of Trent laid down the principle by directing bishops to establish seminaries. The Church had previously taken very little care in the preparation of future priests for the tasks that awaited them, but the example of the Jesuits showed what happy results could be expected from a meticulous and rigorous training such as the Society gave its own members. Nevertheless many years passed before the principle stated in the canon of 1563 became a reality. Where were the necessary teachers to be found? Bishops were unwilling to approach the regulars, who were not perhaps familiar with the precise duties incumbent upon parish priests and curates, and who in any case would be outside episcopal control. This problem was to remain unsolved for half a century, or was only partially resolved. Gregory XIII, who did so much for the colleges, laboured hard on behalf of the Society of Jesus. It was now necessary that in every diocese a single house should shelter, educate and train those destined for the priesthood; about 1620 this result was far from having been achieved, but the impulse had been given. Secular institutes and societies of priests prepared the ground. Among these model nurseries was the Oratory of St Philip Neri, followed by that created in France by Bérulle, then the little community established by the Abbé Bourdoise at Saint-Nicolas du Chardonnet. St Vincent de Paul, with more rapid strides, had already begun that great kneading of the clergy in town and country which was to prove one of the most useful works of his busy life. Gathering around him parish priests and curates, he gave them such pertinent instruction that their sacerdotal life was thereby as it were supernaturalized. The clergy began to understand the beauty of the liturgy and the need for propriety, even in matters of dress, and to deepen their spiritual life through the medium of retreats. Spring was at hand. Fr Condren had joined the Oratory; Jean-Jacques Olier, who in 1622, at the age of fourteen, had already been provided with a small benefice,

[1] Mespelebrunn, Archbishop of Wurzburg, banished those who did not attend Mass, whether Protestants or bad Catholics.

would soon begin to dream of the Society of Saint-Sulpice, which was to forge the *élite* of the French clergy. Let us look ahead forty years, to about 1660, and we shall find seminaries established almost everywhere, and young generations of worthy, well-instructed and capable priests. The grain sown a hundred years earlier will be seen to have yielded a valuable harvest.

During the first quarter of the seventeenth century, which produced so many exemplary figures, this exacting and pure ideal of priesthood, humble but profoundly conscious of its own greatness, was represented in all its fullness by one man, who founded the institution destined to give it universal effect. Pierre de Bérulle (1575–1629) was a grandson of Chancellor Séguier. There was thus a legal tradition in his family, but he himself was brought up as a nobleman. From early childhood he gave signs of a temperament cold, reserved and extremely religious. When told of his father's death he replied without shedding a tear: 'God willed it; I must will it.' That from the lips of a seven-year-old boy was certainly remarkable. Ten years later he astonished his teachers with his talents as a controversialist, and one of the most illustrious Parisian *salons* gladly opened its doors to the young apostle of austere mien and agreeably correct deportment.

This was the *salon* of Mme Acarie, 'la belle Acarie,' the young mother of three daughters whom she was bringing up to resemble herself, and wife of a rather simple-minded counsellor of the Parlement. Around this woman, who was 'much according to the Gospel' and 'intelligent as she was holy,' there gathered many religious persons drawn by the quality of her soul and her exceptional faith, to take part in spiritual colloquies and lofty meditation. At the Acaries' mansion, in the Faubourg Saint-Antoine, one met the Princesse de Longueville, the Marquise de Meignelay, the Marquise de Bréauté, M. du Val, the illustrious orator of the Sorbonne, the venerable M. Gallemant, parish priest of Aumale, and sometimes Fr Coton, the holy Capuchin Benoît de Canfeld or (during his stay in Paris) Francis of Sales. Mme Acarie's *salon* was a veritable 'Hôtel de Rambouillet' of religious questions, a 'blue room' whose members were concerned not with correcting the French language, but with improving the spiritual life of Catholics. Young Pierre de Bérulle, still uncertain as to what mode of the religious life he should adopt, and wondering whether to become a Jesuit, a Capuchin or a Carthusian, discovered in that company his true vocation. It was Dom Beaucousin, vicar of the Charterhouse, who perceived and told him what he ought to do: become a secular priest, but in the fullest sense of the term. Bérulle determined to follow this advice.[1]

---

[1] At about this time, and at Mme Acarie's request, he made an adventurous journey to Spain to arrange for the establishment of the Carmelite Order in France. See the following section.

Not long afterwards he made contact with some French disciples of St Philip Neri, founder of the Roman Oratory.[1] Two little 'Philippine' groups had established themselves in Provence, one at Notre-Dame de Grace, near Cotignac in Var, the other at Cavaillon, a small but go-ahead city, and Archbishop Farugi of Avignon interested himself in their work. Between 1605 and 1609 the community at Cavaillon had become divided on the subject of their future organization. One party, led by Caesar de Bus, wished to form a true congregation with vows; [2] another, under Romillion, desired to remain 'in the purely ecclesiastical state,' that is to say, faithful to the pattern of the Roman Oratory. This latter group had removed to Aix and created an institute *ad instar Oratorii Romani*. Two or three of its members went to Paris, hoping to make a foundation, and there, at their lodgings in the Faubourg Saint-Jacques, they met the Abbé Pierre de Bérulle, who was then living at the Carmelite house. Their exchange of views resulted in a grand idea: to form a society of priests modelled upon the Philippine Oratory, but adapted to the requirements of the apostolate in France.

Thus was quickly born the Oratory of Jesus Christ,[3] so called 'in honour of the prayers offered by Our Lord during His mortal life.' Its members were not religious, but 'pious priests specially dedicated to performing all the duties of sacerdotal life with all possible perfection.' As Fr Condren, one of its most illustrious members, said later, 'the priests who form it are not bound by vows to observe poverty, chastity, obedience and the evangelical counsels. But it embraces all these virtues by undertaking this sublime sacerdotal state, which should sanctify and perfect all other states within the Church, and which therefore presupposes the perfection of all.' The exact rôle assumed by the Oratory is well described by Condren as follows: 'The houses of the Oratory should be, with regard to other priests, what the monasteries are with regard to laymen; for, just as in the days of Christian fervour's decadence God inspired numerous layfolk with the spirit of retirement and thereby gave rise to the monasteries, so now, when the priestly order had in many respects fallen from its pristine perfection, God induced Cardinal de Bérulle to found a congregation of priests, who not only profess to strive for sacerdotal perfection, but also to isolate themselves from all that might deter them therefrom.' Unlike the Jesuits, who worked in some degree from without, like an advance guard, the Oratorians wished to be within the very midst of the priestly ranks, so as to reanimate them and give them back their ancient virtues. Erected upon such foundations, the Oratory would labour with all its strength and by every suitable means to reform the clergy. Bérulle

---

[1] See pp. 126–30.
[2] These were the Doctrinarians, of whom we shall speak in the following section.
[3] It was officially instituted by the Bull *Sacrosanctae* on 10th May 1613.

assigned his sons the threefold task of helping priests in the parishes, organizing retreats at which men dedicated to God might recuperate their spiritual forces, and founding seminaries. His humility led him to look about for a superior to guide his institute,[1] but when the search failed he had to resign himself to its direction. The task was a heavy one: first because the success of the Oratory was rapid, and its growth raised many problems; then because that very success provoked stout resistance and even attack. He had to deal with faction and intrigue. Nothing, however, discouraged that calm, strong-willed man the fundamentals of whose character were revealed in his plain, resolute features, his prominent eyes and heavy lips: the supernatural patience, compounded from resignation and confidence, of one who had given his entire self to Christ and expected nothing in return but strength and success.

In 1631 the Oratory possessed seventy-one houses, including twenty-one colleges and six seminaries. The proportion is surprising, because education had no place in the founder's mind, where the training of priests took precedence of everything else. It was in fact with this training that Bérulle was exclusively concerned, and in 1620 he opened the first official seminary at Paris, in the Rue Saint-Jacques. But two years later, by order of the Pope, he was obliged to interest himself in education. Schools were opened and the Oratory certainly achieved marvellous results. But this task was destined to deflect its members from their original vocation; it would also involve them in a conflict with the Jesuits, in which neither side gave proof of much moderation or Christian charity. Bérulle was created cardinal in 1627, and when he died in 1629 he had the supreme satisfaction of having been God's instrument in setting on foot the indispensable work of recalling the clergy to their vocation and of preparing them for the service of Holy Church. That is his great achievement in the eyes of history.

Bérulle, however, was not the only man to undertake such work. Far removed from him in space, but his brother according to the spirit, Francis of Sales had recently established his 'Sainte Maison' at Thonon, the eventual nucleus of a model congregation very much like the Oratory. André Bourdoise, a rugged and outspoken parish priest, but full of zeal, came with his curates to make a retreat at the Oratory. He left resolved to found a similar community; this was the origin of the Priests of Saint-Nicolas du Chardonnet, who opened a seminary. Another of Bérulle's spiritual sons was Vincent de Paul, 'Monsieur Vincent,' whose Lazarists would found numerous seminaries. And M. Olier, founder of Saint-Sulpice, was a disciple of Fr Condren, the glory of the Oratory and its second Superior-General.

[1] He appealed in vain to Francis of Sales.

12. REFORM OF THE REGULAR CLERGY CONTINUES

Bérulle, Bourdoise, Vincent de Paul, M. Olier—and, let us add among many others, Peter Fourier—are names that will not allow us to forget that the clergy was henceforth in process of transformation. And not the secular priesthood alone, for the regulars also showed manifold signs of improvement. The great revival we noted as having begun long before the Council of Trent, and which was marked particularly by the birth of the Society of Jesus, by the foundation of the Capuchins and by the reform of Carmel, had not weakened. Quite the reverse. There were of course many difficulties. Too many monasteries remained attached to their lamentable routine, and even in some cases to their scandalous ways. Moreover relations between seculars and regulars were often strained; the former reproached the latter with their abuse of exemptions which left them virtually independent of episcopal authority. If many bishops sought to reform the Orders and Congregations within their dioceses,[1] it was only to ensure their more complete subjection, and that alone was not enough. The fact, however, remains that voluntary return to strict observance was making undeniable progress within the ancient Orders themselves.

Among the Black Benedictines the movement was headed by two great Congregations, those of Saint-Vannes and Saint-Maur. Because their histories were 'closely linked, their influence was mutual: Saint-Vannes communicated to Saint-Maur its supernatural character, while Saint-Maur clarified and strengthened the literary movement of Saint-Vannes.'[2] The starting-point was Saint-Vannes in Lorraine, where the banner of reform was raised by Didier de la Cour in about 1600. Very soon afterwards Saint-Hydulphe at Moyenmoutier rallied to the cause, and was followed one after another by some forty monasteries. Several French houses did likewise, among them Saint-Pierre at Jumièges in 1617. But a delicate problem arose. The monasteries of Lorraine and those of France had not the same lay overlord and did not live under the same régime. Dom Bernard, prior of the Collège de Cluny at Paris, therefore took the initiative of founding a new national Benedictine Congregation, which he named after St Maurus, one of St Benedict's first companions. Its success was overwhelming. In 1621 Gregory XV recognized the new Congregation, which soon counted two hundred monasteries, though Cluny sulked and stood apart. The true Cassinese tradition reawoke: intellectual labour was restored to honour by the Maurists, among whom Mabillon was shortly to appear.

[1] See Chapter II, section 11.
[2] Dom de Hemptinne, *L'Ordre de Saint Benoît*.

Similar paths were chosen in Belgium by the abbey of St Hubert, and in Germany by renowned Fulda, which was imperilled by the Swedish invasion during the Thirty Years War. The movement was now well under way.

Meanwhile the same course had been followed among the White Benedictines, the sons of St Bernard. The Feuillant reform, begun by Jean de la Barrière at Toulouse, had made considerable progress since 1575, notwithstanding some furious resistance which reached the point of hand-to-hand fighting. The Order, recognized by Sixtus V, became (c. 1600) a real power in France as well as in Italy; but antagonistic forces were at work, which led to a split between the French and the Italian Feuillants. The reform reached Belgium, where it was adopted by the abbey of Orval. Citeaux, however, refused to follow these good examples, until compelled to do so by the iron hand of Richelieu. No more than seven or eight houses were attached to Clairvaux, which was faithful to the strict observance. There would be plenty of work for M. de Rancé among the White Monks.

Behold now, among the canons regular, a holy man, a veritable saint, worthy to be ranked with the Curé d'Ars whom he resembles in many respects. Peter Fourier (1575–1640) was a Lorrainer, an ardent and apostolic soul who was nephew to no less a person than the Cardinal de Lorraine. The canons of Charmoussy, where he served his novitiate, loaded him in vain with insults, hoping to damp his zeal which they considered out of place. Appointed to Mattaincourt, he showed himself the perfect model of a parish priest, completely dedicated to the welfare of souls. He devoted much care to the Christian education of youth, and founded with Alix Le Clerc the Congregation of Daughters of Our Lady. About 1620, by order of Gregory XV and the Bishop of Toul, he was hard at work reorganizing the Augustinian canons. He assembled their better elements at Lunéville, which he made his headquarters, and soon afterwards founded the Congregation of Our Saviour, whose influence was felt throughout Lorraine and far beyond. The same work was begun in France by Fr Faure at Saint-Vincent de Senlis, and then taken over by Cardinal de Rochefoucauld. In 1622 His Eminence was officially directed by Gregory XV to reform the French canons regular, and soon afterwards, using the convent of Sainte-Geneviève as his centre, he endowed the 'Genovéfaines' with a radiance whose memory is preserved at Paris in the Panthéon and the famous library of Sainte-Geneviève. Finally, the Premonstratensians joined the movement and recovered their ancient loyalty to the Rule of St Norbert. In Spain the reform begun by Didace de Mendieto developed, and Jean des Pruets had it approved by Rome. In Lorraine, that of Didier Picard and Servais de Larnelle, called 'of the ancient rigour,' made progress and established itself in France, especially in

Normandy, and Paul V gave it official recognition. Even the Common Observance, under Abbot Drosios of Pare, was dreaming of reform.

Nor were the Mendicants left behind. The movement here was led by the Capuchins. In 1608 the Pope recognized them as 'true sons of St Francis'; in 1619 they were freed from all dependence on the Conventuals, and allowed a superior-general of their own. Their growth from that date onwards was remarkable; they reached a total of more than eighteen thousand and had houses everywhere. Fr Joseph, Richelieu's 'Grey Eminence,' was a member of their Order, which also produced St Felix of Cantalice, St Laurence of Brindisi and St Fidelis of Sigmaringen, the last of whom was murdered by the Calvinists while he was preaching in Grisons (1622). The Dominicans were perhaps less influential at that date, but they too were riding on the flood-tide of reform both in Spain and France. The French reform in particular was encouraged by the Master-General, Secchi (1612–28), and further developed by his successor Ridolfi, who established a model friary in every province. The 'Discalced Augustinians,' founded in Spain by Thomas of Jesus,[1] installed themselves at Paris, where Notre-Dame des Victoires preserves their memory.

This impressive spectacle offsets the picture afforded by those lax congregations and undisciplined communities which shocked the Cardinal of Florence. The situation was very much the same among female religious, except perhaps that progress was a little slower. Many communities, isolated amid their vast country estates and seldom visited by their spiritual directors, wallowed in somnolence rather than in vice; feminine vanity did whatever else was necessary to restrain better inclinations. But in many cases also the situation was altered by the appointment of a fervent and energetic abbess, often a daughter of the higher nobility, who had received the convent in dower and suddenly resolved to take her duties seriously. A few professed nuns would rally to her side: enclosure was re-established, undesirable guests were refused admission to the parlour and the recalcitrant were ordered to obey or to depart. The result was to create a new centre of religious fervour that would set a good example to its neighbours. This is what happened at Port-Royal under Mère Angélique (formerly Jacqueline Arnauld), who brought her daughters back to the Cistercian observance in 1609 and was followed by the 'Solitaries,' who settled in the neighbourhood. Such also was the case with the Feuillantines at Toulouse, with Marguerite de Beauvilliers at Montmartre, with Antoinette d'Orléans at Fontevrault, and then with the priories of Lancrite and Poitiers, which last gave rise to the Daughters of Calvary.

All this represents a magnificent spirit of revival; but we come now

[1] Thomas of Jesus (1529–82), a Portuguese Hermit of St Augustine, must not be confused with his Spanish namesake, of whom mention has been made on p. 126 above.

to something even more wonderful, an enterprise full of passion and romantic events—the introduction of the Carmelites to France. This idea took shape in the *salon* of Mme Acarie, to whom St Teresa had appeared on two occasions. To establish the reformed Carmelites in Paris was a splendid project, but one that did not please everybody; other Congregations, even the most saintly, were violently opposed to the scheme. Mme Acarie stood her ground, supported by the young Abbé Pierre de Bérulle, who was inspired with apostolic zeal. A Bull was obtained in 1603, and Bérulle set out for Spain in search of spiritual reinforcements. It was not an easy task; Bremond's sparkling pen gives it the appearance of a Quixotic romance. Nothing is lacking, not even a nocturnal abduction; for in order to enable the nuns destined for France to leave Salamanca, the young emissary was obliged to hurry them from their convent before daybreak, so as to avoid resistance. 'This little Dom Pedro,' said one of them, 'would have delighted our holy Mother.' In due course six Spanish Carmelites arrived in France, led by Mother Anne of Jesus, one of St Teresa's favourite daughters. The first Carmel was founded at Paris, and quickly received a flow of vocations drawn in large numbers from the noblest families. Mme Acarie herself subsequently joined the community with her three daughters, and became Blessed Mary of the Incarnation. Among later entrants was Louise de la Vallière, who came to expiate her sins. It was not long before there were Carmels at Pontoise, Amiens, Dijon, Tours and many other places. The seed sown by the saint of Avila yielded some rich harvests.

So much then for the reform of ancient Orders, and the flowering of trees planted in the preceding era. The institutes founded during the Tridentine period were in healthy condition. First and foremost of these were the Jesuits, who now occupied a prominent and even decisive place in the struggle on behalf of God. They were almost ubiquitous, serving as propagandists in Protestant countries, as educators of youth, as confessors of princes and as missionaries. But the seculars, though quite prepared to welcome congregations of other priests, were often hostile to the Fathers. Enemies of the Jesuits were at work and had already won some temporary success. Besides, the giants of the Society were disappearing one after another: Suarez in 1617, Bellarmine in 1621, Lessius in 1623. But the sons of St Ignatius had already acquired such influence that, while no longer maintaining the triumphant rhythm of their early years, continued to infiltrate, to radiate and to open schools. In 1626 they had sixteen thousand members and more than four hundred and fifty houses of instruction. They could face with serenity the trials that lay not far ahead.

The impulse which led to the reform of so many Orders, ancient and more recent, is manifested yet again in the continual emergence of new Orders. The multiplication of institutes and foundations is perhaps one of the most striking, if not the most happy, features of the Tridentine Church and the Catholic revival. We are far from the great medieval unity in which all the regulars were included under a mere half-dozen or so denominations. New contemplative Orders were few and far between: the Benedictines, Poor Clares and Carmelites absorbed the majority of such vocations. However, the *Annunziata Celeste*, founded at Genoa by Vittoria Fornari in 1602, enjoyed some small measure of success, reaching Nancy and Paris in 1616 and 1621 respectively. The Visitandines expanded rapidly, despite the fact that cloistered prayer was not, as we shall see, originally their vocation.

On the other hand new active Orders were numerous, and would increase with the passage of time. About 1620 the Brothers of St John of God were flourishing, and their Hospital of Charity in the Rue des Saints-Pères at Paris was the most important in the French capital.[1] At Rome there appeared an astonishing saint, who had led a fast life in his youth, but had been converted by St Philip Neri. This was St Camillus of Lellis (1550–1614). Devoting himself to incurables, he gathered around him many clerics and laymen who were no less eager to work for the charity of Christ. Such was the origin of the Camillans, or 'Clerks Regular ministering to the Infirm,' [2] whose large red crosses on their black garments soon became familiar. In a single generation these *Crociferi* founded twenty hospitals, and two hundred and twenty of their brethren died of diseases contracted while nursing the sick. At Paris the Hospitallers of Our Lady's Charity, who had opened a hospital near the Place des Vosges, behaved with no less heroism.

Teaching also was one of the major vocations of that age. The Ursulines, founded by Angela Merici and given their final form by St Charles Borromeo, were established in France, at Isle-sur-Sorgne, by François de Bermond and Caesar de Bus under the name 'Sisters of Christian Doctrine.' Coming to Paris in 1604, they were befriended by Mme Acarie, who persuaded Sainte-Beuve [3] and his wife to set them up in the Rue Saint-Jacques. Before long many French towns had Ursuline convents—nearly three hundred in all—where girls of the upper classes received their education. The Daughters of Our Lady of Bordeaux, instituted there by St Jeanne de Lestonnac in 1606, spread in the south-west and west of France, while the canonesses of St Peter Fourier enjoyed similar progress in the east. For the education of boys, the Oratory began to open schools in addition to those run by the Jesuits; their rivalry, though bitter, was none the less useful, and

---

[1] An absurd system of 'town planning' destroyed it in recent times and has given it a miserable substitute.

[2] They were also known as 'Brothers of the Good Death.'

[3] A counsellor of the Parlement.

N

certain bishops imitated them on the local plane. The 'Doctrinarians' of Blessed Caesar de Bus (1544–1607), otherwise known as 'Fathers of Christian Doctrine,' made a brilliant start, which unfortunately did not continue for long. The Piarists, or 'Clerks of the Pious Schools,' founded in Aragon by St Joseph Calasanctius (1556–1648) and approved in 1617, enjoyed a rapid success, which was subsequently thwarted by the rivalry of the Oratorians.

Of all the Orders born after the Council of Trent, the most original and best adapted to the apostolic needs of the age was certainly the *Visitation*, founded in 1610 by that genius whom we meet yet once again—St Francis of Sales. It was a Congregation intended to combine the secular and the religious state, the twin vocations of Martha and Mary; its members, while practising interior recollection, would devote themselves to works of charity. The Bishop of Annecy, with his spiritual daughter St Jeanne de Chantal, tried to make this idea a living reality. But the stupid interference of Cardinal Marguemont, Archbishop of Lyons, obliged the Visitandines to become a cloistered Order of contemplatives under solemn vows. Their empty place, however, was soon afterwards filled, and with what impetuous ardour, by the daughters of M. Vincent, the Sisters of Charity.

13. AMONG THE CHRISTIAN MASSES

On the threshold of the seventeenth century reformation of the clergy is the outstanding characteristic of a Church whose every feature was by no means attractive, but in whom an abundance of goodwill left no doubt as to the future. One problem remained: how to work the new leaven into the Mass of the baptized. That was the task to which the Church devoted her energies from now onwards; her history during the great 'classical' age was that of a persevering effort to accomplish this work of reanimating the very soul of the Christian people. But her instruments were already to hand, or were in course of preparation.

The first of these instruments was *teaching*. It is impossible to overestimate the importance of the place occupied henceforward in the Church by educational interests. St Ignatius clearly explains why. 'Our task,' he says, 'is to reinstate religion, but in order to do that we must first prepare students. This preparation consists in cultivating the intellect through the inferior branches of learning, that is to say, the humanities, philosophy and the sciences.' This was perfectly true. Long before Luther raised the problem of salvation and grace, the great debates concerning human nature had turned largely upon the art of teaching. The humanists had opposed the antiquated methods of the Sorbonne and of the colleges of Montaigu and Navarre.

As early as 1537 Fr Toussaint wrote one short sentence that is worth a complete programme: 'The college will do more for the Gospel than all our sermons.' At Milan, about the same time, Fr Castellino founded the Society of Servants of Little Children; the Barnabites and Somaschi placed education in the front rank of their vocational duties; so did the daughters of Angela Merici. A decree of the Council of Trent, enacted in the fifth session, made teaching obligatory upon the Church: every parish was to have at least one school for the free education of its children. And the great reforming movement led many of the new Orders to devote themselves to this most necessary task: first the Jesuits, then the Oratorians, the Doctrinarians, the Piarists, the Daughters of St Peter Fourier, the Ursulines and others. We may safely say that Catholic education, in which the Church was thenceforward keenly interested, received its impetus and its modern form at that date.

Its methods were laid down principally by the Jesuits, in those 'mixed' colleges where they allowed a few young laymen to benefit by the training given to their own scholastics. Gandia and Messina were the first of these schools; but Frs Le Jay and Francis Xavier quickly realized the importance of this kind of work and the need for its expansion. Separated in due course from the scholasticates, the Jesuit colleges became incomparable smithies for the forging of intellect and character, and their enormous success proved that they answered to a genuine need. The *Ratio Studiorum* of 1598 drew up a programme of studies, as solid as it was logical, of which the humanities were the foundation. But it also introduced fresh techniques, which provided for the children's health [1] and almost abolished the whip as an instrument of pedagogy.[2] The Jesuit colleges produced generations of distinguished men; we need only recite the names of Corneille and Molière, Descartes and Lope de Vega, Bossuet and Flèchier, Lamoignon and Séguier, Luxembourg and Condé, in order to appreciate the quality of the education given and the methods used. After 1621 the Oratorians also entered the educational field and tried to improve still further upon Jesuit methods; e.g. they introduced the study of mathematics and the physical and natural sciences. Among the illustrious pupils of the Oratory were Colbert, Tourville and Villars.

Nor were the children of the poorer classes neglected. With all due deference to Michel Bréal, who maintains that what we should call primary education was 'a fruit of Protestantism,' the Fathers of Trent

---

[1] This had been completely ignored at the Collège de Montaigu in the time of Erasmus and Rabelais.

[2] The *Ratio* expressly states that persuasion is to be preferred. Recourse was had to corporal punishment only as a last resort, and even then it was administered not by a Jesuit, but by a layman attached to the establishment, whom the boys called 'Fr Flogger.' The expression became proverbial. See F. de Daimville, *Les Jésuites et l'Education de la Société Française*, Paris, 1940.

gave particular attention to this subject. Bishops were ordered to see that the parochial schools were properly run, and to pay the masters either in cash or by granting them a benefice. In Italy, St Charles Borromeo set an example: in 1564 he founded at Milan the first primary school, which was quickly followed by hundreds of others. Ursulines and Piarists set to work with the same spirit. In France the national council of Cambrai (1565) included on its agenda a complete scheme of primary education; and thirty years later, when the Cardinal of Florence arrived in the country, he was surprised and filled with admiration at the sight of many parishes paying the village school-master. In Germany this work had been commenced as early as the fourteenth century by Gerard de Groot's Brethren of the Common Life,[1] who were succeeded by teaching congregations and diocesan schools. Everywhere then the Church took charge of the education of millions of children, not of course for the pleasure of teaching them Catholic arithmetic or Catholic grammar, but in order to prepare them for the reception of religious instruction properly so called, which was her first and ultimate concern.

Her main purpose in fact was to spread the truths of faith, to make them known to Catholics who had for too long forgotten them. In 1546 the Council of Trent placed catechism in the forefront of its deliberations. It was essential to halt the progress of religious ignorance, which at that time was grievous beyond words; there were actually certain parts of Europe where Catholics never attended Mass, and were incapable of reciting a prayer or even of making the sign of the cross. But it was also necessary to allay the hunger for knowledge and certitude which Protestantism claimed to satisfy. The need was so intense that in many places, before the Council took steps to deal with the situation, self-appointed catechists used to go about the streets and public squares peddling the Word—often in a manner that left much to be desired from a theological point of view. There were no doubt such men as John of Avila and young Ignatius, but there were also many false visionaries and other misguided teachers.

The Council understood that it must do something to supply the people's wants. The Fathers who took part in its sessions had more or less immediate access to Ponce de la Fuente's *Summa de Doctrina Christiana*, which appeared at Seville in 1543, and the *Esposizione Volgari sopra il simbolo Apostolico* published at Venice by Bishop Lippomano in 1545. Between these dates and the closing of the Council, no fewer than twenty-five treatises purporting to expound the whole of Catholic doctrine came from the presses of France, Italy and Spain. *The Catechism of the Council of Trent*, decided upon by the Assembly and promulgated by St Pius V, was therefore the answer to an urgent need.

---

[1] See *The Protestant Reformation*, Chapter III.

The Tridentine catechism, however, and those splendid treatises were addressed to educated minds, especially to members of the clergy. The next thing to do was to make this huge body of doctrine available in such a form that everyone would be able to enjoy its benefits. Hence the publication of innumerable catechisms of a more popular character. The most successful of all these was St Peter Canisius's *Summary of Christian Doctrine*. The great Jesuit prepared three editions, *major*, *minor* and *minima*, intended for different classes of readers, so that everyone without exception, from small children to educated gentlemen, had at his disposal the necessary means of instruction. Each of the main doctrinal affirmations was skilfully based upon Scripture and the Fathers. The Protestants pretended to make sacred history their private domain, but Canisius broke their monopoly by making it an integral part of his teaching. But his work, which was quickly translated into all languages, was not the only one of its kind to reach the Catholic masses. Bellarmine and Baronius also wrote catechisms, and the Doctrinarians and Piarists had their own. Sound doctrine, hitherto sadly neglected, now possessed the means of finding its way into minds and hearts.

But books of doctrine were not enough, adapted though they were to all ages and conditions; it was not sufficient merely to educate children. It was necessary in addition to re-establish contact between the Gospel and that Christian people who had still to be evangelized and reconquered. This was a long-term job, and at the beginning of the sixteenth century it had scarcely begun; one cannot lure mankind overnight from vagaries that have beguiled them for at least a hundred years. Hasty and startling 'conversions' were no good. In order once again to teach the baptized to think and behave as Christians a combined and prolonged effort would have to be made, an effort that was just beginning at the very end of the period now under consideration.

The idea which was beginning to gain ground and was soon to prove so fruitful was none other than that which our own age believes itself to have discovered. The apostolic institutions applicable to Catholics are no different from those governing the work in pagan territory or in countries dominated by Protestantism; the same effort is required to meet an identical need. It was in fact the *missionary* idea [1] that was coming into favour; missions would have to go not among the pagans, but among the mass of the baptized, aiming not at 'conversions' in the ordinary sense of the term, i.e. of baptism or abjuration, but at that other form of 'conversion' which every Catholic can achieve if he decides to renounce his sinful life and give himself truly to God.

The mission would become the principal weapon of the Church later in the seventeenth century, when St Francis Régis [2] had begun his

---

[1] The word 'mission' was seldom used at this time.
[2] He was twenty-five years old in 1622.

labours in the Vivarais, when St Vincent de Paul had founded his Lazarists, when St John Eudes had taken western France in hand, and so on. But here already are the heralds of this gigantic movement: Fr Auger, a Jesuit, who died in 1591 after rousing Bordeaux and the south-west; Fr Veron (died 1649), who left the Society with a view to greater freedom, and stirred the neighbourhood of Caen; St Alexander Sauli, a Barnabite, who worked so successfully for twenty years in Corsica that the Holy See appointed him to the episcopal see of Aleria. In Brittany, Michel de Noblitz, a simple priest of great eloquence and unshakable determination, went about for forty years stimulating the countryside. His influence is felt there to this day; his hymns are still sung, and a memory survives of the vivid pictures he used to draw in order to illustrate the points of his instruction. Fr Maunoir belonged to his school. Other *de facto* missionaries of the period were St Philip Neri, who talked to the people of Rome in the language best suited to touch them; Charles Borromeo, who made Milan once more a truly Christian city; Peter Canisius, who did not confine himself to combating heresy, but also fascinated Catholic audiences.   To enlighten the baptized, to persuade them with force and delicacy to rise above themselves: such was the task which, for twenty years on the threshold of the new century, claimed the ceaseless devotion of a saint who was also the most human of his kind. We have met him several times before, and we meet him here again: the Bishop of Annecy.

14. St Francis of Sales

St Francis of Sales (1576–1622) seems to have been specially chosen by Providence to embody in his own person and in his fruitful life all the most essential and most decisive elements of that enormous task accomplished by the Church from the time when, awaking to the problems and perils that beset her, she resolved to reform herself from within, to return to her ancient loyalty and to oppose her enemies with the armour of light. We need only recall the various points in the great scheme of renovation carried out by Catholicism during the sixty years following the Council of Trent, and we shall immediately recognize the historical importance of this man. He is in the front rank of those who were called upon to defend the faith; he devoted his early career to the reconquest of lands occupied by heresy; he dedicated twenty strenuous years to clerical reform; he founded a new Order; and when it came to working the true leaven of the Gospel into the heavy Christian lump, no one was more efficient than this tireless preacher and brilliant author of an *Introduction to the Devout Life*.

One might almost say that a hundred and fifty years of Christian history, with their dramatic struggles, had prepared for his coming and made his achievement possible. Christian humanism, of which so many lofty minds had dreamed since the days of Marsilio Ficino and Pico della Mirandola, the doctrine whose foundations had been laid by Lefèvre d'Étaples and Thomas More and the great Erasmus, reached its full maturity, its wisest and most splendid formulation, in Francis of Sales. The excesses of the Renaissance and the opposite excesses of the Protestant Reformation found perfect equilibrium in the bosom of his calm sagacity. All that vast mystical current, which for two hundred years had bathed the Christian soul and prevented it from becoming a desert, flowed at length into this broad, inexhaustible reservoir. All those rivers of life, from the *Imitation* to Lorenzo Scupoli's *Spiritual Combat* (his bedside book), from Teresa of Avila to the master of the *Spiritual Exercises*, with whom he links hands through Molina, meet in him and enable him to draw from them what is purest, most active and best adapted to the common run of men. Francis of Sales is the living embodiment of an era, the reward of three generations' hopes and prayers.

He was born at Thorens in Savoy, a province which for ancient feudal reasons was still dependent on Turin, but already shared fully in the spiritual growth of France, with which it was connected by many ties. The language of Savoy was purest French, such as was then reaching its full perfection; the Pléiade too had friends at Annecy, at Chambéry, and even in the royal abbey of Hautecombe. Francis never, in mind or heart, separated his little fatherland from the beautiful realm adjoining it. It was in Paris moreover that he completed his studies, at the Collège de Clermont, where the Jesuits were skilled in the formation of genuine humanists, lovers of Greek and Latin, as well as fervent Catholics. There was little need to urge him along this road. At the age of eleven he asked for the tonsure, and smiled quietly when his father suggested to him a more ambitious future as a senator or jurisconsult. At Clermont he was so recollected, so agreeable, so eager to communicate each week, that his companions nicknamed him 'the Angel.' There could surely be little question as to his future.

And yet at the age of eighteen he underwent a terrible ordeal, a maelstrom of anguish and uncertainty, a crisis of soul and mind together. It was the dark hour, the painful hour in which every man faced with decisive problems must choose his destiny. These experiences usually take place at the level of instinct, where the victim flounders in putrid slime. Such was not the case with Francis of Sales; his was a conflict of ideas, one in which so many of his contemporaries suffered unspeakable torments from doubt on the subjects of grace, predestination, eternal salvation and everlasting damnation. For several months he strove with theories and hypotheses, but eventually emerged victorious. What brought him safe and sound through this exhausting contest was not intelligence or reasoning, but the impetus of love. He too had his night of fire, sixty-eight years before Pascal. 'O Lord,' he cried, 'if I am not to see You, never permit me to curse and blaspheme You. And if I cannot love You in the other life, since none praises You in hell, let me at least profit by every moment of my brief existence to love You here on earth.' His prayer deserved to be granted, and granted it was with incomparable generosity. He knelt before the statue of Notre-Dame des Grès, and Our Lady received his heart.

He then spent four years at Padua, where he learned to reverence St Thomas Aquinas and was thrilled by his first contact with the mind of St Augustine and other Fathers. Here also he strengthened his vocation amid a crowd of wild youths who were exasperated by his steady ways and bullied him unmercifully. And now it was time for ordination. He received all the minor Orders in a week, the diaconate three months later and the priesthood after another three months. Such rapid advancement might be considered a little unwise but for the fact that St Gregory of Nazianzen's famous words might have been spoken of this young man whom God had visibly chosen for Himself: 'He was a priest before he was a priest.'

And now—to work! No sooner had Francis been ordained than he was fully occupied with his ministry. As provost of the chapter of Annecy he bore a title which carried no more significance than its holder chose to give it. Well, this young canon endowed it with all his ardour and all his charity. He visited the sick, helped the poor, spent long hours in the confessional and discoursed. Indeed he discoursed so much and so frequently that his father M. de Sales was quite indignant; the good man reproached him for never preparing one of those fine sermons, 'with Greek and Latin quotations,' which certainly diverted the congregation, but never lifted them from the rut of habit. This preacher of less than thirty years knew how to stir the hearts of crowds, and his reputation was already increasing. It was a distinction fraught with peril.

Chablais had become Protestant. It was a charming country of mountains and hills, lying between Hermance and Saint-Gingolph on the southern shore of the Lake of Geneva with Thonon as its capital. In 1550 it was occupied by Duke Charles Emmanuel of Savoy, who wished to recover it from the Calvinists. A first attempt ended in fiasco. Then the Bishop of Annecy (who was also titular of Geneva) asked for volunteers, and the young provost was among the first to offer himself. There followed four years of superhuman and literally heroic effort. Time and again the missionary returned to his lodging through ice and deep snow, his feet running with blood. Many a night too he spent in the open, having, like his Master, nowhere to lay his head. He often risked his life in crossing the Dranse on an icy plank, or

THE NEW FACE OF THE CHURCH

in venturing among enemies who were inclined to make free with their daggers. No matter. The Word must be preached and preached it should be. So they would not listen to his sermons? Very well, the forerunner of publicists and patron of journalists had recourse to tracts, and his little controversial leaflets were distributed or posted everywhere. The result was assured. In 1598, when the bishop came to see what had been done, he found that almost the entire population of Chablais had returned to the Catholic fold.

Francis was then thirty-two years of age. His mission to Chablais had made him famous. At Rome, Clement VIII wished to hear him in person; and when the discourse ended, in the presence of eight cardinals and twenty bishops, the Pope arose and embraced the young apostle. The Bishop of Annecy was old and infirm; Francis became his coadjutor with right of succession. In 1602 he stayed for a while in Paris, where he was much admired. Mme Acarié's *salon* made him welcome, and Pierre de Bérulle declared himself his friend. Common people and high-born ladies crowded round his pulpit; and Henri IV, wishing to number him among the clergy of the realm, offered him the co-adjutorship of Paris, which he refused. 'I am already married, Sire, to a poor woman; I cannot leave her for one more rich.' In deliberately choosing this duty he knew well that the call was from God Himself. His bishop died while he was on the way home. He would be nothing more and nothing less than a modest Savoyard bishop.

But what a bishop! It was his good fortune in the first place to occupy his see, like St Charles Borromeo, for a period of twenty years. Slowly and patiently he would be able to plough his furrow and sow his good grain with care. He lived modestly, more like a monk than a prelate, in the little city of Annecy, for Geneva, whose title he bore, was in the hands of Theodore Beza. All who had need of him found him at their service: 'the bishops, those great drinking troughs,' was one of his delightful expressions. He organized catechism classes throughout the diocese, and sometimes found time to instruct the children in person. He ordered such of his priests as had no cure of souls to offer themselves as assistants to the parish priests. Having no money with which to found a seminary he made good this regrettable lack by holding spiritual conferences which lasted for a week and were intended for the clergy; but he also held special conferences at which he made careful inquiry into the vocation of every candidate for the priesthood. He wished to bring the Truth and the Life to all whom God had entrusted to him. He preached every Sunday and the cathedral was always full. These discourses were not so much sermons as familiar talks, introducing anecdotes, comparisons and questions to the congregation, all with infinite simplicity and refinement. Yet he who was so wonderful a preacher took as his guiding principle: 'I don't want people to say "Oh, what a great preacher! Oh, how well he speaks!" but only "My God, how good You are, and just!" and so on.'

He did not of course spend the whole of his time at Annecy. He often left the pleasant little town with its cobbled streets, 'despite bad weather and deep snow,' to ride for weeks on end visiting the twenty sectors of which his diocese was composed. Although the most active of bishops and the very opposite of a stay-at-home, he managed to write innumerable letters (more than two thousand have survived) to his friends, both famous and obscure, and to those men and women who sought his spiritual direction. He also found time to preach at Grenoble and Dijon, as well as at Paris, whither he was invited in 1618. He died at the age of fifty-five, but his twenty years of episcopate were equivalent to twice as many in such a life. There is a mysterious ubiquity which enables genius to accomplish tasks whose magnitude daunts the average man. Few have possessed it to the same extent as did St Francis of Sales.

What qualities of mind and heart were devoted to that tireless activity! He was also a good-looking man, as Jeanne de Chantal tells us.[1] The portraits hardly do him justice; most of them—including that belonging to the hospital at Annecy, which was painted during his lifetime—are insipid and conventional. 'That countenance full of gentleness but also of majesty, restful yet charged with strength,' of which Henri Bordeaux speaks, 'so sweet and luminous that it insensibly poured calm into the most troubled minds,' is certainly the countenance described by his contemporaries and loved by those who knew him well. The most outstanding feature of his character is gentleness, charity ever present in the great as in the small affairs of life, the charity which impelled him to give his shoes to a poor man, and which also prevented him from uttering a single harsh word to a poor girl who had wandered from the paths of virtue. 'I am the most emotional person in the world,' he once admitted, 'and I think I love nothing but God and all souls for His sake.' At this point, however, we must be on our guard. Because he wrote that more flies are caught with a drop of honey than with a barrel of vinegar, we must not think of him as a trapper of pious little creatures. 'I like souls that are independent,' he confesses, 'souls that are vigorous and not effeminate.' His own was exactly of that stamp. He had strength of character with good, plain common sense; he was too wise to be deceived by appearances or to be duped by sentiment. These may be called unassuming qualities, middle-class virtues. 'We are inclined,' says his compatriot Henri Bordeaux again, 'to take him for quite an ordinary man, good, serene, gentle and upright, whose very virtue is undistinguished. But if you walk in his

[1] His beauty was roseate, fascinating. Mme de Chantal adds that it caused her and the weaker sex in general many distractions.

footsteps you suddenly feel yourself flooded with light; his sanctity sweeps down upon you, without your being aware of its approach or of its proofs.' Sainte-Beuve, who was no devout believer, had already noted as much in the penetrating number of *Les Lundi* which he devoted to this great figure: 'In St Francis of Sales there is more than the virtuous man, more than the serviceable man, more than the human being; there is the *saint*, a real thing which, as soon as it becomes manifest, will always be adored among men.' 'Adored' is not perhaps exactly the right word, but this perfect priest undoubtedly deserves our affection and respect. His human virtues, illuminated by the love of Christ, possess undying radiance.

His help was sought by innumerable souls: great ladies and poor girls, men of distinguished intellect and simpletons. All were received with unvarying courtesy. As a spiritual director of women, Francis of Sales devoted himself to everyone who placed herself in his hands as if she alone existed and were mistress of his time. Most beloved of them all was Jeanne de Chantal (1572–1641), whom he guided to sanctity and to whom he was united by 'an affection whiter than snow, purer than the sun.' At first he was inclined to laugh at this young widow's pretended vocation; but he quickly perceived her depth of soul and associated her with his apostolic work; she helped him to found the Order of the Visitation, which he hoped would continue his work and of which she became the first superior. Another of those whom he directed was 'the young lady of pure gold,' Mme de Charmoisy, whose spiritual needs gave rise to his *Introduction to the Devout Life*, a 'memorial erected to a beautiful soul,' which would immortalize her name. And if death had not come too soon, interrupting their spiritual dialogue, it is possible that the impetuous Mère Angélique Arnauld might never have allowed herself to be caught in the dark whirlwind to which M. de Saint-Cyran afterwards enticed her.

The literary work of St Francis of Sales was the fruit of particular occasions; it sprang from his labours in the field of conscience. But he possessed outstanding gifts as a writer, and even more eminent talents as a specialist of the human heart and an explorer of souls. His *Introduction to the Devout Life* (1608) is addressed, through the fictitious person of Philothea, to that innumerable host of faithful whom the Church produced on the morrow of Trent, anxious to live closer to God 'amid the salt waters of this world and fly through the flames of temptation without burning the wings of holy desire.' It has been called a book for beginners, and in a sense it is; but its complement, the *Treatise of Divine Love* (1616), which was certainly written with the same end in view, leads to the highest summits of mystical experience. The *Spiritual Conferences* and letters likewise supplement a work whose true purpose was never to expound a doctrine in the dry terms of dogmatic theology, but to bring it as near as possible to life for the benefit of souls.

Nevertheless that doctrine exists, all the more moving and impressive because it is not high-flown or artificial. Despite geographical proximity, it is far removed from the *Christian Institution* of Master Calvin. In truth, almost unwittingly, Francis of Sales takes the opposite road to Calvin. The Abbé Bremond defines his philosophy as 'devout humanism.' The essential fact is that he makes man his starting-point, the real and complete man, full of defects but created in God's image and likeness. How well he understands psychology! It is as a psychologist rather than a metaphysician that he seeks in the human soul the foundations of divine love. Francis of Sales is a humanist in the full sense of that word, and not merely because he made an exhaustive study of the humanities under Jesuit teachers. 'I am so much a man as to be nothing else.' These famous words express their meaning perfectly. 'Christian humanism,' says Bremond, 'easily accommodates the two mottoes to the dogmas and spirit of the Church. With Terence, and even better than him, he understands full well that nothing human is alien to him—because in everything human he recognizes the image of God and in every man a brother. With Shakespeare, and more loudly than Shakespeare, he proclaims "What a noble thing is man!"—because humanity has been redeemed by God made Man, and because grace elevates it above its natural perfection.'

Here then is fulfilled the glorification of God in man and of man through God, of which all the most Christian humanists had dreamed for one hundred and fifty years. 'Devout humanism': the word 'devout' which has today become so insipid, must be taken in its most exacting sense, as it was understood in the seventeenth century. It implies a humanism dedicated to God, finding in supernatural man its meaning and its justification. It banishes that despair of man which defiles every brand of Protestantism. Francis of Sales was by no means blind to the reality of sin, but he knew also the superior power of grace. Having discovered the secret of wisdom to lie in complete confidence in God, he no longer concerned himself with the problem of predestination which had troubled his eighteenth year. He readily admits 'that he hates all contention and dispute among Catholics,' leaving it to the Almighty to solve problems that are beyond human reason. 'No doubt,' he writes, 'God has prepared Paradise for those alone whom He foresees will be His own . . . But it is within our power to become His own.' The rule of life he offers is confidence in God and a vigorous effort on the part of man; 'to spin the thread of small virtues,' but also to supernaturalize those virtues. It is sufficient that we *try* to give ourselves to God, that we *try* to do good, that we *try* to pray, and above all that we *try* to love. After that there is no more difficulty; divine mercy will respond to this effort, to this expectation, and the mystery of redemption will do its work. *In pace in idipsum*, as we sing at Compline: the rest is heaven's answer.

Is this kind of humanism simply a method of good conduct, or does it lead to the mystical state? The question has been much disputed. While some consider it as nothing more than a technique of practical asceticism, Bremond maintains that in the long run Francis of Sales is and wishes to be only a mystic, his gaze fixed upon the 'fine point,' the unutterable state. Maybe the dispute is one of words alone. It is clear that we do not discover in his works the careful analyses found in the writings of St Teresa and St John of the Cross, let alone the meticulous rules of prayer laid down by St Ignatius. He is in a way less original and less precise; but if the true aim of all mysticism is to deliver the whole man to infinite love, surely it would be impossible to be more of a mystic than Francis of Sales, for whom love is the sole law of religious life. Only his range is more limited than that of the great Spaniards, and his step less rapid. This characteristic belongs to the whole French school of the *grand siècle*, which was somewhat mistrustful of exaltation and flights into the empyrean; it is that of his friend Bérulle, of M. Olier and of the great Visitandine, Mary of the Incarnation.

But his supreme merit lies in his making this brand of mysticism an integral part of daily life; he makes it accessible to all, every one of us can assimilate it. 'The interior and spiritual life,' says Bossuet, 'used to be relegated to the cloister; it was considered too uncouth to appear at court and in society. Francis of Sales was chosen to go and fetch it out of hiding.' This splendid tribute from the Eagle of Meaux is worthy of remembrance. 'It is wrong and even heretical,' exclaims the saint, 'to wish to banish the devout life from the army, the factory, the courts of princes and the homes of married people.' Every woman who so wishes is a potential Philothea, and in this respect many men have eagerly followed the example of their womenfolk. The whole trend of thought which, about 1600, looked for the return of holiness into daily life found its most perfect expression in St Francis of Sales.[1] He may be considered as the ancestor of Catholic Action and the lay apostolate, as

[1] It is in the light of this trend that we must consider his idea of founding with his friend Jeanne de Chantal a new Order. The religious whom he had in mind would belong to a new type. Originally they were to have been called Daughters of St Martha, which gives a clue to their vocation. St Francis of Sales wished them to be apostles, bringing the presence of Christ into the world, visiting the poor and sick as the Blessed Virgin visited her cousin Elizabeth; whence the name *Visitation* which the congregation ultimately assumed. They were to bear material witness of the holiness acquired in a life of renunciation and prayer. The idea was too advanced for the ecclesiastical authorities, who were scared by the prospect of nuns leaving the cloister and coming in contact with men. The Archbishop of Lyons persuaded the saint (and, with more difficulty, Jeanne de Chantal) to make the Visitandines a contemplative Order, serving the world only by the supernatural means of prayer and mortification.

he certainly was of the spiritual life in its modern form, for the doctrine of St Francis of Sales left an indelible imprint upon the Catholicism of his own age and of those which followed. True he was not the first to say that 'Christians are wrong to be as unchristian as they are'; but he said it so well, in so persuasive a manner, that men listened to him and were anxious to follow his advice. His book enjoyed prodigious success; editions poured from the press, sometimes even without his knowledge or consent. The devotions which he advocated became widespread; he did much to propagate devotion to the angels, and to the guardian angel in particular. He did more than anyone else to make frequent communion a normal part of Catholic life. What he offered, with his kindly smile and hand ever raised to bless and absolve, was quite simply that form of Christianity which was best suited to the society of his own age, and is likewise to our own—a form of Christianity whose main features are peace, poise and love.

It may be argued that this doctrine contained some elements of danger, that the trust reposed in human reason by 'devout humanism' would lead to results exactly opposite to those envisaged by St Francis of Sales, to a certain rupture between religion and life. Its adherents were 'devout' (in a sense that was to become deplorable) as regards dogma, but as for the rest ... it may be suggested that the part he assigns to man's will in the work of salvation is excessive, that it impinges upon that of God, and that such total reliance upon grace may lead to quietism. Bossuet, who had so often praised the Bishop of Annecy, came to distrust his influence when he heard Fénelon and his disciples appealing to the saint's authority. Again, it is urged, the sublime familiarity of St Francis of Sales led to sheer tastelessness once it had lost his firm simplicity. The commandments of God were put into quatrains, songs were made of the *Our Father*, and the 'little virtues' degenerated into very small observances. These dangers, however, which critics have been able to discover after the event, did not exist when that doctrine and 'devout humanism' were voiced by a man as wise and well balanced as the author of the *Introduction*. He knew so well how difficult it is to lift the weight off a sinful soul that he would never have trusted to easy-going routine, let alone to quietism. He had learned only too well from Lorenzo Scupoli that Christian experience is a combat.

He himself fought this battle until the very last. In the late autumn of 1622 Francis of Sales set out for Lyons, where he had some business to transact. He was already a sick man, prematurely exhausted by over-work. His *entourage*, who had feared for his life in the previous summer while he was travelling in Maurienne, tried to detain him, but he would not listen. He stopped at Bellay, to visit his old friend Bishop Camus. Then he resumed his journey through the bitter north winds of the Rhône valley, heading for the metropolis of the Gauls. On 28th December an importunate nobleman kept him standing, bare-headed and shivering, in the cathedral square. Next day he was stricken with congestion. Death found him the calm, collected figure he had always been. While strength remained he gave instructions for the government of his Order, then for the conduct of his diocese. His dedicated life ended with the holiest of deaths.

Thus in the year 1622, remarkable from so many points of view, there disappeared one who contributed more than any other to prepare the synthesis of past and future. A whole epoch terminated in him, but from him also much of the succeeding age was born. Scarcely fifty years had passed when he was raised to the altars by Alexander VII (1665). Pius IX declared him a Doctor of the Church in 1877. No Catholic can open the inexhaustible treasury of his book without a friendly feeling for one who taught so well that the glory of God has no better temple than the heart of man, and for the saint whose unshakable common sense appears so simple that one is almost persuaded that one could follow his example.

15. Baroque

As the sixteenth century drew towards its close, merging into the so-called classical era, the glorification of man in God, and of God through man, concerning which the *Introduction* had spoken with such moderation and reserve, expressed itself in another way, very different in tone, but similar in principle. Religious art had by no means lost its vitality, indeed it had received fresh impetus from the Council of Trent. Popes Sixtus V, Clement VIII and Paul V, all of whom helped to complete St Peter's, helped artists, just as their predecessors of the Renaissance [1] had done, by building and adorning new churches. Bishops throughout the Christian world asked for buildings with more space and light than hitherto, and sought to embellish older churches with new splendours. Religious Orders vied with one another in similar fashion, with the secret purpose of glorifying not only God but also the saints who had worn their respective habits. Nor was there any lack of patrons, for secular princes quickly followed this example, especially in countries where Catholicism was officially allied with the civil power. More churches were built, more religious pictures were painted and more sculpture produced during the sixty years following the Council than during the previous sixty years, when genius was at work. The stern Tridentine canons did not sterilize ecclesiastical art, which was in fact reanimated by the great Catholic revival.

[1] Stefano Maderno was a protégé of Clement VIII; Guido Reni and Bernini owed much to Paul V.

It was certainly not the art of the High Renaissance, but it possessed remarkable originality and was fascinating in many ways. Beginning at Rome under the auspices of a restored and regenerate Papacy, it made its way first into the romanesque countries of the South, and then into Austria and those parts of Germany which had remained Catholic. It is often designated by the somewhat equivocal term 'Baroque.' This word was long used in a pejorative sense. 'Baroque: bizarre, both morally and physically,' says the Dictionary of the French Academy. It seems to be derived from the Portuguese *barroco*, which was applied to pearls irregularly shaped and of inferior quality. Baroque was long regarded as a degenerate form of Renaissance art, until it was discovered to be almost the exact reverse. Émile Mâle [1] was the first to show that it was no less absurd to employ the word '*Baroque*' as an epithet of contempt than it was to despise 'Gothic' in the seventeenth century. Today there is an opposite trend: some exalt Baroque as a characteristic form of western civilization, while others see it as a constant of the human mind.

Baroque as an art-form is defined by its exuberance, by a certain mannerism, by its search for effect, by its love of rich materials, by its intentionally pompous ornamentation, and by its striving to express in all their violence feelings that wear the look of passion. Judged by the strict canons of the High Renaissance it undoubtedly appears to be a less perfect art. Anyone studying the masterpieces of the great age might already have perceived that the sculptural beauty of Michelangelo's figures would lead to gesticulating emphasis, and that the purity of Raphael's 'Madonnas' would end in sugared facility.[2] But the characteristics of Baroque in the late sixteenth century were by no means peculiar to itself. They are to be found in other forms of art, at other times and elsewhere, in the hellenistic period, for example, or in the late Roman Empire, and even as far afield as India. We may perhaps consider Baroque as a state through which art passes in course of its development, and it has even been maintained that the 'constants of the human mind govern the evolution of aesthetic cycles,' in which five epochs can be distinguished: that of myth, that of intuitive faith, that of experimental reasoning, that of affective communion and that of practical knowledge. These epochs, at any rate in the Christian West, are designated by five words: Romanesque, Gothic, Renaissance, Baroque and Rococo.

It was then by virtue of an internal law that art assumed (*c.* 1575–1600) the characteristics mentioned above, characteristics which are seen from our present-day viewpoint to be endowed with a positive

---

[1] *Art religieux après le concile de Trente*, 1923. The author never uses the term 'Baroque.'
[2] See Chapter II, section 14.

value and no longer marked with a negative sign. This theory is strengthened by the fact that, simultaneously with Baroque art, there existed a literary Baroque represented in Italy by 'Marinism,' so called after Gian Battista Marina (1569–1629); in Spain by 'Gongorism,' after Luis de Gongora (1561–1627); and in France by the style of the *Astrée*. There was also a musical Baroque, and even a Baroque of daily life with its enchanting gardens, its grottoes and rock-work, its Venetian mirrors, its brocades, and also its strong emotions and unbridled passions. To what must we attribute this development? Apart from the internal law of civilizations already referred to, there were causes that are easily discernible. (1) Society was emerging from a grave crisis, with that ardour for life which follows all great historical dramas and whose sensibility has not yet recovered from the violent shocks it has received. (2) Civilization felt itself to have attained world stature and was intoxicated, as Claudel says, with that 'adventure of the sea' which it had just experienced. The previous century had witnessed the 'Manuelian' Baroque of the Portuguese navigators. (3) The predominant political system tended to create a monarchical and aristocratic state, and, on another level, had its counterpart in a Church more centralized, stronger and more pontifical than erstwhile. (4) Man's intellect had been disturbed by the conflict over reason, and yielded sometimes to the irrational. Such perhaps were the fundamental facts that were about to find expression in Baroque art.

It was this new current which the Church, with her age-long sense of contemporary trends, took up and employed for her own purposes. Baroque art was perfectly adapted to the joy and magnificence of her liturgical ceremonies. Its sumptuousness corresponded well with the splendour of that faith which had been rediscovered and reinvigorated. That the Protestants hated images and pomp in their places of worship was all the more reason for thronging façades, pillars and chapels with statues of the saints, and for covering the walls of God's house with gold, marble and porphyry; besides, nothing was too precious for the All Highest. The creative enthusiasm of artists corresponded to the generous impulse which carried missionaries to the four corners of the earth. This much is proved by the fact that the Society of Jesus, which led the vanguard of the missions, was also the zealous propagator of Baroque.[1]

At the same time those apologetic purposes which, as we have seen,[2] the Council had resolved that art and its practitioners should subserve, were everywhere in evidence. 'The Virgin triumphing over Luther and Calvin' was a fine subject for the Dominicans. The cohorts of saints, male and female, produced by the great movement of Catholic

[1] So much so that Baroque is sometimes called 'Jesuit art.'
[2] See Chapter II, section 14.

reform and canonized by the Church furnished new and stirring scenes:
from St Teresa to St Francis Xavier, and even less familiar but no less
touching figures, e.g. St Aloysius Gonzaga. Mary Immaculate took a
more prominent place than ever before in painting and sculpture; there
was a veritable spate of Madonnas. The Angels—a Baroque motif if
ever there was one!—occupied in stone or on canvas the same place
granted them by such theologians as St Francis of Sales. But this
apologetic of forms proclaimed above all the glory of God and of His
Church; *ad majorem Dei gloriam* was the watchword of the Jesuits.
From his place in church, during the magnificent services of a reformed
liturgy, the worshipper gazed up at the roof, where angels soared amid
the azure of heaven or the gold of constellations. He beheld an
endless line of ornament sweeping along walls and pillars to hold him
with their magic spell. Our Lady and the saints were no longer motion-
less in niches of stone, as in the Gothic porches; they seemed to stride
towards him in order to convince him of their existence and their
power. And the organ, which was then coming into general use, filled
the nave with its voice now gentle, now sonorous. It captivated his
senses, raising him to sacred and unconscious exaltation.

Thus all the arts were associated in this glorification of God and of
His Church. In the field of architecture Vignola, builder of the Gesù,[1]
left two pupils: Giacomo della Porta, who designed Saint-Louis des
Français, and Domenico Fontana. Carlo Maderno lagged a little
behind him, but Bernini, who was still quite young in 1622 (he was
born in 1598), was already dreaming of that wonderful colonnade with
which he afterwards enfolded the piazza of St Peter's. The plastic arts
did even more than architecture to give Baroque its characteristic
features. Bernini was also the leading sculptor; the richness of his
imagination and his amazing facility caused him to be regarded by his
contemporaries as a genius—a judgment that has not been ratified by
posterity. Fra Montorsolo and Raphael Montelupo, pupils of Michelangelo, were not altogether unworthy of so illustrious a master, while
Stefano Maderno's [2] 'Cecilia,' devoid of flowing drapery and swooning
effects, represents all that is most perfect and refined in the sculpture
of that period.

True Baroque, however, attains its zenith in painting. The vast mural
spaces provided by the new architecture offered a challenge and an
opportunity to artists, as also did the demand for enormous, brightly
coloured pictures to be placed above the altars. In all Catholic countries
—or in nearly all, for there was one exception—Baroque painters

---

[1] Note, however, that Vignola himself was not responsible for the exuberant and rather
theatrical interior decoration to be seen in the Gesù today. His own was sober and bare;
the Baroque element was introduced by his successors.

[2] He must not be confused with his namesake Carlo, architect of the façade of St Peter's.

expressed themselves, not always in masterpieces, but at least with extraordinary vigour, and the influence of their style was so great that one writer has even referred to the 'Baroque of the Anti-baroques.' This new style of painting placed itself everywhere at the service of the Church, followed her inspiration and received from her its themes. The Italian centre was Bologna. Here the three Carracchi,[1] all of them illustrious decorators, managed with fair success to combine Michelangelo's arrangement, Titian's colouring and the aerial grace of Correggio. Annibal was the most gifted of the three, and the new art reached its apogee with his Madonnas in glory surrounded by a quivering swarm of angels. There was almost as much of the Baroque in their Bolognese rival Caravaggio (1560–1609) whose realism in the 'Entombment' or the 'Death of the Virgin' was already far removed from the ordinances of the Renaissance. Guido Reni (1575–1642), *il dolce Guido*, that tireless painter of pictures and frescoes for innumerable churches, yielded so completely to Baroque sensitivity that many have reacted unfavourably to his work.

In Spain, with its more tragic spirit, Baroque expressed itself in works of violent pathos representing a keen but sombre faith. Examples are Ribera's (1588–1656) 'Deposition' and his 'Martyrdom of St Bartholomew,' in which latter the instruments of torture are painted with almost sadistic realism. Later came the art of Zurbaran and of Velasquez (1599–1660).

But the true genius of Baroque painting is Peter Paul Rubens (1577–1640); he is indeed its very incarnation. Son of an alderman of Antwerp, he studied in turn at Venice, Mantua, Rome and in Spain before returning to Flanders as official painter to the archduke Albert. There he gave expression to the spirit of the southern Low Countries, which had remained faithful to Catholicism and had become the model of counterreformation. All the exuberance of that age, all its prodigious vitality, is apparent in his work. His figures are as naturally cosmic as they are realistic and true to life. He reveals a sort of concupiscence which no decree of Trent and no article of the catechism could restrain, but which he very often employed in the Catholic cause, to which he was deeply attached. He did an enormous amount of work for the Church: scenes from the life of Christ, and many saints. His purpose was to show forth the glory of God and of the Church, and he did so in such pictures as the 'Dispute of the Blessed Sacrament,' the 'Meeting of St Ambrose and Theodosius,' the 'Miracle of St Ignatius of Loyola' and the 'Assumption.' In his 'Lance Thrust' (1620) the victim he shows is no tortured and vanquished man, but He by whom Death was to be vanquished. Passionately fond of experiment, of unexpected harmonies in colour, of daring and complex composition and of blazing light, it

[1] Louis (1555–1619), Augustine (1557–1602) and Annibal (1560–1609).

was only by sheer genius that he avoided the perils which threatened Baroque. But none has better conveyed the mixture of forces in his time, that law of perpetual evolution in which the Church was able to recognize the ineffable activity of God.

France was the only country that escaped this triumphant wave of Baroque. She was of course no stranger to the great movement that uplifted Catholicism. But she already found within herself a tradition of equilibrium and moderation, of common sense and moral stability, which prevented her from yielding too much to passion or to display of feeling. Baroque architecture properly so called had few representatives in France; Douai perhaps was one of them. From Gothic mingled with Renaissance, such as may still be seen at Saint-Étienne-du-Mont (completed in 1626) or at Saint-Eustache (completed in 1642), there was a direct transition to the classical style. Simon Vouet (1590–1649) alone of French painters can be classed as Baroque. The rest were already in harmony with the spiritual teaching of the 'French School'; they were truer contemporaries of St Francis of Sales and M. Vincent than were the Baroque artists of Italy, Spain and the Low Countries.

It may be that we should hear a note of warning in this French resistance. No doubt the more rational genius of France suspected the insidious dangers that Baroque art carried within itself, and her more moderate faith mistrusted itself. For there were hidden perils in that seductive style. The peril of sensuality is obvious. The expression of feeling attained to a degree of violence that approached morbidity. One recalls the pert observation of President des Brosses in presence of Bernini's 'St Teresa in Ecstasy': 'If that is divine love,' muttered the old rascal, 'it is very familiar to me.' Here we have sensuality bordering on hystero-mysticism, of which there were too many examples. But even among artists far less given to facile expressionism a tinge of paganism mingles irresistibly with the most genuine Christian inspiration, and one no longer knows whether one is intoxicated by Catholic joy or Dionysiac revelry. In Rubens, for instance, pagan themes rival those of Scripture and hagiography. Was art looking back beyond Trent, not to the *forms* of the Renaissance, but to the more suspect elements of its inspiration?

The other danger was of an aesthetic kind, and it was no less serious. There was a risk that the exuberance of Baroque would become overloaded. The luxury in which it delighted tended to affectation and falsehood. Baroque in its best period stemmed from living roots, but it was doomed to slide almost imperceptibly into mere ornament. There was an unconscious decline from Baroque to preciosity, and the end was reached in the eighteenth century with *Rococo*, art of the boudoir, in which Christian faith would have no place.

But about 1620 this lapse had not yet begun. Baroque in its youth was an art of fervour and enthusiasm, corresponding to the ardour of a Church on the flood-tide of reform. That it bore within itself the agency of its own destruction was part of human destiny. Has not the picture of the Church at which we have been looking shown many areas of shadow? But did that prevent her from being sure of her destiny and looking bravely into the future?

16. GLORY OF THE CHURCH IN 1622

The year 1622 is not one of those historic dates that are easily remembered. It does not seem to have the importance of 1610 (assassination of Henri IV) or of 1618 (beginning of the Thirty Years War). The most we can say is that it corresponds in general to that moment when the new century revealed its true features—allowing for the time lag of about two decades behind the centenary years, which seems to be a constant of history.[1] The Thirty Years War had begun in Germany, and men asked themselves whether it would be more than an internal crisis of the Empire and whether, by crushing the Czechs at the White Mountain (1620), Tilly and his Bavarians had not simply restored Catholic order in the states of Ferdinand. But there were many indications that, by wishing to exploit his victory to the full, the emperor was going to turn the Bohemian affair into a European conflict. France, still in a condition of painful disorder, already foresaw that she would be led by young Bishop Richelieu, for whom the queen-mother had demanded a red hat. In England James I, exasperated by the Gunpowder Plot, chose the Protestant camp, a choice, however, which did not enable him to escape from all his difficulties, notably with Parliament. And the Spanish throne, which was still the most powerful of that age, had recently been inherited (1621) by Philip IV, an irresolute weakling whom all the energy of the Duke of Olivares could not deter from dissipating his forces and his power.

For the Church, however, 1622 was an important and significant date. It corresponds to the brief but fruitful pontificate of Gregory XV (1621-3). Among numerous other events resulting from this great pope's activity in every field—diplomacy, Marian theology and the missions—two were of supreme importance for the future: (1) the final organization of the Sacred College and of the Conclave; (2) the establishment of the Congregation of Propaganda, which would henceforward control the entire apostolate. St Francis of Sales died in 1622, and the great Jesuits had vanished from the scene a little while before. But their successors, Bérulle, Vincent de Paul and Olier, were already on the stage. These facts indicated that an era had gone and that

[1] The seventeenth century ends in 1715 with the death of Louis XIV; the eighteenth and its sequel, the revolutionary crisis, in 1815; the nineteenth in 1914-19.

another was at hand. The Church, whose infallible intuition is always able to mark such stages by striking symbols, did so now with incomparable splendour.

On 12th March 1622 there took place in St Peter's at Rome a tremendous ceremony, such as had never yet been seen and has never since been witnessed. The Sovereign Pontiff, that little bent figure of a man in whom nevertheless reposed the overwhelming glory of the Church, proceeded to a fivefold canonization. During the long interval from Adrian VI to Sixtus V, a period of sixty-five years, no saint had been rasied to the altars; it was as if the Church, preoccupied with her struggles and her effort of reform, had not dared to glorify herself in the best of her children. The tradition had been revived in 1588, and each successive pope had had engraved upon his tomb the names of those whom he had canonized. But none of those occasions had been attended by such magnificence as the canonization of these five. It created a sensation throughout the Christian world, and a precious engraving of the scene, made by order of the Pope, was kept in many libraries.

The basilica of St Peter was quite new, only just completed and not yet consecrated.[1] Special arrangements were made for this occasion: the architect Guidotti constructed tribunes draped and fitted with staircases, which not only added to the splendour of the scene, but also enabled the crowd of dignitaries to enjoy a better view. The anonymous engraver aptly described it as a 'theatre.' On top of a kind of rood-screen, which at that time separated the choir from the transept, the beastplates and arms of the papal guards gleamed in the light of chandeliers. From the ceiling fell huge painted banners representing the new saints, and the walls were covered with red hangings and tapestry. A vast crowd filled the nave to overflowing. Silver trumpets rent the heavy air. Applause echoed and re-echoed. Then the solemn liturgy began, supported by the angelic singers of the Sistine Choir. Symbolic gifts were offered to the Pope: the keg of pure wine, the gilded loaves stamped with his arms. The voice which God inspired was uplifted in the silence to declare to the universal Church that five of her children, four men and a woman, were appointed her witnesses in heaven.

Who were they? Four belonged to quite recent times, indeed they had been dead hardly fifty years. All four were of that wonderful Christian generation which gave back to the Church her strength by restoring her to consciousness of her allegiance.[2] The names of these

---

[1] St Peter's was consecrated in 1626, the thirteen hundredth anniversary of the consecration of the earlier basilica.

[2] Six years earlier another of their contemporaries, Charles Borromeo, had been raised to the altars.

four, whose images could be seen on the heavy banners, were Teresa of Avila, Philip Neri, Ignatius of Loyola and Francis Xavier. Each was depicted, as indicated in the Bull of Canonization, in some episode of his or her life, or in an attitude that summarized the fundamentals of their message: the angel of her ecstasy plunged the fiery dart into Teresa's breast; Our Lady appeared to Philip Neri, carrying the Child, who smiled upon him; Ignatius presented the Constitutions of his Order; Francis Xavier, opening his tunic, seemed to wish to allay the interior heat that consumed him, and at the same time to offer mankind his inexhaustible love.

Four saints, of what stature and of what significance! For each of them had had a particular message to bear, and each had faithfully delivered it without thought of self. The mystic of Avila proclaimed that the Church of Christ has no life except in union with Him, and that no earthly effort can have any meaning unless the ultimate goal is attained and God made present in the soul. Philip, with his laughter and untidy dress, personified the perfect joy of the Church, the supernatural joy compounded of hope and faith. The great Basque bears witness to that combative ardour which Catholicism had now regained and with which she would henceforth confront her adversaries, to that effort of self-conquest, to that discipline which the army of Christ like the armies of the world would consider an essential prerequisite of strength. And Francis, the conqueror of Asia, showed not only the Church's power of expansion, but also her unbounded love and the welcome she offers to all men upon earth, of all races and of all conditions. Those four saints sum up and embody the entire work accomplished in nearly one hundred years. What genius for symbolism and what a sense of history must that pope have had who united them in this single act of glory.

We need only look back to the year 1527 to realize the enormous results achieved, and to be filled with admiration. In that year the mercenaries of Frundsberg and Bourbon were masters of Rome; [1] terror, violence and ferocity reigned in the Eternal City, and the Pope, a refugee in the Castle of Sant' Angelo, was but a poor man driven to despair, whom the German emperor thought he held in thrall. Everywhere the ancient edifice of Mother Church was creaking and cracking; already whole sections had started to collapse. Luther was at work in Germany, and the religious revolution which he had let loose was beginning to infiltrate into many countries like an epidemic that had all the appearances of plague. The Mystical Spouse of Christ stood weak and unarmed in presence of this threat. Gone was her fair visage; she was horribly defiled. She had almost forgotten that there existed within her fold men and women whose loyalty was untarnished, and who

[1] See Chapter II, section 1.

would be able on the morrow to help her climb once more into the light. That was in 1527. And now, one hundred years later—these triumphant canonizations in St Peter's. The Church, looking back on that March day in 1622 to her recent past, could be proud of herself and of those who had wrought her salvation.

This, however, did not mean that everything was perfect and that the future held no menace. The victory of the Church over the world is never more than approximate, and can always be challenged. The era just ended had witnessed the unleashing of forces so furiously hostile to Christianity that one might well have asked whether the struggle would not be very soon renewed, and whether these mortal powers would not win the day. Would those saints, whose presence signified that faith was even stronger and whose work had made possible the Catholic Reformation—would those saints tomorrow guide society or would they appear to have been no more than a ransom for the grievous sins of our modern world? St Thomas More and St John Fisher had testified against the dictatorial despotism of kings, but would their lessons prevent the evolution that was driving Europe to absolutist centralization? St Peter Canisius and St Robert Bellarmine had done battle with heresy, but were they the victors? The sovereign gentleness of St Francis Xavier, St Francis of Solano and St Peter Claver had combated colonial exploiters, but would their words of love defeat the aims of self interest and the passion for domination? Above all, St Teresa, St John of the Cross, St Charles Borromeo, St Philip Neri, St Ignatius and St Francis of Sales had in their several ways erected against a humanism founded upon reason, and ending in the exaltation of men against God, an idea of man 'restored in Christ,' who finds in the supernatural the true goal both of his reason and of his life; but which of the two conceptions would prevail? The debate is by no means ended.

On the threshold of the seventeenth century the Church was well aware of this; she knew that her long patient task was still unfinished, for it never will be finished until the end of time. But she had recovered all her fervour, all her hope; she no longer doubted the future, as she had once seemed tempted to do. Difficult days might come; the Word, of which she is the depositary, would conquer, for she had been assured that the gates of hell would never prevail against her.

It was perhaps this supernatural hope that Gregory XV wished to signify when he chose one more saint for the canonization in 1622. For there was a fifth saint whose banner hung from the vaulting of St Peter's on 12th March. He did not belong to the glorious cohort of those who had brought about the reformation of the Church. He lived in the twelfth century (probably 1050–1130) and his name was Isidore the Husbandman. Why was this obscure personage associated with the glorious four? Was it only to please the people of Madrid, whose patron he was? No. His life contains a profound and striking symbol. We read in his 'legend' that this man of God had such great faith that while he was tilling the stark earth of Spain a spring of living water leaped from the open furrow and that an angel came to complete his work. Was it not so with the Church at this very moment? The furrow was open; the spring of living water had sprung from the ancient Christian soil; but it was for God to continue the work and bring it to fruition.

CHRONOLOGICAL TABLE

FOURTEENTH CENTURY

DATE	HISTORY OF THE CHURCH	POLITICAL AND SOCIAL HISTORY	ARTS, LITERATURE AND SCIENCE
1350		The Turks set foot in Europe. John the Good, King of France (1350–63).	Boccaccio (1313–75).
1352	Innocent VI (1352–62).	The Golden Bull does away with all papal participation in imperial elections. Battle of Poitiers.	
1360		Treaty of Bretigny. Murad I, Sultan (1360–89).	
1361	Death of Tauler (b. 1290).		
1363	Urban V (1362–70).	Charles V, King of France (1363–80). In Russia, Prince Dmitri of Moscow (1363–81).	Guillaume de Machaut's *Mass* (1300–77).
1364			Foundation of Cracow University.
1365	Death of Henry Suso (b. 1295).		Foundation of Vienna University.
1366		The Count of Savoy's crusade.	
1369		Death of Peter de Lusignan, King of Cyprus.	
1370	Gregory XI (1370–8).		
1373	Death of St Bridget of Sweden (1302–73).		
1374			Death of Petrarch.
1377	*Return of Gregory XI to Rome, end of the papal exile in Avignon.*	Richard II, King of England (1377–99).	
1378	*Beginning of the Great Schism in the West.* Urban VI, Pope of Rome (1378–89). Clement VII, Pope of Avignon (1378–94).		
1380	Death of St Catherine of Siena (b. 1347).	Charles VI, King of France (1380–1422). The Mongols defeat Dmitri's Russian armies at Kulikovo.	
1381	Birth of St Colette. Death of Ruysbroek (b. 1293).	Peasants' Revolt in England.	
1382	Condemnation of Wyclif (b. 1328, d. 1384).	Flemings crushed at Roosebeke.	
1384	Death of G. de Groot (b. 1340); formation of Brethren of the Common Life.		
1386		Swiss victory at Sempach.	Foundation of Heidelberg University.

DATE	HISTORY OF THE CHURCH	POLITICAL AND SOCIAL HISTORY	ARTS, LITERATURE AND SCIENCE
1387	The canons of Windesheim.		
1389	Boniface IX, Pope of Rome (1389–1404).	Serbs defeated by the Turks at Kossovo. Bajazet becomes Sultan (1389–1402).	
1390	Foundation of the Jeronimites.		P. de Mezières's *The Dream o the Old Pilgrim.*
1391		Manuel II, Emperor of Byzantium (1391–1425).	
1392		Madness of Charles VI of France.	
1394	Benedict XII, Pope of Avignon (deposed 1417; *d.* 1422).		
1396		Death of Emperor John V Palaelogus (1341–96). *Defeat of the Crusade at Nicopolis.*	Claus Sluter (1360–1406).
1399		Accession of the House of Lancaster in England, Henry IV (1399–1413).	Thomas à Kempis (1380– 1471).

FIFTEENTH CENTURY

DATE	HISTORY OF THE CHURCH	POLITICAL AND SOCIAL HISTORY	ARTS, LITERATURE AND SCIENCE
1400			*The Imitation of Jesus Christ.*
1401		Tamerlane defeats Bajazet at Ankara.	*Flamboyant Art* in France. 1400–20, the manuscripts of the Duc de Berry. Jean de Béthencourt sails to the Canaries.
1402	Birth of Denys the Carthusian (*d.* 1471).		
1404	Innocent VII, Pope of Rome (1404–6).		
1405	John Huss (*b.* 1368) preaching in Bohemia.		
1406	Gregory XII, Pope of Rome (deposed 1417).		Brunelleschi (1377–1446), architect of the cupola of St Mary's cathedral, Florence. Giberti (1378–1455). Fra Angelico (1378–1455).
1409	Council of Pisa: three popes now in office at once. Alexander V, Pope of Pisa (1409–10).		Foundation of Leipzig University.
1410	John XXIII, Pope of Pisa (deposed 1415, *d.* 1419). St Bernardine of Siena (1380–1444).	Sigismund, King of Germany, crowned emperor 1432, *d.* 1437. Polish victory at Tannenberg.	Poggio (1380–1459). Pierre d'Ailly's *Mirror of the World.*
1413		Henry V, King of England (1413–22).	
1414	Council of Constance (1414–1417). Execution of John Huss.		

DATE	HISTORY OF THE CHURCH	POLITICAL AND SOCIAL HISTORY	ARTS, LITERATURE AND SCIENCE
1414			Henry the Navigator (1394–1460) established at Sagres. Donatello (1386–1466). The Portuguese reach Cape Bogador.
1417	*End of the Great Schism, election of Martin V* (1417–1431).		
1419	Death of St Vincent Ferrer (b. 1357). St Antoninus (1389–1459).	Beginning of the Hussite Wall (first defenestration of Prague).	The Portuguese in Madeira.
1420		Treaty of Troyes.	Death of Pierre d'Ailly (b. 1350).
1422		Charles VII, King of France (1422–61). Henry VI, King of England (1422–61).	
	St John Capistran (1393–1456).		
1425		John VIII, Emperor of Byzantium (1425–48).	
1429		Capture of Orleans by Joan of Arc. Coronation of Charles VII at Rheims (17th July).	Death of John Gerson (b. 1363).
1430			Death of Christina of Pisa (b. 1367). Luca della Robbia (1400–81).
1431	*Eugenius IV* (1431–47). Council of Basel.	*Death of Joan of Arc, burnt at Rouen* (31st May).	
1434		The Medicis at Florence.	
1436	Foundation of the Oblates by St Frances of Rome.		Alberti (1466–70).
1438	Felix V, the last antipope (1438–43).	Pragmatic Sanction of Bourges.	The first complete manuscript of Plato reaches the West.
1440		The epic stand of John Hunyadi against the Turks. In Germany, Frederick III of Hapsburg (1440–93).	
1444	Death of St Bernardine of Siena (b. 1380).	Christian defeat at Varna.	
1445			The work of Alain Chartier (1390–1450). The Portuguese reach Cape Verde.
1447	Nicholas V (1447–55). Death of St Colette.	St Francis of Paola (1416–1507).	P. della Francesca (1416–92). Creation of the Vatican Library.
1448	Concordat of Vienna.	Constantine XI, last Emperor of Byzantium (1448–53).	
1450			*Invention of the Printing Press.* *The Passion* of Arnould Gréban. Benozzo Gozzoli (1420–97).
1451		Mohammed II, Sultan (1451–1481).	Platina (1421–81) and the Roman Academy.

DATE	HISTORY OF THE CHURCH	POLITICAL AND SOCIAL HISTORY	ARTS, LITERATURE AND SCIENCE
1453		*Capture of Constantinople by the Turks. End of the Hundred Years War* (battle of Castillon).	
1454		League of Lodi.	
1455	Callixtus III Borgia (1455–1458).	In England, the Wars of the Roses (1455–85). Belgrade liberated by John Hunyadi.	
1456	Rehabilitation of Joan of Arc.		
1457		Christian naval victory of Metelina.	
1458	Pius II (Aeneas Sylvius Piccolomini) (1458–64).		
1460			The work of François Villon (1431–6?).
1461		Louis XI, King of France (1461–83).	Bellini (1430–1516). Schongauer (1430–91). Mantegna (1431–1506).
1462		In Russia, Ivan III (1462–1505).	
1464	Paul II (1464–71).		Marsilio Ficino (1433–99). Memling (1433–94). Death of Nicholas of Cusa (*b.* 1401). Verrocchio (1435–1488).
1469		Marriage of Ferdinand of Aragon and Isabella of Castile.	
1471	Sixtus IV (1471–84).	Turkish advance guards in the West (at Otranto in 1480).	The Portuguese cross the Equator.
1472		Ivan III marries Sophia, heiress of the Palaelogi.	
			Bramante (1444–1514). *Botticelli* (1444–1510).
1477	St Catherine of Genoa (1447–1510).	End of the House of Burgundy (death of Charles the Bold).	
1478	Bull instituting the Inquisition in Spain.	Assassination of Giulio dei Medici in Florence.	
1480		End of Mongol domination in Russia.	Signorelli (1450–1523). Hieronymus Bosch (1450–1516).
1481		Death of Mohammed II, rivalry of Bajazet II and Djem.	
			Leonardo da Vinci (1452–1519).
1483	Birth of Luther at Eisleben.		
1484	Innocent VIII (1484–92). Franciscan mission to the Congo.		
1485		Accession of Henry VII Tudor in England. In Florence, striking domination of Lorenzo the Magnificent.	Carpaccio (1455–1526). Reuchlin (1455–1522).

DATE	HISTORY OF THE CHURCH	POLITICAL AND SOCIAL HISTORY	ARTS, LITERATURE AND SCIENCE
1487			Bartholomew Diaz reaches the Cape of Good Hope.
1488	Codification of measures against witchcraft and sorcery.		
1490			Mathias Grünewald (1466–1528).
1491	Appearance of the Blessed Virgin at 'The Three Ears of Corn.' Birth of St Ignatius.	The Capetian Crown annexes Brittany: end of the great fiefs in France. Charles VIII, King of France (1491–1498).	
1492	*Alexander VI Borgia.*	*Capture of Granada by the Catholic kings of Spain.*	*Christopher Columbus discovers North America.*
1493		Alexander VI divides the New World between Spain and Portugal. Beginning of the wars in Italy.	Pico della Mirandola (1463–1494).
1494		Battle of Fornovo.	*Erasmus (1466–1536).* Quentin Matsys (1466–1538). Guillaume Budé (1467–1540).
1497			Cabot discovers Labrador.
1498	Savonarola executed at Florence.	Louis XII, King of France (1498–1515).	Vasco da Gama discovers the maritime route to India.
1499			*Bramante is summoned to Rome to rebuild St Peter's.*

SIXTEENTH CENTURY

DATE	HISTORY OF THE CHURCH	POLITICAL AND SOCIAL HISTORY	ARTS, LITERATURE AND SCIENCE
1500		Birth of Charles V.	Machiavelli (1469–1527). *Albrecht Dürer (1471–1528).* Lucas Cranach (1472–1553).
1503	Pius III (Sept.–Oct.). *Julius II (1503–13).*		
1504	Bartholomew Las Casas (1474–1566) begins his apostleship.		Amerigo Vespucci in 'America.'
1508		League of Cambrai.	*Michelangelo (1475–1564). Titian (1477–1574).*
1509	Birth of Calvin.	French victory at Agnadello. The Holy League against the French. *Henry VIII, King of England (1509–1547).*	
1511	Luther's visit to Rome. Creation of the diocese of San Domingo in the Antilles.		Erasmus's *In Praise of Folly.*
1512	Publication of the Polyglot Bible. Opening of the 5th Oecumenical Lateran Council (1512–17).	Victory and death of Gaston de Foix at Ravenna.	

DATE	HISTORY OF THE CHURCH	POLITICAL AND SOCIAL HISTORY	ARTS, LITERATURE AND SCIENCE
1513	*Leo X* (1513–21). Creation of the first diocese in America (Darien in Panama).		*Raphael* (1483–1520).
1515		*François I, King of France* (1515–47). Victory of Marignano.	
1516	Concordat of Francis I.	Perpetual peace between France and Switzerland.	
1517	*The Affair of the Indulgences* (31st October). At Rome, development of the Oratory of Divine Love.		
1518	*Zwingli* (1484–1531) in Switzerland. Leo X consecrates Henri, the first Negro bishop.		
1519		*Charles V, emperor.*	Magellan sails round the world (1519–22). Fernando Cortez conquers Mexico.
1520	*Luther breaks with Rome.* Bull 'Exsurge Domine.'	Solyman the Magnificent (1520–66).	
1521	Luther translates the Bible at the Wartburg.		
1522	Adrian VI (1522–3).	Marguerite of Navarre (1492–1549) exercises great influence in France.	Luis Vives (1492–1540).
1523	*Clement VII* (1523–34). *Lefèvre d'Étaples* and Briçonnet: the Meaux group. St Ignatius at Manresa.	Gustavus Vasa, King of Sweden (1523–60).	Paracelsus (1493–1541).
1524	Oeclampadius at Basel. Bucer at Strasbourg. Sweden passes to Lutheranism. Creation of the Theatines.		*Corregio* (1494–1534). Erasmus's *Free Will.*
1525	Luther's marriage. The Meaux group is dispersed. St Louis Bertrand in Colombia.	Battle of Pavia. François I taken prisoner. Peasants' War in Germany.	Luther's *Servile Will.* Rabelais (1495–1553).
1526	Foundation of the Capuchins.	Albert of Brandenburg secularizes the estates of the Teutonic Knights. Battle of Mohacs, capture of most of Hungary by the Turks.	Clément Marot (1496–1544)
1527		The sack of Rome.	Melanchthon (1497–1560) *Veronese* (1528–88).
1529	The 'Protestants' in Germany. In France, execution of Louis de Berquin.	Diet of Speyer.	
1530	*Confession of Augsburg.* Protestantism penetrates France.		
1531		War of the Swiss cantons. Death of Zwingli. In Germany, the Schmalkaldic League.	

DATE	HISTORY OF THE CHURCH	POLITICAL AND SOCIAL HISTORY	ARTS, LITERATURE AND SCIENCE
1532		Peace of Nuremberg between the emperor and the German princes.	First book of *Gargantua*. Pizarro and Almagro in Peru.
1533	Henry VIII of England breaks with Rome. Calvin is converted to Protestantism. Foundation of the Barnabites. In India, creation of the bishopric of Goa.		
1534	*Paul III* (1534–49). *The Placard Affair in Paris.* St Ignatius at Montmartre.	The 'Capitulations' assure France's position in the Middle East.	Jacques Cartier in Canada. Primatizzio (1504–70).
1535	The Anabaptist tragedy in Münster. Calvin at Basel. Denmark becomes Lutheran. Martyrdom of St Thomas More.		Melanchthon's *Loci communes.*
1536	Calvin publishes the *Christian Institution* in Latin. First period in Geneva (1536–8).	New war between Charles V and François I. François I allies with the Turks.	
1537	*St Ignatius Loyola founds the Society of Jesus.*	*Ivan IV the Terrible is 'Tsar' of Russia* (1537–84).	
1538	Calvin at Strasbourg, where he prepares the French translation of the *Christian Institution* (published 1541).	Truce of Nice between Charles V and François I.	
1540	Foundation of the Brethren of St John of God. Paul III authorizes Society of Jesus. *St Francis Xavier* (1506–1552) sets off on his mission.		Jean Goujon (1510?–1568). Pierre Lescot (1510–76). Bernard Palissy (1510–1590). Goudimel (1510–1572).
1541	Calvin again at Geneva.	Charles V's defeat before Algiers. Interim of Ratisbon between Charles V and the princes.	
1542	Creation of the *Roman Inquisition.*		
1544		Peace of Crépy between Charles V and François I.	
1545	*Council of Trent* (13th December, first session).		Philibert Delorme (1515–1570).
1546	Death of Luther (18th February). Massacre of the Waldenses in Provence.	Charles V fights the German Lutheran princes.	
1547		*Henri II, King of France* (1547–59). Edward VI, King of England (1547–1553).	Ambroise Paré (1517–90).
1549	The first 'Prayer Book.' England glides towards heresy. St Francis Xavier goes to Japan.	Beginning of the 'Reductions' in Paraguay.	
1550	*Julius III* (1550–55).		
1551		Edict of Châteaubriant.	
1552	Suspension of the Council of Trent. Deaths of St Ignatius and St Francis Xavier.		Joachim du Bellay (1522–1560).

O

DATE	HISTORY OF THE CHURCH	POLITICAL AND SOCIAL HISTORY	ARTS, LITERATURE AND SCIENCE
1553	Calvin secures the condemnation of Michael Servetus at Geneva. The 'Conversion of St Teresa of Avila.'	Mary Tudor, Queen of England (1553–8).	
1555	Marcellus II (April). *Paul IV* (1555–9). Defeat of Mary Tudor's attempt to restore Catholicism in England.		Ronsard (1524–85).
1556		Charles V retires to Yuste. *Philip II* (1556–89), King of Spain. Ferdinand in Austria, then emperor.	*Palestrina's* masterpieces (1526–94).
1557	Calvinism triumphs in Hungary.	French defeat at St Quentin.	
1558	The Index.	*Death of Charles V. Elizabeth I, Queen of England* (1558–1603).	Paul IV has the nudes in Michelangelo's frescoes veiled.
1559	*Pius IV* (1559–65). In France, rigorous measures against the Protestants, who hold their first Synod. John Knox in Scotland.	Treaty of Cateau-Cambrésis. François II, King of France (1559–60).	
1560	The Oratory is constituted around St Philip Neri.	Protestant conspiracy of Amboise. Charles X, King of France (1560–74), regency of Catherine dei Medici.	La Boétie (1530–63).
1561	Failure of the Conference of Poissy.		
1562	Guy de Bray introduces Calvinism into the Low Countries. New meeting of the Council of Trent. *St Teresa* (1515–82) founds the first reformed Carmelite house.	The riot at Vassy starts the Wars of Religion in France.	
1563	Close of the Council of Trent (4th December). In England, the Thirty-Nine Articles.		*Montaigne* (1533–92)
1564	Death of Calvin (27th May).		Death of Michelangelo.
1566	*St Pius V* (1566–72). Publication of the Tridentine Catechism.	Revolt of the Low Countries.	*Molina* (1536–1600).
1568	St Charles Borromeo (1538–1584). *St John of the Cross* (1542–91) founds the Development of Catholicism.		Vignola (1507–73) begins the Gesù at Rome.
1570			Treatise by Molanus on sacred art. *Baronius* (1538–1607).
1571		Christian victory at Lepanto.	
1572	Gregory XIII (1572–85).	*Massacre of St Bartholomew*, death of Admiral de Coligny.	The Gregorian calendar.
1573	As from this date many nunciatures opened.		

DATE	HISTORY OF THE CHURCH	POLITICAL AND SOCIAL HISTORY	ARTS, LITERATURE AND SCIENCE
1574	St Peter Canisius (1521–97) in Germany.	*Henri III, King of France* (1574–89).	
1576	St Robert Bellarmine (1542–1621).	Rudolf II, emperor (1576–1611). Henry Bathory (1576–86), restorer of Catholicism in Poland.	Death of Titian. *Cervantes* (1547–1616). *El Greco* (1547–1614).
1579			*Suarez* (1548–1617).
1580	St Camillus of Lellis (1550–1614).	Portugal annexed by Spain (until 1641).	The *Essays* of Montaigne.
1581	Fr Matteo Ricci (1552–1610) in China. Martyrdom of Bl. Edmund Campion in England.	Independence of the United Provinces (William of Orange, 1537–84).	Agrippa d'Aubigné (1552–1630). *The Ascent of Mount Carmel* by St John of the Cross.
1585	Sixtus V (1585–90).		
1586	Organization of the Sacred College (70 cardinals). St Joseph Calasanctius (1566–1648).		
1587	Creation of the *Roman Congregations*.	Death of Mary Stuart	
1588	Moscow created a patriarchate.	Defeat of the Armada. Assassination of the Duc de Guise.	
1589		Assassination of Henri III. *Henri IV* (1589–1610). Battle of Arques.	Bacon (1559–1626).
1590	Urban VII (in September). Gregory XIV (1590–91).	Battle of Ivry.	The Caracchi (1555–1619). Caravaggio (1560–1609).
1591	Innocent IX (Oct.–Dec.)		Gongora (1561–1627).
1592	Clement VIII (1591–1605). The Sixto-Clementine Bible.		Death of *Montaigne* (1533–1592).
1593		Abjuration of Henri IV.	
1594	Mission of St Francis of Sales in Chablais.		Death of Tintoretto. *Shakespeare* (1564–1616). *Galileo* (1564–1642).
1595	The Ruthenians return to the Catholic Church.		
1596	Persecution in Japan.		
1598	*Edict of Nantes.*	Treaty of Vervins. Philip III of Spain (1598–1621).	Birth of Bernini. Marina (1569–1629). Birth of Velasquez.
1599	Mission of the Carmelites in Persia. Marc Lescarbot in Acadie.	Execution of Giordano Bruno.	

SEVENTEENTH CENTURY

DATE	HISTORY OF THE CHURCH	POLITICAL AND SOCIAL HISTORY	ARTS, LITERATURE AND SCIENCE
1603	Samuel de Champlain (1567–1635) in Canada.	*James I of England* (1603–25).	
1604	Fr de Nobili (1577–1656) in India.		
1605	Leo XI (in April), *Paul V* (1605–21). The 'Schism' of Venice. Beginnings of *Fr de Bérulle* (1575–1629), St Peter Fourier (1575–1640).		Guido Reni (1575–1642).

DATE	HISTORY OF THE CHURCH	POLITICAL AND SOCIAL HISTORY	ARTS, LITERATURE AND SCIENCE
1607	Death of St Rose of Lima (1587–1607). St Francis Solano in Argentina.		Publication of the *Astrée* (1607–28). *Rubens* (1577–1640). Harvey (1578–1658), circulation of the blood.
1609	St Francis of Sales (1567–1622). Bl. Martin Porres (1569–1639) in America. St Peter Claver (1580–1614). Foundation of the *Visitation* (1610) by *St Jeanne de Chantal* (1572–1641).		
1611		*Gustavus Adolfus, King of Sweden* (1611–32).	
1612		Mathias, emperor (1612–19).	Completion of St Peter's (consecrated 1626).
1613	The French Oratory.	*Accession of Czar Michael Romanov.*	Galileo's *History of Solar Phenomena.*
1614	Catholicism banished from Japan.		Franz Hals (1584–1666).
1615	The Recollects in Canada.		First trial of Galileo.
1617	Seville inaugurates the feast of the Immaculate Conception.		
1618	The Benedictines of Saint-Maur.	Beginning of the Thirty Years War. Rebellion of the Czechs against the Emperor Mathias.	Ribera (1588–1656).
1619		Ferdinand II, emperor (1619–1635).	
1620		The Puritans in *Mayflower* to America. Battle of the White Mountain in Bohemia.	Simon Vouet (1590–1649).
1621	*Gregory XV* (1621–3).	Philip IV of Spain.	
1622	*Congregation of Propaganda founded.* Quadruple canonization of St Ignatius of Loyola, S. Philip Neri, St Teresa and St Francis Xavier.		

SELECT BIBLIOGRAPHY

These are the most important works cited by the author in his extensive bibliographical notes. I have substituted English translations wherever possible. For the benefit of readers to whom the numerous French and German works may be inaccessible, I have added a short supplement of English books covering much of the same field.

GENERAL

A. Dufourcq: *Histoire moderne de l'église*, vol. xviii, 7th ed., 1933.

L. von Pastor: *History of the Popes since the End of the Middle Ages* (Eng. trans., 1891–1938).

Chapter I. THE AWAKENING OF THE CATHOLIC SOUL: ST IGNATIUS OF LOYOLA

P. Pourrat: *La Spiritualité chrétienne*, 2 vols, 1921.

M. Bataillon: *Erasme et l'Espagne*, 1937.

D. Barrand: *Les Ideés philosophiques de Bernardin Ochin*, 1924.

M. de la Clavière: *Saint Gaetan*, 1902.

G. Chastel: *Saint Antoine-Marie Zaccaria, Barnabite*, 1930.

J. Cherprenet: Preface to translation of John of Avila's *Audi Filia*.

P. Dominique: *La Politique des Jésuites*, 1955.

A. Brou: *Les Jésuites de la Légende*, 2 vols., 1906–7.

H. Pinard de la Boullaye: *La Spiritualité Ignatienne*, 1936.

J. Gautier: *La Spiritualité Catholique*, 1953.

P. Suau: *Histoire de Saint François Borgia*, 1910.

Chapter II. THE COUNCIL OF TRENT AND THE WORK OF THE SAINTS

L. Cristiani: *L'Église à l'époque du Concile de Trente*, 1948.

C. J. Hefele–H. Leclercq: *Histoire des Conciles*, vols. ix, x, 1930–8.

Dom Ancel: *L'Activité reformatrice de Paul IV*, 1909; *La Disgrace et le procès des Carafa*, 1909.

P. Richard: *Le Concile de Trente*, 1930–31.

G. Grente: *Saint Pie V*, 1914.

C. Hirschauer: *Politique de Sainte Pie V en France*, 1922.

R. Deslandres: *Saint Pie V et l'Islamisme*, 1911.

R. Hoonaert: *Sainte Thérèse*, 1925.

J. Galzy: *Sainte Thérèse d'Avila*, 1927.

L. Bertrand: *Sainte Thérèse*, 1927.

Fr. Bruno, o.d.c., *St John of the Cross* (Eng. trans., 1933).

L. Ponnelle and L. Bordet: *St Philip Neri and the Roman Society of his Times* (Eng. trans., 1937).

E. Mâle: *L'Art religieux après le Concile de Trente*, 1932; republished as *L'Art religieux de la fin du XVIᵉ Siècle*, 1951.

P. Fierens: *L'Art Flamand*, 1945.

Chapter III. THE RENDING OF CHRISTIAN EUROPE

N. Paulus: *Protestantism und Toleranz in 16. Jahrhundert*, 1911.

F. Buisson: *Sébastien Castellion*, 1892.

E. Girau: *Sébastien Castellion et la Réforme Calviniste*, 1916.

S. Zweig: *The Right to Heresy: Castellion against Calvin* (Eng. trans., 1936).

Duc de Levis Mirepoix: *Les Guerres de religion*, 1950.

Reinhart: *Henri IV ou la France Sauvée*, 1924.

R. Ritter (ed.): *Lettres du Cardinal de Florence*, 1955.

L. Bertrand: *Philippe II à l'Escorial*, 1929; *Philippe II, Une Ténébreuse Affaire*, 1929 (both favourable).

J. Cassou: *La Vie de Philippe II*, 1929 (unfavourable).

H. Pirenne: *Histoire de Belgique*, 1923–4.

X. Carton de Wiart: *Marguerite d'Autriche, Régente des Pays-Bas*, 1939; *La Jeunesse du Taciturne*, 1945.

J. Neale: *Queen Elizabeth*, 1934.

M. Humber-Seller: *Elizabeth I, Reine d'Angleterre*, 1953.

J. Chastenet: *Elizabeth I*, 1951.

E. Waugh: *Edmund Campion*, 1935.

W. L. Mathieson: *Politics and Religion in Scotland*, 1902.

R. Chauviré: *Le Secret de Marie Stuart*, 1937.

J. B. Bossuet: *History of the Variations of the Protestant Churches* (Eng. trans., 1829).

P. Janin: *Les Églises séparées d'Orient*, 1937.

Chapter IV. DE PROPAGANDA FIDE

F. A. Plattner: *Quand l'Europe cherchait l'Asie*, 1954.

L. J. M. Cros: *Saint François Xavier*, 1900.

R. Streit: *Bibliotheca Missionum*, vols. iv and v, 1939.

G. Goyau: *Missions et missionaires*, 1929; *L'Église en marche*, 5 vols., 1928–34; *Apôtres du Christ et de Rome*, 1938.

J. Descola: *Les Conquistadors*, 1954.

C. de la Roncière: *Histoire de la découverte de la Terre*, 1938.

J. Godechot: *Histoire de l'Atlantique*, 1948.

F. Brandel: *La Méditerranée et le monde méditérranéen à l'époque de Philippe II*, 1949.

R. Richard: *La 'Conquête Spirituelle' de Mexique*, 1933.

J. Brodrick: *The Origin of the Jesuits*, 1940; *The Progress of the Jesuits*, 1946.

Leon-Dufour: *Saint François Xavier*, 1953.

L. Delplace: *Le Catholicisme au Japan*, 1909–10.

B. Matîre: *P. Mathieu Ricci et la société chinoise de son temps*, 1937.

P. Dahmen: *Un Jésuite brahme, le Père Nobili*, 1931.

Abbé de Vaumas: *L'Éveil missionaire de la France*, 1942.

G. Goyau: *Origines religieuses du Canada*, 1924.

Chapter V. THE NEW FACE OF THE CHURCH

J. A. Hübner: *Life and Times of Sixtus V* (Eng. trans., 1872).

L. Cristiani: *Saint Pierre Canisius*, 1925.

Dom Guépin: *Saint Josaphat et l'Église Grecque Unie en Pologne*, 1897.

P. Polman: *L'Élément historique dans la controverse religieuse du XVIe Siècle*, 1932.

J. Brodrick: *Robert Bellarmine: Saint and Scholar*, 1961.

A. Kerr: *Baronius*, 1890.

F. X. Jansen: *Baïus et Baïanisme*, 1927.

G. Lanson: *Les Essais de Montaigne, étude et analyse*, 1930.

J. Plattard: *Montaigne et son temps*, 1933.

H. Bremond: *Literary History of Religious Thought in France* (Eng. trans.), vol. iii.

P. Broutin: *L'Évêque dans la tradition pastorale du XVIe Siècle*, 1953.

L. Pingaud: *Saint Pierre Fourier*, 1902.

C. Goutier: *Saint Camille de Lellis*, 1926.

H. Bordeaux: *Saint François de Sales et Notre Cœur de Chair*, 1924.

C. Roffat: *À l'École de Saint François de Sales*, 1948.

F. Vincent: *Saint François de Sales Directeur des Âmes*, 1923.

F. Hermans: *Histoire doctrinale de l'humanisme*, 4 vols., 1948.

G. Schnürer: *Katholische Kirche und Kultur in der Barokzeit*, 1937.

SUPPLEMENT

P. Hughes: *A History of the Church* (2nd ed.), 1948; *A Popular History of the Reformation*, 1957.

P. A. Kunkel: *The Theatines in the History of Catholic Reform*, 1941.

C. Hollis: *St Ignatius*, 1931.

W. H. Longridge (ed. and trans.): *The Spiritual Exercises*, 1919.

T. J. Campbell: *The Jesuits, 1534–1921*, 1932.

M. P. Harvey: *The Jesuits in History*, 1941.

A. M. CLARKE: *The Life of St Francis Borgia*, 1894.

C. C. MARTINDALE: *In God's Army*, vol. ii, 1917.

C. M. ANTONY: *The Life of St Pius V*, 1911.

M. YEO: *A Prince of Pastors: St Charles Borromeos*, 1938.

E. A. PEERS: *Mother of Carmel*, 1945; *St John of the Cross*, 1932; *Spirit of Flame*, 1943.

R. H. ALLPOST: *Henry of Navarre*, 1920.

G. SLOCOMBE: *Henry of Navarre*, 1931.

D. LOTH: *Philip II of Spain*, 1932.

W. WALSH: *Philip II*, 1938.

C. V. WEDGWOOD: *William the Silent*, 1944.

E. LINKLATER: *Mary, Queen of Scots*, 1933.

S. ZWEIG: *Mary Stuart* (Eng. trans., 1935).

V. CRONIN: *The Wise Man from the West* [Fr. M. Ricci], 1955; *A Pearl to India: The Life of Roberto de Nobili*, 1959.

C. F. LUMMIS: *Spanish Pioneers*, 1930.

H. BIGGAR (ed.): *The Voyages of Jacques Cartier*, 1924.

J. BRODRICK: *St Peter Canisius*, 1935.

A. M. BOASE: *The Fortunes of Montaigne*, 1935.

C. C. MARTINDALE: *Life of St Camillus*, 1946.

H. BURTON: *Life of St Francis de Sales*, 2 vols., 1925–9.

M. DE LA BEDOYÈRE: *St Francis de Sales*, 1959.

M. S. BRIGGS: *Baroque Architecture*, 1913.

S. SITWELL: *Southern Baroque Art*, 1924.

INDEX OF PRINCIPAL NAMES